5

Doonesbury's GREATEST HITS

Other Doonesbury Books

Still a Few Bugs in the System
The President Is a Lot Smarter Than You Think
But This War Had Such Promise
Call Me When You Find America
Guilty, Guilty, Guilty!
''What Do We Have for the Witnesses, Johnnie?''
Dare To Be Great, Ms. Caucus
Wouldn't a Gremlin Have Been More Sensible?
''Speaking of Inalienable Rights, Amy . . .''
You're Never Too Old for Nuts and Berries
An Especially Tricky People
As the Kid Goes for Broke
Stalking the Perfect Tan
''Any Grooming Hints for Your Fans, Rollie?''

Also in large format

The Doonesbury Chronicles
A Doonesbury Special

Doonesbury's GREATEST HITS

G. B. Trudeau

Holt, Rinehart and Winston/New York

Published simultaneously in Canada by Holt, Rinehart
and Winston of Canada, Limited.

Library of Congress Catalog Card Number: 78-53780

ISBN Hardbound: 0-03-044851-4
ISBN Paperback: 0-03-044856-5

First Edition

Designer: Libra Graphics, Inc.
Printed in the United States of America
10 9 8 7 6 5 4 3 2 1

"If that's art, then I'm a Hottentot."

—Harry S. Truman

Overture

It was graduation day at Yale and I flicked through the official program to the page that would give the names of the people fetching honorary degrees. Subconsciously one looks for a Surprise. Marshal Ky would have qualified in 1976. I noticed the name of Trudeau, and uttered a silent prayer of gratitude for Yale's tradition against speeches by endoctored celebrities. It turned out of course to be another Trudeau, one of whom I had not heard; only a year or two older than my graduating son. I assumed he was a local divinity of sorts, indeed he was so treated—I think I remember rightly that only he received a standing ovation from the graduating class when his name was called out. Perhaps he had invented the neutron bomb? I remembered somebody telling me that all geniuses in the physical sciences discover their fourth dimensions when they are twenty-two years old. My surprise was genuine, upon hearing the citation, to deduce that he was an artist, or social critic; indeed he was festooned so lavishly by the president of Yale that I wondered how it could be that I had not heard his name before. On mentioning this later to my astonished son I was made to feel as though I had not heard of an entire world war. I strained to see, but from mid-crowd everyone wearing reading glasses and an academic gown looks pretty much the same—and anyway, what did it matter? I did not suppose that merely *looking* at G.B. Trudeau would make me laugh, the way merely looking at Jack Benny used to make me laugh. I have dug up the citation read out at New Haven that springy afternoon, and search it out now for the hyperbole that usually breaks one's back in the rhetoric of honorary degrees. Listen . . .

"Yale's image, as the hucksters would say, would never be the same after what you have done to your classmates and your President. Happily, too, your country will never look at itself quite as self-seriously, certainly not as self-righteously, thanks to your satiric insights into the foibles and pretensions of both the notorious and the obscure. For helping keep us sane even when the times seem crazed, Yale, with pride and delight, confers upon her recent son the degree of Doctor of Humane Letters."

I made a note to look out for what I was informed went out to the newspapers of the world six times a week under the rubric *Doonesbury*. But since I tend to read only *The New York Times,* my resolution flagged; and it was not until receiving this invitation to review his work that I undertook the assignment industriously. I think it is in one way unfair to Mr. Trudeau to have done this to him. Last year a mad musician performed all thirty-two sonatas of Ludwig van Beethoven without interruption, and I cannot imagine anyone doing this as a true act of homage. Yet during the past two weeks every time I have traveled it has been with a briefcase crammed full of *Doonesbury*. People of all ages have certainly thought me reverted to infantilism as they see the comic strips spread about me. But those who looked me in the eye would have detected that I share Yale's pride and delight.

What is there to say about *Doonesbury,* or even about the comic-strip mode? Never having studied a strip before, it is conceivable that I notice things that are generally unnoticed by those continuingly familiar with the genre, even as I notice the loud noise at rock concerts. There is, for instance, the nagging mechanical—and therefore artistic—problem of reintroducing the reader to the synoptic point at which he was dropped the day before. In a collection this is more aggravating than if twenty-four hours have gone by since arriving at the point where the artist left you, and you need a little nudge. Trudeau handles this very deftly, usually by introducing into the panel a tilt of some sort that takes the reader slightly beyond where he was left yesterday, so that he is relieved of that awful sensation of turning wheels without moving forward.

The other problem is the presumptive requirement of the climax—the gag—at the end of every strip. This cadence no artist can hope to satisfy, although they must all make the effort. A collection runs the risk of maximizing the disharmonies. Imagine reading a collection of the last paragraphs of Art Buchwald's columns. Or, as Zonker would put it, Imagine! Which digression brings me to note the awful overuse of the intensifier in Mr. Trudeau's captions. Nothing appears so workaday as to be merely remarkable. Everything is *arresting*! Now this is in sharp stylistic contrast with the very nearly expressionless faces Mr. Trudeau tends to draw. Nobody ever smiles, or hardly ever; and the effect is wonderful, insofar as it reminds the reader that no experience, no absurdity, no observation, is truly new. But nearly everything spoken must be punctuated with exclamation points and served up in boldface type. I am as unconvinced that this is necessary as I am persuaded that Trudeau scores remarkably well in wrenching a climax of sorts out of almost every one of his strips. There are the anticlimaxes; but the reader forgives them indulgently; he is well enough nourished, all the more so since there is all that wonderful assonant humor and derision in mid-panel: indeed, not infrequently the true climaxes come in the penultimate panel, and the rest is lagniappe.

And then—there is a sense of rhetorical leisure in Trudeau. *Whatever* is the *hurry*? It is very pleasurable, the more so when one realizes how compressive the form is by nature, like smoking a cigar on a parachute jump. After reading three years' worth of *Doonesbury* I am certain I have read as many words as are in *War and Peace*. The artist gives off a great air of authority by this device, rather like those notices in *The New Yorker* magazine in which even the most conventional abbreviations are spurned ("Closed on Sundays and holidays, except for Thanksgiving").

Consider the treatment of an essentially banal exchange. If it were honed less finely, it would not work. One of the characters is watching a television screen, whence the words sound out:

"At the very root of the Big Apple's problems seems to be the endless exodus of the middle class. 'Good Night, New York' is fortunate to have with us tonight Mr. Jamie Dodd, one such fugitive.

"Jamie, I take it you and your wife have always been anxious to leave New York? . . ."

"Oh no, not at all, Geraldo—in fact, at first the city seemed a marvelous place for an upwardly mobile couple like us! [Note the exclamation point.] But then one day last fall I was promoted to a $45,000 job. That same day my wife was assaulted in the park. The power went off, and the garbage people went on strike . . . And suddenly! Right! Suddenly Darien made *loads* of sense!"

It requires a hypnotic self-assurance to bring off (as Trudeau does) that sequence. As so often, he relies heavily on his meiotic pen to do it.

The longueurs are sometimes almost teasingly didactic. Who else in the funny-paper business would attempt the following?

[Again, the action is coming out of the television set.]

"Mr. Finkles, as one of New York's past comptrollers, how were you able to build up such a whopping deficit?"

"Well Geraldo, we had *many* great tricks. The most common one was selling city bonds on the strength of inflated estimates of anticipated federal funding. This device was very popular among top city money wizards. But let me show you my personal favorite. See Column B here? This is where we charged the final wage period of one fiscal year to the budget of the next! In so doing, we built up a hidden deficit of *two billion dollars*!"

"Wow!"

"Now I must caution the folks at home from trying this . . ."

Note the touch of the anticlimax in the last line, inserted in the way that Oliphant permits the kitten or the mouse to pronounce the moral coda. But the unapologetically literate account of the exact character of the financial hanky-panky gives a rollicking sense of reality to the episode.

Note also: "Geraldo." Trudeau likes to identify his characters, and he is quite willing to be personal.

"Good morning. [We see a telephone receptionist.] *New York Daily News* promotion department."

"Yes, hello. I'm about to kill someone and I'd like to talk to somebody about coverage."

"Yes sir. Would this be an isolated crime of passion, or will you be making a habit of it?"

"Uh, I don't know . . . I'm not sure . . . I mean I don't know my long-range plans yet . . ."

"I'm sorry, sir, but we have to know what sort of story yours is."

"Mine is a story of hopelessness and shattered dreams in the city they call New York."

"Fine. That would be Mr. Breslin. Please hold."

Duke, recalled as ambassador from China, is trying to go back to free-lance journalism, but he is in despair. "Wenner won't even return my calls, so I guess a job at *Rolling Stone* is out."

"Amazing. After all you've been through you'd think he'd at least lend a hand."

"Nope. He needs them both for social climbing."

Duke, by the way, is relieved as chargé in China by Leonard Woodcock. "Leonard Woodcock! I just can't get over it! Whatever could have possessed Carter to pick Woodcock for China?"

"Well, sir [says his Chinese interpreter], maybe it's because Mr.Woodcock's career has been one of great sensitivity to the plight of the working class!"

"Honey, all labor leaders are sensitive to the working class. That's how they avoid belonging to it."

The willingness to criticize the union bureaucracy reminds us with relief that Trudeau, who sprang from the loins of the Vietnam antinomianism, quickly achieved perspective. There is the radio phone-in talk show. The host is talking:

"Was our squalid, cynical mission in Vietnam ever really worth the price? Was it ever worth the . . ."

RING! RING!

"Hello, this is a listener, and I'm sick of your autopsy! Get off it and stop dwelling in the past! It's *over*, hear me?—It's over!"

"Lissen, buddy, the Vietnam debacle rightly occasions a reassessment of our national purposes. We're doin' this gig for the future. We're doin' it for your children!"

"My children? They're in bed."

Indeed, let the coopters beware (remember Al Capp?). G.B. Trudeau isn't thirty yet, and listen to this indoctrination class in Saigon now that the FLN have taken over.

"Yes?" [The teacher is responding to a question from a trainee.]

"Excuse me, sir, but I don't think I belong in this class. I already know most of this stuff."

"What's your name? I'll check the printout."

"Tho. I'm a former commissioned officer."

"Tho? Lou Tho, Jr.? You were assigned to this class?"

"Yup."

"That's funny—you were meant to be shot."

"No, that's Dad—Lou, Sr."

Those in search of the meaning of humane letters need go no further than to *Doonesbury*.

William F. Buckley, Jr.

Doonesbury's Greatest Hits

ACT ONE

Time: 1975 (Early Post-Watergate)

Selected Scenes

"Tales from the Margaret Mead Taproom".....	Duke, Zonker
"Little Orphan Kimmy"	The Rosenthals
"Last Plane from Saigon"	Phred, B.D.
Bicentennial Interlude: "The Birth of a Nation" (Nate's version)	The Harrises, Minutemen
"Operation Frequent Manhood" (Dance Macabre)	Duke, MacArthur, U.S. Marines
"Courts and Torts"	Joanie, Ginny, Woody
"You're Never Too Old for Nuts and Berries" ..	Zonker, Mike, Mr. Harris
Bicentennial Interlude: "The Birth of a Nation" (Amy's version)............................	The Harrises, Paul Revere
"I'm Gay, I'm Cheerful"	Andy, Joanie

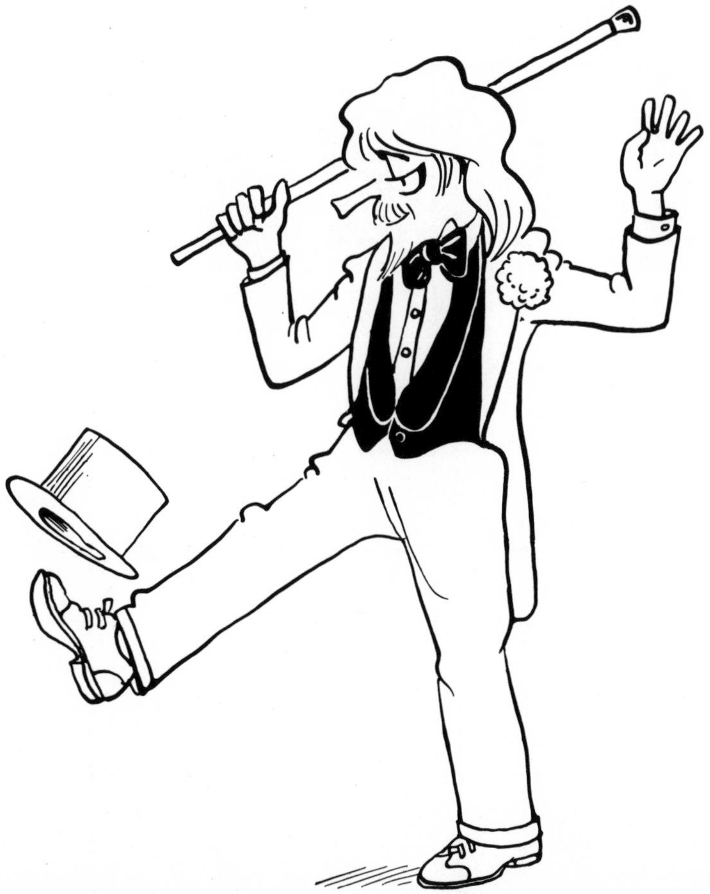

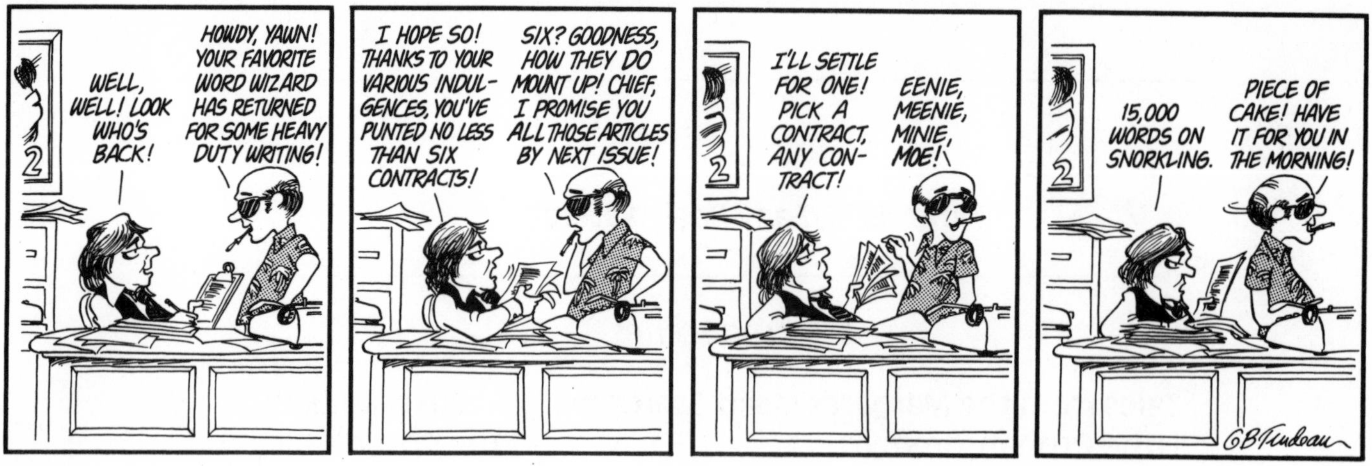
WELL, WELL! LOOK WHO'S BACK!
HOWDY, YAWN! YOUR FAVORITE WORD WIZARD HAS RETURNED FOR SOME HEAVY DUTY WRITING!
I HOPE SO! THANKS TO YOUR VARIOUS INDULGENCES, YOU'VE PUNTED NO LESS THAN SIX CONTRACTS!
SIX? GOODNESS, HOW THEY DO MOUNT UP! CHIEF, I PROMISE YOU ALL THOSE ARTICLES BY NEXT ISSUE!
I'LL SETTLE FOR ONE! PICK A CONTRACT, ANY CONTRACT!
EENIE, MEENIE, MINIE, MOE!
15,000 WORDS ON SNORKLING.
PIECE OF CAKE! HAVE IT FOR YOU IN THE MORNING!
GBTrudeau

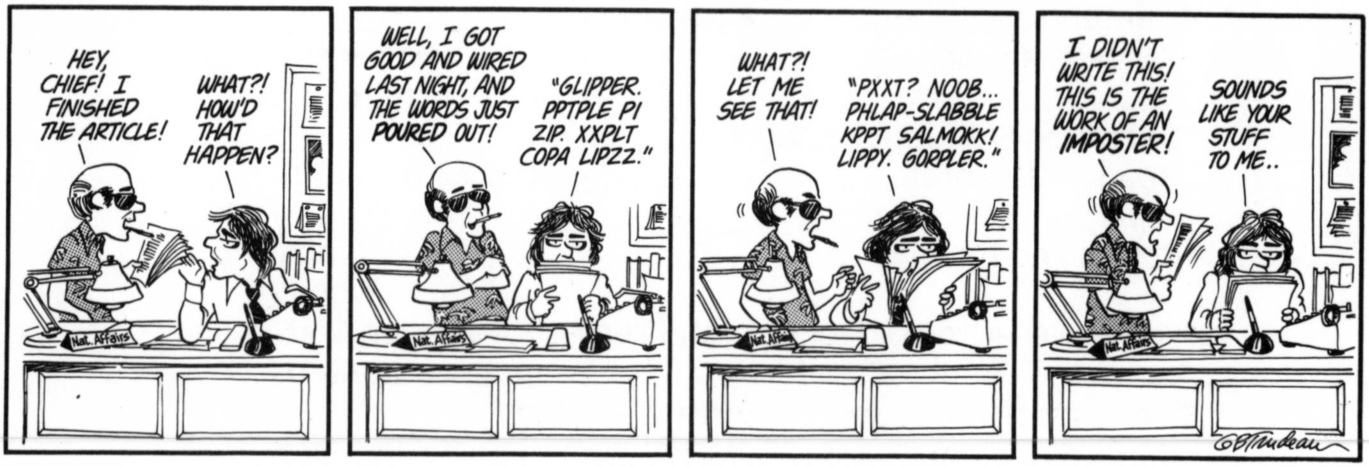
HEY, CHIEF! I FINISHED THE ARTICLE!
WHAT?! HOW'D THAT HAPPEN?
Nat. Affairs
WELL, I GOT GOOD AND WIRED LAST NIGHT, AND THE WORDS JUST POURED OUT!
"GLIPPER. PPTPLE PI ZIP. XXPLT COPA LIPZZ."
WHAT?! LET ME SEE THAT!
"PXXT? NOOB... PHLAP-SLABBLE KPPT SALMOKK! LIPPY. GORPLER."
I DIDN'T WRITE THIS! THIS IS THE WORK OF AN IMPOSTER!
SOUNDS LIKE YOUR STUFF TO ME..
GBTrudeau

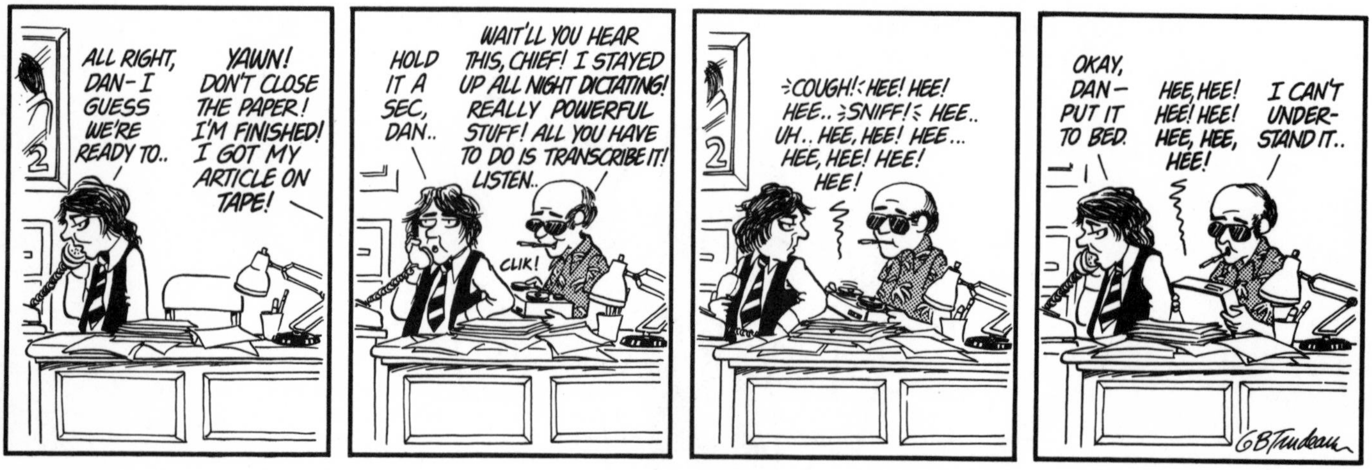
ALL RIGHT, DAN– I GUESS WE'RE READY TO..
YAWN! DON'T CLOSE THE PAPER! I'M FINISHED! I GOT MY ARTICLE ON TAPE!
HOLD IT A SEC, DAN..
WAIT'LL YOU HEAR THIS, CHIEF! I STAYED UP ALL NIGHT DICTATING! REALLY POWERFUL STUFF! ALL YOU HAVE TO DO IS TRANSCRIBE IT! LISTEN..
CLIK!
COUGH! HEE! HEE! HEE.. SNIFF! HEE.. UH.. HEE, HEE! HEE... HEE, HEE! HEE! HEE!
OKAY, DAN– PUT IT TO BED.
HEE, HEE! HEE! HEE! HEE, HEE, HEE!
I CAN'T UNDERSTAND IT..
GBTrudeau

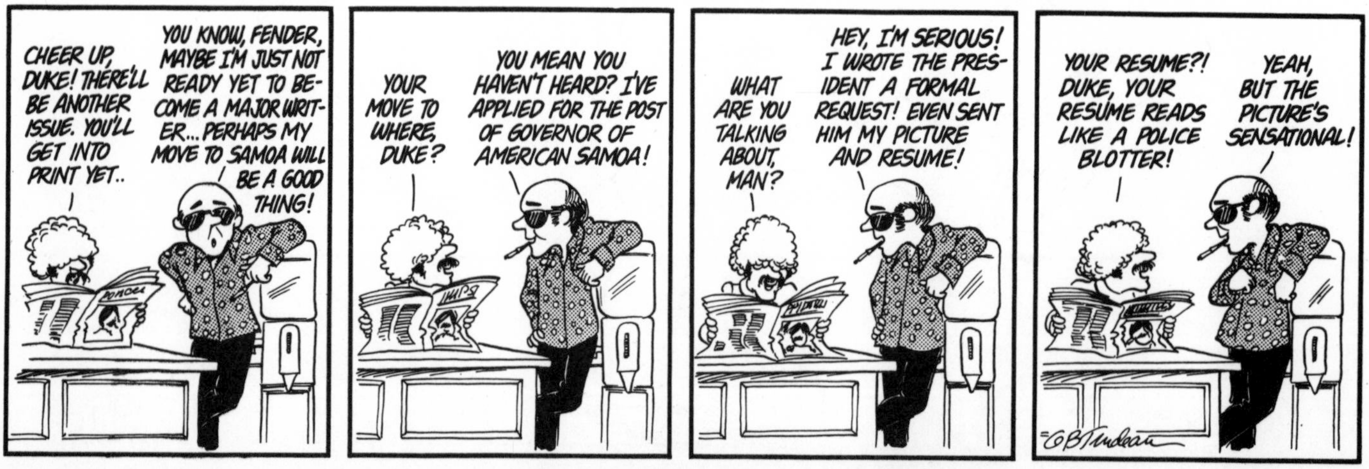
CHEER UP, DUKE! THERE'LL BE ANOTHER ISSUE. YOU'LL GET INTO PRINT YET..
YOU KNOW, FENDER, MAYBE I'M JUST NOT READY YET TO BECOME A MAJOR WRITER... PERHAPS MY MOVE TO SAMOA WILL BE A GOOD THING!
YOUR MOVE TO WHERE, DUKE?
YOU MEAN YOU HAVEN'T HEARD? I'VE APPLIED FOR THE POST OF GOVERNOR OF AMERICAN SAMOA!
WHAT ARE YOU TALKING ABOUT, MAN?
HEY, I'M SERIOUS! I WROTE THE PRESIDENT A FORMAL REQUEST! EVEN SENT HIM MY PICTURE AND RESUME!
YOUR RESUME?! DUKE, YOUR RESUME READS LIKE A POLICE BLOTTER!
YEAH, BUT THE PICTURE'S SENSATIONAL!
GBTrudeau

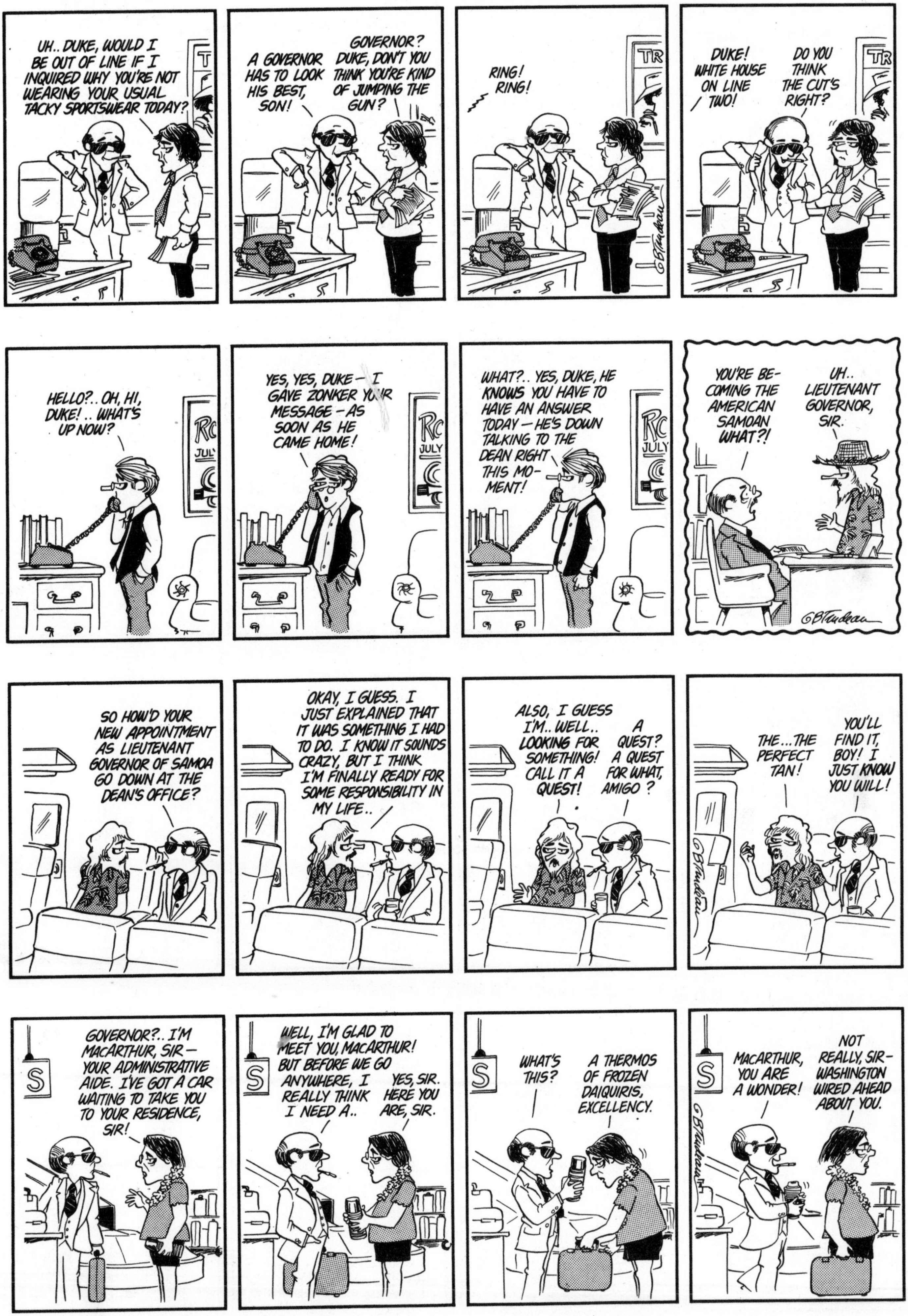
UH.. DUKE, WOULD I BE OUT OF LINE IF I INQUIRED WHY YOU'RE NOT WEARING YOUR USUAL TACKY SPORTSWEAR TODAY?
A GOVERNOR HAS TO LOOK HIS BEST, SON!
GOVERNOR? DUKE, DON'T YOU THINK YOU'RE KIND OF JUMPING THE GUN?
RING! RING!
DUKE! WHITE HOUSE ON LINE TWO!
DO YOU THINK THE CUT'S RIGHT?
HELLO?.. OH, HI, DUKE! .. WHAT'S UP NOW?
YES, YES, DUKE — I GAVE ZONKER YOUR MESSAGE — AS SOON AS HE CAME HOME!
WHAT?.. YES, DUKE, HE KNOWS YOU HAVE TO HAVE AN ANSWER TODAY — HE'S DOWN TALKING TO THE DEAN RIGHT THIS MOMENT!
YOU'RE BECOMING THE AMERICAN SAMOAN WHAT?!
UH.. LIEUTENANT GOVERNOR, SIR.
SO HOW'D YOUR NEW APPOINTMENT AS LIEUTENANT GOVERNOR OF SAMOA GO DOWN AT THE DEAN'S OFFICE?
OKAY, I GUESS. I JUST EXPLAINED THAT IT WAS SOMETHING I HAD TO DO. I KNOW IT SOUNDS CRAZY, BUT I THINK I'M FINALLY READY FOR SOME RESPONSIBILITY IN MY LIFE..
ALSO, I GUESS I'M.. WELL.. LOOKING FOR SOMETHING! CALL IT A QUEST!
A QUEST? A QUEST FOR WHAT, AMIGO?
THE... THE PERFECT TAN!
YOU'LL FIND IT, BOY! I JUST KNOW YOU WILL!
GOVERNOR?.. I'M MACARTHUR, SIR — YOUR ADMINISTRATIVE AIDE. I'VE GOT A CAR WAITING TO TAKE YOU TO YOUR RESIDENCE, SIR!
WELL, I'M GLAD TO MEET YOU, MACARTHUR! BUT BEFORE WE GO ANYWHERE, I REALLY THINK I NEED A..
YES, SIR. HERE YOU ARE, SIR.
WHAT'S THIS?
A THERMOS OF FROZEN DAIQUIRIS, EXCELLENCY.
MACARTHUR, YOU ARE A WONDER!
NOT REALLY, SIR — WASHINGTON WIRED AHEAD ABOUT YOU.

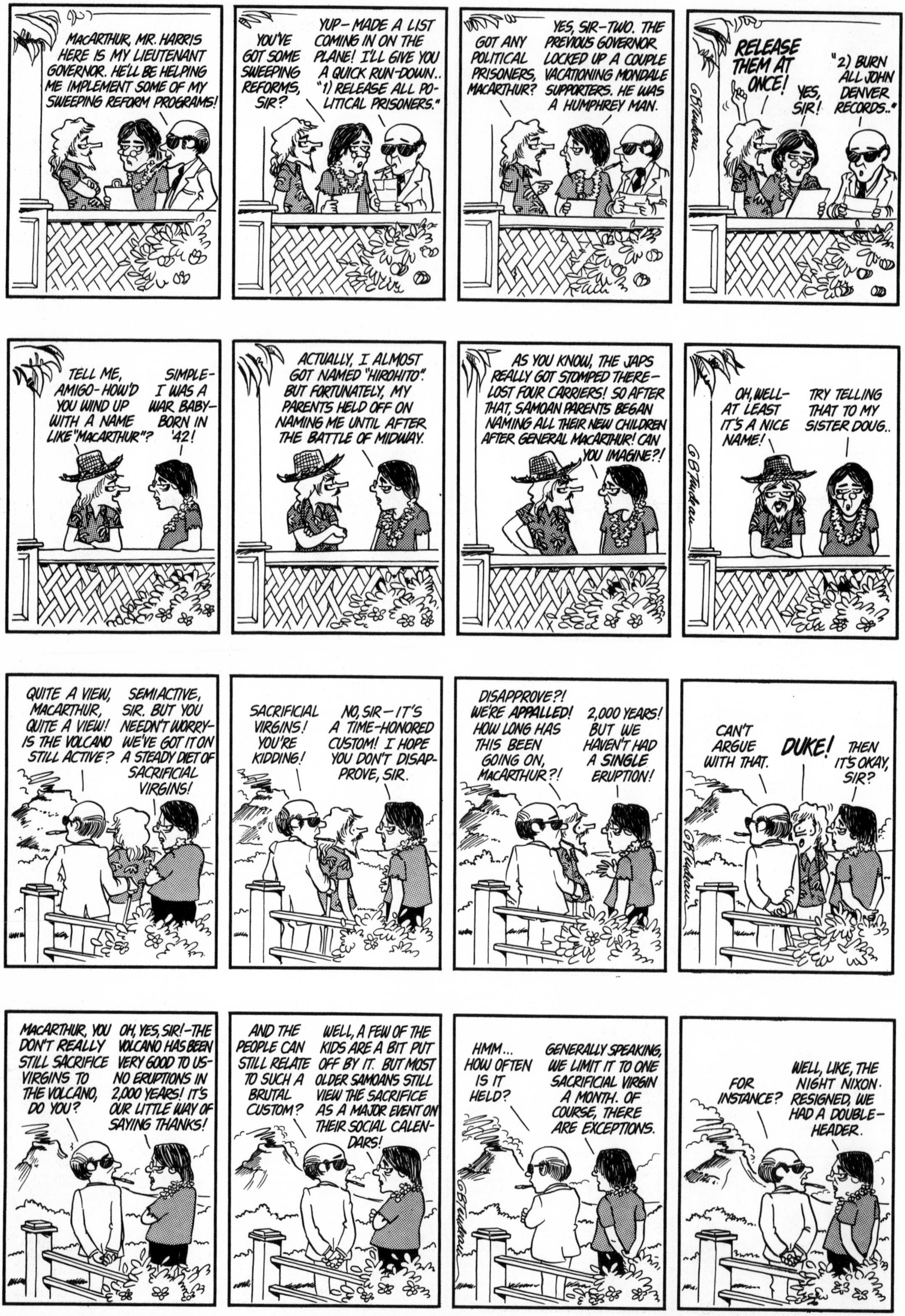
MACARTHUR, MR. HARRIS HERE IS MY LIEUTENANT GOVERNOR. HE'LL BE HELPING ME IMPLEMENT SOME OF MY SWEEPING REFORM PROGRAMS!
YOU'VE GOT SOME SWEEPING REFORMS, SIR?
YUP—MADE A LIST COMING IN ON THE PLANE! I'LL GIVE YOU A QUICK RUN-DOWN.. "1) RELEASE ALL POLITICAL PRISONERS."
GOT ANY POLITICAL PRISONERS, MACARTHUR?
YES, SIR—TWO. THE PREVIOUS GOVERNOR LOCKED UP A COUPLE VACATIONING MONDALE SUPPORTERS. HE WAS A HUMPHREY MAN.
RELEASE THEM AT ONCE!
YES, SIR!
"2) BURN ALL JOHN DENVER RECORDS.."
TELL ME, AMIGO—HOW'D YOU WIND UP WITH A NAME LIKE "MACARTHUR"?
SIMPLE—I WAS A WAR BABY—BORN IN '42!
ACTUALLY, I ALMOST GOT NAMED "HIROHITO". BUT FORTUNATELY, MY PARENTS HELD OFF ON NAMING ME UNTIL AFTER THE BATTLE OF MIDWAY.
AS YOU KNOW, THE JAPS REALLY GOT STOMPED THERE—LOST FOUR CARRIERS! SO AFTER THAT, SAMOAN PARENTS BEGAN NAMING ALL THEIR NEW CHILDREN AFTER GENERAL MACARTHUR! CAN YOU IMAGINE?!
OH, WELL—AT LEAST IT'S A NICE NAME!
TRY TELLING THAT TO MY SISTER DOUG..
QUITE A VIEW, MACARTHUR, QUITE A VIEW! IS THE VOLCANO STILL ACTIVE?
SEMIACTIVE, SIR. BUT YOU NEEDN'T WORRY—WE'VE GOT IT ON A STEADY DIET OF SACRIFICIAL VIRGINS!
SACRIFICIAL VIRGINS! YOU'RE KIDDING!
NO, SIR—IT'S A TIME-HONORED CUSTOM! I HOPE YOU DON'T DISAPPROVE, SIR.
DISAPPROVE?! WE'RE APPALLED! HOW LONG HAS THIS BEEN GOING ON, MACARTHUR?!
2,000 YEARS! BUT WE HAVEN'T HAD A SINGLE ERUPTION!
CAN'T ARGUE WITH THAT.
DUKE!
THEN IT'S OKAY, SIR?
MACARTHUR, YOU DON'T REALLY STILL SACRIFICE VIRGINS TO THE VOLCANO, DO YOU?
OH, YES, SIR!—THE VOLCANO HAS BEEN VERY GOOD TO US—NO ERUPTIONS IN 2,000 YEARS! IT'S OUR LITTLE WAY OF SAYING THANKS!
AND THE PEOPLE CAN STILL RELATE TO SUCH A BRUTAL CUSTOM?
WELL, A FEW OF THE KIDS ARE A BIT PUT OFF BY IT. BUT MOST OLDER SAMOANS STILL VIEW THE SACRIFICE AS A MAJOR EVENT ON THEIR SOCIAL CALENDARS!
HMM... HOW OFTEN IS IT HELD?
GENERALLY SPEAKING, WE LIMIT IT TO ONE SACRIFICIAL VIRGIN A MONTH. OF COURSE, THERE ARE EXCEPTIONS.
FOR INSTANCE?
WELL, LIKE, THE NIGHT NIXON RESIGNED, WE HAD A DOUBLE-HEADER.

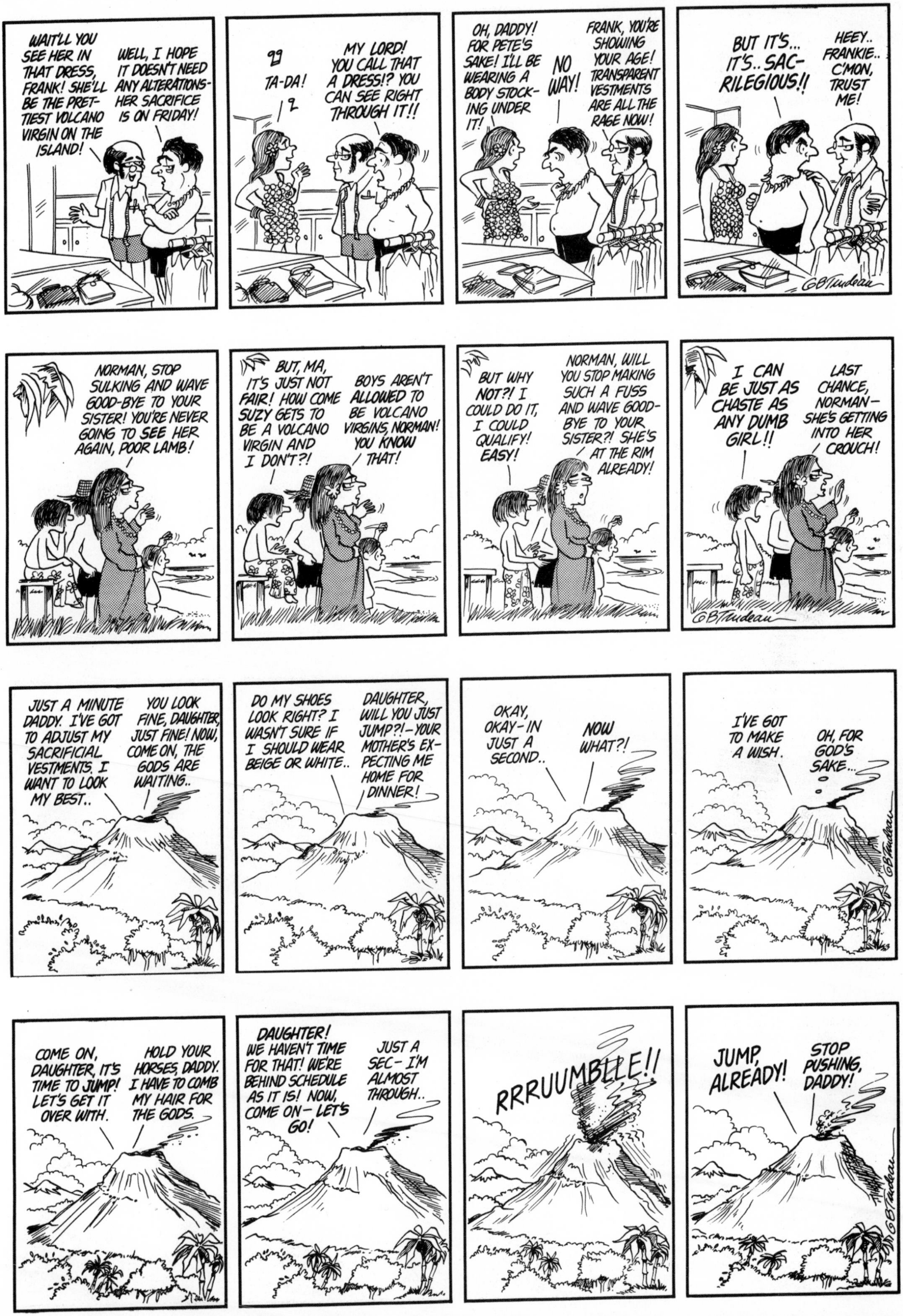

WAIT'LL YOU SEE HER IN THAT DRESS, FRANK! SHE'LL BE THE PRETTIEST VOLCANO VIRGIN ON THE ISLAND!
WELL, I HOPE IT DOESN'T NEED ANY ALTERATIONS- HER SACRIFICE IS ON FRIDAY!
TA-DA!
MY LORD! YOU CALL THAT A DRESS!? YOU CAN SEE RIGHT THROUGH IT!!
OH, DADDY! FOR PETE'S SAKE! I'LL BE WEARING A BODY STOCKING UNDER IT!
NO WAY!
FRANK, YOU'RE SHOWING YOUR AGE! TRANSPARENT VESTMENTS ARE ALL THE RAGE NOW!
BUT IT'S... IT'S.. SACRILEGIOUS!!
HEEY.. FRANKIE.. C'MON, TRUST ME!
©GBTrudeau
NORMAN, STOP SULKING AND WAVE GOOD-BYE TO YOUR SISTER! YOU'RE NEVER GOING TO SEE HER AGAIN, POOR LAMB!
BUT, MA, IT'S JUST NOT FAIR! HOW COME SUZY GETS TO BE A VOLCANO VIRGIN AND I DON'T?!
BOYS AREN'T ALLOWED TO BE VOLCANO VIRGINS, NORMAN! YOU KNOW THAT!
BUT WHY NOT?! I COULD DO IT, I COULD QUALIFY! EASY!
NORMAN, WILL YOU STOP MAKING SUCH A FUSS AND WAVE GOOD-BYE TO YOUR SISTER?! SHE'S AT THE RIM ALREADY!
I CAN BE JUST AS CHASTE AS ANY DUMB GIRL!!
LAST CHANCE, NORMAN- SHE'S GETTING INTO HER CROUCH!
©GBTrudeau
JUST A MINUTE DADDY. I'VE GOT TO ADJUST MY SACRIFICIAL VESTMENTS. I WANT TO LOOK MY BEST..
YOU LOOK FINE, DAUGHTER, JUST FINE! NOW, COME ON, THE GODS ARE WAITING..
DO MY SHOES LOOK RIGHT? I WASN'T SURE IF I SHOULD WEAR BEIGE OR WHITE..
DAUGHTER, WILL YOU JUST JUMP?!-YOUR MOTHER'S EXPECTING ME HOME FOR DINNER!
OKAY, OKAY-IN JUST A SECOND..
NOW WHAT?!
I'VE GOT TO MAKE A WISH.
OH, FOR GOD'S SAKE...
©GBTrudeau
COME ON, DAUGHTER, IT'S TIME TO JUMP! LET'S GET IT OVER WITH.
HOLD YOUR HORSES, DADDY. I HAVE TO COMB MY HAIR FOR THE GODS.
DAUGHTER! WE HAVEN'T TIME FOR THAT! WE'RE BEHIND SCHEDULE AS IT IS! NOW, COME ON- LET'S GO!
JUST A SEC- I'M ALMOST THROUGH..
RRRUUMBLLE!!
JUMP, ALREADY!
STOP PUSHING, DADDY!
©GBTrudeau

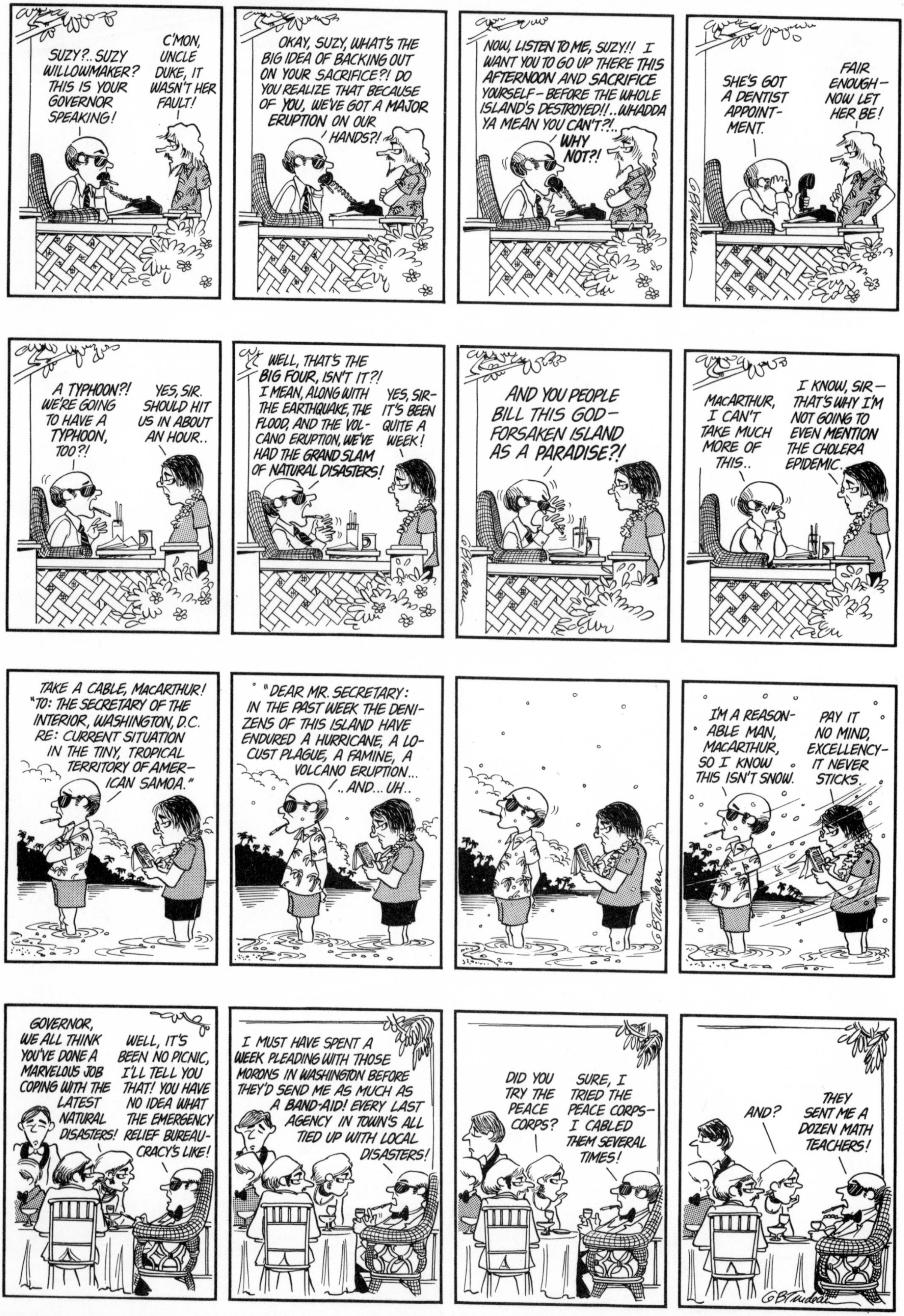
SUZY?.. SUZY WILLOWMAKER? THIS IS YOUR GOVERNOR SPEAKING!
C'MON, UNCLE DUKE, IT WASN'T HER FAULT!
OKAY, SUZY, WHAT'S THE BIG IDEA OF BACKING OUT ON YOUR SACRIFICE?! DO YOU REALIZE THAT BECAUSE OF YOU, WE'VE GOT A MAJOR ERUPTION ON OUR HANDS?!
NOW, LISTEN TO ME, SUZY!! I WANT YOU TO GO UP THERE THIS AFTERNOON AND SACRIFICE YOURSELF – BEFORE THE WHOLE ISLAND'S DESTROYED!!.. WHADDA YA MEAN YOU CAN'T?!.. WHY NOT?!
SHE'S GOT A DENTIST APPOINTMENT.
FAIR ENOUGH – NOW LET HER BE!
A TYPHOON?! WE'RE GOING TO HAVE A TYPHOON, TOO?!
YES, SIR. SHOULD HIT US IN ABOUT AN HOUR..
WELL, THAT'S THE BIG FOUR, ISN'T IT?! I MEAN, ALONG WITH THE EARTHQUAKE, THE FLOOD, AND THE VOLCANO ERUPTION, WE'VE HAD THE GRAND SLAM OF NATURAL DISASTERS!
YES, SIR – IT'S BEEN QUITE A WEEK!
AND YOU PEOPLE BILL THIS GOD-FORSAKEN ISLAND AS A PARADISE?!
MACARTHUR, I CAN'T TAKE MUCH MORE OF THIS..
I KNOW, SIR – THAT'S WHY I'M NOT GOING TO EVEN MENTION THE CHOLERA EPIDEMIC.
TAKE A CABLE, MACARTHUR! "TO: THE SECRETARY OF THE INTERIOR, WASHINGTON, D.C. RE: CURRENT SITUATION IN THE TINY, TROPICAL TERRITORY OF AMERICAN SAMOA."
"DEAR MR. SECRETARY: IN THE PAST WEEK THE DENIZENS OF THIS ISLAND HAVE ENDURED A HURRICANE, A LOCUST PLAGUE, A FAMINE, A VOLCANO ERUPTION...
.. AND... UH..
I'M A REASONABLE MAN, MACARTHUR, SO I KNOW THIS ISN'T SNOW.
PAY IT NO MIND, EXCELLENCY – IT NEVER STICKS.
GOVERNOR, WE ALL THINK YOU'VE DONE A MARVELOUS JOB COPING WITH THE LATEST NATURAL DISASTERS!
WELL, IT'S BEEN NO PICNIC, I'LL TELL YOU THAT! YOU HAVE NO IDEA WHAT THE EMERGENCY RELIEF BUREAUCRACY'S LIKE!
I MUST HAVE SPENT A WEEK PLEADING WITH THOSE MORONS IN WASHINGTON BEFORE THEY'D SEND ME AS MUCH AS A BAND-AID! EVERY LAST AGENCY IN TOWN'S ALL TIED UP WITH LOCAL DISASTERS!
DID YOU TRY THE PEACE CORPS?
SURE, I TRIED THE PEACE CORPS – I CABLED THEM SEVERAL TIMES!
AND?
THEY SENT ME A DOZEN MATH TEACHERS!

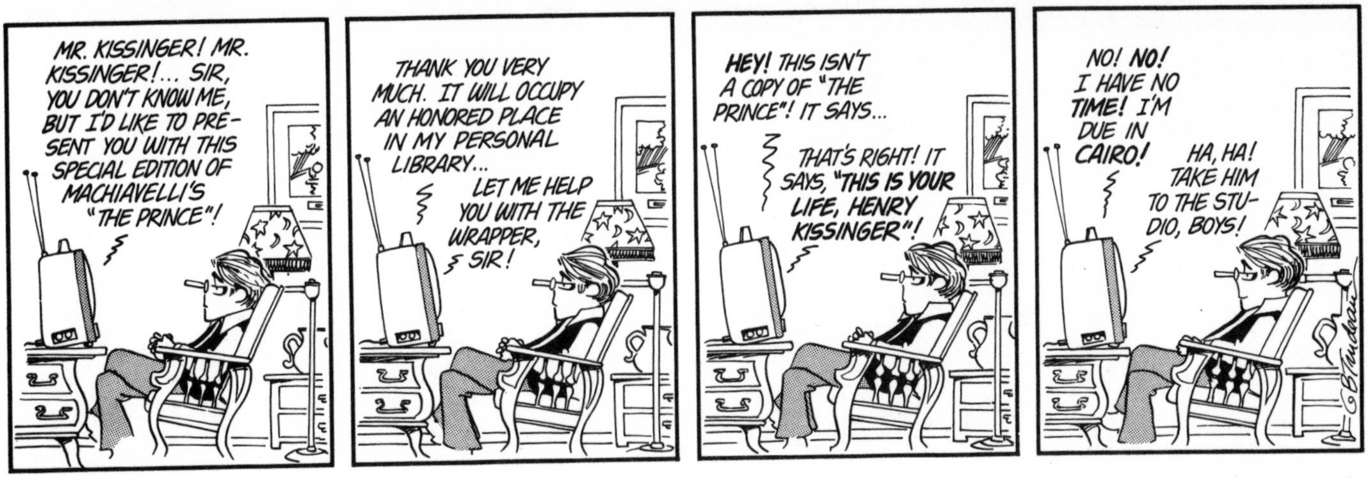
MR. KISSINGER! MR. KISSINGER!... SIR, YOU DON'T KNOW ME, BUT I'D LIKE TO PRESENT YOU WITH THIS SPECIAL EDITION OF MACHIAVELLI'S "THE PRINCE"!
THANK YOU VERY MUCH. IT WILL OCCUPY AN HONORED PLACE IN MY PERSONAL LIBRARY...
LET ME HELP YOU WITH THE WRAPPER, SIR!
HEY! THIS ISN'T A COPY OF "THE PRINCE"! IT SAYS...
THAT'S RIGHT! IT SAYS, "THIS IS YOUR LIFE, HENRY KISSINGER"!
NO! NO! I HAVE NO TIME! I'M DUE IN CAIRO!
HA, HA! TAKE HIM TO THE STUDIO, BOYS!
©BTrudeau

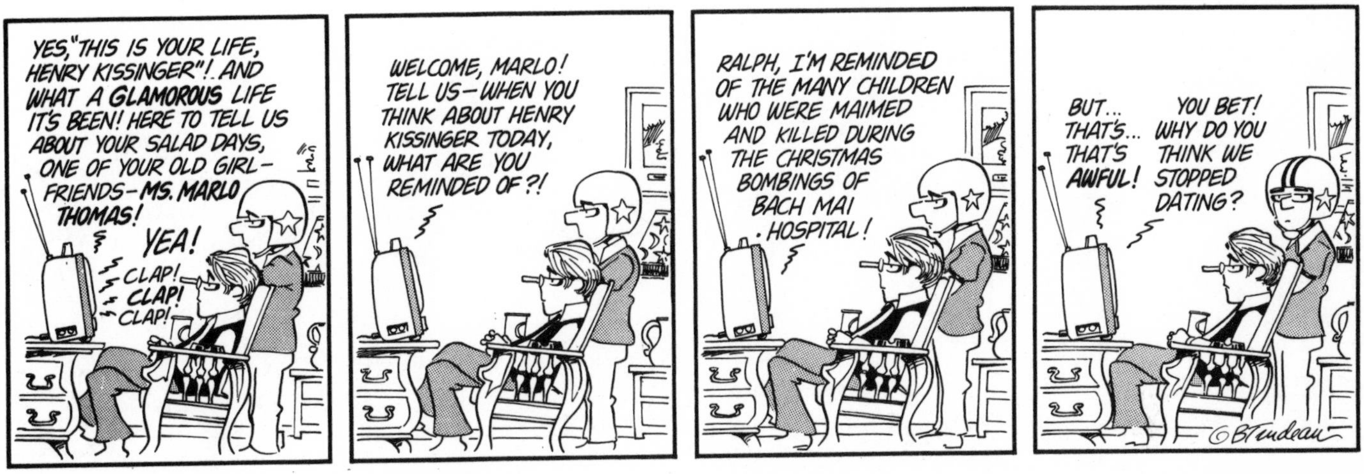
YES, "THIS IS YOUR LIFE, HENRY KISSINGER"! AND WHAT A GLAMOROUS LIFE IT'S BEEN! HERE TO TELL US ABOUT YOUR SALAD DAYS, ONE OF YOUR OLD GIRLFRIENDS–MS. MARLO THOMAS!
YEA!
CLAP! CLAP! CLAP!
WELCOME, MARLO! TELL US–WHEN YOU THINK ABOUT HENRY KISSINGER TODAY, WHAT ARE YOU REMINDED OF?!
RALPH, I'M REMINDED OF THE MANY CHILDREN WHO WERE MAIMED AND KILLED DURING THE CHRISTMAS BOMBINGS OF BACH MAI HOSPITAL!
BUT... THAT'S... THAT'S AWFUL!
YOU BET! WHY DO YOU THINK WE STOPPED DATING?
©BTrudeau

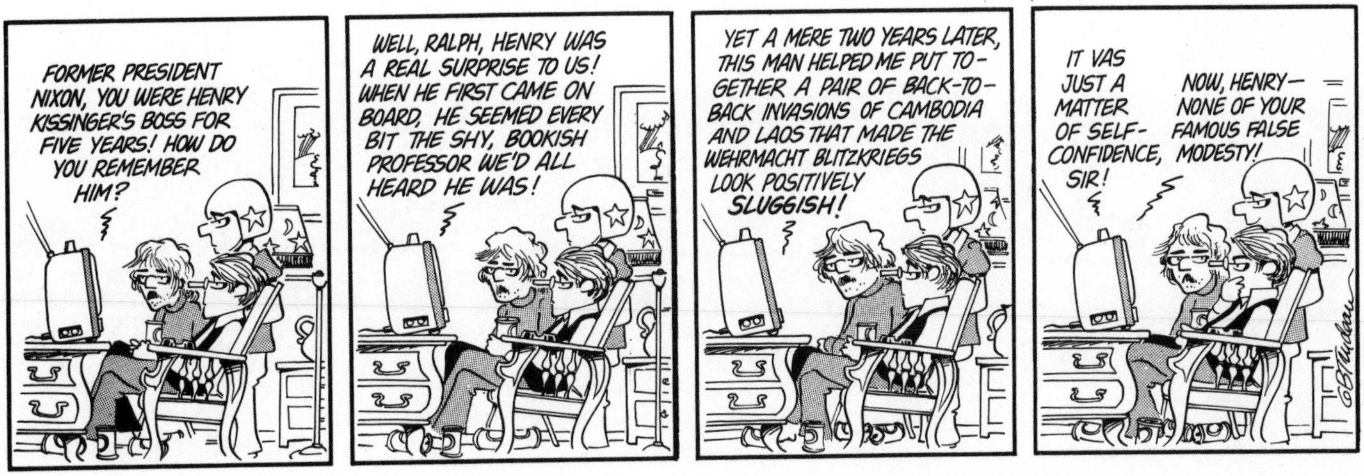
FORMER PRESIDENT NIXON, YOU WERE HENRY KISSINGER'S BOSS FOR FIVE YEARS! HOW DO YOU REMEMBER HIM?
WELL, RALPH, HENRY WAS A REAL SURPRISE TO US! WHEN HE FIRST CAME ON BOARD, HE SEEMED EVERY BIT THE SHY, BOOKISH PROFESSOR WE'D ALL HEARD HE WAS!
YET A MERE TWO YEARS LATER, THIS MAN HELPED ME PUT TOGETHER A PAIR OF BACK-TO-BACK INVASIONS OF CAMBODIA AND LAOS THAT MADE THE WEHRMACHT BLITZKRIEGS LOOK POSITIVELY SLUGGISH!
IT VAS JUST A MATTER OF SELF-CONFIDENCE, SIR!
NOW, HENRY–NONE OF YOUR FAMOUS FALSE MODESTY!
©BTrudeau

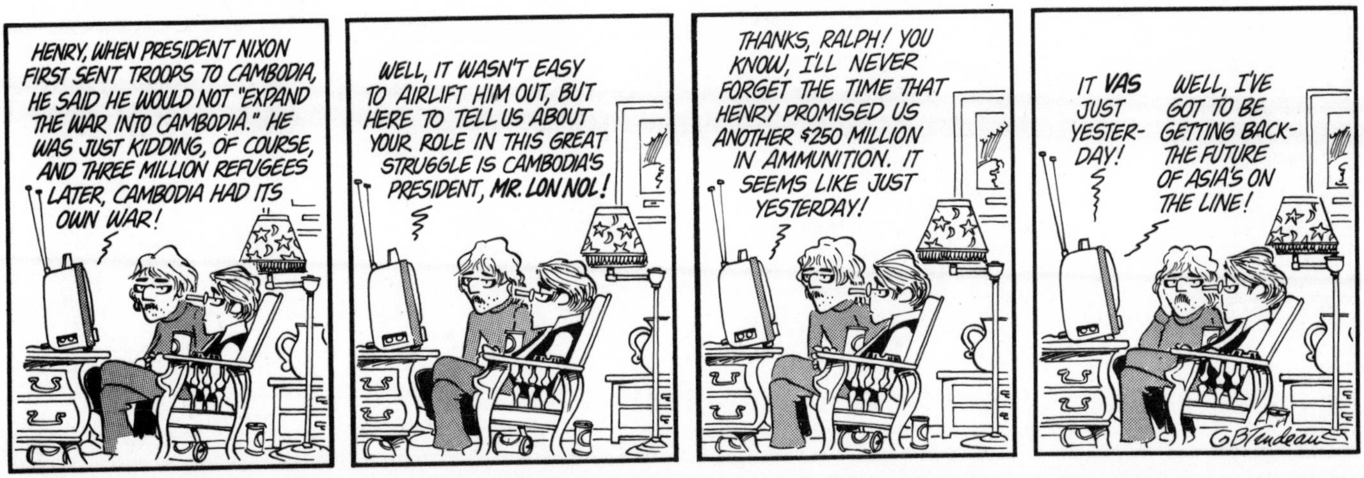
HENRY, WHEN PRESIDENT NIXON FIRST SENT TROOPS TO CAMBODIA, HE SAID HE WOULD NOT "EXPAND THE WAR INTO CAMBODIA." HE WAS JUST KIDDING, OF COURSE, AND THREE MILLION REFUGEES LATER, CAMBODIA HAD ITS OWN WAR!
WELL, IT WASN'T EASY TO AIRLIFT HIM OUT, BUT HERE TO TELL US ABOUT YOUR ROLE IN THIS GREAT STRUGGLE IS CAMBODIA'S PRESIDENT, MR. LON NOL!
THANKS, RALPH! YOU KNOW, I'LL NEVER FORGET THE TIME THAT HENRY PROMISED US ANOTHER $250 MILLION IN AMMUNITION. IT SEEMS LIKE JUST YESTERDAY!
IT VAS JUST YESTERDAY!
WELL, I'VE GOT TO BE GETTING BACK–THE FUTURE OF ASIA'S ON THE LINE!
©BTrudeau

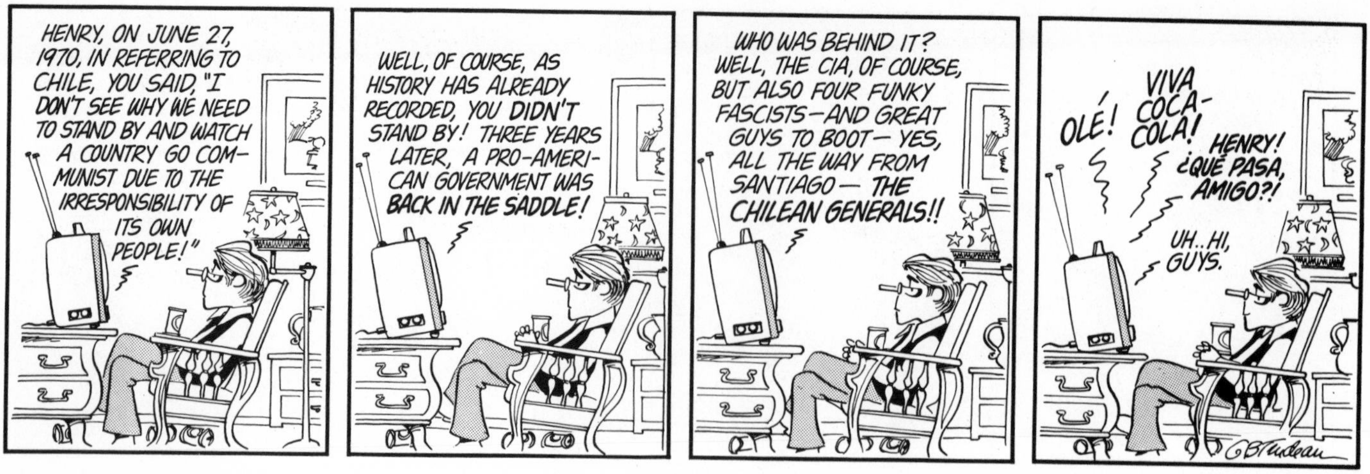
HENRY, ON JUNE 27, 1970, IN REFERRING TO CHILE, YOU SAID, "I DON'T SEE WHY WE NEED TO STAND BY AND WATCH A COUNTRY GO COMMUNIST DUE TO THE IRRESPONSIBILITY OF ITS OWN PEOPLE!"
WELL, OF COURSE, AS HISTORY HAS ALREADY RECORDED, YOU DIDN'T STAND BY! THREE YEARS LATER, A PRO-AMERICAN GOVERNMENT WAS BACK IN THE SADDLE!
WHO WAS BEHIND IT? WELL, THE CIA, OF COURSE, BUT ALSO FOUR FUNKY FASCISTS—AND GREAT GUYS TO BOOT—YES, ALL THE WAY FROM SANTIAGO—THE CHILEAN GENERALS!!
OLÉ!
VIVA COCA-COLA!
HENRY! ¿QUÉ PASA, AMIGO?!
UH..HI, GUYS.
GBTrudeau

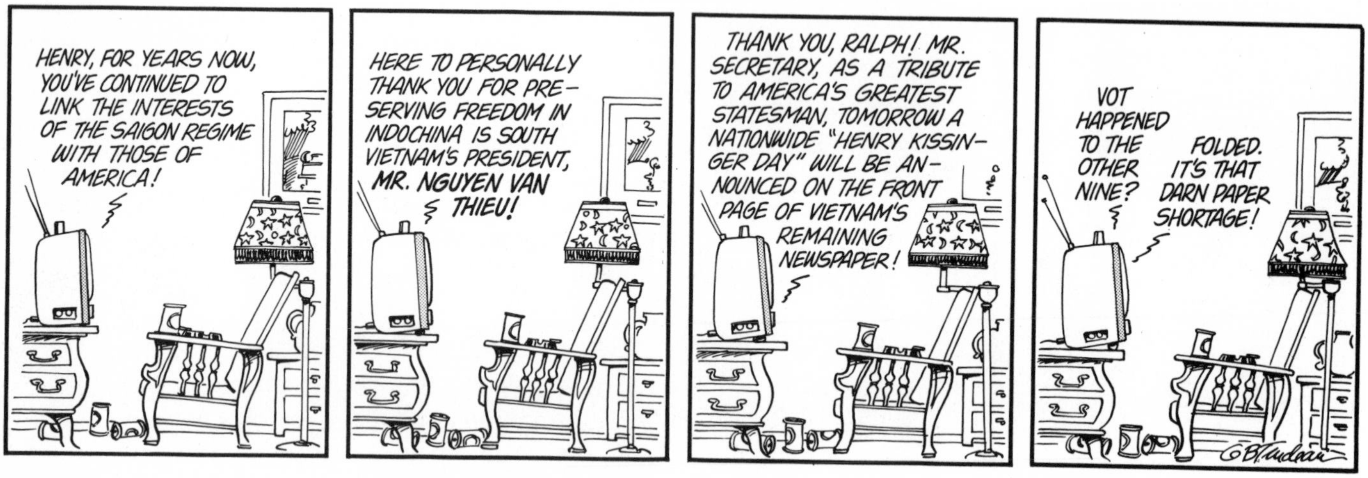
HENRY, FOR YEARS NOW, YOU'VE CONTINUED TO LINK THE INTERESTS OF THE SAIGON REGIME WITH THOSE OF AMERICA!
HERE TO PERSONALLY THANK YOU FOR PRESERVING FREEDOM IN INDOCHINA IS SOUTH VIETNAM'S PRESIDENT, MR. NGUYEN VAN THIEU!
THANK YOU, RALPH! MR. SECRETARY, AS A TRIBUTE TO AMERICA'S GREATEST STATESMAN, TOMORROW A NATIONWIDE "HENRY KISSINGER DAY" WILL BE ANNOUNCED ON THE FRONT PAGE OF VIETNAM'S REMAINING NEWSPAPER!
VOT HAPPENED TO THE OTHER NINE?
FOLDED. IT'S THAT DARN PAPER SHORTAGE!
GBTrudeau

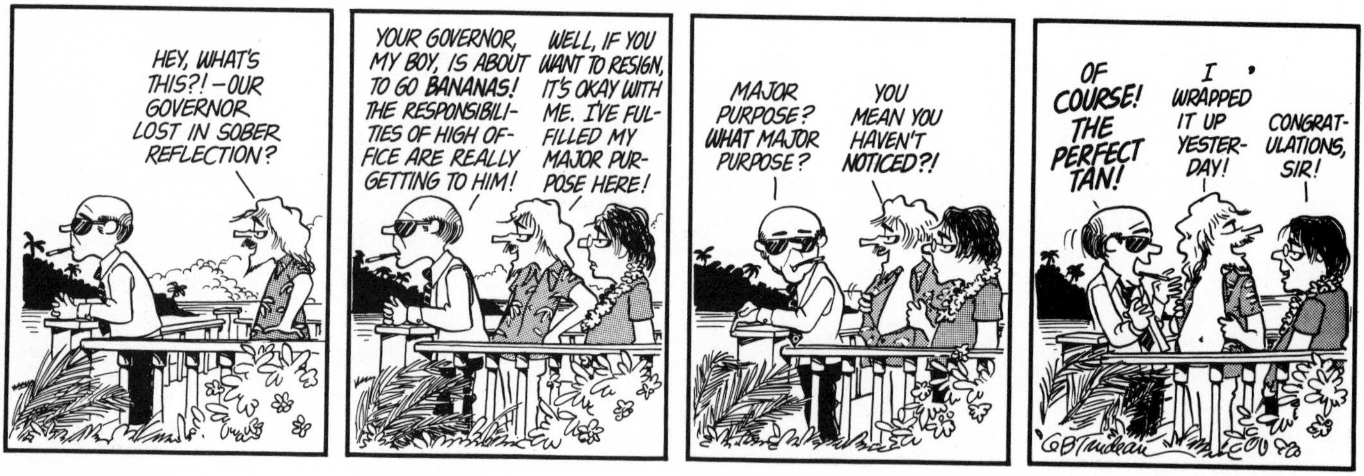
HEY, WHAT'S THIS?!—OUR GOVERNOR LOST IN SOBER REFLECTION?
YOUR GOVERNOR, MY BOY, IS ABOUT TO GO BANANAS! THE RESPONSIBILITIES OF HIGH OFFICE ARE REALLY GETTING TO HIM!
WELL, IF YOU WANT TO RESIGN, IT'S OKAY WITH ME. I'VE FULFILLED MY MAJOR PURPOSE HERE!
MAJOR PURPOSE? WHAT MAJOR PURPOSE?
YOU MEAN YOU HAVEN'T NOTICED?!
OF COURSE! THE PERFECT TAN!
I WRAPPED IT UP YESTERDAY!
CONGRATULATIONS, SIR!
GBTrudeau

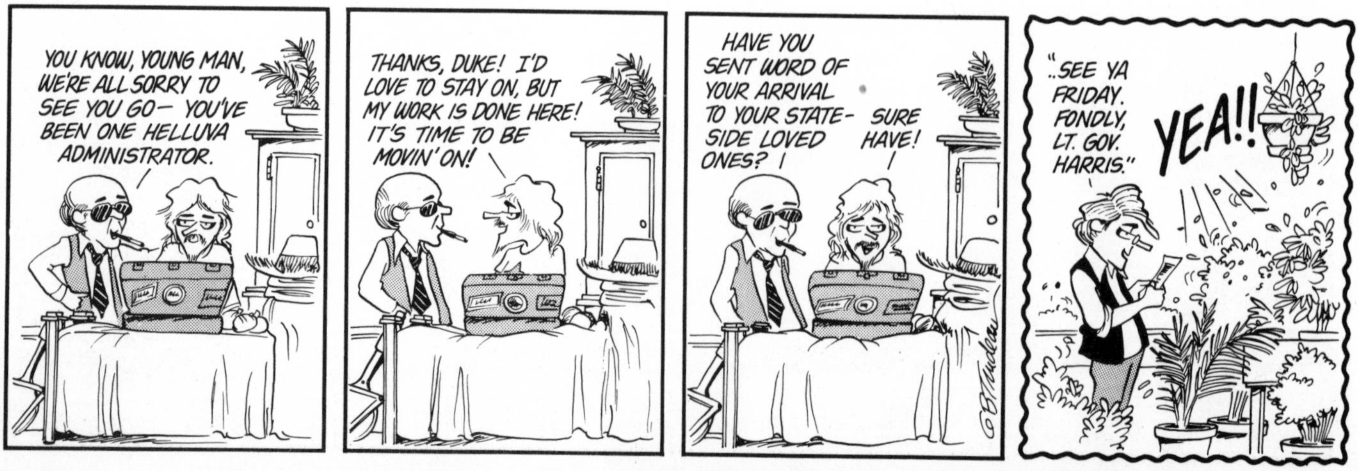
YOU KNOW, YOUNG MAN, WE'RE ALL SORRY TO SEE YOU GO—YOU'VE BEEN ONE HELLUVA ADMINISTRATOR.
THANKS, DUKE! I'D LOVE TO STAY ON, BUT MY WORK IS DONE HERE! IT'S TIME TO BE MOVIN' ON!
HAVE YOU SENT WORD OF YOUR ARRIVAL TO YOUR STATESIDE LOVED ONES?
SURE HAVE!
GBTrudeau
"..SEE YA FRIDAY. FONDLY, LT. GOV. HARRIS."
YEA!!

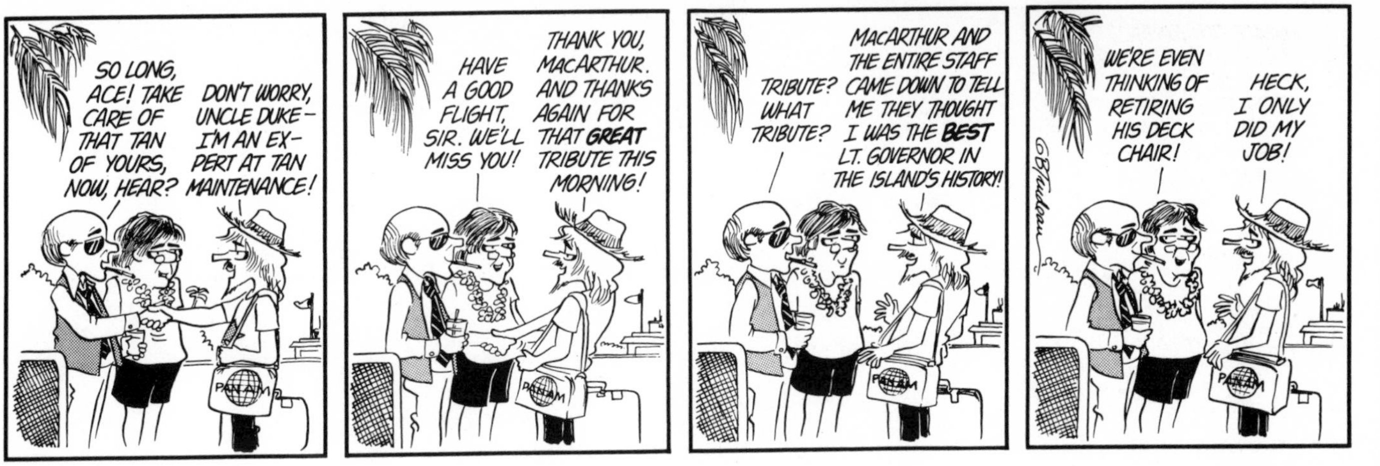
SO LONG, ACE! TAKE CARE OF THAT TAN OF YOURS, NOW, HEAR?
DON'T WORRY, UNCLE DUKE–I'M AN EXPERT AT TAN MAINTENANCE!
HAVE A GOOD FLIGHT, SIR. WE'LL MISS YOU!
THANK YOU, MACARTHUR. AND THANKS AGAIN FOR THAT **GREAT** TRIBUTE THIS MORNING!
TRIBUTE? WHAT TRIBUTE?
MACARTHUR AND THE ENTIRE STAFF CAME DOWN TO TELL ME THEY THOUGHT I WAS THE **BEST** LT. GOVERNOR IN THE ISLAND'S HISTORY!
WE'RE EVEN THINKING OF RETIRING HIS DECK CHAIR!
HECK, I ONLY DID MY JOB!

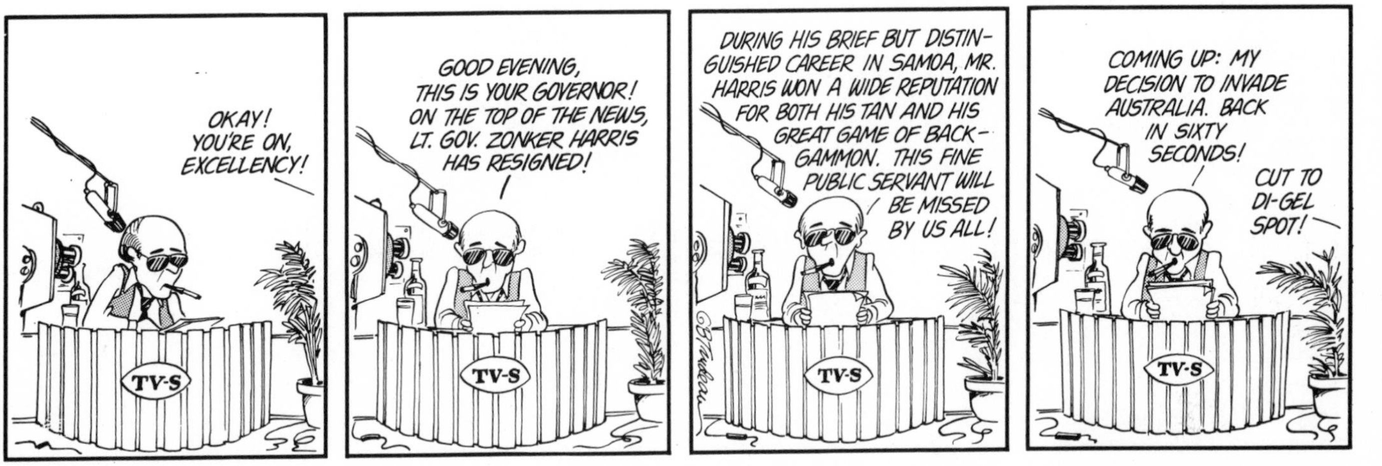
OKAY! YOU'RE ON, EXCELLENCY!
GOOD EVENING, THIS IS YOUR GOVERNOR! ON THE TOP OF THE NEWS, LT. GOV. ZONKER HARRIS HAS RESIGNED!
DURING HIS BRIEF BUT DISTINGUISHED CAREER IN SAMOA, MR. HARRIS WON A WIDE REPUTATION FOR BOTH HIS TAN AND HIS GREAT GAME OF BACKGAMMON. THIS FINE PUBLIC SERVANT WILL BE MISSED BY US ALL!
COMING UP: MY DECISION TO INVADE AUSTRALIA. BACK IN SIXTY SECONDS!
CUT TO DI-GEL SPOT!

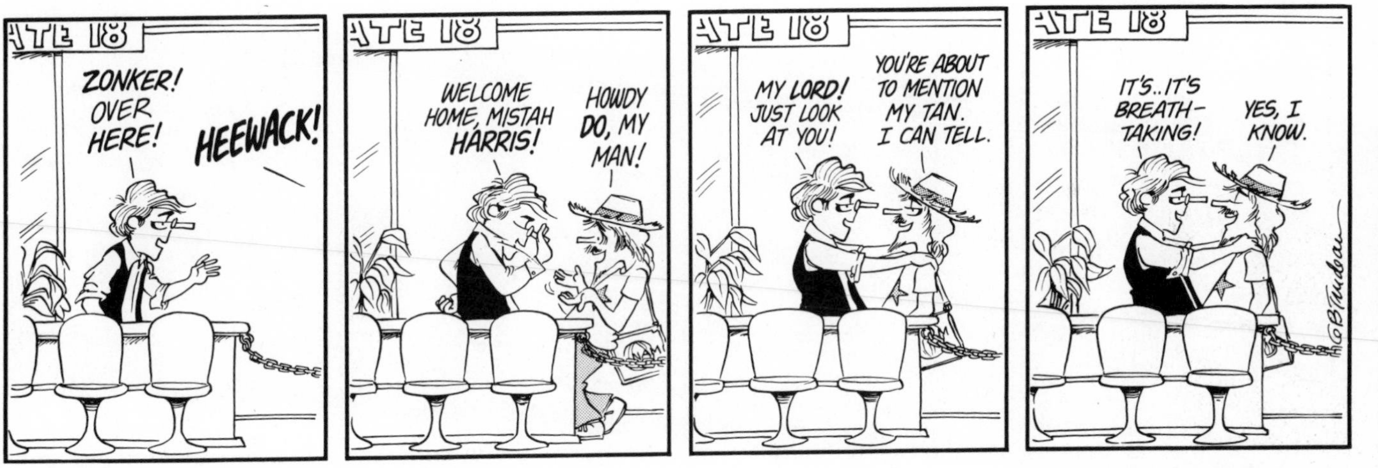
ZONKER! OVER HERE!
HEEWACK!
WELCOME HOME, MISTAH **HARRIS**!
HOWDY **DO**, MY MAN!
MY **LORD**! JUST LOOK AT YOU!
YOU'RE ABOUT TO MENTION MY TAN. I CAN TELL.
IT'S..IT'S BREATHTAKING!
YES, I KNOW.

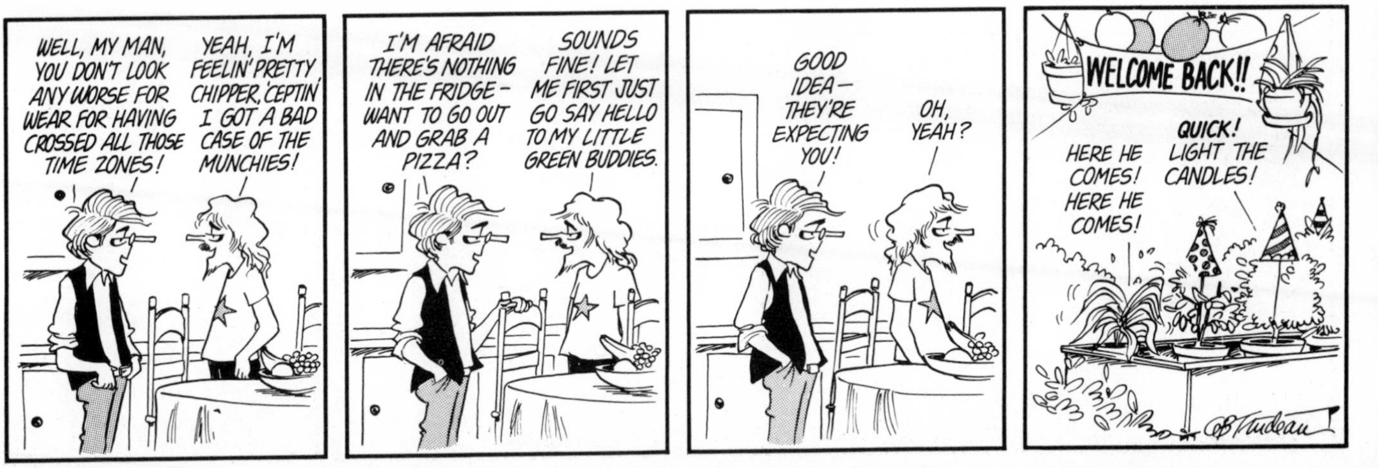
WELL, MY MAN, YOU DON'T LOOK ANY WORSE FOR WEAR FOR HAVING CROSSED ALL THOSE TIME ZONES!
YEAH, I'M FEELIN' PRETTY CHIPPER, 'CEPTIN' I GOT A BAD CASE OF THE MUNCHIES!
I'M AFRAID THERE'S NOTHING IN THE FRIDGE–WANT TO GO OUT AND GRAB A PIZZA?
SOUNDS FINE! LET ME FIRST JUST GO SAY HELLO TO MY LITTLE GREEN BUDDIES.
GOOD IDEA–THEY'RE EXPECTING YOU!
OH, YEAH?
WELCOME BACK!!
HERE HE COMES! HERE HE COMES!
QUICK! LIGHT THE CANDLES!

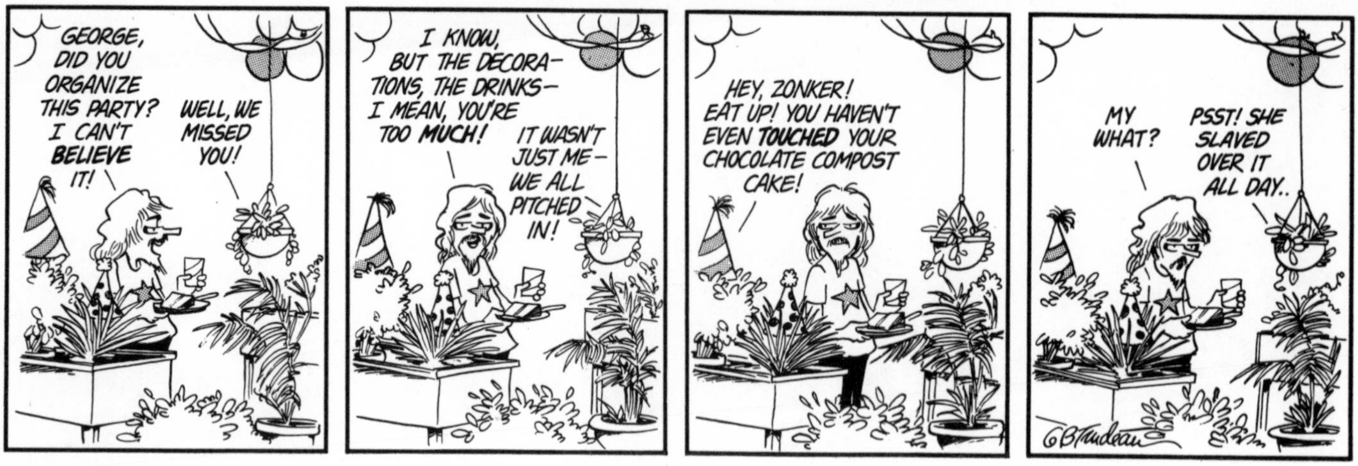
GEORGE, DID YOU ORGANIZE THIS PARTY? I CAN'T **BELIEVE** IT!
WELL, WE MISSED YOU!
I KNOW, BUT THE DECORATIONS, THE DRINKS— I MEAN, YOU'RE TOO **MUCH**!
IT WASN'T JUST ME— WE ALL PITCHED IN!
HEY, ZONKER! EAT UP! YOU HAVEN'T EVEN **TOUCHED** YOUR CHOCOLATE COMPOST CAKE!
MY WHAT?
PSST! SHE SLAVED OVER IT ALL DAY..

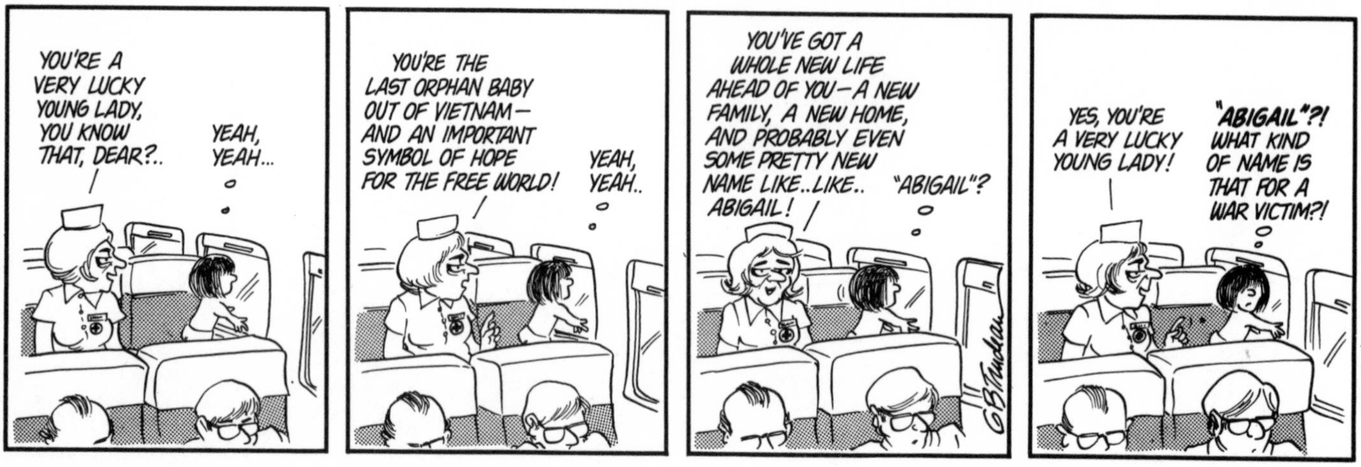
YOU'RE A VERY LUCKY YOUNG LADY, YOU KNOW THAT, DEAR?..
YEAH, YEAH...
YOU'RE THE LAST ORPHAN BABY OUT OF VIETNAM— AND AN IMPORTANT SYMBOL OF HOPE FOR THE FREE WORLD!
YEAH, YEAH..
YOU'VE GOT A WHOLE NEW LIFE AHEAD OF YOU—A NEW FAMILY, A NEW HOME, AND PROBABLY EVEN SOME PRETTY NEW NAME LIKE..LIKE.. ABIGAIL!
"ABIGAIL"?
YES, YOU'RE A VERY LUCKY YOUNG LADY!
"ABIGAIL"?! WHAT KIND OF NAME IS THAT FOR A WAR VICTIM?!

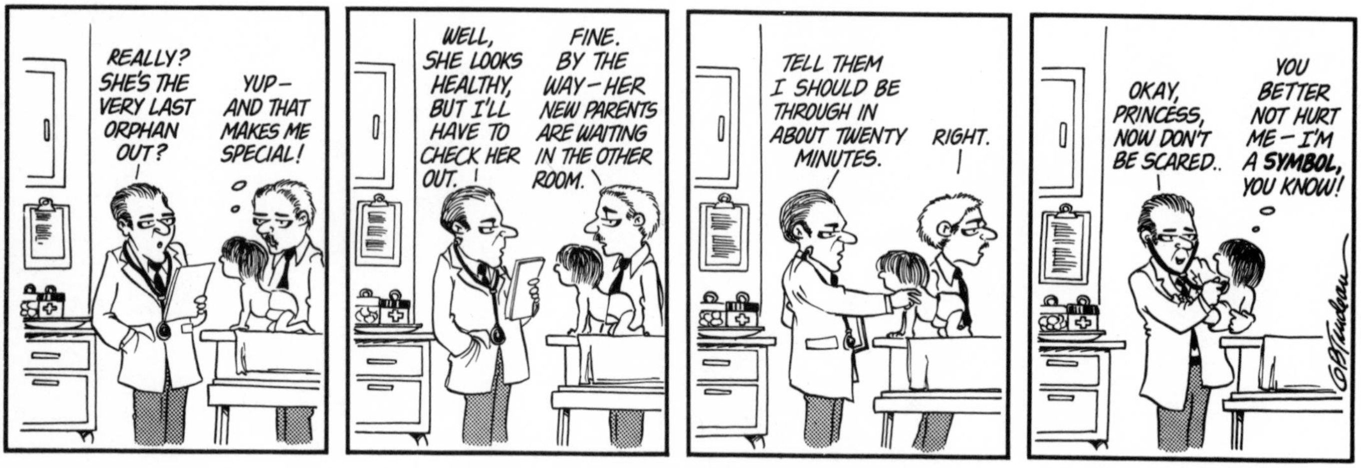
REALLY? SHE'S THE VERY LAST ORPHAN OUT?
YUP— AND THAT MAKES ME SPECIAL!
WELL, SHE LOOKS HEALTHY, BUT I'LL HAVE TO CHECK HER OUT.
FINE. BY THE WAY—HER NEW PARENTS ARE WAITING IN THE OTHER ROOM.
TELL THEM I SHOULD BE THROUGH IN ABOUT TWENTY MINUTES.
RIGHT.
OKAY, PRINCESS, NOW DON'T BE SCARED..
YOU BETTER NOT HURT ME—I'M A **SYMBOL**, YOU KNOW!

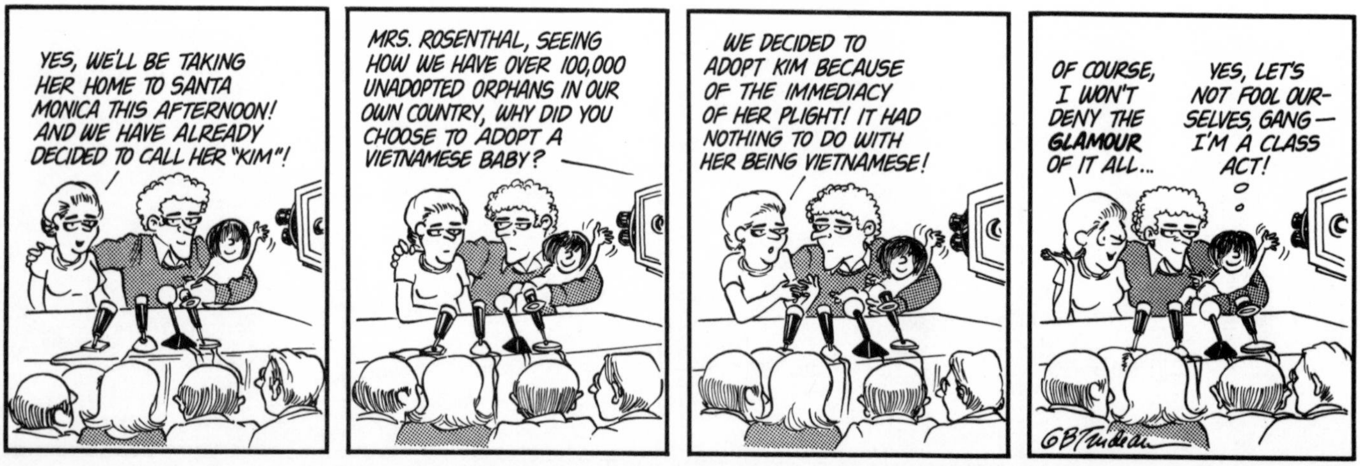
YES, WE'LL BE TAKING HER HOME TO SANTA MONICA THIS AFTERNOON! AND WE HAVE ALREADY DECIDED TO CALL HER "KIM"!
MRS. ROSENTHAL, SEEING HOW WE HAVE OVER 100,000 UNADOPTED ORPHANS IN OUR OWN COUNTRY, WHY DID YOU CHOOSE TO ADOPT A VIETNAMESE BABY?
WE DECIDED TO ADOPT KIM BECAUSE OF THE IMMEDIACY OF HER PLIGHT! IT HAD NOTHING TO DO WITH HER BEING VIETNAMESE!
OF COURSE, I WON'T DENY THE **GLAMOUR** OF IT ALL...
YES, LET'S NOT FOOL OURSELVES, GANG— I'M A CLASS ACT!

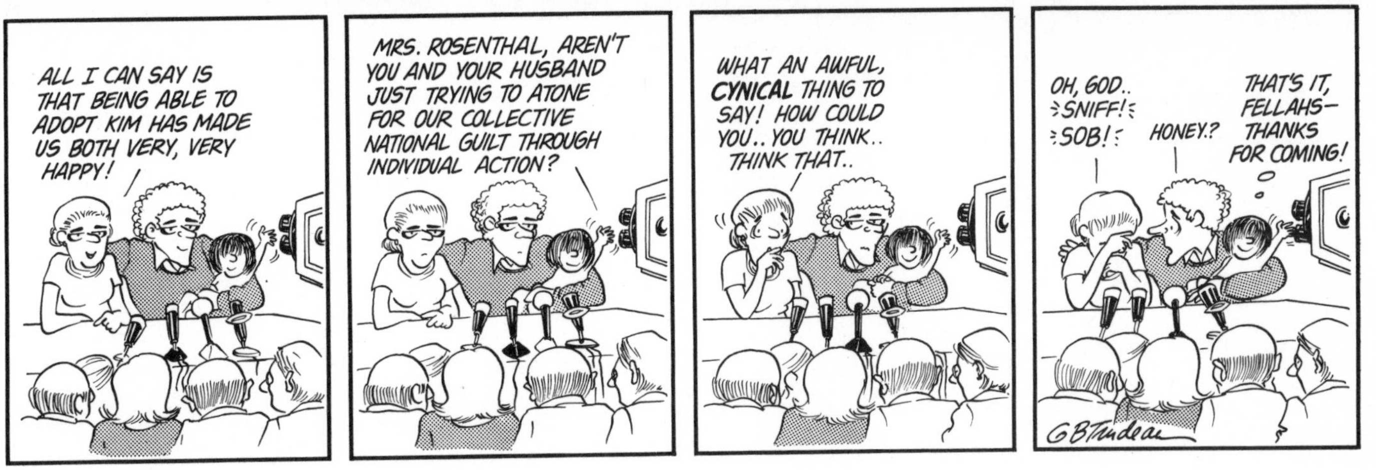
ALL I CAN SAY IS THAT BEING ABLE TO ADOPT KIM HAS MADE US BOTH VERY, VERY HAPPY!
MRS. ROSENTHAL, AREN'T YOU AND YOUR HUSBAND JUST TRYING TO ATONE FOR OUR COLLECTIVE NATIONAL GUILT THROUGH INDIVIDUAL ACTION?
WHAT AN AWFUL, CYNICAL THING TO SAY! HOW COULD YOU.. YOU THINK.. THINK THAT..
OH, GOD.. SNIFF! SOB!
HONEY.?
THAT'S IT, FELLAHS— THANKS FOR COMING!
GBTrudeau

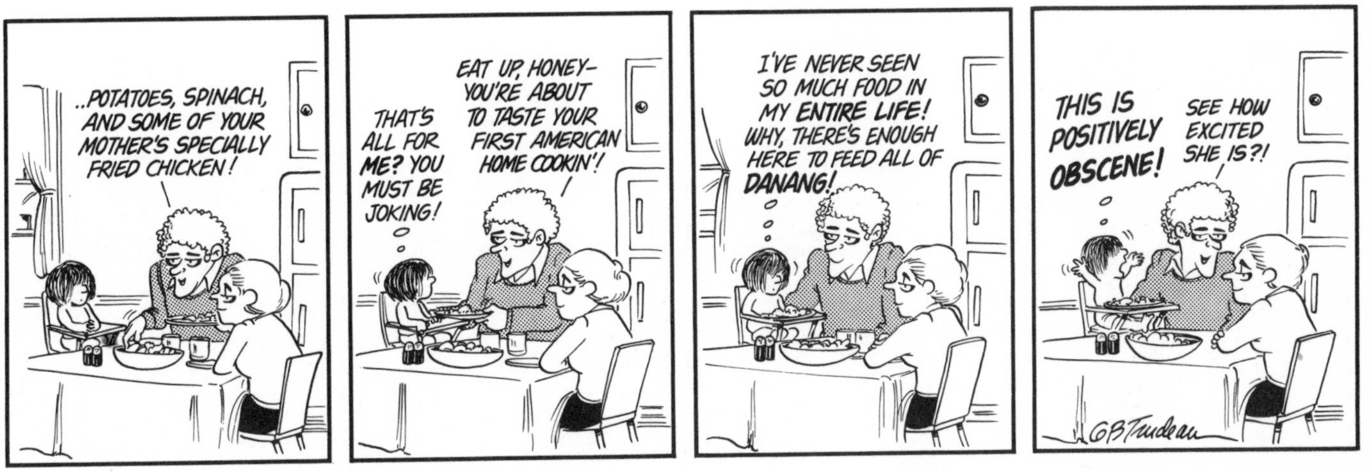
..POTATOES, SPINACH, AND SOME OF YOUR MOTHER'S SPECIALLY FRIED CHICKEN!
EAT UP, HONEY— YOU'RE ABOUT TO TASTE YOUR FIRST AMERICAN HOME COOKIN'!
THAT'S ALL FOR ME? YOU MUST BE JOKING!
I'VE NEVER SEEN SO MUCH FOOD IN MY ENTIRE LIFE! WHY, THERE'S ENOUGH HERE TO FEED ALL OF DANANG!
THIS IS POSITIVELY OBSCENE!
SEE HOW EXCITED SHE IS?!
GBTrudeau

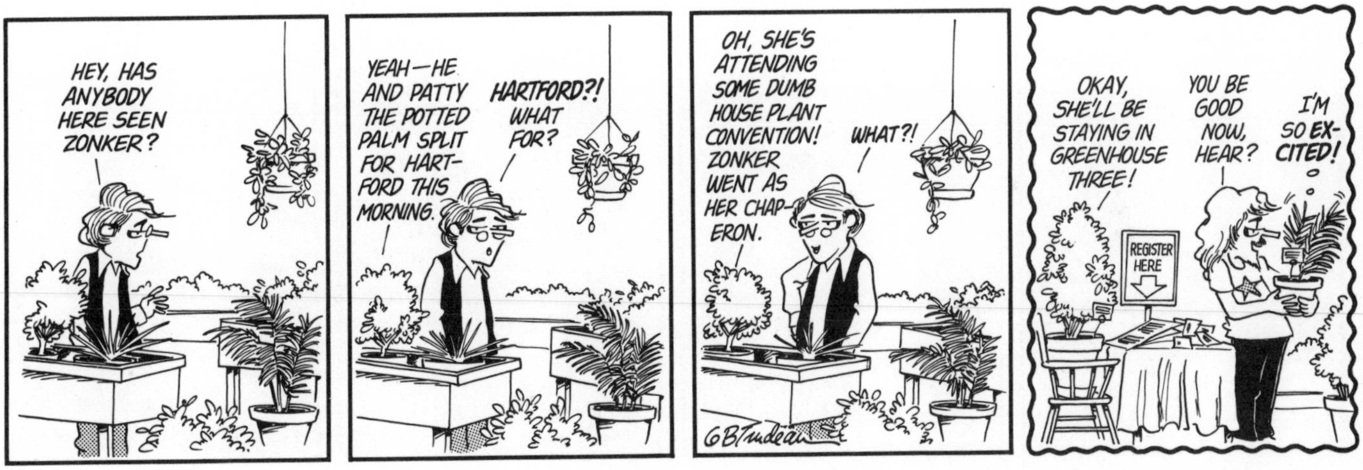
HEY, HAS ANYBODY HERE SEEN ZONKER?
YEAH—HE AND PATTY THE POTTED PALM SPLIT FOR HARTFORD THIS MORNING.
HARTFORD?! WHAT FOR?
OH, SHE'S ATTENDING SOME DUMB HOUSE PLANT CONVENTION! ZONKER WENT AS HER CHAPERON.
WHAT?!
GBTrudeau
OKAY, SHE'LL BE STAYING IN GREENHOUSE THREE!
REGISTER HERE
YOU BE GOOD NOW, HEAR?
I'M SO EXCITED!

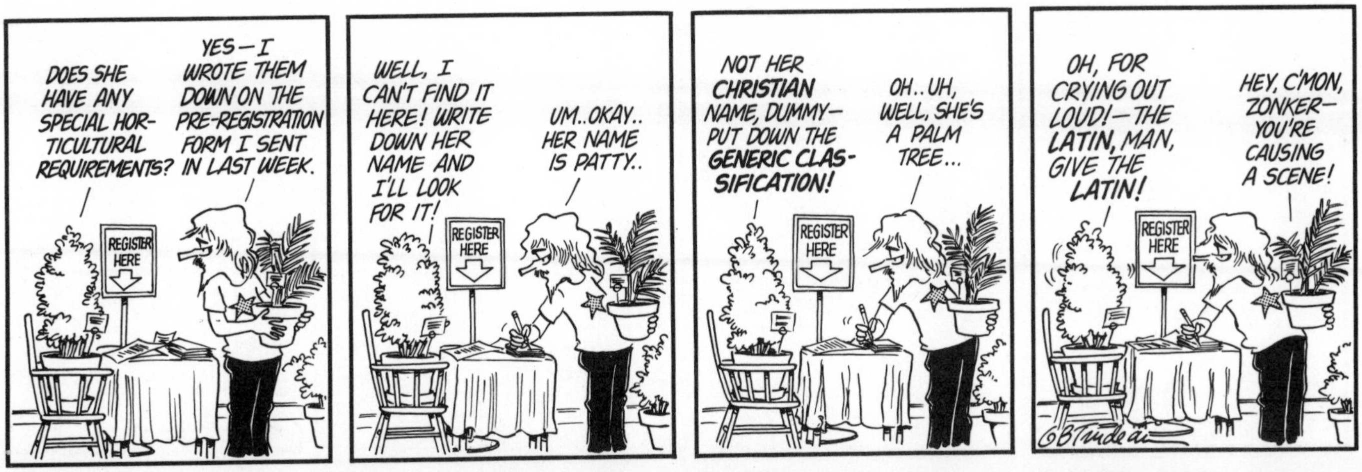
DOES SHE HAVE ANY SPECIAL HORTICULTURAL REQUIREMENTS?
YES—I WROTE THEM DOWN ON THE PRE-REGISTRATION FORM I SENT IN LAST WEEK.
REGISTER HERE
WELL, I CAN'T FIND IT HERE! WRITE DOWN HER NAME AND I'LL LOOK FOR IT!
UM..OKAY.. HER NAME IS PATTY..
REGISTER HERE
NOT HER CHRISTIAN NAME, DUMMY— PUT DOWN THE GENERIC CLASSIFICATION!
OH..UH, WELL, SHE'S A PALM TREE...
REGISTER HERE
OH, FOR CRYING OUT LOUD!—THE LATIN, MAN, GIVE THE LATIN!
HEY, C'MON, ZONKER— YOU'RE CAUSING A SCENE!
REGISTER HERE
GBTrudeau

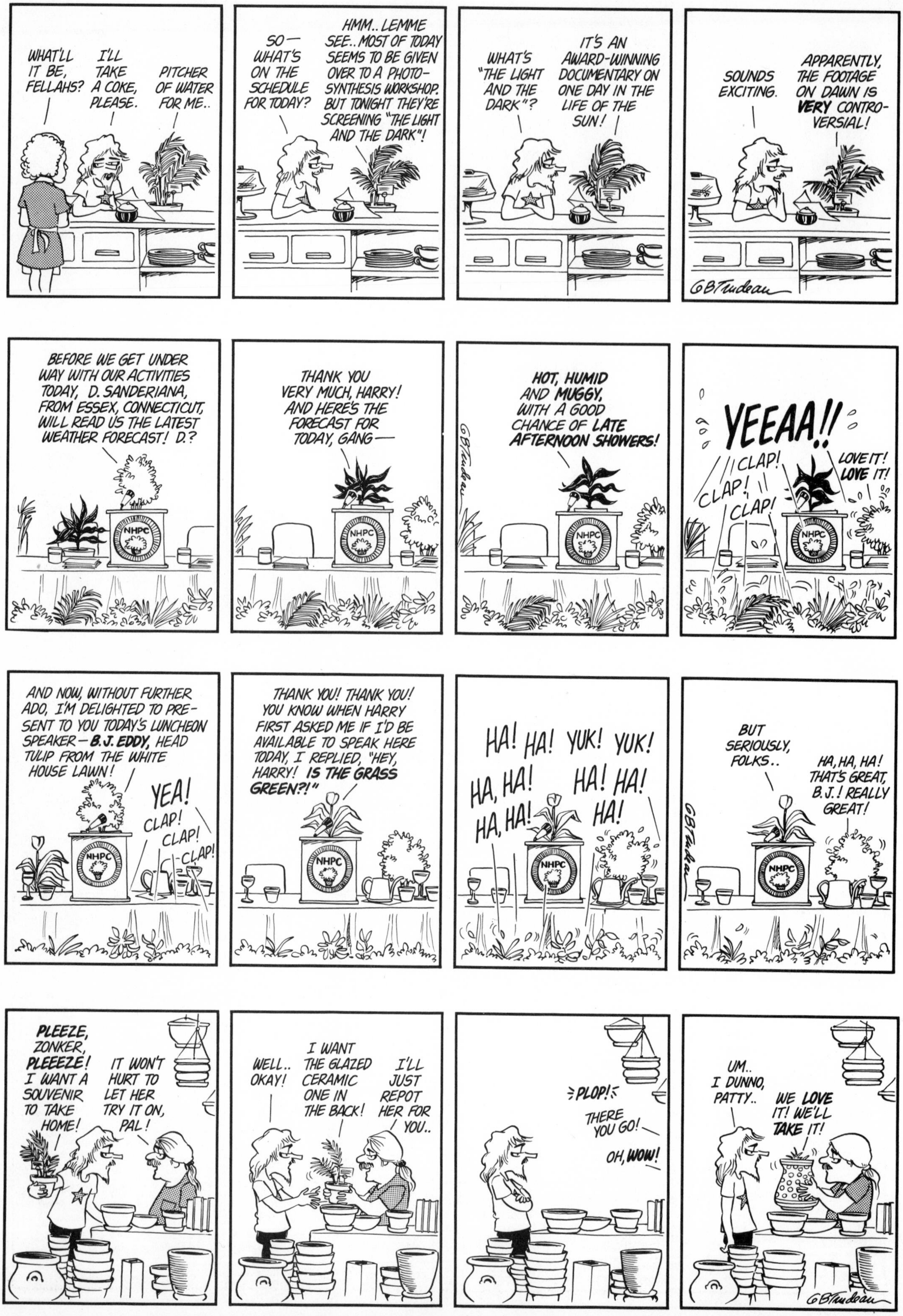
WHAT'LL IT BE, FELLAHS?
I'LL TAKE A COKE, PLEASE.
PITCHER OF WATER FOR ME..
SO— WHAT'S ON THE SCHEDULE FOR TODAY?
HMM.. LEMME SEE.. MOST OF TODAY SEEMS TO BE GIVEN OVER TO A PHOTO-SYNTHESIS WORKSHOP. BUT TONIGHT THEY'RE SCREENING "THE LIGHT AND THE DARK"!
WHAT'S "THE LIGHT AND THE DARK"?
IT'S AN AWARD-WINNING DOCUMENTARY ON ONE DAY IN THE LIFE OF THE SUN!
SOUNDS EXCITING.
APPARENTLY, THE FOOTAGE ON DAWN IS **VERY** CONTRO-VERSIAL!
GBTrudeau
BEFORE WE GET UNDER WAY WITH OUR ACTIVITIES TODAY, D. SANDERIANA, FROM ESSEX, CONNECTICUT, WILL READ US THE LATEST WEATHER FORECAST! D.?
NHPC
THANK YOU VERY MUCH, HARRY! AND HERE'S THE FORECAST FOR TODAY, GANG—
GBTrudeau
HOT, HUMID AND **MUGGY**, WITH A GOOD CHANCE OF **LATE AFTERNOON SHOWERS!**
YEEAA!!
CLAP! CLAP! CLAP!
LOVE IT! **LOVE** IT!
AND NOW, WITHOUT FURTHER ADO, I'M DELIGHTED TO PRE-SENT TO YOU TODAY'S LUNCHEON SPEAKER—**B. J. EDDY,** HEAD TULIP FROM THE WHITE HOUSE LAWN!
YEA!
CLAP! CLAP! CLAP!
THANK YOU! THANK YOU! YOU KNOW WHEN HARRY FIRST ASKED ME IF I'D BE AVAILABLE TO SPEAK HERE TODAY, I REPLIED, "HEY, HARRY! **IS THE GRASS GREEN?!"**
HA! HA! YUK! YUK!
HA, HA! HA, HA! HA! HA! HA!
GBTrudeau
BUT SERIOUSLY, FOLKS..
HA, HA, HA! THAT'S GREAT, B.J.! REALLY GREAT!
PLEEZE, ZONKER, **PLEEEZE!** I WANT A SOUVENIR TO TAKE HOME!
IT WON'T HURT TO LET HER TRY IT ON, PAL!
WELL.. OKAY!
I WANT THE GLAZED CERAMIC ONE IN THE BACK!
I'LL JUST REPOT HER FOR YOU..
PLOP!
THERE YOU GO!
OH, **WOW!**
UM.. I DUNNO, PATTY..
WE **LOVE** IT! WE'LL **TAKE** IT!
GBTrudeau

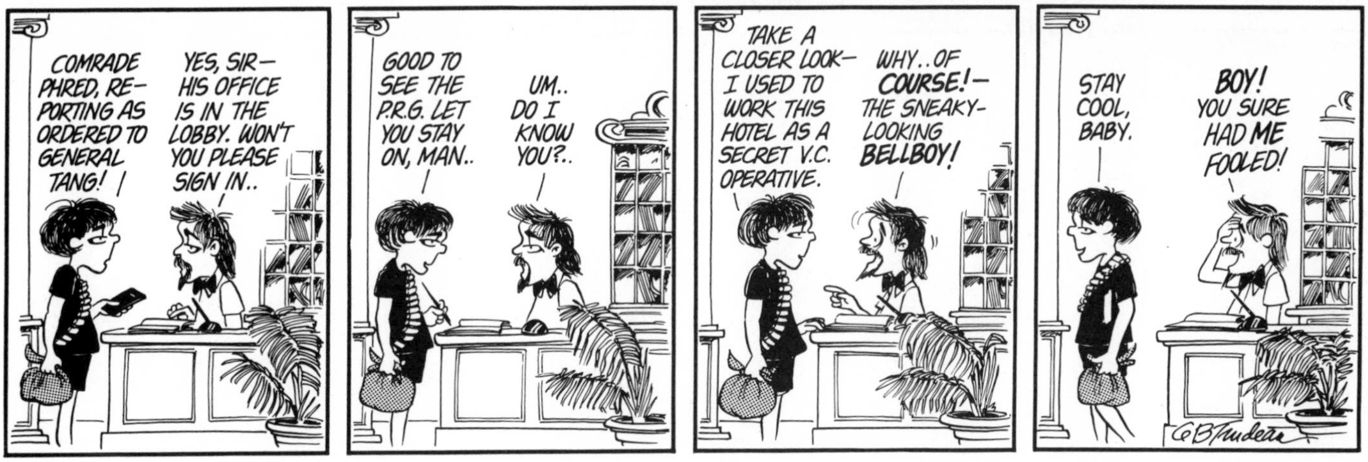
COMRADE PHRED, REPORTING AS ORDERED TO GENERAL TANG!
YES, SIR— HIS OFFICE IS IN THE LOBBY. WON'T YOU PLEASE SIGN IN..
GOOD TO SEE THE P.R.G. LET YOU STAY ON, MAN..
UM.. DO I KNOW YOU?..
TAKE A CLOSER LOOK— I USED TO WORK THIS HOTEL AS A SECRET V.C. OPERATIVE.
WHY..OF COURSE!— THE SNEAKY-LOOKING BELLBOY!
STAY COOL, BABY.
BOY! YOU SURE HAD ME FOOLED!
GBTrudeau

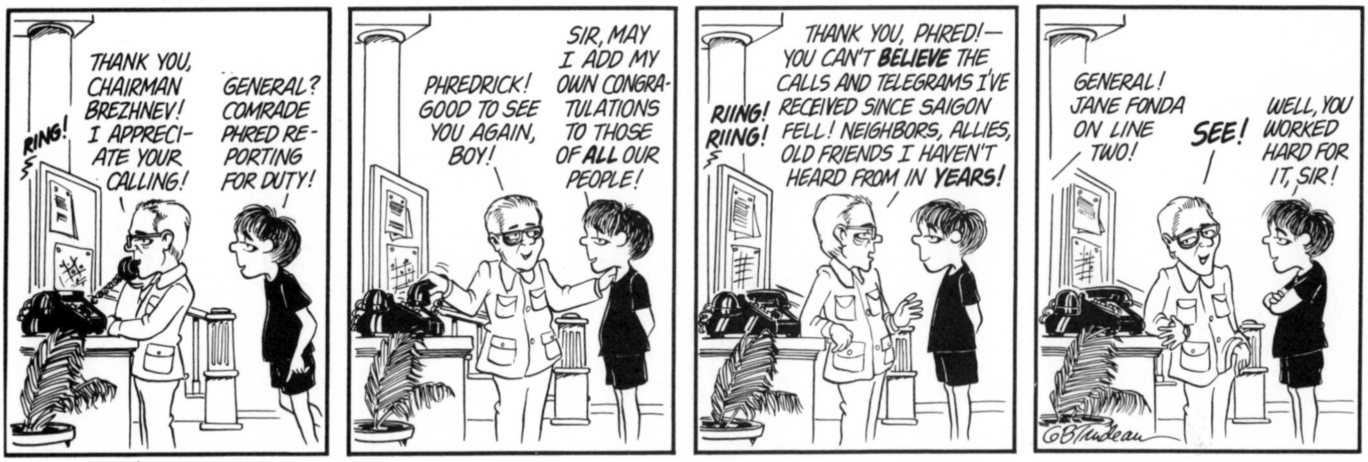
RING!
THANK YOU, CHAIRMAN BREZHNEV! I APPRECIATE YOUR CALLING!
GENERAL? COMRADE PHRED REPORTING FOR DUTY!
PHREDRICK! GOOD TO SEE YOU AGAIN, BOY!
SIR, MAY I ADD MY OWN CONGRATULATIONS TO THOSE OF ALL OUR PEOPLE!
RIING! RIING!
THANK YOU, PHRED!— YOU CAN'T BELIEVE THE CALLS AND TELEGRAMS I'VE RECEIVED SINCE SAIGON FELL! NEIGHBORS, ALLIES, OLD FRIENDS I HAVEN'T HEARD FROM IN YEARS!
GENERAL! JANE FONDA ON LINE TWO!
SEE!
WELL, YOU WORKED HARD FOR IT, SIR!
GBTrudeau

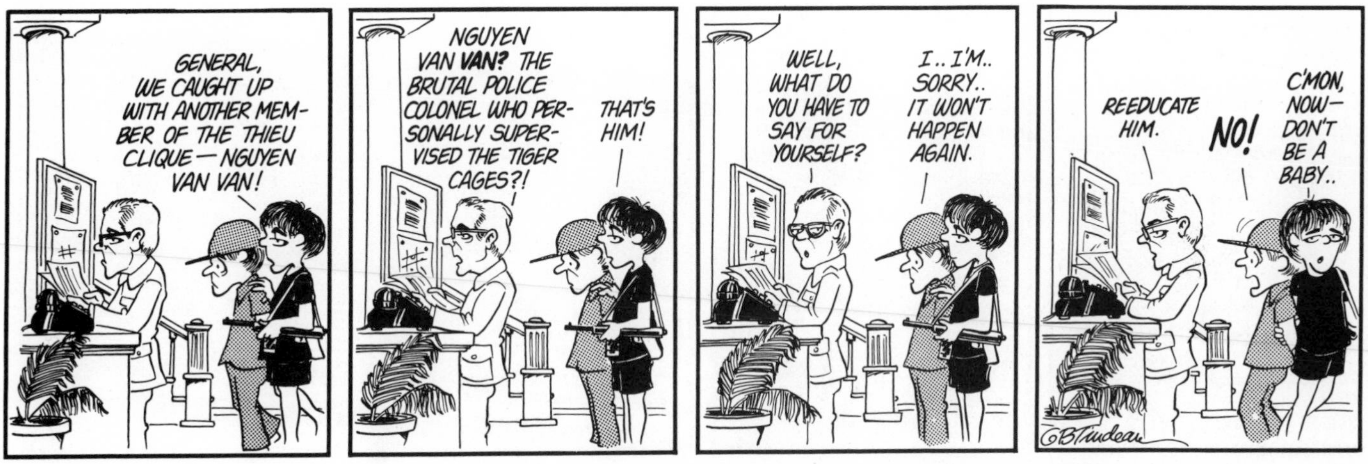
GENERAL, WE CAUGHT UP WITH ANOTHER MEMBER OF THE THIEU CLIQUE— NGUYEN VAN VAN!
NGUYEN VAN VAN? THE BRUTAL POLICE COLONEL WHO PERSONALLY SUPERVISED THE TIGER CAGES?!
THAT'S HIM!
WELL, WHAT DO YOU HAVE TO SAY FOR YOURSELF?
I.. I'M.. SORRY.. IT WON'T HAPPEN AGAIN.
REEDUCATE HIM.
NO!
C'MON, NOW— DON'T BE A BABY..
GBTrudeau

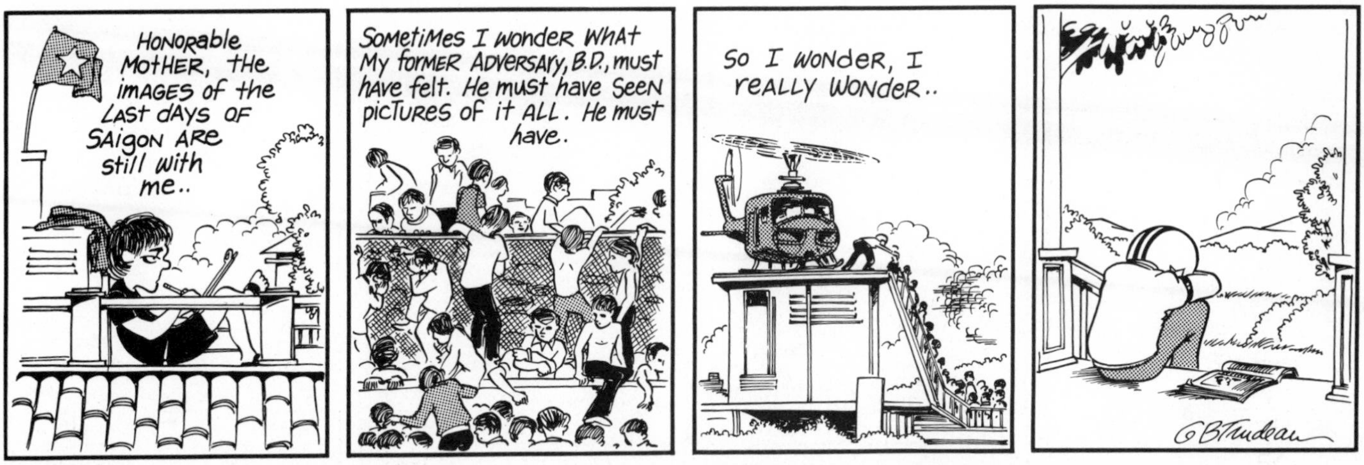
Honorable Mother, the images of the last days of Saigon are still with me..
Sometimes I wonder what my former adversary, B.D., must have felt. He must have seen pictures of it ALL. He must have.
So I wonder, I really wonder..
GBTrudeau

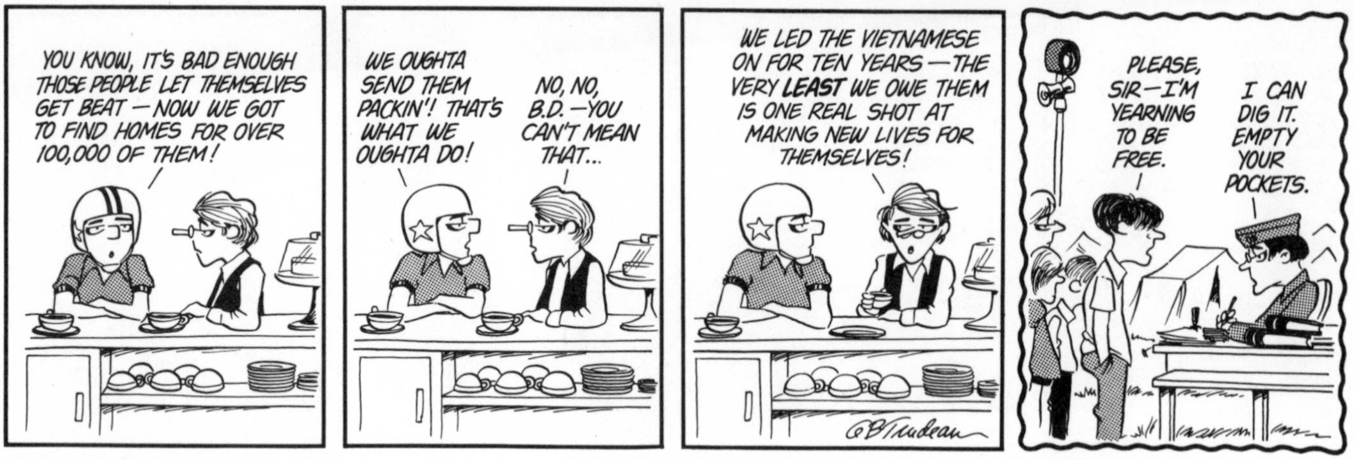
YOU KNOW, IT'S BAD ENOUGH THOSE PEOPLE LET THEMSELVES GET BEAT — NOW WE GOT TO FIND HOMES FOR OVER 100,000 OF THEM!
WE OUGHTA SEND THEM PACKIN'! THAT'S WHAT WE OUGHTA DO!
NO, NO, B.D.—YOU CAN'T MEAN THAT...
WE LED THE VIETNAMESE ON FOR TEN YEARS — THE VERY LEAST WE OWE THEM IS ONE REAL SHOT AT MAKING NEW LIVES FOR THEMSELVES!
PLEASE, SIR—I'M YEARNING TO BE FREE.
I CAN DIG IT. EMPTY YOUR POCKETS.

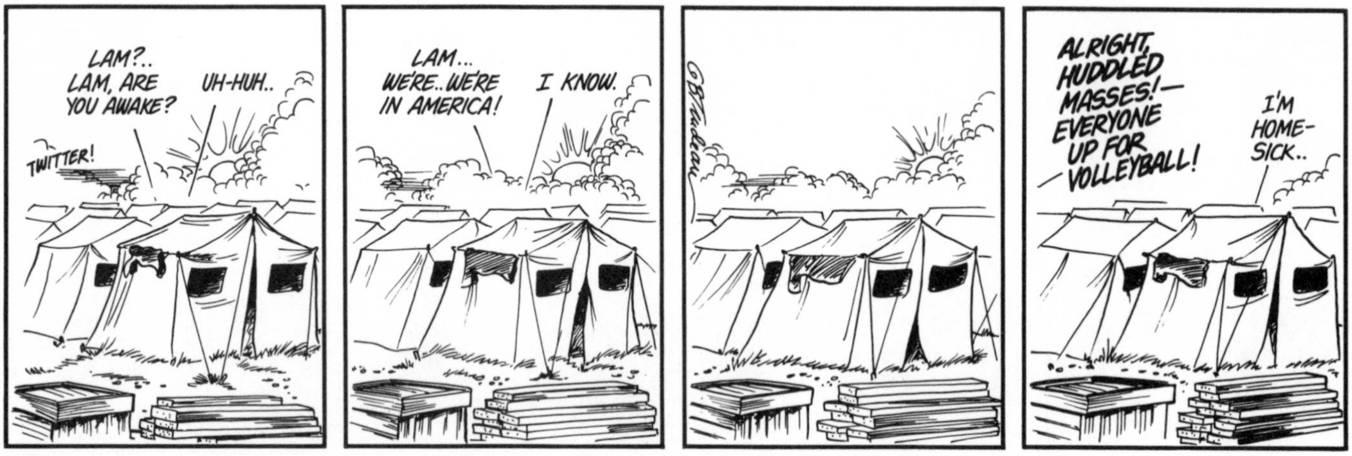
LAM?.. LAM, ARE YOU AWAKE?
UH-HUH..
TWITTER!
LAM... WE'RE.. WE'RE IN AMERICA!
I KNOW.
ALRIGHT, HUDDLED MASSES!— EVERYONE UP FOR VOLLEYBALL!
I'M HOME-SICK..

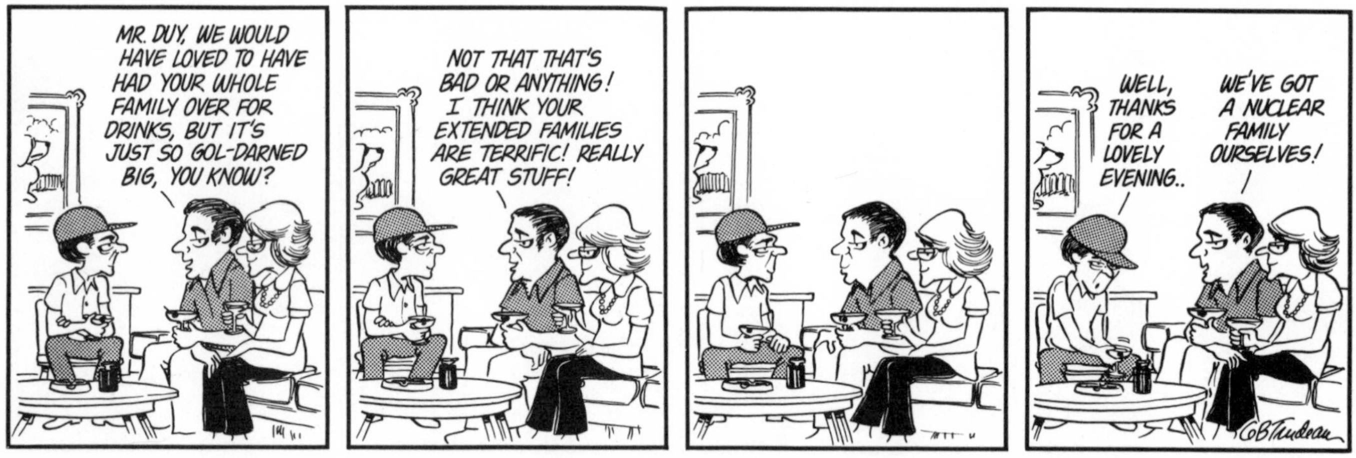
MR. DUY, WE WOULD HAVE LOVED TO HAVE HAD YOUR WHOLE FAMILY OVER FOR DRINKS, BUT IT'S JUST SO GOL-DARNED BIG, YOU KNOW?
NOT THAT THAT'S BAD OR ANYTHING! I THINK YOUR EXTENDED FAMILIES ARE TERRIFIC! REALLY GREAT STUFF!
WELL, THANKS FOR A LOVELY EVENING..
WE'VE GOT A NUCLEAR FAMILY OURSELVES!

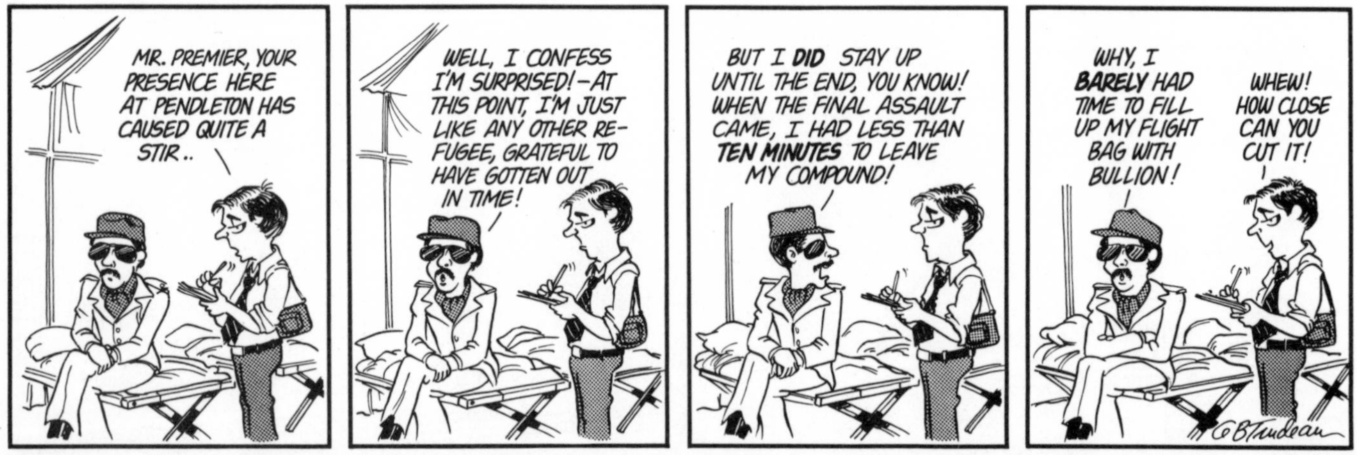
MR. PREMIER, YOUR PRESENCE HERE AT PENDLETON HAS CAUSED QUITE A STIR..
WELL, I CONFESS I'M SURPRISED!—AT THIS POINT, I'M JUST LIKE ANY OTHER RE-FUGEE, GRATEFUL TO HAVE GOTTEN OUT IN TIME!
BUT I DID STAY UP UNTIL THE END, YOU KNOW! WHEN THE FINAL ASSAULT CAME, I HAD LESS THAN TEN MINUTES TO LEAVE MY COMPOUND!
WHY, I BARELY HAD TIME TO FILL UP MY FLIGHT BAG WITH BULLION!
WHEW! HOW CLOSE CAN YOU CUT IT!

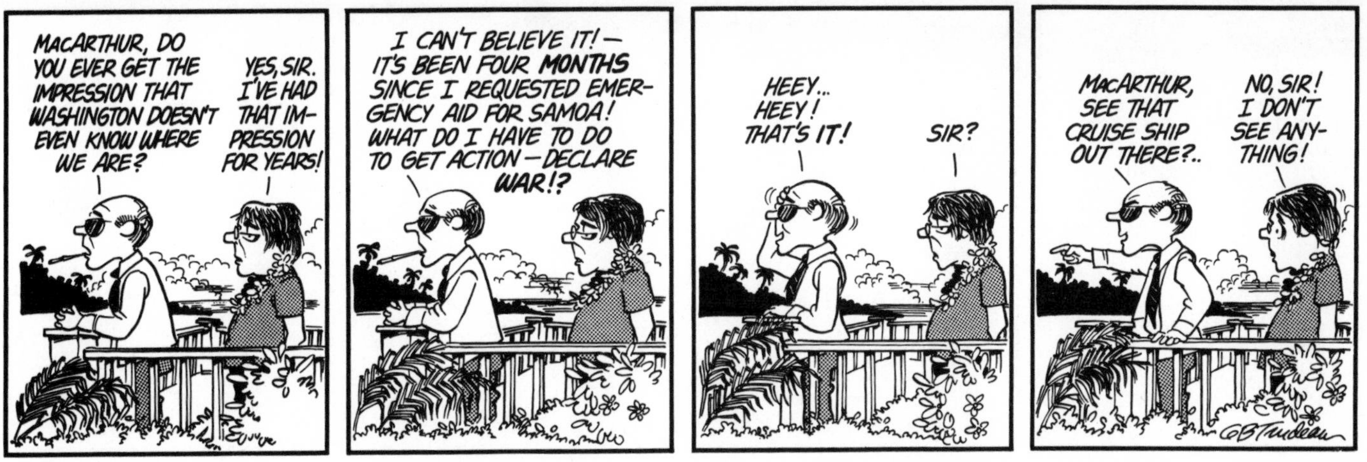
MacARTHUR, DO YOU EVER GET THE IMPRESSION THAT WASHINGTON DOESN'T EVEN KNOW WHERE WE ARE?
YES, SIR. I'VE HAD THAT IMPRESSION FOR YEARS!
I CAN'T BELIEVE IT!—IT'S BEEN FOUR **MONTHS** SINCE I REQUESTED EMERGENCY AID FOR SAMOA! WHAT DO I HAVE TO DO TO GET ACTION—DECLARE **WAR!?**
HEEY... HEEY! THAT'S **IT!**
SIR?
MacARTHUR, SEE THAT CRUISE SHIP OUT THERE?..
NO, SIR! I DON'T SEE ANYTHING!
GBTrudeau

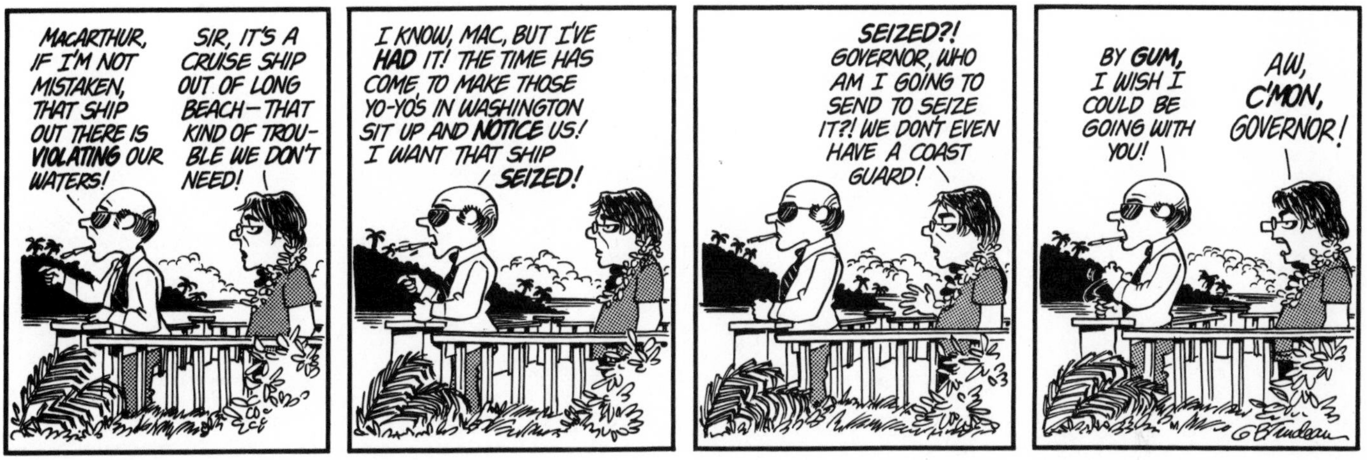
MacARTHUR, IF I'M NOT MISTAKEN, THAT SHIP OUT THERE IS **VIOLATING** OUR WATERS!
SIR, IT'S A CRUISE SHIP OUT OF LONG BEACH—THAT KIND OF TROUBLE WE DON'T NEED!
I KNOW, MAC, BUT I'VE **HAD** IT! THE TIME HAS COME TO MAKE THOSE YO-YO'S IN WASHINGTON SIT UP AND **NOTICE** US! I WANT THAT SHIP **SEIZED!**
SEIZED?! GOVERNOR, WHO AM I GOING TO SEND TO SEIZE IT?! WE DON'T EVEN HAVE A COAST GUARD!
BY **GUM**, I WISH I COULD BE GOING WITH YOU!
AW, **C'MON**, GOVERNOR!
GBTrudeau

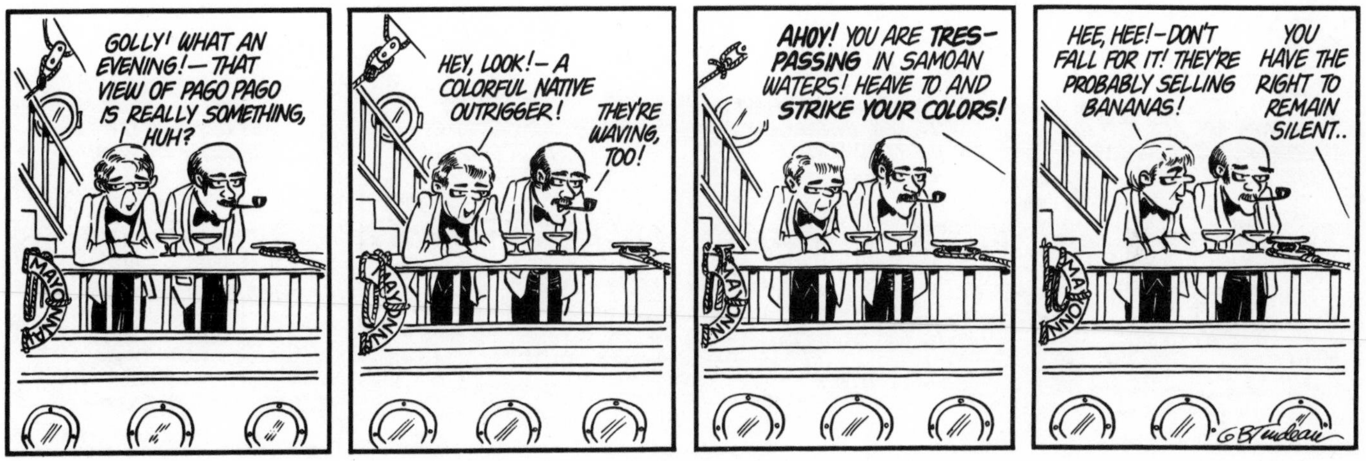
GOLLY! WHAT AN EVENING!—THAT VIEW OF PAGO PAGO IS REALLY SOMETHING, HUH?
HEY, LOOK!—A COLORFUL NATIVE OUTRIGGER!
THEY'RE WAVING, TOO!
AHOY! YOU ARE **TRESPASSING** IN SAMOAN WATERS! HEAVE TO AND **STRIKE YOUR COLORS!**
HEE, HEE!—DON'T FALL FOR IT! THEY'RE PROBABLY SELLING BANANAS!
YOU HAVE THE RIGHT TO REMAIN SILENT..
GBTrudeau

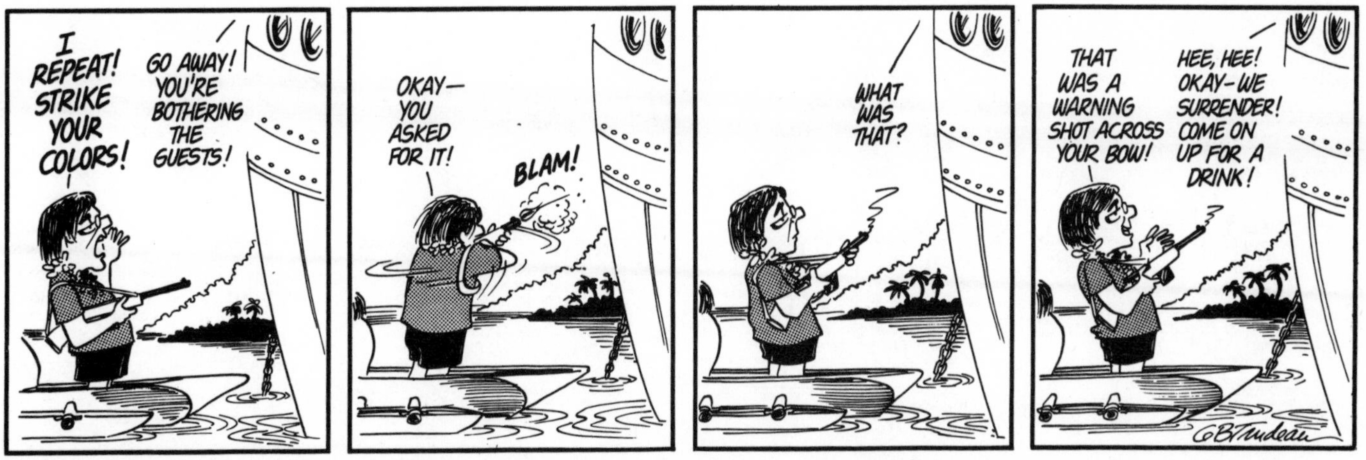
I REPEAT! STRIKE YOUR COLORS!
GO AWAY! YOU'RE BOTHERING THE GUESTS!
OKAY—YOU ASKED FOR IT!
BLAM!
WHAT WAS THAT?
THAT WAS A WARNING SHOT ACROSS YOUR BOW!
HEE, HEE! OKAY—WE SURRENDER! COME ON UP FOR A DRINK!
GBTrudeau

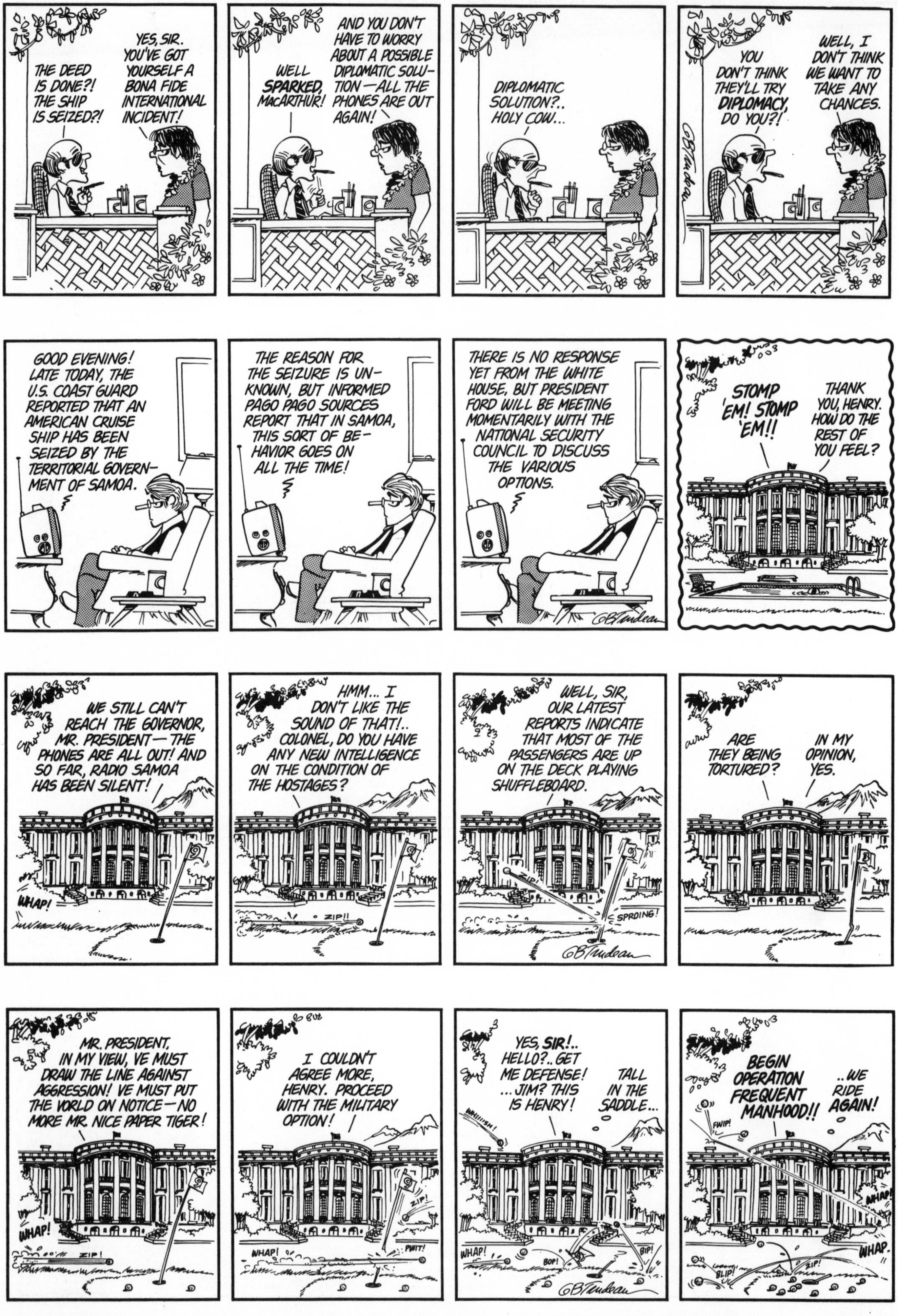

THE DEED IS DONE?! THE SHIP IS SEIZED?!
YES, SIR. YOU'VE GOT YOURSELF A BONA FIDE INTERNATIONAL INCIDENT!
WELL **SPARKED,** MacARTHUR!
AND YOU DON'T HAVE TO WORRY ABOUT A POSSIBLE DIPLOMATIC SOLUTION—ALL THE PHONES ARE OUT AGAIN!
DIPLOMATIC SOLUTION?.. HOLY COW...
YOU DON'T THINK THEY'LL TRY **DIPLOMACY,** DO YOU?!
WELL, I DON'T THINK WE WANT TO TAKE ANY CHANCES.
GOOD EVENING! LATE TODAY, THE U.S. COAST GUARD REPORTED THAT AN AMERICAN CRUISE SHIP HAS BEEN SEIZED BY THE TERRITORIAL GOVERNMENT OF SAMOA.
THE REASON FOR THE SEIZURE IS UNKNOWN, BUT INFORMED PAGO PAGO SOURCES REPORT THAT IN SAMOA, THIS SORT OF BEHAVIOR GOES ON ALL THE TIME!
THERE IS NO RESPONSE YET FROM THE WHITE HOUSE, BUT PRESIDENT FORD WILL BE MEETING MOMENTARILY WITH THE NATIONAL SECURITY COUNCIL TO DISCUSS THE VARIOUS OPTIONS.
STOMP 'EM! STOMP 'EM!!
THANK YOU, HENRY. HOW DO THE REST OF YOU FEEL?
WE STILL CAN'T REACH THE GOVERNOR, MR. PRESIDENT—THE PHONES ARE ALL OUT! AND SO FAR, RADIO SAMOA HAS BEEN SILENT!
WHAP!
HMM... I DON'T LIKE THE SOUND OF THAT!.. COLONEL, DO YOU HAVE ANY NEW INTELLIGENCE ON THE CONDITION OF THE HOSTAGES?
ZIP!!
WELL, SIR, OUR LATEST REPORTS INDICATE THAT MOST OF THE PASSENGERS ARE UP ON THE DECK PLAYING SHUFFLEBOARD.
SPROING!
ARE THEY BEING TORTURED?
IN MY OPINION, YES.
MR. PRESIDENT, IN MY VIEW, VE MUST DRAW THE LINE AGAINST AGGRESSION! VE MUST PUT THE VORLD ON NOTICE—NO MORE MR. NICE PAPER TIGER!
WHAP!
ZIP!
I COULDN'T AGREE MORE, HENRY. PROCEED WITH THE MILITARY OPTION!
ZIP!
WHAP!
PWIT!
YES, **SIR!**.. HELLO?.. GET ME DEFENSE! ... JIM? THIS IS HENRY!
TALL IN THE SADDLE...
WHAP!
BOP!
BIP!
BEGIN OPERATION FREQUENT MANHOOD!!
.. WE RIDE AGAIN!
FWIP!
WHAP!
WHAP.
BLIP!
ZIP!

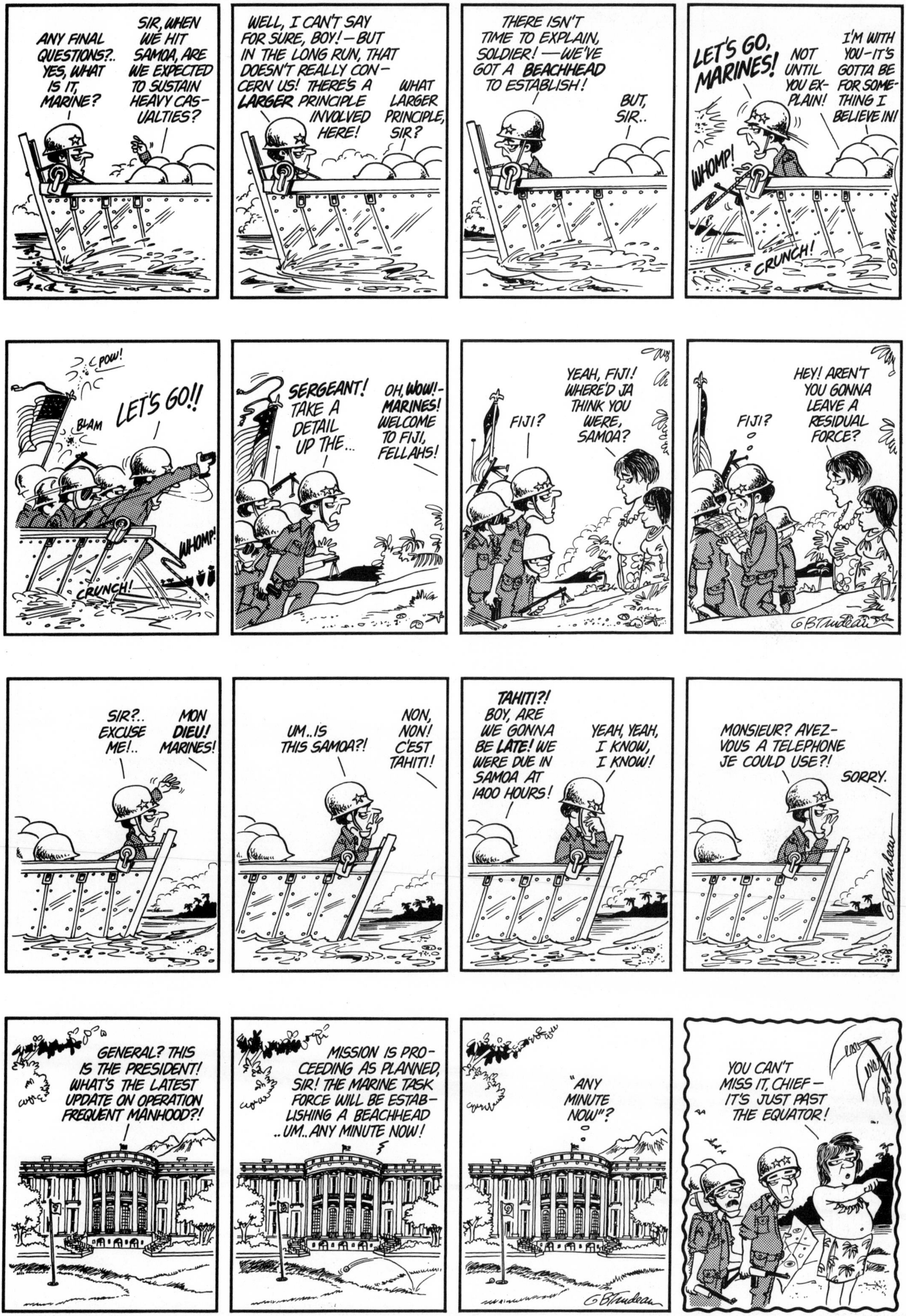

ANY FINAL QUESTIONS?.. YES, WHAT IS IT, MARINE?
SIR, WHEN WE HIT SAMOA, ARE WE EXPECTED TO SUSTAIN HEAVY CASUALTIES?
WELL, I CAN'T SAY FOR SURE, BOY! — BUT IN THE LONG RUN, THAT DOESN'T REALLY CONCERN US! THERE'S A LARGER PRINCIPLE INVOLVED HERE!
WHAT LARGER PRINCIPLE, SIR?
THERE ISN'T TIME TO EXPLAIN, SOLDIER! — WE'VE GOT A BEACHHEAD TO ESTABLISH!
BUT, SIR..
LET'S GO, MARINES!
NOT UNTIL YOU EXPLAIN!
I'M WITH YOU — IT'S GOTTA BE FOR SOMETHING I BELIEVE IN!
WHOMP!
CRUNCH!
POW!
BLAM
LET'S GO!!
WHOMP!
CRUNCH!
SERGEANT! TAKE A DETAIL UP THE...
OH, WOW! — MARINES! WELCOME TO FIJI, FELLAHS!
FIJI?
YEAH, FIJI! WHERE'D JA THINK YOU WERE, SAMOA?
FIJI?
HEY! AREN'T YOU GONNA LEAVE A RESIDUAL FORCE?
SIR?.. EXCUSE ME!..
MON DIEU! MARINES!
UM..IS THIS SAMOA?!
NON, NON! C'EST TAHITI!
TAHITI?! BOY, ARE WE GONNA BE LATE! WE WERE DUE IN SAMOA AT 1400 HOURS!
YEAH, YEAH, I KNOW, I KNOW!
MONSIEUR? AVEZ-VOUS A TELEPHONE JE COULD USE?!
SORRY.
GENERAL? THIS IS THE PRESIDENT! WHAT'S THE LATEST UPDATE ON OPERATION FREQUENT MANHOOD?!
MISSION IS PROCEEDING AS PLANNED, SIR! THE MARINE TASK FORCE WILL BE ESTABLISHING A BEACHHEAD ..UM.. ANY MINUTE NOW!
"ANY MINUTE NOW"?
YOU CAN'T MISS IT, CHIEF — IT'S JUST PAST THE EQUATOR!

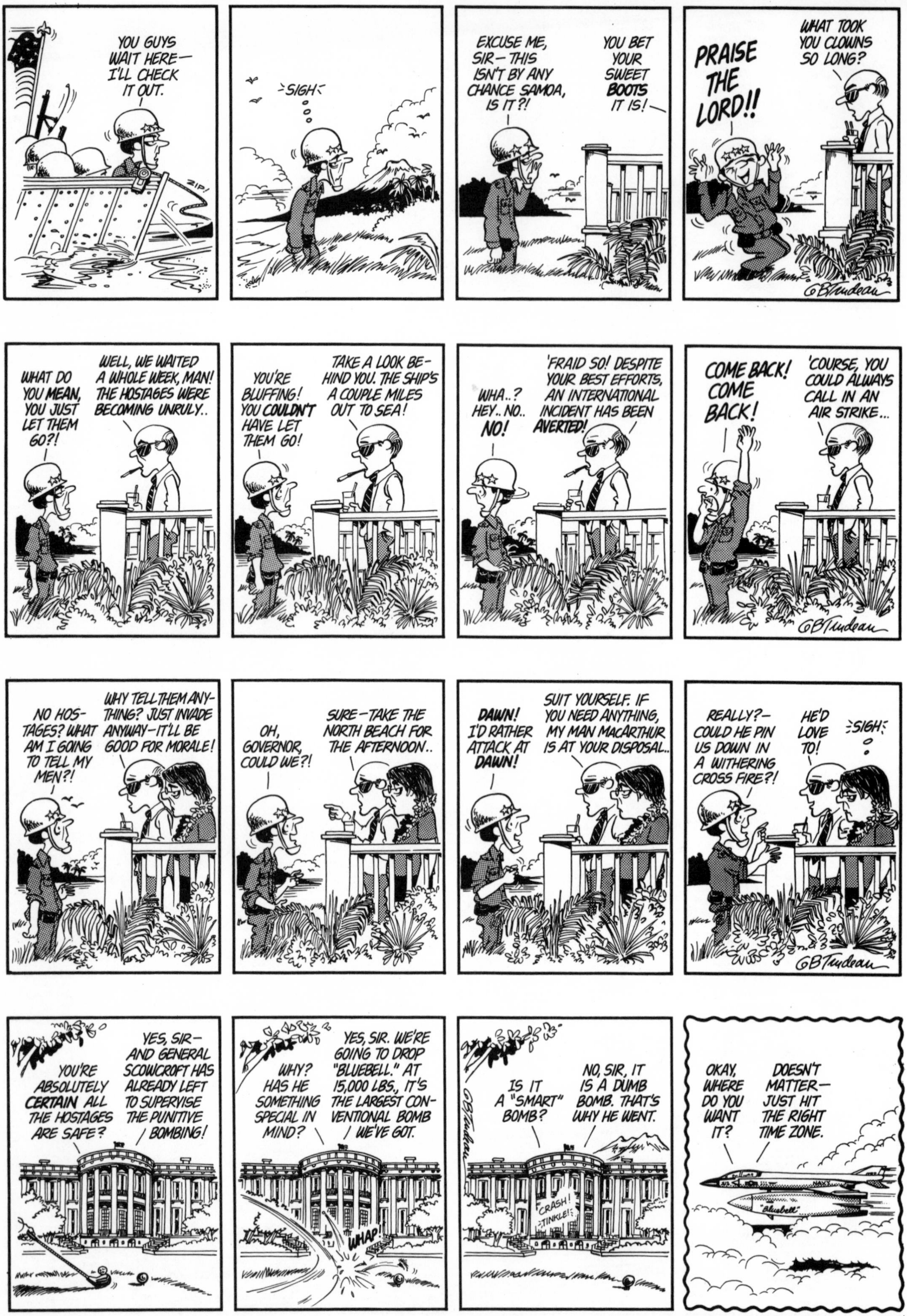
YOU GUYS WAIT HERE— I'LL CHECK IT OUT.
ZIP!
SIGH
EXCUSE ME, SIR— THIS ISN'T BY ANY CHANCE SAMOA, IS IT?!
YOU BET YOUR SWEET BOOTS IT IS!
PRAISE THE LORD!!
WHAT TOOK YOU CLOWNS SO LONG?
WHAT DO YOU MEAN, YOU JUST LET THEM GO?!
WELL, WE WAITED A WHOLE WEEK, MAN! THE HOSTAGES WERE BECOMING UNRULY..
YOU'RE BLUFFING! YOU COULDN'T HAVE LET THEM GO!
TAKE A LOOK BEHIND YOU. THE SHIP'S A COUPLE MILES OUT TO SEA!
WHA..? HEY.. NO.. NO!
'FRAID SO! DESPITE YOUR BEST EFFORTS, AN INTERNATIONAL INCIDENT HAS BEEN AVERTED!
COME BACK! COME BACK!
'COURSE, YOU COULD ALWAYS CALL IN AN AIR STRIKE...
NO HOSTAGES? WHAT AM I GOING TO TELL MY MEN?!
WHY TELL THEM ANYTHING? JUST INVADE ANYWAY—IT'LL BE GOOD FOR MORALE!
OH, GOVERNOR, COULD WE?!
SURE—TAKE THE NORTH BEACH FOR THE AFTERNOON..
DAWN! I'D RATHER ATTACK AT DAWN!
SUIT YOURSELF. IF YOU NEED ANYTHING, MY MAN MACARTHUR IS AT YOUR DISPOSAL..
REALLY?— COULD HE PIN US DOWN IN A WITHERING CROSS FIRE?!
HE'D LOVE TO!
SIGH
YOU'RE ABSOLUTELY CERTAIN ALL THE HOSTAGES ARE SAFE?
YES, SIR— AND GENERAL SCOWCROFT HAS ALREADY LEFT TO SUPERVISE THE PUNITIVE BOMBING!
WHY? HAS HE SOMETHING SPECIAL IN MIND?
YES, SIR. WE'RE GOING TO DROP "BLUEBELL." AT 15,000 LBS., IT'S THE LARGEST CONVENTIONAL BOMB WE'VE GOT.
WHAP!
IS IT A "SMART" BOMB?
NO, SIR, IT IS A DUMB BOMB. THAT'S WHY HE WENT.
CRASH! TINKLE!
OKAY, WHERE DO YOU WANT IT?
DOESN'T MATTER— JUST HIT THE RIGHT TIME ZONE.
NAVY
"bluebell"

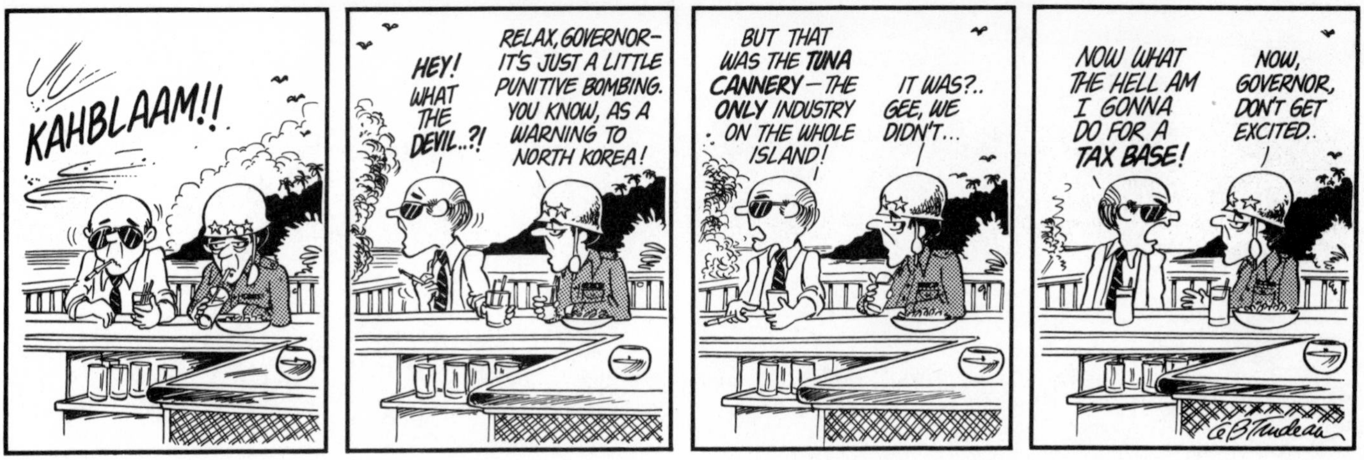
KAHBLAAM!!
HEY! WHAT THE DEVIL..?!
RELAX, GOVERNOR—IT'S JUST A LITTLE PUNITIVE BOMBING. YOU KNOW, AS A WARNING TO NORTH KOREA!
BUT THAT WAS THE TUNA CANNERY—THE ONLY INDUSTRY ON THE WHOLE ISLAND!
IT WAS?.. GEE, WE DIDN'T...
NOW WHAT THE HELL AM I GONNA DO FOR A TAX BASE!
NOW, GOVERNOR, DON'T GET EXCITED..
GBTrudeau

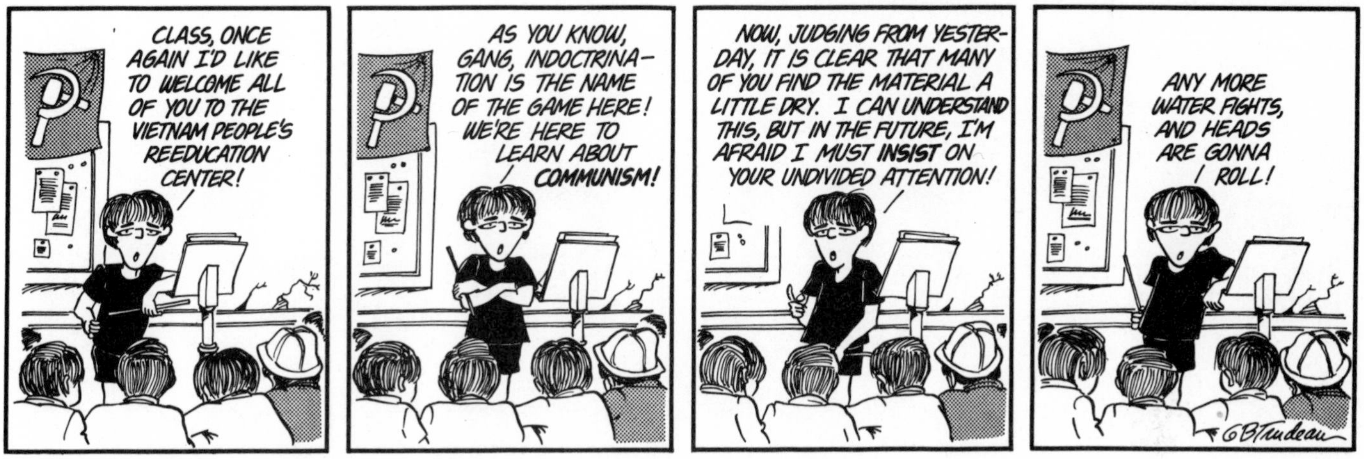
CLASS, ONCE AGAIN I'D LIKE TO WELCOME ALL OF YOU TO THE VIETNAM PEOPLE'S REEDUCATION CENTER!
AS YOU KNOW, GANG, INDOCTRINATION IS THE NAME OF THE GAME HERE! WE'RE HERE TO LEARN ABOUT COMMUNISM!
NOW, JUDGING FROM YESTERDAY, IT IS CLEAR THAT MANY OF YOU FIND THE MATERIAL A LITTLE DRY. I CAN UNDERSTAND THIS, BUT IN THE FUTURE, I'M AFRAID I MUST INSIST ON YOUR UNDIVIDED ATTENTION!
ANY MORE WATER FIGHTS, AND HEADS ARE GONNA ROLL!
GBTrudeau

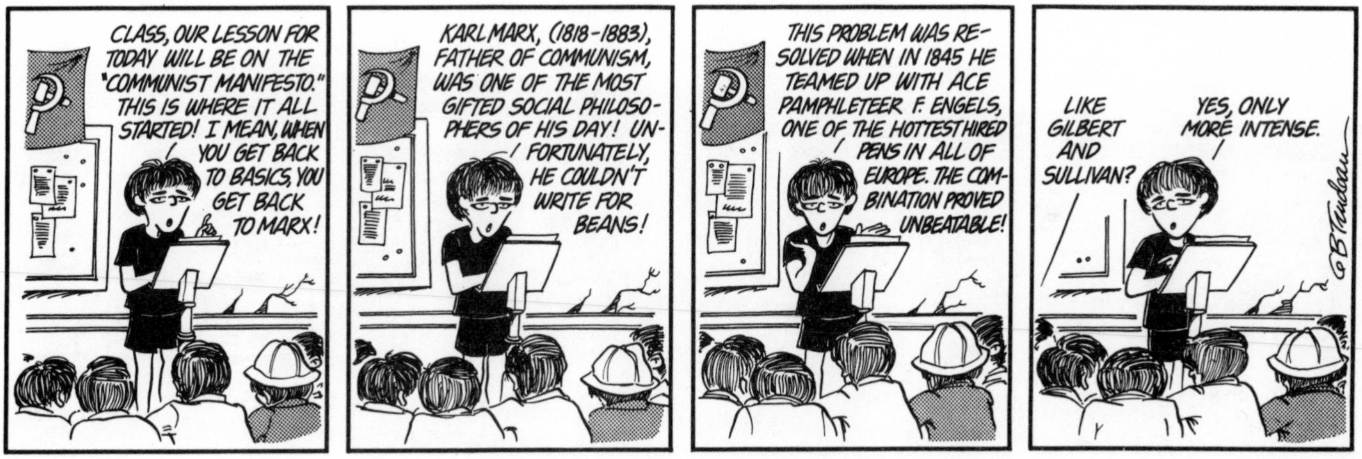
CLASS, OUR LESSON FOR TODAY WILL BE ON THE "COMMUNIST MANIFESTO." THIS IS WHERE IT ALL STARTED! I MEAN, WHEN YOU GET BACK TO BASICS, YOU GET BACK TO MARX!
KARL MARX, (1818-1883), FATHER OF COMMUNISM, WAS ONE OF THE MOST GIFTED SOCIAL PHILOSOPHERS OF HIS DAY! UNFORTUNATELY, HE COULDN'T WRITE FOR BEANS!
THIS PROBLEM WAS RESOLVED WHEN IN 1845 HE TEAMED UP WITH ACE PAMPHLETEER F. ENGELS, ONE OF THE HOTTEST HIRED PENS IN ALL OF EUROPE. THE COMBINATION PROVED UNBEATABLE!
LIKE GILBERT AND SULLIVAN?
YES, ONLY MORE INTENSE.
GBTrudeau

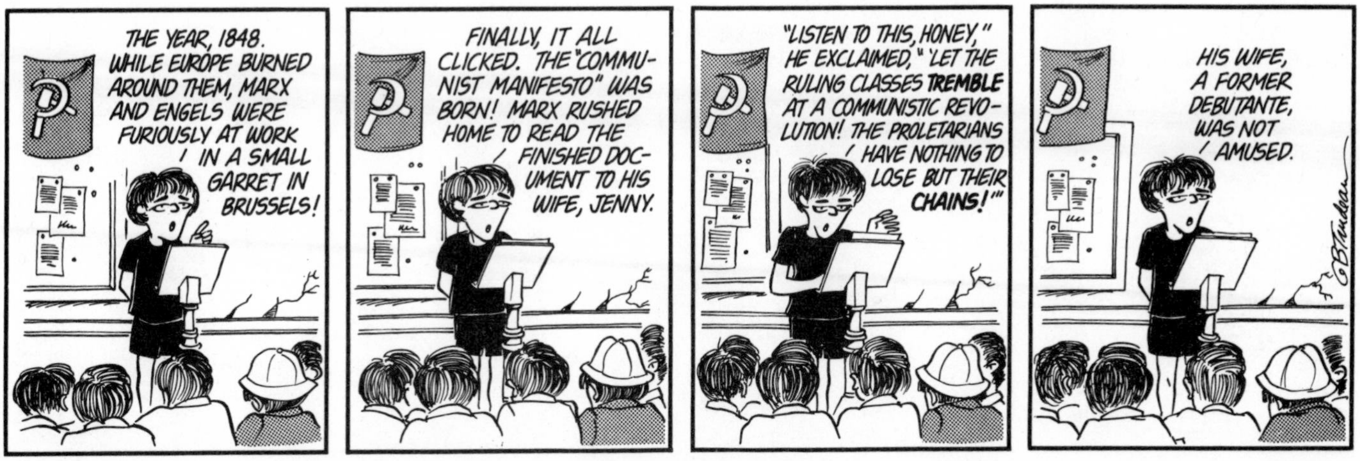
THE YEAR, 1848. WHILE EUROPE BURNED AROUND THEM, MARX AND ENGELS WERE FURIOUSLY AT WORK IN A SMALL GARRET IN BRUSSELS!
FINALLY, IT ALL CLICKED. THE "COMMUNIST MANIFESTO" WAS BORN! MARX RUSHED HOME TO READ THE FINISHED DOCUMENT TO HIS WIFE, JENNY.
"LISTEN TO THIS, HONEY," HE EXCLAIMED, "'LET THE RULING CLASSES TREMBLE AT A COMMUNISTIC REVOLUTION! THE PROLETARIANS HAVE NOTHING TO LOSE BUT THEIR CHAINS!'"
HIS WIFE, A FORMER DEBUTANTE, WAS NOT AMUSED.
GBTrudeau

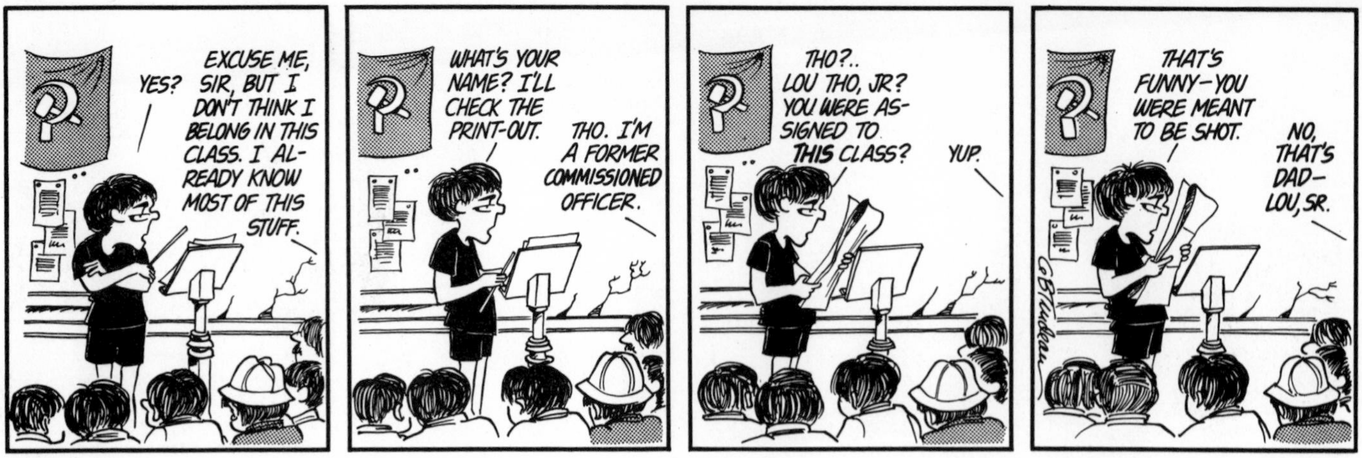
YES?
EXCUSE ME, SIR, BUT I DON'T THINK I BELONG IN THIS CLASS. I ALREADY KNOW MOST OF THIS STUFF.
WHAT'S YOUR NAME? I'LL CHECK THE PRINT-OUT.
THO. I'M A FORMER COMMISSIONED OFFICER.
THO?.. LOU THO, JR? YOU WERE ASSIGNED TO **THIS** CLASS?
YUP.
THAT'S FUNNY—YOU WERE MEANT TO BE SHOT.
NO, THAT'S DAD-LOU, SR.
G.B.Trudeau

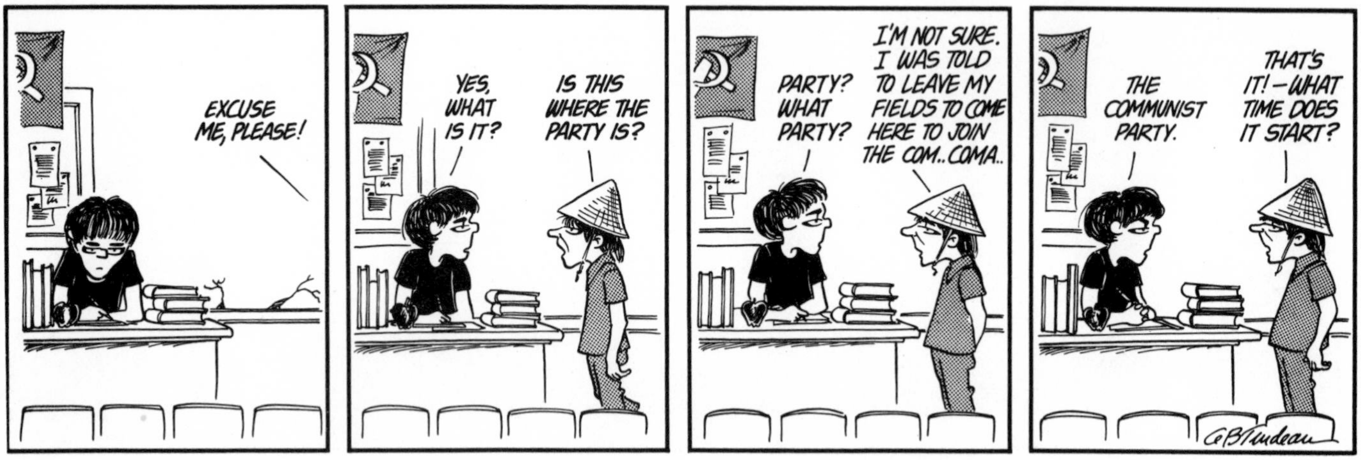
EXCUSE ME, PLEASE!
YES, WHAT IS IT?
IS THIS WHERE THE PARTY IS?
PARTY? WHAT PARTY?
I'M NOT SURE. I WAS TOLD TO LEAVE MY FIELDS TO COME HERE TO JOIN THE COM..COMA..
THE COMMUNIST PARTY.
THAT'S IT!—WHAT TIME DOES IT START?
G.B.Trudeau

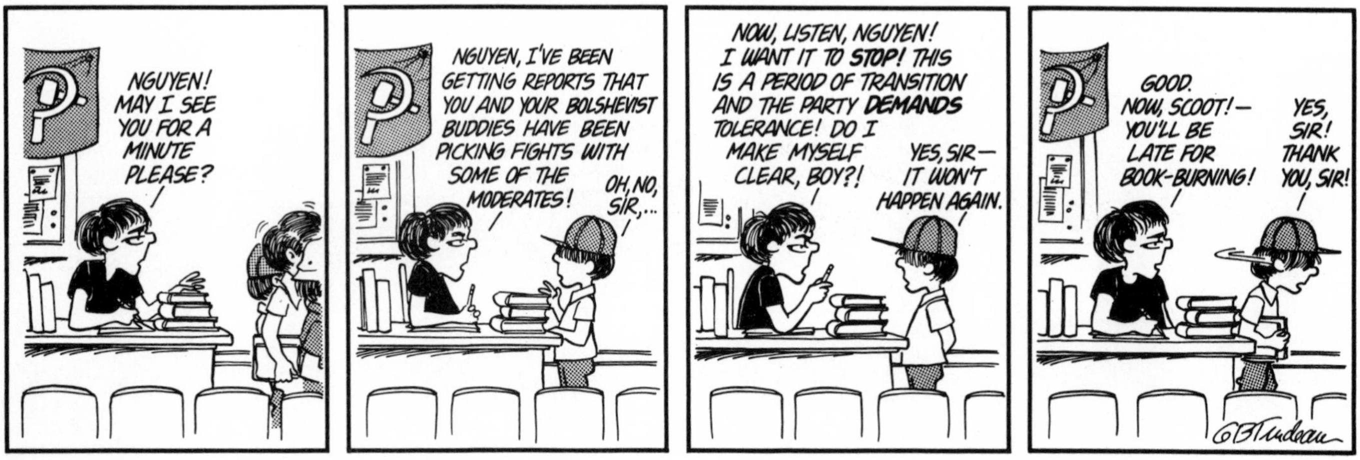
NGUYEN! MAY I SEE YOU FOR A MINUTE PLEASE?
NGUYEN, I'VE BEEN GETTING REPORTS THAT YOU AND YOUR BOLSHEVIST BUDDIES HAVE BEEN PICKING FIGHTS WITH SOME OF THE MODERATES!
OH, NO, SIR,...
NOW, LISTEN, NGUYEN! I WANT IT TO **STOP!** THIS IS A PERIOD OF TRANSITION AND THE PARTY **DEMANDS** TOLERANCE! DO I MAKE MYSELF CLEAR, BOY?!
YES, SIR—IT WON'T HAPPEN AGAIN.
GOOD. NOW, SCOOT!—YOU'LL BE LATE FOR BOOK-BURNING!
YES, SIR! THANK YOU, SIR!
G.B.Trudeau

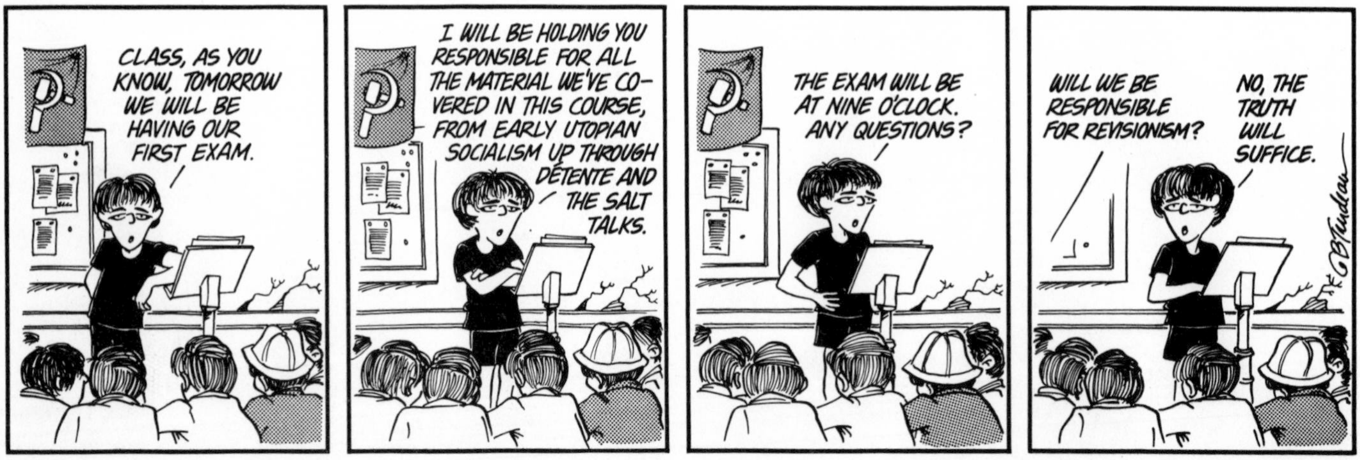
CLASS, AS YOU KNOW, TOMORROW WE WILL BE HAVING OUR FIRST EXAM.
I WILL BE HOLDING YOU RESPONSIBLE FOR ALL THE MATERIAL WE'VE COVERED IN THIS COURSE, FROM EARLY UTOPIAN SOCIALISM UP THROUGH DÉTENTE AND THE SALT TALKS.
THE EXAM WILL BE AT NINE O'CLOCK. ANY QUESTIONS?
WILL WE BE RESPONSIBLE FOR REVISIONISM?
NO, THE TRUTH WILL SUFFICE.
G.B.Trudeau

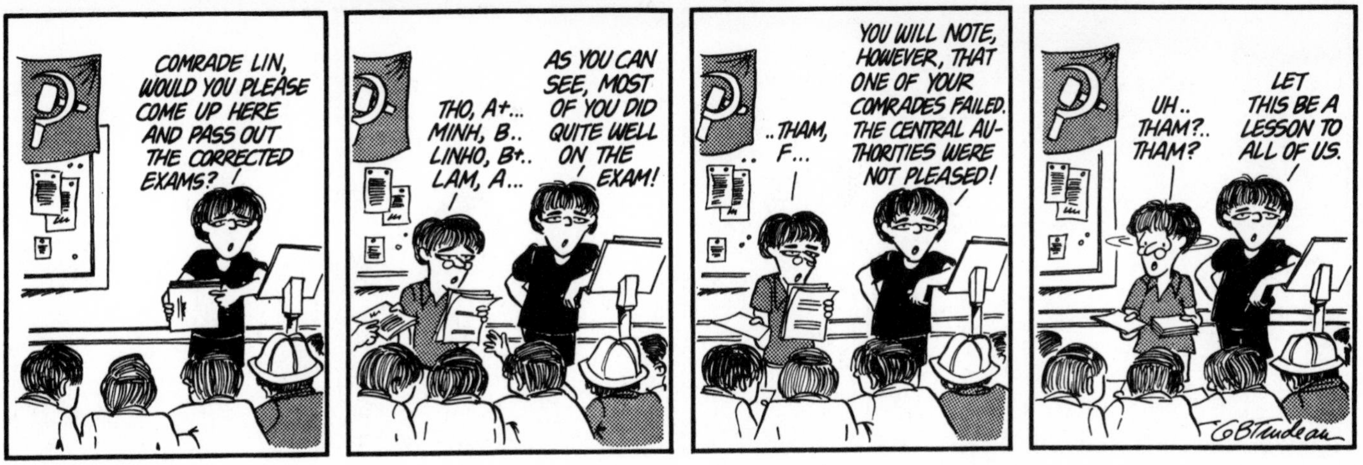
COMRADE LIN, WOULD YOU PLEASE COME UP HERE AND PASS OUT THE CORRECTED EXAMS?
THO, A+... MINH, B.. LINHO, B+.. LAM, A...
AS YOU CAN SEE, MOST OF YOU DID QUITE WELL ON THE EXAM!
..THAM, F...
YOU WILL NOTE, HOWEVER, THAT ONE OF YOUR COMRADES FAILED. THE CENTRAL AUTHORITIES WERE NOT PLEASED!
UH.. THAM?.. THAM?
LET THIS BE A LESSON TO ALL OF US.
GBTrudeau

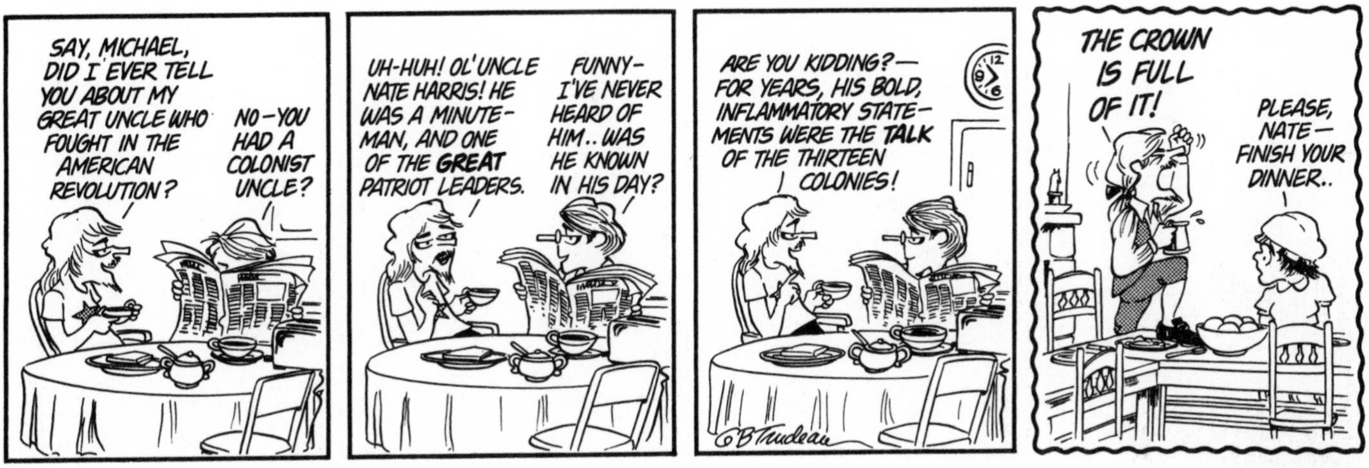
SAY, MICHAEL, DID I EVER TELL YOU ABOUT MY GREAT UNCLE WHO FOUGHT IN THE AMERICAN REVOLUTION?
NO—YOU HAD A COLONIST UNCLE?
UH-HUH! OL' UNCLE NATE HARRIS! HE WAS A MINUTEMAN, AND ONE OF THE GREAT PATRIOT LEADERS.
FUNNY—I'VE NEVER HEARD OF HIM.. WAS HE KNOWN IN HIS DAY?
ARE YOU KIDDING?—FOR YEARS, HIS BOLD, INFLAMMATORY STATEMENTS WERE THE TALK OF THE THIRTEEN COLONIES!
GBTrudeau
THE CROWN IS FULL OF IT!
PLEASE, NATE—FINISH YOUR DINNER..

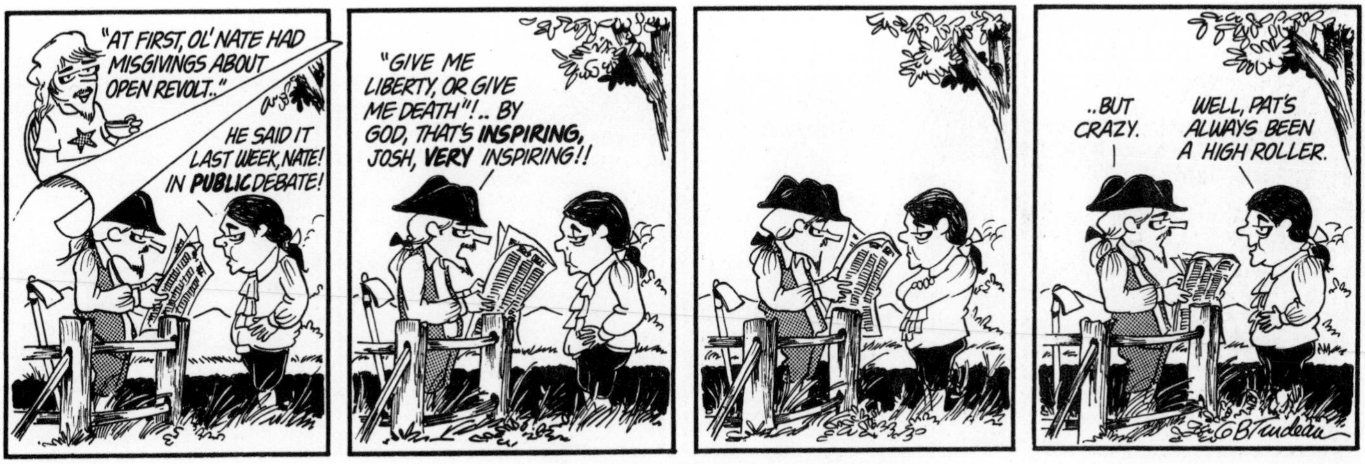
"AT FIRST, OL' NATE HAD MISGIVINGS ABOUT OPEN REVOLT."
HE SAID IT LAST WEEK, NATE! IN PUBLIC DEBATE!
"GIVE ME LIBERTY, OR GIVE ME DEATH"!.. BY GOD, THAT'S INSPIRING, JOSH, VERY INSPIRING!!
..BUT CRAZY.
WELL, PAT'S ALWAYS BEEN A HIGH ROLLER.
GBTrudeau

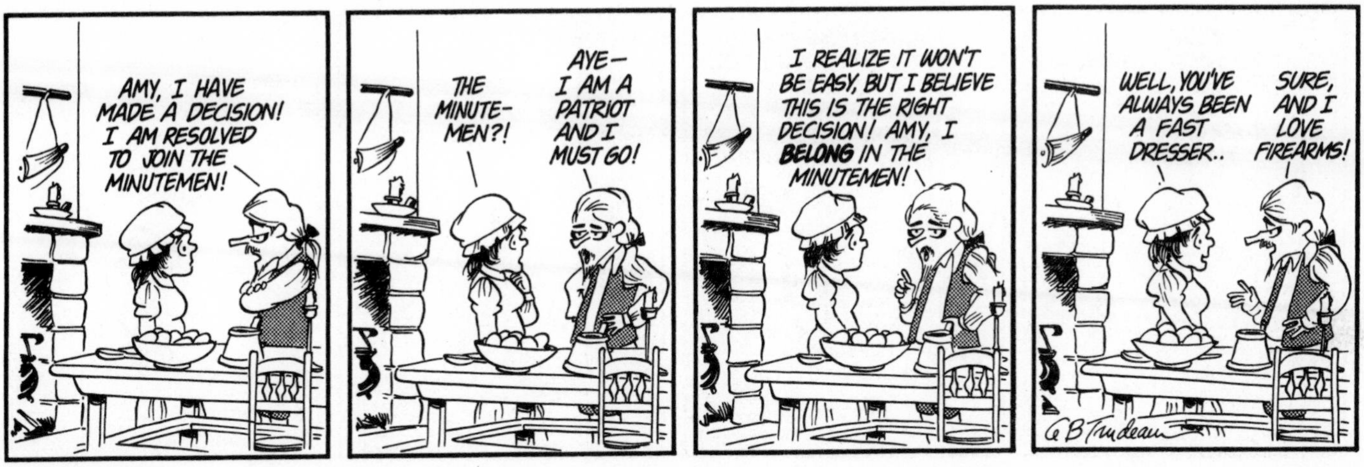
AMY, I HAVE MADE A DECISION! I AM RESOLVED TO JOIN THE MINUTEMEN!
THE MINUTEMEN?!
AYE—I AM A PATRIOT AND I MUST GO!
I REALIZE IT WON'T BE EASY, BUT I BELIEVE THIS IS THE RIGHT DECISION! AMY, I BELONG IN THE MINUTEMEN!
WELL, YOU'VE ALWAYS BEEN A FAST DRESSER..
SURE, AND I LOVE FIREARMS!
GBTrudeau

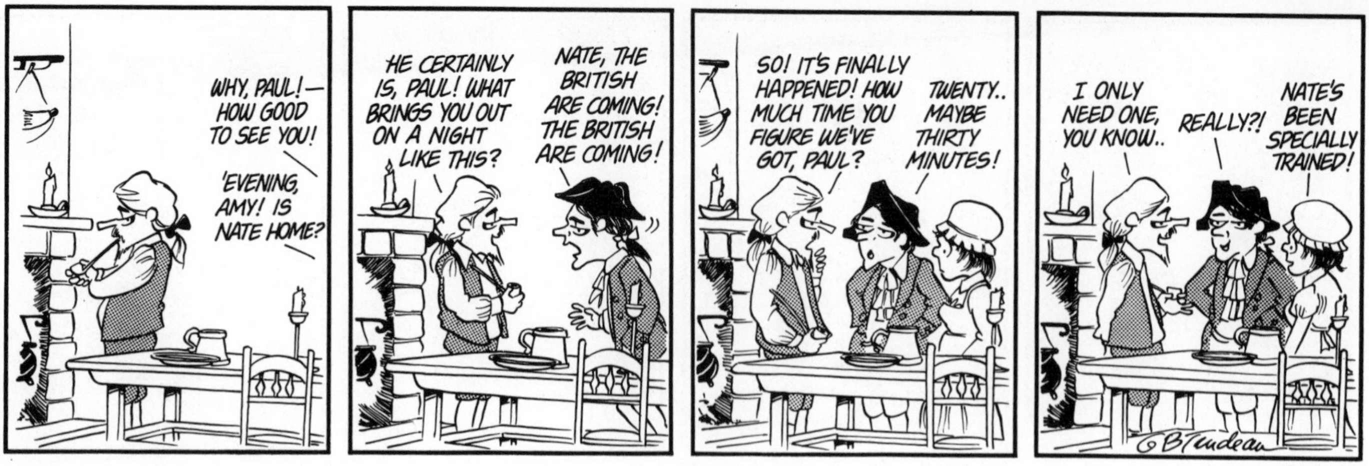
WHY, PAUL!— HOW GOOD TO SEE YOU!
'EVENING, AMY! IS NATE HOME?
HE CERTAINLY IS, PAUL! WHAT BRINGS YOU OUT ON A NIGHT LIKE THIS?
NATE, THE BRITISH ARE COMING! THE BRITISH ARE COMING!
SO! IT'S FINALLY HAPPENED! HOW MUCH TIME YOU FIGURE WE'VE GOT, PAUL?
TWENTY.. MAYBE THIRTY MINUTES!
I ONLY NEED ONE, YOU KNOW..
REALLY?!
NATE'S BEEN SPECIALLY TRAINED!

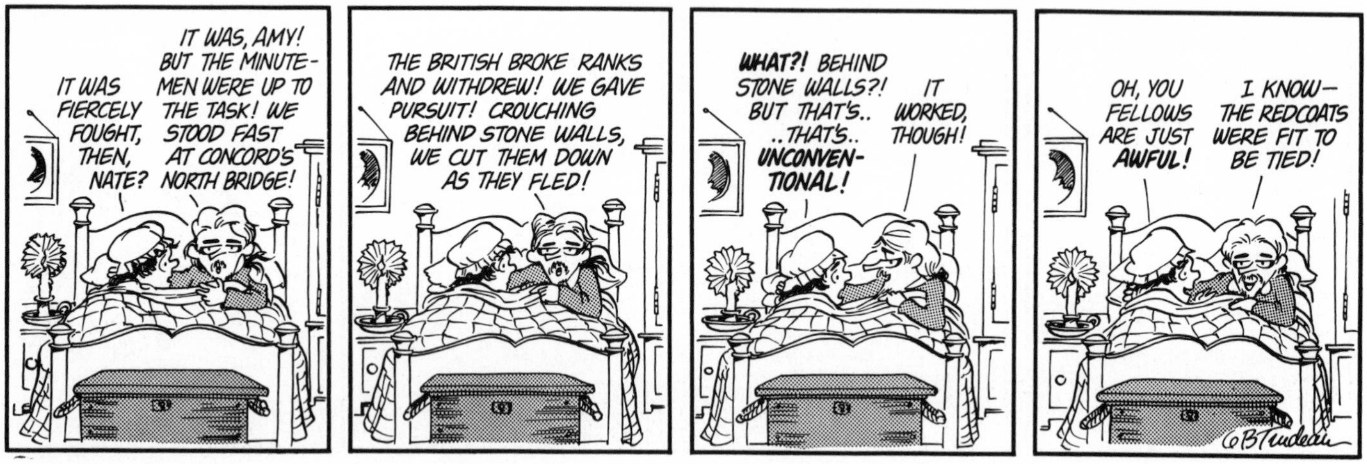
IT WAS FIERCELY FOUGHT, THEN, NATE?
IT WAS, AMY! BUT THE MINUTE-MEN WERE UP TO THE TASK! WE STOOD FAST AT CONCORD'S NORTH BRIDGE!
THE BRITISH BROKE RANKS AND WITHDREW! WE GAVE PURSUIT! CROUCHING BEHIND STONE WALLS, WE CUT THEM DOWN AS THEY FLED!
WHAT?! BEHIND STONE WALLS?! BUT THAT'S.. ..THAT'S.. UNCONVEN-TIONAL!
IT WORKED, THOUGH!
OH, YOU FELLOWS ARE JUST AWFUL!
I KNOW— THE REDCOATS WERE FIT TO BE TIED!

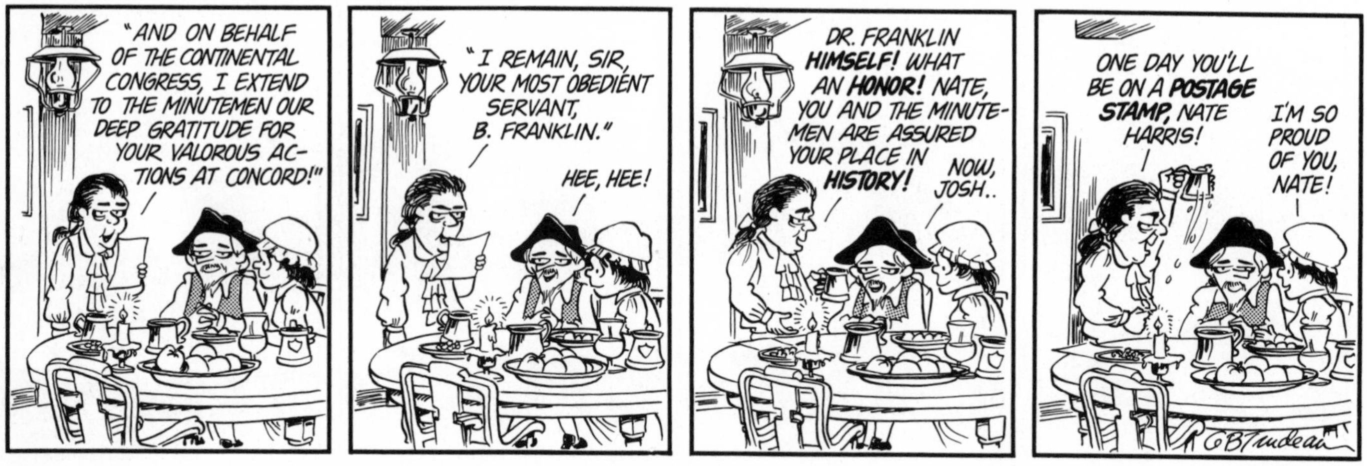
"AND ON BEHALF OF THE CONTINENTAL CONGRESS, I EXTEND TO THE MINUTEMEN OUR DEEP GRATITUDE FOR YOUR VALOROUS AC-TIONS AT CONCORD!"
"I REMAIN, SIR, YOUR MOST OBEDIENT SERVANT, B. FRANKLIN."
HEE, HEE!
DR. FRANKLIN HIMSELF! WHAT AN HONOR! NATE, YOU AND THE MINUTE-MEN ARE ASSURED YOUR PLACE IN HISTORY!
NOW, JOSH..
ONE DAY YOU'LL BE ON A POSTAGE STAMP, NATE HARRIS!
I'M SO PROUD OF YOU, NATE!

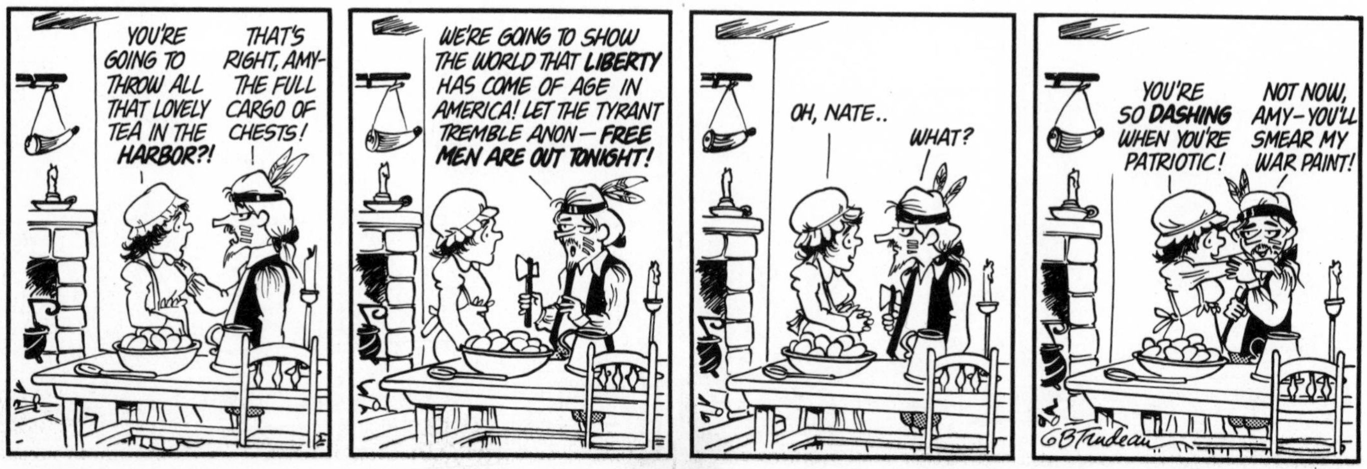
YOU'RE GOING TO THROW ALL THAT LOVELY TEA IN THE HARBOR?!
THAT'S RIGHT, AMY- THE FULL CARGO OF CHESTS!
WE'RE GOING TO SHOW THE WORLD THAT LIBERTY HAS COME OF AGE IN AMERICA! LET THE TYRANT TREMBLE ANON— FREE MEN ARE OUT TONIGHT!
OH, NATE..
WHAT?
YOU'RE SO DASHING WHEN YOU'RE PATRIOTIC!
NOT NOW, AMY–YOU'LL SMEAR MY WAR PAINT!

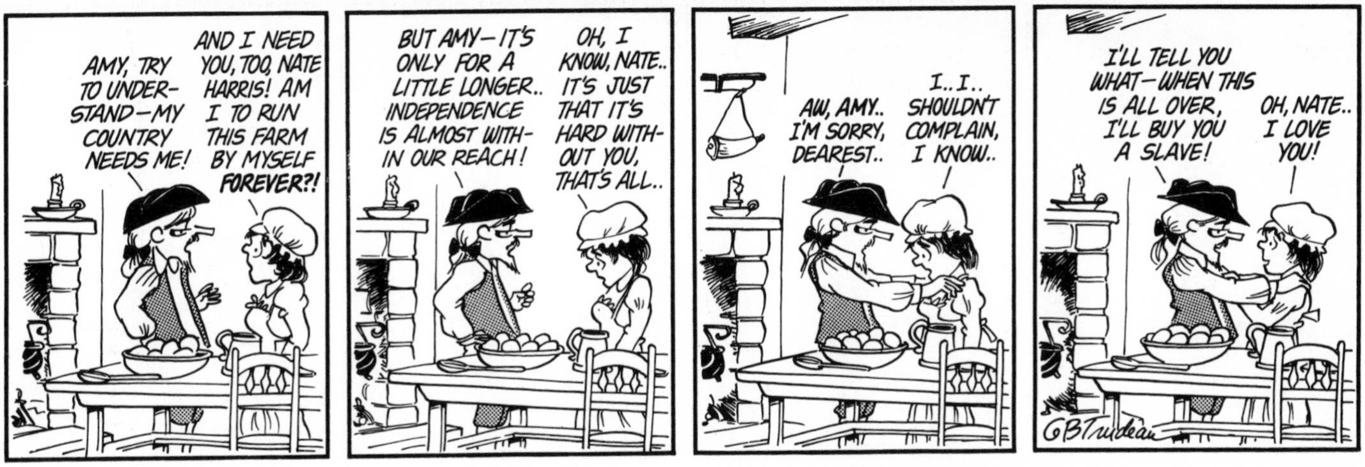
AMY, TRY TO UNDER-STAND—MY COUNTRY NEEDS ME!
AND I NEED YOU, TOO, NATE HARRIS! AM I TO RUN THIS FARM BY MYSELF FOREVER?!
BUT AMY—IT'S ONLY FOR A LITTLE LONGER.. INDEPENDENCE IS ALMOST WITH-IN OUR REACH!
OH, I KNOW, NATE.. IT'S JUST THAT IT'S HARD WITH-OUT YOU, THAT'S ALL..
AW, AMY.. I'M SORRY, DEAREST..
I.. I.. SHOULDN'T COMPLAIN, I KNOW..
I'LL TELL YOU WHAT—WHEN THIS IS ALL OVER, I'LL BUY YOU A SLAVE!
OH, NATE.. I LOVE YOU!
GBTrudeau

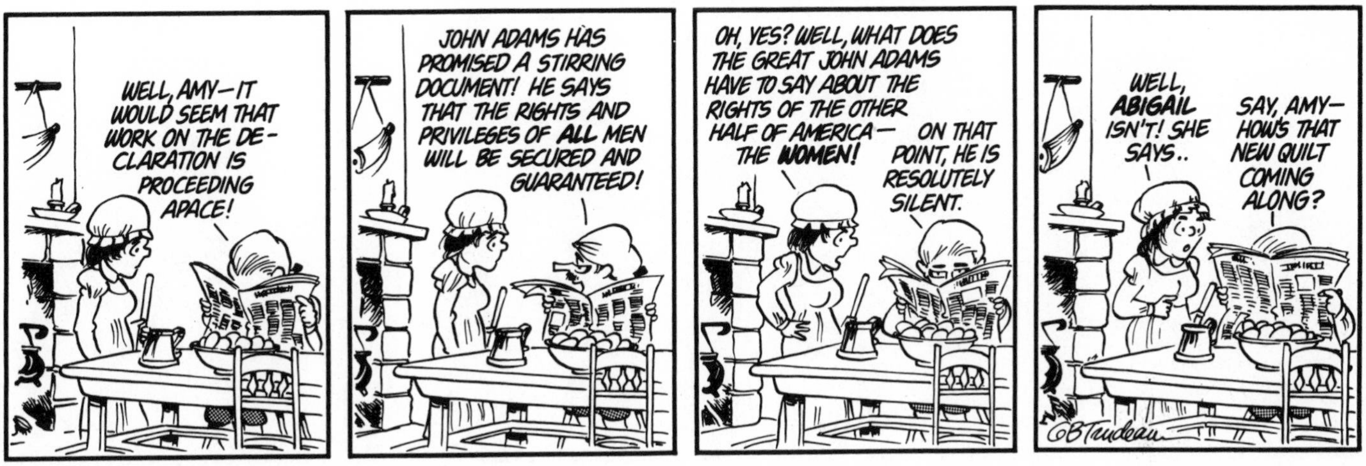
WELL, AMY—IT WOULD SEEM THAT WORK ON THE DE-CLARATION IS PROCEEDING APACE!
JOHN ADAMS HAS PROMISED A STIRRING DOCUMENT! HE SAYS THAT THE RIGHTS AND PRIVILEGES OF ALL MEN WILL BE SECURED AND GUARANTEED!
OH, YES? WELL, WHAT DOES THE GREAT JOHN ADAMS HAVE TO SAY ABOUT THE RIGHTS OF THE OTHER HALF OF AMERICA—THE WOMEN!
ON THAT POINT, HE IS RESOLUTELY SILENT.
WELL, ABIGAIL ISN'T! SHE SAYS..
SAY, AMY—HOW'S THAT NEW QUILT COMING ALONG?
GBTrudeau

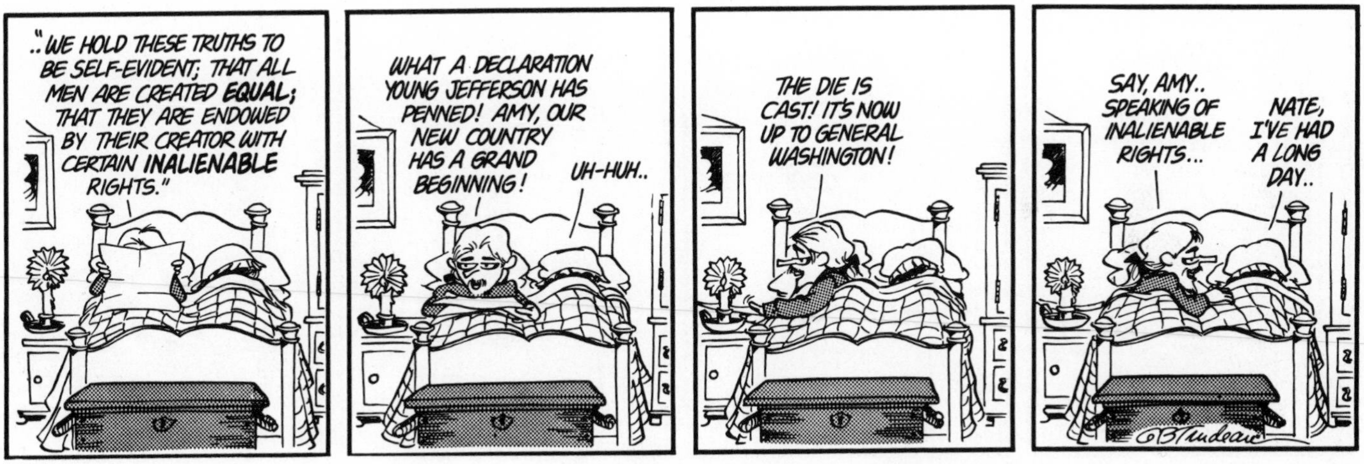
"..WE HOLD THESE TRUTHS TO BE SELF-EVIDENT; THAT ALL MEN ARE CREATED EQUAL; THAT THEY ARE ENDOWED BY THEIR CREATOR WITH CERTAIN INALIENABLE RIGHTS."
WHAT A DECLARATION YOUNG JEFFERSON HAS PENNED! AMY, OUR NEW COUNTRY HAS A GRAND BEGINNING!
UH-HUH..
THE DIE IS CAST! IT'S NOW UP TO GENERAL WASHINGTON!
SAY, AMY.. SPEAKING OF INALIENABLE RIGHTS...
NATE, I'VE HAD A LONG DAY..
GBTrudeau

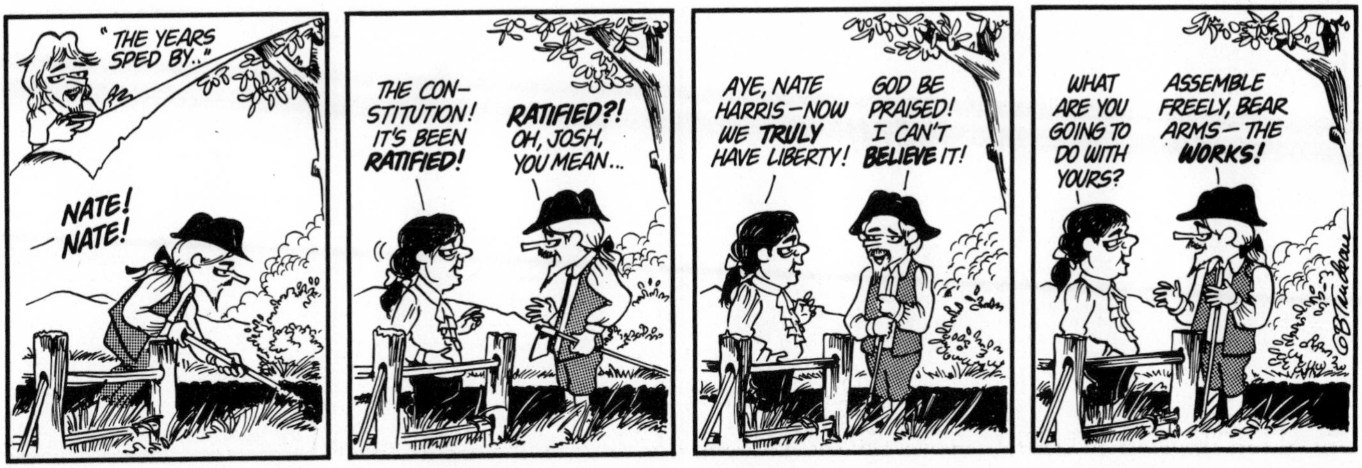
"THE YEARS SPED BY.."
NATE! NATE!
THE CON-STITUTION! IT'S BEEN RATIFIED!
RATIFIED?! OH, JOSH, YOU MEAN...
AYE, NATE HARRIS—NOW WE TRULY HAVE LIBERTY!
GOD BE PRAISED! I CAN'T BELIEVE IT!
WHAT ARE YOU GOING TO DO WITH YOURS?
ASSEMBLE FREELY, BEAR ARMS—THE WORKS!
GBTrudeau

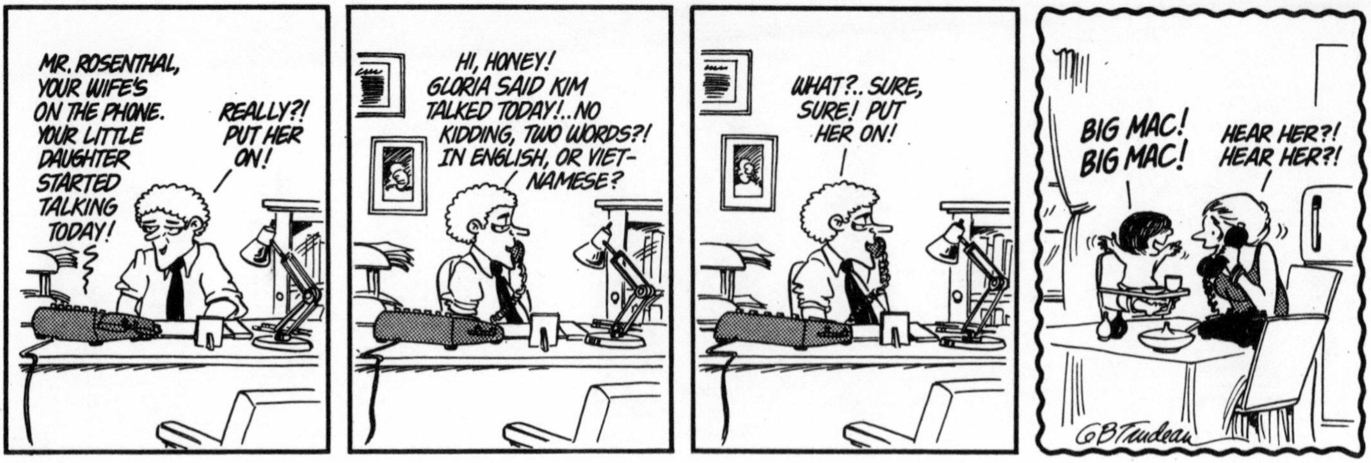
MR. ROSENTHAL, YOUR WIFE'S ON THE PHONE. YOUR LITTLE DAUGHTER STARTED TALKING TODAY!
REALLY?! PUT HER ON!
HI, HONEY! GLORIA SAID KIM TALKED TODAY!..NO KIDDING, TWO WORDS?! IN ENGLISH, OR VIET-NAMESE?
WHAT?.. SURE, SURE! PUT HER ON!
BIG MAC! BIG MAC!
HEAR HER?! HEAR HER?!
GBTrudeau

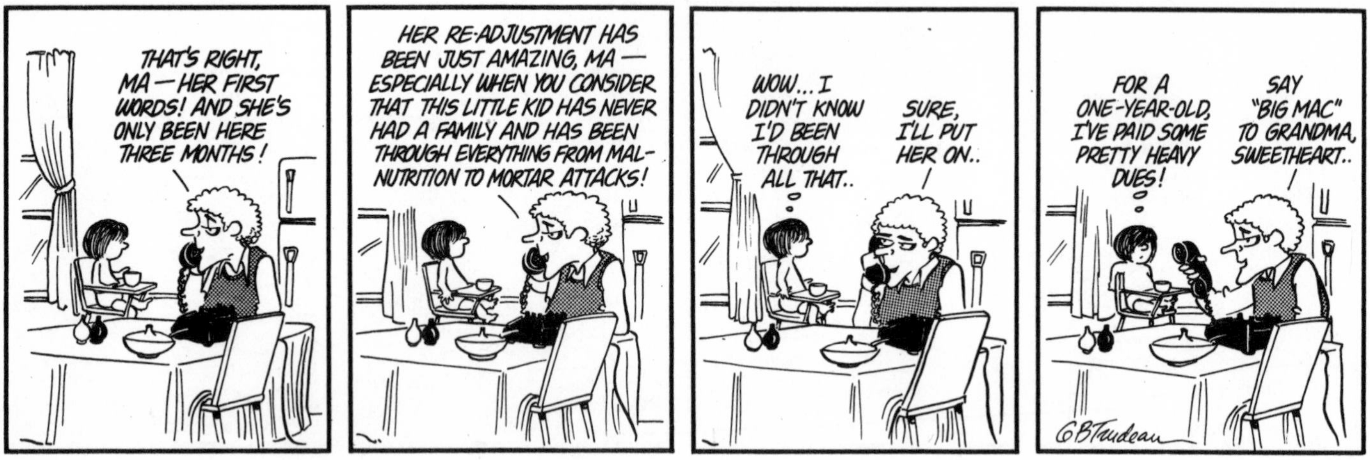
THAT'S RIGHT, MA — HER FIRST WORDS! AND SHE'S ONLY BEEN HERE THREE MONTHS!
HER RE-ADJUSTMENT HAS BEEN JUST AMAZING, MA — ESPECIALLY WHEN YOU CONSIDER THAT THIS LITTLE KID HAS NEVER HAD A FAMILY AND HAS BEEN THROUGH EVERYTHING FROM MAL-NUTRITION TO MORTAR ATTACKS!
WOW... I DIDN'T KNOW I'D BEEN THROUGH ALL THAT..
SURE, I'LL PUT HER ON..
FOR A ONE-YEAR-OLD, I'VE PAID SOME PRETTY HEAVY DUES!
SAY "BIG MAC" TO GRANDMA, SWEETHEART..
GBTrudeau

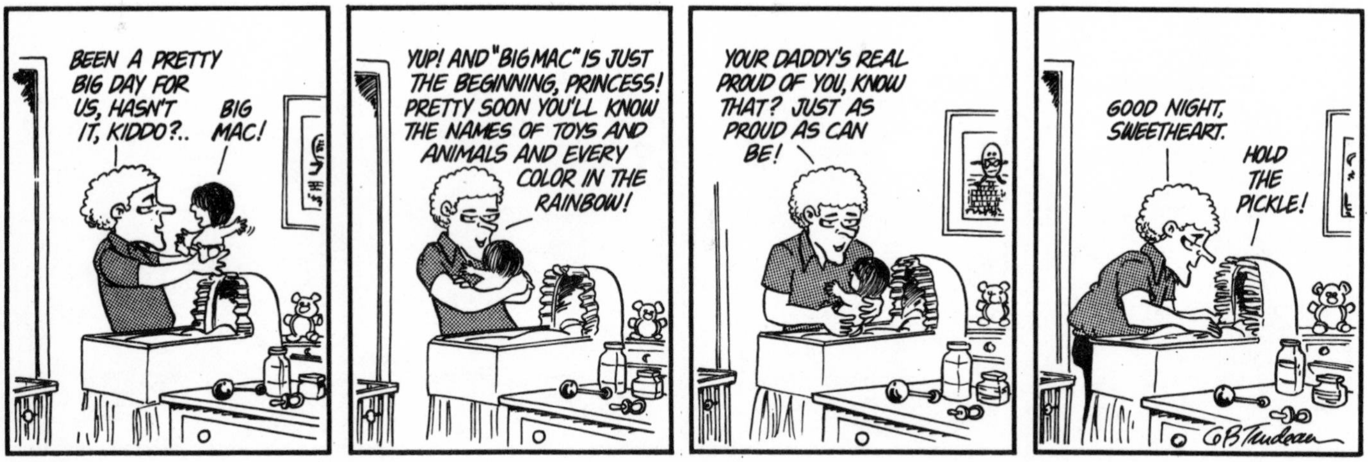
BEEN A PRETTY BIG DAY FOR US, HASN'T IT, KIDDO?..
BIG MAC!
YUP! AND "BIG MAC" IS JUST THE BEGINNING, PRINCESS! PRETTY SOON YOU'LL KNOW THE NAMES OF TOYS AND ANIMALS AND EVERY COLOR IN THE RAINBOW!
YOUR DADDY'S REAL PROUD OF YOU, KNOW THAT? JUST AS PROUD AS CAN BE!
GOOD NIGHT, SWEETHEART.
HOLD THE PICKLE!
GBTrudeau

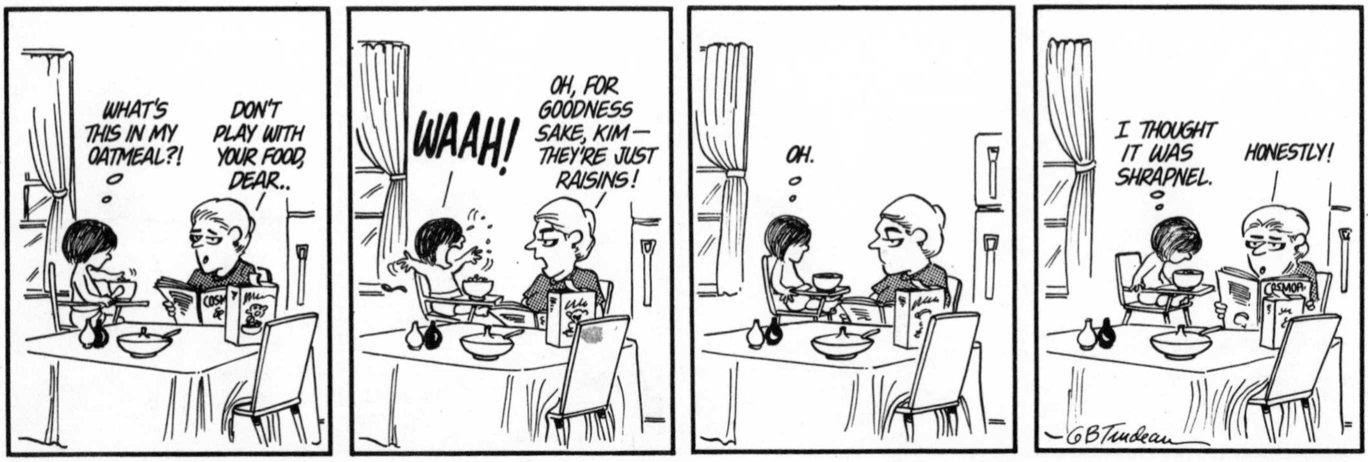
WHAT'S THIS IN MY OATMEAL?!
DON'T PLAY WITH YOUR FOOD, DEAR..
WAAH!
OH, FOR GOODNESS SAKE, KIM — THEY'RE JUST RAISINS!
OH.
I THOUGHT IT WAS SHRAPNEL.
HONESTLY!
GBTrudeau

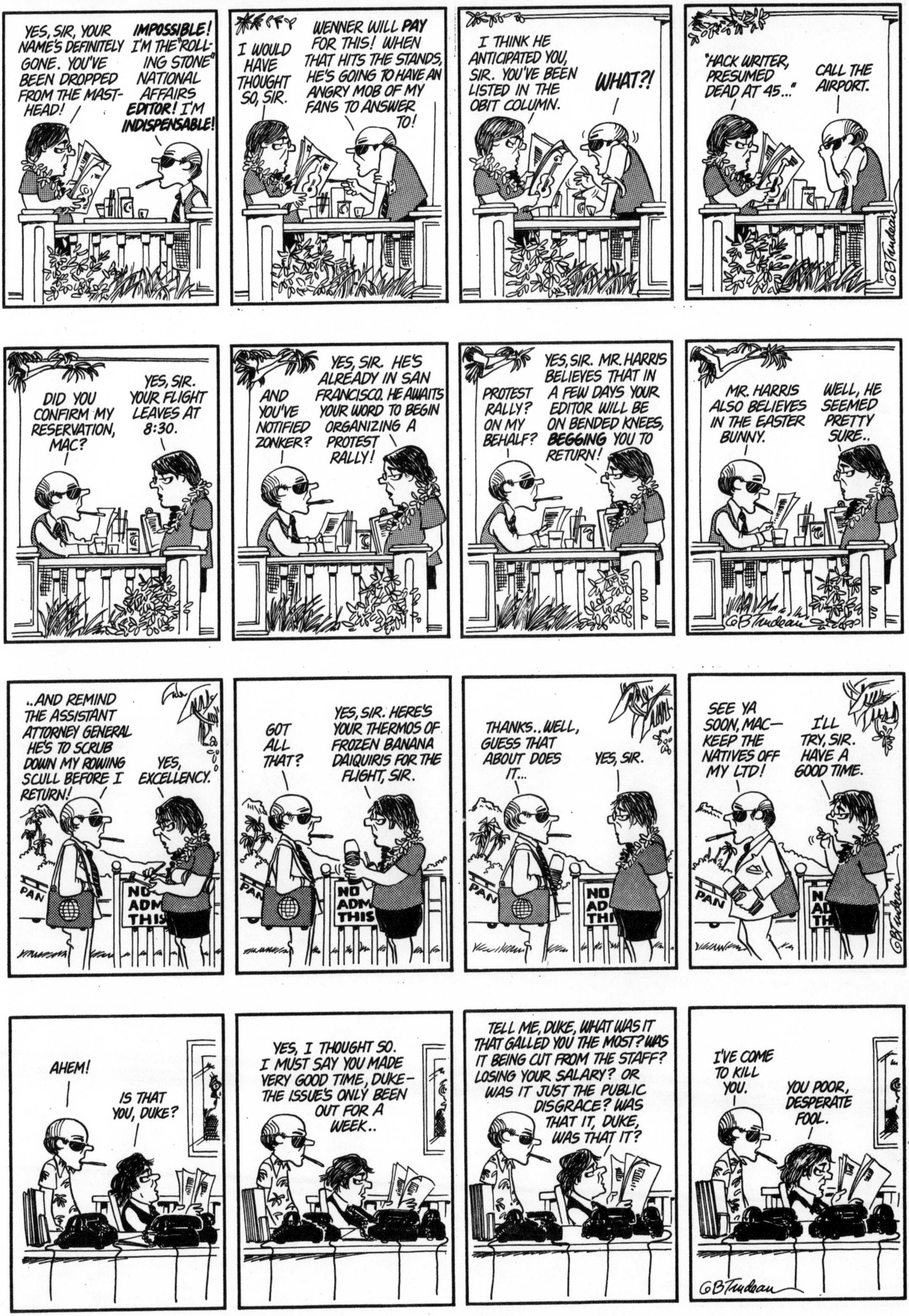
YES, SIR, YOUR NAME'S DEFINITELY GONE. YOU'VE BEEN DROPPED FROM THE MAST-HEAD!
IMPOSSIBLE! I'M THE "ROLLING STONE" NATIONAL AFFAIRS EDITOR! I'M INDISPENSABLE!
I WOULD HAVE THOUGHT SO, SIR.
WENNER WILL PAY FOR THIS! WHEN THAT HITS THE STANDS, HE'S GOING TO HAVE AN ANGRY MOB OF MY FANS TO ANSWER TO!
I THINK HE ANTICIPATED YOU, SIR. YOU'VE BEEN LISTED IN THE OBIT COLUMN.
WHAT?!
"HACK WRITER, PRESUMED DEAD AT 45..."
CALL THE AIRPORT.
GBTrudeau
DID YOU CONFIRM MY RESERVATION, MAC?
YES, SIR. YOUR FLIGHT LEAVES AT 8:30.
AND YOU'VE NOTIFIED ZONKER?
YES, SIR. HE'S ALREADY IN SAN FRANCISCO. HE AWAITS YOUR WORD TO BEGIN ORGANIZING A PROTEST RALLY!
PROTEST RALLY? ON MY BEHALF?
YES, SIR. MR. HARRIS BELIEVES THAT IN A FEW DAYS YOUR EDITOR WILL BE ON BENDED KNEES, BEGGING YOU TO RETURN!
MR. HARRIS ALSO BELIEVES IN THE EASTER BUNNY.
WELL, HE SEEMED PRETTY SURE..
GBTrudeau
..AND REMIND THE ASSISTANT ATTORNEY GENERAL HE'S TO SCRUB DOWN MY ROWING SCULL BEFORE I RETURN!
YES, EXCELLENCY.
PAN
NO
GOT ALL THAT?
YES, SIR. HERE'S YOUR THERMOS OF FROZEN BANANA DAIQUIRIS FOR THE FLIGHT, SIR.
THANKS.. WELL, GUESS THAT ABOUT DOES IT...
YES, SIR.
SEE YA SOON, MAC– KEEP THE NATIVES OFF MY LTD!
I'LL TRY, SIR. HAVE A GOOD TIME.
GBTrudeau
AHEM!
IS THAT YOU, DUKE?
YES, I THOUGHT SO. I MUST SAY YOU MADE VERY GOOD TIME, DUKE– THE ISSUE'S ONLY BEEN OUT FOR A WEEK..
TELL ME, DUKE, WHAT WAS IT THAT GALLED YOU THE MOST? WAS IT BEING CUT FROM THE STAFF? LOSING YOUR SALARY? OR WAS IT JUST THE PUBLIC DISGRACE? WAS THAT IT, DUKE, WAS THAT IT?
I'VE COME TO KILL YOU.
YOU POOR, DESPERATE FOOL.
GBTrudeau

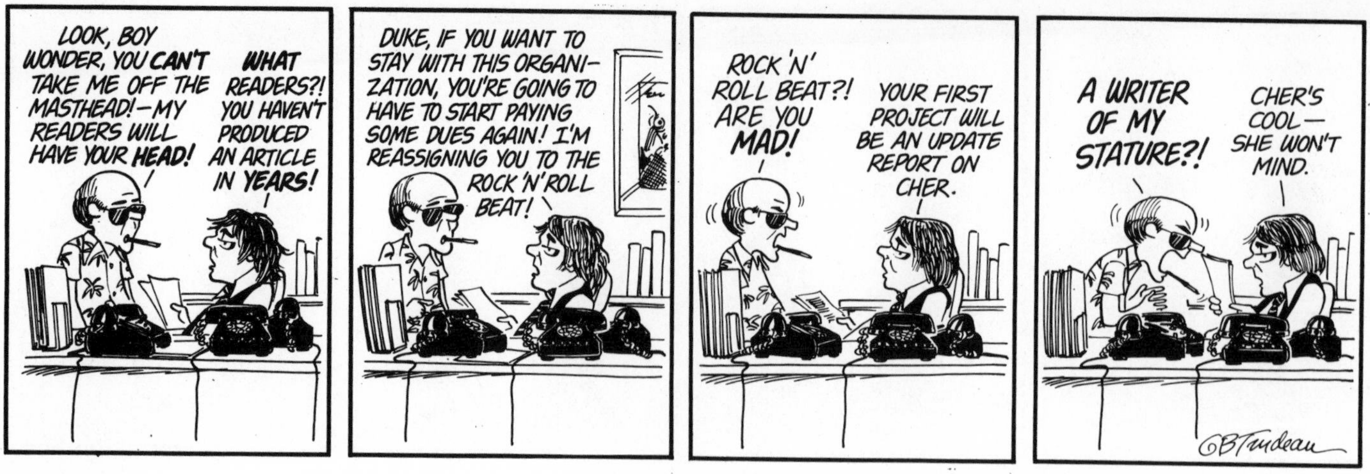
LOOK, BOY WONDER, YOU CAN'T TAKE ME OFF THE MASTHEAD!—MY READERS WILL HAVE YOUR HEAD!
WHAT READERS?! YOU HAVEN'T PRODUCED AN ARTICLE IN YEARS!
DUKE, IF YOU WANT TO STAY WITH THIS ORGANIZATION, YOU'RE GOING TO HAVE TO START PAYING SOME DUES AGAIN! I'M REASSIGNING YOU TO THE ROCK 'N' ROLL BEAT!
ROCK 'N' ROLL BEAT?! ARE YOU MAD!
YOUR FIRST PROJECT WILL BE AN UPDATE REPORT ON CHER.
A WRITER OF MY STATURE?!
CHER'S COOL—SHE WON'T MIND.
GBTrudeau

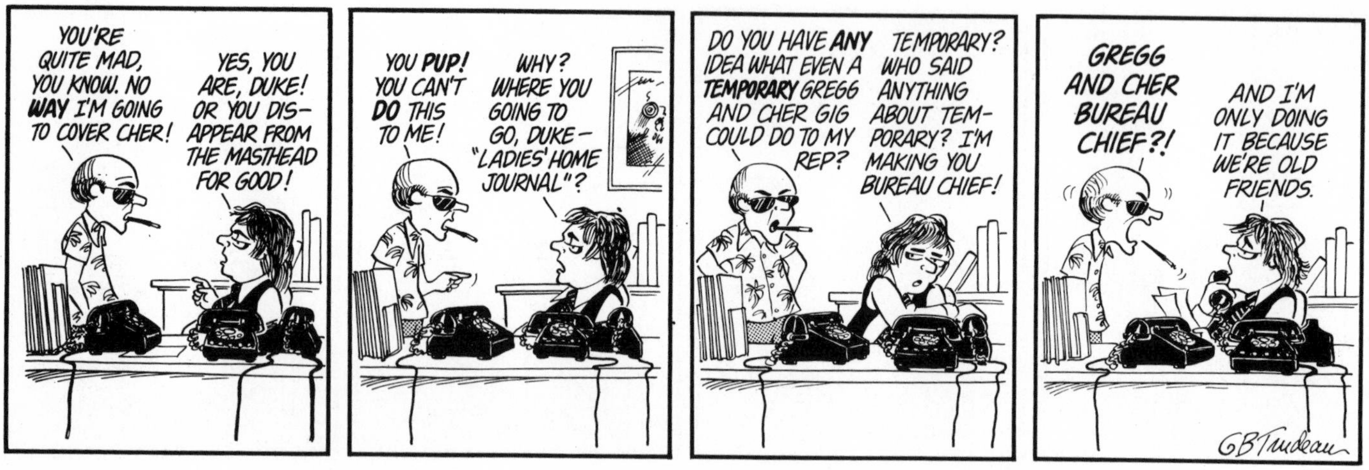
YOU'RE QUITE MAD, YOU KNOW. NO WAY I'M GOING TO COVER CHER!
YES, YOU ARE, DUKE! OR YOU DISAPPEAR FROM THE MASTHEAD FOR GOOD!
YOU PUP! YOU CAN'T DO THIS TO ME!
WHY? WHERE YOU GOING TO GO, DUKE—"LADIES' HOME JOURNAL"?
DO YOU HAVE ANY IDEA WHAT EVEN A TEMPORARY GREGG AND CHER GIG COULD DO TO MY REP?
TEMPORARY? WHO SAID ANYTHING ABOUT TEMPORARY? I'M MAKING YOU BUREAU CHIEF!
GREGG AND CHER BUREAU CHIEF?!
AND I'M ONLY DOING IT BECAUSE WE'RE OLD FRIENDS.
GBTrudeau

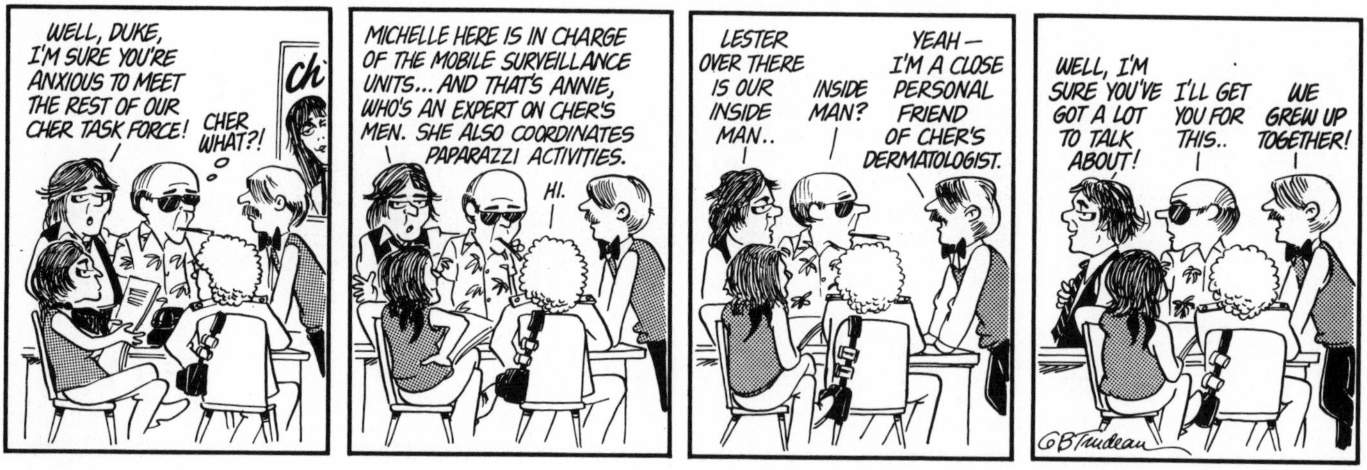
WELL, DUKE, I'M SURE YOU'RE ANXIOUS TO MEET THE REST OF OUR CHER TASK FORCE!
CHER WHAT?!
MICHELLE HERE IS IN CHARGE OF THE MOBILE SURVEILLANCE UNITS... AND THAT'S ANNIE, WHO'S AN EXPERT ON CHER'S MEN. SHE ALSO COORDINATES PAPARAZZI ACTIVITIES.
HI.
LESTER OVER THERE IS OUR INSIDE MAN..
INSIDE MAN?
YEAH—I'M A CLOSE PERSONAL FRIEND OF CHER'S DERMATOLOGIST.
WELL, I'M SURE YOU'VE GOT A LOT TO TALK ABOUT!
I'LL GET YOU FOR THIS..
WE GREW UP TOGETHER!
GBTrudeau

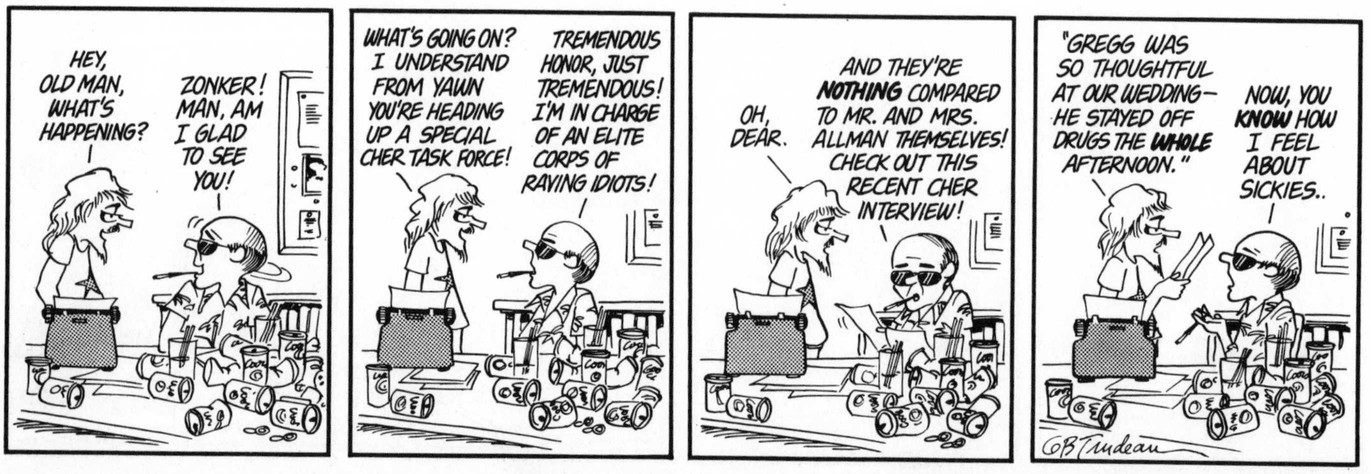
HEY, OLD MAN, WHAT'S HAPPENING?
ZONKER! MAN, AM I GLAD TO SEE YOU!
WHAT'S GOING ON? I UNDERSTAND FROM YAWN YOU'RE HEADING UP A SPECIAL CHER TASK FORCE!
TREMENDOUS HONOR, JUST TREMENDOUS! I'M IN CHARGE OF AN ELITE CORPS OF RAVING IDIOTS!
OH, DEAR.
AND THEY'RE NOTHING COMPARED TO MR. AND MRS. ALLMAN THEMSELVES! CHECK OUT THIS RECENT CHER INTERVIEW!
"GREGG WAS SO THOUGHTFUL AT OUR WEDDING—HE STAYED OFF DRUGS THE WHOLE AFTERNOON."
NOW, YOU KNOW HOW I FEEL ABOUT SICKIES..
GBTrudeau

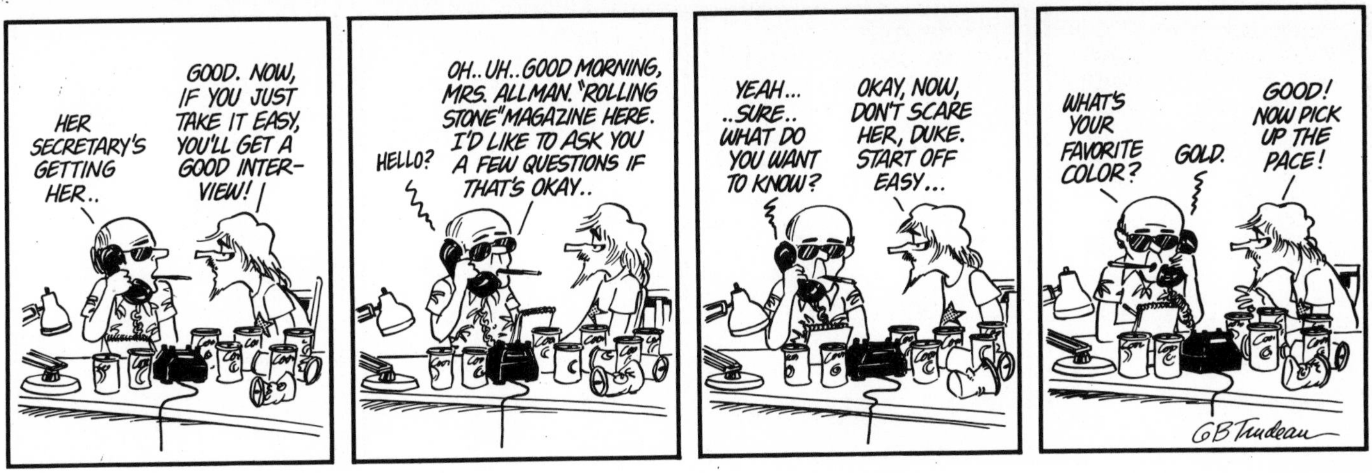
HER SECRETARY'S GETTING HER..
GOOD. NOW, IF YOU JUST TAKE IT EASY, YOU'LL GET A GOOD INTERVIEW!
HELLO?
OH..UH..GOOD MORNING, MRS. ALLMAN. "ROLLING STONE" MAGAZINE HERE. I'D LIKE TO ASK YOU A FEW QUESTIONS IF THAT'S OKAY..
YEAH... ..SURE.. WHAT DO YOU WANT TO KNOW?
OKAY, NOW, DON'T SCARE HER, DUKE. START OFF EASY...
WHAT'S YOUR FAVORITE COLOR?
GOLD.
GOOD! NOW PICK UP THE PACE!
GBTrudeau

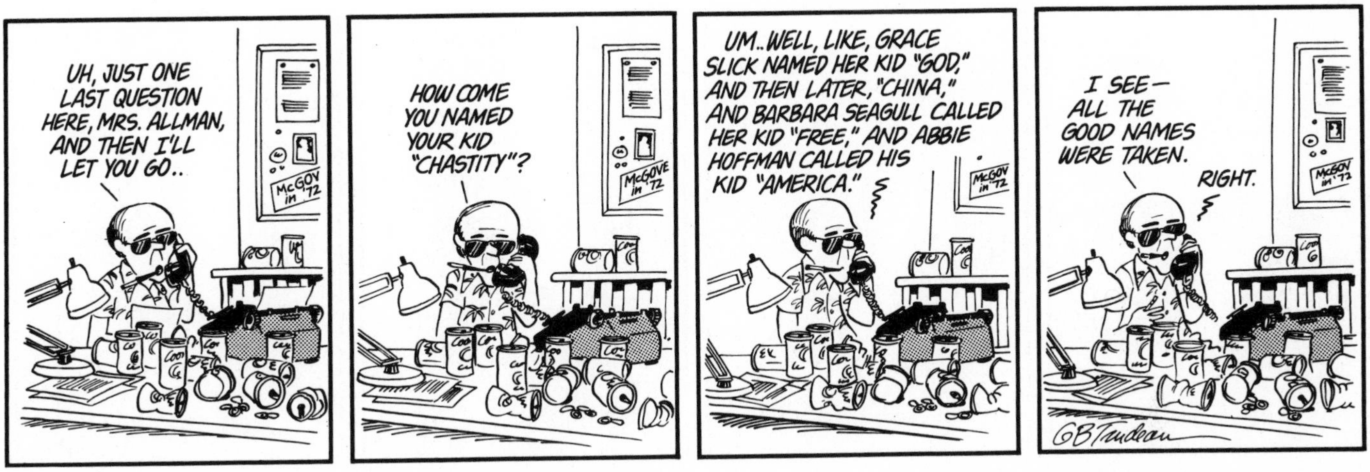
UH, JUST ONE LAST QUESTION HERE, MRS. ALLMAN, AND THEN I'LL LET YOU GO..
McGOV in '72
HOW COME YOU NAMED YOUR KID "CHASTITY"?
UM..WELL, LIKE, GRACE SLICK NAMED HER KID "GOD," AND THEN LATER, "CHINA," AND BARBARA SEAGULL CALLED HER KID "FREE," AND ABBIE HOFFMAN CALLED HIS KID "AMERICA."
I SEE— ALL THE GOOD NAMES WERE TAKEN.
RIGHT.
GBTrudeau

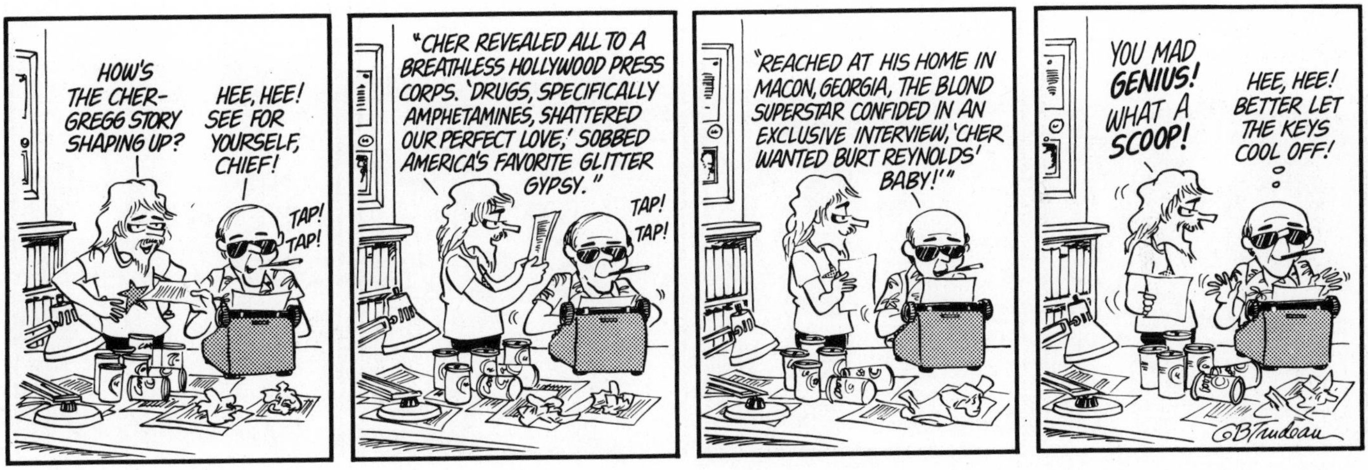
HOW'S THE CHER-GREGG STORY SHAPING UP?
HEE, HEE! SEE FOR YOURSELF, CHIEF!
TAP! TAP!
"CHER REVEALED ALL TO A BREATHLESS HOLLYWOOD PRESS CORPS. 'DRUGS, SPECIFICALLY AMPHETAMINES, SHATTERED OUR PERFECT LOVE,' SOBBED AMERICA'S FAVORITE GLITTER GYPSY."
TAP! TAP!
"REACHED AT HIS HOME IN MACON, GEORGIA, THE BLOND SUPERSTAR CONFIDED IN AN EXCLUSIVE INTERVIEW, 'CHER WANTED BURT REYNOLDS' BABY!'"
YOU MAD GENIUS! WHAT A SCOOP!
HEE, HEE! BETTER LET THE KEYS COOL OFF!
GBTrudeau

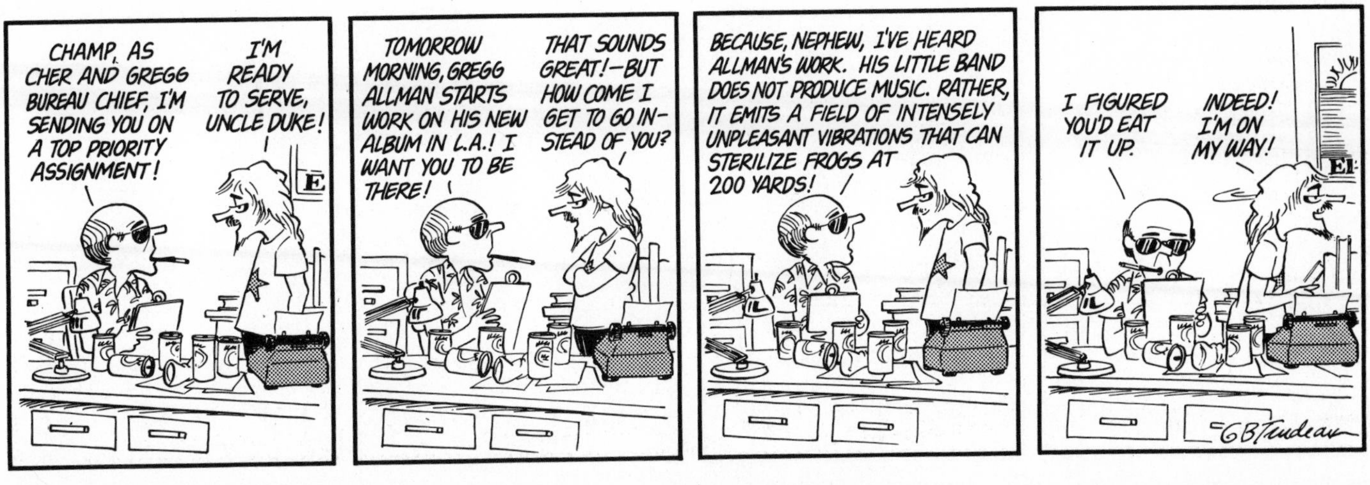
CHAMP, AS CHER AND GREGG BUREAU CHIEF, I'M SENDING YOU ON A TOP PRIORITY ASSIGNMENT!
I'M READY TO SERVE, UNCLE DUKE!
TOMORROW MORNING, GREGG ALLMAN STARTS WORK ON HIS NEW ALBUM IN L.A.! I WANT YOU TO BE THERE!
THAT SOUNDS GREAT!—BUT HOW COME I GET TO GO INSTEAD OF YOU?
BECAUSE, NEPHEW, I'VE HEARD ALLMAN'S WORK. HIS LITTLE BAND DOES NOT PRODUCE MUSIC. RATHER, IT EMITS A FIELD OF INTENSELY UNPLEASANT VIBRATIONS THAT CAN STERILIZE FROGS AT 200 YARDS!
I FIGURED YOU'D EAT IT UP.
INDEED! I'M ON MY WAY!
GBTrudeau

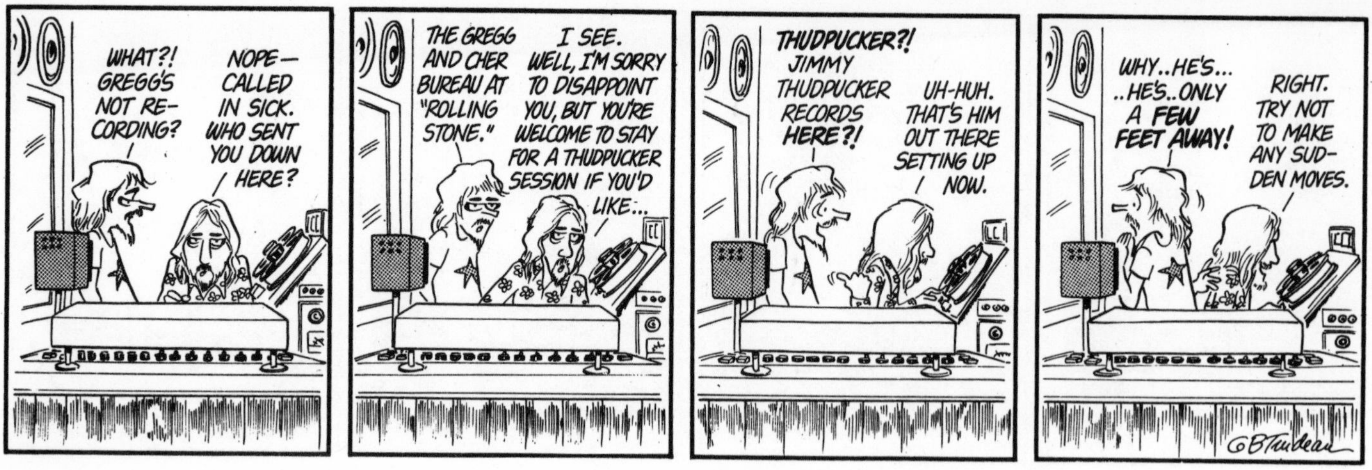
WHAT?! GREGG'S NOT RE-CORDING?
NOPE— CALLED IN SICK. WHO SENT YOU DOWN HERE?
THE GREGG AND CHER BUREAU AT "ROLLING STONE."
I SEE. WELL, I'M SORRY TO DISAPPOINT YOU, BUT YOU'RE WELCOME TO STAY FOR A THUDPUCKER SESSION IF YOU'D LIKE...
THUDPUCKER?! JIMMY THUDPUCKER RECORDS HERE?!
UH-HUH. THAT'S HIM OUT THERE SETTING UP NOW.
WHY..HE'S... ..HE'S..ONLY A FEW FEET AWAY!
RIGHT. TRY NOT TO MAKE ANY SUD-DEN MOVES.
GBTrudeau

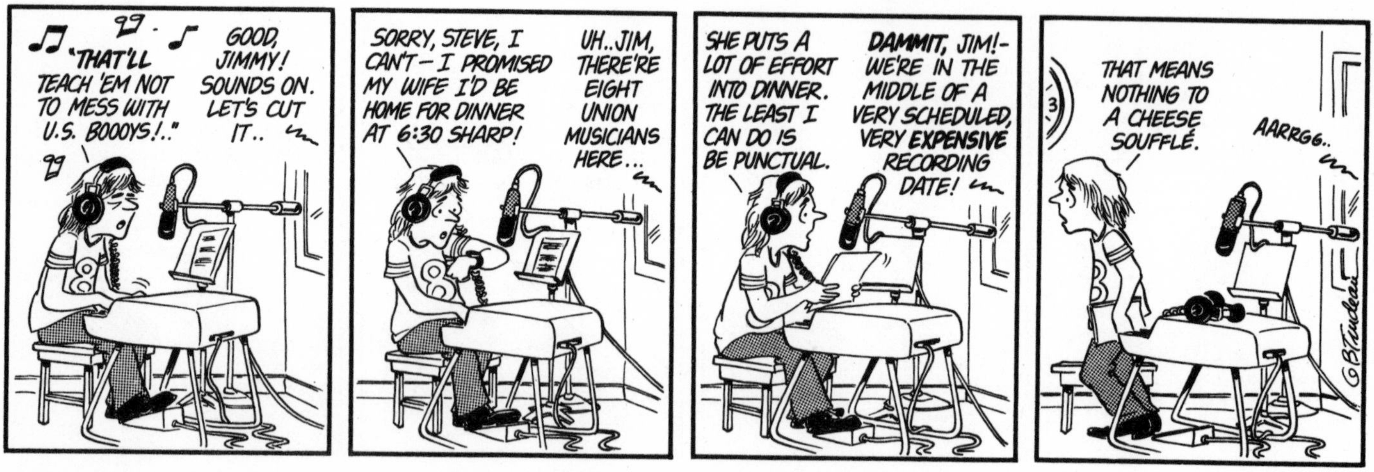
"THAT'LL TEACH 'EM NOT TO MESS WITH U.S. BOOOYS!.."
GOOD, JIMMY! SOUNDS ON. LET'S CUT IT..
SORRY, STEVE, I CAN'T—I PROMISED MY WIFE I'D BE HOME FOR DINNER AT 6:30 SHARP!
UH..JIM, THERE'RE EIGHT UNION MUSICIANS HERE...
SHE PUTS A LOT OF EFFORT INTO DINNER. THE LEAST I CAN DO IS BE PUNCTUAL.
DAMMIT, JIM!- WE'RE IN THE MIDDLE OF A VERY SCHEDULED, VERY EXPENSIVE RECORDING DATE!
THAT MEANS NOTHING TO A CHEESE SOUFFLÉ.
AARRGG..
GBTrudeau

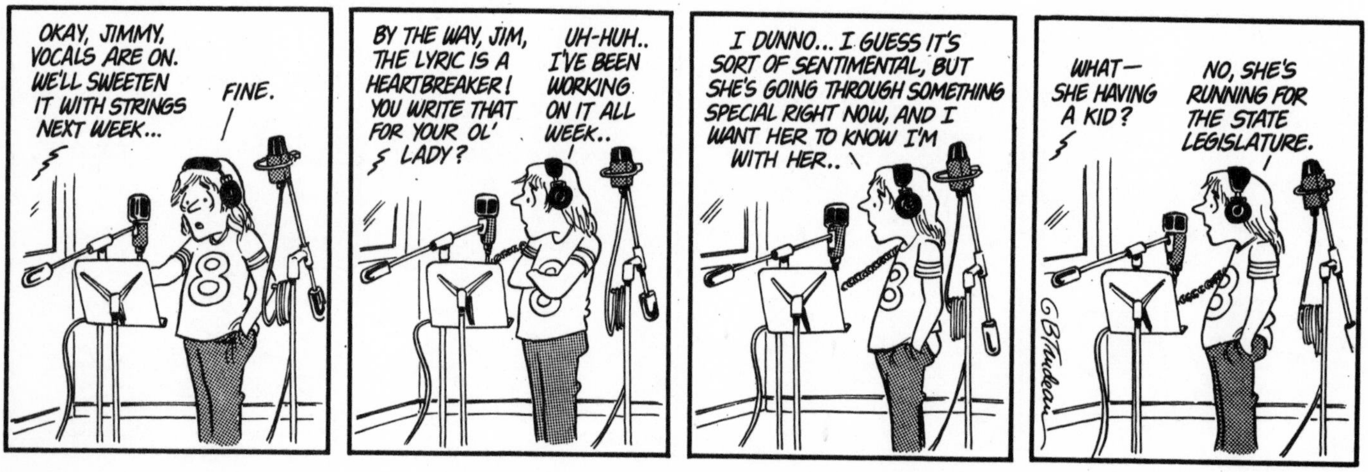
OKAY, JIMMY, VOCALS ARE ON. WE'LL SWEETEN IT WITH STRINGS NEXT WEEK...
FINE.
BY THE WAY, JIM, THE LYRIC IS A HEARTBREAKER! YOU WRITE THAT FOR YOUR OL' LADY?
UH-HUH.. I'VE BEEN WORKING ON IT ALL WEEK..
I DUNNO... I GUESS IT'S SORT OF SENTIMENTAL, BUT SHE'S GOING THROUGH SOMETHING SPECIAL RIGHT NOW, AND I WANT HER TO KNOW I'M WITH HER..
WHAT— SHE HAVING A KID?
NO, SHE'S RUNNING FOR THE STATE LEGISLATURE.
GBTrudeau

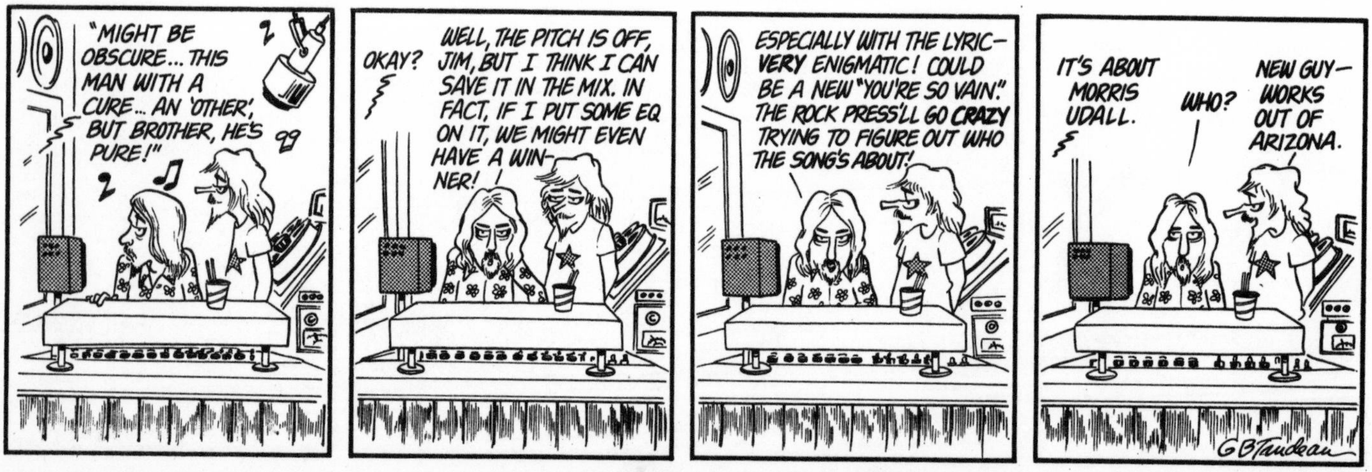
"MIGHT BE OBSCURE... THIS MAN WITH A CURE... AN 'OTHER', BUT BROTHER, HE'S PURE!"
OKAY?
WELL, THE PITCH IS OFF, JIM, BUT I THINK I CAN SAVE IT IN THE MIX. IN FACT, IF I PUT SOME EQ ON IT, WE MIGHT EVEN HAVE A WIN-NER!
ESPECIALLY WITH THE LYRIC- VERY ENIGMATIC! COULD BE A NEW "YOU'RE SO VAIN." THE ROCK PRESS'LL GO CRAZY TRYING TO FIGURE OUT WHO THE SONG'S ABOUT!
IT'S ABOUT MORRIS UDALL.
WHO?
NEW GUY— WORKS OUT OF ARIZONA.
GBTrudeau

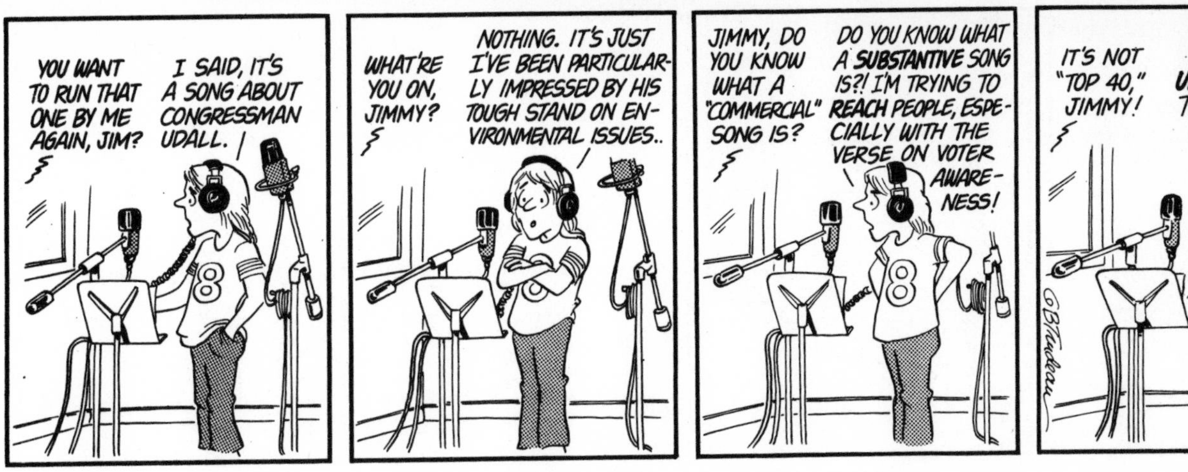
YOU WANT TO RUN THAT ONE BY ME AGAIN, JIM?
I SAID, IT'S A SONG ABOUT CONGRESSMAN UDALL.
WHAT'RE YOU ON, JIMMY?
NOTHING. IT'S JUST I'VE BEEN PARTICULARLY IMPRESSED BY HIS TOUGH STAND ON ENVIRONMENTAL ISSUES..
JIMMY, DO YOU KNOW WHAT A "COMMERCIAL" SONG IS?
DO YOU KNOW WHAT A SUBSTANTIVE SONG IS?! I'M TRYING TO REACH PEOPLE, ESPECIALLY WITH THE VERSE ON VOTER AWARENESS!
IT'S NOT "TOP 40," JIMMY!
NEITHER'S UDALL, FOOL—THAT'S THE POINT!
GBTrudeau

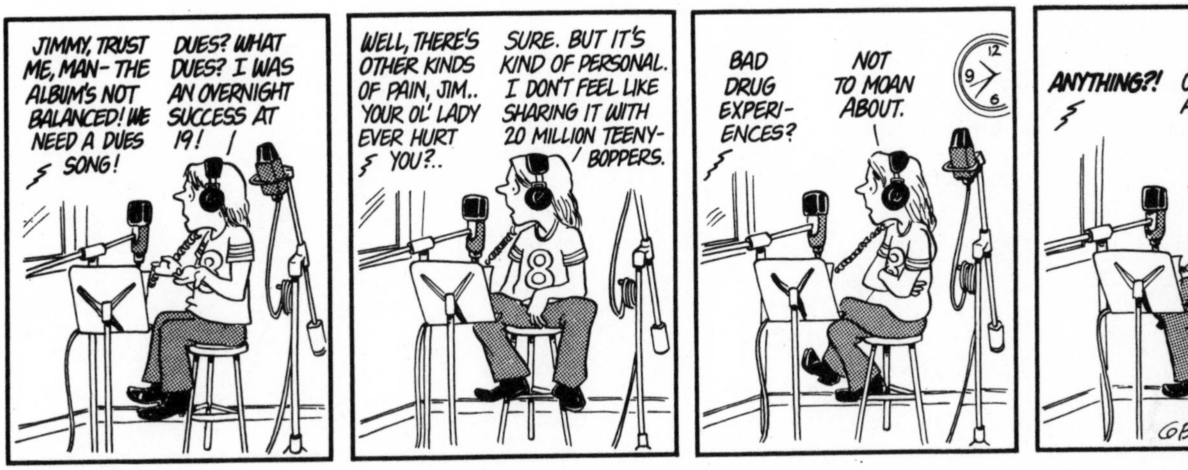
JIMMY, TRUST ME, MAN—THE ALBUM'S NOT BALANCED! WE NEED A DUES SONG!
DUES? WHAT DUES? I WAS AN OVERNIGHT SUCCESS AT 19!
WELL, THERE'S OTHER KINDS OF PAIN, JIM.. YOUR OL' LADY EVER HURT YOU?..
SURE. BUT IT'S KIND OF PERSONAL. I DON'T FEEL LIKE SHARING IT WITH 20 MILLION TEENY-BOPPERS.
BAD DRUG EXPERIENCES?
NOT TO MOAN ABOUT.
ANYTHING?!
WELL, I ONCE HAD MY APPENDIX OUT..
GBTrudeau

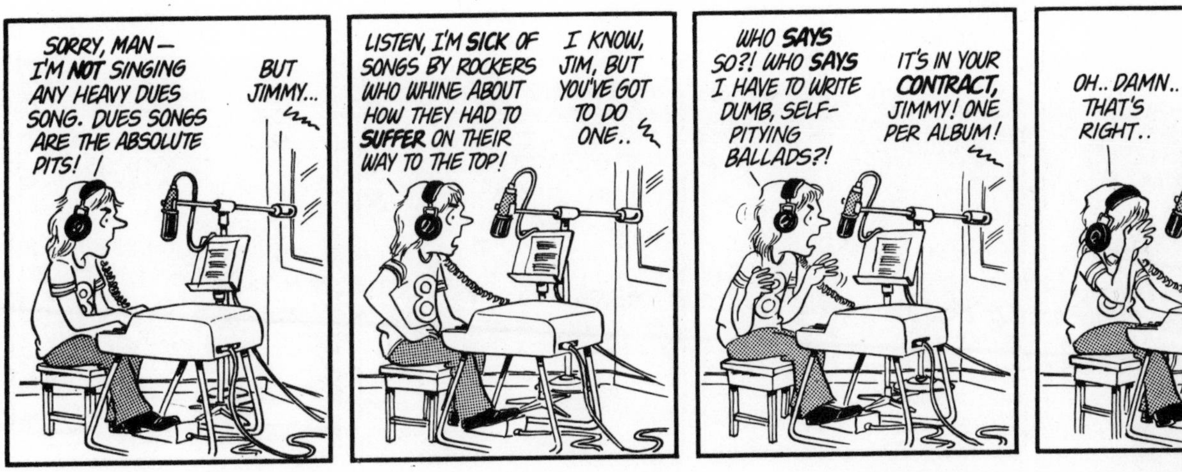
SORRY, MAN—I'M NOT SINGING ANY HEAVY DUES SONG. DUES SONGS ARE THE ABSOLUTE PITS!
BUT JIMMY...
LISTEN, I'M SICK OF SONGS BY ROCKERS WHO WHINE ABOUT HOW THEY HAD TO SUFFER ON THEIR WAY TO THE TOP!
I KNOW, JIM, BUT YOU'VE GOT TO DO ONE..
WHO SAYS SO?! WHO SAYS I HAVE TO WRITE DUMB, SELF-PITYING BALLADS?!
IT'S IN YOUR CONTRACT, JIMMY! ONE PER ALBUM!
OH.. DAMN.. THAT'S RIGHT..
NOW, C'MON—YOU WANT YOUR FANS TO THINK YOU'RE SHALLOW?
GBTrudeau

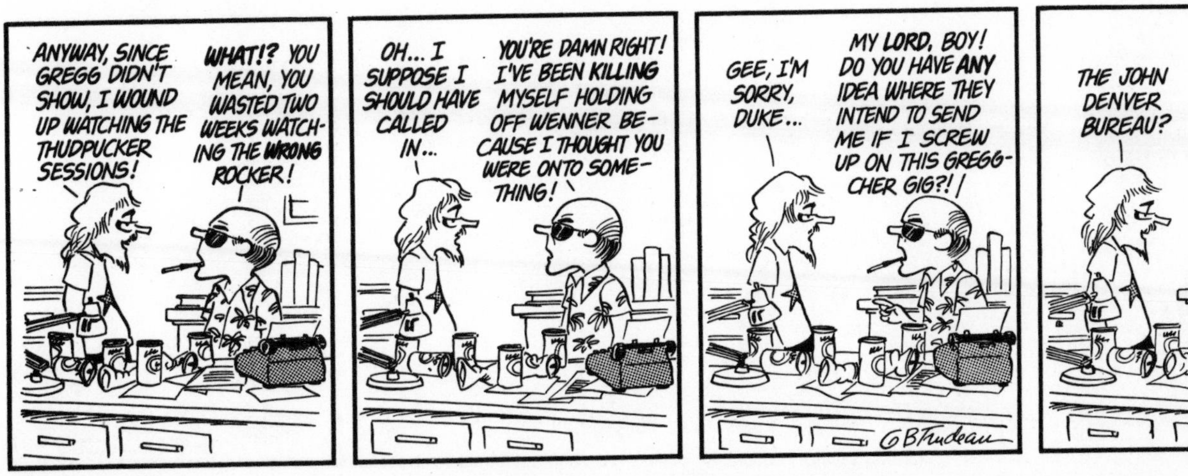
ANYWAY, SINCE GREGG DIDN'T SHOW, I WOUND UP WATCHING THE THUDPUCKER SESSIONS!
WHAT!? YOU MEAN, YOU WASTED TWO WEEKS WATCHING THE WRONG ROCKER!
OH... I SUPPOSE I SHOULD HAVE CALLED IN...
YOU'RE DAMN RIGHT! I'VE BEEN KILLING MYSELF HOLDING OFF WENNER BECAUSE I THOUGHT YOU WERE ONTO SOMETHING!
GEE, I'M SORRY, DUKE...
MY LORD, BOY! DO YOU HAVE ANY IDEA WHERE THEY INTEND TO SEND ME IF I SCREW UP ON THIS GREGG-CHER GIG?!
THE JOHN DENVER BUREAU?
I BREAK INTO HIVES JUST THINKING ABOUT IT..
GBTrudeau

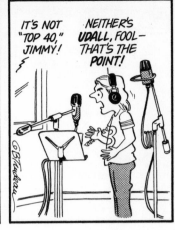

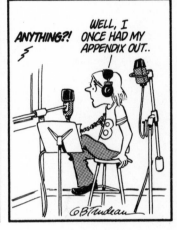

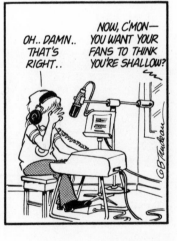

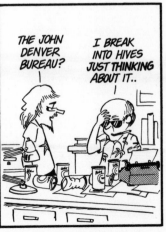

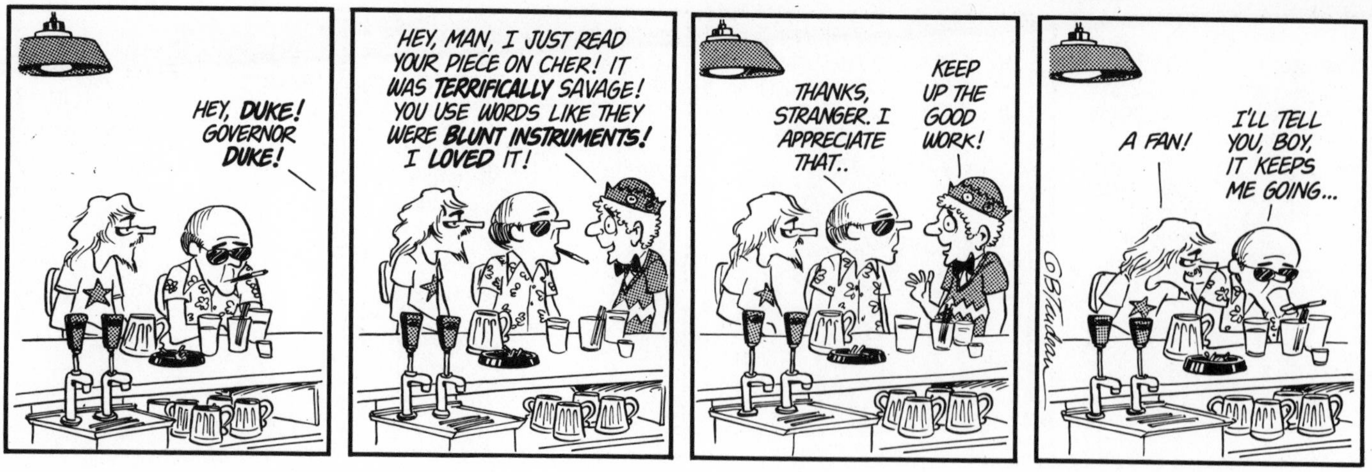
HEY, DUKE! GOVERNOR DUKE!
HEY, MAN, I JUST READ YOUR PIECE ON CHER! IT WAS TERRIFICALLY SAVAGE! YOU USE WORDS LIKE THEY WERE BLUNT INSTRUMENTS! I LOVED IT!
THANKS, STRANGER. I APPRECIATE THAT..
KEEP UP THE GOOD WORK!
A FAN!
I'LL TELL YOU, BOY, IT KEEPS ME GOING...

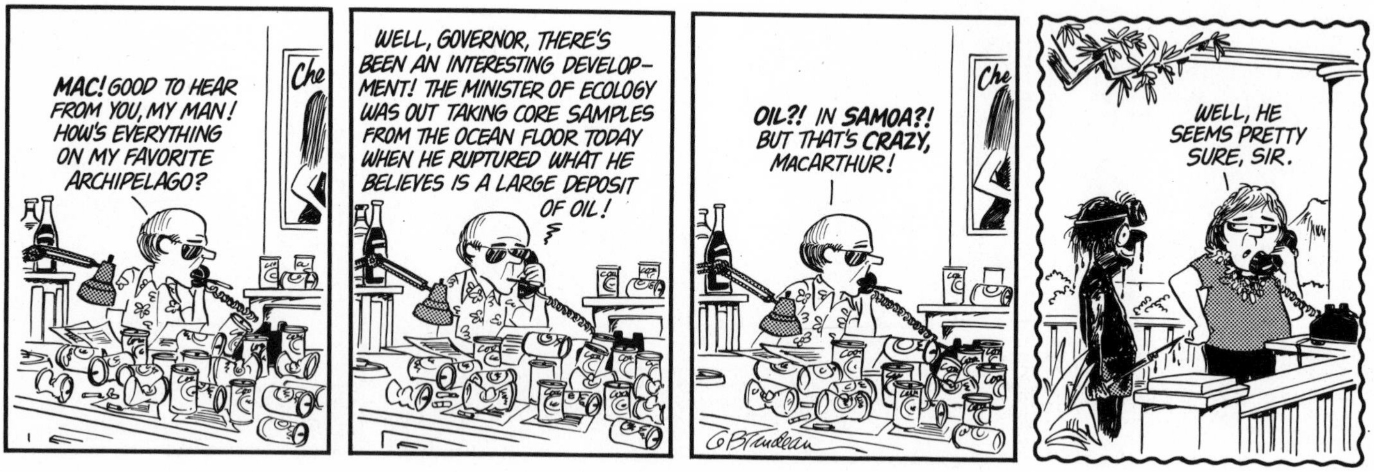
MAC! GOOD TO HEAR FROM YOU, MY MAN! HOW'S EVERYTHING ON MY FAVORITE ARCHIPELAGO?
WELL, GOVERNOR, THERE'S BEEN AN INTERESTING DEVELOPMENT! THE MINISTER OF ECOLOGY WAS OUT TAKING CORE SAMPLES FROM THE OCEAN FLOOR TODAY WHEN HE RUPTURED WHAT HE BELIEVES IS A LARGE DEPOSIT OF OIL!
OIL?! IN SAMOA?! BUT THAT'S CRAZY, MACARTHUR!
WELL, HE SEEMS PRETTY SURE, SIR.

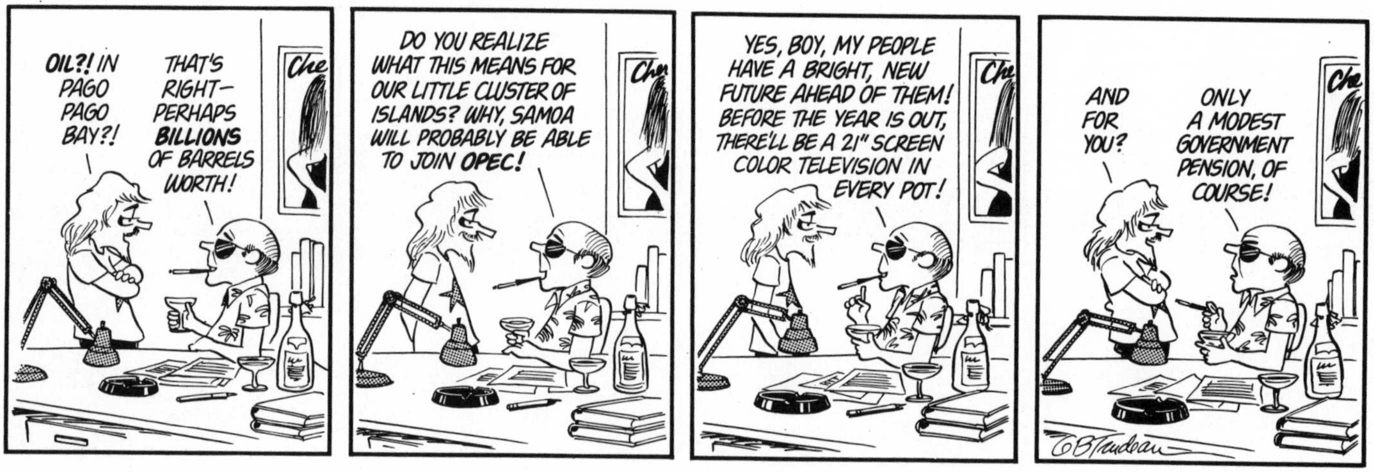
OIL?! IN PAGO PAGO BAY?!
THAT'S RIGHT— PERHAPS BILLIONS OF BARRELS WORTH!
DO YOU REALIZE WHAT THIS MEANS FOR OUR LITTLE CLUSTER OF ISLANDS? WHY, SAMOA WILL PROBABLY BE ABLE TO JOIN OPEC!
YES, BOY, MY PEOPLE HAVE A BRIGHT, NEW FUTURE AHEAD OF THEM! BEFORE THE YEAR IS OUT, THERE'LL BE A 21" SCREEN COLOR TELEVISION IN EVERY POT!
AND FOR YOU?
ONLY A MODEST GOVERNMENT PENSION, OF COURSE!

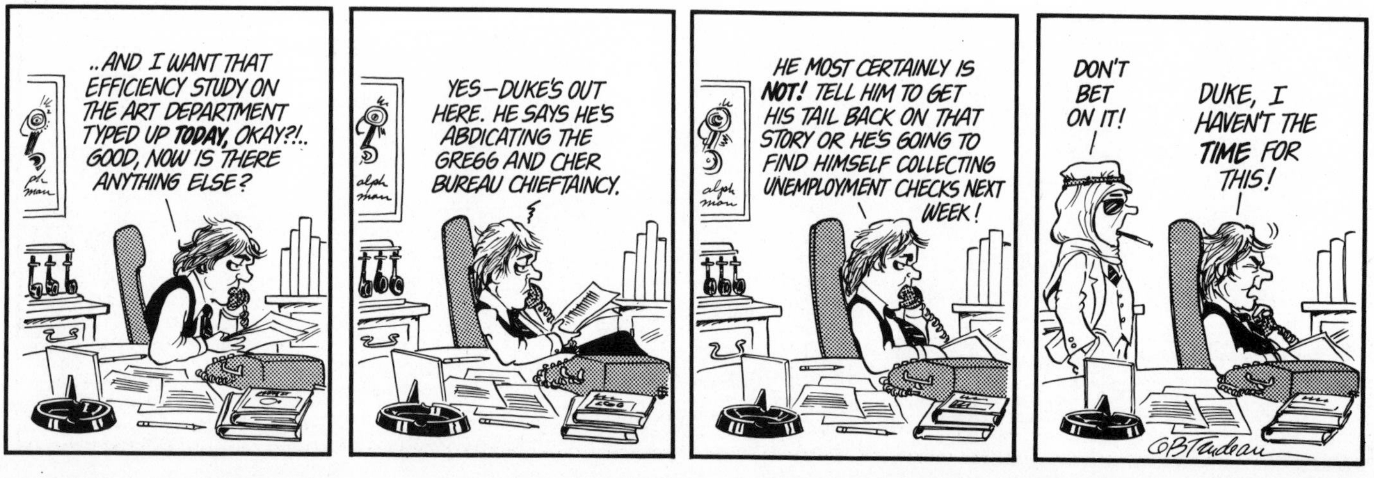
..AND I WANT THAT EFFICIENCY STUDY ON THE ART DEPARTMENT TYPED UP TODAY, OKAY?!.. GOOD, NOW IS THERE ANYTHING ELSE?
YES—DUKE'S OUT HERE. HE SAYS HE'S ABDICATING THE GREGG AND CHER BUREAU CHIEFTAINCY.
HE MOST CERTAINLY IS NOT! TELL HIM TO GET HIS TAIL BACK ON THAT STORY OR HE'S GOING TO FIND HIMSELF COLLECTING UNEMPLOYMENT CHECKS NEXT WEEK!
DON'T BET ON IT!
DUKE, I HAVEN'T THE TIME FOR THIS!

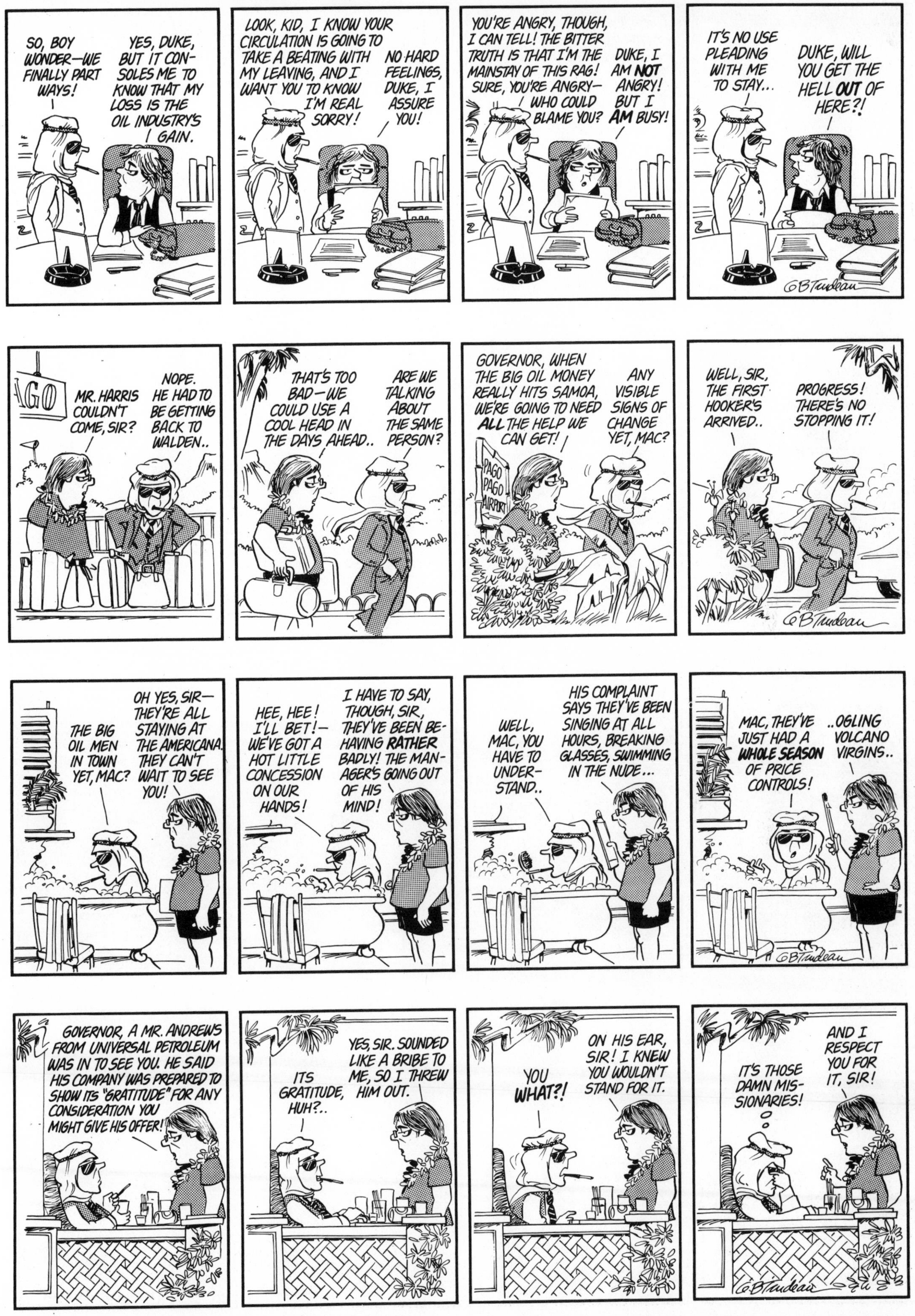
SO, BOY WONDER—WE FINALLY PART WAYS!
YES, DUKE, BUT IT CONSOLES ME TO KNOW THAT MY LOSS IS THE OIL INDUSTRY'S GAIN.
LOOK, KID, I KNOW YOUR CIRCULATION IS GOING TO TAKE A BEATING WITH MY LEAVING, AND I WANT YOU TO KNOW I'M REAL SORRY!
NO HARD FEELINGS, DUKE, I ASSURE YOU!
YOU'RE ANGRY, THOUGH, I CAN TELL! THE BITTER TRUTH IS THAT I'M THE MAINSTAY OF THIS RAG! SURE, YOU'RE ANGRY—WHO COULD BLAME YOU?
DUKE, I AM **NOT** ANGRY! BUT I **AM** BUSY!
IT'S NO USE PLEADING WITH ME TO STAY...
DUKE, WILL YOU GET THE HELL **OUT** OF HERE?!
G.B.Trudeau
AGO
MR. HARRIS COULDN'T COME, SIR?
NOPE. HE HAD TO BE GETTING BACK TO WALDEN..
THAT'S TOO BAD—WE COULD USE A COOL HEAD IN THE DAYS AHEAD..
ARE WE TALKING ABOUT THE SAME PERSON?
GOVERNOR, WHEN THE BIG OIL MONEY REALLY HITS SAMOA, WE'RE GOING TO NEED **ALL** THE HELP WE CAN GET!
PAGO PAGO AIRPORT
ANY VISIBLE SIGNS OF CHANGE YET, MAC?
WELL, SIR, THE FIRST HOOKER'S ARRIVED..
PROGRESS! THERE'S NO STOPPING IT!
G.B.Trudeau
THE BIG OIL MEN IN TOWN YET, MAC?
OH YES, SIR—THEY'RE ALL STAYING AT THE AMERICANA. THEY CAN'T WAIT TO SEE YOU!
HEE, HEE! I'LL BET!—WE'VE GOT A HOT LITTLE CONCESSION ON OUR HANDS!
I HAVE TO SAY, THOUGH, SIR, THEY'VE BEEN BEHAVING **RATHER** BADLY! THE MANAGER'S GOING OUT OF HIS MIND!
WELL, MAC, YOU HAVE TO UNDERSTAND..
HIS COMPLAINT SAYS THEY'VE BEEN SINGING AT ALL HOURS, BREAKING GLASSES, SWIMMING IN THE NUDE...
MAC, THEY'VE JUST HAD A **WHOLE SEASON** OF PRICE CONTROLS!
..OGLING VOLCANO VIRGINS..
G.B.Trudeau
GOVERNOR, A MR. ANDREWS FROM UNIVERSAL PETROLEUM WAS IN TO SEE YOU. HE SAID HIS COMPANY WAS PREPARED TO SHOW ITS "GRATITUDE" FOR ANY CONSIDERATION YOU MIGHT GIVE HIS OFFER!
ITS GRATITUDE, HUH?..
YES, SIR. SOUNDED LIKE A BRIBE TO ME, SO I THREW HIM OUT.
YOU **WHAT?!**
ON HIS EAR, SIR! I KNEW YOU WOULDN'T STAND FOR IT.
IT'S THOSE DAMN MISSIONARIES!
AND I RESPECT YOU FOR IT, SIR!
G.B.Trudeau

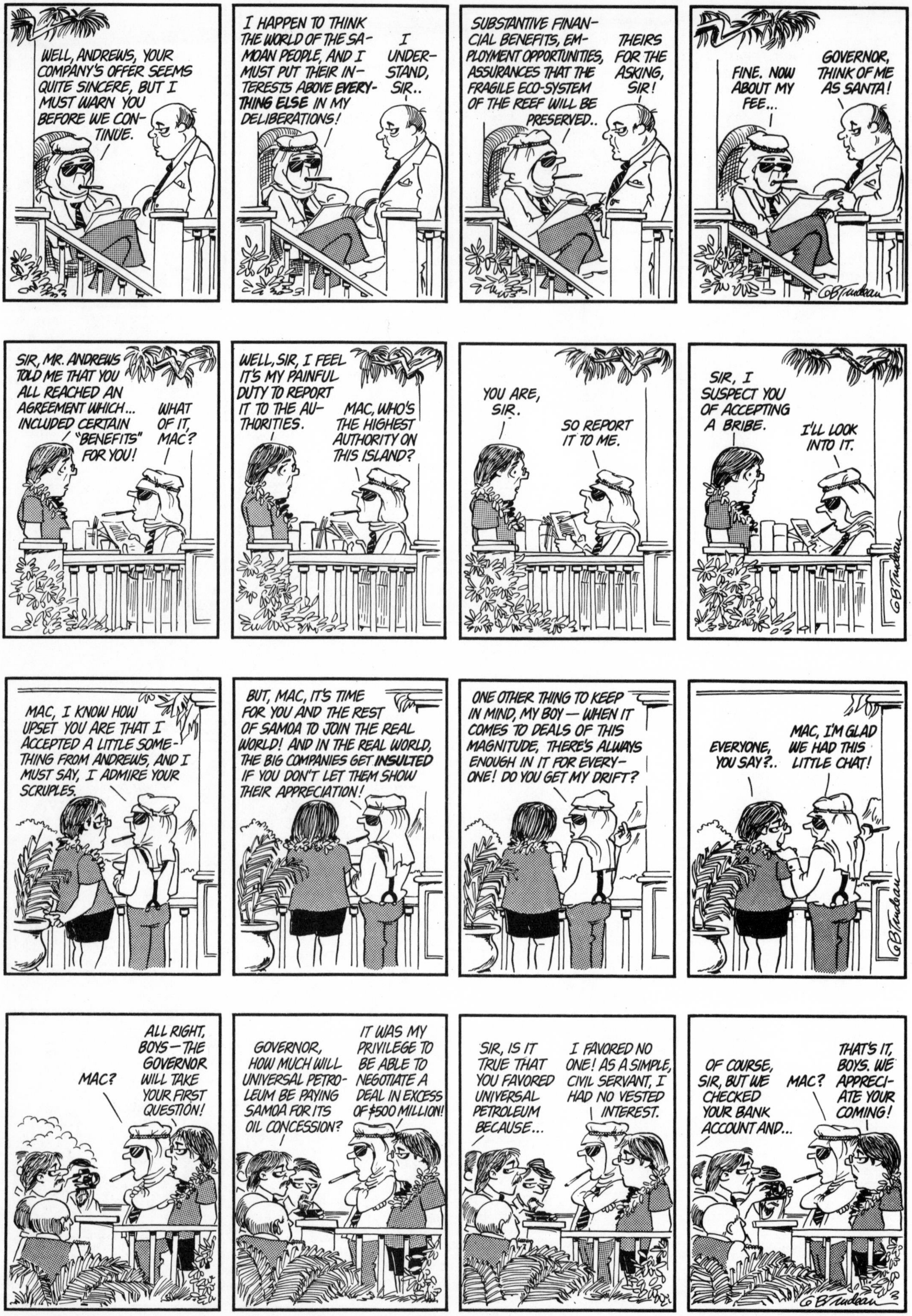

WELL, ANDREWS, YOUR COMPANY'S OFFER SEEMS QUITE SINCERE, BUT I MUST WARN YOU BEFORE WE CONTINUE.
I HAPPEN TO THINK THE WORLD OF THE SAMOAN PEOPLE, AND I MUST PUT THEIR INTERESTS ABOVE **EVERYTHING ELSE** IN MY DELIBERATIONS!
I UNDERSTAND, SIR..
SUBSTANTIVE FINANCIAL BENEFITS, EMPLOYMENT OPPORTUNITIES, ASSURANCES THAT THE FRAGILE ECO-SYSTEM OF THE REEF WILL BE PRESERVED..
THEIRS FOR THE ASKING, SIR!
FINE. NOW ABOUT MY FEE...
GOVERNOR, THINK OF ME AS SANTA!
SIR, MR. ANDREWS TOLD ME THAT YOU ALL REACHED AN AGREEMENT WHICH... INCLUDED CERTAIN "BENEFITS" FOR YOU!
WHAT OF IT, MAC?
WELL, SIR, I FEEL IT'S MY PAINFUL DUTY TO REPORT IT TO THE AUTHORITIES.
MAC, WHO'S THE HIGHEST AUTHORITY ON THIS ISLAND?
YOU ARE, SIR.
SO REPORT IT TO ME.
SIR, I SUSPECT YOU OF ACCEPTING A BRIBE.
I'LL LOOK INTO IT.
MAC, I KNOW HOW UPSET YOU ARE THAT I ACCEPTED A LITTLE SOMETHING FROM ANDREWS, AND I MUST SAY, I ADMIRE YOUR SCRUPLES.
BUT, MAC, IT'S TIME FOR YOU AND THE REST OF SAMOA TO JOIN THE REAL WORLD! AND IN THE REAL WORLD, THE BIG COMPANIES GET **INSULTED** IF YOU DON'T LET THEM SHOW THEIR APPRECIATION!
ONE OTHER THING TO KEEP IN MIND, MY BOY — **WHEN IT** COMES TO DEALS OF THIS MAGNITUDE, THERE'S ALWAYS ENOUGH IN IT FOR EVERYONE! DO YOU GET MY DRIFT?
EVERYONE, YOU SAY?..
MAC, I'M GLAD WE HAD THIS LITTLE CHAT!
MAC?
ALL RIGHT, BOYS — THE GOVERNOR WILL TAKE YOUR FIRST QUESTION!
GOVERNOR, HOW MUCH WILL UNIVERSAL PETROLEUM BE PAYING SAMOA FOR ITS OIL CONCESSION?
IT WAS MY PRIVILEGE TO BE ABLE TO NEGOTIATE A DEAL IN EXCESS OF $500 MILLION!
SIR, IS IT TRUE THAT YOU FAVORED UNIVERSAL PETROLEUM BECAUSE...
I FAVORED NO ONE! AS A SIMPLE, CIVIL SERVANT, I HAD NO VESTED INTEREST.
OF COURSE, SIR, BUT WE CHECKED YOUR BANK ACCOUNT AND...
MAC?
THAT'S IT, BOYS. WE APPRECIATE YOUR COMING!

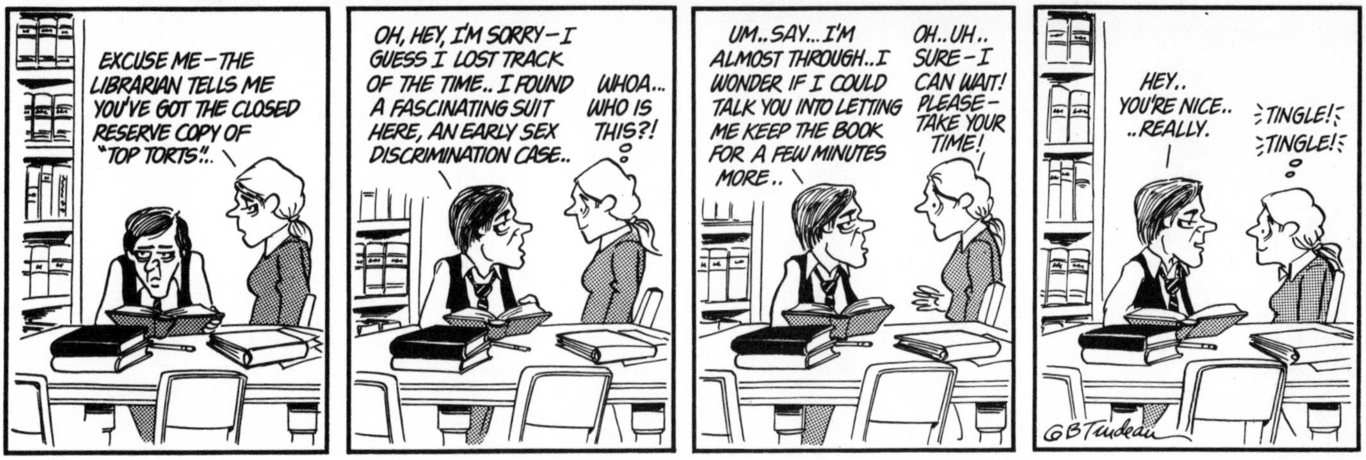
EXCUSE ME—THE LIBRARIAN TELLS ME YOU'VE GOT THE CLOSED RESERVE COPY OF "TOP TORTS"..
OH, HEY, I'M SORRY—I GUESS I LOST TRACK OF THE TIME.. I FOUND A FASCINATING SUIT HERE, AN EARLY SEX DISCRIMINATION CASE..
WHOA... WHO IS THIS?!
UM.. SAY... I'M ALMOST THROUGH.. I WONDER IF I COULD TALK YOU INTO LETTING ME KEEP THE BOOK FOR A FEW MINUTES MORE..
OH.. UH.. SURE—I CAN WAIT! PLEASE—TAKE YOUR TIME!
HEY.. YOU'RE NICE.. ..REALLY.
TINGLE! TINGLE!
GBTrudeau

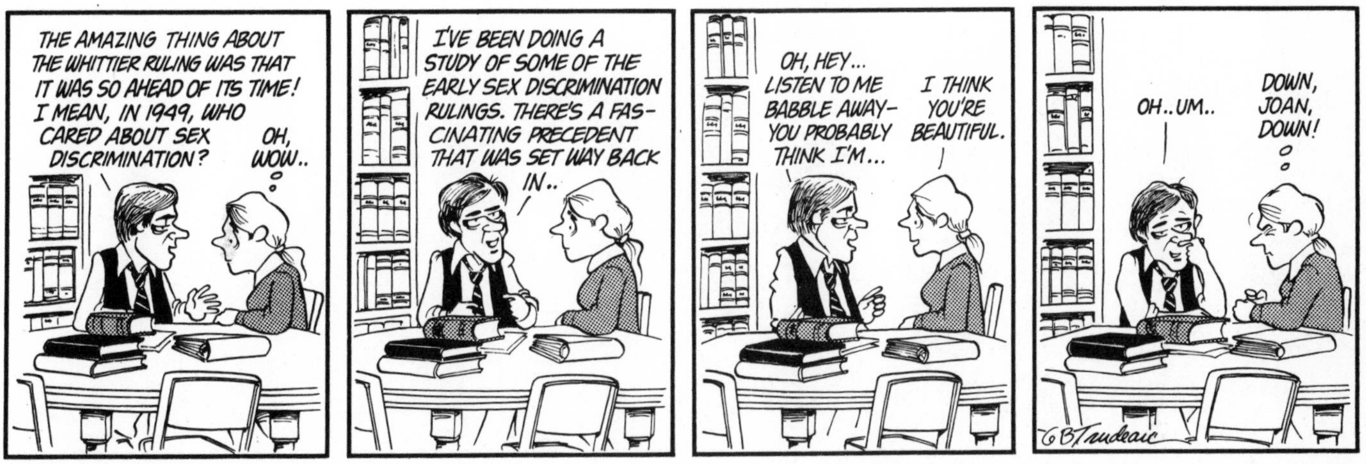
THE AMAZING THING ABOUT THE WHITTIER RULING WAS THAT IT WAS SO AHEAD OF ITS TIME! I MEAN, IN 1949, WHO CARED ABOUT SEX DISCRIMINATION?
OH, WOW..
I'VE BEEN DOING A STUDY OF SOME OF THE EARLY SEX DISCRIMINATION RULINGS. THERE'S A FASCINATING PRECEDENT THAT WAS SET WAY BACK IN..
OH, HEY... LISTEN TO ME BABBLE AWAY—YOU PROBABLY THINK I'M...
I THINK YOU'RE BEAUTIFUL.
OH.. UM..
DOWN, JOAN, DOWN!
GBTrudeau

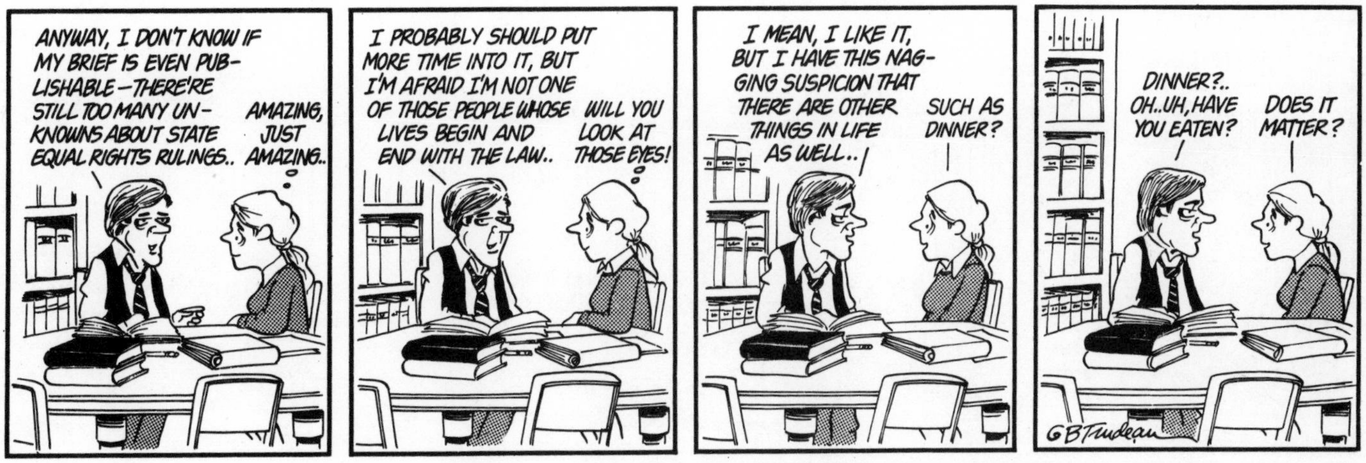
ANYWAY, I DON'T KNOW IF MY BRIEF IS EVEN PUBLISHABLE—THERE'RE STILL TOO MANY UNKNOWNS ABOUT STATE EQUAL RIGHTS RULINGS..
AMAZING, JUST AMAZING..
I PROBABLY SHOULD PUT MORE TIME INTO IT, BUT I'M AFRAID I'M NOT ONE OF THOSE PEOPLE WHOSE LIVES BEGIN AND END WITH THE LAW..
WILL YOU LOOK AT THOSE EYES!
I MEAN, I LIKE IT, BUT I HAVE THIS NAGGING SUSPICION THAT THERE ARE OTHER THINGS IN LIFE AS WELL..
SUCH AS DINNER?
DINNER?.. OH.. UH, HAVE YOU EATEN?
DOES IT MATTER?
GBTrudeau

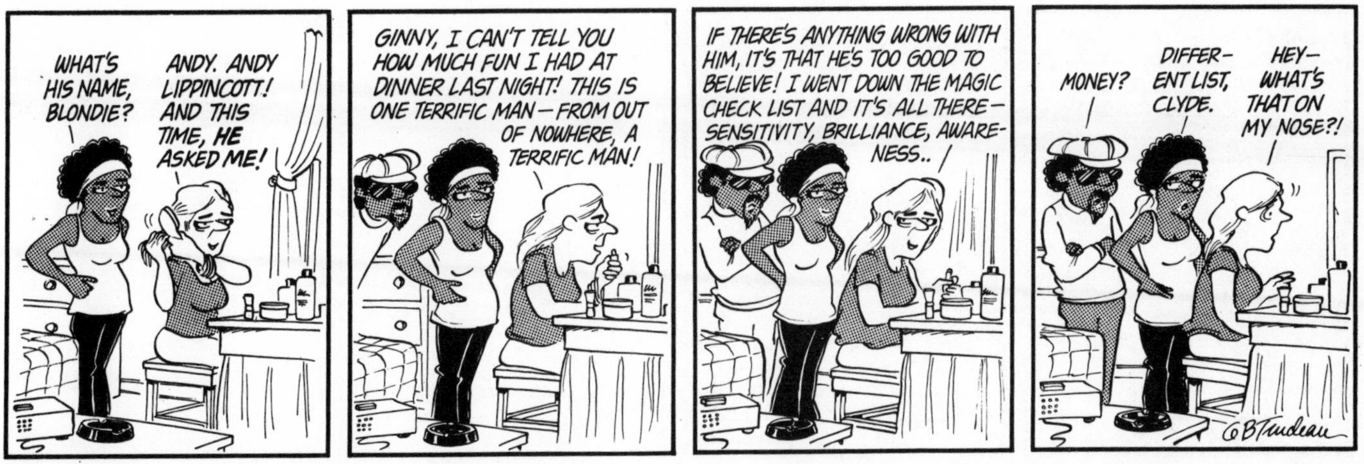
WHAT'S HIS NAME, BLONDIE?
ANDY. ANDY LIPPINCOTT! AND THIS TIME, HE ASKED ME!
GINNY, I CAN'T TELL YOU HOW MUCH FUN I HAD AT DINNER LAST NIGHT! THIS IS ONE TERRIFIC MAN—FROM OUT OF NOWHERE, A TERRIFIC MAN!
IF THERE'S ANYTHING WRONG WITH HIM, IT'S THAT HE'S TOO GOOD TO BELIEVE! I WENT DOWN THE MAGIC CHECK LIST AND IT'S ALL THERE—SENSITIVITY, BRILLIANCE, AWARENESS..
MONEY?
DIFFERENT LIST, CLYDE.
HEY—WHAT'S THAT ON MY NOSE?!
GBTrudeau

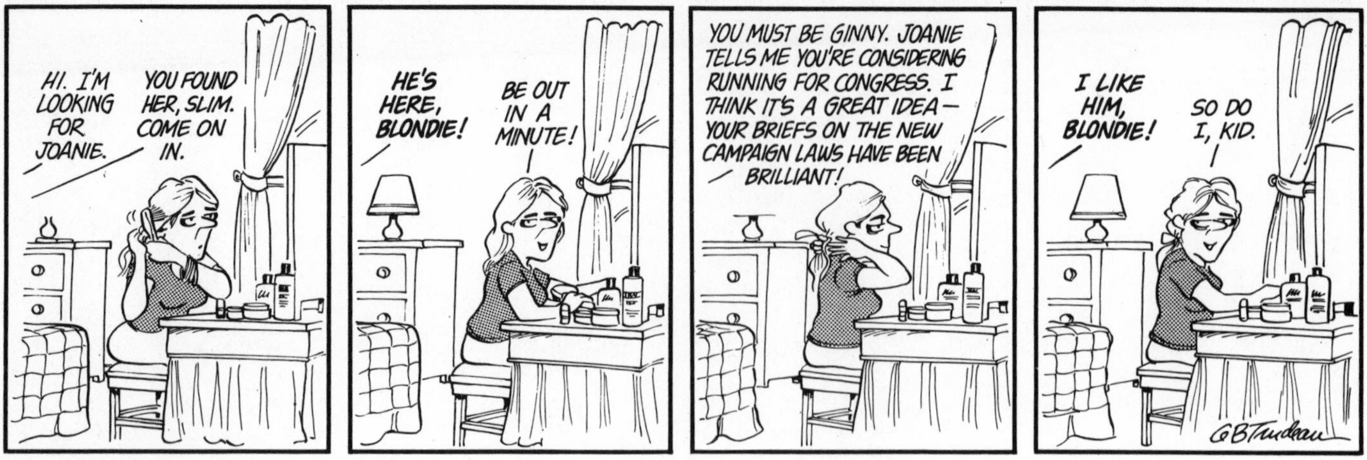
HI. I'M LOOKING FOR JOANIE.
YOU FOUND HER, SLIM. COME ON IN.
HE'S HERE, BLONDIE!
BE OUT IN A MINUTE!
YOU MUST BE GINNY. JOANIE TELLS ME YOU'RE CONSIDERING RUNNING FOR CONGRESS. I THINK IT'S A GREAT IDEA— YOUR BRIEFS ON THE NEW CAMPAIGN LAWS HAVE BEEN BRILLIANT!
I LIKE HIM, BLONDIE!
SO DO I, KID.
GBTrudeau

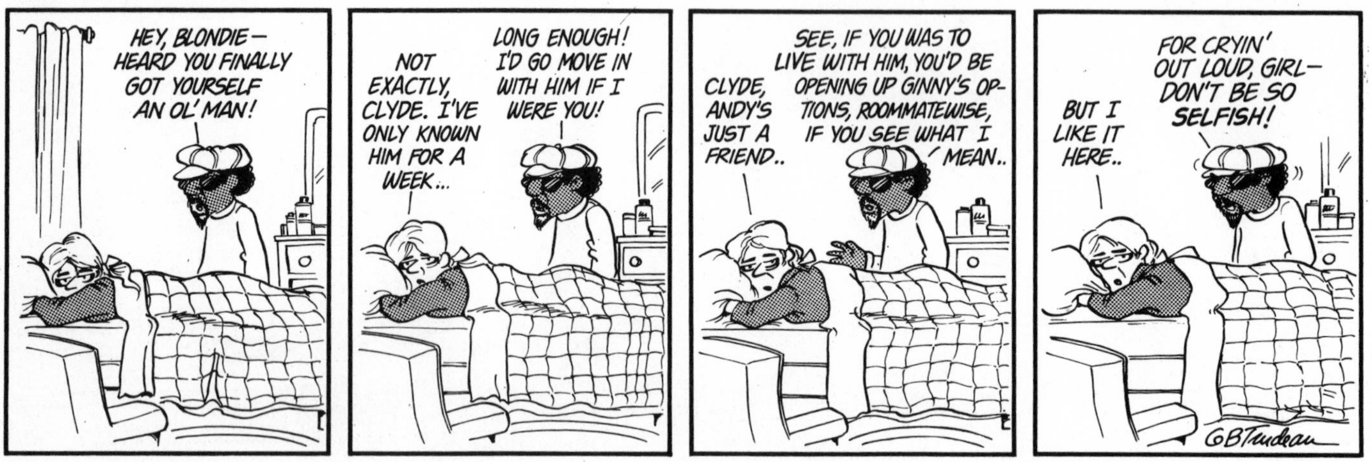
HEY, BLONDIE— HEARD YOU FINALLY GOT YOURSELF AN OL' MAN!
NOT EXACTLY, CLYDE. I'VE ONLY KNOWN HIM FOR A WEEK...
LONG ENOUGH! I'D GO MOVE IN WITH HIM IF I WERE YOU!
CLYDE, ANDY'S JUST A FRIEND..
SEE, IF YOU WAS TO LIVE WITH HIM, YOU'D BE OPENING UP GINNY'S OPTIONS, ROOMMATEWISE, IF YOU SEE WHAT I MEAN..
BUT I LIKE IT HERE..
FOR CRYIN' OUT LOUD, GIRL— DON'T BE SO SELFISH!
GBTrudeau

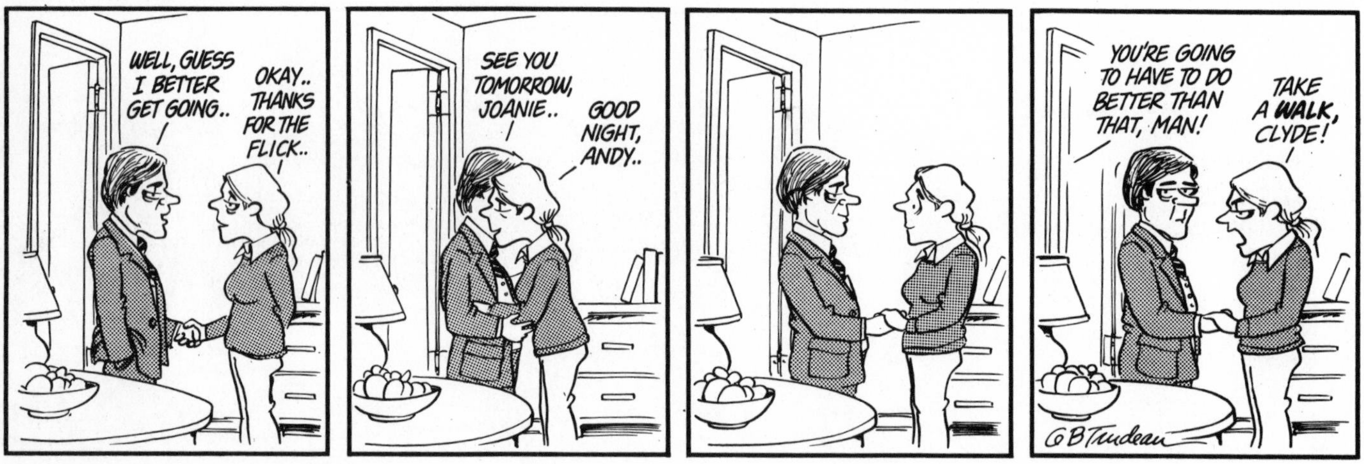
WELL, GUESS I BETTER GET GOING..
OKAY.. THANKS FOR THE FLICK..
SEE YOU TOMORROW, JOANIE..
GOOD NIGHT, ANDY..
YOU'RE GOING TO HAVE TO DO BETTER THAN THAT, MAN!
TAKE A WALK, CLYDE!
GBTrudeau

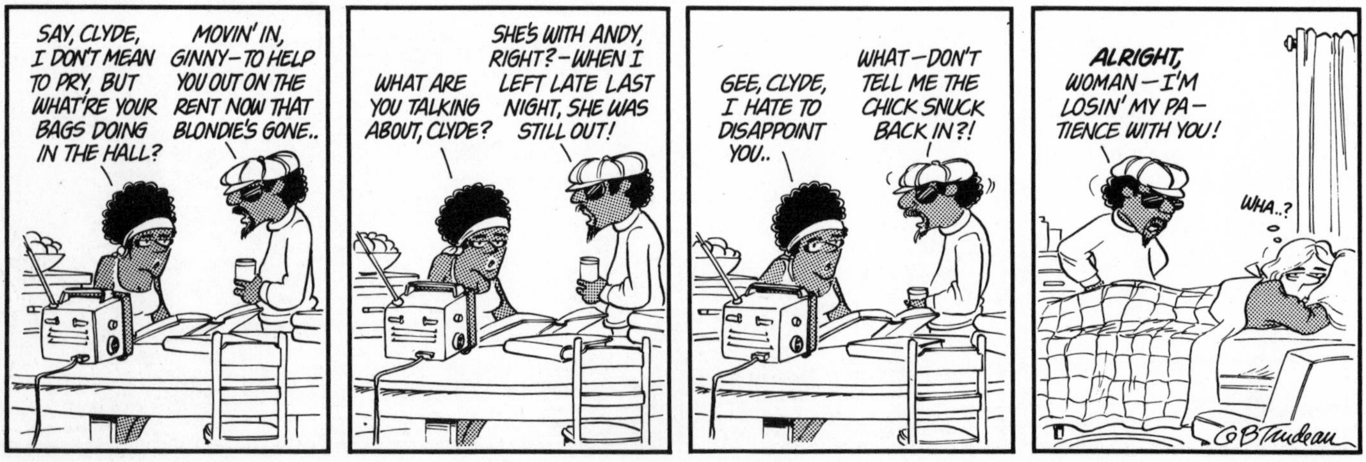
SAY, CLYDE, I DON'T MEAN TO PRY, BUT WHAT'RE YOUR BAGS DOING IN THE HALL?
MOVIN' IN, GINNY— TO HELP YOU OUT ON THE RENT NOW THAT BLONDIE'S GONE..
WHAT ARE YOU TALKING ABOUT, CLYDE?
SHE'S WITH ANDY, RIGHT?— WHEN I LEFT LATE LAST NIGHT, SHE WAS STILL OUT!
GEE, CLYDE, I HATE TO DISAPPOINT YOU..
WHAT— DON'T TELL ME THE CHICK SNUCK BACK IN?!
ALRIGHT, WOMAN— I'M LOSIN' MY PATIENCE WITH YOU!
WHA..?
GBTrudeau

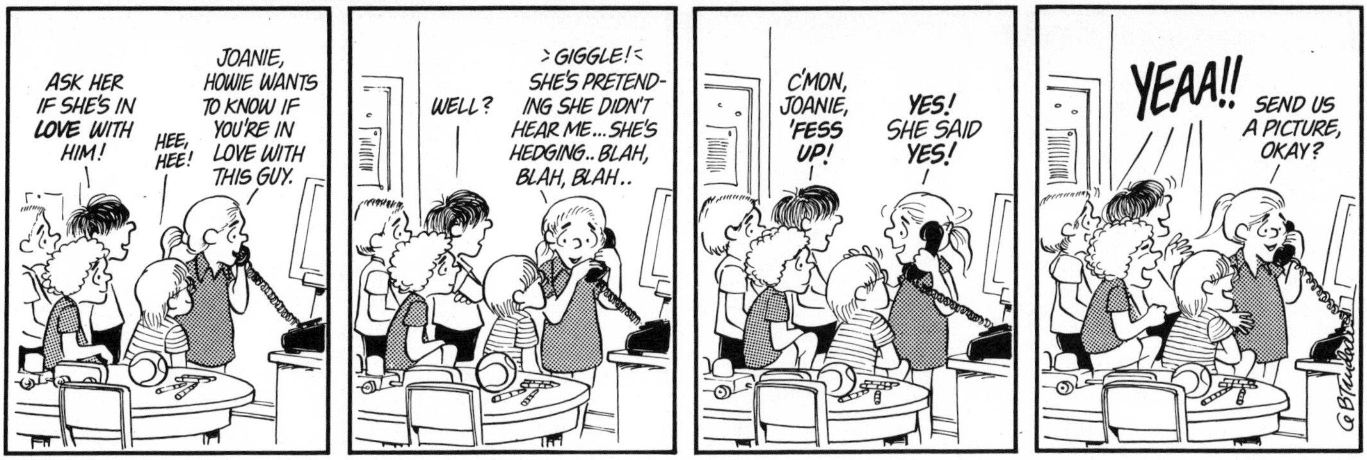
ASK HER IF SHE'S IN LOVE WITH HIM!
HEE, HEE!
JOANIE, HOWIE WANTS TO KNOW IF YOU'RE IN LOVE WITH THIS GUY.
WELL?
>GIGGLE!< SHE'S PRETENDING SHE DIDN'T HEAR ME... SHE'S HEDGING.. BLAH, BLAH, BLAH..
C'MON, JOANIE, 'FESS UP!
YES! SHE SAID YES!
YEAA!!
SEND US A PICTURE, OKAY?
© B Trudeau

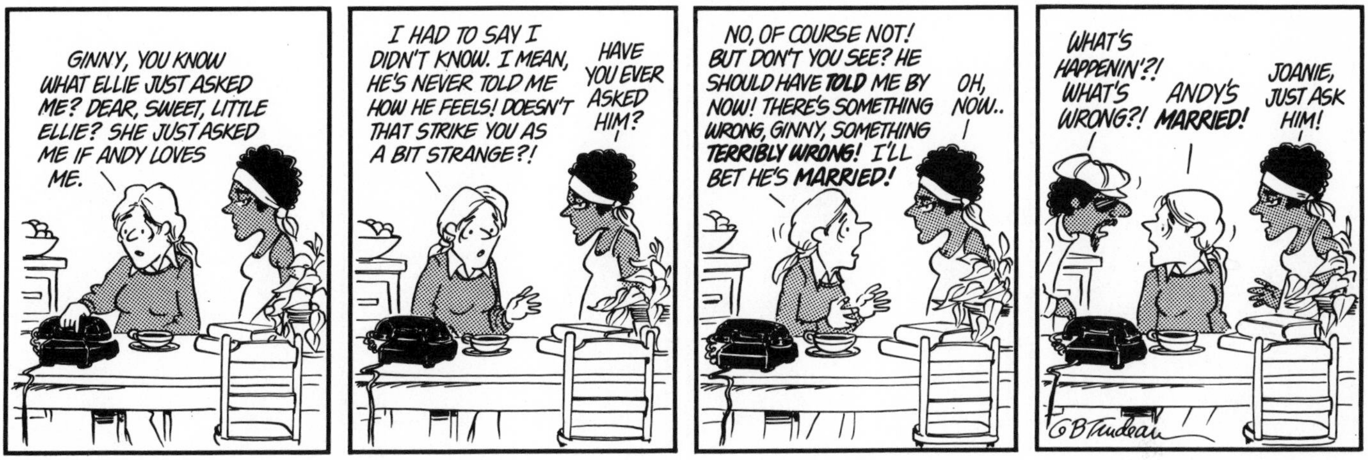
GINNY, YOU KNOW WHAT ELLIE JUST ASKED ME? DEAR, SWEET, LITTLE ELLIE? SHE JUST ASKED ME IF ANDY LOVES ME.
I HAD TO SAY I DIDN'T KNOW. I MEAN, HE'S NEVER TOLD ME HOW HE FEELS! DOESN'T THAT STRIKE YOU AS A BIT STRANGE?!
HAVE YOU EVER ASKED HIM?
NO, OF COURSE NOT! BUT DON'T YOU SEE? HE SHOULD HAVE TOLD ME BY NOW! THERE'S SOMETHING WRONG, GINNY, SOMETHING TERRIBLY WRONG! I'LL BET HE'S MARRIED!
OH, NOW..
WHAT'S HAPPENIN'?! WHAT'S WRONG?!
ANDY'S MARRIED!
JOANIE, JUST ASK HIM!
© B Trudeau

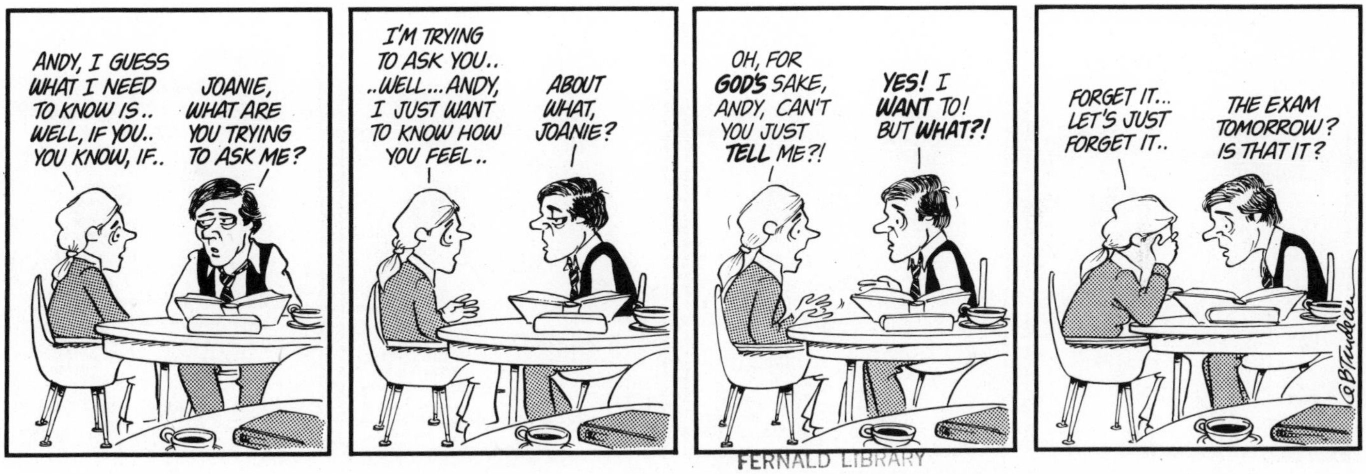
ANDY, I GUESS WHAT I NEED TO KNOW IS.. WELL, IF YOU.. YOU KNOW, IF..
JOANIE, WHAT ARE YOU TRYING TO ASK ME?
I'M TRYING TO ASK YOU.. ..WELL... ANDY, I JUST WANT TO KNOW HOW YOU FEEL..
ABOUT WHAT, JOANIE?
OH, FOR GOD'S SAKE, ANDY, CAN'T YOU JUST TELL ME?!
YES! I WANT TO! BUT WHAT?!
FORGET IT... LET'S JUST FORGET IT..
THE EXAM TOMORROW? IS THAT IT?
© B Trudeau

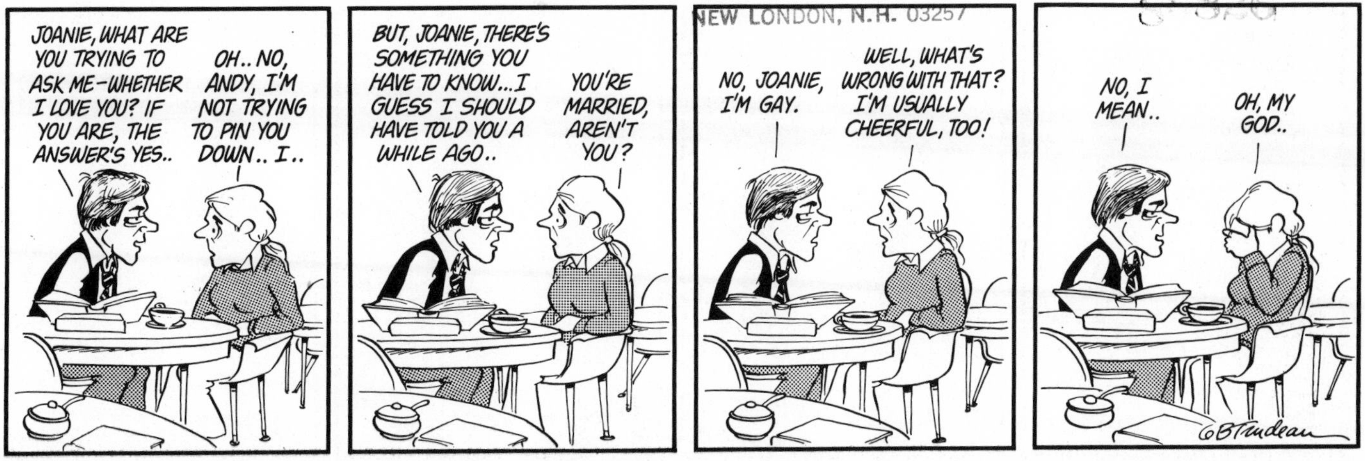
JOANIE, WHAT ARE YOU TRYING TO ASK ME—WHETHER I LOVE YOU? IF YOU ARE, THE ANSWER'S YES..
OH.. NO, ANDY, I'M NOT TRYING TO PIN YOU DOWN.. I..
BUT, JOANIE, THERE'S SOMETHING YOU HAVE TO KNOW... I GUESS I SHOULD HAVE TOLD YOU A WHILE AGO..
YOU'RE MARRIED, AREN'T YOU?
NO, JOANIE, I'M GAY.
WELL, WHAT'S WRONG WITH THAT? I'M USUALLY CHEERFUL, TOO!
NO, I MEAN..
OH, MY GOD..
© B Trudeau

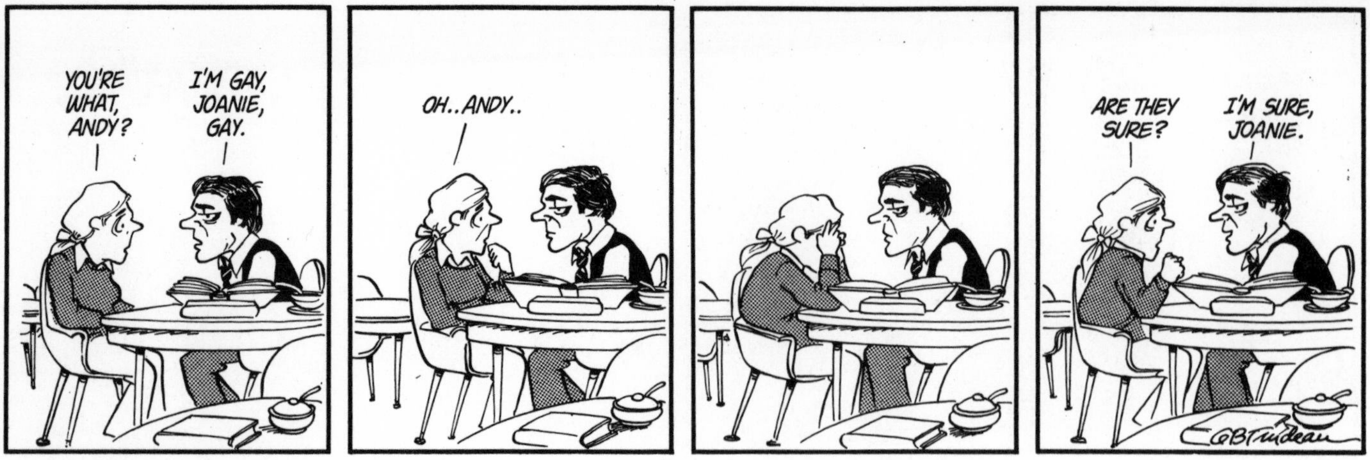
YOU'RE WHAT, ANDY?
I'M GAY, JOANIE, GAY.
OH.. ANDY..
ARE THEY SURE?
I'M SURE, JOANIE.

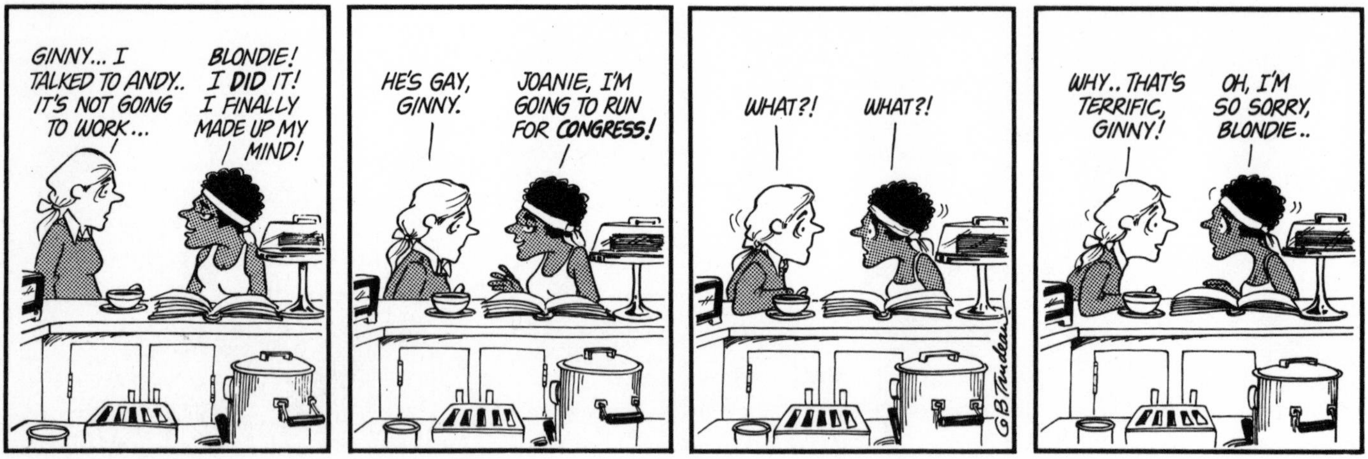
GINNY... I TALKED TO ANDY.. IT'S NOT GOING TO WORK...
BLONDIE! I DID IT! I FINALLY MADE UP MY MIND!
HE'S GAY, GINNY.
JOANIE, I'M GOING TO RUN FOR CONGRESS!
WHAT?!
WHAT?!
WHY.. THAT'S TERRIFIC, GINNY!
OH, I'M SO SORRY, BLONDIE..

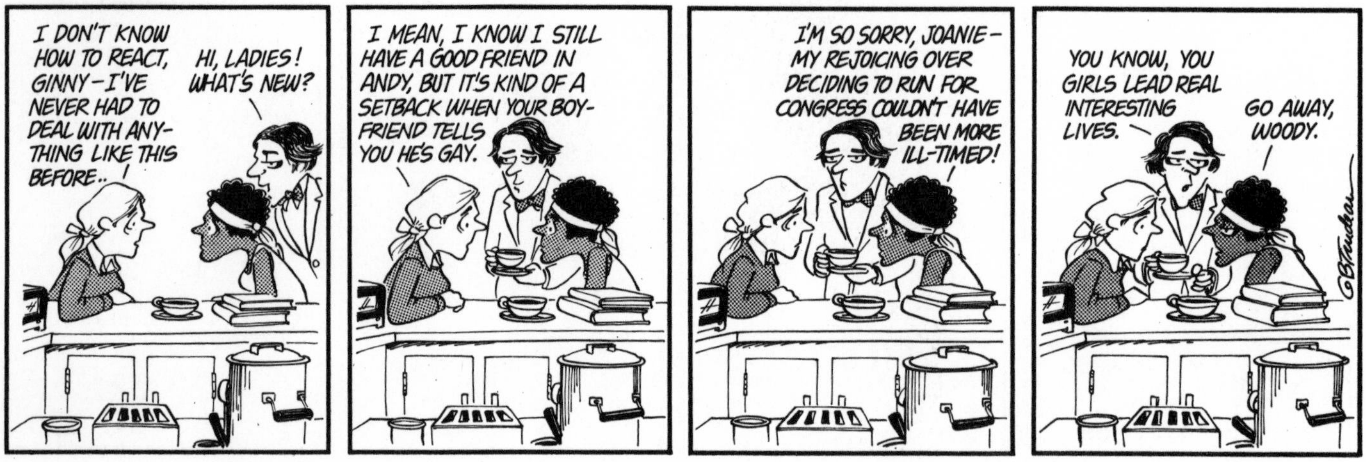
I DON'T KNOW HOW TO REACT, GINNY–I'VE NEVER HAD TO DEAL WITH ANY-THING LIKE THIS BEFORE..
HI, LADIES! WHAT'S NEW?
I MEAN, I KNOW I STILL HAVE A GOOD FRIEND IN ANDY, BUT IT'S KIND OF A SETBACK WHEN YOUR BOY-FRIEND TELLS YOU HE'S GAY.
I'M SO SORRY, JOANIE– MY REJOICING OVER DECIDING TO RUN FOR CONGRESS COULDN'T HAVE BEEN MORE ILL-TIMED!
YOU KNOW, YOU GIRLS LEAD REAL INTERESTING LIVES.
GO AWAY, WOODY.

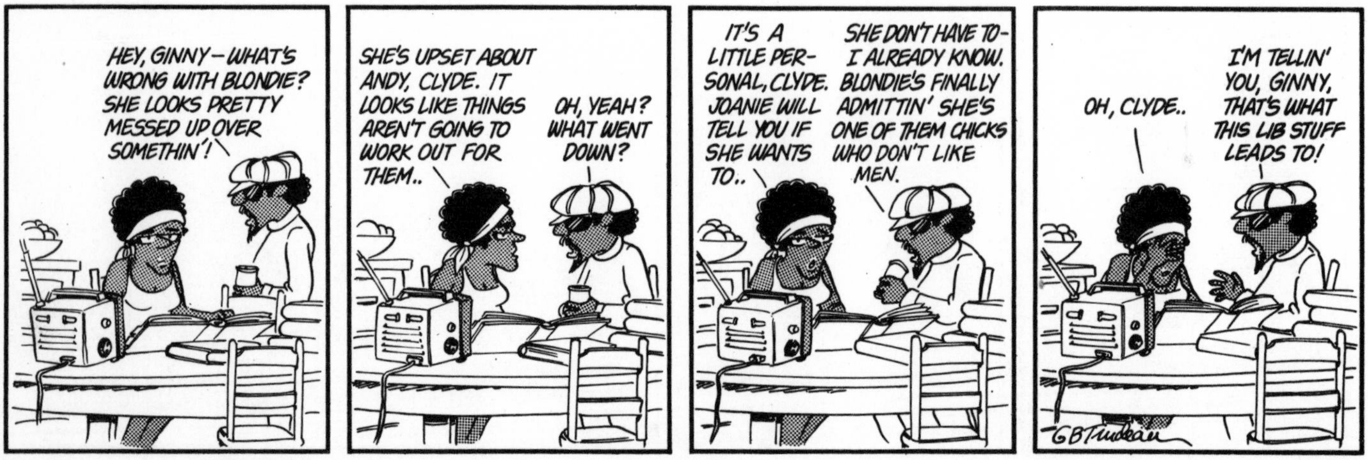
HEY, GINNY–WHAT'S WRONG WITH BLONDIE? SHE LOOKS PRETTY MESSED UP OVER SOMETHIN'!
SHE'S UPSET ABOUT ANDY, CLYDE. IT LOOKS LIKE THINGS AREN'T GOING TO WORK OUT FOR THEM..
OH, YEAH? WHAT WENT DOWN?
IT'S A LITTLE PER-SONAL, CLYDE. JOANIE WILL TELL YOU IF SHE WANTS TO..
SHE DON'T HAVE TO– I ALREADY KNOW. BLONDIE'S FINALLY ADMITTIN' SHE'S ONE OF THEM CHICKS WHO DON'T LIKE MEN.
OH, CLYDE..
I'M TELLIN' YOU, GINNY, THAT'S WHAT THIS LIB STUFF LEADS TO!

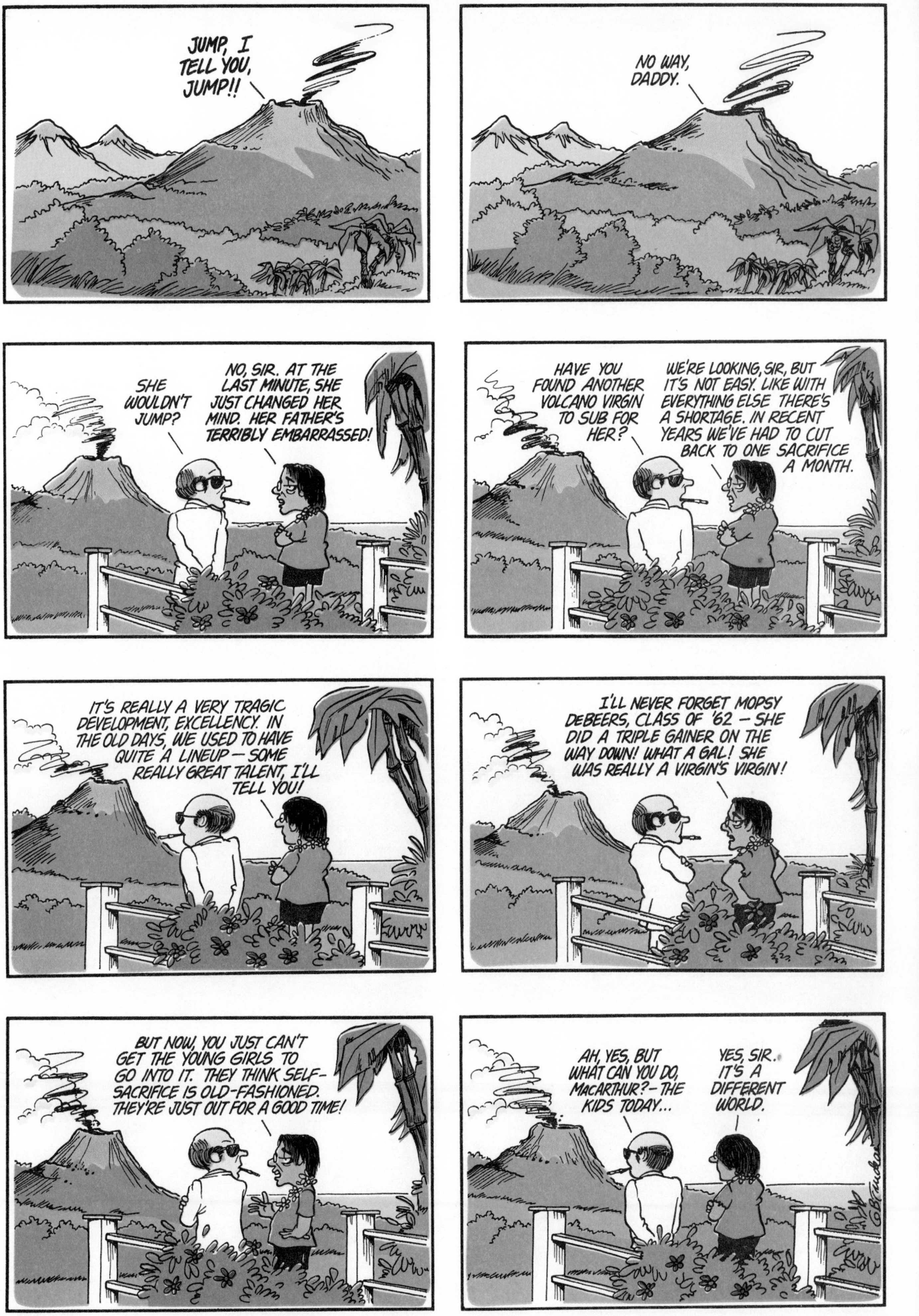
JUMP, I TELL YOU, JUMP!!
NO WAY, DADDY.
SHE WOULDN'T JUMP?
NO, SIR. AT THE LAST MINUTE, SHE JUST CHANGED HER MIND. HER FATHER'S TERRIBLY EMBARRASSED!
HAVE YOU FOUND ANOTHER VOLCANO VIRGIN TO SUB FOR HER?
WE'RE LOOKING, SIR, BUT IT'S NOT EASY. LIKE WITH EVERYTHING ELSE THERE'S A SHORTAGE. IN RECENT YEARS WE'VE HAD TO CUT BACK TO ONE SACRIFICE A MONTH.
IT'S REALLY A VERY TRAGIC DEVELOPMENT, EXCELLENCY. IN THE OLD DAYS, WE USED TO HAVE QUITE A LINEUP — SOME REALLY GREAT TALENT, I'LL TELL YOU!
I'LL NEVER FORGET MOPSY DEBEERS, CLASS OF '62 — SHE DID A TRIPLE GAINER ON THE WAY DOWN! WHAT A GAL! SHE WAS REALLY A VIRGIN'S VIRGIN!
BUT NOW, YOU JUST CAN'T GET THE YOUNG GIRLS TO GO INTO IT. THEY THINK SELF-SACRIFICE IS OLD-FASHIONED. THEY'RE JUST OUT FOR A GOOD TIME!
AH, YES, BUT WHAT CAN YOU DO, MACARTHUR?— THE KIDS TODAY...
YES, SIR. IT'S A DIFFERENT WORLD.

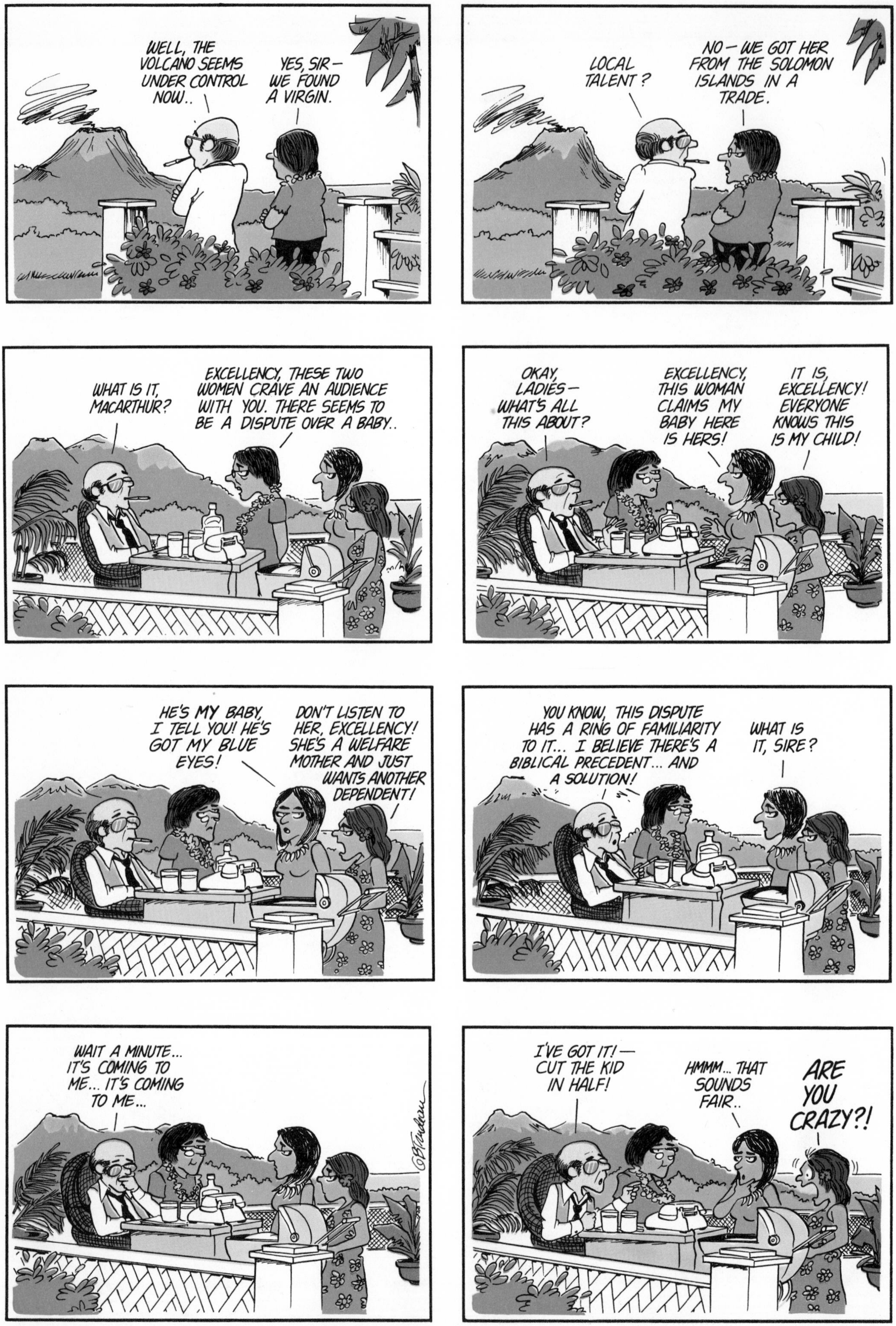
WELL, THE VOLCANO SEEMS UNDER CONTROL NOW..
YES, SIR— WE FOUND A VIRGIN.
LOCAL TALENT?
NO— WE GOT HER FROM THE SOLOMON ISLANDS IN A TRADE.
WHAT IS IT, MACARTHUR?
EXCELLENCY, THESE TWO WOMEN CRAVE AN AUDIENCE WITH YOU. THERE SEEMS TO BE A DISPUTE OVER A BABY..
OKAY, LADIES— WHAT'S ALL THIS ABOUT?
EXCELLENCY, THIS WOMAN CLAIMS MY BABY HERE IS HERS!
IT IS, EXCELLENCY! EVERYONE KNOWS THIS IS MY CHILD!
HE'S MY BABY, I TELL YOU! HE'S GOT MY BLUE EYES!
DON'T LISTEN TO HER, EXCELLENCY! SHE'S A WELFARE MOTHER AND JUST WANTS ANOTHER DEPENDENT!
YOU KNOW, THIS DISPUTE HAS A RING OF FAMILIARITY TO IT... I BELIEVE THERE'S A BIBLICAL PRECEDENT... AND A SOLUTION!
WHAT IS IT, SIRE?
WAIT A MINUTE... IT'S COMING TO ME... IT'S COMING TO ME...
I'VE GOT IT!— CUT THE KID IN HALF!
HMMM... THAT SOUNDS FAIR..
ARE YOU CRAZY?!

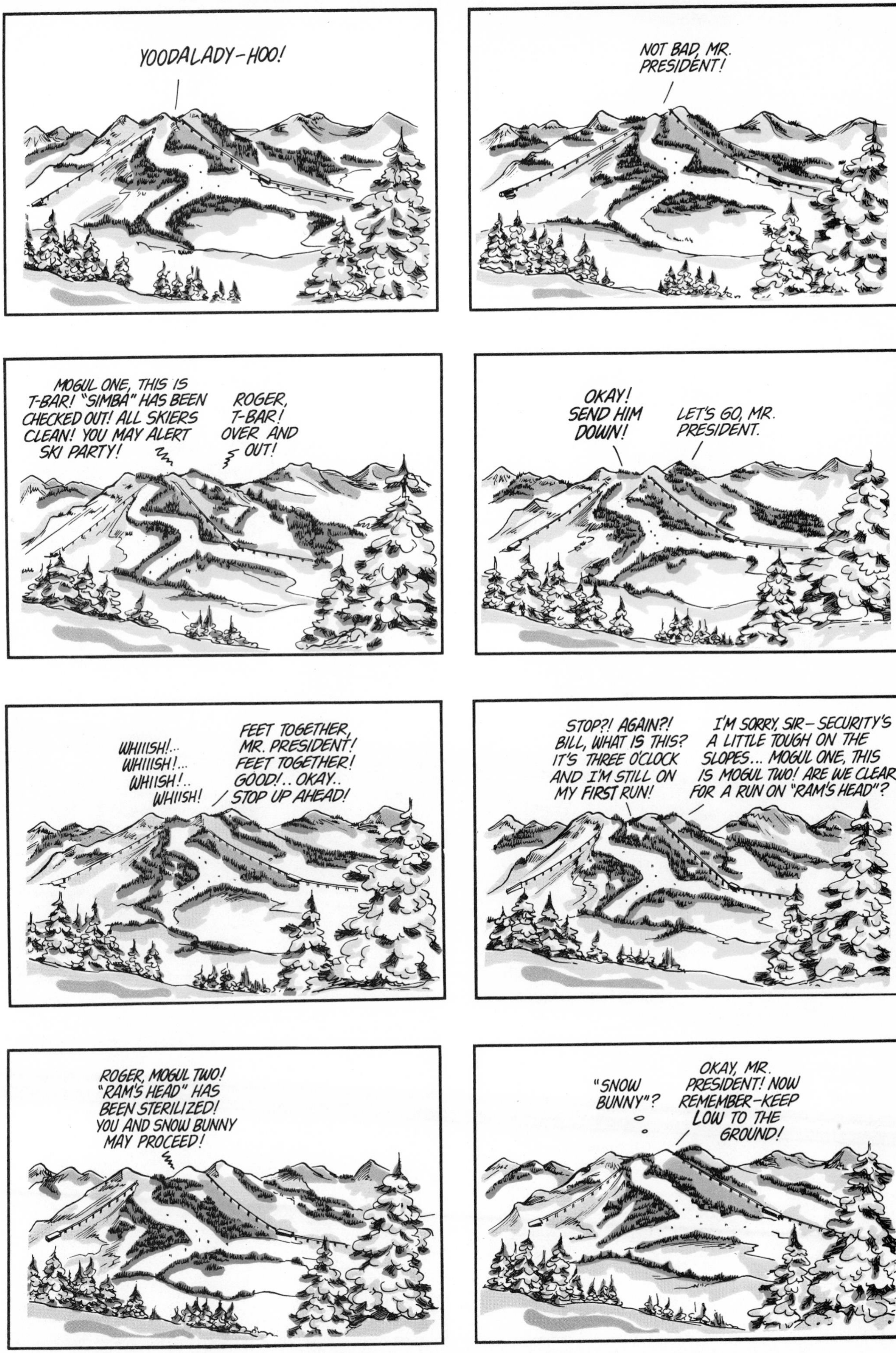
YOODALADY-HOO!
NOT BAD, MR. PRESIDENT!
MOGUL ONE, THIS IS T-BAR! "SIMBA" HAS BEEN CHECKED OUT! ALL SKIERS CLEAN! YOU MAY ALERT SKI PARTY!
ROGER, T-BAR! OVER AND OUT!
OKAY! SEND HIM DOWN!
LET'S GO, MR. PRESIDENT.
WHIISH!.. WHIISH!.. WHIISH!.. WHIISH!
FEET TOGETHER, MR. PRESIDENT! FEET TOGETHER! GOOD!.. OKAY.. STOP UP AHEAD!
STOP?! AGAIN?! BILL, WHAT IS THIS? IT'S THREE O'CLOCK AND I'M STILL ON MY FIRST RUN!
I'M SORRY, SIR– SECURITY'S A LITTLE TOUGH ON THE SLOPES... MOGUL ONE, THIS IS MOGUL TWO! ARE WE CLEAR FOR A RUN ON "RAM'S HEAD"?
ROGER, MOGUL TWO! "RAM'S HEAD" HAS BEEN STERILIZED! YOU AND SNOW BUNNY MAY PROCEED!
"SNOW BUNNY"?
OKAY, MR. PRESIDENT! NOW REMEMBER–KEEP LOW TO THE GROUND!

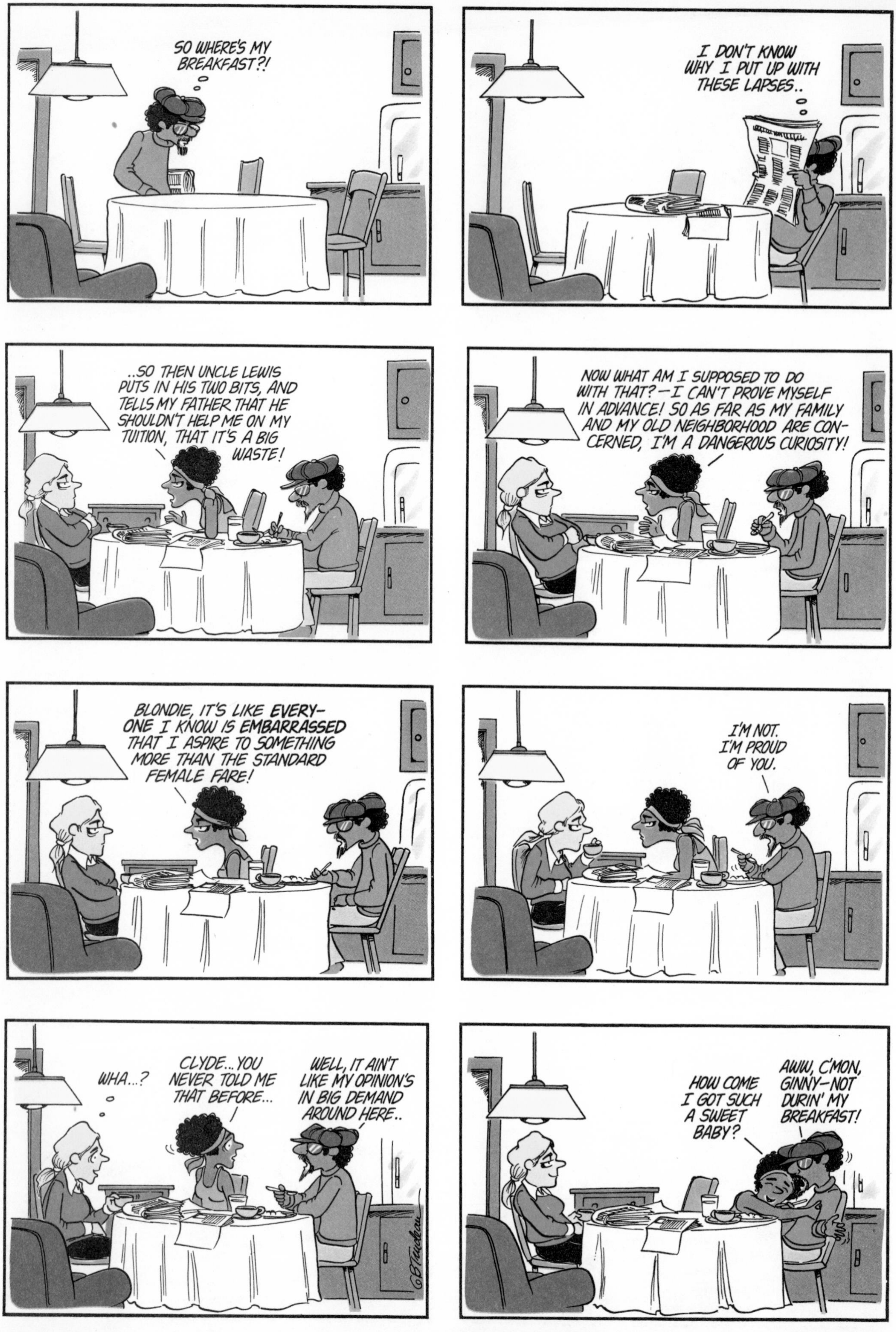
SO WHERE'S MY BREAKFAST?!
I DON'T KNOW WHY I PUT UP WITH THESE LAPSES..
...SO THEN UNCLE LEWIS PUTS IN HIS TWO BITS, AND TELLS MY FATHER THAT HE SHOULDN'T HELP ME ON MY TUITION, THAT IT'S A BIG WASTE!
NOW WHAT AM I SUPPOSED TO DO WITH THAT? — I CAN'T PROVE MYSELF IN ADVANCE! SO AS FAR AS MY FAMILY AND MY OLD NEIGHBORHOOD ARE CONCERNED, I'M A DANGEROUS CURIOSITY!
BLONDIE, IT'S LIKE EVERYONE I KNOW IS EMBARRASSED THAT I ASPIRE TO SOMETHING MORE THAN THE STANDARD FEMALE FARE!
I'M NOT. I'M PROUD OF YOU.
WHA...?
CLYDE...YOU NEVER TOLD ME THAT BEFORE...
WELL, IT AIN'T LIKE MY OPINION'S IN BIG DEMAND AROUND HERE..
HOW COME I GOT SUCH A SWEET BABY?
AWW, C'MON, GINNY—NOT DURIN' MY BREAKFAST!

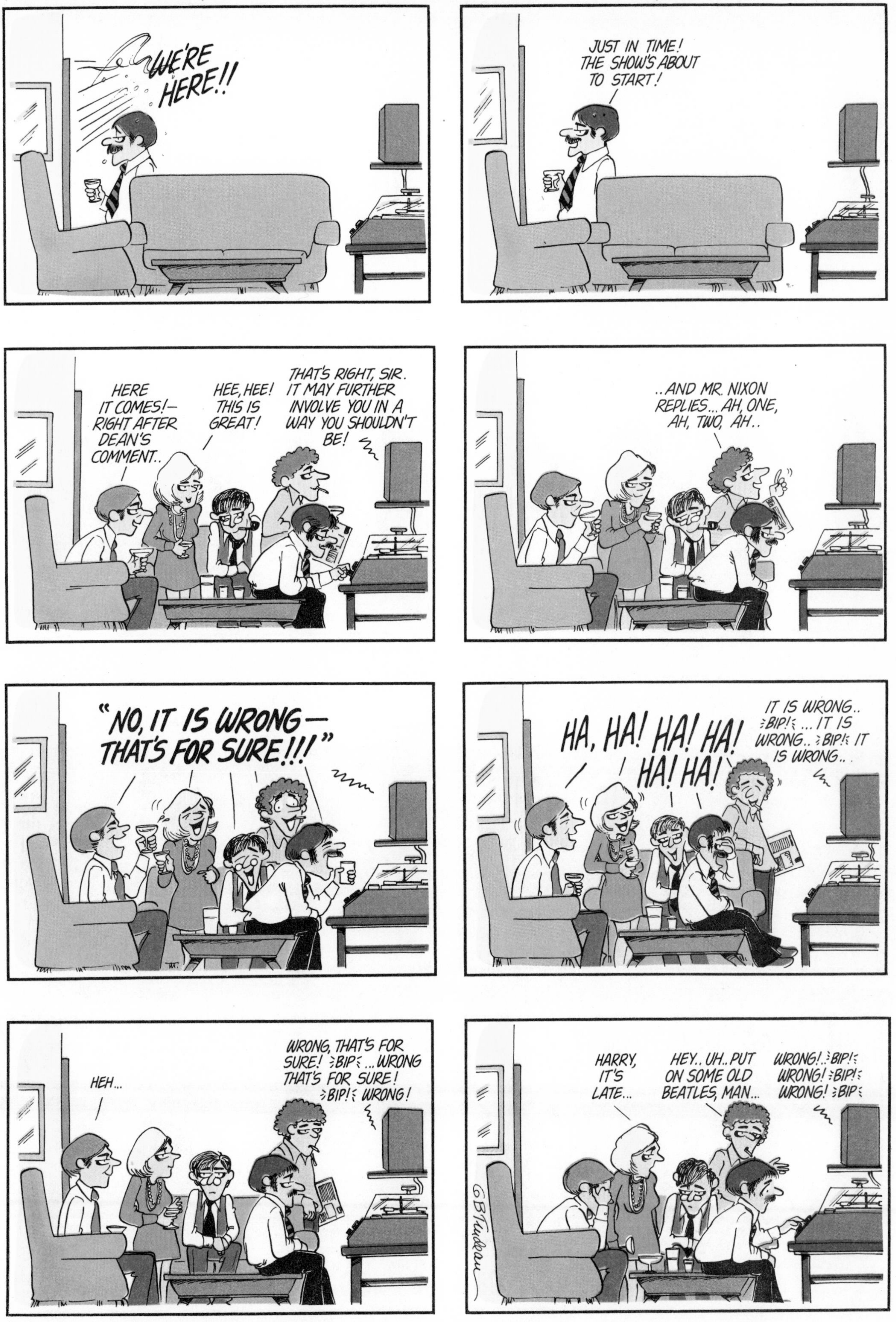
WE'RE HERE!!
JUST IN TIME! THE SHOW'S ABOUT TO START!
HERE IT COMES!— RIGHT AFTER DEAN'S COMMENT..
HEE, HEE! THIS IS GREAT!
THAT'S RIGHT, SIR. IT MAY FURTHER INVOLVE YOU IN A WAY YOU SHOULDN'T BE!
..AND MR. NIXON REPLIES... AH, ONE, AH, TWO, AH..
"NO, IT IS WRONG— THAT'S FOR SURE!!!"
HA, HA! HA! HA! HA! HA!
IT IS WRONG.. BIP! ... IT IS WRONG.. BIP! IT IS WRONG..
HEH...
WRONG, THAT'S FOR SURE! BIP ... WRONG THAT'S FOR SURE! BIP! WRONG!
HARRY, IT'S LATE...
HEY.. UH.. PUT ON SOME OLD BEATLES, MAN...
WRONG!.. BIP! WRONG! BIP! WRONG! BIP

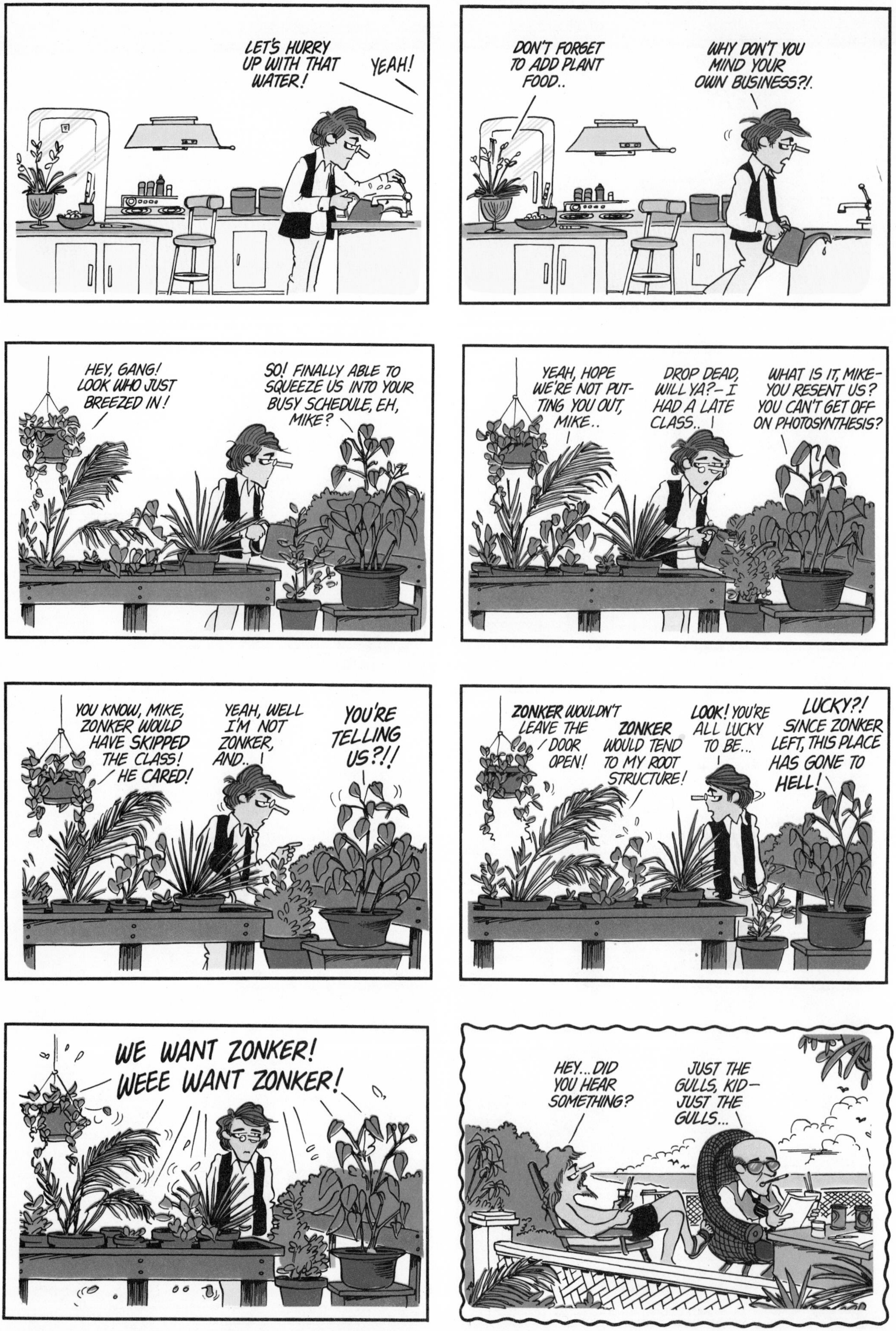
LET'S HURRY UP WITH THAT WATER!
YEAH!
DON'T FORGET TO ADD PLANT FOOD..
WHY DON'T YOU MIND YOUR OWN BUSINESS?!.
HEY, GANG! LOOK WHO JUST BREEZED IN!
SO! FINALLY ABLE TO SQUEEZE US INTO YOUR BUSY SCHEDULE, EH, MIKE?
YEAH, HOPE WE'RE NOT PUTTING YOU OUT, MIKE..
DROP DEAD, WILL YA?– I HAD A LATE CLASS..
WHAT IS IT, MIKE– YOU RESENT US? YOU CAN'T GET OFF ON PHOTOSYNTHESIS?
YOU KNOW, MIKE, ZONKER WOULD HAVE SKIPPED THE CLASS! HE CARED!
YEAH, WELL I'M NOT ZONKER, AND..
YOU'RE TELLING US?!!
ZONKER WOULDN'T LEAVE THE DOOR OPEN!
ZONKER WOULD TEND TO MY ROOT STRUCTURE!
LOOK! YOU'RE ALL LUCKY TO BE...
LUCKY?! SINCE ZONKER LEFT, THIS PLACE HAS GONE TO HELL!
WE WANT ZONKER!
WEEE WANT ZONKER!
HEY...DID YOU HEAR SOMETHING?
JUST THE GULLS, KID– JUST THE GULLS...

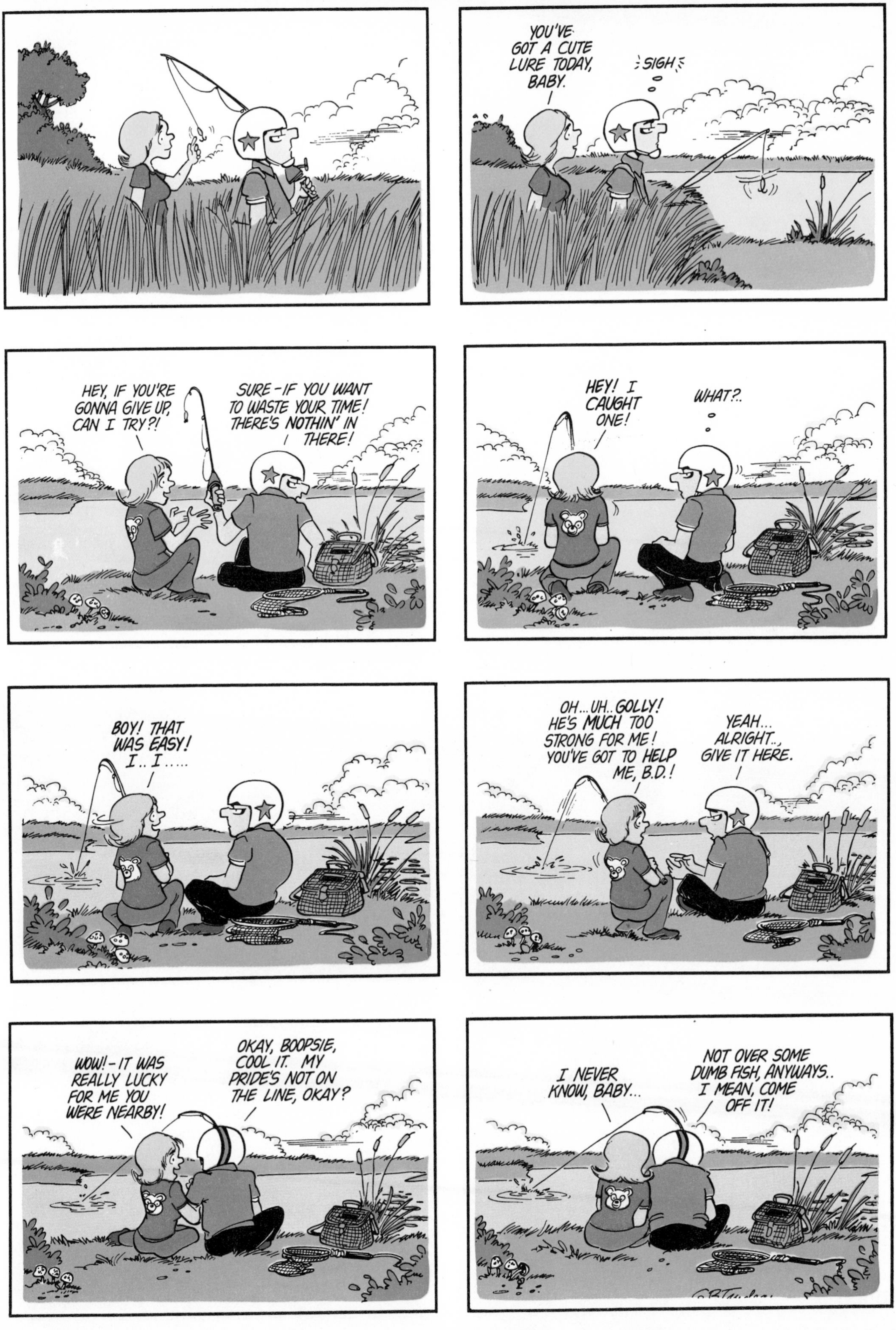
YOU'VE GOT A CUTE LURE TODAY, BABY.
SIGH
HEY, IF YOU'RE GONNA GIVE UP, CAN I TRY?!
SURE - IF YOU WANT TO WASTE YOUR TIME! THERE'S NOTHIN' IN THERE!
HEY! I CAUGHT ONE!
WHAT?..
BOY! THAT WAS EASY! I.. I.....
OH... UH.. GOLLY! HE'S MUCH TOO STRONG FOR ME! YOU'VE GOT TO HELP ME, B.D.!
YEAH... ALRIGHT.., GIVE IT HERE.
WOW! - IT WAS REALLY LUCKY FOR ME YOU WERE NEARBY!
OKAY, BOOPSIE, COOL IT. MY PRIDE'S NOT ON THE LINE, OKAY?
I NEVER KNOW, BABY...
NOT OVER SOME DUMB FISH, ANYWAYS.. I MEAN, COME OFF IT!

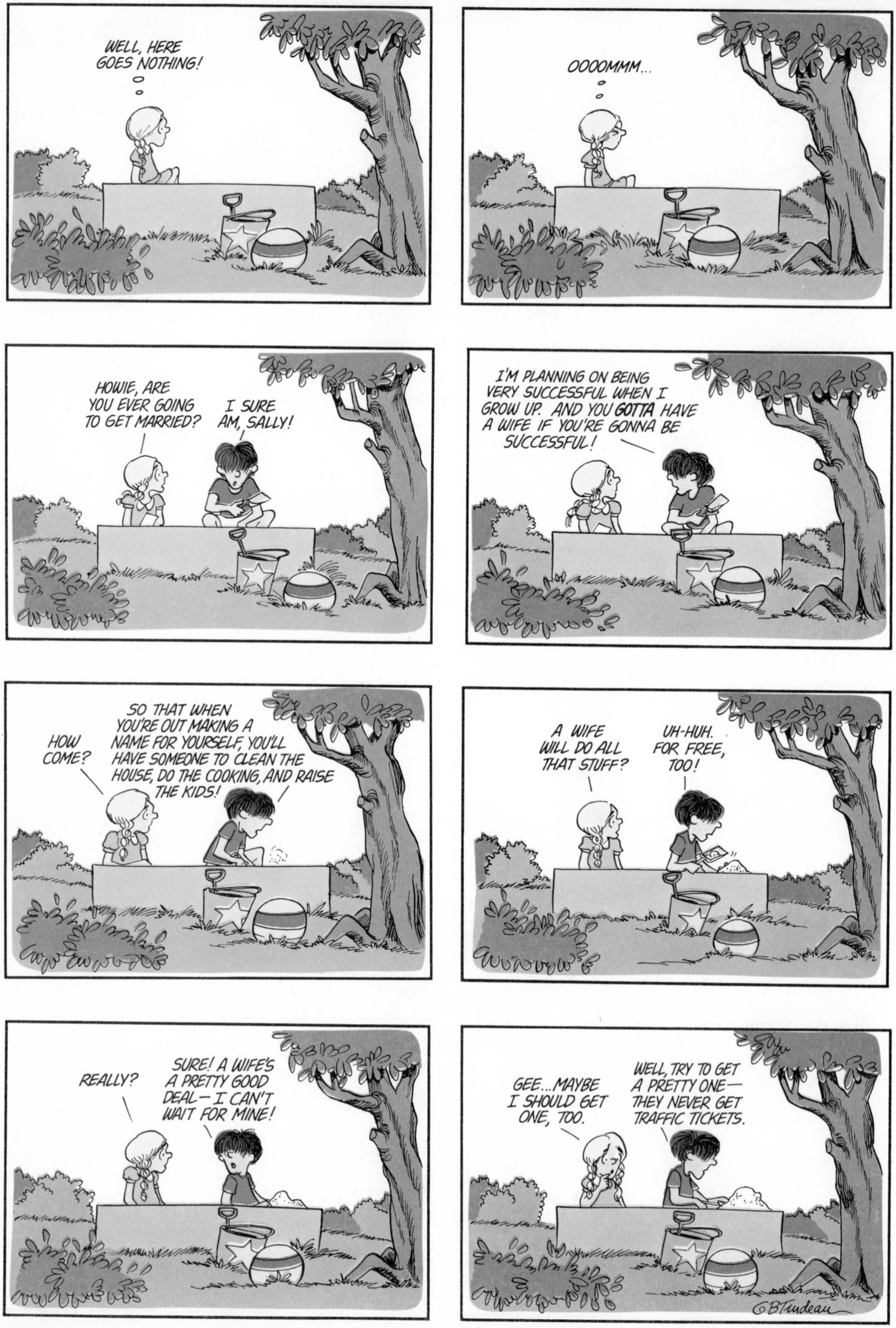
WELL, HERE GOES NOTHING!
OOOOMMM...
HOWIE, ARE YOU EVER GOING TO GET MARRIED?
I SURE AM, SALLY!
I'M PLANNING ON BEING VERY SUCCESSFUL WHEN I GROW UP. AND YOU GOTTA HAVE A WIFE IF YOU'RE GONNA BE SUCCESSFUL!
HOW COME?
SO THAT WHEN YOU'RE OUT MAKING A NAME FOR YOURSELF, YOU'LL HAVE SOMEONE TO CLEAN THE HOUSE, DO THE COOKING, AND RAISE THE KIDS!
A WIFE WILL DO ALL THAT STUFF?
UH-HUH. FOR FREE, TOO!
REALLY?
SURE! A WIFE'S A PRETTY GOOD DEAL— I CAN'T WAIT FOR MINE!
GEE...MAYBE I SHOULD GET ONE, TOO.
WELL, TRY TO GET A PRETTY ONE— THEY NEVER GET TRAFFIC TICKETS.
GBTrudeau

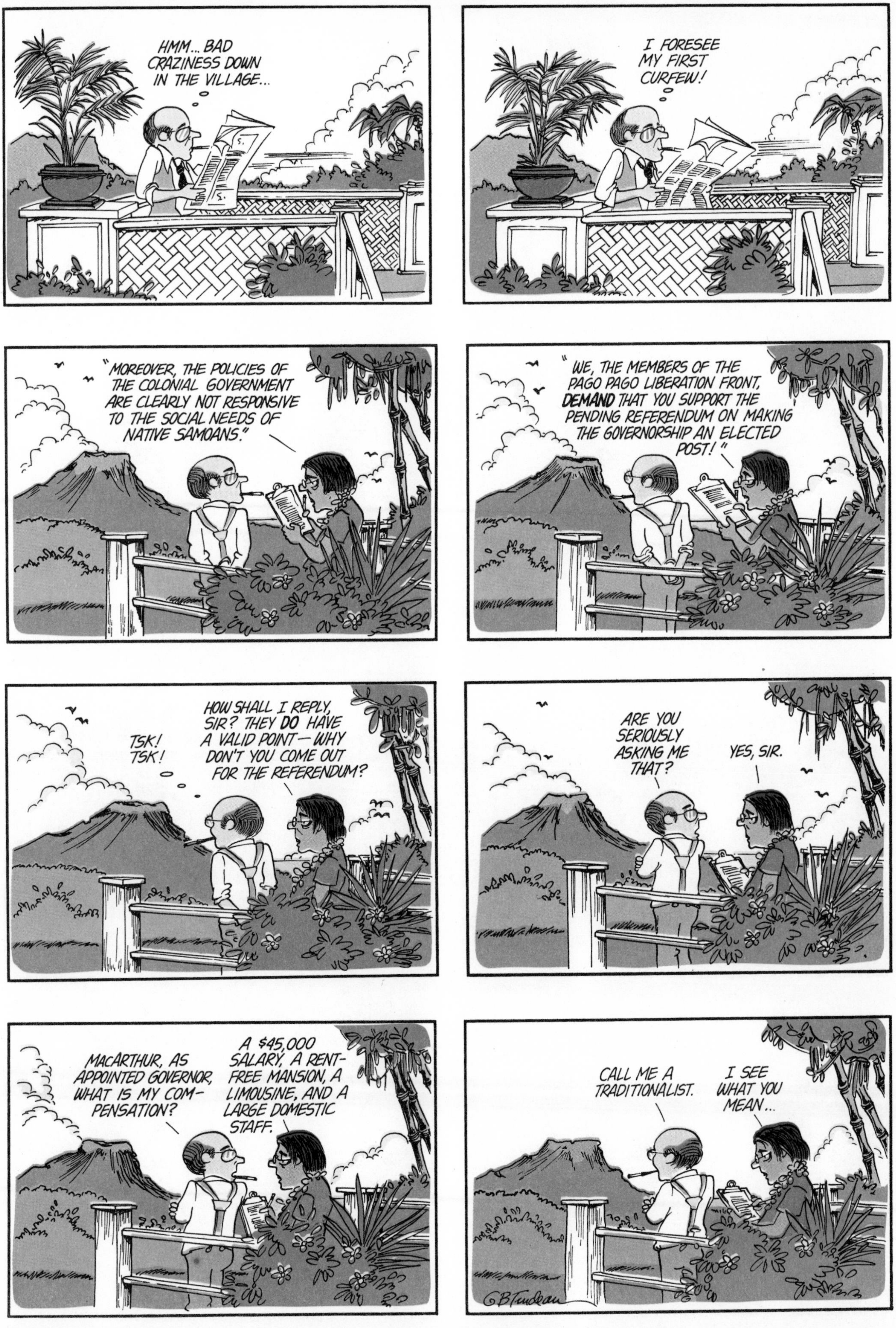
HMM... BAD CRAZINESS DOWN IN THE VILLAGE...
I FORESEE MY FIRST CURFEW!
"MOREOVER, THE POLICIES OF THE COLONIAL GOVERNMENT ARE CLEARLY NOT RESPONSIVE TO THE SOCIAL NEEDS OF NATIVE SAMOANS."
"WE, THE MEMBERS OF THE PAGO PAGO LIBERATION FRONT, DEMAND THAT YOU SUPPORT THE PENDING REFERENDUM ON MAKING THE GOVERNORSHIP AN ELECTED POST!"
TSK! TSK!
HOW SHALL I REPLY, SIR? THEY DO HAVE A VALID POINT—WHY DON'T YOU COME OUT FOR THE REFERENDUM?
ARE YOU SERIOUSLY ASKING ME THAT?
YES, SIR.
MacARTHUR, AS APPOINTED GOVERNOR, WHAT IS MY COM-PENSATION?
A $45,000 SALARY, A RENT-FREE MANSION, A LIMOUSINE, AND A LARGE DOMESTIC STAFF.
CALL ME A TRADITIONALIST.
I SEE WHAT YOU MEAN...
GBTrudeau

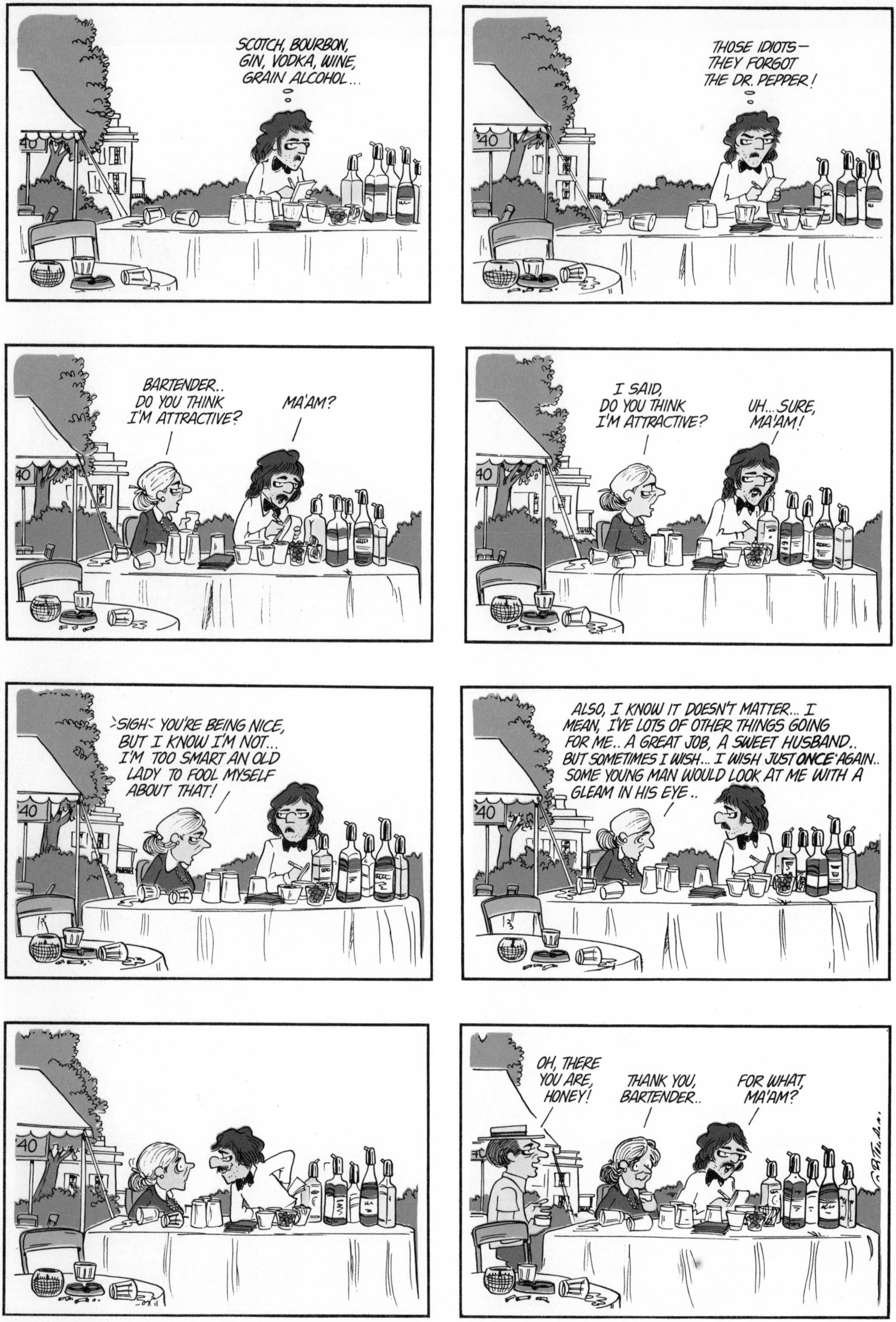
SCOTCH, BOURBON, GIN, VODKA, WINE, GRAIN ALCOHOL...
THOSE IDIOTS— THEY FORGOT THE DR. PEPPER!
BARTENDER.. DO YOU THINK I'M ATTRACTIVE?
MA'AM?
I SAID, DO YOU THINK I'M ATTRACTIVE?
UH... SURE, MA'AM!
>SIGH< YOU'RE BEING NICE, BUT I KNOW I'M NOT... I'M TOO SMART AN OLD LADY TO FOOL MYSELF ABOUT THAT!
ALSO, I KNOW IT DOESN'T MATTER... I MEAN, I'VE LOTS OF OTHER THINGS GOING FOR ME.. A GREAT JOB, A SWEET HUSBAND.. BUT SOMETIMES I WISH... I WISH JUST ONCE AGAIN.. SOME YOUNG MAN WOULD LOOK AT ME WITH A GLEAM IN HIS EYE..
OH, THERE YOU ARE, HONEY!
THANK YOU, BARTENDER..
FOR WHAT, MA'AM?

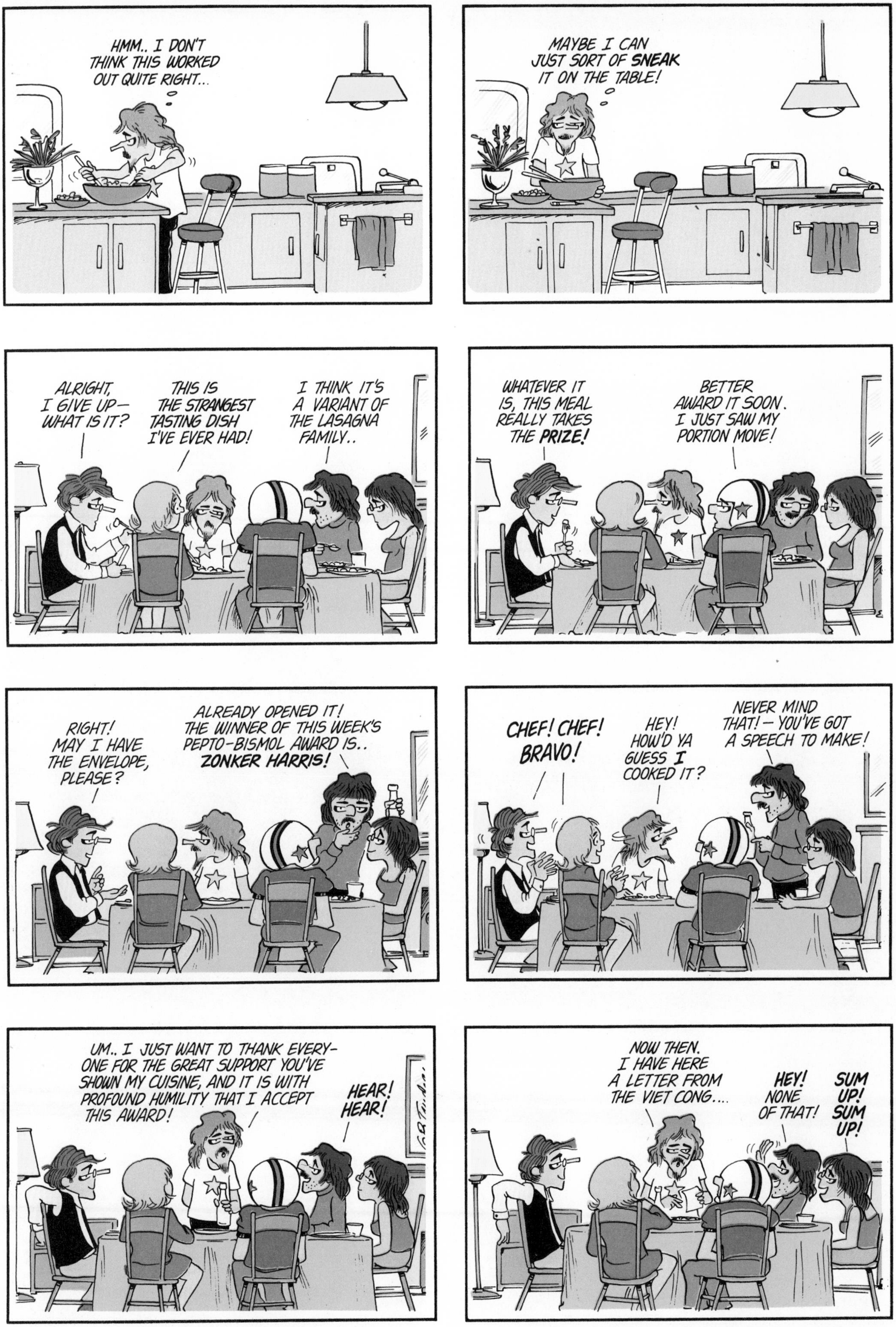
HMM.. I DON'T THINK THIS WORKED OUT QUITE RIGHT...
MAYBE I CAN JUST SORT OF SNEAK IT ON THE TABLE!
ALRIGHT, I GIVE UP— WHAT IS IT?
THIS IS THE STRANGEST TASTING DISH I'VE EVER HAD!
I THINK IT'S A VARIANT OF THE LASAGNA FAMILY..
WHATEVER IT IS, THIS MEAL REALLY TAKES THE PRIZE!
BETTER AWARD IT SOON. I JUST SAW MY PORTION MOVE!
RIGHT! MAY I HAVE THE ENVELOPE, PLEASE?
ALREADY OPENED IT! THE WINNER OF THIS WEEK'S PEPTO-BISMOL AWARD IS.. ZONKER HARRIS!
CHEF! CHEF! BRAVO!
HEY! HOW'D YA GUESS I COOKED IT?
NEVER MIND THAT! — YOU'VE GOT A SPEECH TO MAKE!
UM.. I JUST WANT TO THANK EVERY-ONE FOR THE GREAT SUPPORT YOU'VE SHOWN MY CUISINE, AND IT IS WITH PROFOUND HUMILITY THAT I ACCEPT THIS AWARD!
HEAR! HEAR!
NOW THEN. I HAVE HERE A LETTER FROM THE VIET CONG....
HEY! NONE OF THAT!
SUM UP! SUM UP!

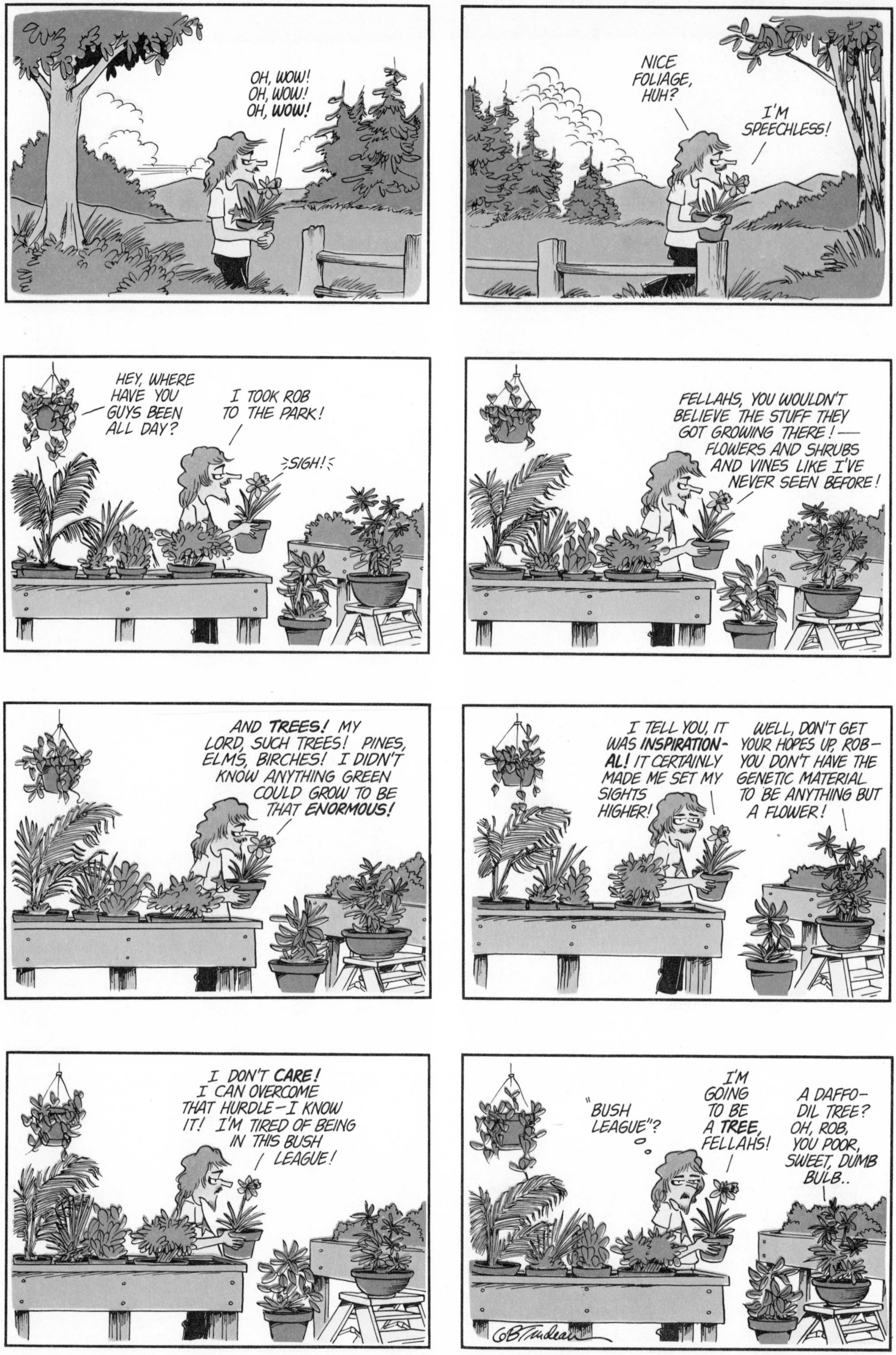
OH, WOW! OH, WOW! OH, WOW!
NICE FOLIAGE, HUH?
I'M SPEECHLESS!
HEY, WHERE HAVE YOU GUYS BEEN ALL DAY?
I TOOK ROB TO THE PARK!
SIGH!
FELLAHS, YOU WOULDN'T BELIEVE THE STUFF THEY GOT GROWING THERE!— FLOWERS AND SHRUBS AND VINES LIKE I'VE NEVER SEEN BEFORE!
AND TREES! MY LORD, SUCH TREES! PINES, ELMS, BIRCHES! I DIDN'T KNOW ANYTHING GREEN COULD GROW TO BE THAT ENORMOUS!
I TELL YOU, IT WAS INSPIRATION-AL! IT CERTAINLY MADE ME SET MY SIGHTS HIGHER!
WELL, DON'T GET YOUR HOPES UP, ROB— YOU DON'T HAVE THE GENETIC MATERIAL TO BE ANYTHING BUT A FLOWER!
I DON'T CARE! I CAN OVERCOME THAT HURDLE—I KNOW IT! I'M TIRED OF BEING IN THIS BUSH LEAGUE!
"BUSH LEAGUE"?
I'M GOING TO BE A TREE, FELLAHS!
A DAFFO-DIL TREE? OH, ROB, YOU POOR, SWEET, DUMB BULB..
GBTrudeau

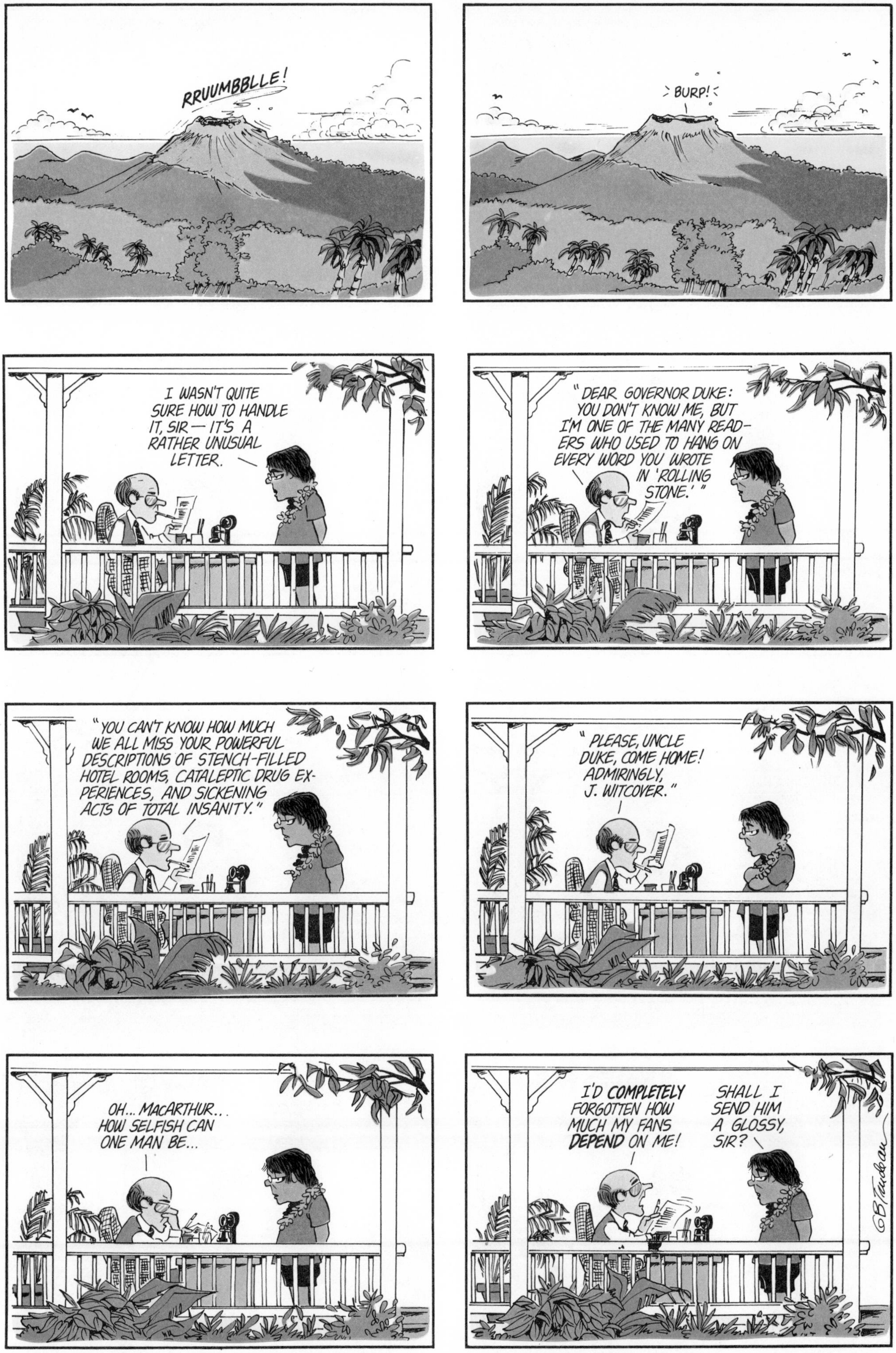
RRUUMBBLLE!
BURP!
I WASN'T QUITE SURE HOW TO HANDLE IT, SIR — IT'S A RATHER UNUSUAL LETTER.
"DEAR GOVERNOR DUKE: YOU DON'T KNOW ME, BUT I'M ONE OF THE MANY READERS WHO USED TO HANG ON EVERY WORD YOU WROTE IN 'ROLLING STONE.'"
"YOU CAN'T KNOW HOW MUCH WE ALL MISS YOUR POWERFUL DESCRIPTIONS OF STENCH-FILLED HOTEL ROOMS, CATALEPTIC DRUG EXPERIENCES, AND SICKENING ACTS OF TOTAL INSANITY."
"PLEASE, UNCLE DUKE, COME HOME! ADMIRINGLY, J. WITCOVER."
OH... MacARTHUR... HOW SELFISH CAN ONE MAN BE...
I'D COMPLETELY FORGOTTEN HOW MUCH MY FANS DEPEND ON ME!
SHALL I SEND HIM A GLOSSY, SIR?
©BTrudeau

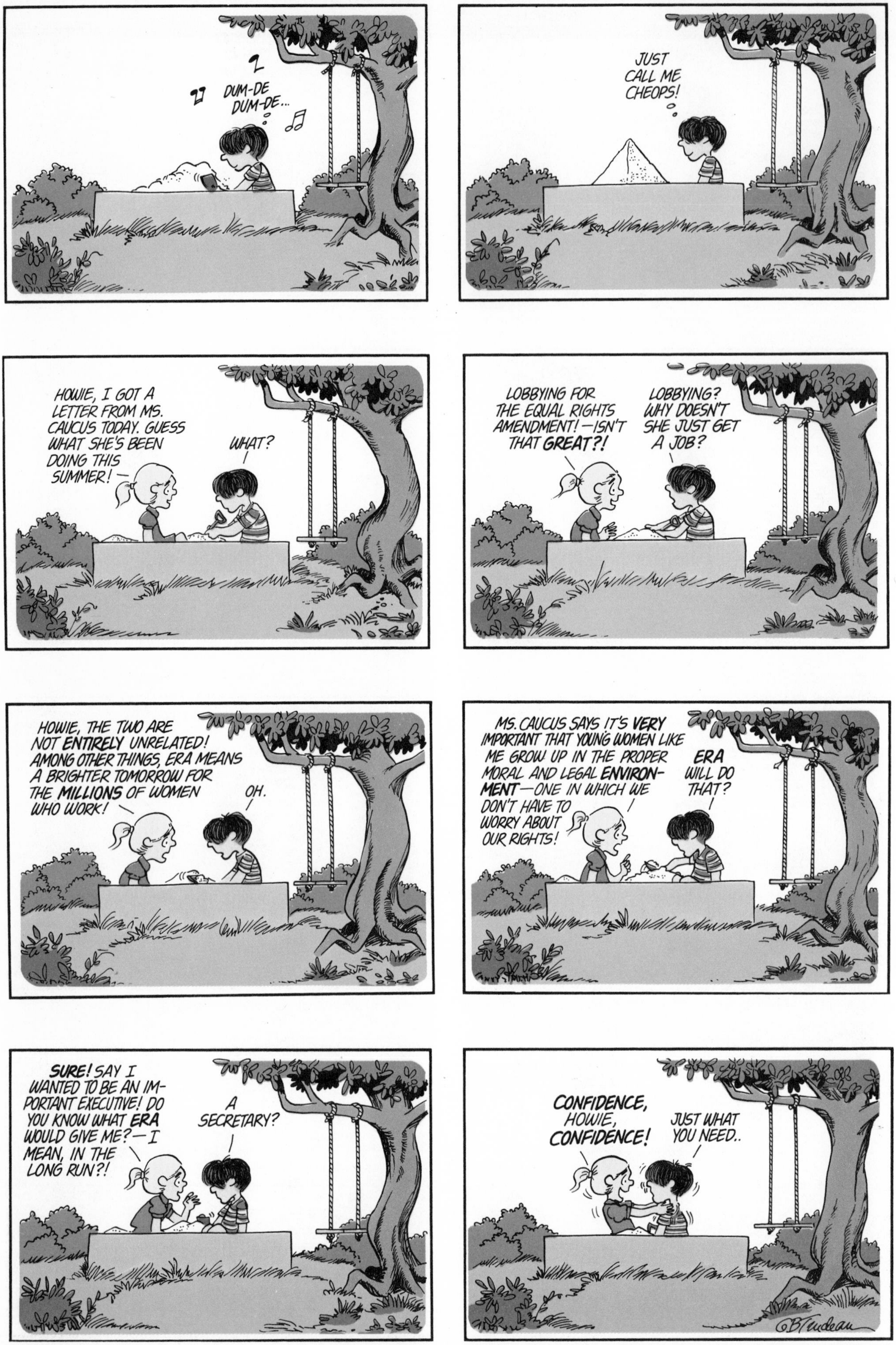
DUM-DE
DUM-DE...
JUST CALL ME CHEOPS!
HOWIE, I GOT A LETTER FROM MS. CAUCUS TODAY. GUESS WHAT SHE'S BEEN DOING THIS SUMMER!
WHAT?
LOBBYING FOR THE EQUAL RIGHTS AMENDMENT!—ISN'T THAT GREAT?!
LOBBYING? WHY DOESN'T SHE JUST GET A JOB?
HOWIE, THE TWO ARE NOT ENTIRELY UNRELATED! AMONG OTHER THINGS, ERA MEANS A BRIGHTER TOMORROW FOR THE MILLIONS OF WOMEN WHO WORK!
OH.
MS. CAUCUS SAYS IT'S VERY IMPORTANT THAT YOUNG WOMEN LIKE ME GROW UP IN THE PROPER MORAL AND LEGAL ENVIRON-MENT—ONE IN WHICH WE DON'T HAVE TO WORRY ABOUT OUR RIGHTS!
ERA WILL DO THAT?
SURE! SAY I WANTED TO BE AN IM-PORTANT EXECUTIVE! DO YOU KNOW WHAT ERA WOULD GIVE ME?—I MEAN, IN THE LONG RUN?!
A SECRETARY?
CONFIDENCE, HOWIE, CONFIDENCE!
JUST WHAT YOU NEED..
GBTrudeau

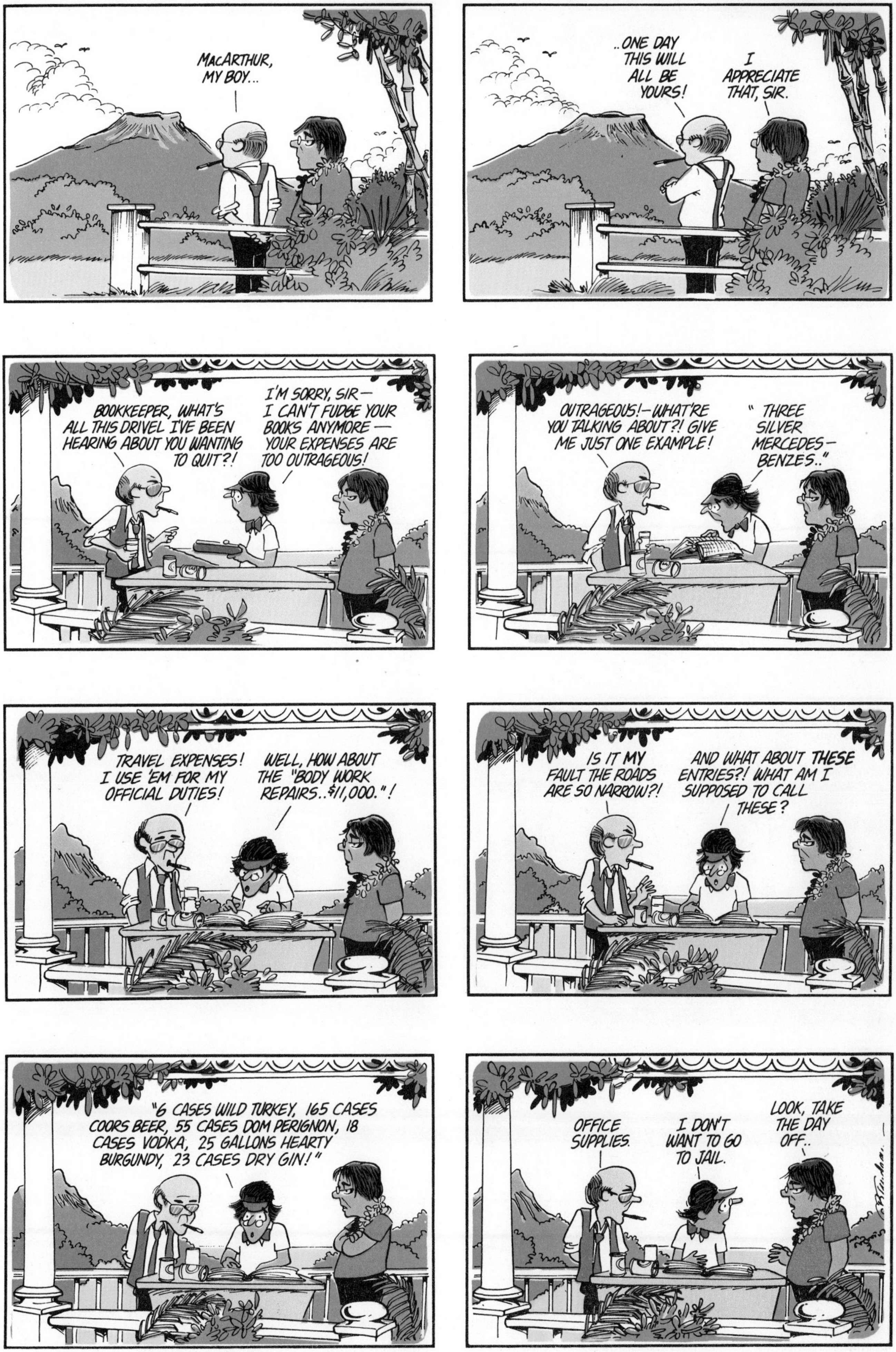
MacARTHUR, MY BOY...
..ONE DAY THIS WILL ALL BE YOURS!
I APPRECIATE THAT, SIR.
BOOKKEEPER, WHAT'S ALL THIS DRIVEL I'VE BEEN HEARING ABOUT YOU WANTING TO QUIT?!
I'M SORRY, SIR— I CAN'T FUDGE YOUR BOOKS ANYMORE— YOUR EXPENSES ARE TOO OUTRAGEOUS!
OUTRAGEOUS!—WHAT'RE YOU TALKING ABOUT?! GIVE ME JUST ONE EXAMPLE!
" THREE SILVER MERCEDES-BENZES.."
TRAVEL EXPENSES! I USE 'EM FOR MY OFFICIAL DUTIES!
WELL, HOW ABOUT THE "BODY WORK REPAIRS..$11,000." !
IS IT MY FAULT THE ROADS ARE SO NARROW?!
AND WHAT ABOUT THESE ENTRIES?! WHAT AM I SUPPOSED TO CALL THESE?
"6 CASES WILD TURKEY, 165 CASES COORS BEER, 55 CASES DOM PERIGNON, 18 CASES VODKA, 25 GALLONS HEARTY BURGUNDY, 23 CASES DRY GIN!"
OFFICE SUPPLIES.
I DON'T WANT TO GO TO JAIL.
LOOK, TAKE THE DAY OFF..

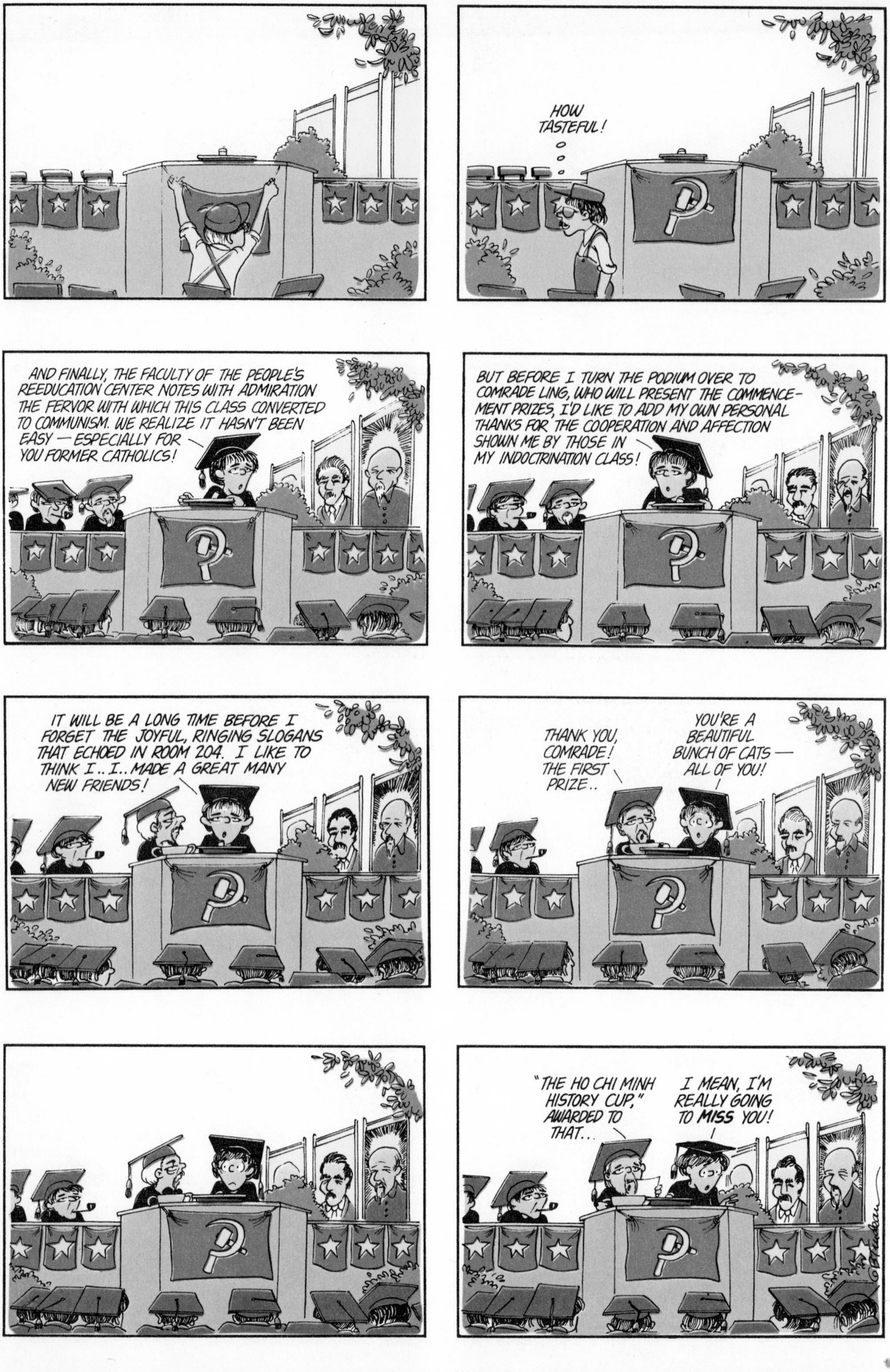
HOW TASTEFUL!
AND FINALLY, THE FACULTY OF THE PEOPLE'S REEDUCATION CENTER NOTES WITH ADMIRATION THE FERVOR WITH WHICH THIS CLASS CONVERTED TO COMMUNISM. WE REALIZE IT HASN'T BEEN EASY — ESPECIALLY FOR YOU FORMER CATHOLICS!
BUT BEFORE I TURN THE PODIUM OVER TO COMRADE LING, WHO WILL PRESENT THE COMMENCEMENT PRIZES, I'D LIKE TO ADD MY OWN PERSONAL THANKS FOR THE COOPERATION AND AFFECTION SHOWN ME BY THOSE IN MY INDOCTRINATION CLASS!
IT WILL BE A LONG TIME BEFORE I FORGET THE JOYFUL, RINGING SLOGANS THAT ECHOED IN ROOM 204. I LIKE TO THINK I.. I.. MADE A GREAT MANY NEW FRIENDS!
THANK YOU, COMRADE! THE FIRST PRIZE..
YOU'RE A BEAUTIFUL BUNCH OF CATS — ALL OF YOU!
"THE HO CHI MINH HISTORY CUP," AWARDED TO THAT...
I MEAN, I'M REALLY GOING TO **MISS** YOU!

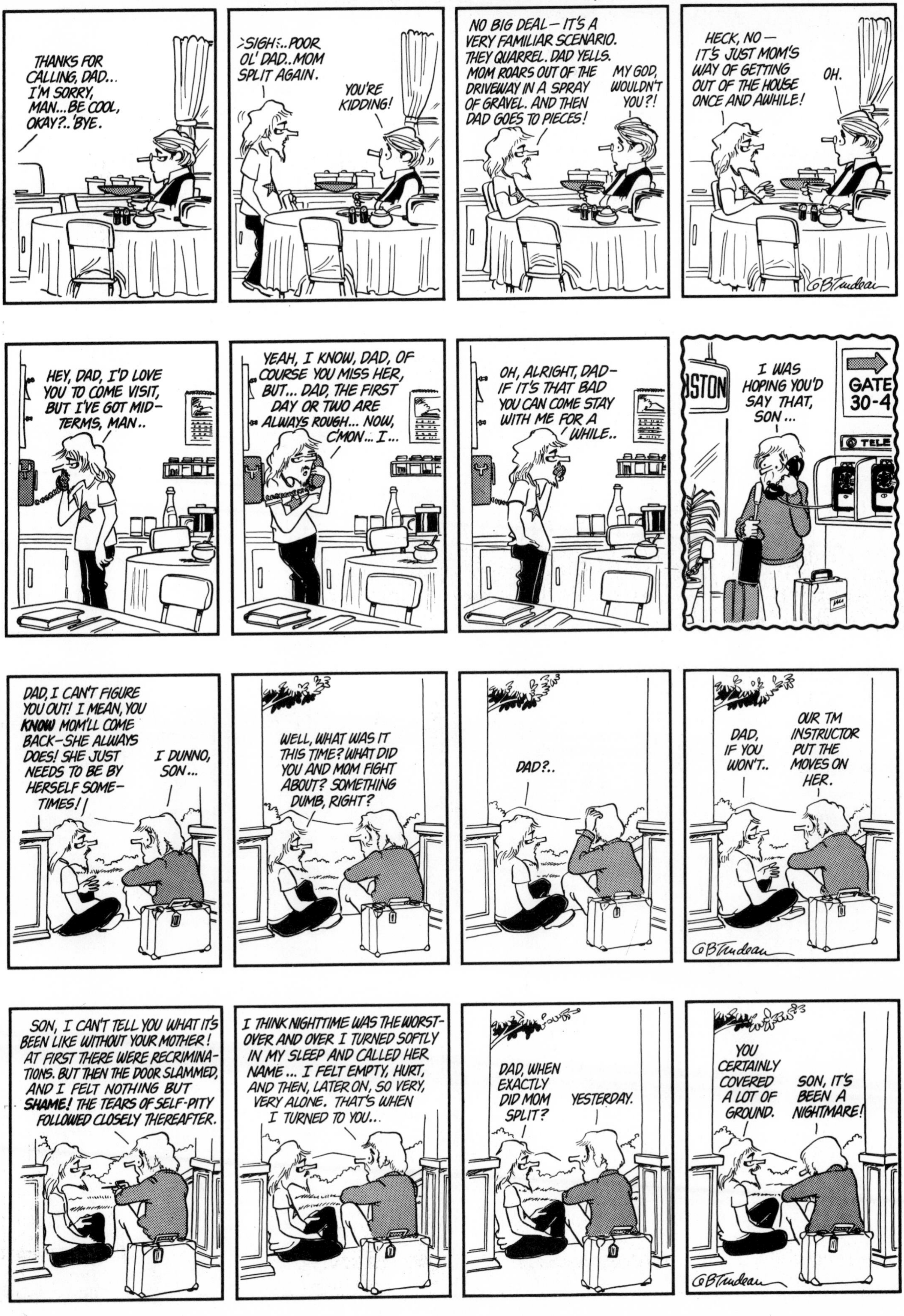
THANKS FOR CALLING, DAD... I'M SORRY, MAN... BE COOL, OKAY?.. 'BYE.
≥SIGH≤.. POOR OL' DAD.. MOM SPLIT AGAIN.
YOU'RE KIDDING!
NO BIG DEAL — IT'S A VERY FAMILIAR SCENARIO. THEY QUARREL. DAD YELLS. MOM ROARS OUT OF THE DRIVEWAY IN A SPRAY OF GRAVEL. AND THEN DAD GOES TO PIECES!
MY GOD, WOULDN'T YOU?!
HECK, NO — IT'S JUST MOM'S WAY OF GETTING OUT OF THE HOUSE ONCE AND AWHILE!
OH.
HEY, DAD, I'D LOVE YOU TO COME VISIT, BUT I'VE GOT MID-TERMS, MAN..
YEAH, I KNOW, DAD, OF COURSE YOU MISS HER, BUT... DAD, THE FIRST DAY OR TWO ARE ALWAYS ROUGH... NOW, C'MON... I...
OH, ALRIGHT, DAD- IF IT'S THAT BAD YOU CAN COME STAY WITH ME FOR A WHILE..
STON
I WAS HOPING YOU'D SAY THAT, SON...
GATE 30-4
TELE
DAD, I CAN'T FIGURE YOU OUT! I MEAN, YOU KNOW MOM'LL COME BACK—SHE ALWAYS DOES! SHE JUST NEEDS TO BE BY HERSELF SOME-TIMES!
I DUNNO, SON...
WELL, WHAT WAS IT THIS TIME? WHAT DID YOU AND MOM FIGHT ABOUT? SOMETHING DUMB, RIGHT?
DAD?..
DAD, IF YOU WON'T..
OUR TM INSTRUCTOR PUT THE MOVES ON HER.
SON, I CAN'T TELL YOU WHAT IT'S BEEN LIKE WITHOUT YOUR MOTHER! AT FIRST THERE WERE RECRIMINA-TIONS. BUT THEN THE DOOR SLAMMED, AND I FELT NOTHING BUT SHAME! THE TEARS OF SELF-PITY FOLLOWED CLOSELY THEREAFTER.
I THINK NIGHTTIME WAS THE WORST- OVER AND OVER I TURNED SOFTLY IN MY SLEEP AND CALLED HER NAME... I FELT EMPTY, HURT, AND THEN, LATER ON, SO VERY, VERY ALONE. THAT'S WHEN I TURNED TO YOU...
DAD, WHEN EXACTLY DID MOM SPLIT?
YESTERDAY.
YOU CERTAINLY COVERED A LOT OF GROUND.
SON, IT'S BEEN A NIGHTMARE!

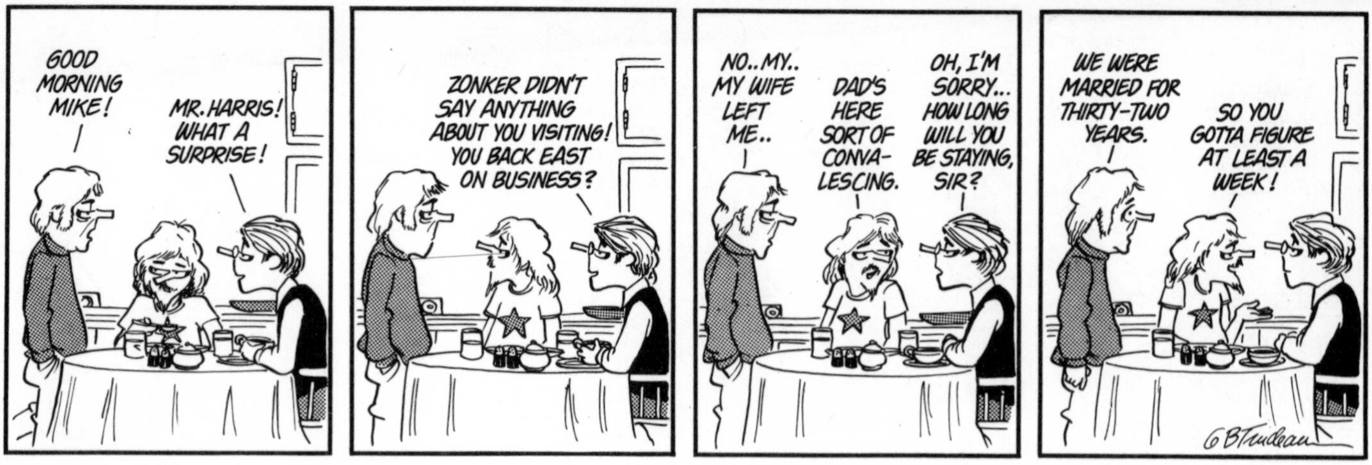
GOOD MORNING MIKE!
MR. HARRIS! WHAT A SURPRISE!
ZONKER DIDN'T SAY ANYTHING ABOUT YOU VISITING! YOU BACK EAST ON BUSINESS?
NO.. MY.. MY WIFE LEFT ME..
DAD'S HERE SORT OF CONVA-LESCING.
OH, I'M SORRY... HOW LONG WILL YOU BE STAYING, SIR?
WE WERE MARRIED FOR THIRTY-TWO YEARS.
SO YOU GOTTA FIGURE AT LEAST A WEEK!
GBTrudeau

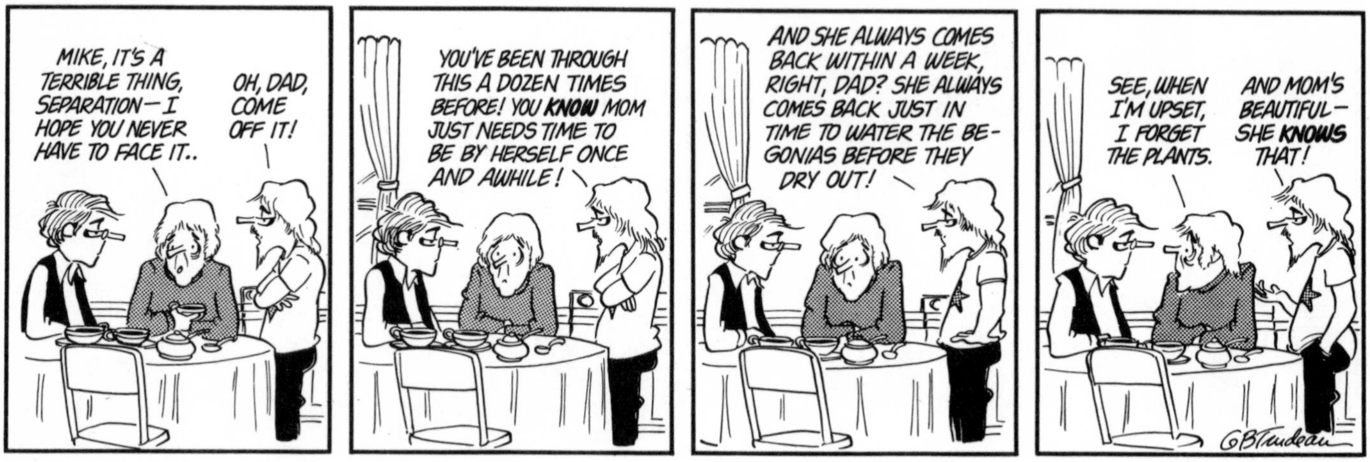
MIKE, IT'S A TERRIBLE THING, SEPARATION— I HOPE YOU NEVER HAVE TO FACE IT..
OH, DAD, COME OFF IT!
YOU'VE BEEN THROUGH THIS A DOZEN TIMES BEFORE! YOU KNOW MOM JUST NEEDS TIME TO BE BY HERSELF ONCE AND AWHILE!
AND SHE ALWAYS COMES BACK WITHIN A WEEK, RIGHT, DAD? SHE ALWAYS COMES BACK JUST IN TIME TO WATER THE BE-GONIAS BEFORE THEY DRY OUT!
SEE, WHEN I'M UPSET, I FORGET THE PLANTS.
AND MOM'S BEAUTIFUL— SHE KNOWS THAT!
GBTrudeau

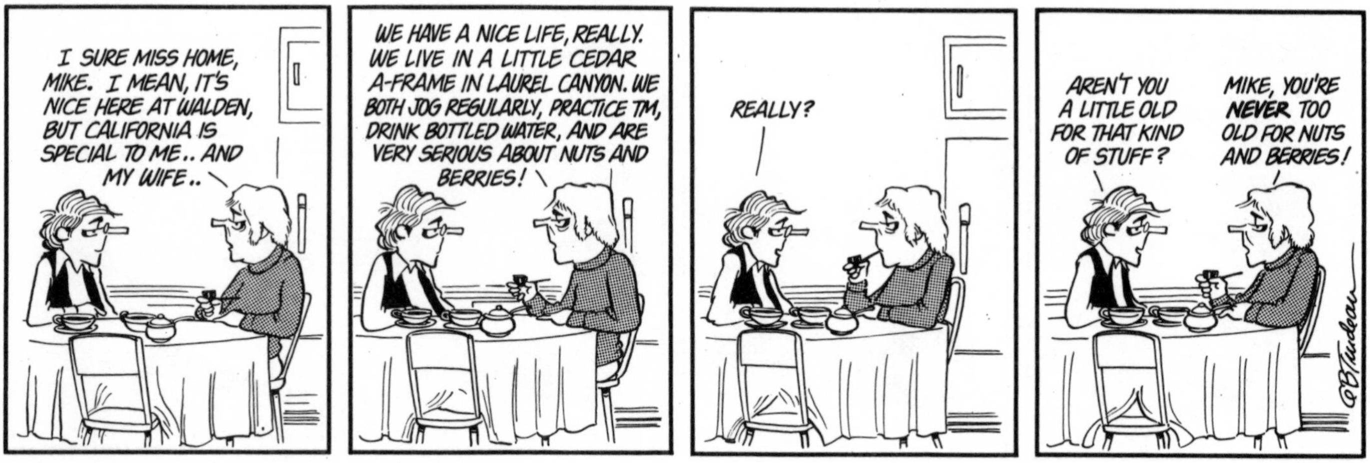
I SURE MISS HOME, MIKE. I MEAN, IT'S NICE HERE AT WALDEN, BUT CALIFORNIA IS SPECIAL TO ME.. AND MY WIFE..
WE HAVE A NICE LIFE, REALLY. WE LIVE IN A LITTLE CEDAR A-FRAME IN LAUREL CANYON. WE BOTH JOG REGULARLY, PRACTICE TM, DRINK BOTTLED WATER, AND ARE VERY SERIOUS ABOUT NUTS AND BERRIES!
REALLY?
AREN'T YOU A LITTLE OLD FOR THAT KIND OF STUFF?
MIKE, YOU'RE NEVER TOO OLD FOR NUTS AND BERRIES!
GBTrudeau

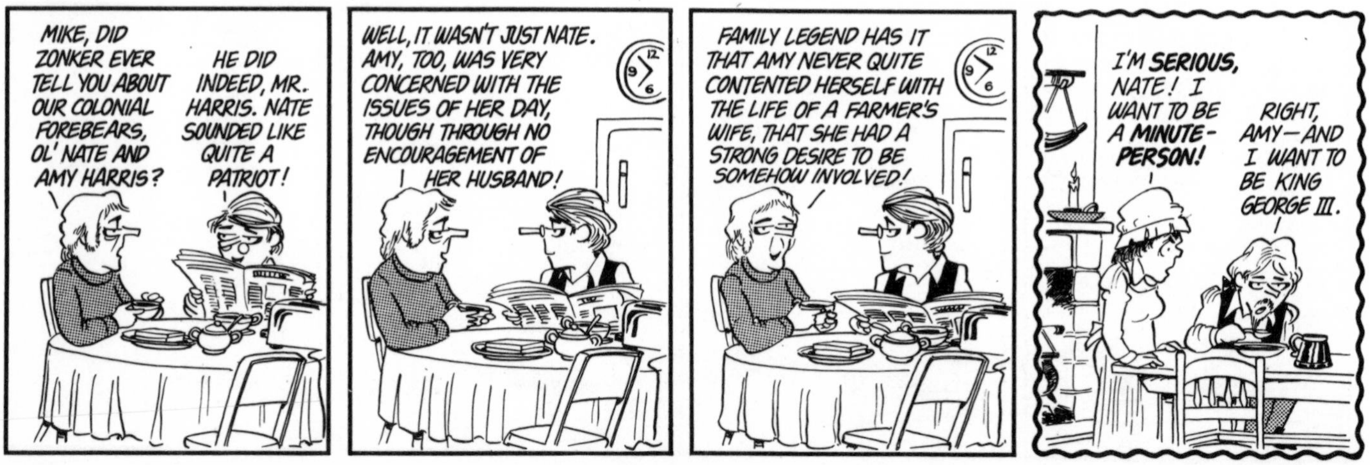
MIKE, DID ZONKER EVER TELL YOU ABOUT OUR COLONIAL FOREBEARS, OL' NATE AND AMY HARRIS?
HE DID INDEED, MR. HARRIS. NATE SOUNDED LIKE QUITE A PATRIOT!
WELL, IT WASN'T JUST NATE. AMY, TOO, WAS VERY CONCERNED WITH THE ISSUES OF HER DAY, THOUGH THROUGH NO ENCOURAGEMENT OF HER HUSBAND!
FAMILY LEGEND HAS IT THAT AMY NEVER QUITE CONTENTED HERSELF WITH THE LIFE OF A FARMER'S WIFE, THAT SHE HAD A STRONG DESIRE TO BE SOMEHOW INVOLVED!
I'M SERIOUS, NATE! I WANT TO BE A MINUTE-PERSON!
RIGHT, AMY— AND I WANT TO BE KING GEORGE III.

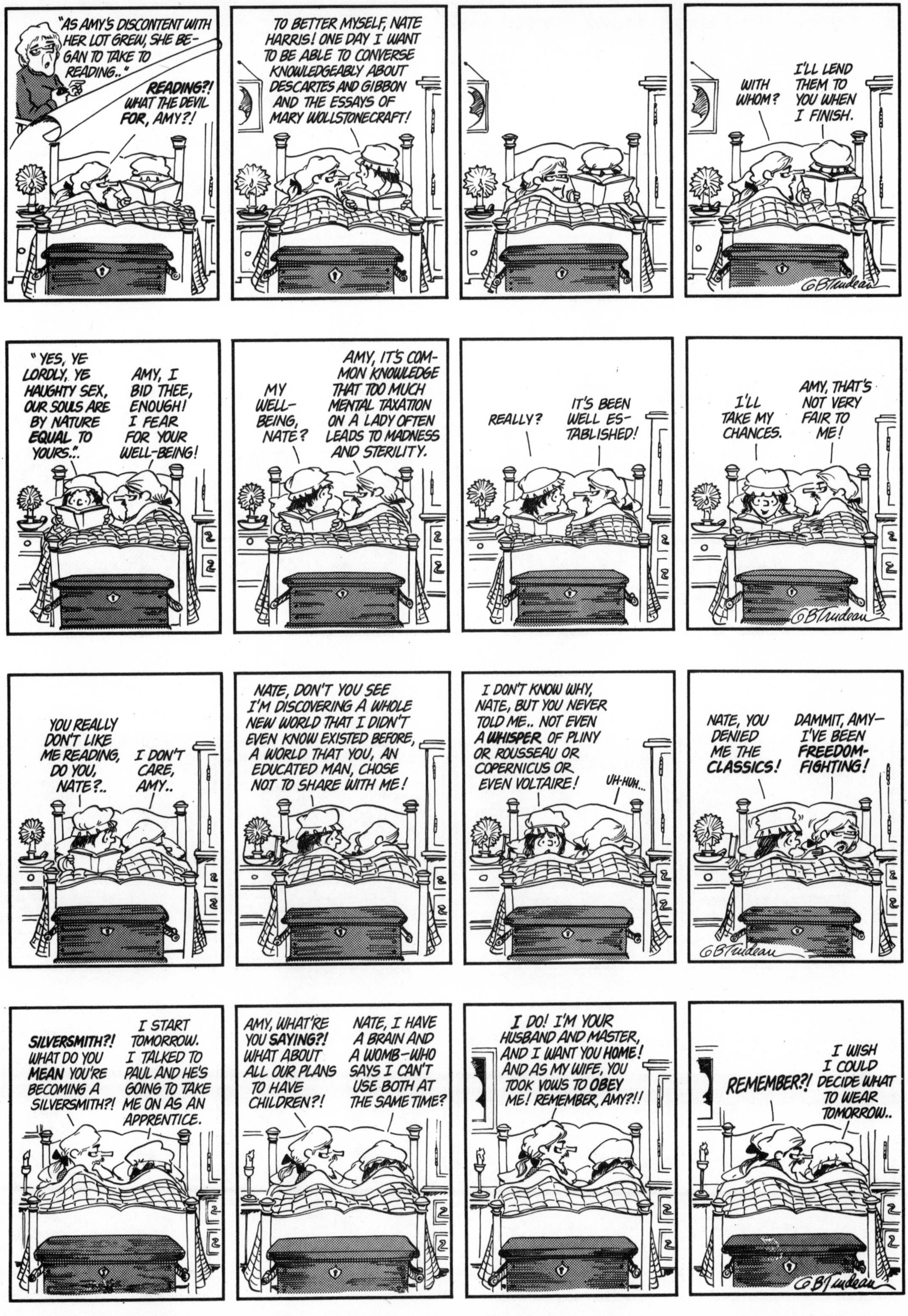
"AS AMY'S DISCONTENT WITH HER LOT GREW, SHE BEGAN TO TAKE TO READING.."
READING?! WHAT THE DEVIL FOR, AMY?!
TO BETTER MYSELF, NATE HARRIS! ONE DAY I WANT TO BE ABLE TO CONVERSE KNOWLEDGEABLY ABOUT DESCARTES AND GIBBON AND THE ESSAYS OF MARY WOLLSTONECRAFT!
WITH WHOM?
I'LL LEND THEM TO YOU WHEN I FINISH.
"YES, YE LORDLY, YE HAUGHTY SEX, OUR SOULS ARE BY NATURE EQUAL TO YOURS.."
AMY, I BID THEE, ENOUGH! I FEAR FOR YOUR WELL-BEING!
MY WELL-BEING, NATE?
AMY, IT'S COMMON KNOWLEDGE THAT TOO MUCH MENTAL TAXATION ON A LADY OFTEN LEADS TO MADNESS AND STERILITY.
REALLY?
IT'S BEEN WELL ESTABLISHED!
I'LL TAKE MY CHANCES.
AMY, THAT'S NOT VERY FAIR TO ME!
YOU REALLY DON'T LIKE ME READING, DO YOU, NATE?..
I DON'T CARE, AMY..
NATE, DON'T YOU SEE I'M DISCOVERING A WHOLE NEW WORLD THAT I DIDN'T EVEN KNOW EXISTED BEFORE, A WORLD THAT YOU, AN EDUCATED MAN, CHOSE NOT TO SHARE WITH ME!
I DON'T KNOW WHY, NATE, BUT YOU NEVER TOLD ME.. NOT EVEN A WHISPER OF PLINY OR ROUSSEAU OR COPERNICUS OR EVEN VOLTAIRE!
UH-HUH...
NATE, YOU DENIED ME THE CLASSICS!
DAMMIT, AMY—I'VE BEEN FREEDOM-FIGHTING!
SILVERSMITH?! WHAT DO YOU MEAN YOU'RE BECOMING A SILVERSMITH?!
I START TOMORROW. I TALKED TO PAUL AND HE'S GOING TO TAKE ME ON AS AN APPRENTICE.
AMY, WHAT'RE YOU SAYING?! WHAT ABOUT ALL OUR PLANS TO HAVE CHILDREN?!
NATE, I HAVE A BRAIN AND A WOMB—WHO SAYS I CAN'T USE BOTH AT THE SAME TIME?
I DO! I'M YOUR HUSBAND AND MASTER, AND I WANT YOU HOME! AND AS MY WIFE, YOU TOOK VOWS TO OBEY ME! REMEMBER, AMY?!!
REMEMBER?!
I WISH I COULD DECIDE WHAT TO WEAR TOMORROW..
©GBTrudeau

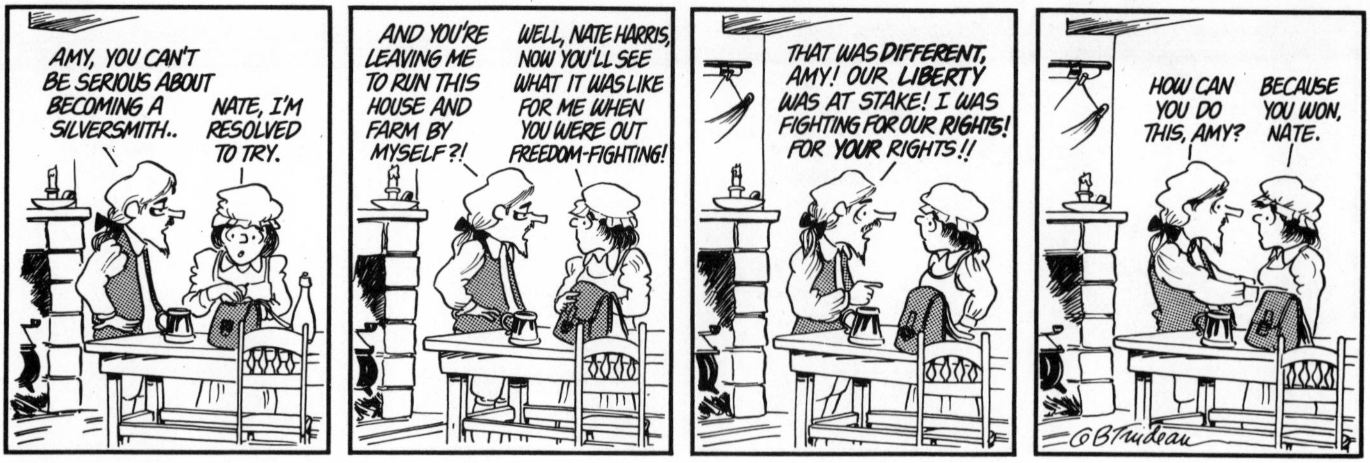
AMY, YOU CAN'T BE SERIOUS ABOUT BECOMING A SILVERSMITH..
NATE, I'M RESOLVED TO TRY.
AND YOU'RE LEAVING ME TO RUN THIS HOUSE AND FARM BY MYSELF?!
WELL, NATE HARRIS, NOW YOU'LL SEE WHAT IT WAS LIKE FOR ME WHEN YOU WERE OUT FREEDOM-FIGHTING!
THAT WAS **DIFFERENT**, AMY! OUR **LIBERTY** WAS AT STAKE! I WAS FIGHTING FOR OUR **RIGHTS**! FOR **YOUR** RIGHTS!!
HOW CAN YOU DO THIS, AMY?
BECAUSE YOU WON, NATE.

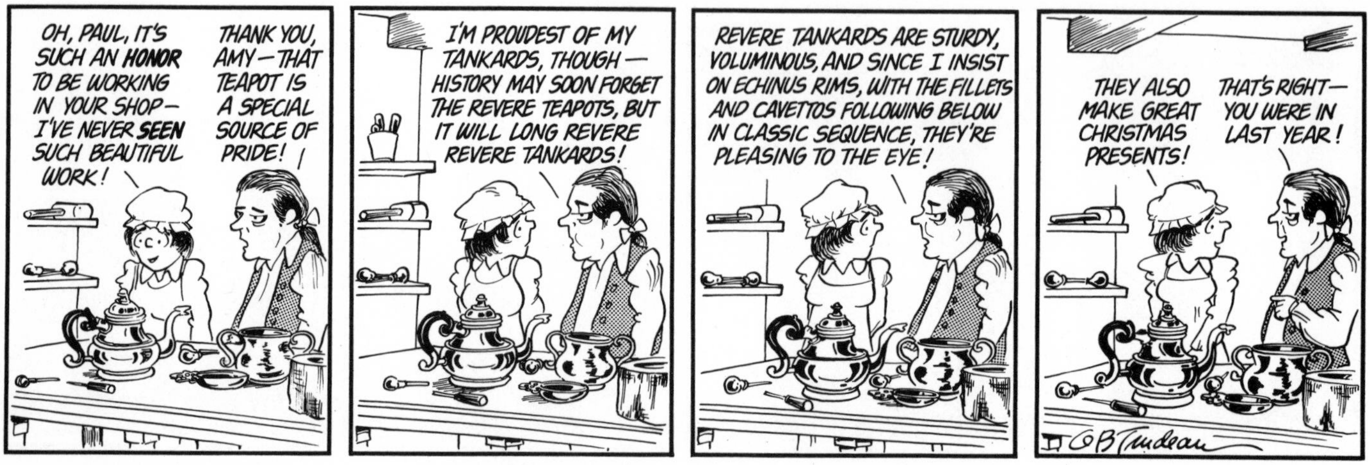
OH, PAUL, IT'S SUCH AN **HONOR** TO BE WORKING IN YOUR SHOP— I'VE NEVER **SEEN** SUCH BEAUTIFUL WORK!
THANK YOU, AMY—THAT TEAPOT IS A SPECIAL SOURCE OF PRIDE!
I'M PROUDEST OF MY TANKARDS, THOUGH— HISTORY MAY SOON FORGET THE REVERE TEAPOTS, BUT IT WILL LONG REVERE REVERE TANKARDS!
REVERE TANKARDS ARE STURDY, VOLUMINOUS, AND SINCE I INSIST ON ECHINUS RIMS, WITH THE FILLETS AND CAVETTOS FOLLOWING BELOW IN CLASSIC SEQUENCE, THEY'RE PLEASING TO THE EYE!
THEY ALSO MAKE GREAT CHRISTMAS PRESENTS!
THAT'S RIGHT— YOU WERE IN LAST YEAR!

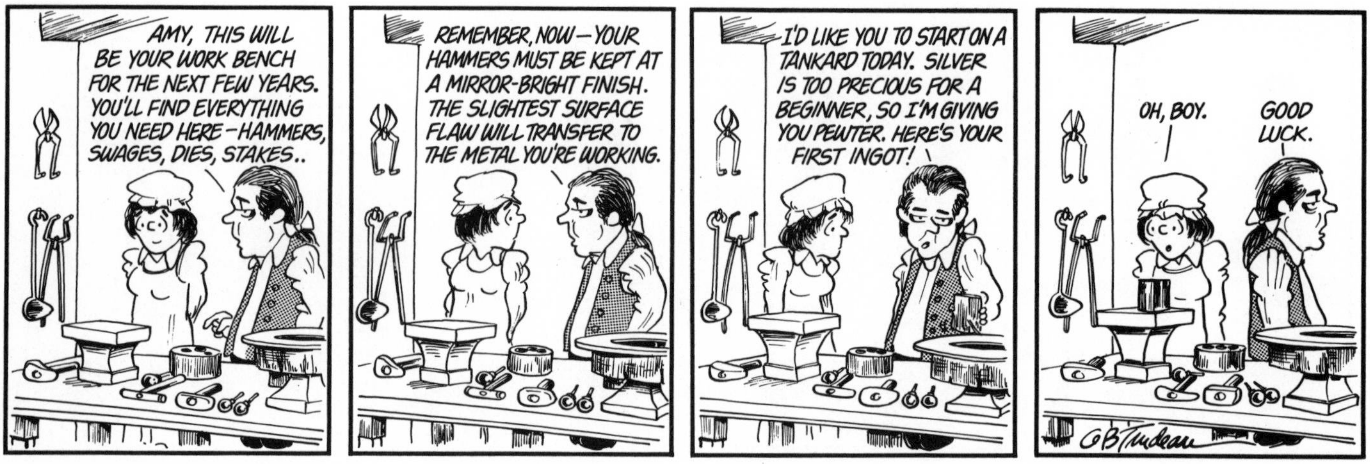
AMY, THIS WILL BE YOUR WORK BENCH FOR THE NEXT FEW YEARS. YOU'LL FIND EVERYTHING YOU NEED HERE—HAMMERS, SWAGES, DIES, STAKES..
REMEMBER, NOW—YOUR HAMMERS MUST BE KEPT AT A MIRROR-BRIGHT FINISH. THE SLIGHTEST SURFACE FLAW WILL TRANSFER TO THE METAL YOU'RE WORKING.
I'D LIKE YOU TO START ON A TANKARD TODAY. SILVER IS TOO PRECIOUS FOR A BEGINNER, SO I'M GIVING YOU PEWTER. HERE'S YOUR FIRST INGOT!
OH, BOY.
GOOD LUCK.

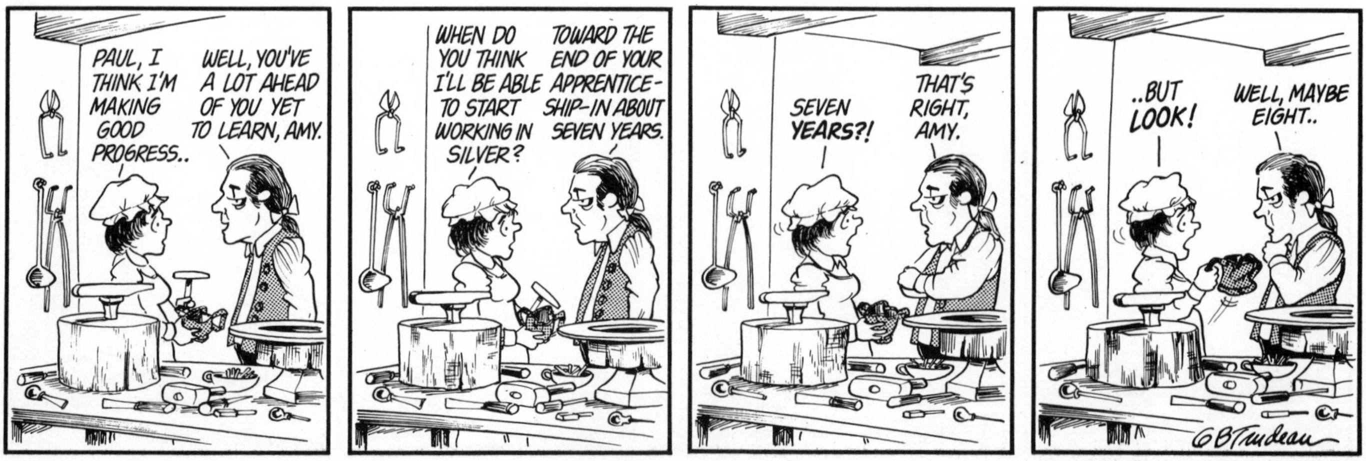
PAUL, I THINK I'M MAKING GOOD PROGRESS..
WELL, YOU'VE A LOT AHEAD OF YOU YET TO LEARN, AMY.
WHEN DO YOU THINK I'LL BE ABLE TO START WORKING IN SILVER?
TOWARD THE END OF YOUR APPRENTICE-SHIP—IN ABOUT SEVEN YEARS.
SEVEN **YEARS**?!
THAT'S RIGHT, AMY.
..BUT **LOOK**!
WELL, MAYBE EIGHT..

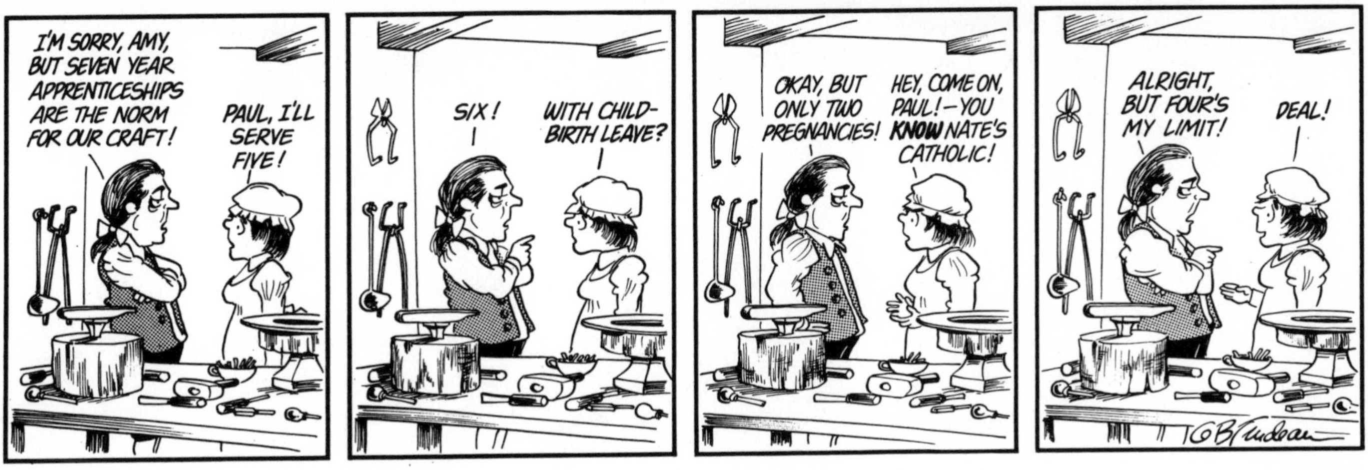
I'M SORRY, AMY, BUT SEVEN YEAR APPRENTICESHIPS ARE THE NORM FOR OUR CRAFT!
PAUL, I'LL SERVE FIVE!
SIX!
WITH CHILD-BIRTH LEAVE?
OKAY, BUT ONLY TWO PREGNANCIES!
HEY, COME ON, PAUL!—YOU **KNOW** NATE'S CATHOLIC!
ALRIGHT, BUT FOUR'S MY LIMIT!
DEAL!
GBTrudeau

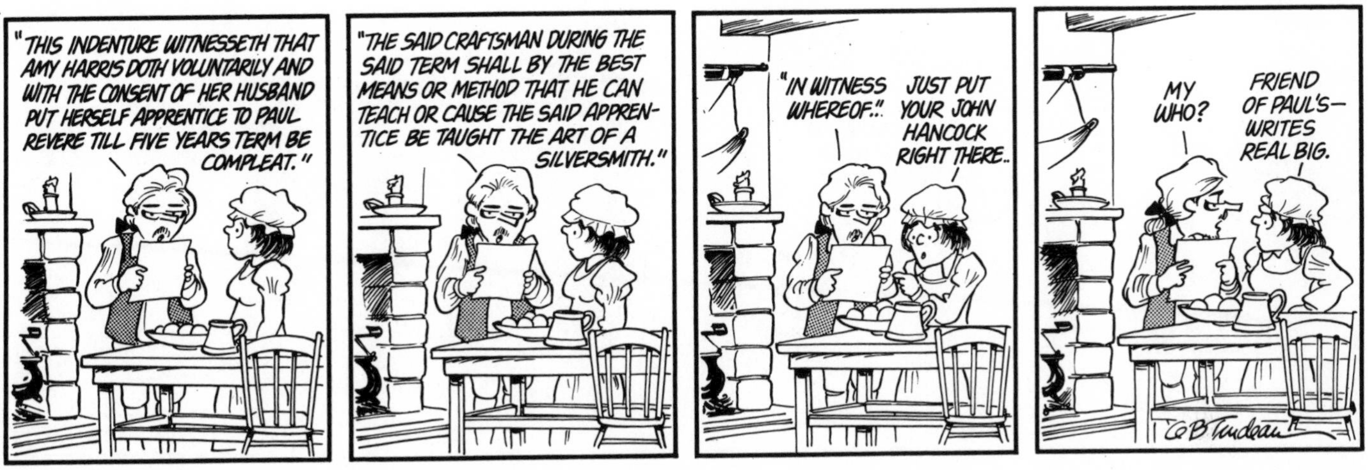
"THIS INDENTURE WITNESSETH THAT AMY HARRIS DOTH VOLUNTARILY AND WITH THE CONSENT OF HER HUSBAND PUT HERSELF APPRENTICE TO PAUL REVERE TILL FIVE YEARS TERM BE COMPLEAT."
"THE SAID CRAFTSMAN DURING THE SAID TERM SHALL BY THE BEST MEANS OR METHOD THAT HE CAN TEACH OR CAUSE THE SAID APPRENTICE BE TAUGHT THE ART OF A SILVERSMITH."
"IN WITNESS WHEREOF..."
JUST PUT YOUR JOHN HANCOCK RIGHT THERE..
MY WHO?
FRIEND OF PAUL'S—WRITES REAL BIG.
GBTrudeau

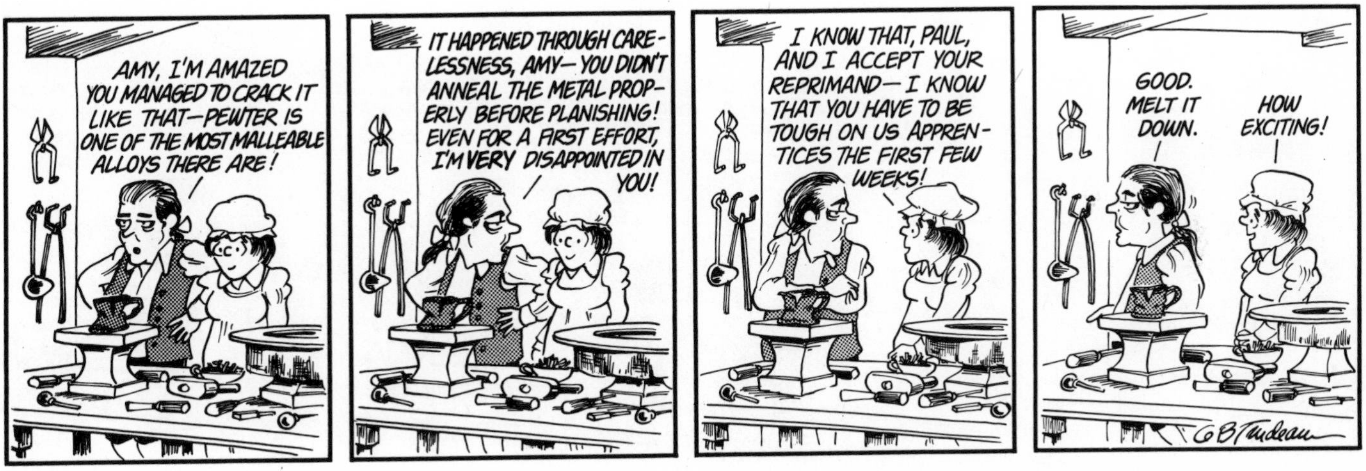
AMY, I'M AMAZED YOU MANAGED TO CRACK IT LIKE THAT—PEWTER IS ONE OF THE MOST MALLEABLE ALLOYS THERE ARE!
IT HAPPENED THROUGH CARELESSNESS, AMY—YOU DIDN'T ANNEAL THE METAL PROPERLY BEFORE PLANISHING! EVEN FOR A FIRST EFFORT, I'M **VERY** DISAPPOINTED IN YOU!
I KNOW THAT, PAUL, AND I ACCEPT YOUR REPRIMAND—I KNOW THAT YOU HAVE TO BE TOUGH ON US APPRENTICES THE FIRST FEW WEEKS!
GOOD. MELT IT DOWN.
HOW EXCITING!
GBTrudeau

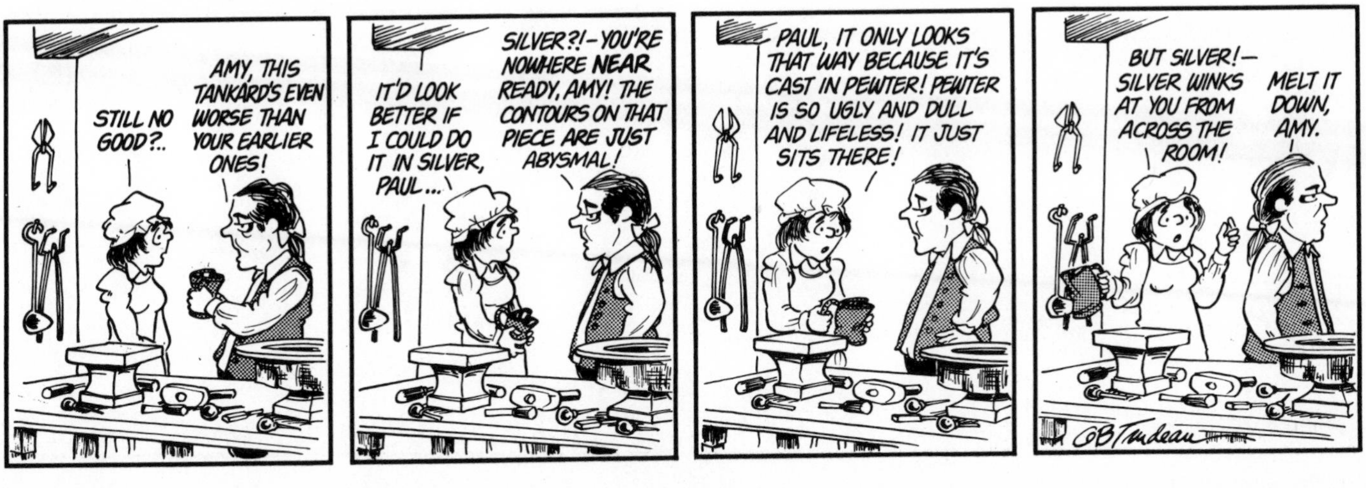
STILL NO GOOD?..
AMY, THIS TANKARD'S EVEN WORSE THAN YOUR EARLIER ONES!
IT'D LOOK BETTER IF I COULD DO IT IN SILVER, PAUL...
SILVER?!—YOU'RE NOWHERE **NEAR** READY, AMY! THE CONTOURS ON THAT PIECE ARE JUST ABYSMAL!
PAUL, IT ONLY LOOKS THAT WAY BECAUSE IT'S CAST IN PEWTER! PEWTER IS SO UGLY AND DULL AND LIFELESS! IT JUST SITS THERE!
BUT SILVER!—SILVER WINKS AT YOU FROM ACROSS THE ROOM!
MELT IT DOWN, AMY.
GBTrudeau

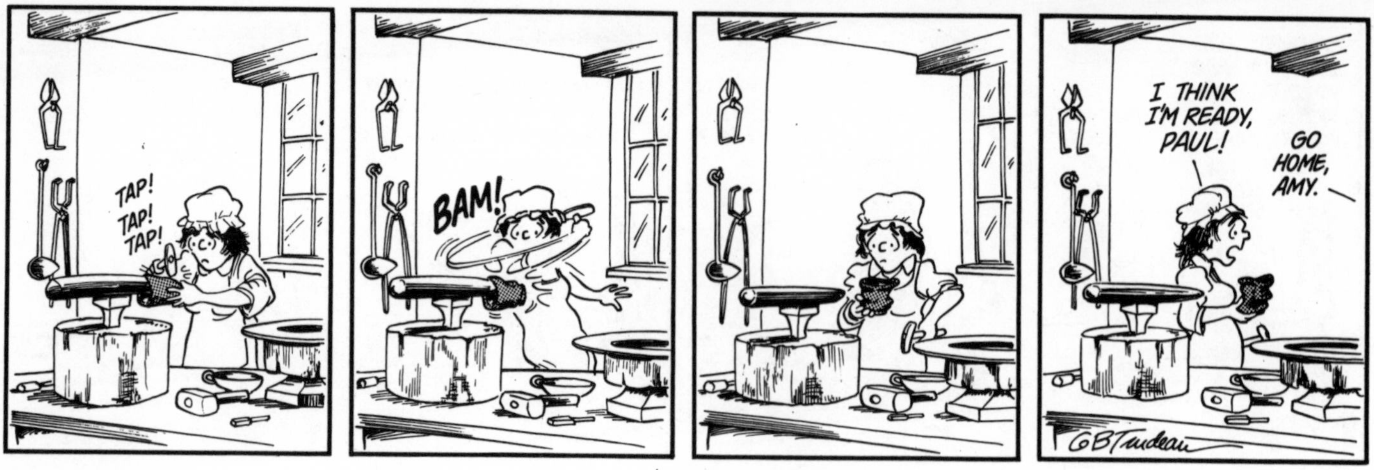
TAP! TAP! TAP!
BAM!
I THINK I'M READY, PAUL!
GO HOME, AMY.
GBTrudeau

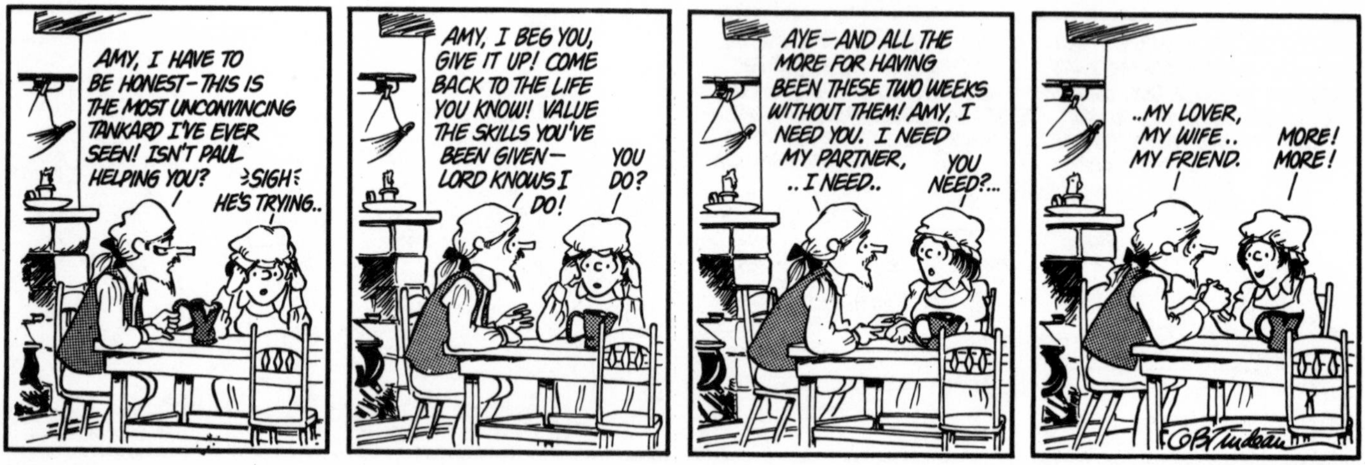
AMY, I HAVE TO BE HONEST—THIS IS THE MOST UNCONVINCING TANKARD I'VE EVER SEEN! ISN'T PAUL HELPING YOU?
SIGH HE'S TRYING..
AMY, I BEG YOU, GIVE IT UP! COME BACK TO THE LIFE YOU KNOW! VALUE THE SKILLS YOU'VE BEEN GIVEN—LORD KNOWS I DO!
YOU DO?
AYE—AND ALL THE MORE FOR HAVING BEEN THESE TWO WEEKS WITHOUT THEM! AMY, I NEED YOU. I NEED MY PARTNER, .. I NEED..
YOU NEED?...
..MY LOVER, MY WIFE.. MY FRIEND.
MORE! MORE!
GBTrudeau

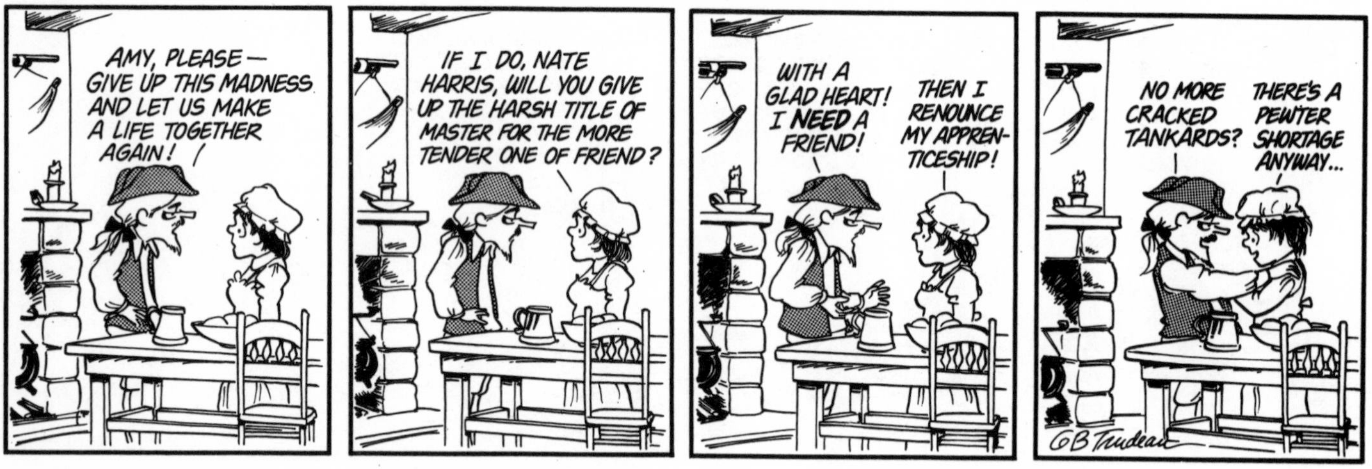
AMY, PLEASE— GIVE UP THIS MADNESS AND LET US MAKE A LIFE TOGETHER AGAIN!
IF I DO, NATE HARRIS, WILL YOU GIVE UP THE HARSH TITLE OF MASTER FOR THE MORE TENDER ONE OF FRIEND?
WITH A GLAD HEART! I NEED A FRIEND!
THEN I RENOUNCE MY APPRENTICESHIP!
NO MORE CRACKED TANKARDS?
THERE'S A PEWTER SHORTAGE ANYWAY...
GBTrudeau

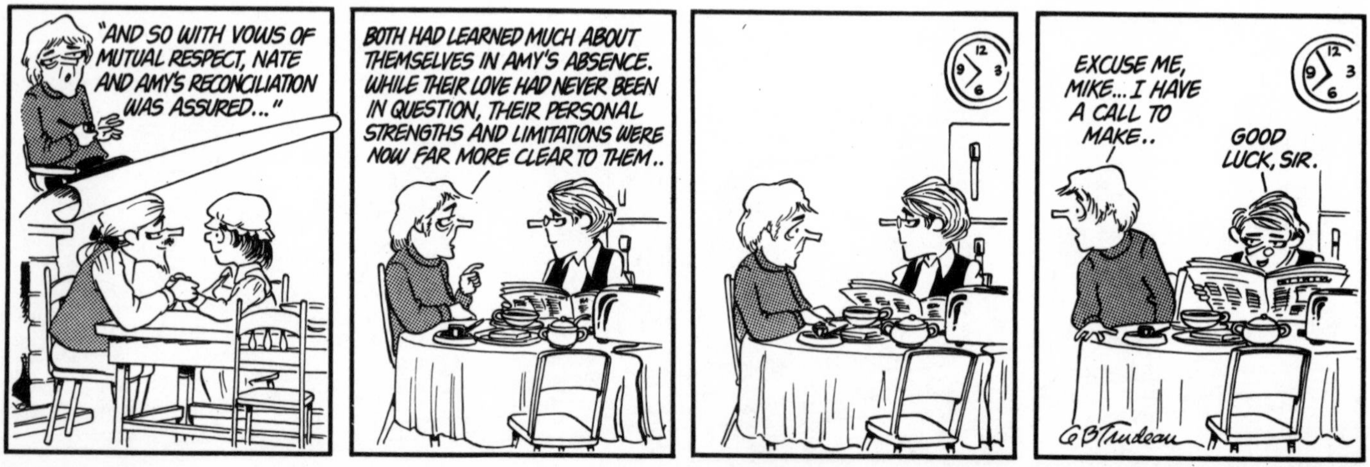
"AND SO WITH VOWS OF MUTUAL RESPECT, NATE AND AMY'S RECONCILIATION WAS ASSURED..."
BOTH HAD LEARNED MUCH ABOUT THEMSELVES IN AMY'S ABSENCE. WHILE THEIR LOVE HAD NEVER BEEN IN QUESTION, THEIR PERSONAL STRENGTHS AND LIMITATIONS WERE NOW FAR MORE CLEAR TO THEM..
EXCUSE ME, MIKE... I HAVE A CALL TO MAKE..
GOOD LUCK, SIR.
GBTrudeau

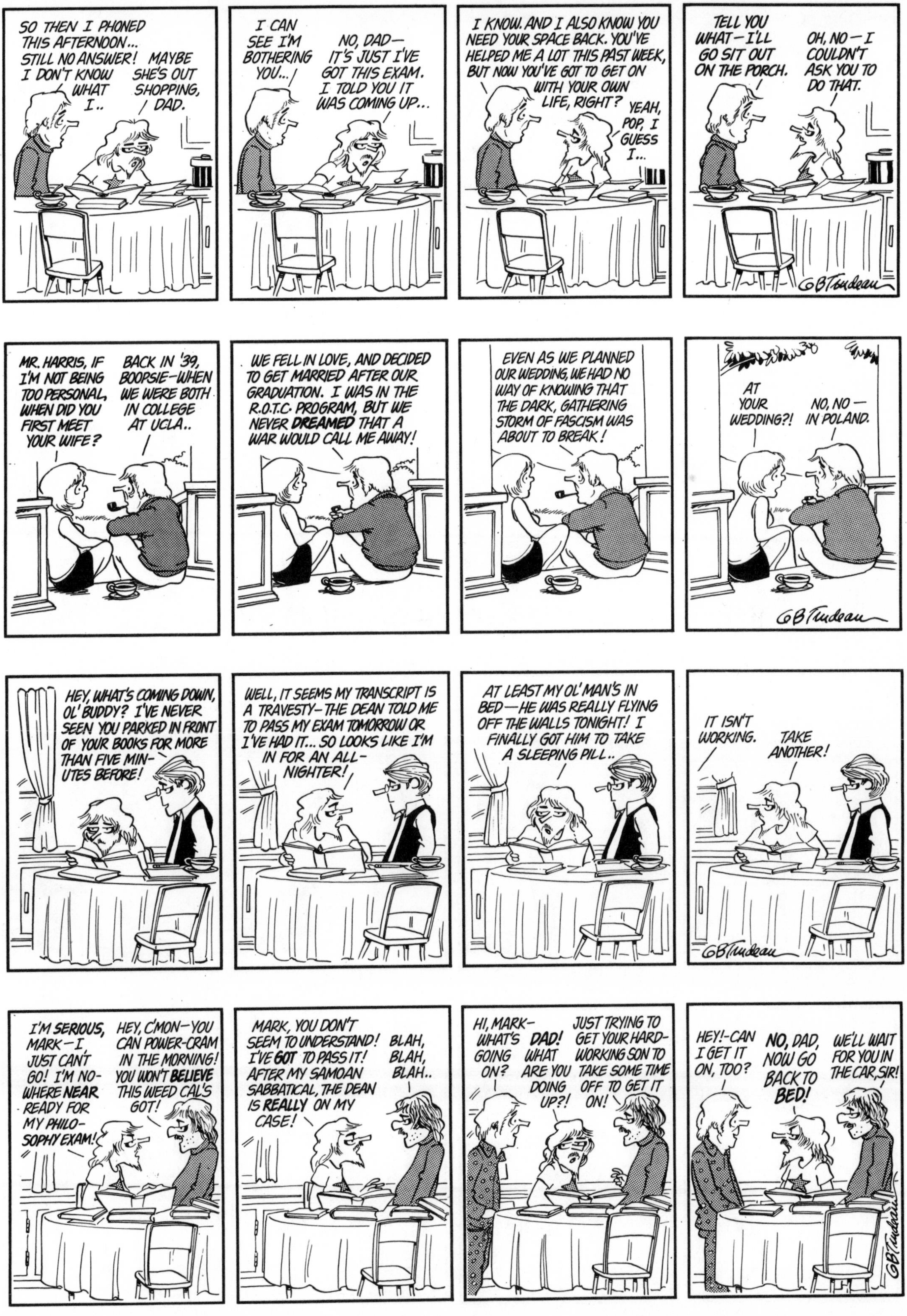
SO THEN I PHONED THIS AFTERNOON... STILL NO ANSWER! I DON'T KNOW WHAT I..
MAYBE SHE'S OUT SHOPPING, DAD.
I CAN SEE I'M BOTHERING YOU...
NO, DAD— IT'S JUST I'VE GOT THIS EXAM. I TOLD YOU IT WAS COMING UP...
I KNOW. AND I ALSO KNOW YOU NEED YOUR SPACE BACK. YOU'VE HELPED ME A LOT THIS PAST WEEK, BUT NOW YOU'VE GOT TO GET ON WITH YOUR OWN LIFE, RIGHT?
YEAH, POP, I GUESS I...
TELL YOU WHAT—I'LL GO SIT OUT ON THE PORCH.
OH, NO—I COULDN'T ASK YOU TO DO THAT.
MR. HARRIS, IF I'M NOT BEING TOO PERSONAL, WHEN DID YOU FIRST MEET YOUR WIFE?
BACK IN '39, BOOPSIE—WHEN WE WERE BOTH IN COLLEGE AT UCLA..
WE FELL IN LOVE, AND DECIDED TO GET MARRIED AFTER OUR GRADUATION. I WAS IN THE R.O.T.C. PROGRAM, BUT WE NEVER DREAMED THAT A WAR WOULD CALL ME AWAY!
EVEN AS WE PLANNED OUR WEDDING, WE HAD NO WAY OF KNOWING THAT THE DARK, GATHERING STORM OF FASCISM WAS ABOUT TO BREAK!
AT YOUR WEDDING?!
NO, NO— IN POLAND.
HEY, WHAT'S COMING DOWN, OL' BUDDY? I'VE NEVER SEEN YOU PARKED IN FRONT OF YOUR BOOKS FOR MORE THAN FIVE MINUTES BEFORE!
WELL, IT SEEMS MY TRANSCRIPT IS A TRAVESTY—THE DEAN TOLD ME TO PASS MY EXAM TOMORROW OR I'VE HAD IT... SO LOOKS LIKE I'M IN FOR AN ALL-NIGHTER!
AT LEAST MY OL' MAN'S IN BED—HE WAS REALLY FLYING OFF THE WALLS TONIGHT! I FINALLY GOT HIM TO TAKE A SLEEPING PILL..
IT ISN'T WORKING.
TAKE ANOTHER!
I'M SERIOUS, MARK—I JUST CAN'T GO! I'M NOWHERE NEAR READY FOR MY PHILOSOPHY EXAM!
HEY, C'MON—YOU CAN POWER-CRAM IN THE MORNING! YOU WON'T BELIEVE THIS WEED CAL'S GOT!
MARK, YOU DON'T SEEM TO UNDERSTAND! I'VE GOT TO PASS IT! AFTER MY SAMOAN SABBATICAL, THE DEAN IS REALLY ON MY CASE!
BLAH, BLAH, BLAH..
HI, MARK— WHAT'S GOING ON?
DAD! WHAT ARE YOU DOING UP?!
JUST TRYING TO GET YOUR HARD-WORKING SON TO TAKE SOME TIME OFF TO GET IT ON!
HEY!-CAN I GET IT ON, TOO?
NO, DAD, NOW GO BACK TO BED!
WE'LL WAIT FOR YOU IN THE CAR, SIR!

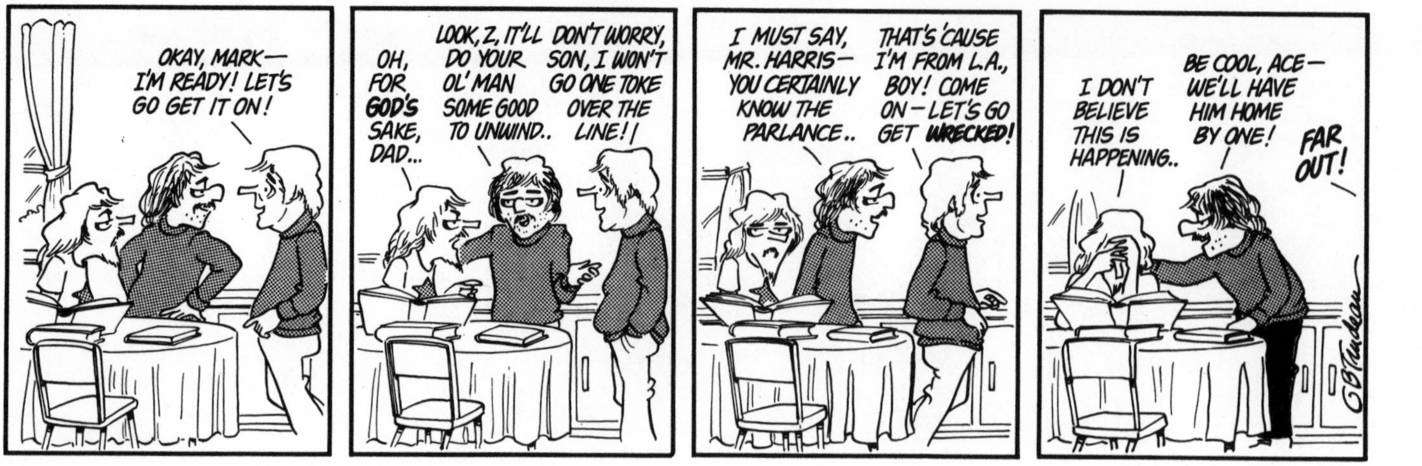
OKAY, MARK— I'M READY! LET'S GO GET IT ON!
OH, FOR GOD'S SAKE, DAD...
LOOK, Z, IT'LL DO YOUR OL' MAN SOME GOOD TO UNWIND..
DON'T WORRY, SON, I WON'T GO ONE TOKE OVER THE LINE!
I MUST SAY, MR. HARRIS— YOU CERTAINLY KNOW THE PARLANCE..
THAT'S 'CAUSE I'M FROM L.A., BOY! COME ON—LET'S GO GET WRECKED!
I DON'T BELIEVE THIS IS HAPPENING..
BE COOL, ACE— WE'LL HAVE HIM HOME BY ONE!
FAR OUT!
GBTrudeau

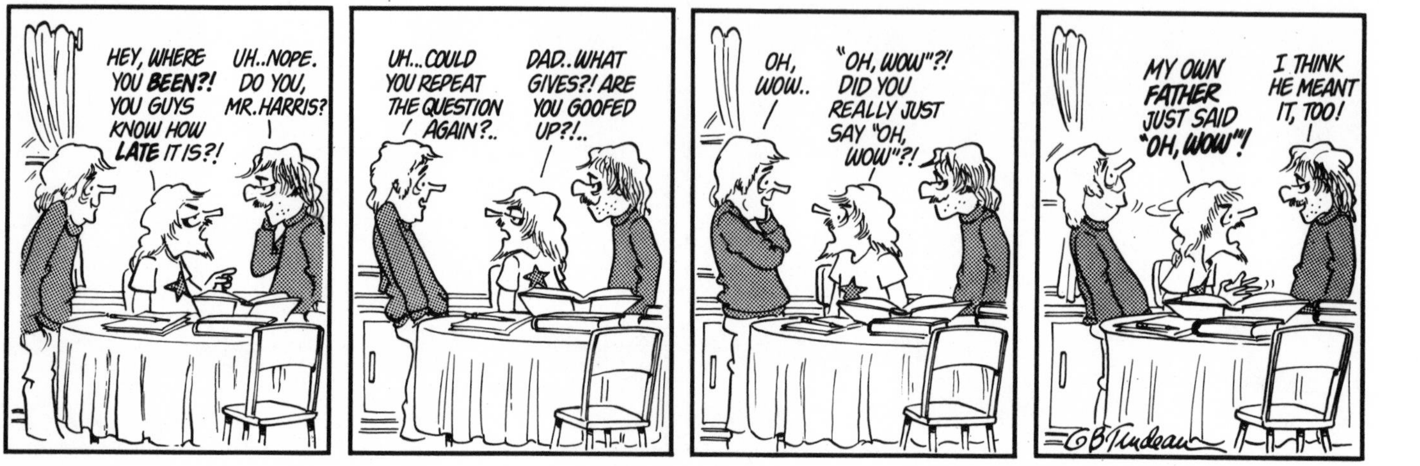
HEY, WHERE YOU BEEN?! YOU GUYS KNOW HOW LATE IT IS?!
UH..NOPE. DO YOU, MR. HARRIS?
UH...COULD YOU REPEAT THE QUESTION AGAIN?..
DAD..WHAT GIVES?! ARE YOU GOOFED UP?!..
OH, WOW..
"OH, WOW"?! DID YOU REALLY JUST SAY "OH, WOW"?!
MY OWN FATHER JUST SAID "OH, WOW"!
I THINK HE MEANT IT, TOO!
GBTrudeau

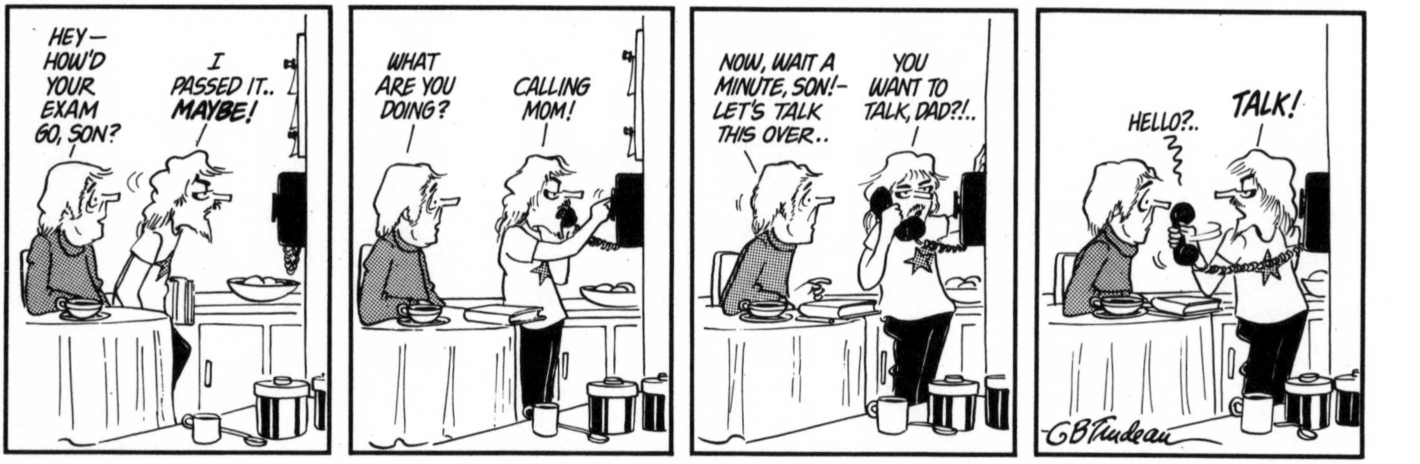
HEY— HOW'D YOUR EXAM GO, SON?
I PASSED IT.. MAYBE!
WHAT ARE YOU DOING?
CALLING MOM!
NOW, WAIT A MINUTE, SON!— LET'S TALK THIS OVER..
YOU WANT TO TALK, DAD?!..
HELLO?..
TALK!
GBTrudeau

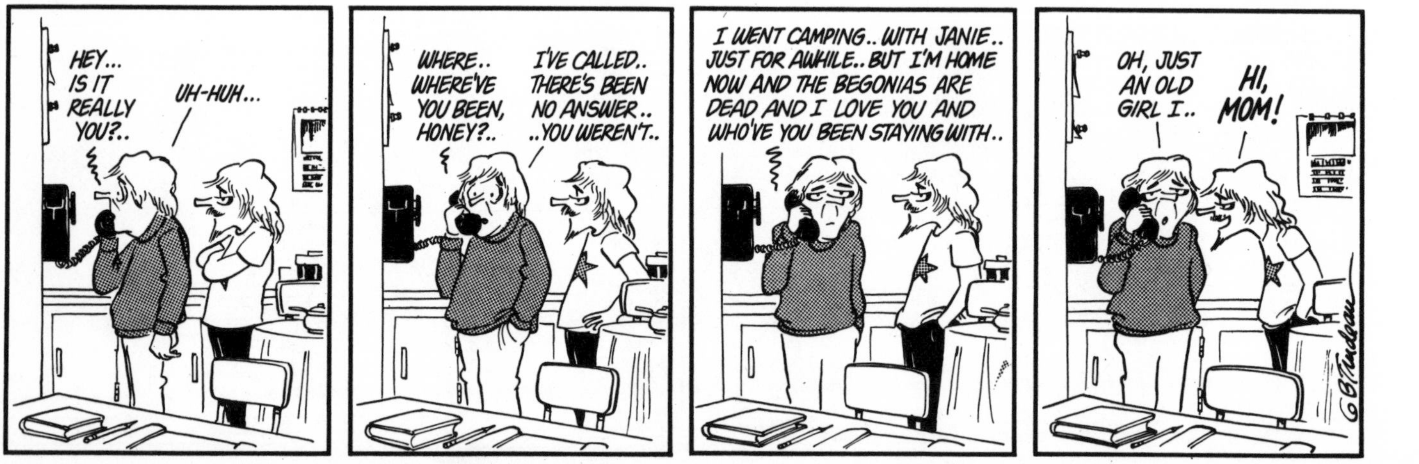
HEY... IS IT REALLY YOU?..
UH-HUH...
WHERE.. WHERE'VE YOU BEEN, HONEY?..
I'VE CALLED.. THERE'S BEEN NO ANSWER.. ..YOU WEREN'T..
I WENT CAMPING.. WITH JANIE.. JUST FOR AWHILE.. BUT I'M HOME NOW AND THE BEGONIAS ARE DEAD AND I LOVE YOU AND WHO'VE YOU BEEN STAYING WITH..
OH, JUST AN OLD GIRL I..
HI, MOM!
GBTrudeau

ACT TWO

Time: 1976 (The Year of the Dragon)

Selected Scenes

"An Especially Tricky People" . . . . Duke, Chinese
dignitaries

"Ginny's Song" (pop version) . . . . Jimmy Thudpucker

"Going the Contrition Route" . . . . The Watergators,
Scott Meredith

"Ginny's Song" (disco version) . . . . Jimmy Thudpucker,
Walden West
Rhythm Section

"The Rains in Plains" . . . . Jimmy Carter, Jerry
Ford, reporters

"Bluestockings Blues" . . . . Ginny, Lacey

"As the Kid Goes for Broke" . . . . Joanie, Rick

"Everybody Does It" . . . . Senator Ventura,
Miss Tibbet,
Dan Rather

"The Walls Tell All" . . . . Duke, Honey

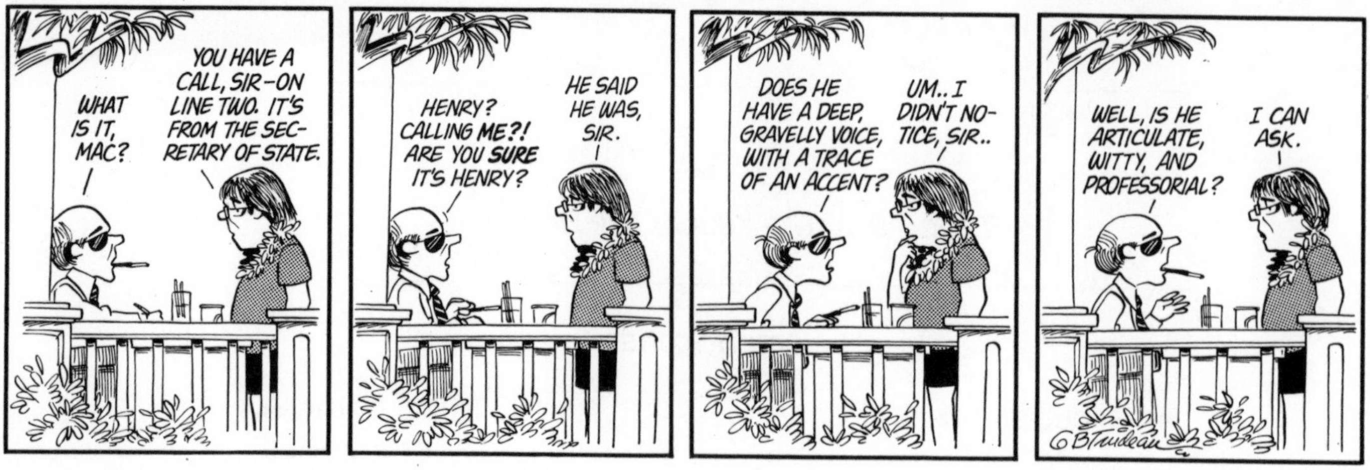
WHAT IS IT, MAC?
YOU HAVE A CALL, SIR—ON LINE TWO. IT'S FROM THE SECRETARY OF STATE.
HENRY? CALLING **ME?!** ARE YOU **SURE** IT'S HENRY?
HE SAID HE WAS, SIR.
DOES HE HAVE A DEEP, GRAVELLY VOICE, WITH A TRACE OF AN ACCENT?
UM.. I DIDN'T NOTICE, SIR..
WELL, IS HE ARTICULATE, WITTY, AND PROFESSORIAL?
I CAN ASK.
© BTrudeau

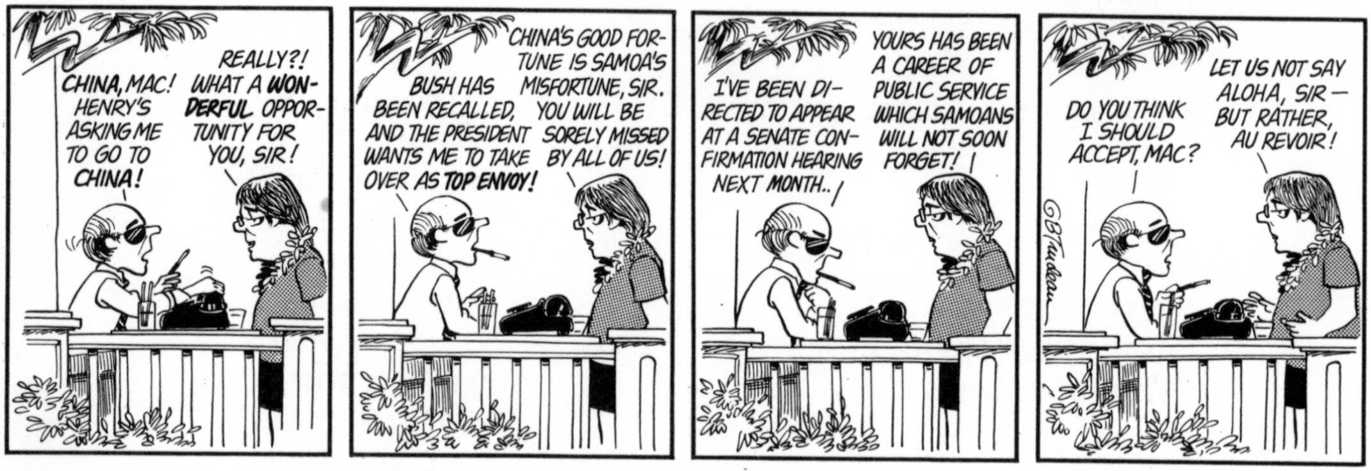
CHINA, MAC! HENRY'S ASKING ME TO GO TO **CHINA!**
REALLY?! WHAT A **WONDERFUL** OPPORTUNITY FOR YOU, SIR!
BUSH HAS BEEN RECALLED, AND THE PRESIDENT WANTS ME TO TAKE OVER AS **TOP ENVOY!**
CHINA'S GOOD FORTUNE IS SAMOA'S MISFORTUNE, SIR. YOU WILL BE SORELY MISSED BY ALL OF US!
I'VE BEEN DIRECTED TO APPEAR AT A SENATE CONFIRMATION HEARING NEXT MONTH..
YOURS HAS BEEN A CAREER OF PUBLIC SERVICE WHICH SAMOANS WILL NOT SOON FORGET!
DO YOU THINK I SHOULD ACCEPT, MAC?
LET US NOT SAY ALOHA, SIR—BUT RATHER, AU REVOIR!
© BTrudeau

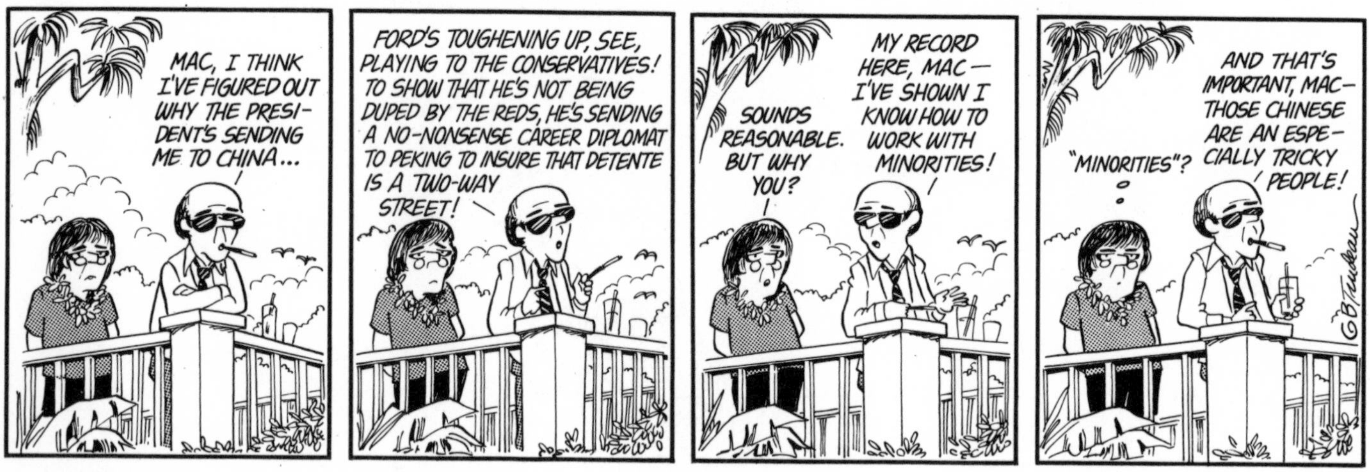
MAC, I THINK I'VE FIGURED OUT WHY THE PRESIDENT'S SENDING ME TO CHINA...
FORD'S TOUGHENING UP, SEE, PLAYING TO THE CONSERVATIVES! TO SHOW THAT HE'S NOT BEING DUPED BY THE REDS, HE'S SENDING A NO-NONSENSE CAREER DIPLOMAT TO PEKING TO INSURE THAT DETENTE IS A TWO-WAY STREET!
SOUNDS REASONABLE. BUT WHY YOU?
MY RECORD HERE, MAC—I'VE SHOWN I KNOW HOW TO WORK WITH MINORITIES!
"MINORITIES"?
AND THAT'S IMPORTANT, MAC—THOSE CHINESE ARE AN ESPECIALLY TRICKY PEOPLE!
© BTrudeau

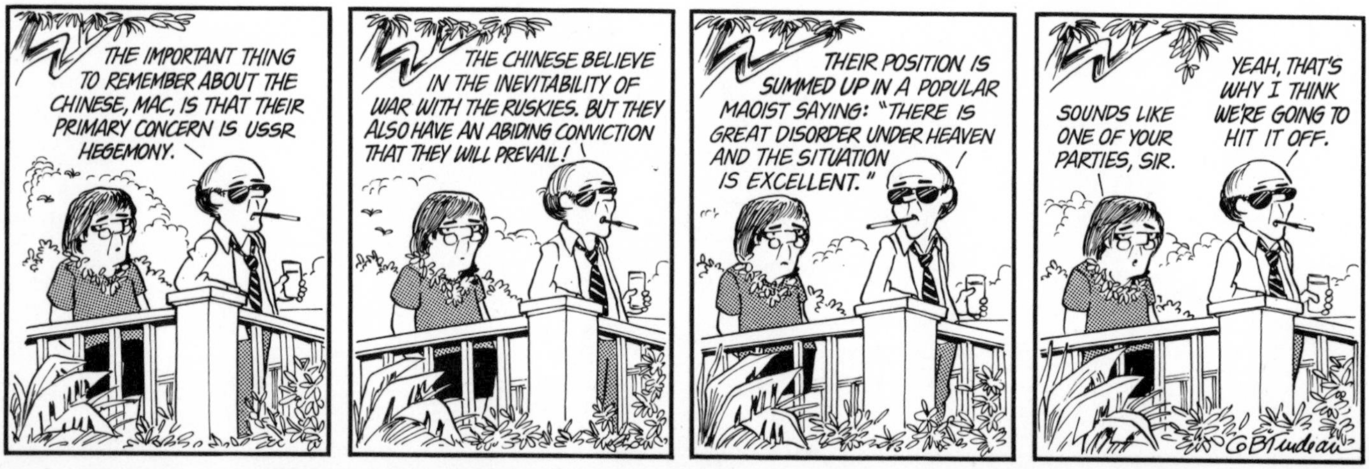
THE IMPORTANT THING TO REMEMBER ABOUT THE CHINESE, MAC, IS THAT THEIR PRIMARY CONCERN IS USSR HEGEMONY.
THE CHINESE BELIEVE IN THE INEVITABILITY OF WAR WITH THE RUSKIES. BUT THEY ALSO HAVE AN ABIDING CONVICTION THAT THEY WILL PREVAIL!
THEIR POSITION IS **SUMMED UP** IN A POPULAR MAOIST SAYING: "THERE IS GREAT DISORDER UNDER HEAVEN AND THE SITUATION IS EXCELLENT."
SOUNDS LIKE ONE OF YOUR PARTIES, SIR.
YEAH, THAT'S WHY I THINK WE'RE GOING TO HIT IT OFF.
© BTrudeau

A FAREWELL GIFT? FOR ME?!

YES, SIR—I TOOK UP A COLLECTION FROM ALL 7,652 SAMOAN GOVERNMENT EMPLOYEES!

AW.. MAC, YOU SHOULDN'T HAVE..

THE RESPONSE WAS TERRIFIC, SO WE GOT YOU SOMETHING REALLY SPECIAL— AND APPROPRIATE!

MAC...I'M.. I'M.. OVERWHELMED!

CHOPSTICKS!

NO, I'M NOT.

THEY'RE SOLID WOOD, SIR!

MAC, BEFORE WE GO, I'D LIKE YOU TO TYPE UP A LIST OF MY MAJOR ACHIEVEMENTS— TO SHOW THE COMMITTEE.

ACHIEVEMENTS, SIR?

RIGHT. A MODEST INVENTORY OF THE MANY SIGNIFICANT CONTRIBUTIONS MADE DURING MY TENURE IN SAMOA!

UM..

OH, C'MON, MAC, DON'T LOOK SO PUT OUT. IT WON'T TAKE YOU THAT LONG!

I WAS JUST THINKING THAT, SIR..

GOD, I PITY THE POOR SUCKER WHO'S GOTTA FOLLOW MY ACT!

HOW'S THAT LIST OF MY MAJOR ACHIEVEMENTS SHAPING UP, MACARTHUR?

WELL, SIR, I'M MAKING PROGRESS..

WHY DON'T YOU READ IT BACK TO ME—I PROBABLY SHOULD CHECK IT FOR ACCURACY.

"A COMPREHENSIVE LIST OF THE MANY ACHIEVEMENTS INFLICTED ON SAMOA BY HIS EXCELLENCY, GOVERNOR DUKE.."

"INFLICTED"?! MAC, YOU LUNKHEAD— YOU DON'T MEAN "INFLICTED"!

WHAT—IS THE TENSE WRONG?

AND YOU CALL YOURSELF FLUENT IN ENGLISH!

LISTEN, GEORGE, I'LL TELL YOU WHY I CALLED— I'M TRYING TO CRANK UP FOR THOSE HEARINGS. ANY IDEA WHAT I CAN EXPECT?

"MAJOR ACHIEVEMENTS OF GOVERNOR DUKE:"

WELL, YES, DUKE, I DID TALK TO SOME OF THE COMMITTEE MEMBERS YESTERDAY. THEY'RE GOING TO WANT TO HEAR ABOUT RECENT ALLEGATIONS OF EXTORTION AND OIL KICKBACKS..

UH-HUH.

TAP! TAP!

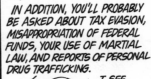
IN ADDITION, YOU'LL PROBABLY BE ASKED ABOUT TAX EVASION, MISAPPROPRIATION OF FEDERAL FUNDS, YOUR USE OF MARTIAL LAW, AND REPORTS OF PERSONAL DRUG TRAFFICKING.

I SEE.

TAP! TAP! TAP!

SO THESE ARE THE KINDS OF THINGS I'D BE ON THE LOOK-OUT FOR..

RIGHT. WELL, THANKS, GEORGE.

"I. COMPLETE RESTORATION OF THE EXECUTIVE MANSION PATIO BAR.."

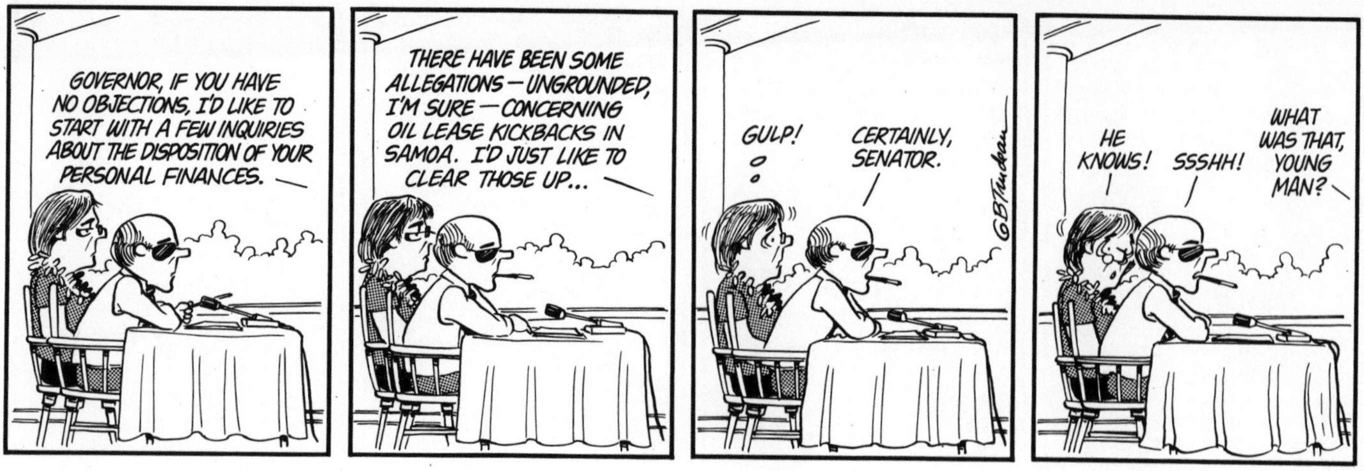
GOVERNOR, IF YOU HAVE NO OBJECTIONS, I'D LIKE TO START WITH A FEW INQUIRIES ABOUT THE DISPOSITION OF YOUR PERSONAL FINANCES.
THERE HAVE BEEN SOME ALLEGATIONS — UNGROUNDED, I'M SURE — CONCERNING OIL LEASE KICKBACKS IN SAMOA. I'D JUST LIKE TO CLEAR THOSE UP...
GULP!
CERTAINLY, SENATOR.
HE KNOWS!
SSSHH!
WHAT WAS THAT, YOUNG MAN?

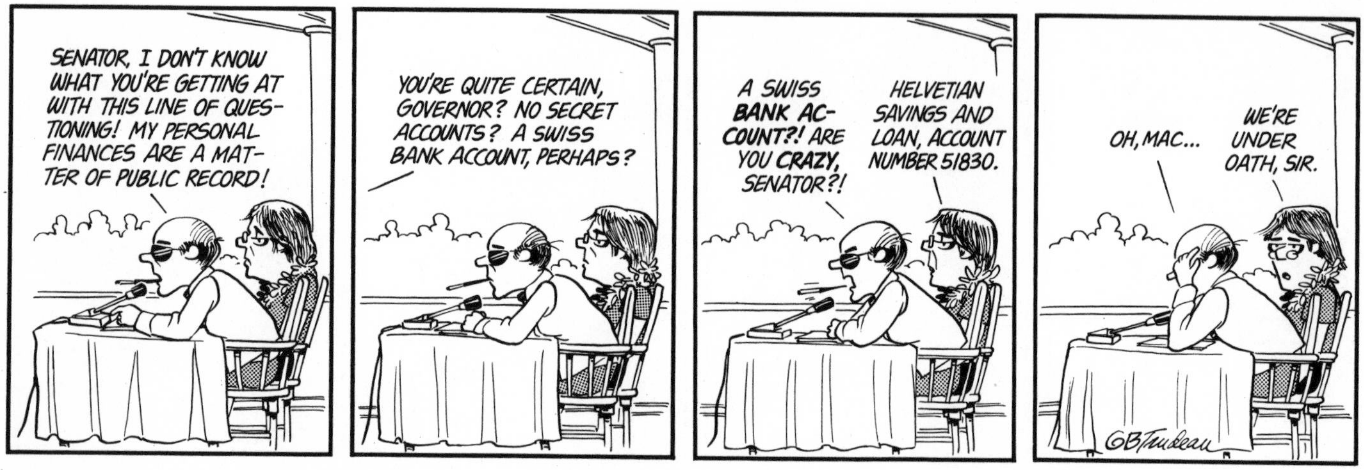
SENATOR, I DON'T KNOW WHAT YOU'RE GETTING AT WITH THIS LINE OF QUESTIONING! MY PERSONAL FINANCES ARE A MATTER OF PUBLIC RECORD!
YOU'RE QUITE CERTAIN, GOVERNOR? NO SECRET ACCOUNTS? A SWISS BANK ACCOUNT, PERHAPS?
A SWISS BANK ACCOUNT?! ARE YOU CRAZY, SENATOR?!
HELVETIAN SAVINGS AND LOAN, ACCOUNT NUMBER 51830.
OH, MAC...
WE'RE UNDER OATH, SIR.

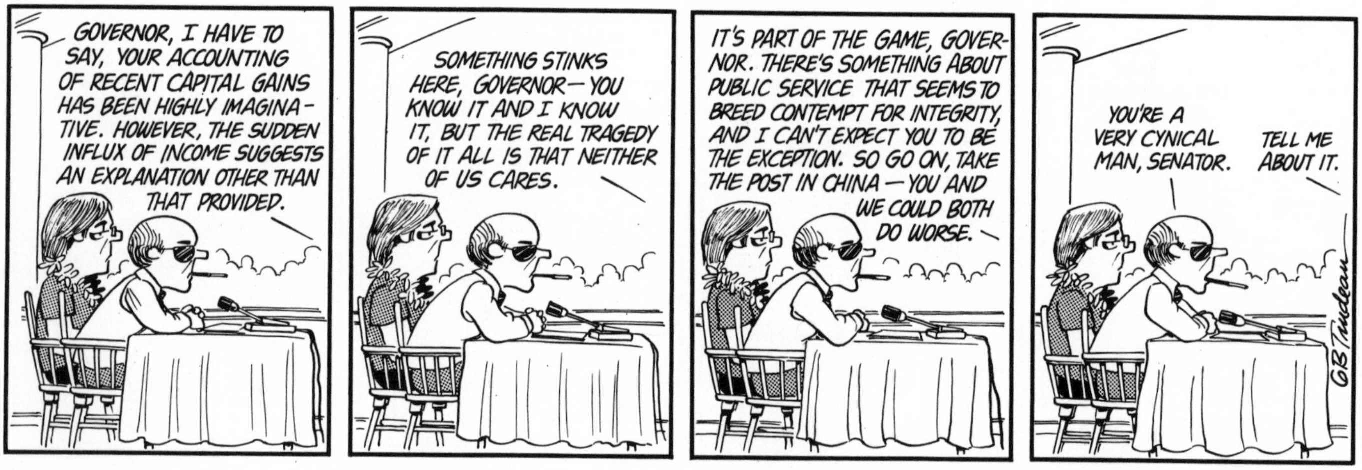
GOVERNOR, I HAVE TO SAY, YOUR ACCOUNTING OF RECENT CAPITAL GAINS HAS BEEN HIGHLY IMAGINATIVE. HOWEVER, THE SUDDEN INFLUX OF INCOME SUGGESTS AN EXPLANATION OTHER THAN THAT PROVIDED.
SOMETHING STINKS HERE, GOVERNOR — YOU KNOW IT AND I KNOW IT, BUT THE REAL TRAGEDY OF IT ALL IS THAT NEITHER OF US CARES.
IT'S PART OF THE GAME, GOVERNOR. THERE'S SOMETHING ABOUT PUBLIC SERVICE THAT SEEMS TO BREED CONTEMPT FOR INTEGRITY, AND I CAN'T EXPECT YOU TO BE THE EXCEPTION. SO GO ON, TAKE THE POST IN CHINA — YOU AND WE COULD BOTH DO WORSE.
YOU'RE A VERY CYNICAL MAN, SENATOR.
TELL ME ABOUT IT.

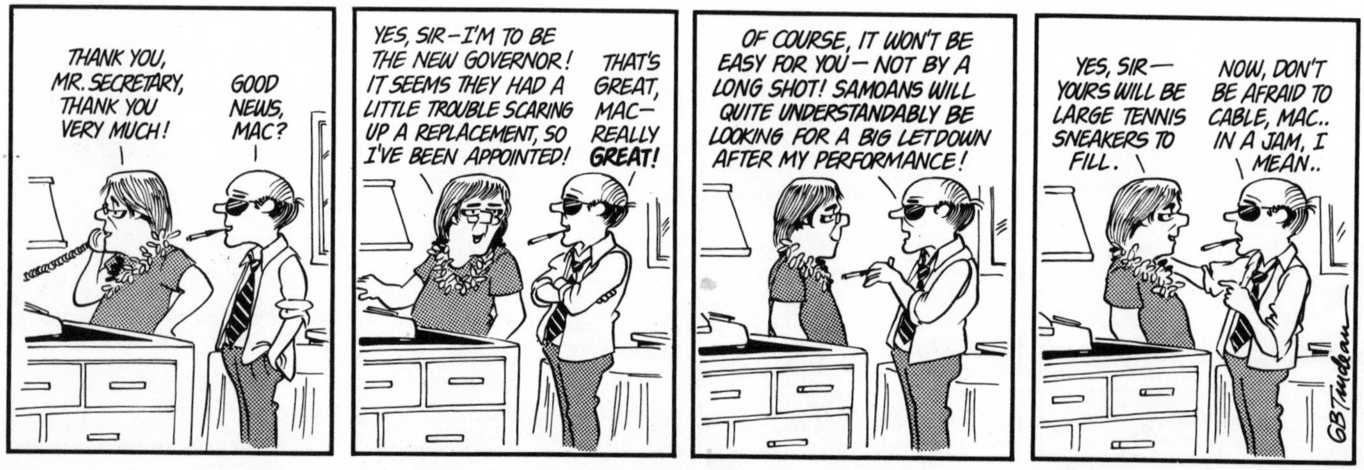
THANK YOU, MR. SECRETARY, THANK YOU VERY MUCH!
GOOD NEWS, MAC?
YES, SIR – I'M TO BE THE NEW GOVERNOR! IT SEEMS THEY HAD A LITTLE TROUBLE SCARING UP A REPLACEMENT, SO I'VE BEEN APPOINTED!
THAT'S GREAT, MAC – REALLY GREAT!
OF COURSE, IT WON'T BE EASY FOR YOU — NOT BY A LONG SHOT! SAMOANS WILL QUITE UNDERSTANDABLY BE LOOKING FOR A BIG LETDOWN AFTER MY PERFORMANCE!
YES, SIR — YOURS WILL BE LARGE TENNIS SNEAKERS TO FILL.
NOW, DON'T BE AFRAID TO CABLE, MAC.. IN A JAM, I MEAN..

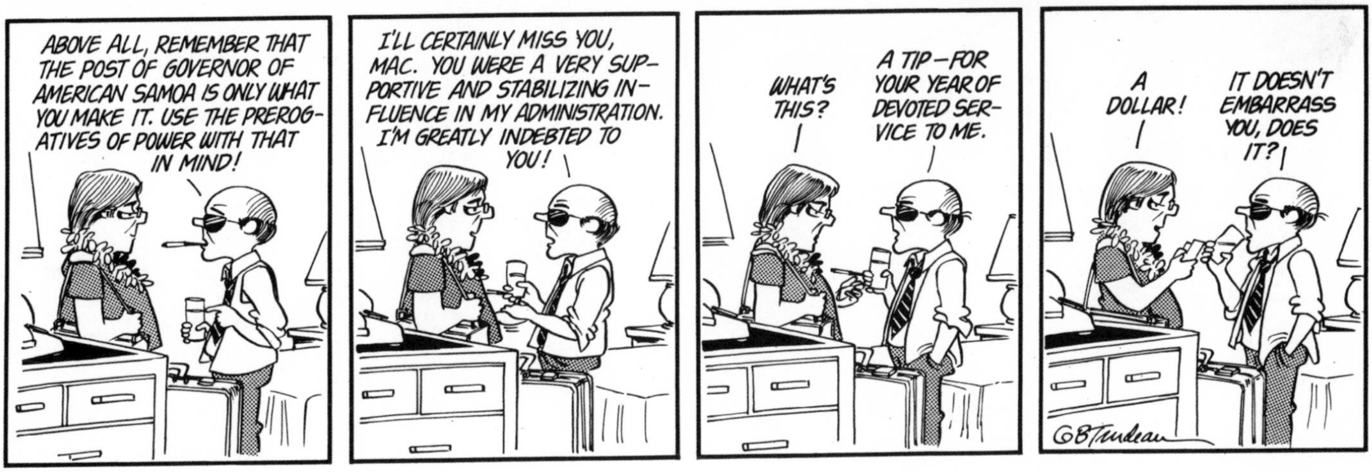
ABOVE ALL, REMEMBER THAT THE POST OF GOVERNOR OF AMERICAN SAMOA IS ONLY WHAT YOU MAKE IT. USE THE PREROGATIVES OF POWER WITH THAT IN MIND!
I'LL CERTAINLY MISS YOU, MAC. YOU WERE A VERY SUPPORTIVE AND STABILIZING INFLUENCE IN MY ADMINISTRATION. I'M GREATLY INDEBTED TO YOU!
WHAT'S THIS?
A TIP—FOR YOUR YEAR OF DEVOTED SERVICE TO ME.
A DOLLAR!
IT DOESN'T EMBARRASS YOU, DOES IT?
GBTrudeau

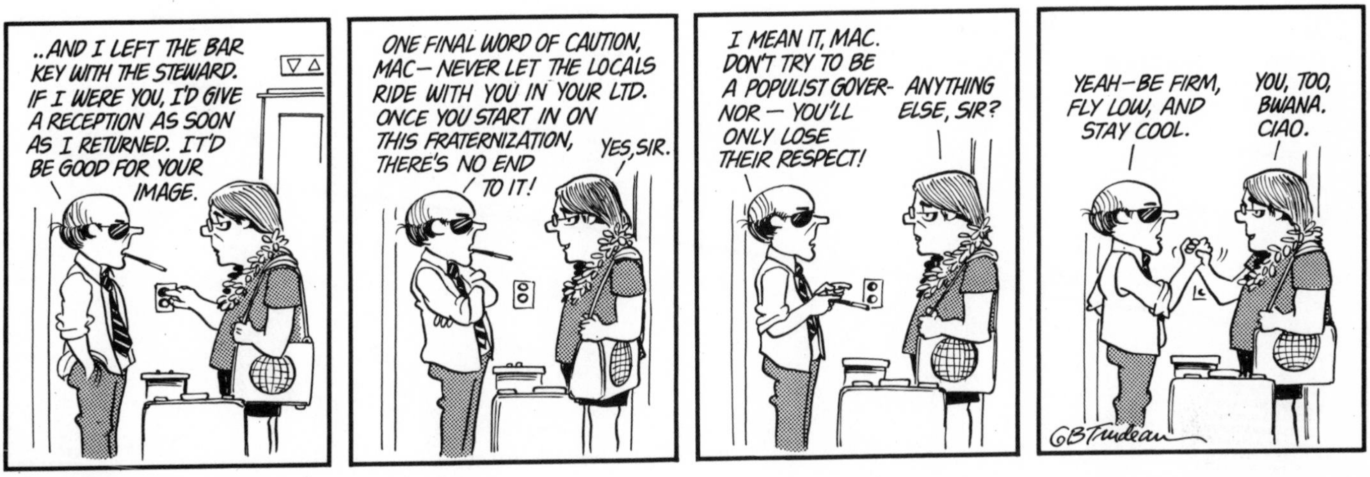
..AND I LEFT THE BAR KEY WITH THE STEWARD. IF I WERE YOU, I'D GIVE A RECEPTION AS SOON AS I RETURNED. IT'D BE GOOD FOR YOUR IMAGE.
ONE FINAL WORD OF CAUTION, MAC—NEVER LET THE LOCALS RIDE WITH YOU IN YOUR LTD. ONCE YOU START IN ON THIS FRATERNIZATION, THERE'S NO END TO IT!
YES, SIR.
I MEAN IT, MAC. DON'T TRY TO BE A POPULIST GOVERNOR—YOU'LL ONLY LOSE THEIR RESPECT!
ANYTHING ELSE, SIR?
YEAH—BE FIRM, FLY LOW, AND STAY COOL.
YOU, TOO, BWANA. CIAO.
GBTrudeau

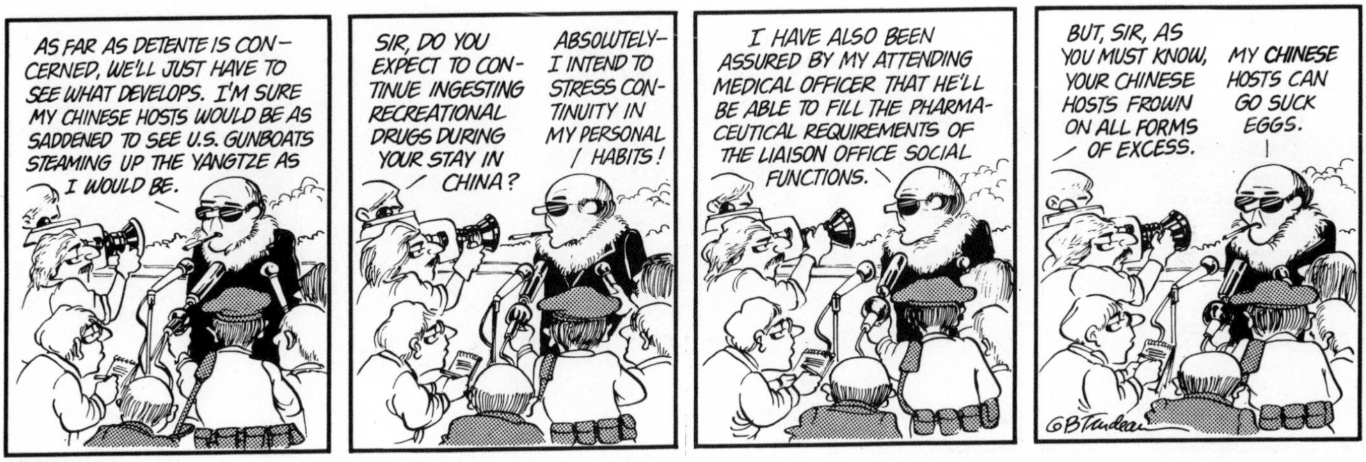
AS FAR AS DETENTE IS CONCERNED, WE'LL JUST HAVE TO SEE WHAT DEVELOPS. I'M SURE MY CHINESE HOSTS WOULD BE AS SADDENED TO SEE U.S. GUNBOATS STEAMING UP THE YANGTZE AS I WOULD BE.
SIR, DO YOU EXPECT TO CONTINUE INGESTING RECREATIONAL DRUGS DURING YOUR STAY IN CHINA?
ABSOLUTELY—I INTEND TO STRESS CONTINUITY IN MY PERSONAL HABITS!
I HAVE ALSO BEEN ASSURED BY MY ATTENDING MEDICAL OFFICER THAT HE'LL BE ABLE TO FILL THE PHARMACEUTICAL REQUIREMENTS OF THE LIAISON OFFICE SOCIAL FUNCTIONS.
BUT, SIR, AS YOU MUST KNOW, YOUR CHINESE HOSTS FROWN ON ALL FORMS OF EXCESS.
MY CHINESE HOSTS CAN GO SUCK EGGS.
GBTrudeau

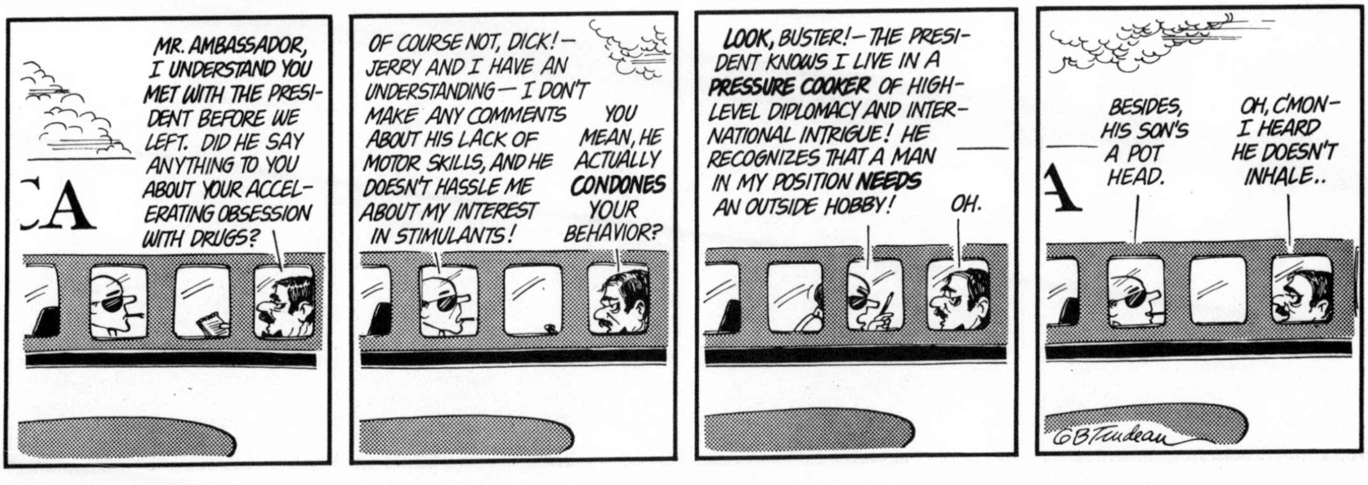
MR. AMBASSADOR, I UNDERSTAND YOU MET WITH THE PRESIDENT BEFORE WE LEFT. DID HE SAY ANYTHING TO YOU ABOUT YOUR ACCELERATING OBSESSION WITH DRUGS?
CA
OF COURSE NOT, DICK!—JERRY AND I HAVE AN UNDERSTANDING—I DON'T MAKE ANY COMMENTS ABOUT HIS LACK OF MOTOR SKILLS, AND HE DOESN'T HASSLE ME ABOUT MY INTEREST IN STIMULANTS!
YOU MEAN, HE ACTUALLY CONDONES YOUR BEHAVIOR?
LOOK, BUSTER!—THE PRESIDENT KNOWS I LIVE IN A PRESSURE COOKER OF HIGH-LEVEL DIPLOMACY AND INTERNATIONAL INTRIGUE! HE RECOGNIZES THAT A MAN IN MY POSITION NEEDS AN OUTSIDE HOBBY!
OH.
BESIDES, HIS SON'S A POT HEAD.
OH, C'MON—I HEARD HE DOESN'T INHALE..
GBTrudeau

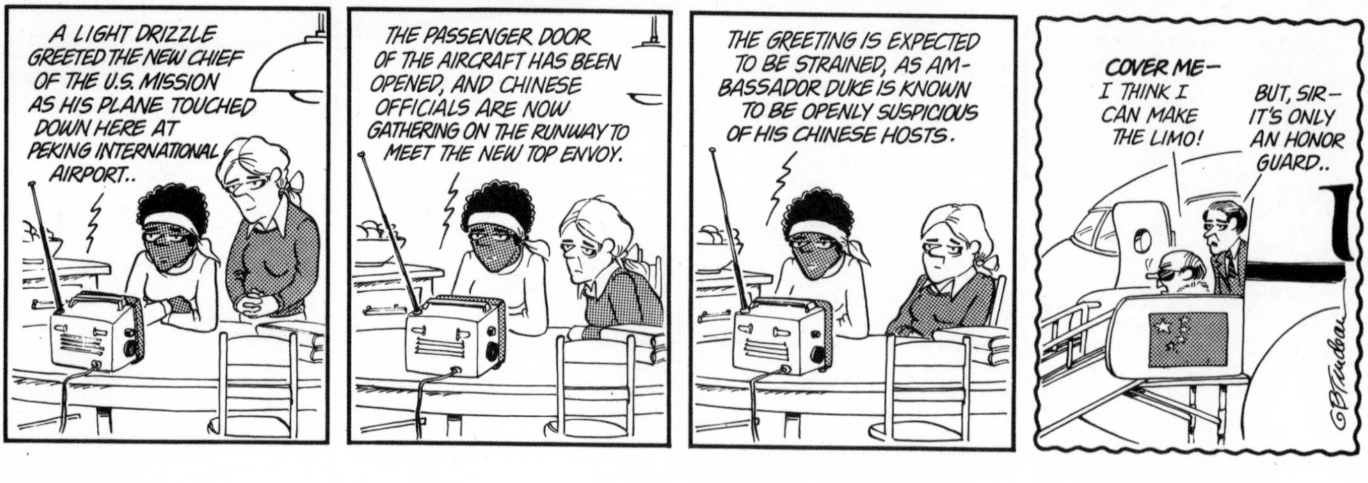
A LIGHT DRIZZLE GREETED THE NEW CHIEF OF THE U.S. MISSION AS HIS PLANE TOUCHED DOWN HERE AT PEKING INTERNATIONAL AIRPORT..
THE PASSENGER DOOR OF THE AIRCRAFT HAS BEEN OPENED, AND CHINESE OFFICIALS ARE NOW GATHERING ON THE RUNWAY TO MEET THE NEW TOP ENVOY.
THE GREETING IS EXPECTED TO BE STRAINED, AS AMBASSADOR DUKE IS KNOWN TO BE OPENLY SUSPICIOUS OF HIS CHINESE HOSTS.
COVER ME— I THINK I CAN MAKE THE LIMO!
BUT, SIR— IT'S ONLY AN HONOR GUARD..
GBTrudeau

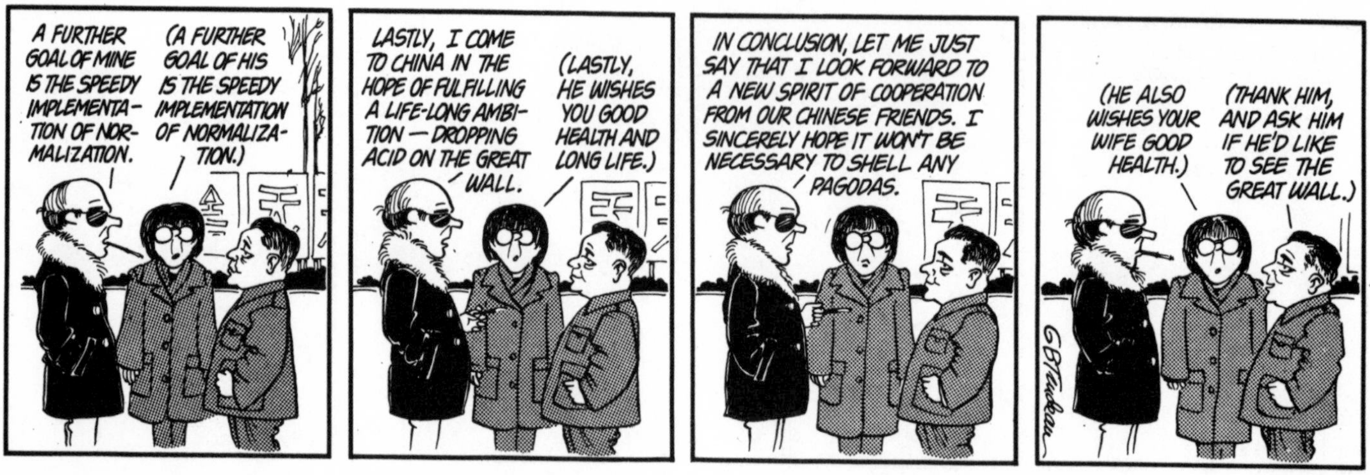
A FURTHER GOAL OF MINE IS THE SPEEDY IMPLEMENTATION OF NORMALIZATION.
(A FURTHER GOAL OF HIS IS THE SPEEDY IMPLEMENTATION OF NORMALIZATION.)
LASTLY, I COME TO CHINA IN THE HOPE OF FULFILLING A LIFE-LONG AMBITION — DROPPING ACID ON THE GREAT WALL.
(LASTLY, HE WISHES YOU GOOD HEALTH AND LONG LIFE.)
IN CONCLUSION, LET ME JUST SAY THAT I LOOK FORWARD TO A NEW SPIRIT OF COOPERATION FROM OUR CHINESE FRIENDS. I SINCERELY HOPE IT WON'T BE NECESSARY TO SHELL ANY PAGODAS.
(HE ALSO WISHES YOUR WIFE GOOD HEALTH.)
(THANK HIM, AND ASK HIM IF HE'D LIKE TO SEE THE GREAT WALL.)
GBTrudeau

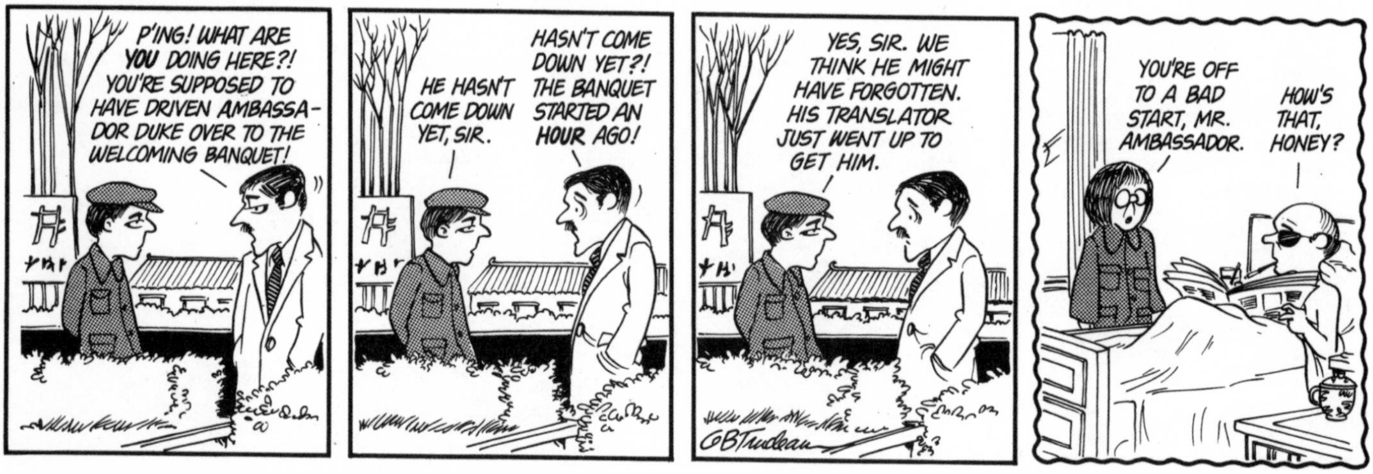
P'ING! WHAT ARE YOU DOING HERE?! YOU'RE SUPPOSED TO HAVE DRIVEN AMBASSADOR DUKE OVER TO THE WELCOMING BANQUET!
HE HASN'T COME DOWN YET, SIR.
HASN'T COME DOWN YET?! THE BANQUET STARTED AN HOUR AGO!
YES, SIR. WE THINK HE MIGHT HAVE FORGOTTEN. HIS TRANSLATOR JUST WENT UP TO GET HIM.
GBTrudeau
YOU'RE OFF TO A BAD START, MR. AMBASSADOR.
HOW'S THAT, HONEY?

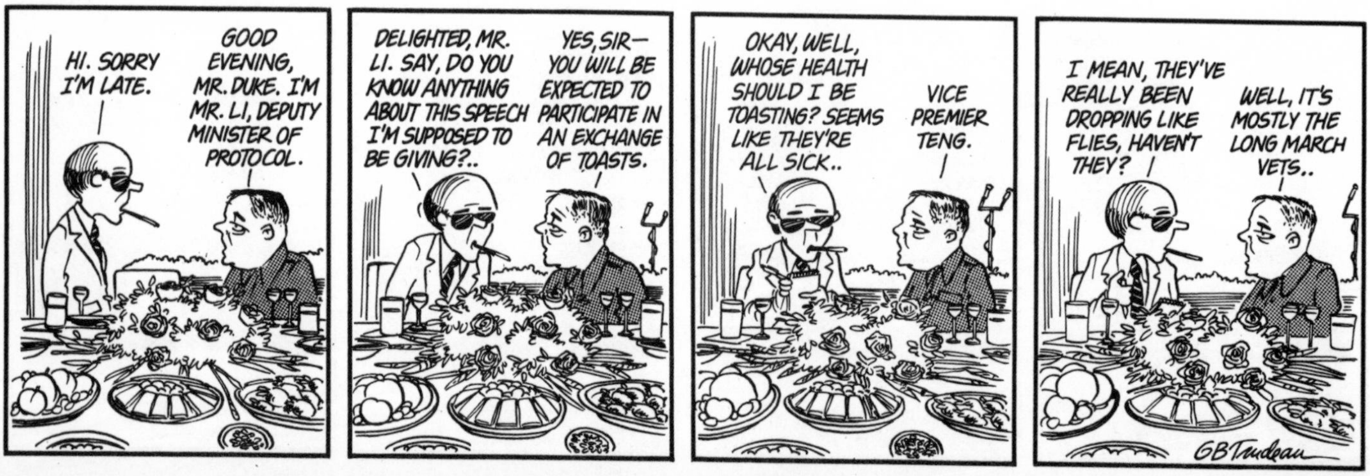
HI. SORRY I'M LATE.
GOOD EVENING, MR. DUKE. I'M MR. LI, DEPUTY MINISTER OF PROTOCOL.
DELIGHTED, MR. LI. SAY, DO YOU KNOW ANYTHING ABOUT THIS SPEECH I'M SUPPOSED TO BE GIVING?..
YES, SIR— YOU WILL BE EXPECTED TO PARTICIPATE IN AN EXCHANGE OF TOASTS.
OKAY, WELL, WHOSE HEALTH SHOULD I BE TOASTING? SEEMS LIKE THEY'RE ALL SICK..
VICE PREMIER TENG.
I MEAN, THEY'VE REALLY BEEN DROPPING LIKE FLIES, HAVEN'T THEY?
WELL, IT'S MOSTLY THE LONG MARCH VETS..
GBTrudeau

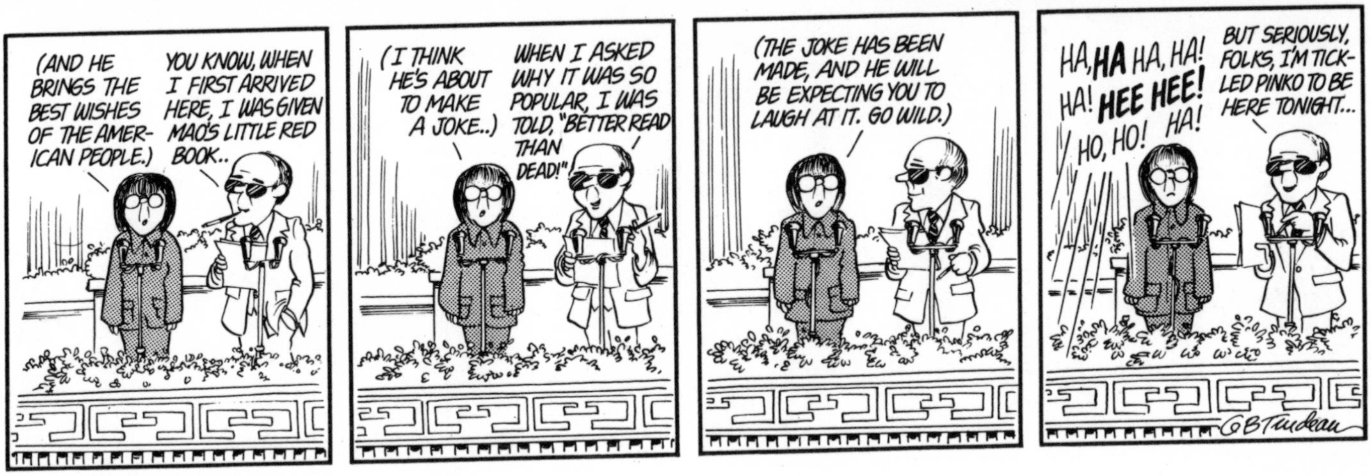
(AND HE BRINGS THE BEST WISHES OF THE AMERICAN PEOPLE.)
YOU KNOW, WHEN I FIRST ARRIVED HERE, I WAS GIVEN MAO'S LITTLE RED BOOK..
(I THINK HE'S ABOUT TO MAKE A JOKE..)
WHEN I ASKED WHY IT WAS SO POPULAR, I WAS TOLD, "BETTER READ THAN DEAD!"
(THE JOKE HAS BEEN MADE, AND HE WILL BE EXPECTING YOU TO LAUGH AT IT. GO WILD.)
HA, HA HA, HA! HA! HEE HEE! HO, HO! HA!
BUT SERIOUSLY, FOLKS, I'M TICKLED PINKO TO BE HERE TONIGHT...
GBTrudeau

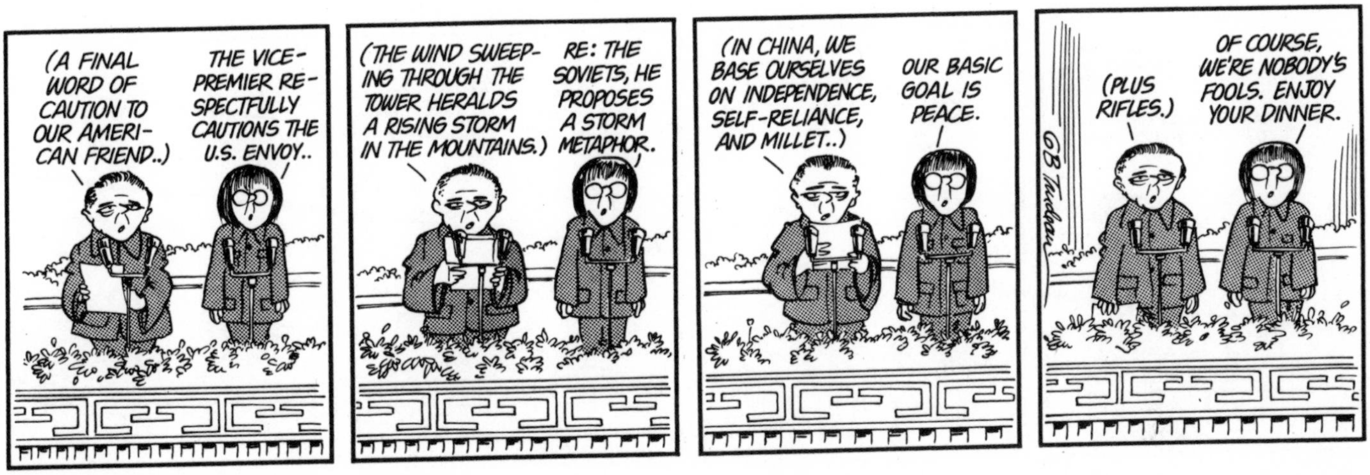
(A FINAL WORD OF CAUTION TO OUR AMERICAN FRIEND..)
THE VICE-PREMIER RESPECTFULLY CAUTIONS THE U.S. ENVOY..
(THE WIND SWEEPING THROUGH THE TOWER HERALDS A RISING STORM IN THE MOUNTAINS.)
RE: THE SOVIETS, HE PROPOSES A STORM METAPHOR.
(IN CHINA, WE BASE OURSELVES ON INDEPENDENCE, SELF-RELIANCE, AND MILLET..)
OUR BASIC GOAL IS PEACE.
(PLUS RIFLES.)
OF COURSE, WE'RE NOBODY'S FOOLS. ENJOY YOUR DINNER.
GBTrudeau

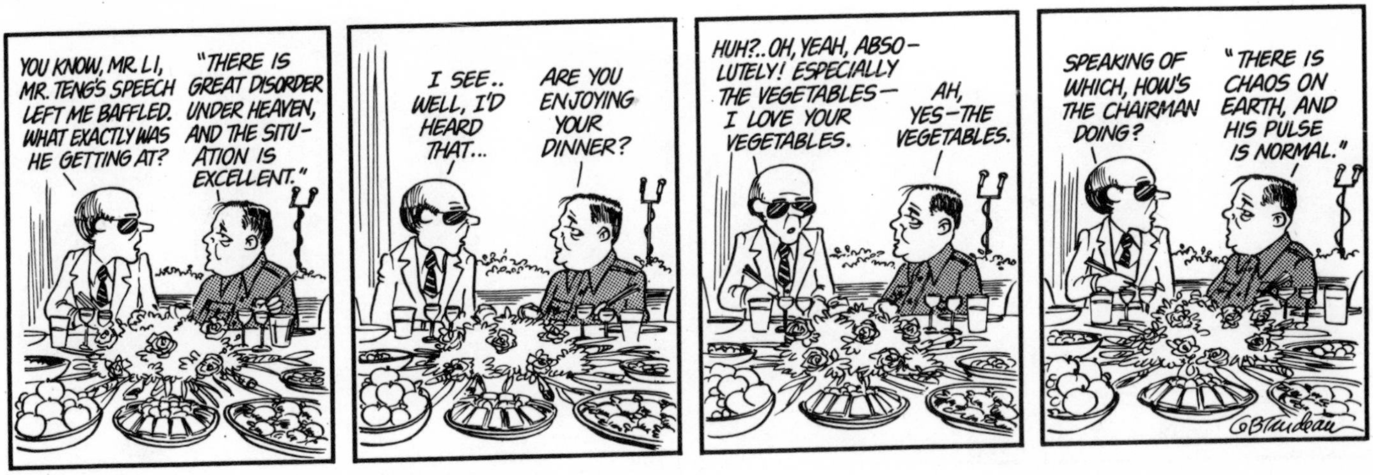
YOU KNOW, MR. LI, MR. TENG'S SPEECH LEFT ME BAFFLED. WHAT EXACTLY WAS HE GETTING AT?
"THERE IS GREAT DISORDER UNDER HEAVEN, AND THE SITUATION IS EXCELLENT."
I SEE.. WELL, I'D HEARD THAT...
ARE YOU ENJOYING YOUR DINNER?
HUH?..OH, YEAH, ABSOLUTELY! ESPECIALLY THE VEGETABLES— I LOVE YOUR VEGETABLES.
AH, YES—THE VEGETABLES.
SPEAKING OF WHICH, HOW'S THE CHAIRMAN DOING?
"THERE IS CHAOS ON EARTH, AND HIS PULSE IS NORMAL."
GBTrudeau

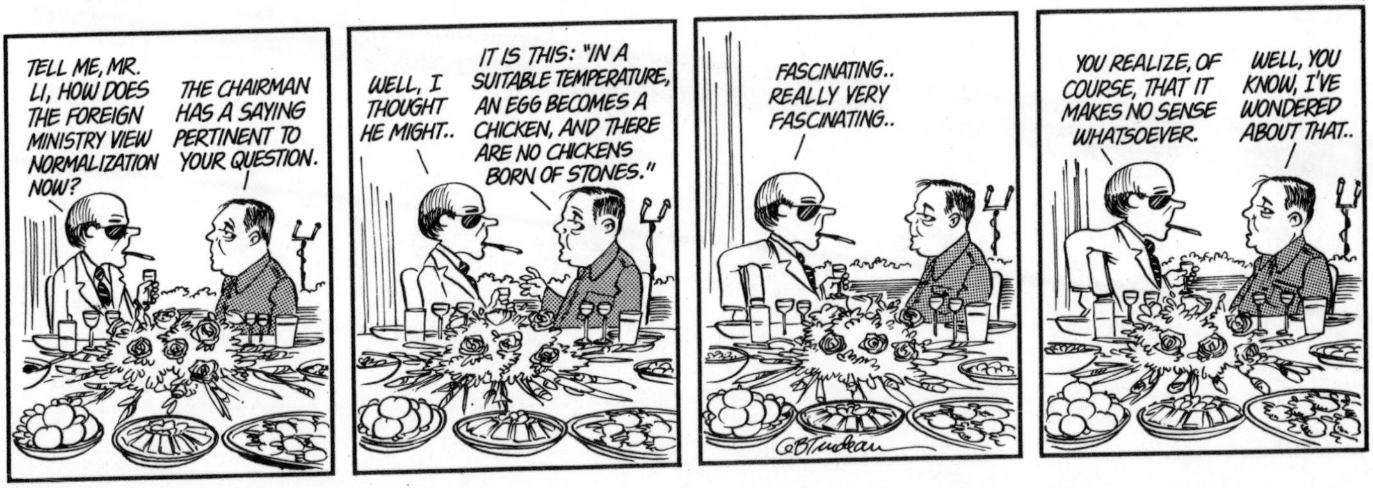
TELL ME, MR. LI, HOW DOES THE FOREIGN MINISTRY VIEW NORMALIZATION NOW?
THE CHAIRMAN HAS A SAYING PERTINENT TO YOUR QUESTION.
WELL, I THOUGHT HE MIGHT..
IT IS THIS: "IN A SUITABLE TEMPERATURE, AN EGG BECOMES A CHICKEN, AND THERE ARE NO CHICKENS BORN OF STONES."
FASCINATING.. REALLY VERY FASCINATING..
GBTrudeau
YOU REALIZE, OF COURSE, THAT IT MAKES NO SENSE WHATSOEVER.
WELL, YOU KNOW, I'VE WONDERED ABOUT THAT..

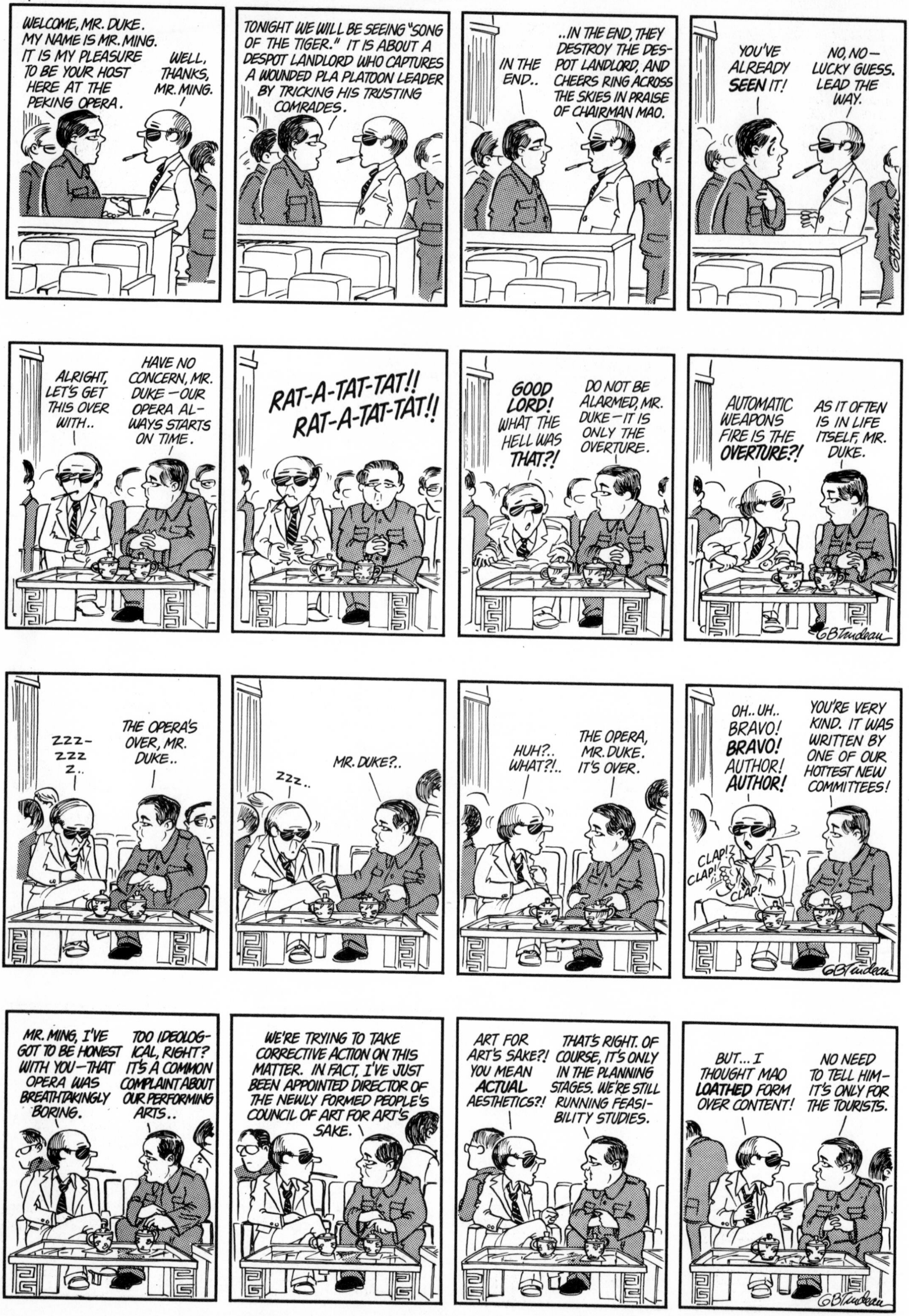
WELCOME, MR. DUKE. MY NAME IS MR. MING. IT IS MY PLEASURE TO BE YOUR HOST HERE AT THE PEKING OPERA.
WELL, THANKS, MR. MING.
TONIGHT WE WILL BE SEEING "SONG OF THE TIGER." IT IS ABOUT A DESPOT LANDLORD WHO CAPTURES A WOUNDED PLA PLATOON LEADER BY TRICKING HIS TRUSTING COMRADES.
IN THE END..
..IN THE END, THEY DESTROY THE DESPOT LANDLORD, AND CHEERS RING ACROSS THE SKIES IN PRAISE OF CHAIRMAN MAO.
YOU'VE ALREADY SEEN IT!
NO, NO—LUCKY GUESS. LEAD THE WAY.
GBTrudeau
ALRIGHT, LET'S GET THIS OVER WITH..
HAVE NO CONCERN, MR. DUKE—OUR OPERA ALWAYS STARTS ON TIME.
RAT-A-TAT-TAT!! RAT-A-TAT-TAT!!
GOOD LORD! WHAT THE HELL WAS THAT?!
DO NOT BE ALARMED, MR. DUKE—IT IS ONLY THE OVERTURE.
AUTOMATIC WEAPONS FIRE IS THE OVERTURE?!
AS IT OFTEN IS IN LIFE ITSELF, MR. DUKE.
GBTrudeau
ZZZ- ZZZ Z..
THE OPERA'S OVER, MR. DUKE..
ZZZ..
MR. DUKE?..
HUH?.. WHAT?!..
THE OPERA, MR. DUKE. IT'S OVER.
OH.. UH.. BRAVO! BRAVO! AUTHOR! AUTHOR!
YOU'RE VERY KIND. IT WAS WRITTEN BY ONE OF OUR HOTTEST NEW COMMITTEES!
CLAP! CLAP! CLAP!
GBTrudeau
MR. MING, I'VE GOT TO BE HONEST WITH YOU—THAT OPERA WAS BREATHTAKINGLY BORING.
TOO IDEOLOGICAL, RIGHT? IT'S A COMMON COMPLAINT ABOUT OUR PERFORMING ARTS..
WE'RE TRYING TO TAKE CORRECTIVE ACTION ON THIS MATTER. IN FACT, I'VE JUST BEEN APPOINTED DIRECTOR OF THE NEWLY FORMED PEOPLE'S COUNCIL OF ART FOR ART'S SAKE.
ART FOR ART'S SAKE?! YOU MEAN ACTUAL AESTHETICS?!
THAT'S RIGHT. OF COURSE, IT'S ONLY IN THE PLANNING STAGES. WE'RE STILL RUNNING FEASIBILITY STUDIES.
BUT... I THOUGHT MAO LOATHED FORM OVER CONTENT!
NO NEED TO TELL HIM—IT'S ONLY FOR THE TOURISTS.
GBTrudeau

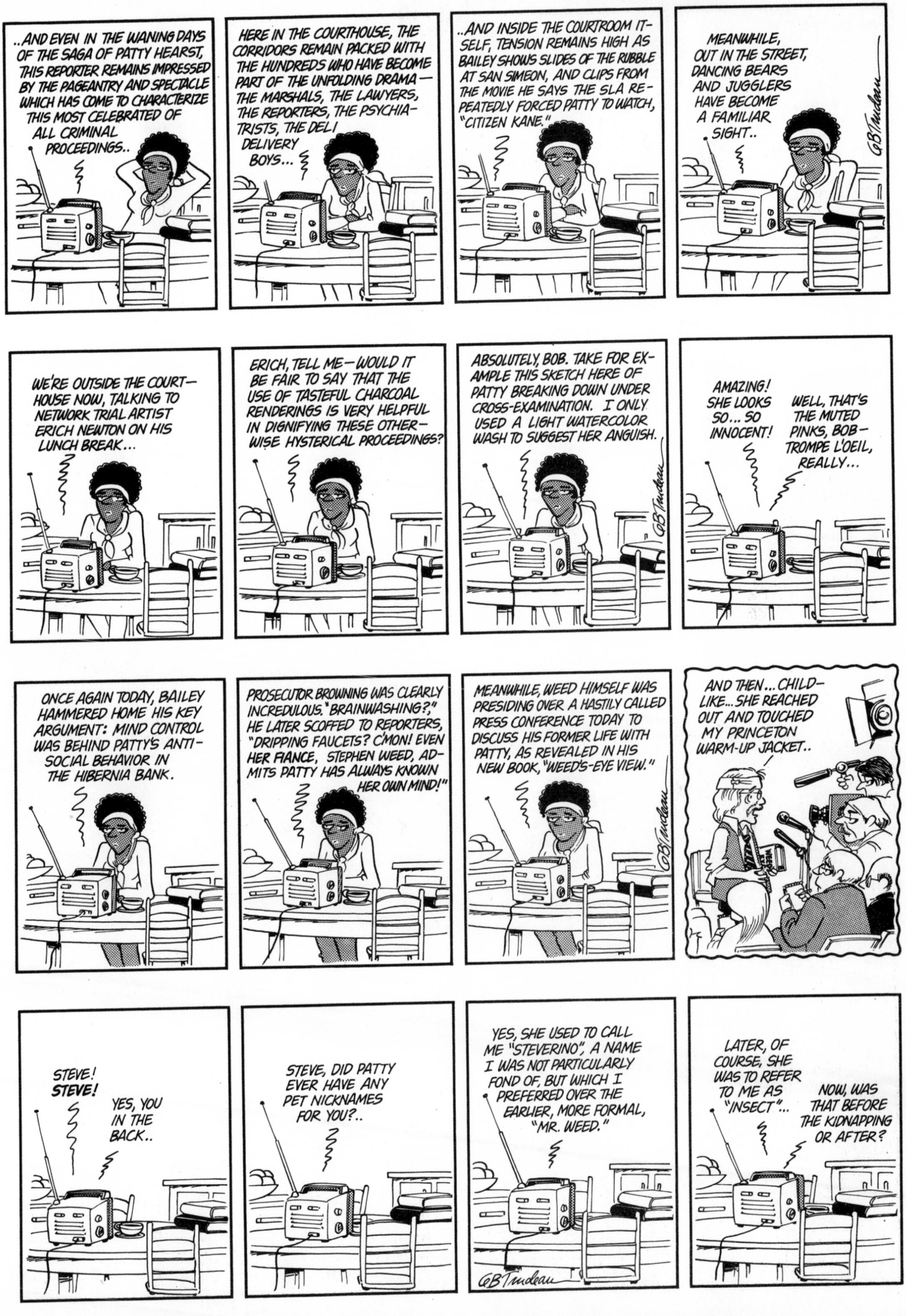
..AND EVEN IN THE WANING DAYS OF THE SAGA OF PATTY HEARST, THIS REPORTER REMAINS IMPRESSED BY THE PAGEANTRY AND SPECTACLE WHICH HAS COME TO CHARACTERIZE THIS MOST CELEBRATED OF ALL CRIMINAL PROCEEDINGS..
HERE IN THE COURTHOUSE, THE CORRIDORS REMAIN PACKED WITH THE HUNDREDS WHO HAVE BECOME PART OF THE UNFOLDING DRAMA — THE MARSHALS, THE LAWYERS, THE REPORTERS, THE PSYCHIATRISTS, THE DELI DELIVERY BOYS...
..AND INSIDE THE COURTROOM ITSELF, TENSION REMAINS HIGH AS BAILEY SHOWS SLIDES OF THE RUBBLE AT SAN SIMEON, AND CLIPS FROM THE MOVIE HE SAYS THE SLA REPEATEDLY FORCED PATTY TO WATCH, "CITIZEN KANE."
MEANWHILE, OUT IN THE STREET, DANCING BEARS AND JUGGLERS HAVE BECOME A FAMILIAR SIGHT..
GBTrudeau
WE'RE OUTSIDE THE COURTHOUSE NOW, TALKING TO NETWORK TRIAL ARTIST ERICH NEWTON ON HIS LUNCH BREAK...
ERICH, TELL ME — WOULD IT BE FAIR TO SAY THAT THE USE OF TASTEFUL CHARCOAL RENDERINGS IS VERY HELPFUL IN DIGNIFYING THESE OTHERWISE HYSTERICAL PROCEEDINGS?
ABSOLUTELY, BOB. TAKE FOR EXAMPLE THIS SKETCH HERE OF PATTY BREAKING DOWN UNDER CROSS-EXAMINATION. I ONLY USED A LIGHT WATERCOLOR WASH TO SUGGEST HER ANGUISH.
GBTrudeau
AMAZING! SHE LOOKS SO... SO INNOCENT!
WELL, THAT'S THE MUTED PINKS, BOB — TROMPE L'OEIL, REALLY...
ONCE AGAIN TODAY, BAILEY HAMMERED HOME HIS KEY ARGUMENT: MIND CONTROL WAS BEHIND PATTY'S ANTI-SOCIAL BEHAVIOR IN THE HIBERNIA BANK.
PROSECUTOR BROWNING WAS CLEARLY INCREDULOUS. "BRAINWASHING?," HE LATER SCOFFED TO REPORTERS, "DRIPPING FAUCETS? C'MON! EVEN HER FIANCE, STEPHEN WEED, ADMITS PATTY HAS ALWAYS KNOWN HER OWN MIND!"
MEANWHILE, WEED HIMSELF WAS PRESIDING OVER A HASTILY CALLED PRESS CONFERENCE TODAY TO DISCUSS HIS FORMER LIFE WITH PATTY, AS REVEALED IN HIS NEW BOOK, "WEED'S-EYE VIEW."
GBTrudeau
AND THEN... CHILD-LIKE... SHE REACHED OUT AND TOUCHED MY PRINCETON WARM-UP JACKET..
STEVE! STEVE!
YES, YOU IN THE BACK..
STEVE, DID PATTY EVER HAVE ANY PET NICKNAMES FOR YOU?..
YES, SHE USED TO CALL ME "STEVERINO", A NAME I WAS NOT PARTICULARLY FOND OF, BUT WHICH I PREFERRED OVER THE EARLIER, MORE FORMAL, "MR. WEED."
GBTrudeau
LATER, OF COURSE, SHE WAS TO REFER TO ME AS "INSECT"...
NOW, WAS THAT BEFORE THE KIDNAPPING OR AFTER?

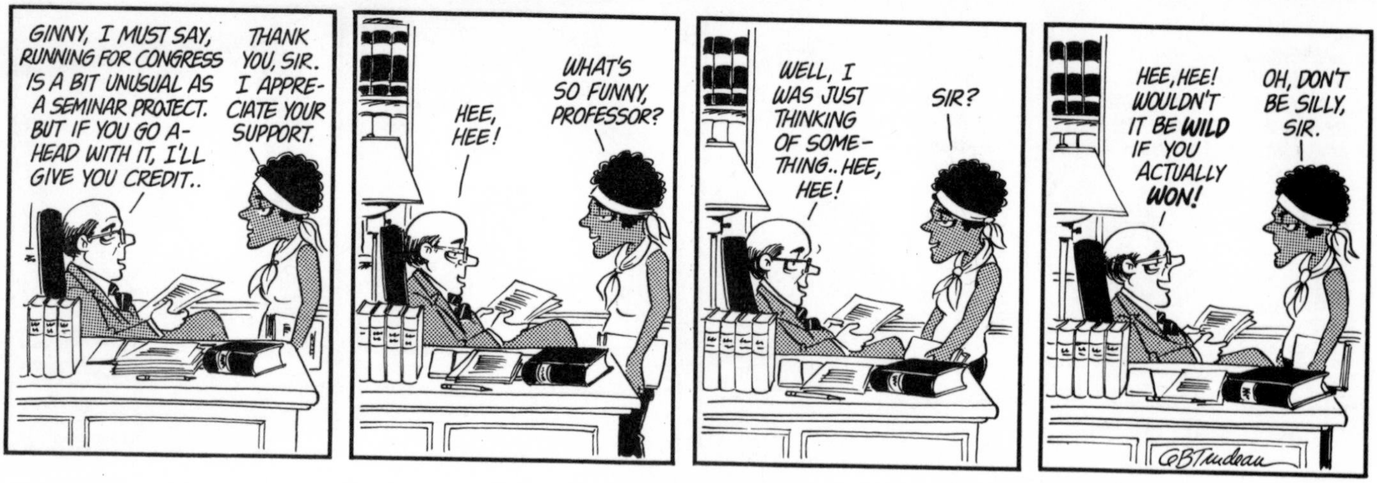
GINNY, I MUST SAY, RUNNING FOR CONGRESS IS A BIT UNUSUAL AS A SEMINAR PROJECT. BUT IF YOU GO A-HEAD WITH IT, I'LL GIVE YOU CREDIT..
THANK YOU, SIR. I APPRE-CIATE YOUR SUPPORT.
HEE, HEE!
WHAT'S SO FUNNY, PROFESSOR?
WELL, I WAS JUST THINKING OF SOME-THING.. HEE, HEE!
SIR?
HEE, HEE! WOULDN'T IT BE **WILD** IF YOU ACTUALLY **WON!**
OH, DON'T BE SILLY, SIR.
GBTrudeau

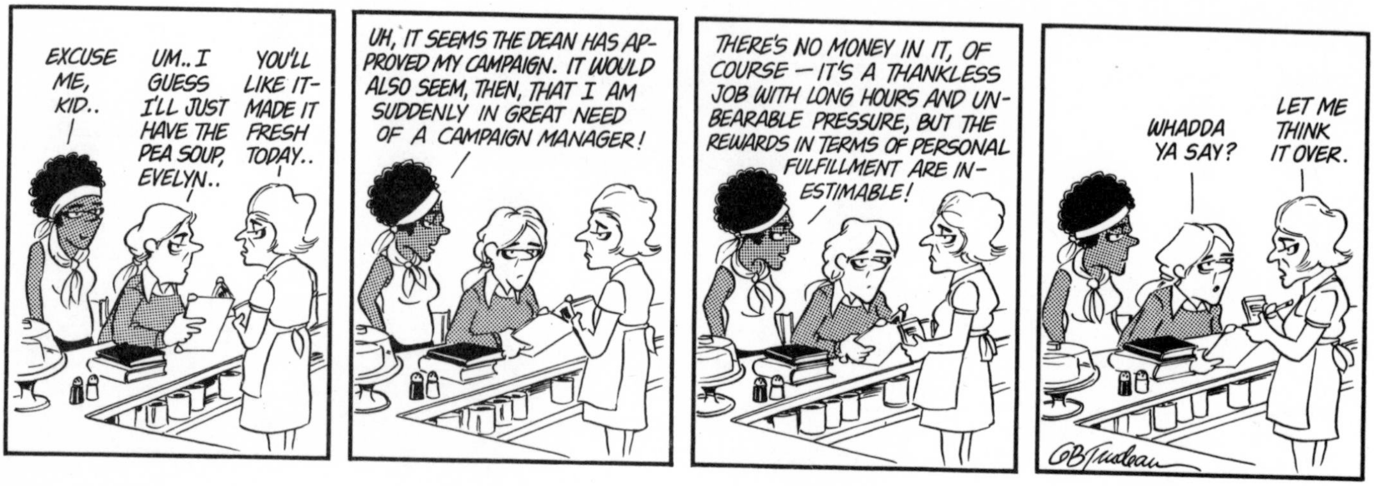
EXCUSE ME, KID..
UM.. I GUESS I'LL JUST HAVE THE PEA SOUP, EVELYN..
YOU'LL LIKE IT- MADE IT FRESH TODAY..
UH, IT SEEMS THE DEAN HAS AP-PROVED MY CAMPAIGN. IT WOULD ALSO SEEM, THEN, THAT I AM SUDDENLY IN GREAT NEED OF A CAMPAIGN MANAGER!
THERE'S NO MONEY IN IT, OF COURSE — IT'S A THANKLESS JOB WITH LONG HOURS AND UN-BEARABLE PRESSURE, BUT THE REWARDS IN TERMS OF PERSONAL FULFILLMENT ARE IN-ESTIMABLE!
WHADDA YA SAY?
LET ME THINK IT OVER.
GBTrudeau

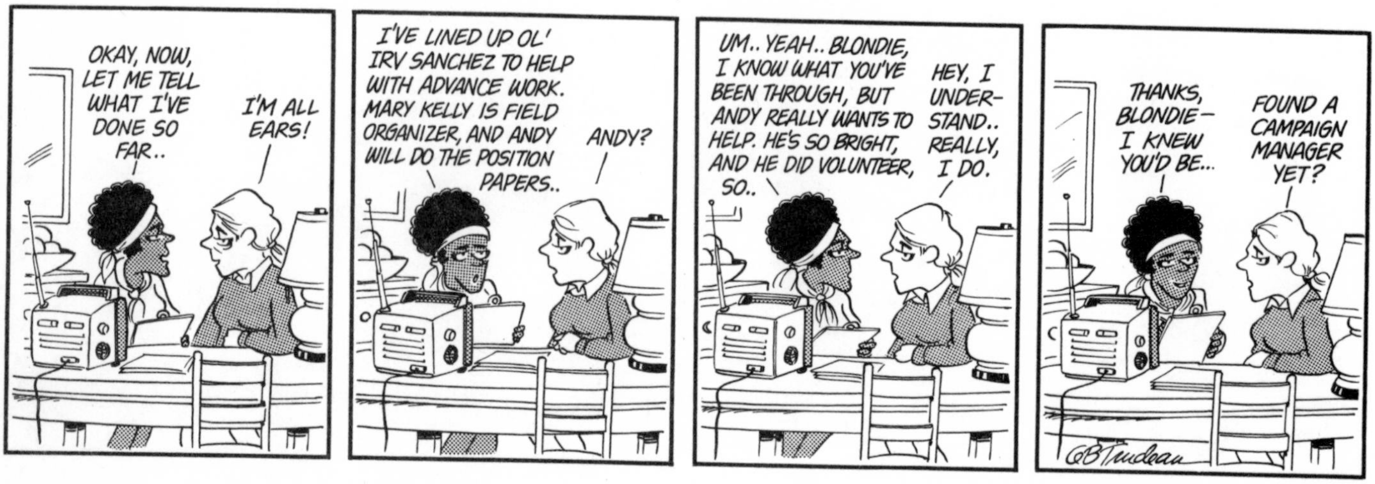
OKAY, NOW, LET ME TELL WHAT I'VE DONE SO FAR..
I'M ALL EARS!
I'VE LINED UP OL' IRV SANCHEZ TO HELP WITH ADVANCE WORK. MARY KELLY IS FIELD ORGANIZER, AND ANDY WILL DO THE POSITION PAPERS..
ANDY?
UM.. YEAH.. BLONDIE, I KNOW WHAT YOU'VE BEEN THROUGH, BUT ANDY REALLY WANTS TO HELP. HE'S SO BRIGHT, AND HE DID VOLUNTEER, SO..
HEY, I UNDER-STAND.. REALLY, I DO.
THANKS, BLONDIE- I KNEW YOU'D BE...
FOUND A CAMPAIGN MANAGER YET?
GBTrudeau

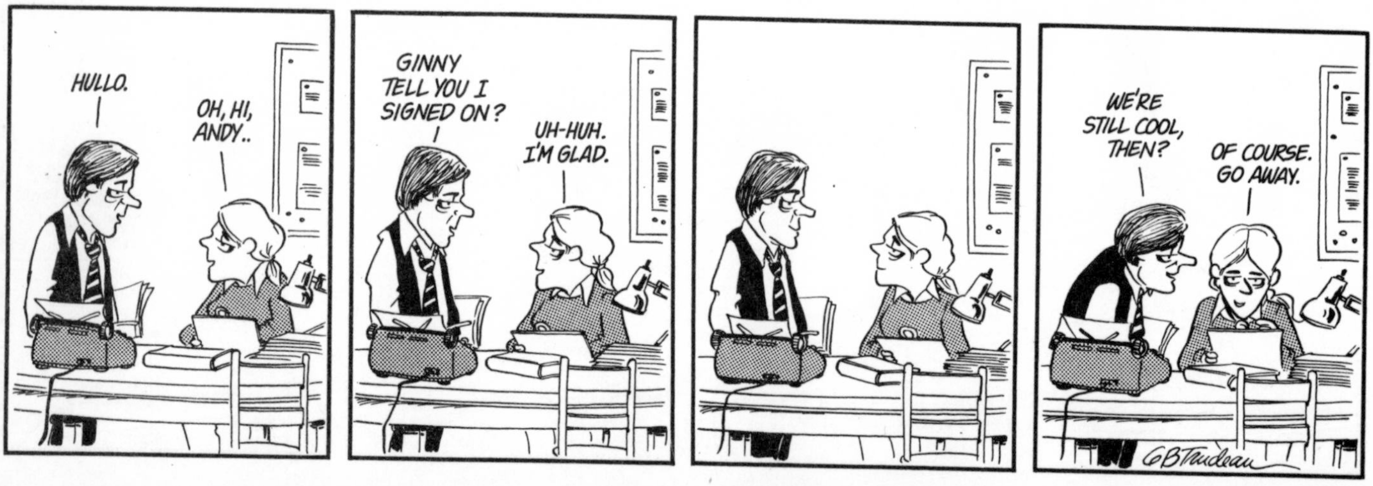
HULLO.
OH, HI, ANDY..
GINNY TELL YOU I SIGNED ON?
UH-HUH. I'M GLAD.
WE'RE STILL COOL, THEN?
OF COURSE. GO AWAY.
GBTrudeau

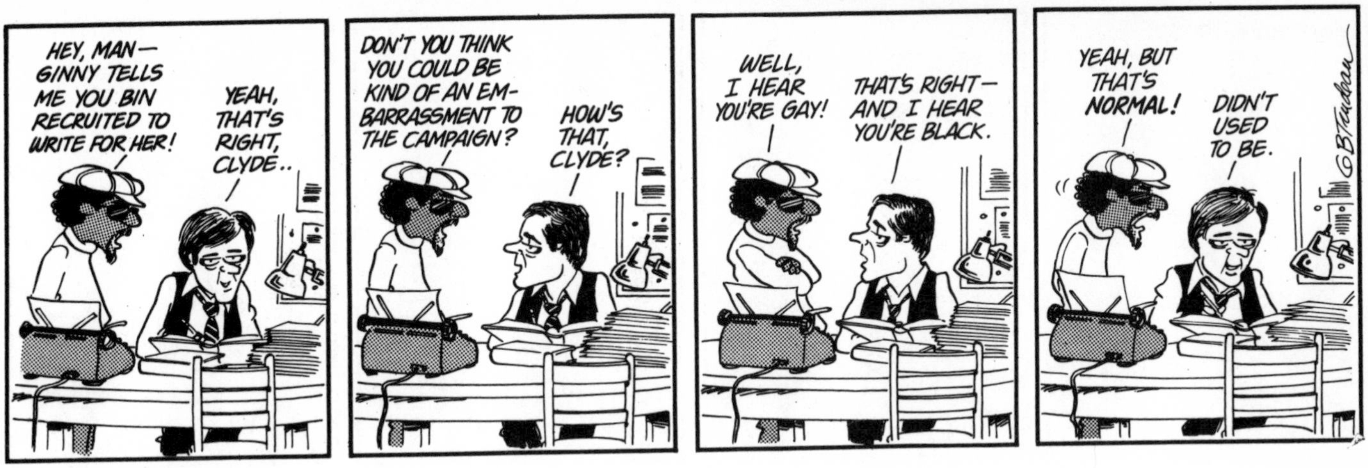
HEY, MAN— GINNY TELLS ME YOU BIN RECRUITED TO WRITE FOR HER!
YEAH, THAT'S RIGHT, CLYDE..
DON'T YOU THINK YOU COULD BE KIND OF AN EMBARRASSMENT TO THE CAMPAIGN?
HOW'S THAT, CLYDE?
WELL, I HEAR YOU'RE GAY!
THAT'S RIGHT— AND I HEAR YOU'RE BLACK.
YEAH, BUT THAT'S **NORMAL!**
DIDN'T USED TO BE.

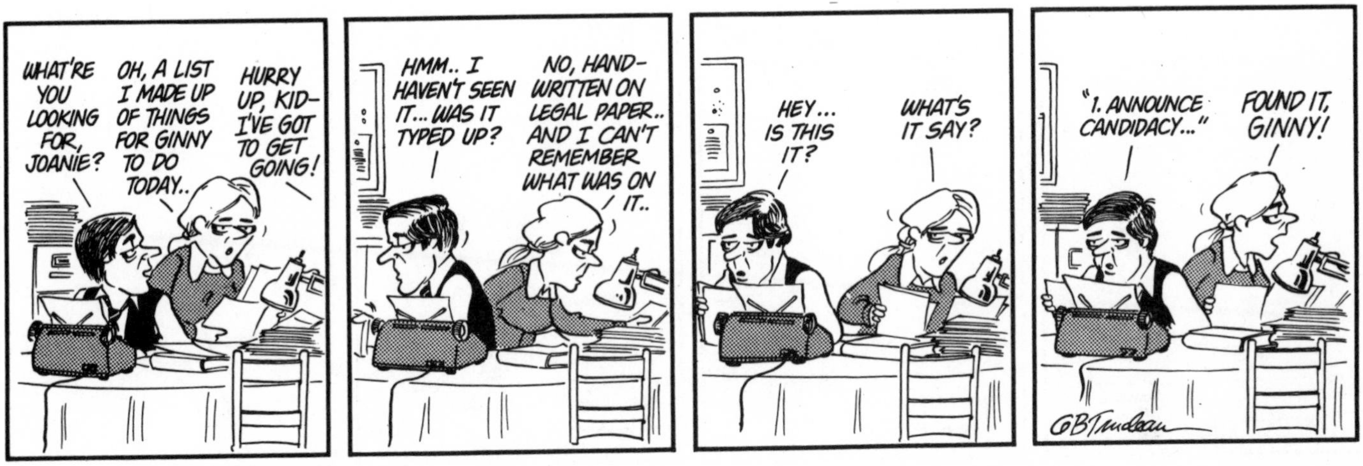
WHAT'RE YOU LOOKING FOR, JOANIE?
OH, A LIST I MADE UP OF THINGS FOR GINNY TO DO TODAY..
HURRY UP, KID— I'VE GOT TO GET GOING!
HMM.. I HAVEN'T SEEN IT... WAS IT TYPED UP?
NO, HANDWRITTEN ON LEGAL PAPER.. AND I CAN'T REMEMBER WHAT WAS ON IT..
HEY... IS THIS IT?
WHAT'S IT SAY?
"1. ANNOUNCE CANDIDACY..."
FOUND IT, GINNY!

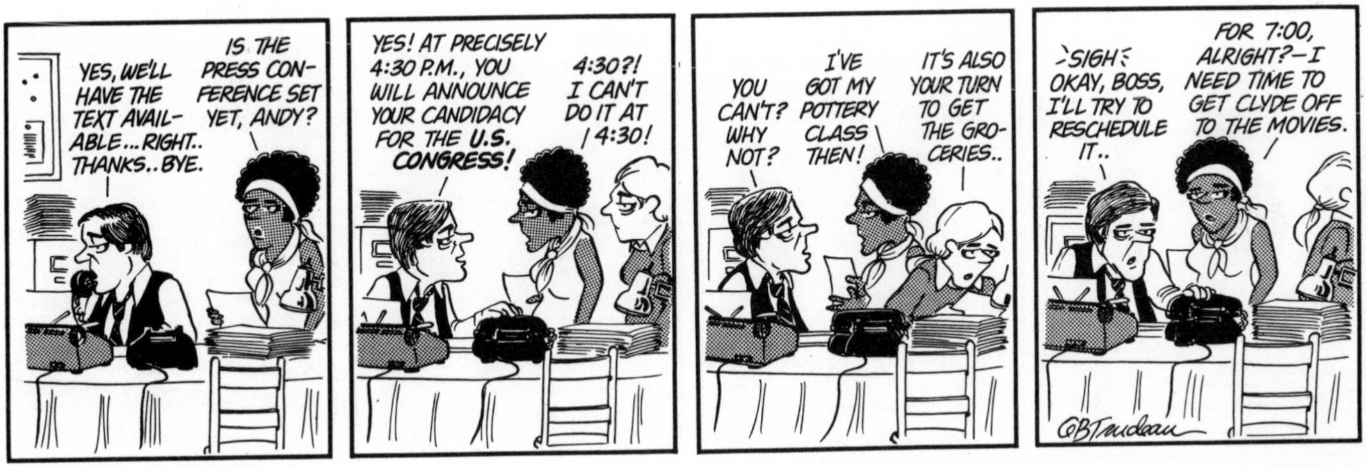
YES, WE'LL HAVE THE TEXT AVAILABLE... RIGHT.. THANKS.. BYE.
IS THE PRESS CONFERENCE SET YET, ANDY?
YES! AT PRECISELY 4:30 P.M., YOU WILL ANNOUNCE YOUR CANDIDACY FOR THE **U.S. CONGRESS!**
4:30?! I CAN'T DO IT AT 4:30!
YOU CAN'T? WHY NOT?
I'VE GOT MY POTTERY CLASS THEN!
IT'S ALSO YOUR TURN TO GET THE GROCERIES..
SIGH OKAY, BOSS, I'LL TRY TO RESCHEDULE IT..
FOR 7:00, ALRIGHT?— I NEED TIME TO GET CLYDE OFF TO THE MOVIES.

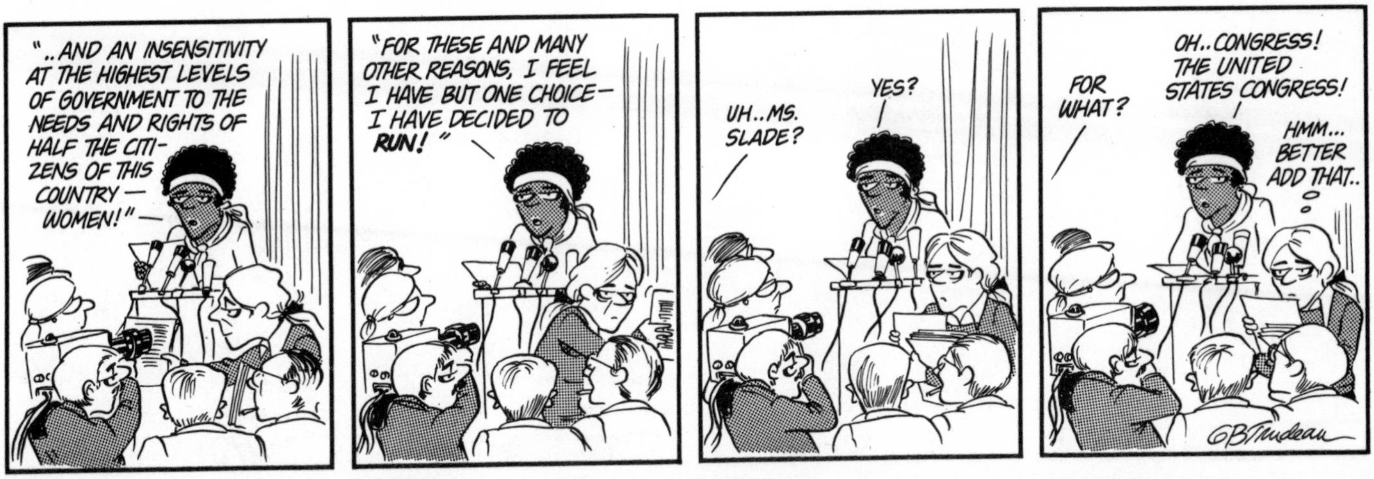
"..AND AN INSENSITIVITY AT THE HIGHEST LEVELS OF GOVERNMENT TO THE NEEDS AND RIGHTS OF HALF THE CITIZENS OF THIS COUNTRY— WOMEN!"
"FOR THESE AND MANY OTHER REASONS, I FEEL I HAVE BUT ONE CHOICE— I HAVE DECIDED TO **RUN!**"
UH..MS. SLADE?
YES?
FOR WHAT?
OH..CONGRESS! THE UNITED STATES CONGRESS!
HMM... BETTER ADD THAT..

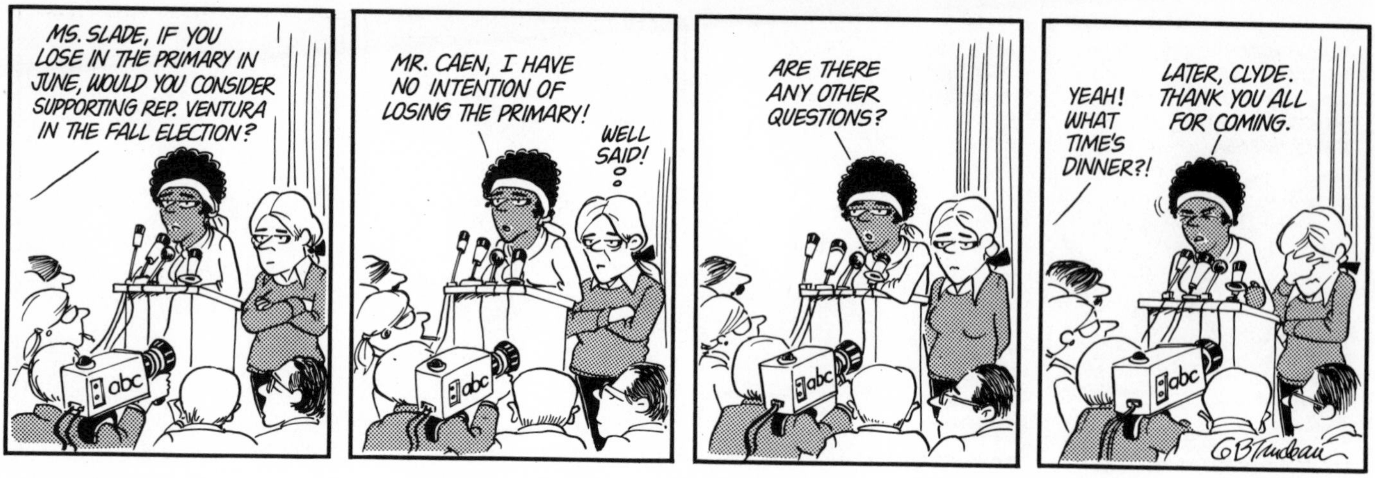
MS. SLADE, IF YOU LOSE IN THE PRIMARY IN JUNE, WOULD YOU CONSIDER SUPPORTING REP. VENTURA IN THE FALL ELECTION?
abc
MR. CAEN, I HAVE NO INTENTION OF LOSING THE PRIMARY!
WELL SAID!
abc
ARE THERE ANY OTHER QUESTIONS?
abc
YEAH! WHAT TIME'S DINNER?!
LATER, CLYDE. THANK YOU ALL FOR COMING.
abc

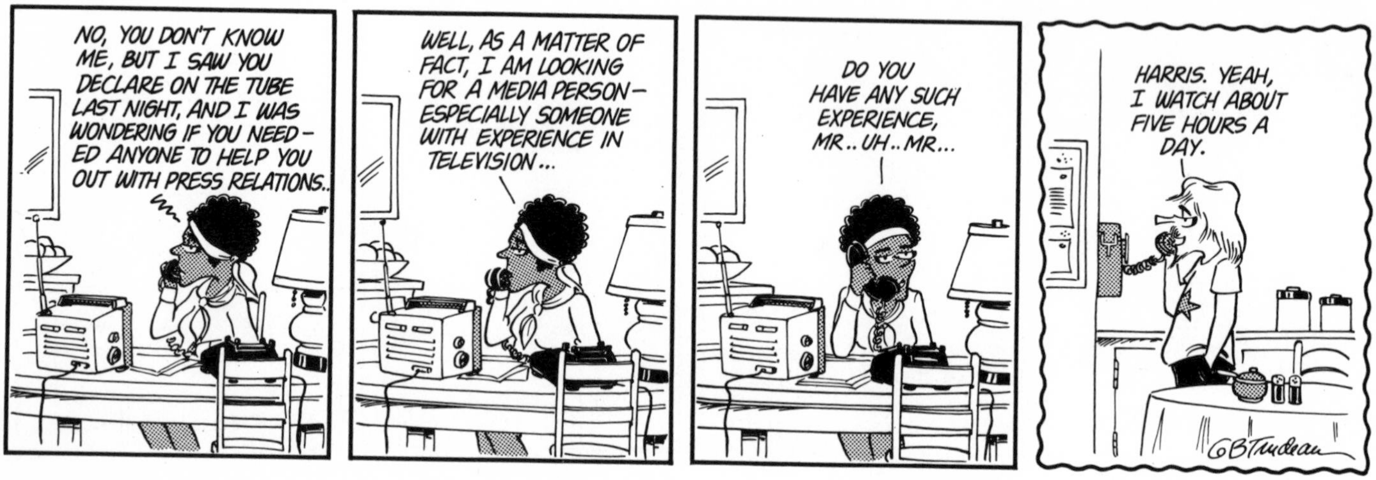
NO, YOU DON'T KNOW ME, BUT I SAW YOU DECLARE ON THE TUBE LAST NIGHT, AND I WAS WONDERING IF YOU NEEDED ANYONE TO HELP YOU OUT WITH PRESS RELATIONS..
WELL, AS A MATTER OF FACT, I AM LOOKING FOR A MEDIA PERSON— ESPECIALLY SOMEONE WITH EXPERIENCE IN TELEVISION...
DO YOU HAVE ANY SUCH EXPERIENCE, MR.. UH.. MR...
HARRIS. YEAH, I WATCH ABOUT FIVE HOURS A DAY.

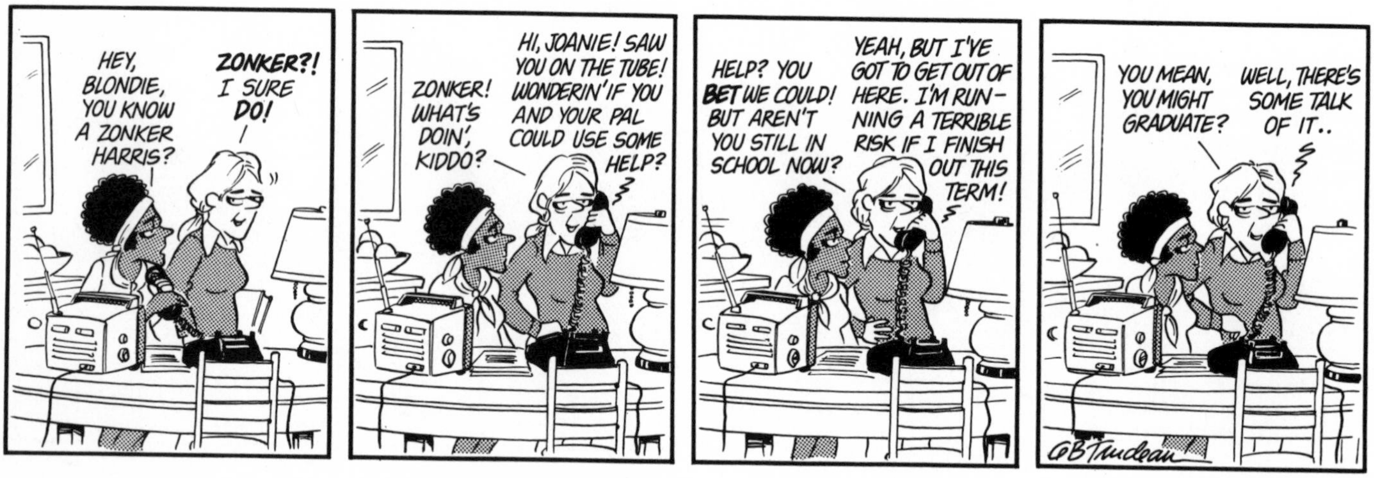
HEY, BLONDIE, YOU KNOW A ZONKER HARRIS?
ZONKER?! I SURE **DO!**
ZONKER! WHAT'S DOIN', KIDDO?
HI, JOANIE! SAW YOU ON THE TUBE! WONDERIN' IF YOU AND YOUR PAL COULD USE SOME HELP?
HELP? YOU **BET** WE COULD! BUT AREN'T YOU STILL IN SCHOOL NOW?
YEAH, BUT I'VE GOT TO GET OUT OF HERE. I'M RUNNING A TERRIBLE RISK IF I FINISH OUT THIS TERM!
YOU MEAN, YOU MIGHT GRADUATE?
WELL, THERE'S SOME TALK OF IT..

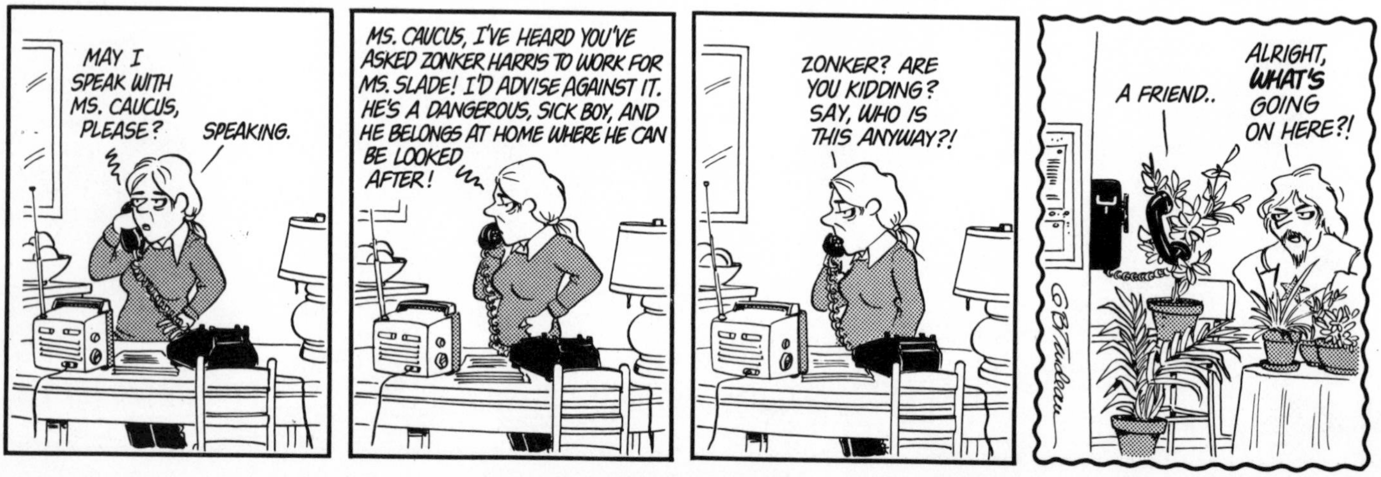
MAY I SPEAK WITH MS. CAUCUS, PLEASE?
SPEAKING.
MS. CAUCUS, I'VE HEARD YOU'VE ASKED ZONKER HARRIS TO WORK FOR MS. SLADE! I'D ADVISE AGAINST IT. HE'S A DANGEROUS, SICK BOY, AND HE BELONGS AT HOME WHERE HE CAN BE LOOKED AFTER!
ZONKER? ARE YOU KIDDING? SAY, WHO IS THIS ANYWAY?!
A FRIEND..
ALRIGHT, **WHAT'S** GOING ON HERE?!

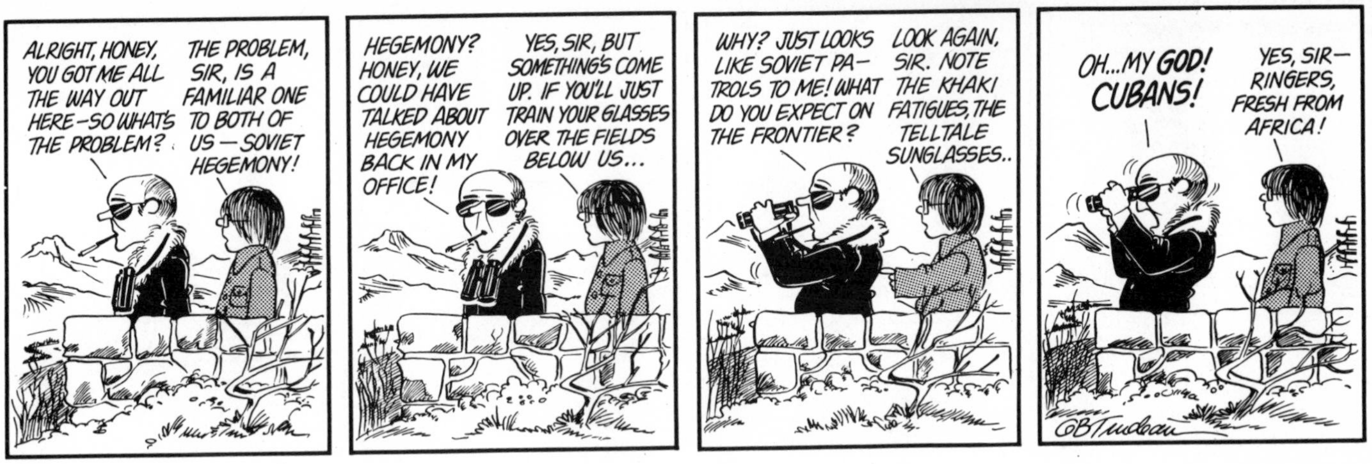
ALRIGHT, HONEY, YOU GOT ME ALL THE WAY OUT HERE—SO WHAT'S THE PROBLEM?
THE PROBLEM, SIR, IS A FAMILIAR ONE TO BOTH OF US—SOVIET HEGEMONY!
HEGEMONY? HONEY, WE COULD HAVE TALKED ABOUT HEGEMONY BACK IN MY OFFICE!
YES, SIR, BUT SOMETHING'S COME UP. IF YOU'LL JUST TRAIN YOUR GLASSES OVER THE FIELDS BELOW US...
WHY? JUST LOOKS LIKE SOVIET PATROLS TO ME! WHAT DO YOU EXPECT ON THE FRONTIER?
LOOK AGAIN, SIR. NOTE THE KHAKI FATIGUES, THE TELLTALE SUNGLASSES..
OH...MY GOD! CUBANS!
YES, SIR—RINGERS, FRESH FROM AFRICA!
©BTrudeau

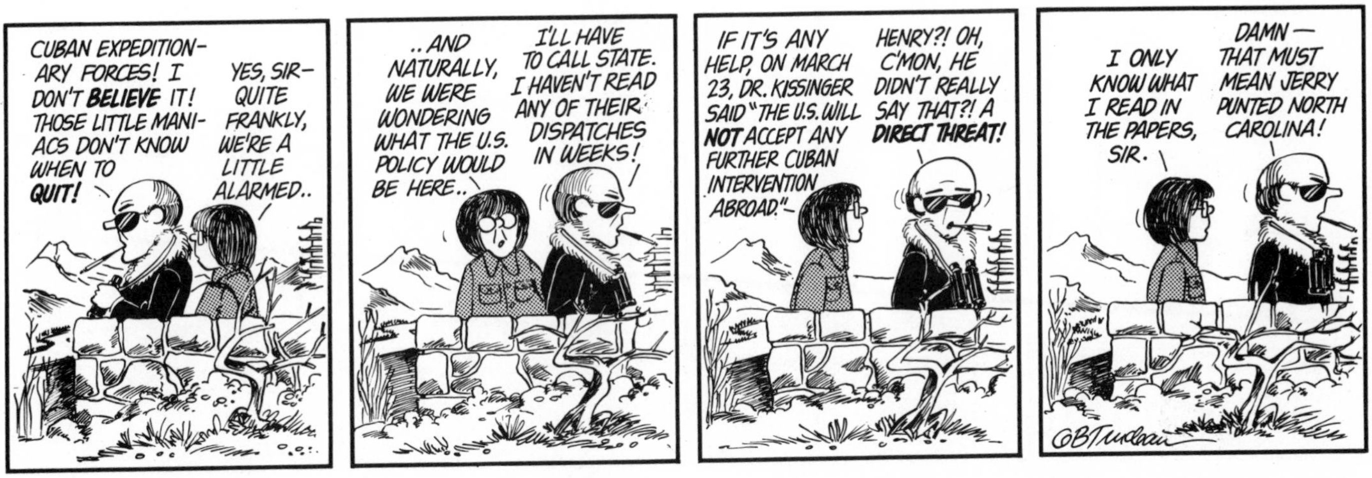
CUBAN EXPEDITIONARY FORCES! I DON'T BELIEVE IT! THOSE LITTLE MANIACS DON'T KNOW WHEN TO QUIT!
YES, SIR—QUITE FRANKLY, WE'RE A LITTLE ALARMED..
..AND NATURALLY, WE WERE WONDERING WHAT THE U.S. POLICY WOULD BE HERE..
I'LL HAVE TO CALL STATE. I HAVEN'T READ ANY OF THEIR DISPATCHES IN WEEKS!
IF IT'S ANY HELP, ON MARCH 23, DR. KISSINGER SAID "THE U.S. WILL NOT ACCEPT ANY FURTHER CUBAN INTERVENTION ABROAD."—
HENRY?! OH, C'MON, HE DIDN'T REALLY SAY THAT?! A DIRECT THREAT!
I ONLY KNOW WHAT I READ IN THE PAPERS, SIR.
DAMN—THAT MUST MEAN JERRY PUNTED NORTH CAROLINA!
©BTrudeau

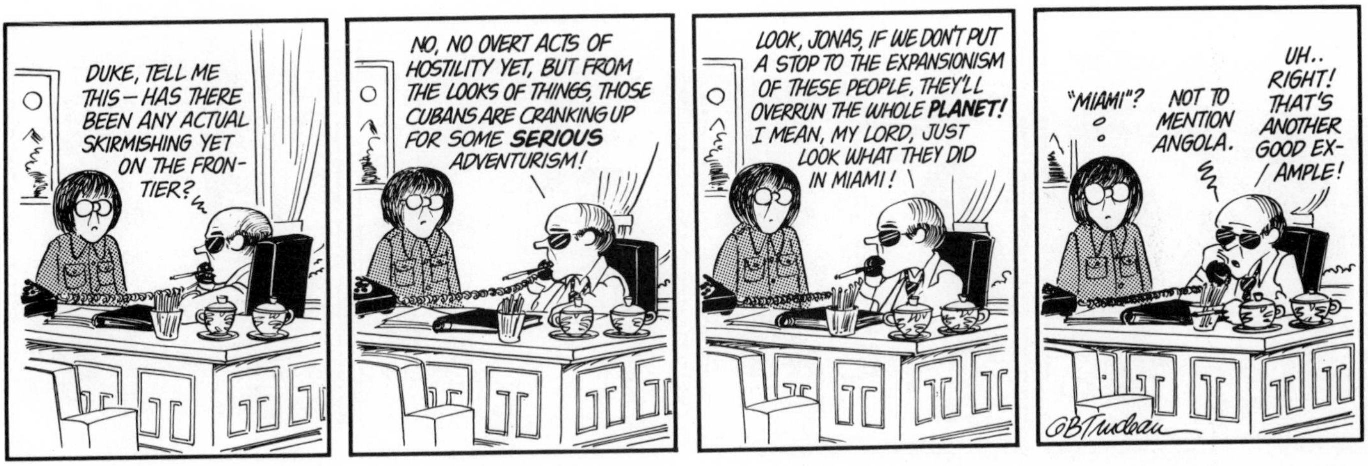
DUKE, TELL ME THIS—HAS THERE BEEN ANY ACTUAL SKIRMISHING YET ON THE FRONTIER?
NO, NO OVERT ACTS OF HOSTILITY YET, BUT FROM THE LOOKS OF THINGS, THOSE CUBANS ARE CRANKING UP FOR SOME SERIOUS ADVENTURISM!
LOOK, JONAS, IF WE DON'T PUT A STOP TO THE EXPANSIONISM OF THESE PEOPLE, THEY'LL OVERRUN THE WHOLE PLANET! I MEAN, MY LORD, JUST LOOK WHAT THEY DID IN MIAMI!
"MIAMI"?
NOT TO MENTION ANGOLA.
UH.. RIGHT! THAT'S ANOTHER GOOD EXAMPLE!
©BTrudeau

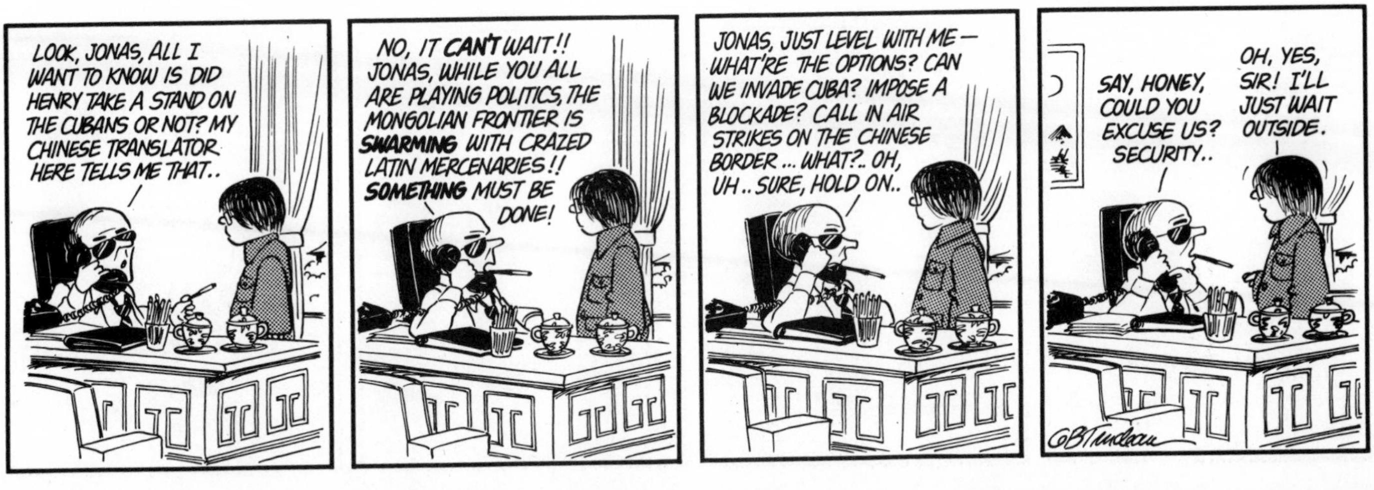
LOOK, JONAS, ALL I WANT TO KNOW IS DID HENRY TAKE A STAND ON THE CUBANS OR NOT? MY CHINESE TRANSLATOR HERE TELLS ME THAT..
NO, IT CAN'T WAIT!! JONAS, WHILE YOU ALL ARE PLAYING POLITICS, THE MONGOLIAN FRONTIER IS SWARMING WITH CRAZED LATIN MERCENARIES!! SOMETHING MUST BE DONE!
JONAS, JUST LEVEL WITH ME—WHAT'RE THE OPTIONS? CAN WE INVADE CUBA? IMPOSE A BLOCKADE? CALL IN AIR STRIKES ON THE CHINESE BORDER ... WHAT?.. OH, UH.. SURE, HOLD ON..
SAY, HONEY, COULD YOU EXCUSE US? SECURITY..
OH, YES, SIR! I'LL JUST WAIT OUTSIDE.
©BTrudeau

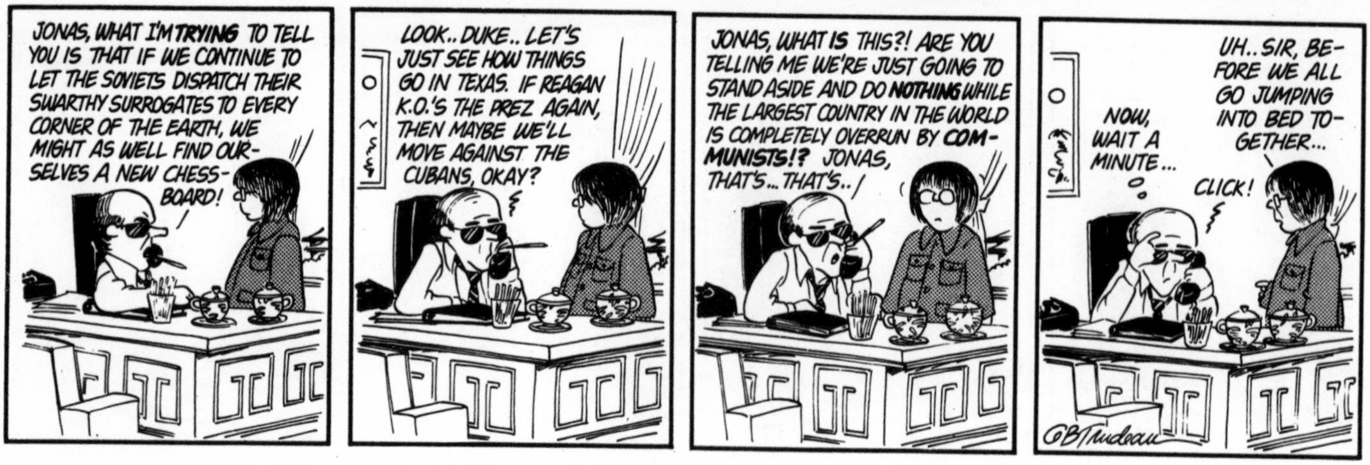
JONAS, WHAT I'M **TRYING** TO TELL YOU IS THAT IF **WE** CONTINUE TO LET THE SOVIETS DISPATCH THEIR SWARTHY SURROGATES TO EVERY CORNER OF THE EARTH, WE MIGHT AS WELL FIND OURSELVES A NEW CHESS-BOARD!
LOOK.. DUKE.. LET'S JUST SEE HOW THINGS GO IN TEXAS. IF REAGAN K.O.'S THE PREZ AGAIN, THEN MAYBE WE'LL MOVE AGAINST THE CUBANS, OKAY?
JONAS, WHAT **IS** THIS?! ARE YOU TELLING ME WE'RE JUST GOING TO STAND ASIDE AND DO **NOTHING** WHILE THE LARGEST COUNTRY IN THE WORLD IS COMPLETELY OVERRUN BY **COMMUNISTS!?** JONAS, THAT'S... THAT'S..
NOW, WAIT A MINUTE...
UH.. SIR, BEFORE WE ALL GO JUMPING INTO BED TOGETHER...
CLICK!

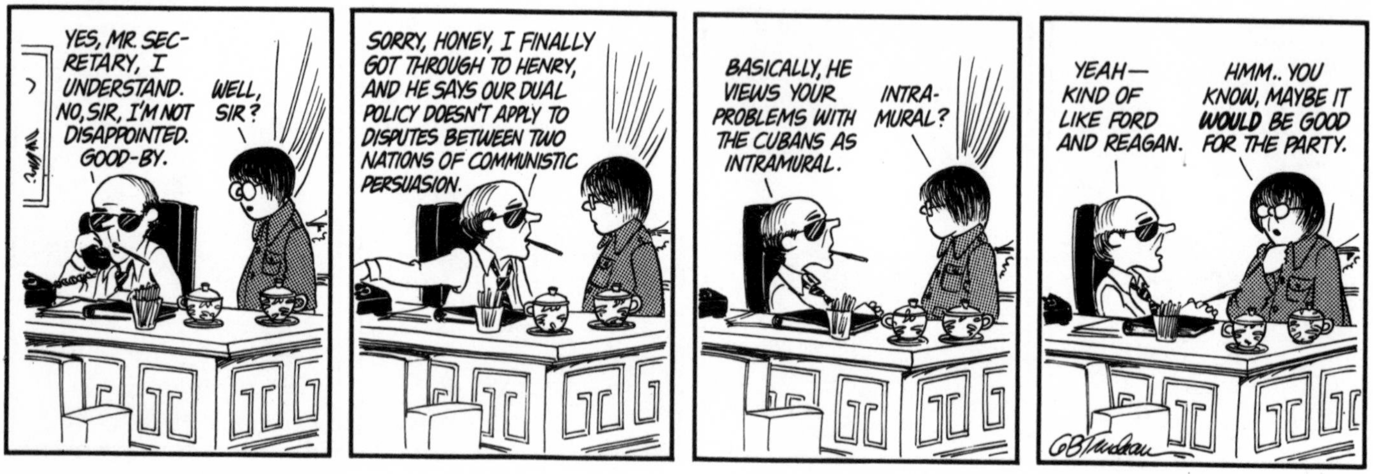
YES, MR. SECRETARY, I UNDERSTAND. NO, SIR, I'M NOT DISAPPOINTED. GOOD-BY.
WELL, SIR?
SORRY, HONEY, I FINALLY GOT THROUGH TO HENRY, AND HE SAYS OUR DUAL POLICY DOESN'T APPLY TO DISPUTES BETWEEN TWO NATIONS OF COMMUNISTIC PERSUASION.
BASICALLY, HE VIEWS YOUR PROBLEMS WITH THE CUBANS AS INTRAMURAL.
INTRAMURAL?
YEAH— KIND OF LIKE FORD AND REAGAN.
HMM.. YOU KNOW, MAYBE IT **WOULD** BE GOOD FOR THE PARTY.

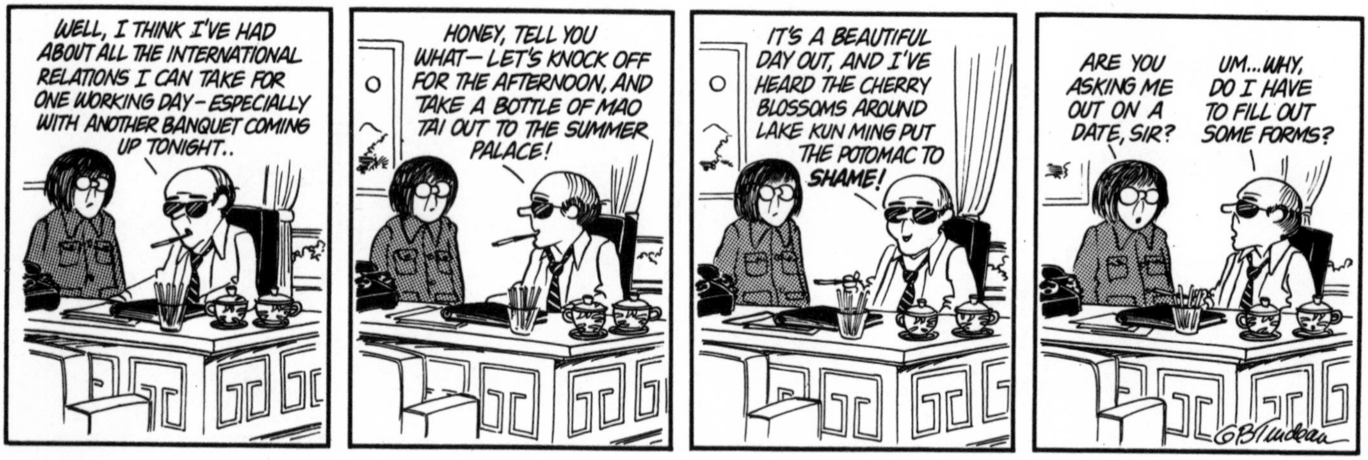
WELL, I THINK I'VE HAD ABOUT ALL THE INTERNATIONAL RELATIONS I CAN TAKE FOR ONE WORKING DAY - ESPECIALLY WITH ANOTHER BANQUET COMING UP TONIGHT..
HONEY, TELL YOU WHAT— LET'S KNOCK OFF FOR THE AFTERNOON, AND TAKE A BOTTLE OF MAO TAI OUT TO THE SUMMER PALACE!
IT'S A BEAUTIFUL DAY OUT, AND I'VE HEARD THE CHERRY BLOSSOMS AROUND LAKE KUN MING PUT THE POTOMAC TO **SHAME!**
ARE YOU ASKING ME OUT ON A DATE, SIR?
UM... WHY, DO I HAVE TO FILL OUT SOME FORMS?

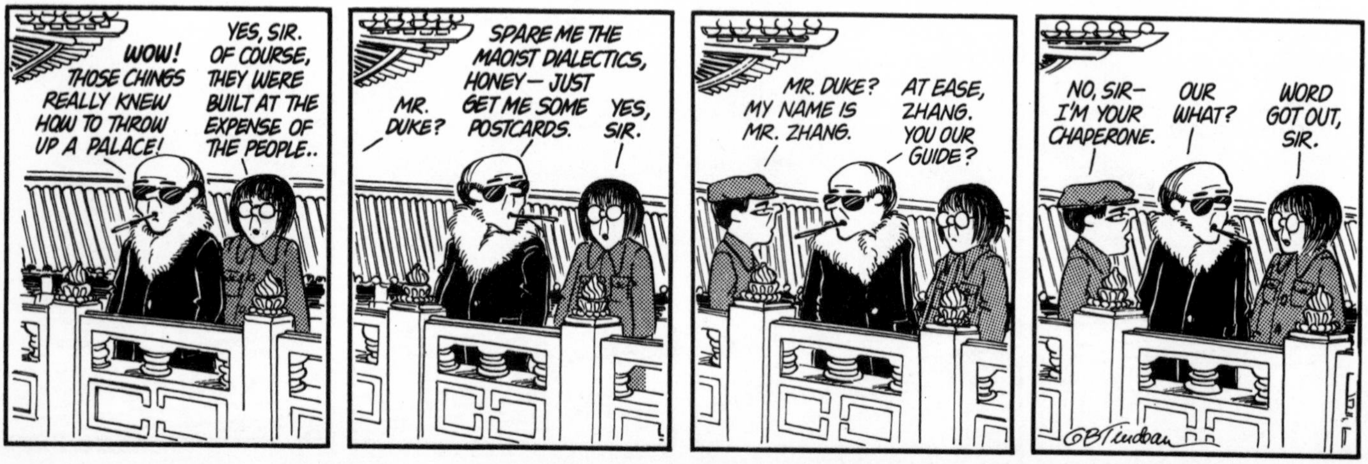
WOW! THOSE CHINGS REALLY KNEW HOW TO THROW UP A PALACE!
YES, SIR. OF COURSE, THEY WERE BUILT AT THE EXPENSE OF THE PEOPLE..
MR. DUKE?
SPARE ME THE MAOIST DIALECTICS, HONEY— JUST GET ME SOME POSTCARDS.
YES, SIR.
MR. DUKE? MY NAME IS MR. ZHANG.
AT EASE, ZHANG. YOU OUR GUIDE?
NO, SIR— I'M YOUR CHAPERONE.
OUR WHAT?
WORD GOT OUT, SIR.

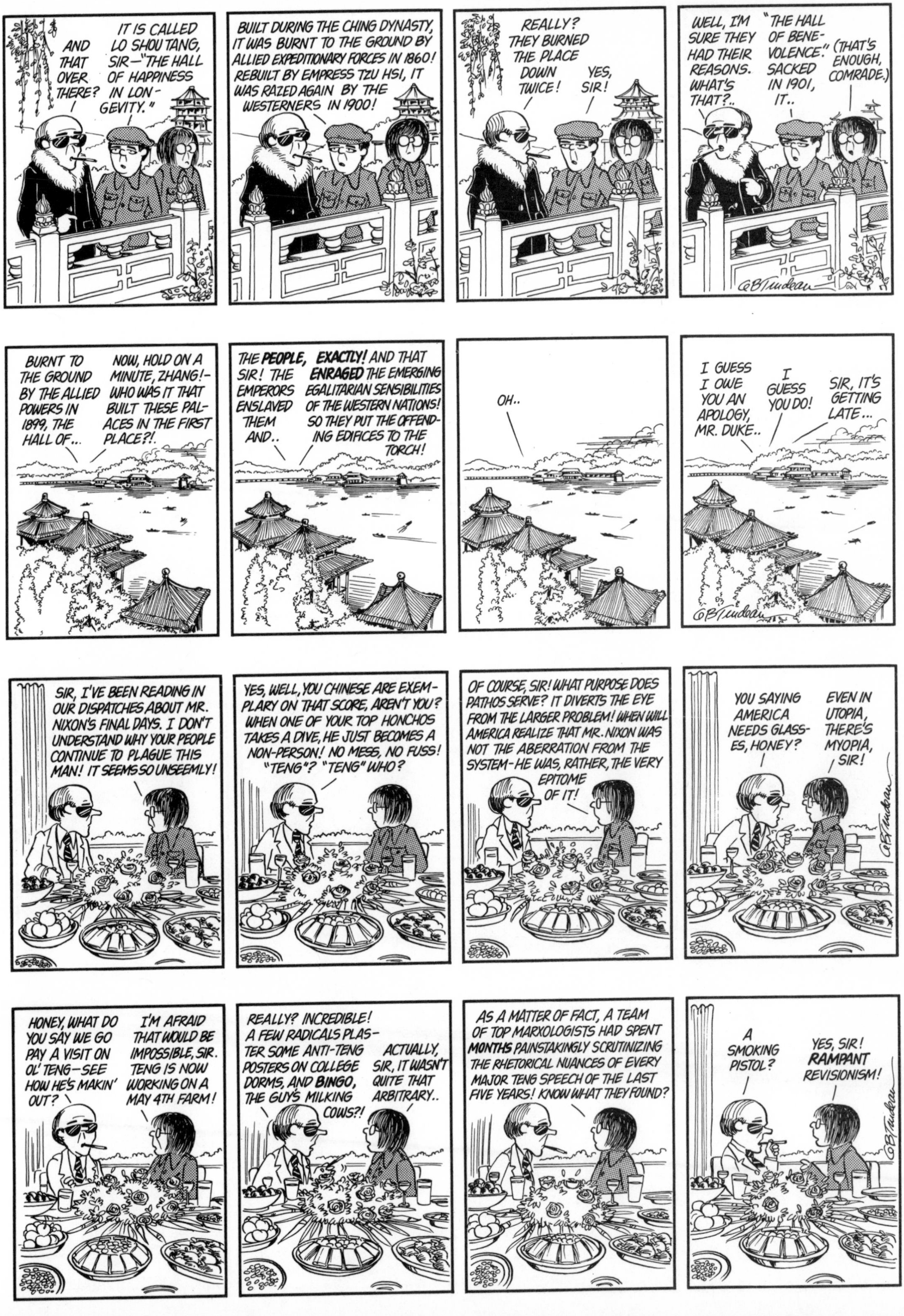
AND THAT OVER THERE?
IT IS CALLED LO SHOU TANG, SIR—"THE HALL OF HAPPINESS IN LONGEVITY."
BUILT DURING THE CHING DYNASTY, IT WAS BURNT TO THE GROUND BY ALLIED EXPEDITIONARY FORCES IN 1860! REBUILT BY EMPRESS TZU HSI, IT WAS RAZED AGAIN BY THE WESTERNERS IN 1900!
REALLY? THEY BURNED THE PLACE DOWN TWICE!
YES, SIR!
WELL, I'M SURE THEY HAD THEIR REASONS. WHAT'S THAT?..
"THE HALL OF BENEVOLENCE." SACKED IN 1901, IT..
(THAT'S ENOUGH, COMRADE.)
BURNT TO THE GROUND BY THE ALLIED POWERS IN 1899, THE HALL OF...
NOW, HOLD ON A MINUTE, ZHANG!- WHO WAS IT THAT BUILT THESE PALACES IN THE FIRST PLACE?!
THE PEOPLE, SIR! THE EMPERORS ENSLAVED THEM AND..
EXACTLY! AND THAT ENRAGED THE EMERGING EGALITARIAN SENSIBILITIES OF THE WESTERN NATIONS! SO THEY PUT THE OFFENDING EDIFICES TO THE TORCH!
OH..
I GUESS I OWE YOU AN APOLOGY, MR. DUKE..
I GUESS YOU DO!
SIR, IT'S GETTING LATE...
SIR, I'VE BEEN READING IN OUR DISPATCHES ABOUT MR. NIXON'S FINAL DAYS. I DON'T UNDERSTAND WHY YOUR PEOPLE CONTINUE TO PLAGUE THIS MAN! IT SEEMS SO UNSEEMLY!
YES, WELL, YOU CHINESE ARE EXEMPLARY ON THAT SCORE, AREN'T YOU? WHEN ONE OF YOUR TOP HONCHOS TAKES A DIVE, HE JUST BECOMES A NON-PERSON! NO MESS, NO FUSS! "TENG"? "TENG" WHO?
OF COURSE, SIR! WHAT PURPOSE DOES PATHOS SERVE? IT DIVERTS THE EYE FROM THE LARGER PROBLEM! WHEN WILL AMERICA REALIZE THAT MR. NIXON WAS NOT THE ABERRATION FROM THE SYSTEM-HE WAS, RATHER, THE VERY EPITOME OF IT!
YOU SAYING AMERICA NEEDS GLASSES, HONEY?
EVEN IN UTOPIA, THERE'S MYOPIA, SIR!
HONEY, WHAT DO YOU SAY WE GO PAY A VISIT ON OL' TENG—SEE HOW HE'S MAKIN' OUT?
I'M AFRAID THAT WOULD BE IMPOSSIBLE, SIR. TENG IS NOW WORKING ON A MAY 4TH FARM!
REALLY? INCREDIBLE! A FEW RADICALS PLASTER SOME ANTI-TENG POSTERS ON COLLEGE DORMS, AND BINGO, THE GUY'S MILKING COWS?!
ACTUALLY, SIR, IT WASN'T QUITE THAT ARBITRARY..
AS A MATTER OF FACT, A TEAM OF TOP MARXOLOGISTS HAD SPENT MONTHS PAINSTAKINGLY SCRUTINIZING THE RHETORICAL NUANCES OF EVERY MAJOR TENG SPEECH OF THE LAST FIVE YEARS! KNOW WHAT THEY FOUND?
A SMOKING PISTOL?
YES, SIR! RAMPANT REVISIONISM!

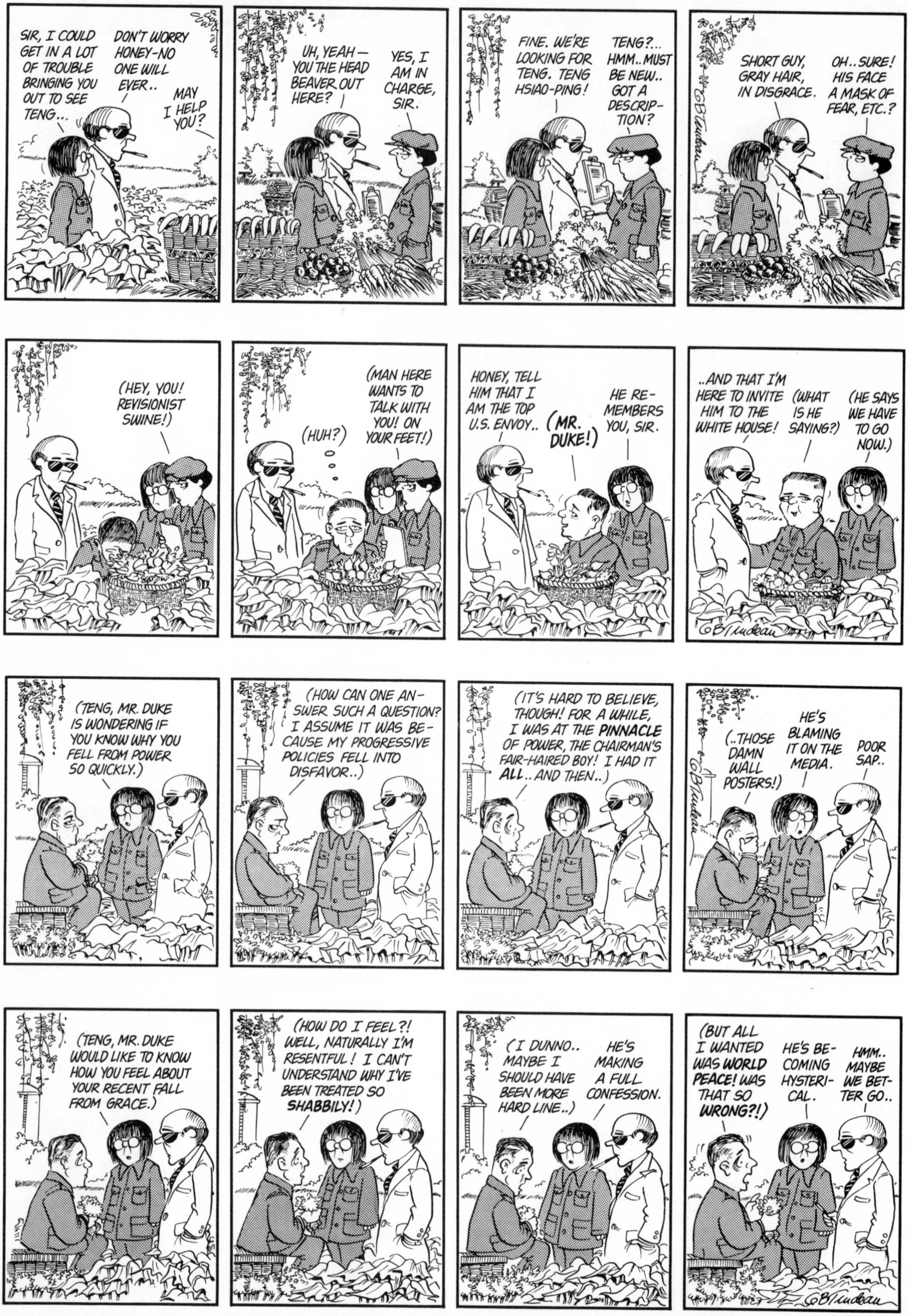
SIR, I COULD GET IN A LOT OF TROUBLE BRINGING YOU OUT TO SEE TENG...
DON'T WORRY HONEY–NO ONE WILL EVER..
MAY I HELP YOU?
UH, YEAH — YOU THE HEAD BEAVER OUT HERE?
YES, I AM IN CHARGE, SIR.
FINE. WE'RE LOOKING FOR TENG. TENG HSIAO-PING!
TENG?... HMM.. MUST BE NEW.. GOT A DESCRIPTION?
SHORT GUY, GRAY HAIR, IN DISGRACE.
OH.. SURE! HIS FACE A MASK OF FEAR, ETC.?
(HEY, YOU! REVISIONIST SWINE!)
(HUH?)
(MAN HERE WANTS TO TALK WITH YOU! ON YOUR FEET!)
HONEY, TELL HIM THAT I AM THE TOP U.S. ENVOY..
(MR. DUKE!)
HE REMEMBERS YOU, SIR.
..AND THAT I'M HERE TO INVITE HIM TO THE WHITE HOUSE!
(WHAT IS HE SAYING?)
(HE SAYS WE HAVE TO GO NOW.)
(TENG, MR. DUKE IS WONDERING IF YOU KNOW WHY YOU FELL FROM POWER SO QUICKLY.)
(HOW CAN ONE ANSWER SUCH A QUESTION? I ASSUME IT WAS BECAUSE MY PROGRESSIVE POLICIES FELL INTO DISFAVOR..)
(IT'S HARD TO BELIEVE, THOUGH! FOR A WHILE, I WAS AT THE **PINNACLE** OF POWER, THE CHAIRMAN'S FAIR-HAIRED BOY! I HAD IT **ALL**.. AND THEN..)
(..THOSE DAMN WALL POSTERS!)
HE'S BLAMING IT ON THE MEDIA.
POOR SAP..
(TENG, MR. DUKE WOULD LIKE TO KNOW HOW YOU FEEL ABOUT YOUR RECENT FALL FROM GRACE.)
(HOW DO I FEEL?! WELL, NATURALLY I'M RESENTFUL! I CAN'T UNDERSTAND WHY I'VE BEEN TREATED SO **SHABBILY!**)
(I DUNNO.. MAYBE I SHOULD HAVE BEEN MORE HARD LINE..)
HE'S MAKING A FULL CONFESSION.
(BUT ALL I WANTED WAS **WORLD PEACE!** WAS THAT SO **WRONG?!**)
HE'S BECOMING HYSTERICAL.
HMM.. MAYBE WE BETTER GO..

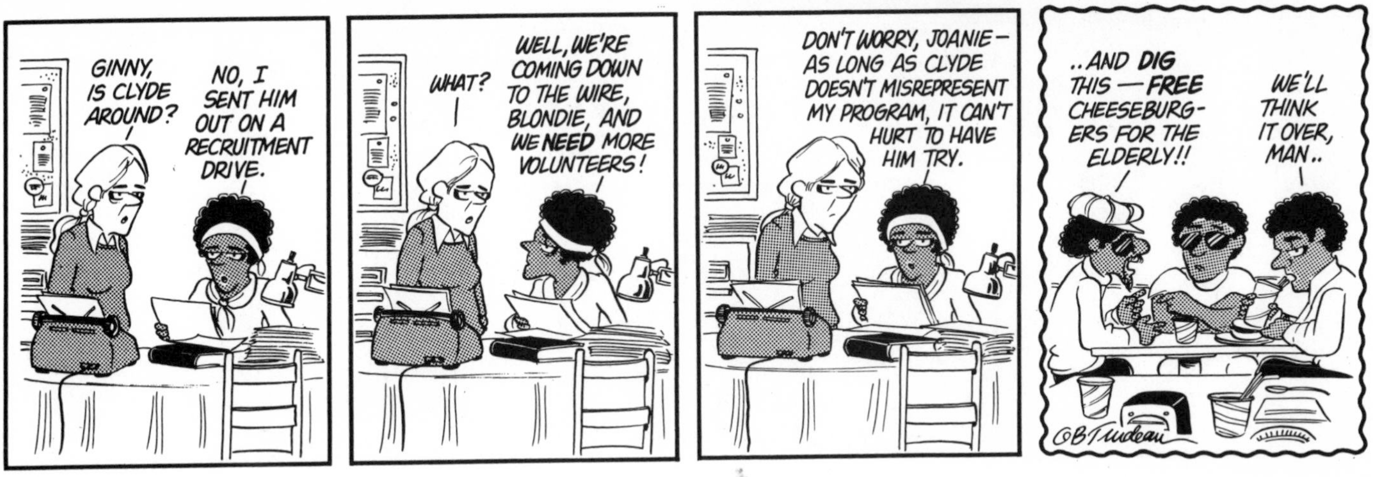
GINNY, IS CLYDE AROUND?
NO, I SENT HIM OUT ON A RECRUITMENT DRIVE.
WHAT?
WELL, WE'RE COMING DOWN TO THE WIRE, BLONDIE, AND WE NEED MORE VOLUNTEERS!
DON'T WORRY, JOANIE - AS LONG AS CLYDE DOESN'T MISREPRESENT MY PROGRAM, IT CAN'T HURT TO HAVE HIM TRY.
..AND DIG THIS — FREE CHEESEBURGERS FOR THE ELDERLY!!
WE'LL THINK IT OVER, MAN..
©GBTrudeau

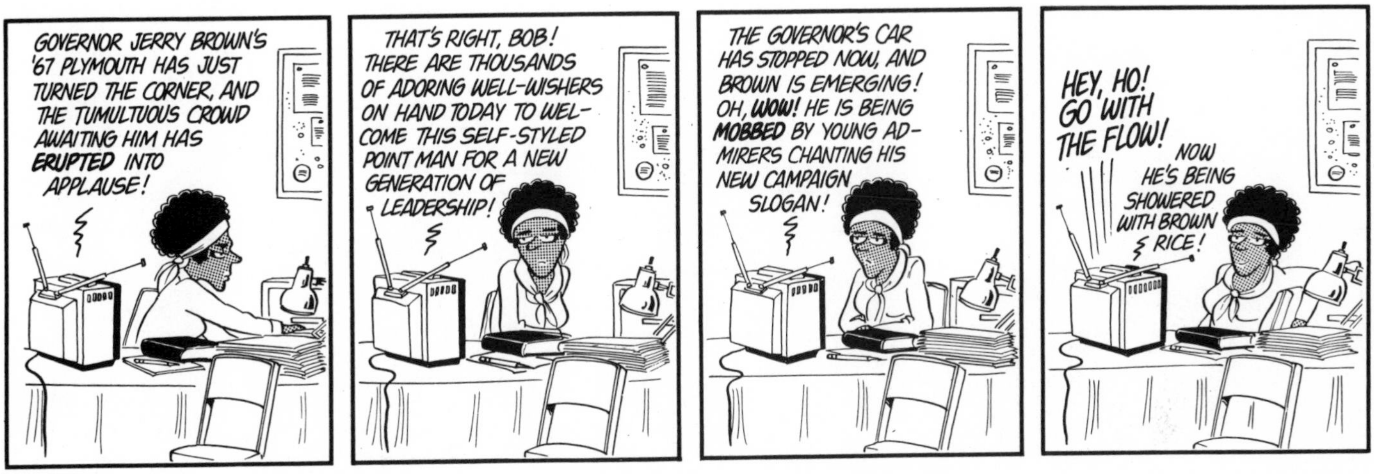
GOVERNOR JERRY BROWN'S '67 PLYMOUTH HAS JUST TURNED THE CORNER, AND THE TUMULTUOUS CROWD AWAITING HIM HAS ERUPTED INTO APPLAUSE!
THAT'S RIGHT, BOB! THERE ARE THOUSANDS OF ADORING WELL-WISHERS ON HAND TODAY TO WELCOME THIS SELF-STYLED POINT MAN FOR A NEW GENERATION OF LEADERSHIP!
THE GOVERNOR'S CAR HAS STOPPED NOW, AND BROWN IS EMERGING! OH, WOW! HE IS BEING MOBBED BY YOUNG ADMIRERS CHANTING HIS NEW CAMPAIGN SLOGAN!
HEY, HO! GO WITH THE FLOW!
NOW HE'S BEING SHOWERED WITH BROWN RICE!

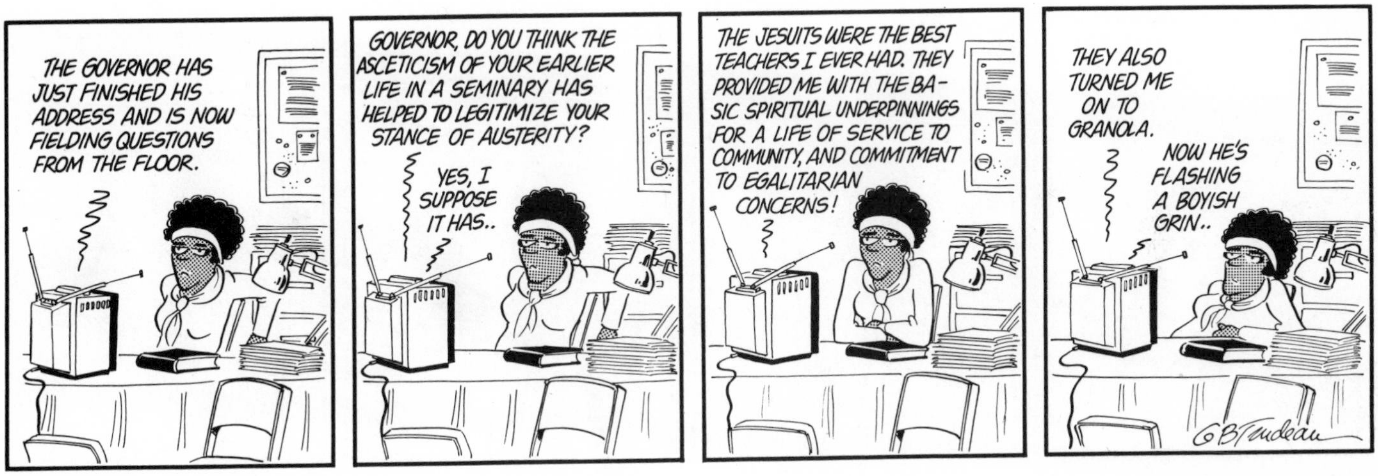
THE GOVERNOR HAS JUST FINISHED HIS ADDRESS AND IS NOW FIELDING QUESTIONS FROM THE FLOOR.
GOVERNOR, DO YOU THINK THE ASCETICISM OF YOUR EARLIER LIFE IN A SEMINARY HAS HELPED TO LEGITIMIZE YOUR STANCE OF AUSTERITY?
YES, I SUPPOSE IT HAS..
THE JESUITS WERE THE BEST TEACHERS I EVER HAD. THEY PROVIDED ME WITH THE BASIC SPIRITUAL UNDERPINNINGS FOR A LIFE OF SERVICE TO COMMUNITY, AND COMMITMENT TO EGALITARIAN CONCERNS!
THEY ALSO TURNED ME ON TO GRANOLA.
NOW HE'S FLASHING A BOYISH GRIN..
©GBTrudeau

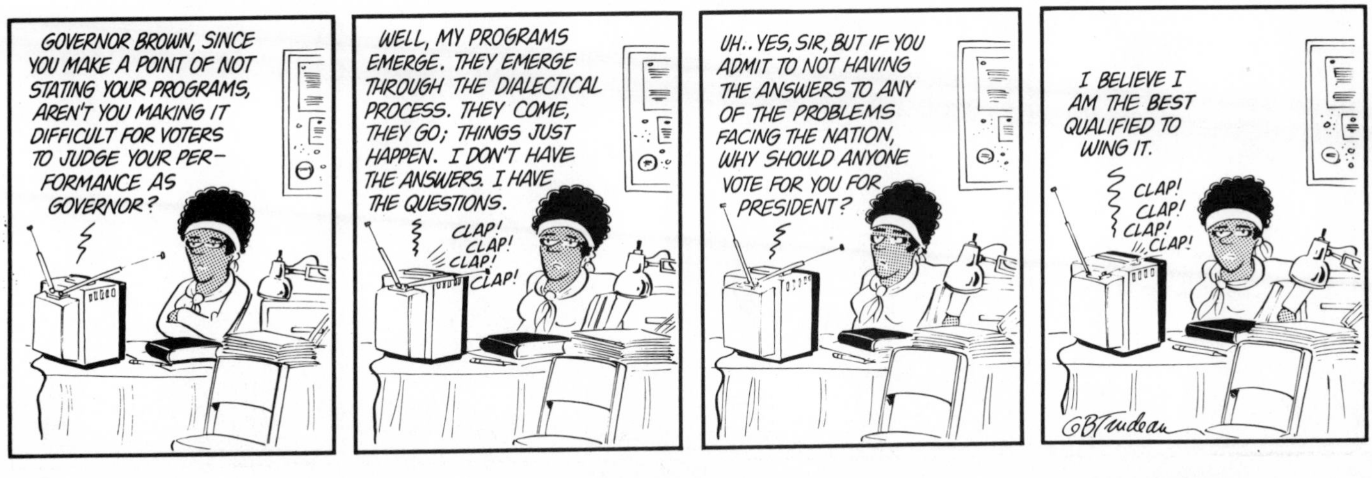
GOVERNOR BROWN, SINCE YOU MAKE A POINT OF NOT STATING YOUR PROGRAMS, AREN'T YOU MAKING IT DIFFICULT FOR VOTERS TO JUDGE YOUR PERFORMANCE AS GOVERNOR?
WELL, MY PROGRAMS EMERGE. THEY EMERGE THROUGH THE DIALECTICAL PROCESS. THEY COME, THEY GO; THINGS JUST HAPPEN. I DON'T HAVE THE ANSWERS. I HAVE THE QUESTIONS.
CLAP! CLAP! CLAP! CLAP!
UH..YES, SIR, BUT IF YOU ADMIT TO NOT HAVING THE ANSWERS TO ANY OF THE PROBLEMS FACING THE NATION, WHY SHOULD ANYONE VOTE FOR YOU FOR PRESIDENT?
I BELIEVE I AM THE BEST QUALIFIED TO WING IT.
CLAP! CLAP! CLAP! CLAP!
©GBTrudeau

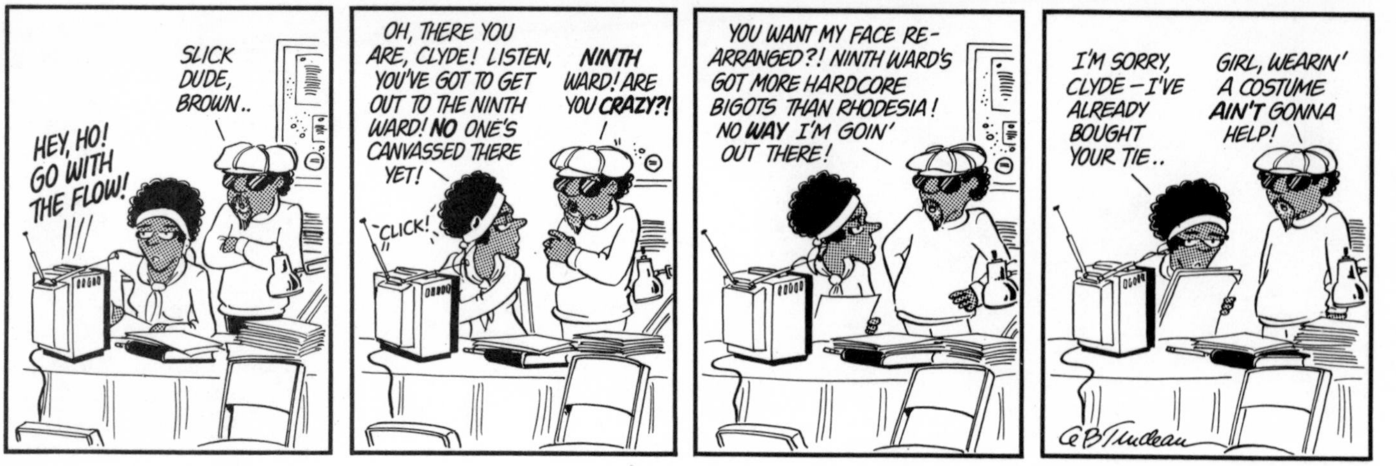

HEY, HO! GO WITH THE FLOW!
SLICK DUDE, BROWN..
OH, THERE YOU ARE, CLYDE! LISTEN, YOU'VE GOT TO GET OUT TO THE NINTH WARD! **NO** ONE'S CANVASSED THERE YET!
CLICK!
NINTH WARD! ARE YOU **CRAZY?!**
YOU WANT MY FACE RE-ARRANGED?! NINTH WARD'S GOT MORE HARDCORE BIGOTS THAN RHODESIA! NO **WAY** I'M GOIN' OUT THERE!
I'M SORRY, CLYDE – I'VE ALREADY BOUGHT YOUR TIE..
GIRL, WEARIN' A COSTUME **AIN'T** GONNA HELP!

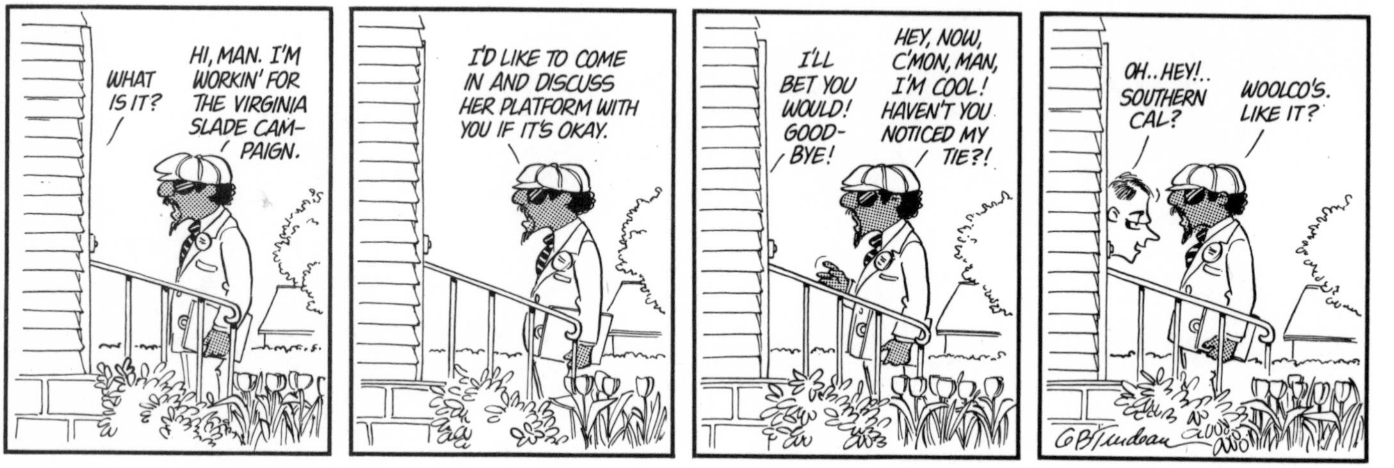

WHAT IS IT?
HI, MAN. I'M WORKIN' FOR THE VIRGINIA SLADE CAMPAIGN.
I'D LIKE TO COME IN AND DISCUSS HER PLATFORM WITH YOU IF IT'S OKAY.
I'LL BET YOU WOULD! GOOD-BYE!
HEY, NOW, C'MON, MAN, I'M COOL! HAVEN'T YOU NOTICED MY TIE?!
OH.. HEY!.. SOUTHERN CAL?
WOOLCO'S. LIKE IT?

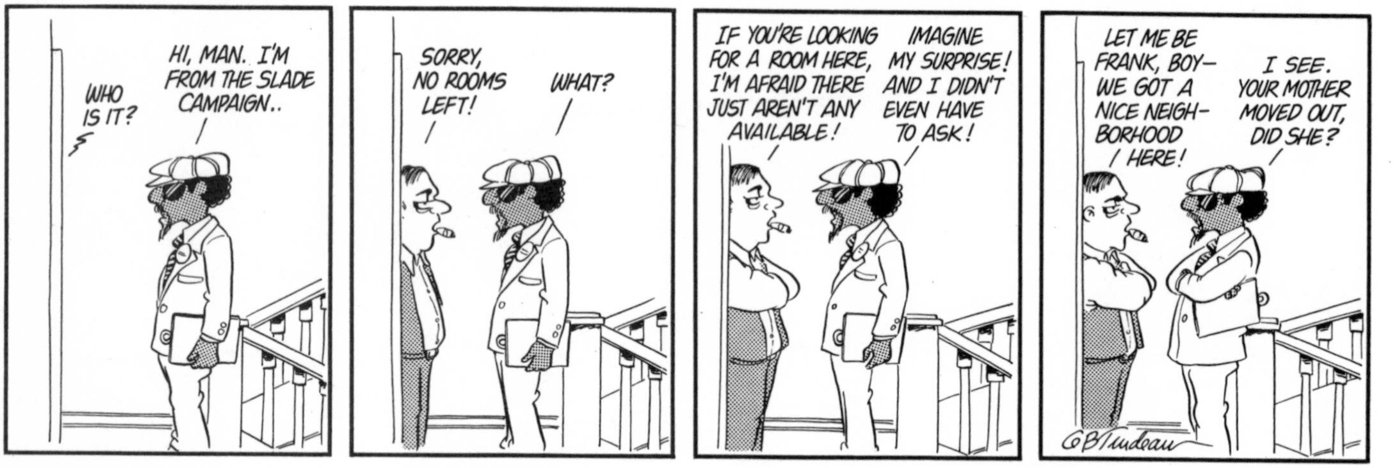

WHO IS IT?
HI, MAN. I'M FROM THE SLADE CAMPAIGN..
SORRY, NO ROOMS LEFT!
WHAT?
IF YOU'RE LOOKING FOR A ROOM HERE, I'M AFRAID THERE JUST AREN'T ANY AVAILABLE!
IMAGINE MY SURPRISE! AND I DIDN'T EVEN HAVE TO ASK!
LET ME BE FRANK, BOY– WE GOT A NICE NEIGHBORHOOD HERE!
I SEE. YOUR MOTHER MOVED OUT, DID SHE?

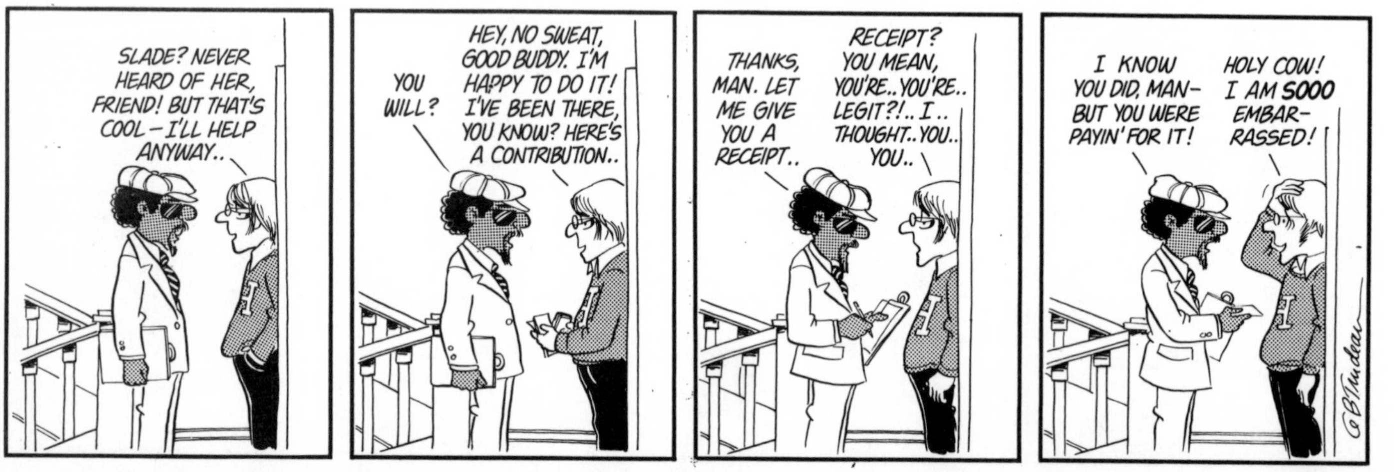

SLADE? NEVER HEARD OF HER, FRIEND! BUT THAT'S COOL – I'LL HELP ANYWAY..
YOU WILL?
HEY, NO SWEAT, GOOD BUDDY. I'M HAPPY TO DO IT! I'VE BEEN THERE, YOU KNOW? HERE'S A CONTRIBUTION..
THANKS, MAN. LET ME GIVE YOU A RECEIPT..
RECEIPT? YOU MEAN, YOU'RE.. YOU'RE.. LEGIT?!.. I.. THOUGHT.. YOU.. YOU..
I KNOW YOU DID, MAN– BUT YOU WERE PAYIN' FOR IT!
HOLY COW! I AM **SOOO** EMBARRASSED!

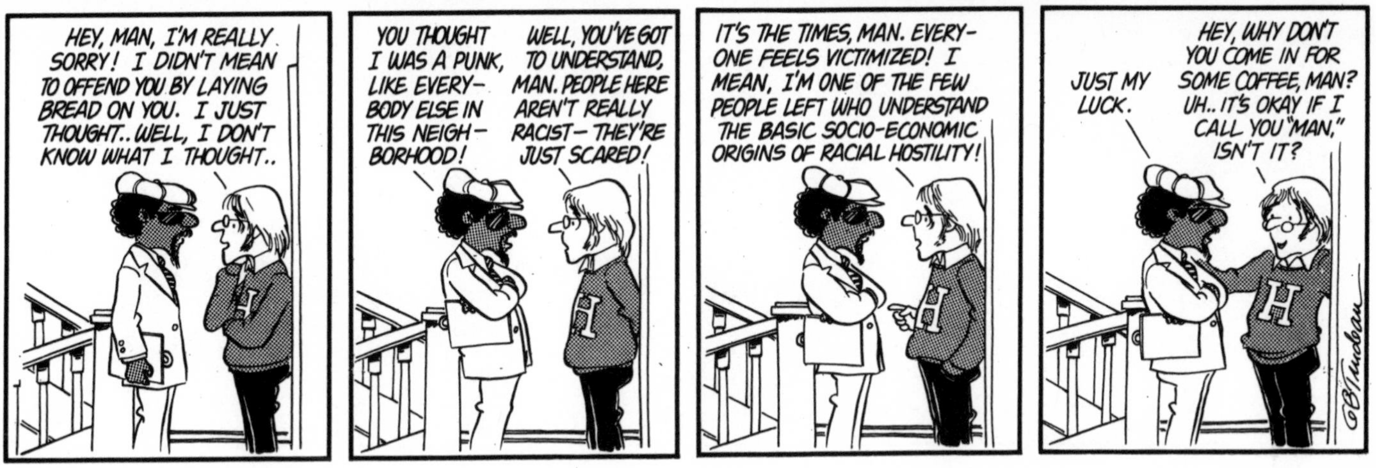
HEY, MAN, I'M REALLY SORRY! I DIDN'T MEAN TO OFFEND YOU BY LAYING BREAD ON YOU. I JUST THOUGHT.. WELL, I DON'T KNOW WHAT I THOUGHT..
YOU THOUGHT I WAS A PUNK, LIKE EVERYBODY ELSE IN THIS NEIGHBORHOOD!
WELL, YOU'VE GOT TO UNDERSTAND, MAN. PEOPLE HERE AREN'T REALLY RACIST— THEY'RE JUST SCARED!
IT'S THE TIMES, MAN. EVERYONE FEELS VICTIMIZED! I MEAN, I'M ONE OF THE FEW PEOPLE LEFT WHO UNDERSTAND THE BASIC SOCIO-ECONOMIC ORIGINS OF RACIAL HOSTILITY!
JUST MY LUCK.
HEY, WHY DON'T YOU COME IN FOR SOME COFFEE, MAN? UH.. IT'S OKAY IF I CALL YOU "MAN," ISN'T IT?
GBTrudeau
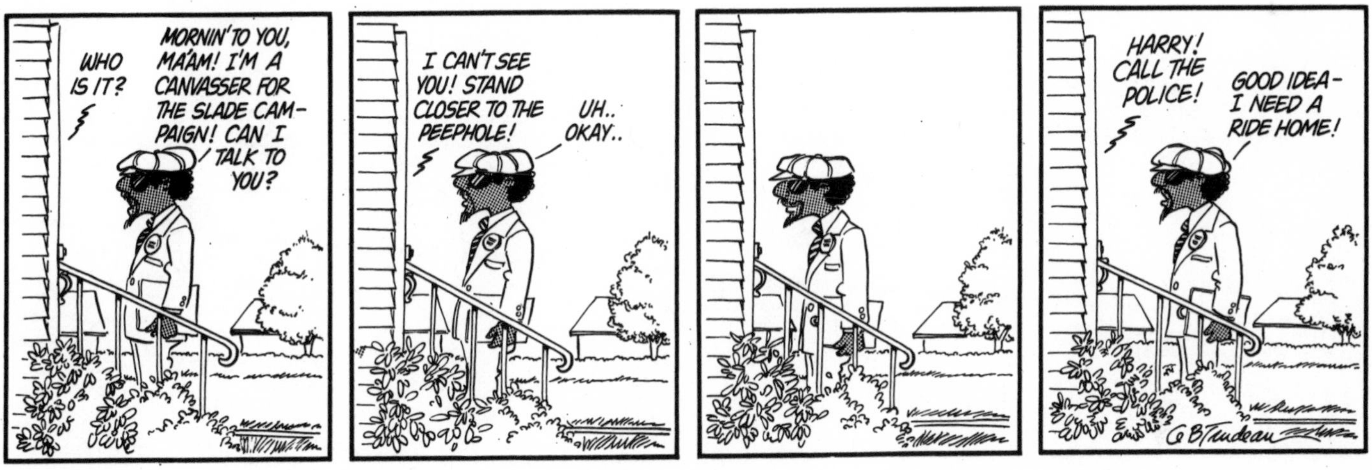
WHO IS IT?
MORNIN' TO YOU, MA'AM! I'M A CANVASSER FOR THE SLADE CAMPAIGN! CAN I TALK TO YOU?
I CAN'T SEE YOU! STAND CLOSER TO THE PEEPHOLE!
UH.. OKAY..
HARRY! CALL THE POLICE!
GOOD IDEA— I NEED A RIDE HOME!
GBTrudeau
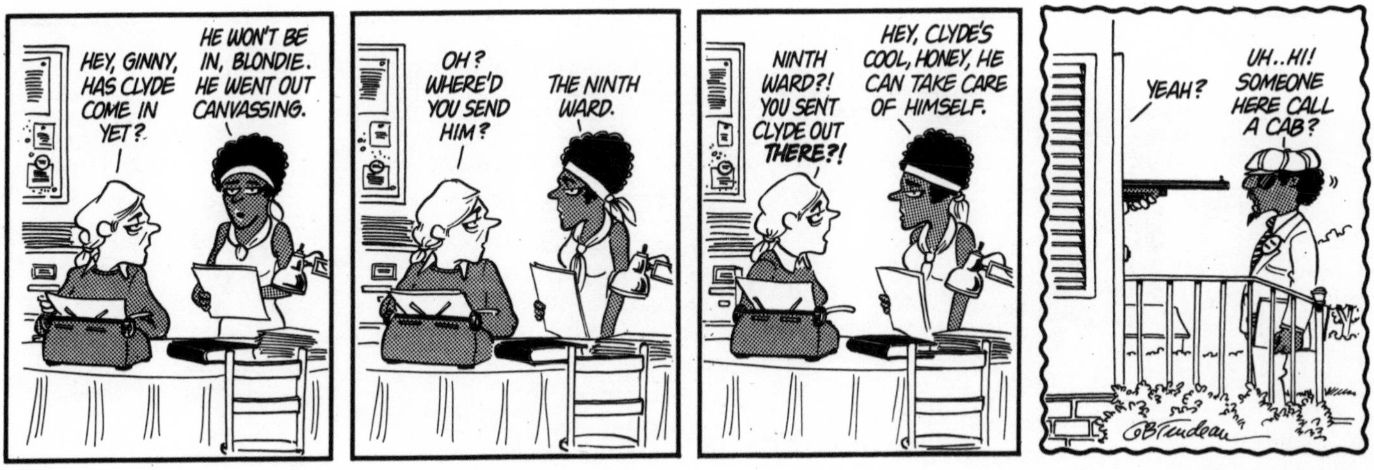
HEY, GINNY, HAS CLYDE COME IN YET?
HE WON'T BE IN, BLONDIE. HE WENT OUT CANVASSING.
OH? WHERE'D YOU SEND HIM?
THE NINTH WARD.
NINTH WARD?! YOU SENT CLYDE OUT **THERE?!**
HEY, CLYDE'S COOL, HONEY, HE CAN TAKE CARE OF HIMSELF.
YEAH?
UH..HI! SOMEONE HERE CALL A CAB?
GBTrudeau
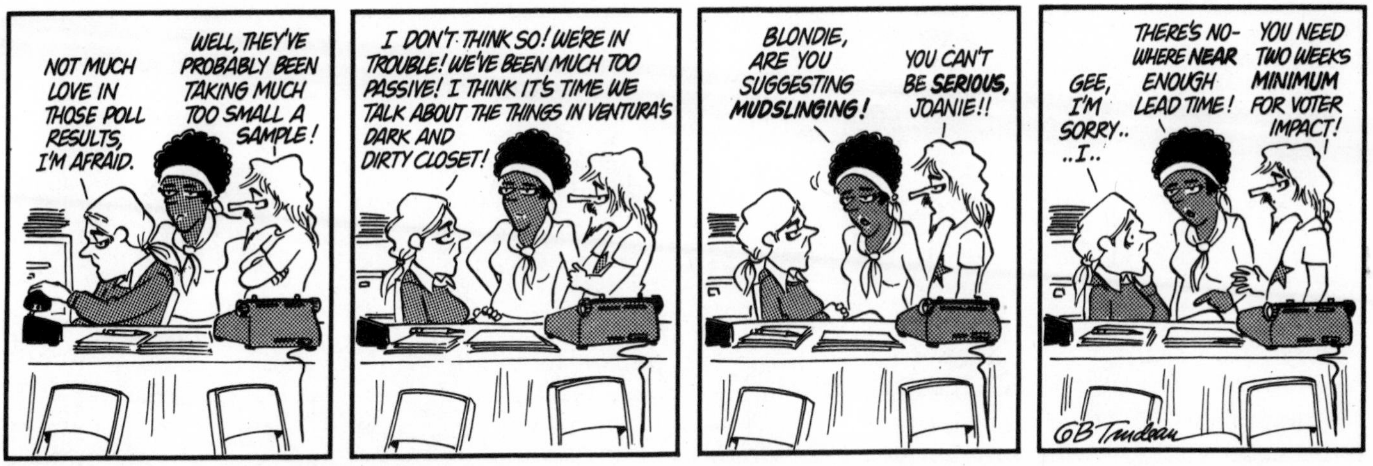
NOT MUCH LOVE IN THOSE POLL RESULTS, I'M AFRAID.
WELL, THEY'VE PROBABLY BEEN TAKING MUCH TOO SMALL A SAMPLE!
I DON'T THINK SO! WE'RE IN TROUBLE! WE'VE BEEN MUCH TOO PASSIVE! I THINK IT'S TIME WE TALK ABOUT THE THINGS IN VENTURA'S DARK AND DIRTY CLOSET!
BLONDIE, ARE YOU SUGGESTING **MUDSLINGING!**
YOU CAN'T BE **SERIOUS,** JOANIE!!
GEE, I'M SORRY.. ..I..
THERE'S NOWHERE **NEAR** ENOUGH LEAD TIME!
YOU NEED TWO WEEKS **MINIMUM** FOR VOTER IMPACT!
GBTrudeau

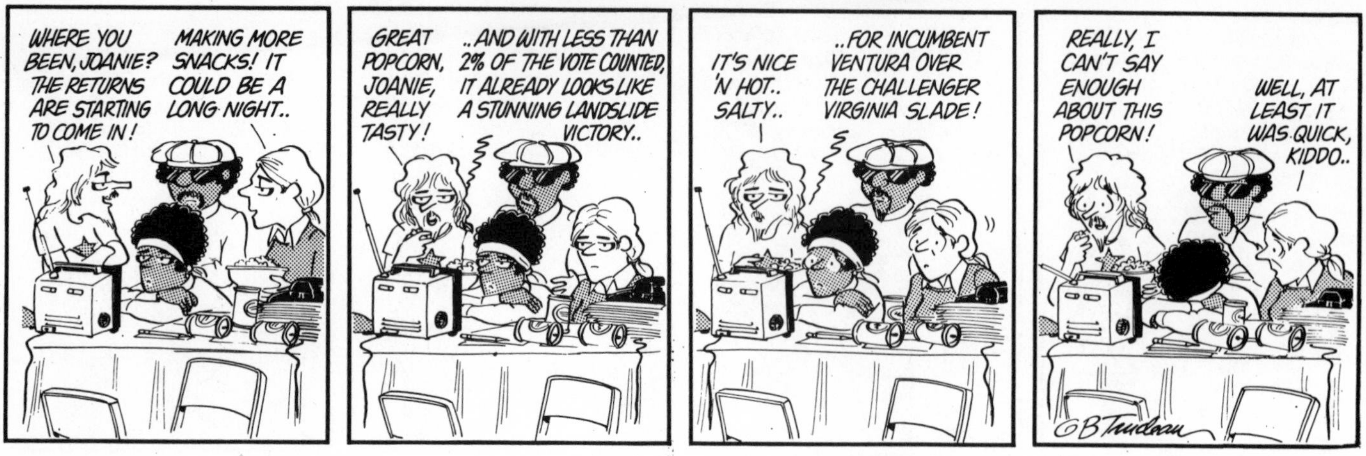
WHERE YOU BEEN, JOANIE? THE RETURNS ARE STARTING TO COME IN!
MAKING MORE SNACKS! IT COULD BE A LONG NIGHT..
GREAT POPCORN, JOANIE, REALLY TASTY!
..AND WITH LESS THAN 2% OF THE VOTE COUNTED, IT ALREADY LOOKS LIKE A STUNNING LANDSLIDE VICTORY..
IT'S NICE 'N HOT.. SALTY..
..FOR INCUMBENT VENTURA OVER THE CHALLENGER VIRGINIA SLADE!
REALLY, I CAN'T SAY ENOUGH ABOUT THIS POPCORN!
WELL, AT LEAST IT WAS QUICK, KIDDO..
©B Trudeau

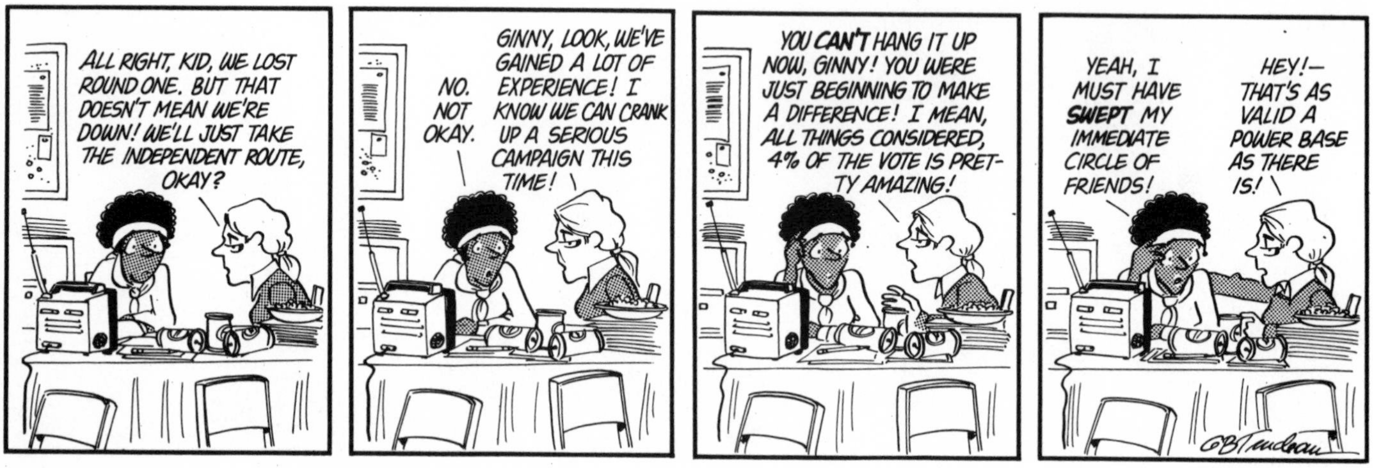
ALL RIGHT, KID, WE LOST ROUND ONE. BUT THAT DOESN'T MEAN WE'RE DOWN! WE'LL JUST TAKE THE INDEPENDENT ROUTE, OKAY?
NO. NOT OKAY.
GINNY, LOOK, WE'VE GAINED A LOT OF EXPERIENCE! I KNOW WE CAN CRANK UP A SERIOUS CAMPAIGN THIS TIME!
YOU CAN'T HANG IT UP NOW, GINNY! YOU WERE JUST BEGINNING TO MAKE A DIFFERENCE! I MEAN, ALL THINGS CONSIDERED, 4% OF THE VOTE IS PRETTY AMAZING!
YEAH, I MUST HAVE SWEPT MY IMMEDIATE CIRCLE OF FRIENDS!
HEY!— THAT'S AS VALID A POWER BASE AS THERE IS!
©B Trudeau

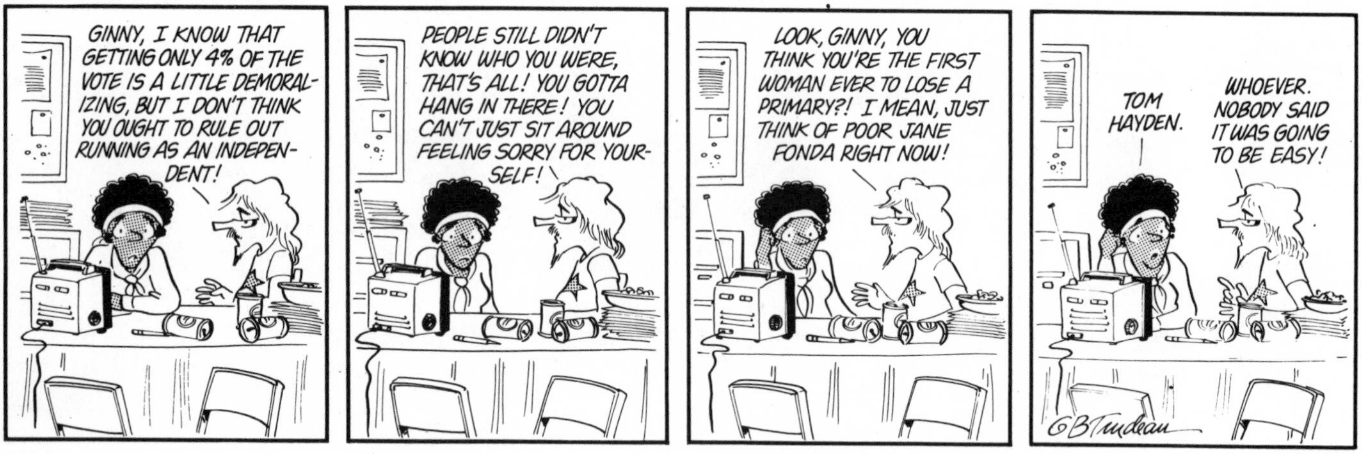
GINNY, I KNOW THAT GETTING ONLY 4% OF THE VOTE IS A LITTLE DEMORALIZING, BUT I DON'T THINK YOU OUGHT TO RULE OUT RUNNING AS AN INDEPENDENT!
PEOPLE STILL DIDN'T KNOW WHO YOU WERE, THAT'S ALL! YOU GOTTA HANG IN THERE! YOU CAN'T JUST SIT AROUND FEELING SORRY FOR YOURSELF!
LOOK, GINNY, YOU THINK YOU'RE THE FIRST WOMAN EVER TO LOSE A PRIMARY?! I MEAN, JUST THINK OF POOR JANE FONDA RIGHT NOW!
TOM HAYDEN.
WHOEVER. NOBODY SAID IT WAS GOING TO BE EASY!
©B Trudeau

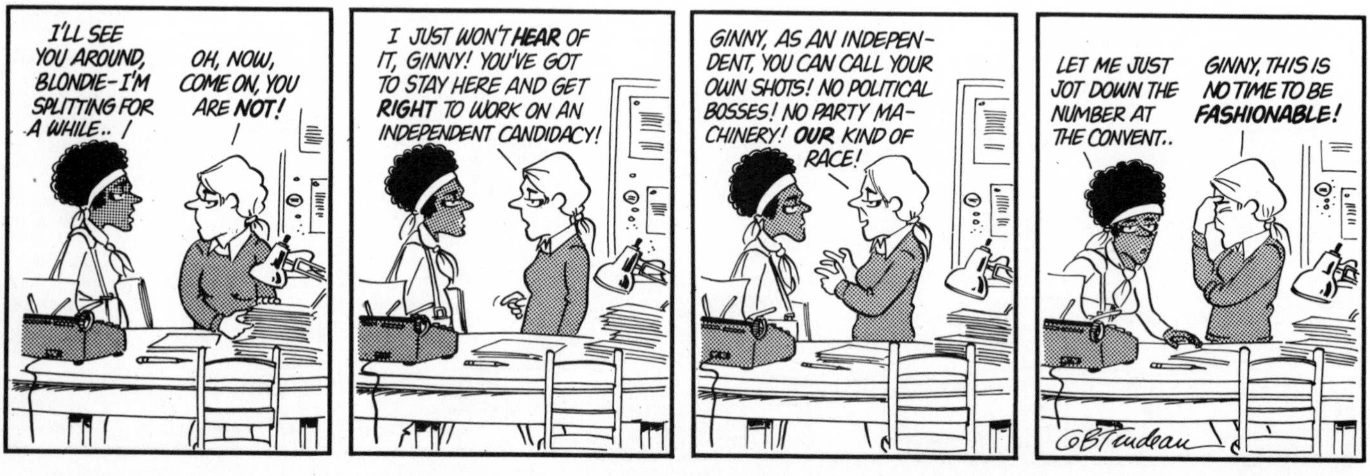
I'LL SEE YOU AROUND, BLONDIE–I'M SPLITTING FOR A WHILE..!
OH, NOW, COME ON, YOU ARE NOT!
I JUST WON'T HEAR OF IT, GINNY! YOU'VE GOT TO STAY HERE AND GET RIGHT TO WORK ON AN INDEPENDENT CANDIDACY!
GINNY, AS AN INDEPENDENT, YOU CAN CALL YOUR OWN SHOTS! NO POLITICAL BOSSES! NO PARTY MACHINERY! OUR KIND OF RACE!
LET ME JUST JOT DOWN THE NUMBER AT THE CONVENT..
GINNY, THIS IS NO TIME TO BE FASHIONABLE!
©B Trudeau

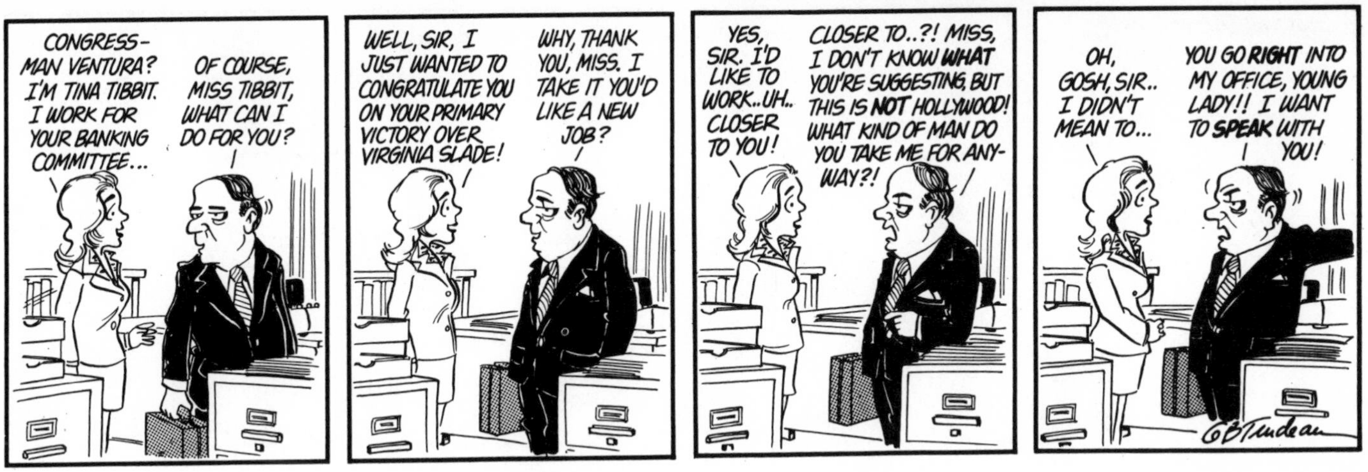
CONGRESSMAN VENTURA? I'M TINA TIBBIT. I WORK FOR YOUR BANKING COMMITTEE...
OF COURSE, MISS TIBBIT, WHAT CAN I DO FOR YOU?
WELL, SIR, I JUST WANTED TO CONGRATULATE YOU ON YOUR PRIMARY VICTORY OVER VIRGINIA SLADE!
WHY, THANK YOU, MISS. I TAKE IT YOU'D LIKE A NEW JOB?
YES, SIR. I'D LIKE TO WORK..UH.. CLOSER TO YOU!
CLOSER TO..?! MISS, I DON'T KNOW WHAT YOU'RE SUGGESTING, BUT THIS IS NOT HOLLYWOOD! WHAT KIND OF MAN DO YOU TAKE ME FOR ANYWAY?!
OH, GOSH, SIR.. I DIDN'T MEAN TO...
YOU GO RIGHT INTO MY OFFICE, YOUNG LADY!! I WANT TO SPEAK WITH YOU!
GBTrudeau

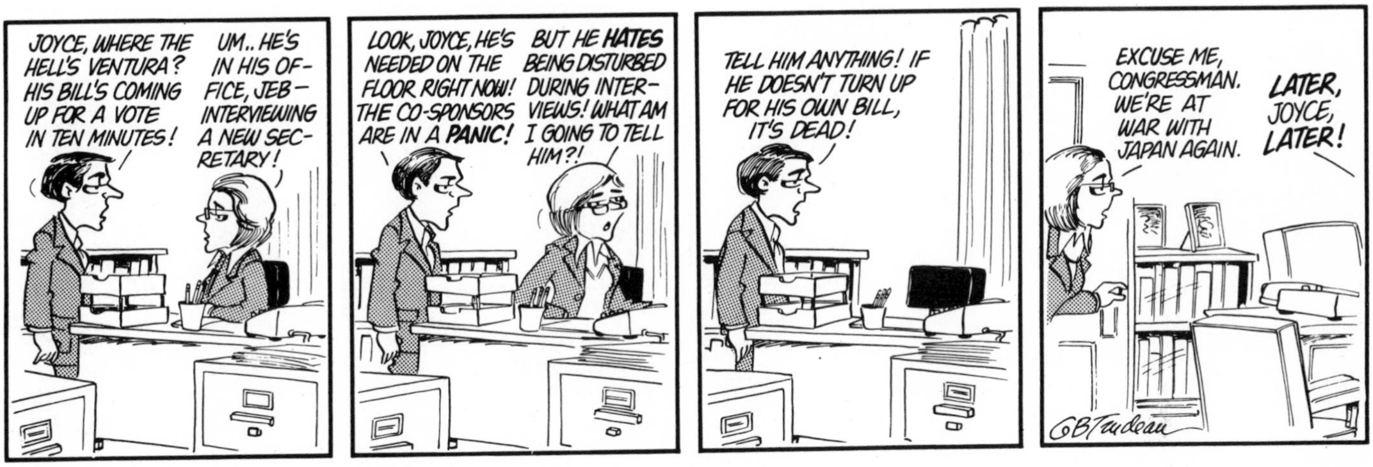
JOYCE, WHERE THE HELL'S VENTURA? HIS BILL'S COMING UP FOR A VOTE IN TEN MINUTES!
UM.. HE'S IN HIS OFFICE, JEB– INTERVIEWING A NEW SECRETARY!
LOOK, JOYCE, HE'S NEEDED ON THE FLOOR RIGHT NOW! THE CO-SPONSORS ARE IN A PANIC!
BUT HE HATES BEING DISTURBED DURING INTERVIEWS! WHAT AM I GOING TO TELL HIM?!
TELL HIM ANYTHING! IF HE DOESN'T TURN UP FOR HIS OWN BILL, IT'S DEAD!
EXCUSE ME, CONGRESSMAN. WE'RE AT WAR WITH JAPAN AGAIN.
LATER, JOYCE, LATER!
GBTrudeau

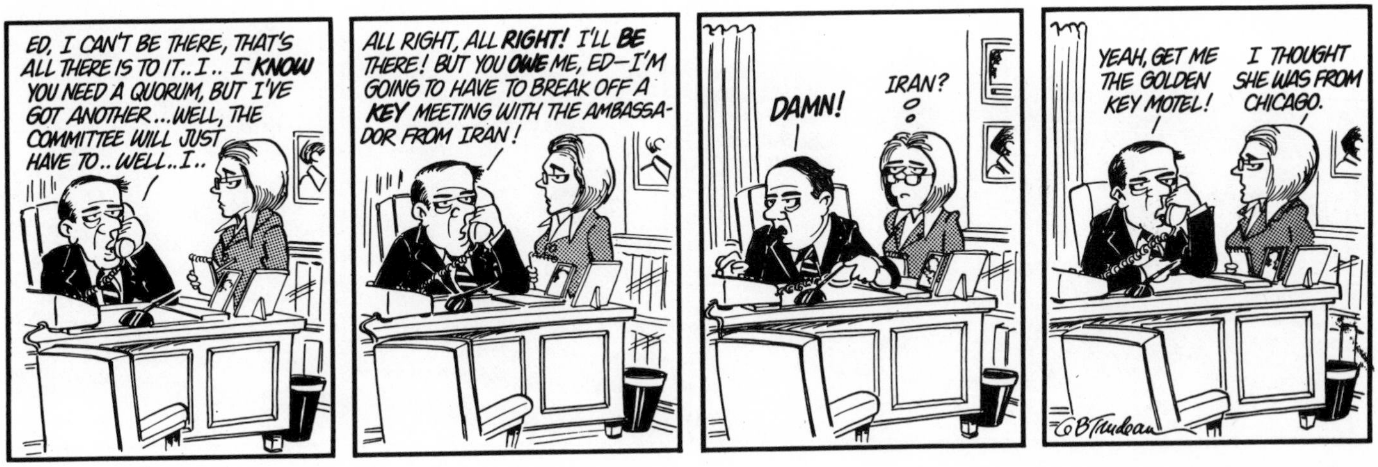
ED, I CAN'T BE THERE, THAT'S ALL THERE IS TO IT..I.. I KNOW YOU NEED A QUORUM, BUT I'VE GOT ANOTHER...WELL, THE COMMITTEE WILL JUST HAVE TO.. WELL..I..
ALL RIGHT, ALL RIGHT! I'LL BE THERE! BUT YOU OWE ME, ED—I'M GOING TO HAVE TO BREAK OFF A KEY MEETING WITH THE AMBASSADOR FROM IRAN!
DAMN!
IRAN?
YEAH, GET ME THE GOLDEN KEY MOTEL!
I THOUGHT SHE WAS FROM CHICAGO.
GBTrudeau

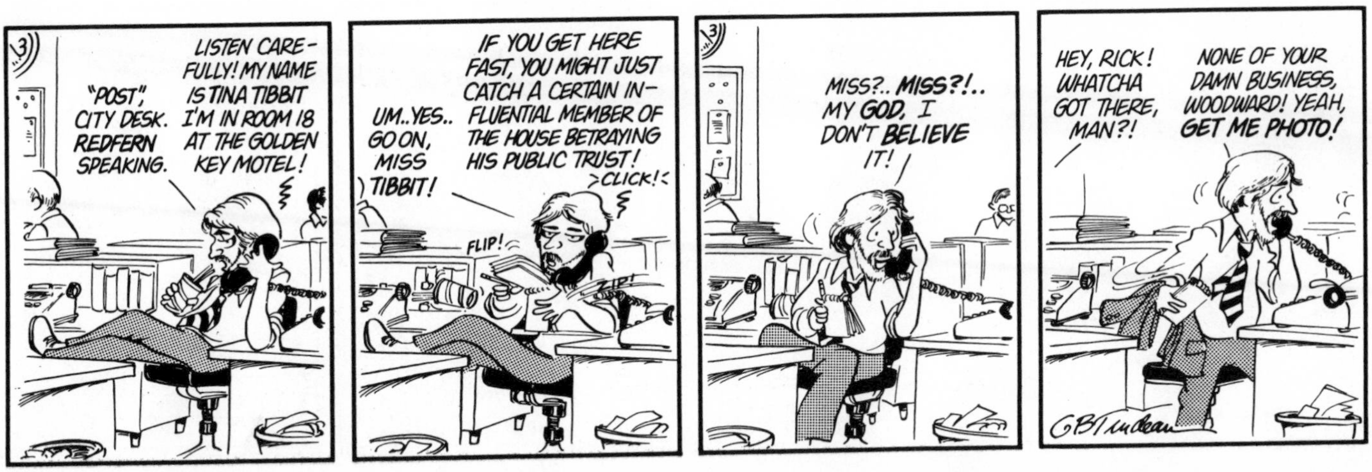
"POST", CITY DESK. REDFERN SPEAKING.
LISTEN CAREFULLY! MY NAME IS TINA TIBBIT I'M IN ROOM 18 AT THE GOLDEN KEY MOTEL!
UM..YES.. GO ON, MISS TIBBIT!
IF YOU GET HERE FAST, YOU MIGHT JUST CATCH A CERTAIN INFLUENTIAL MEMBER OF THE HOUSE BETRAYING HIS PUBLIC TRUST!
CLICK!
FLIP!
MISS?.. MISS?!.. MY GOD, I DON'T BELIEVE IT!
HEY, RICK! WHATCHA GOT THERE, MAN?!
NONE OF YOUR DAMN BUSINESS, WOODWARD! YEAH, GET ME PHOTO!
GBTrudeau

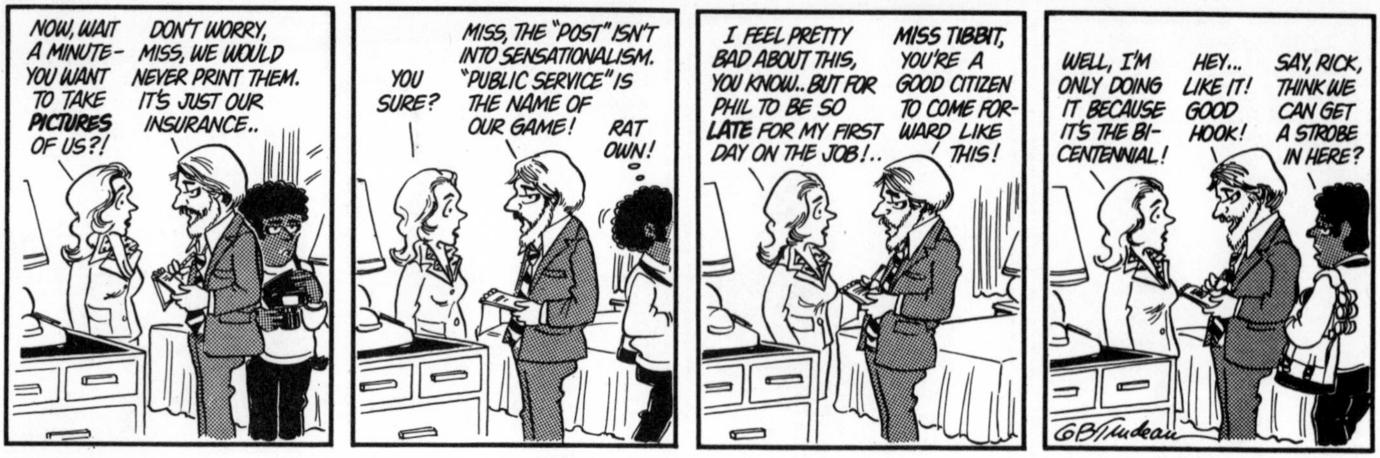
NOW, WAIT A MINUTE- YOU WANT TO TAKE PICTURES OF US?!
DON'T WORRY, MISS, WE WOULD NEVER PRINT THEM. IT'S JUST OUR INSURANCE..
YOU SURE?
MISS, THE "POST" ISN'T INTO SENSATIONALISM. "PUBLIC SERVICE" IS THE NAME OF OUR GAME!
RAT OWN!
I FEEL PRETTY BAD ABOUT THIS, YOU KNOW.. BUT FOR PHIL TO BE SO LATE FOR MY FIRST DAY ON THE JOB!..
MISS TIBBIT, YOU'RE A GOOD CITIZEN TO COME FORWARD LIKE THIS!
WELL, I'M ONLY DOING IT BECAUSE IT'S THE BICENTENNIAL!
HEY... LIKE IT! GOOD HOOK!
SAY, RICK, THINK WE CAN GET A STROBE IN HERE?
GBTrudeau

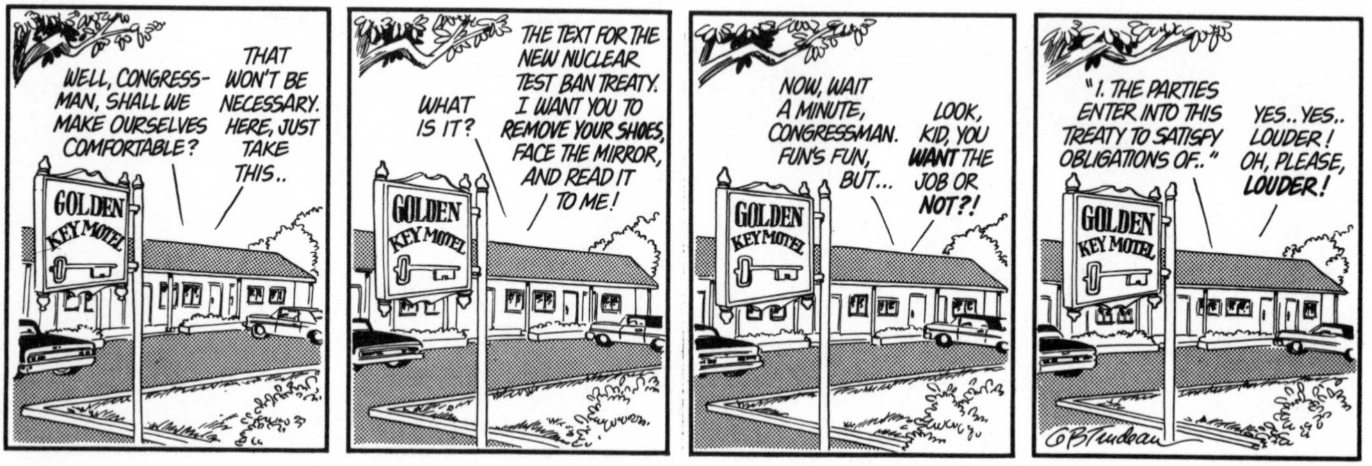
WELL, CONGRESSMAN, SHALL WE MAKE OURSELVES COMFORTABLE?
THAT WON'T BE NECESSARY. HERE, JUST TAKE THIS..
GOLDEN KEY MOTEL
WHAT IS IT?
THE TEXT FOR THE NEW NUCLEAR TEST BAN TREATY. I WANT YOU TO REMOVE YOUR SHOES, FACE THE MIRROR, AND READ IT TO ME!
NOW, WAIT A MINUTE, CONGRESSMAN. FUN'S FUN, BUT...
LOOK, KID, YOU WANT THE JOB OR NOT?!
"I. THE PARTIES ENTER INTO THIS TREATY TO SATISFY OBLIGATIONS OF.."
YES.. YES.. LOUDER! OH, PLEASE, LOUDER!
GBTrudeau

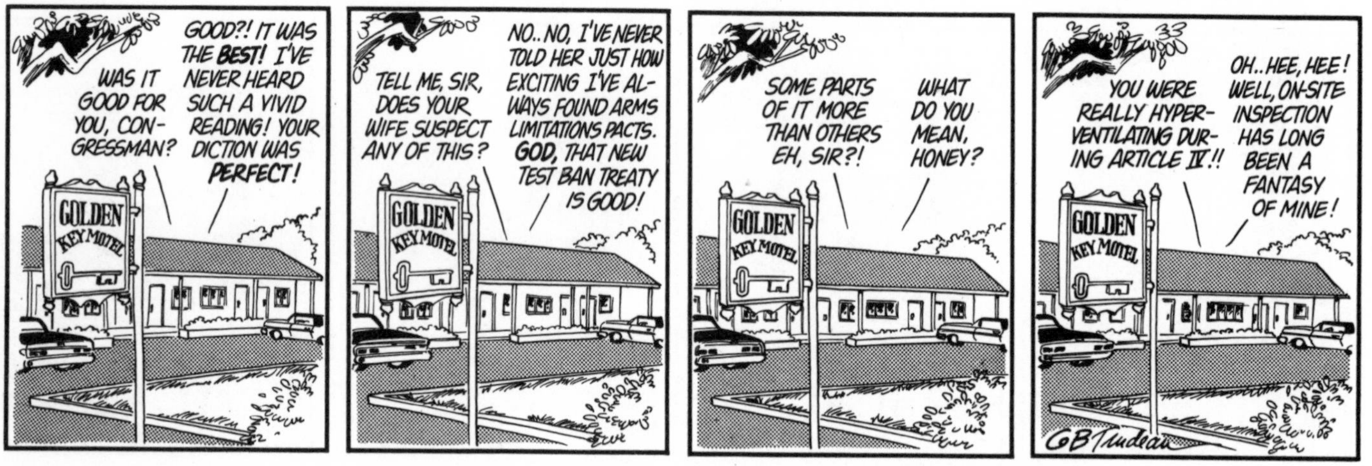
WAS IT GOOD FOR YOU, CONGRESSMAN?
GOOD?! IT WAS THE BEST! I'VE NEVER HEARD SUCH A VIVID READING! YOUR DICTION WAS PERFECT!
GOLDEN KEY MOTEL
TELL ME, SIR, DOES YOUR WIFE SUSPECT ANY OF THIS?
NO.. NO, I'VE NEVER TOLD HER JUST HOW EXCITING I'VE ALWAYS FOUND ARMS LIMITATIONS PACTS. GOD, THAT NEW TEST BAN TREATY IS GOOD!
SOME PARTS OF IT MORE THAN OTHERS EH, SIR?!
WHAT DO YOU MEAN, HONEY?
YOU WERE REALLY HYPERVENTILATING DURING ARTICLE IV!!
OH.. HEE, HEE! WELL, ON-SITE INSPECTION HAS LONG BEEN A FANTASY OF MINE!
GBTrudeau

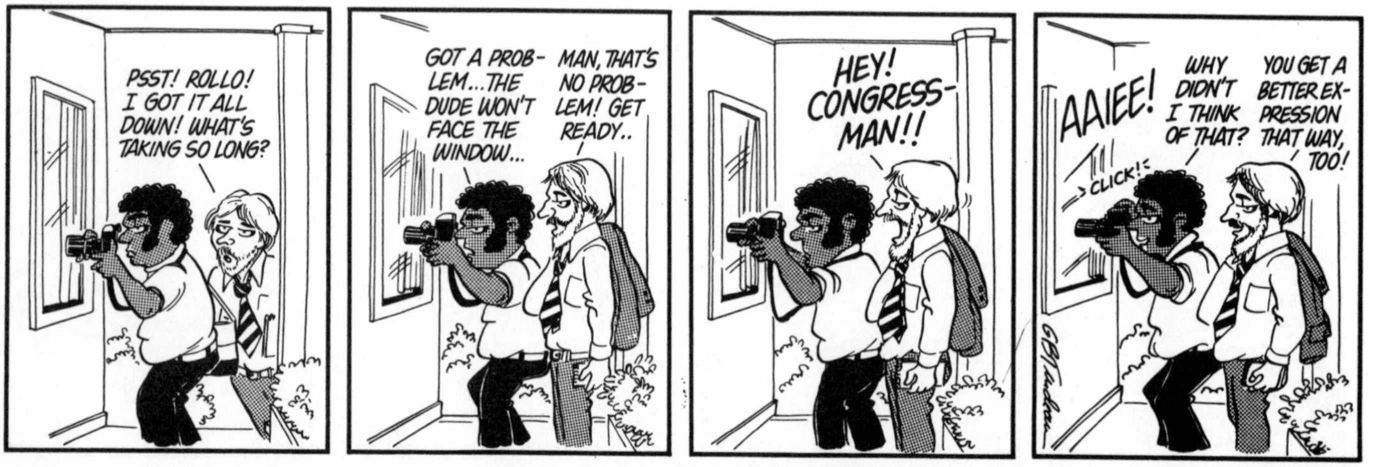
PSST! ROLLO! I GOT IT ALL DOWN! WHAT'S TAKING SO LONG?
GOT A PROBLEM... THE DUDE WON'T FACE THE WINDOW...
MAN, THAT'S NO PROBLEM! GET READY..
HEY! CONGRESSMAN!!
AAIEE!
CLICK!
WHY DIDN'T I THINK OF THAT?
YOU GET A BETTER EXPRESSION THAT WAY, TOO!
GBTrudeau

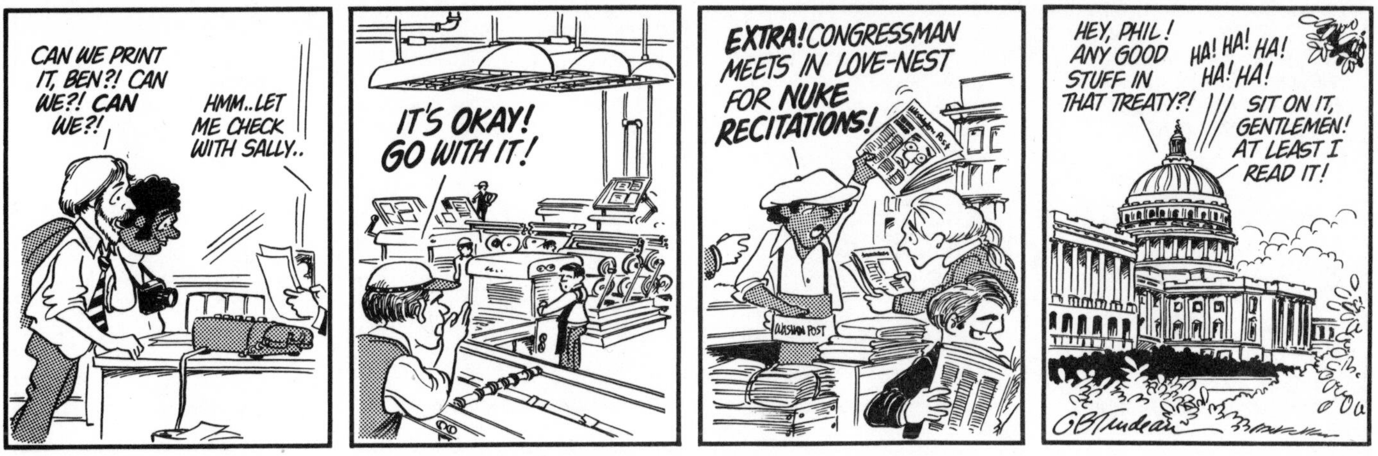
CAN WE PRINT IT, BEN?! CAN WE?! CAN WE?!
HMM..LET ME CHECK WITH SALLY..
IT'S OKAY! GO WITH IT!
EXTRA! CONGRESSMAN MEETS IN LOVE-NEST FOR NUKE RECITATIONS!
WASHINGTON POST
HEY, PHIL! ANY GOOD STUFF IN THAT TREATY?!
HA! HA! HA! HA! HA!
SIT ON IT, GENTLEMEN! AT LEAST I READ IT!
GBTrudeau

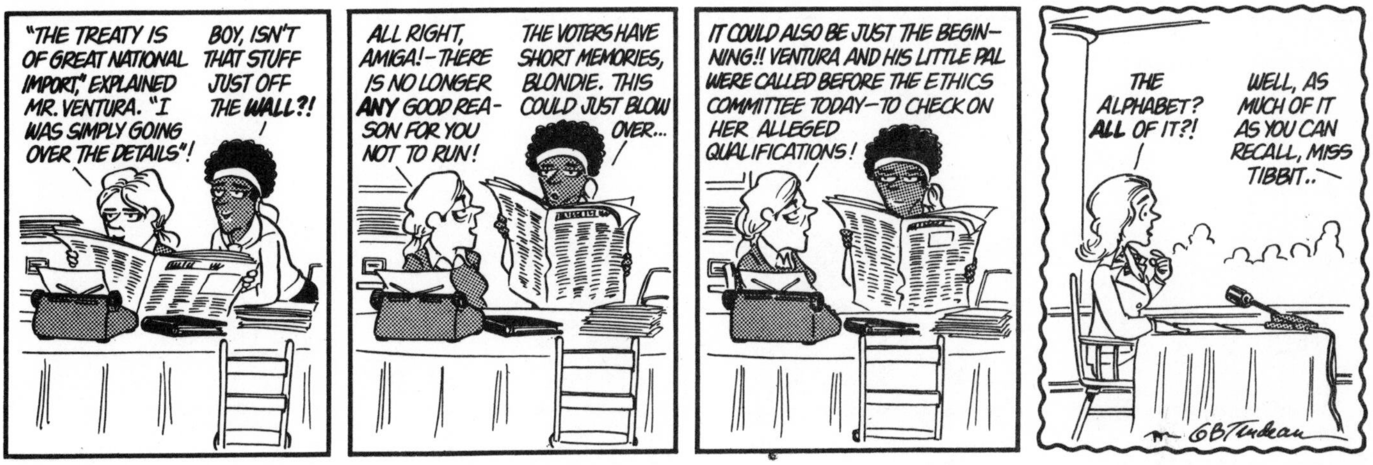
"THE TREATY IS OF GREAT NATIONAL IMPORT," EXPLAINED MR. VENTURA. "I WAS SIMPLY GOING OVER THE DETAILS"!
BOY, ISN'T THAT STUFF JUST OFF THE WALL?!
ALL RIGHT, AMIGA!—THERE IS NO LONGER ANY GOOD REASON FOR YOU NOT TO RUN!
THE VOTERS HAVE SHORT MEMORIES, BLONDIE. THIS COULD JUST BLOW OVER...
IT COULD ALSO BE JUST THE BEGINNING!! VENTURA AND HIS LITTLE PAL WERE CALLED BEFORE THE ETHICS COMMITTEE TODAY—TO CHECK ON HER ALLEGED QUALIFICATIONS!
THE ALPHABET? ALL OF IT?!
WELL, AS MUCH OF IT AS YOU CAN RECALL, MISS TIBBIT..
GBTrudeau

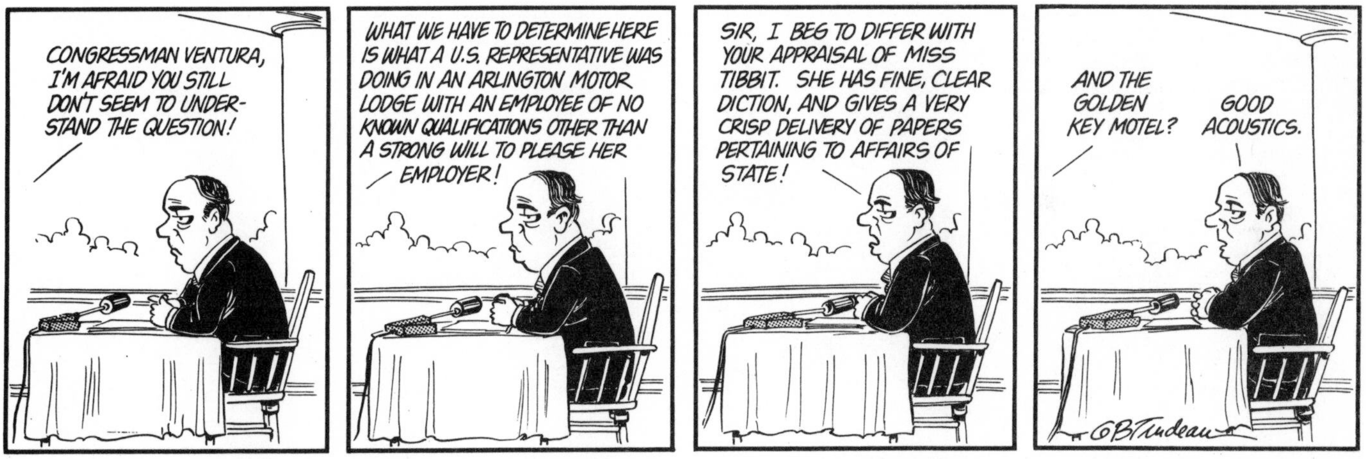
CONGRESSMAN VENTURA, I'M AFRAID YOU STILL DON'T SEEM TO UNDERSTAND THE QUESTION!
WHAT WE HAVE TO DETERMINE HERE IS WHAT A U.S. REPRESENTATIVE WAS DOING IN AN ARLINGTON MOTOR LODGE WITH AN EMPLOYEE OF NO KNOWN QUALIFICATIONS OTHER THAN A STRONG WILL TO PLEASE HER EMPLOYER!
SIR, I BEG TO DIFFER WITH YOUR APPRAISAL OF MISS TIBBIT. SHE HAS FINE, CLEAR DICTION, AND GIVES A VERY CRISP DELIVERY OF PAPERS PERTAINING TO AFFAIRS OF STATE!
AND THE GOLDEN KEY MOTEL?
GOOD ACOUSTICS.
GBTrudeau

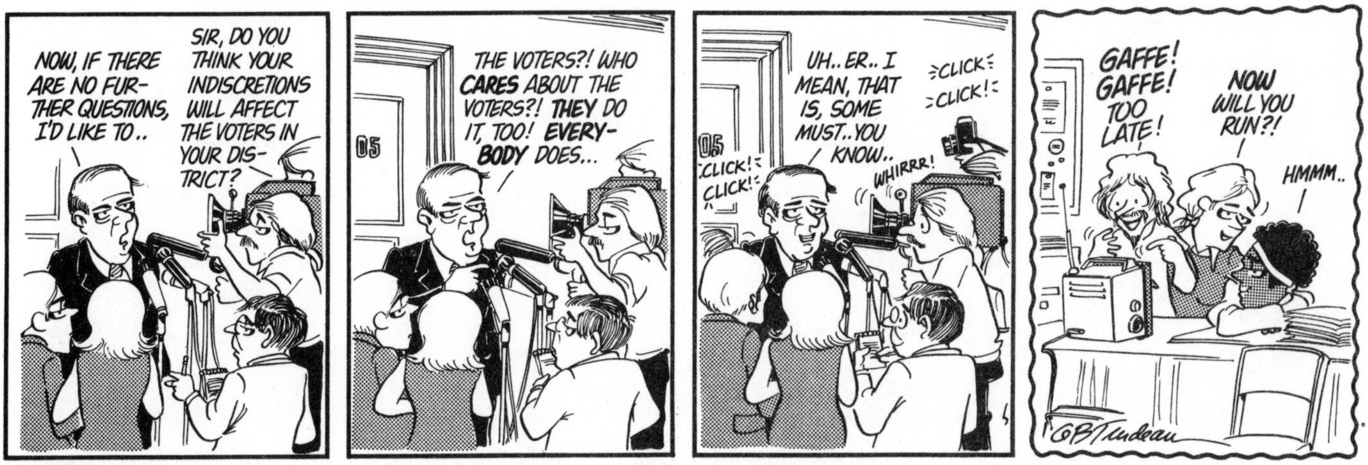
NOW, IF THERE ARE NO FURTHER QUESTIONS, I'D LIKE TO..
SIR, DO YOU THINK YOUR INDISCRETIONS WILL AFFECT THE VOTERS IN YOUR DISTRICT?
THE VOTERS?! WHO CARES ABOUT THE VOTERS?! THEY DO IT, TOO! EVERYBODY DOES...
UH.. ER.. I MEAN, THAT IS, SOME MUST..YOU KNOW..
CLICK! CLICK!
CLICK! CLICK!
WHIRRR!
GAFFE! GAFFE! TOO LATE!
NOW WILL YOU RUN?!
HMMM..
GBTrudeau

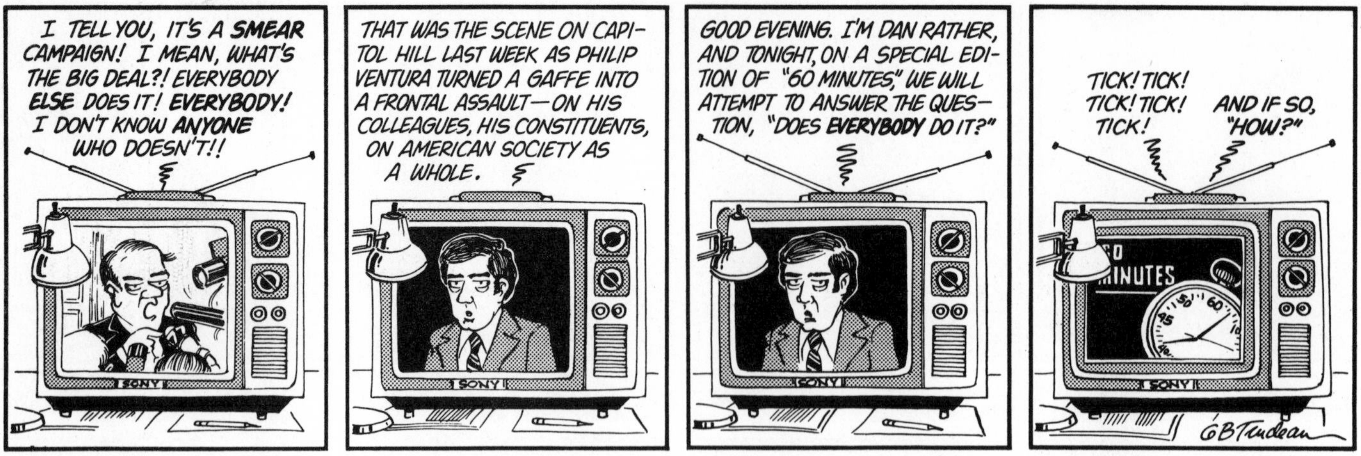
I TELL YOU, IT'S A SMEAR CAMPAIGN! I MEAN, WHAT'S THE BIG DEAL?! EVERYBODY ELSE DOES IT! EVERYBODY! I DON'T KNOW ANYONE WHO DOESN'T!!
SONY
THAT WAS THE SCENE ON CAPITOL HILL LAST WEEK AS PHILIP VENTURA TURNED A GAFFE INTO A FRONTAL ASSAULT—ON HIS COLLEAGUES, HIS CONSTITUENTS, ON AMERICAN SOCIETY AS A WHOLE.
SONY
GOOD EVENING. I'M DAN RATHER, AND TONIGHT, ON A SPECIAL EDITION OF "60 MINUTES," WE WILL ATTEMPT TO ANSWER THE QUESTION, "DOES EVERYBODY DO IT?"
SONY
TICK! TICK! TICK! TICK! TICK!
AND IF SO, "HOW?"
60 MINUTES
SONY
GBTrudeau

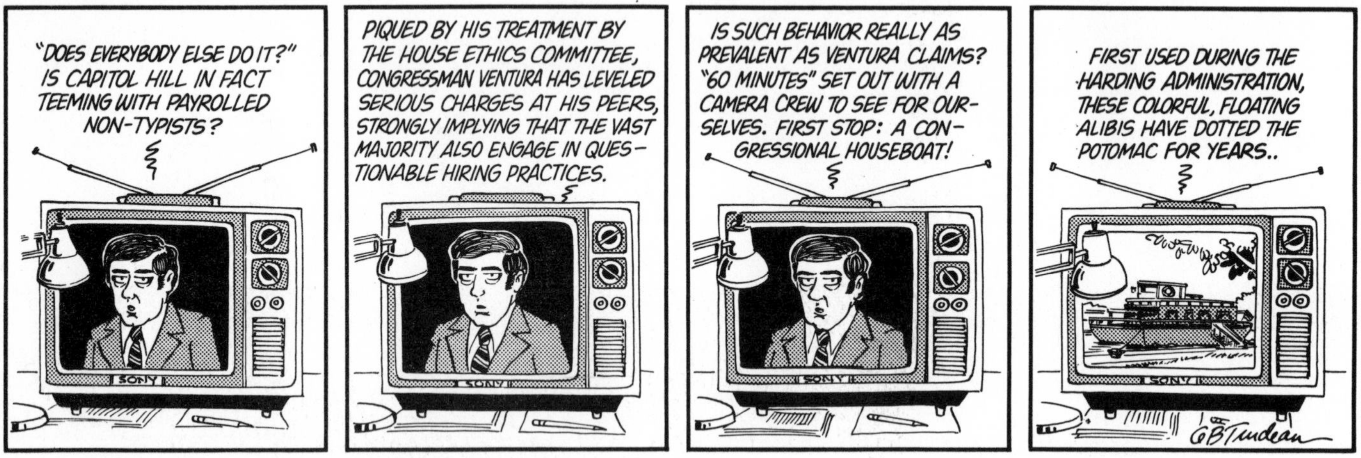
"DOES EVERYBODY ELSE DO IT?" IS CAPITOL HILL IN FACT TEEMING WITH PAYROLLED NON-TYPISTS?
SONY
PIQUED BY HIS TREATMENT BY THE HOUSE ETHICS COMMITTEE, CONGRESSMAN VENTURA HAS LEVELED SERIOUS CHARGES AT HIS PEERS, STRONGLY IMPLYING THAT THE VAST MAJORITY ALSO ENGAGE IN QUESTIONABLE HIRING PRACTICES.
SONY
IS SUCH BEHAVIOR REALLY AS PREVALENT AS VENTURA CLAIMS? "60 MINUTES" SET OUT WITH A CAMERA CREW TO SEE FOR OURSELVES. FIRST STOP: A CONGRESSIONAL HOUSEBOAT!
SONY
FIRST USED DURING THE HARDING ADMINISTRATION, THESE COLORFUL, FLOATING ALIBIS HAVE DOTTED THE POTOMAC FOR YEARS..
SONY
GBTrudeau

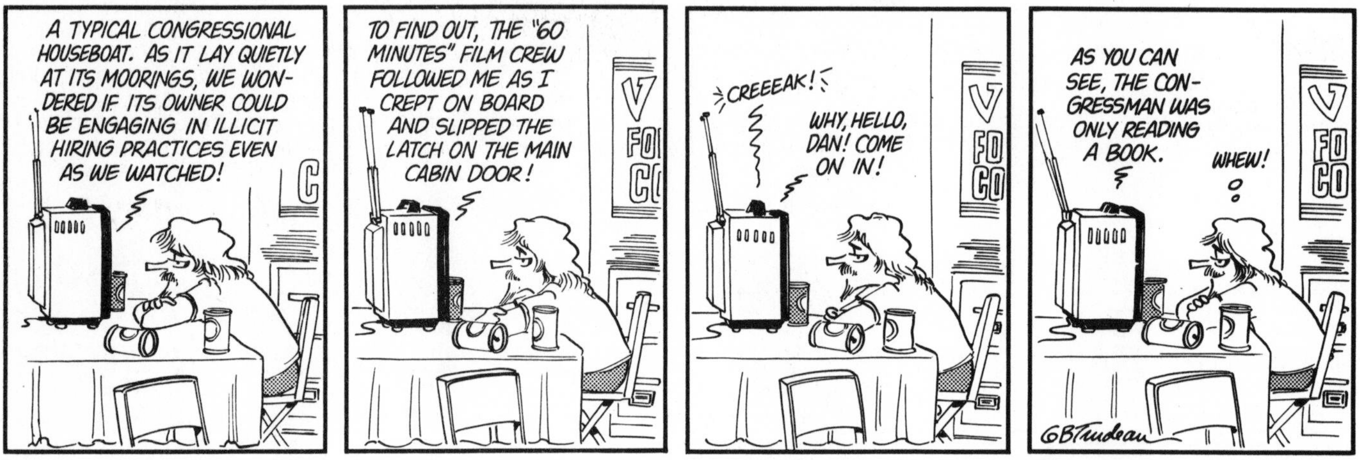
A TYPICAL CONGRESSIONAL HOUSEBOAT. AS IT LAY QUIETLY AT ITS MOORINGS, WE WONDERED IF ITS OWNER COULD BE ENGAGING IN ILLICIT HIRING PRACTICES EVEN AS WE WATCHED!
TO FIND OUT, THE "60 MINUTES" FILM CREW FOLLOWED ME AS I CREPT ON BOARD AND SLIPPED THE LATCH ON THE MAIN CABIN DOOR!
CREEEAK!
WHY, HELLO, DAN! COME ON IN!
AS YOU CAN SEE, THE CONGRESSMAN WAS ONLY READING A BOOK.
WHEW!
GBTrudeau

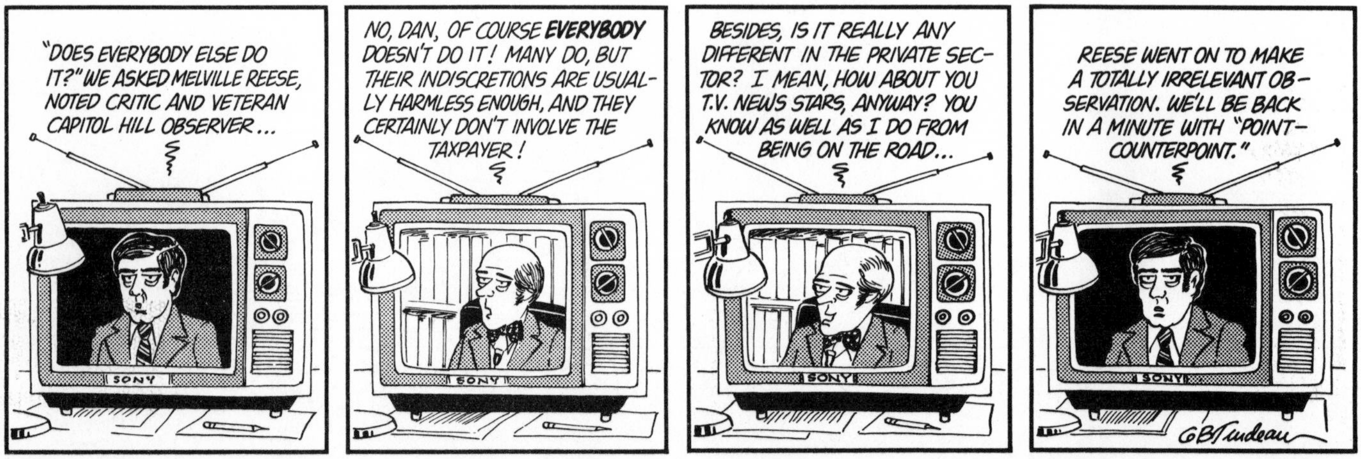
"DOES EVERYBODY ELSE DO IT?" WE ASKED MELVILLE REESE, NOTED CRITIC AND VETERAN CAPITOL HILL OBSERVER...
SONY
NO, DAN, OF COURSE EVERYBODY DOESN'T DO IT! MANY DO, BUT THEIR INDISCRETIONS ARE USUALLY HARMLESS ENOUGH, AND THEY CERTAINLY DON'T INVOLVE THE TAXPAYER!
SONY
BESIDES, IS IT REALLY ANY DIFFERENT IN THE PRIVATE SECTOR? I MEAN, HOW ABOUT YOU T.V. NEWS STARS, ANYWAY? YOU KNOW AS WELL AS I DO FROM BEING ON THE ROAD...
SONY
REESE WENT ON TO MAKE A TOTALLY IRRELEVANT OBSERVATION. WE'LL BE BACK IN A MINUTE WITH "POINT-COUNTERPOINT."
SONY
GBTrudeau

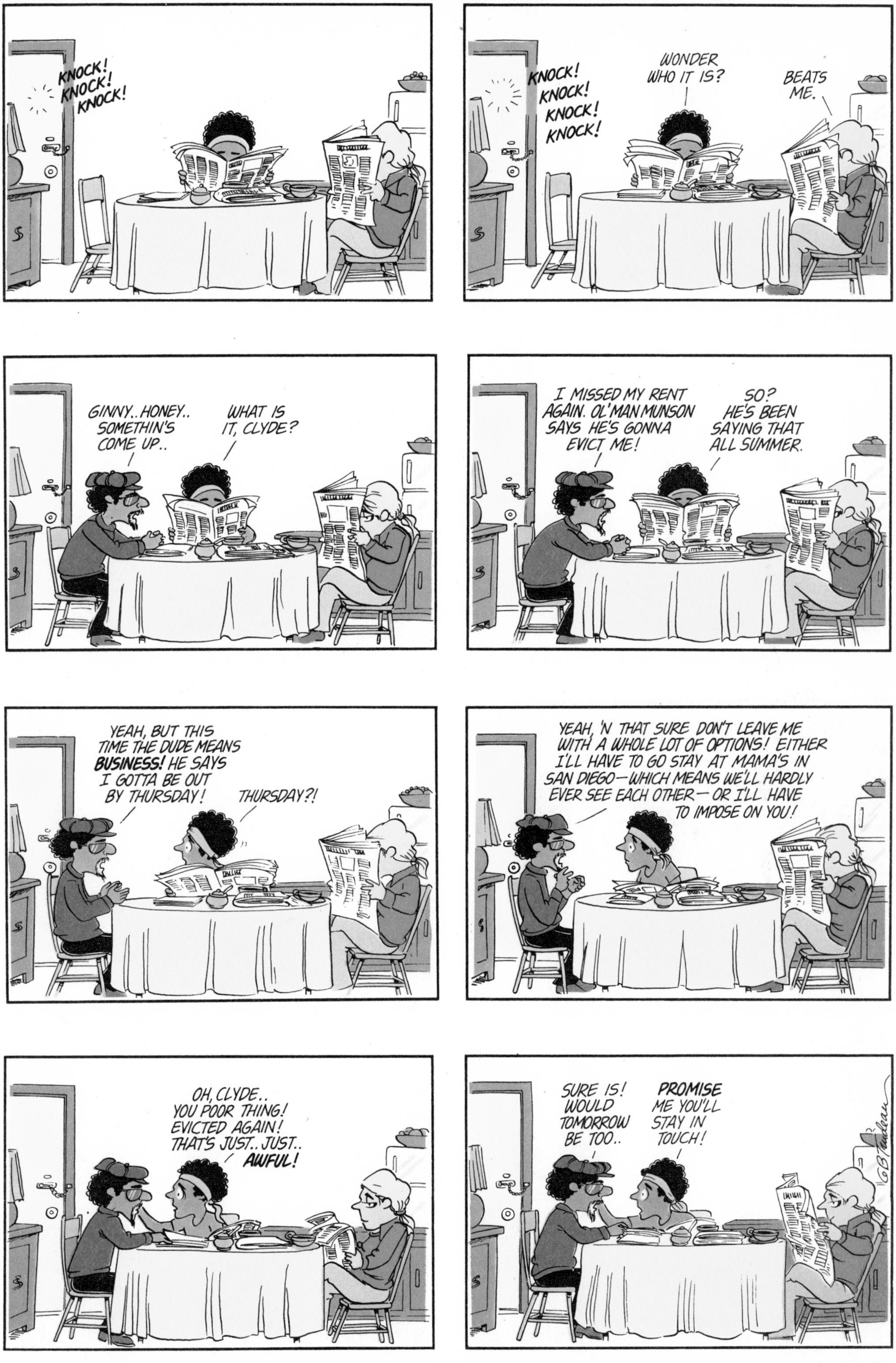
KNOCK! KNOCK! KNOCK!
KNOCK! KNOCK! KNOCK! KNOCK!
WONDER WHO IT IS?
BEATS ME.
GINNY.. HONEY.. SOMETHIN'S COME UP..
WHAT IS IT, CLYDE?
I MISSED MY RENT AGAIN. OL' MAN MUNSON SAYS HE'S GONNA EVICT ME!
SO? HE'S BEEN SAYING THAT ALL SUMMER.
YEAH, BUT THIS TIME THE DUDE MEANS BUSINESS! HE SAYS I GOTTA BE OUT BY THURSDAY!
THURSDAY?!
YEAH, 'N THAT SURE DON'T LEAVE ME WITH A WHOLE LOT OF OPTIONS! EITHER I'LL HAVE TO GO STAY AT MAMA'S IN SAN DIEGO—WHICH MEANS WE'LL HARDLY EVER SEE EACH OTHER—OR I'LL HAVE TO IMPOSE ON YOU!
OH, CLYDE.. YOU POOR THING! EVICTED AGAIN! THAT'S JUST.. JUST.. AWFUL!
SURE IS! WOULD TOMORROW BE TOO..
PROMISE ME YOU'LL STAY IN TOUCH!

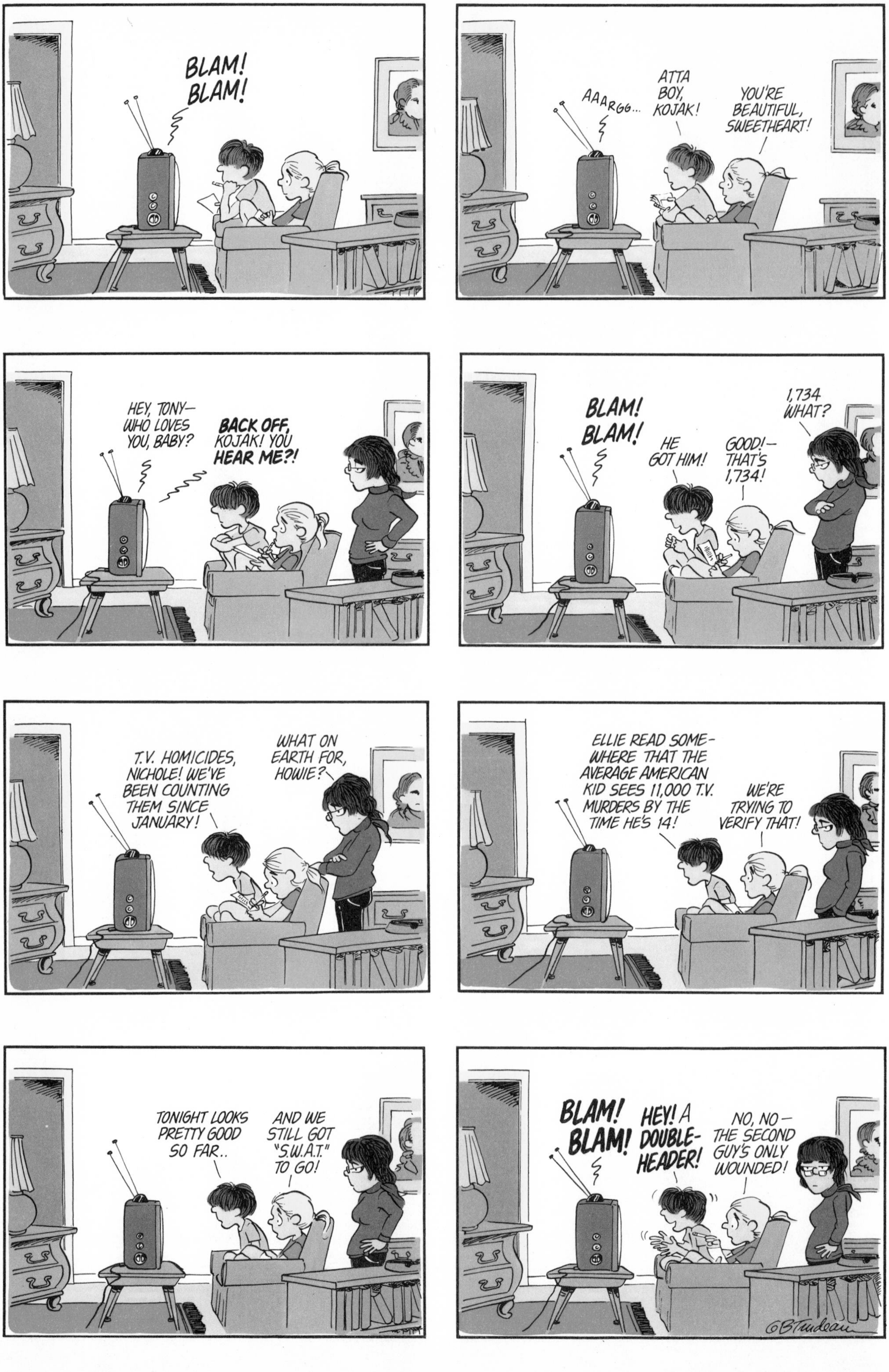
BLAM! BLAM!
AAARGG...
ATTA BOY, KOJAK!
YOU'RE BEAUTIFUL, SWEETHEART!
HEY, TONY— WHO LOVES YOU, BABY?
BACK OFF, KOJAK! YOU HEAR ME?!
BLAM! BLAM!
HE GOT HIM!
GOOD!— THAT'S 1,734!
1,734 WHAT?
T.V. HOMICIDES, NICHOLE! WE'VE BEEN COUNTING THEM SINCE JANUARY!
WHAT ON EARTH FOR, HOWIE?
ELLIE READ SOME-WHERE THAT THE AVERAGE AMERICAN KID SEES 11,000 T.V. MURDERS BY THE TIME HE'S 14!
WE'RE TRYING TO VERIFY THAT!
TONIGHT LOOKS PRETTY GOOD SO FAR..
AND WE STILL GOT "S.W.A.T." TO GO!
BLAM! BLAM!
HEY! A DOUBLE-HEADER!
NO, NO— THE SECOND GUY'S ONLY WOUNDED!
GBTrudeau

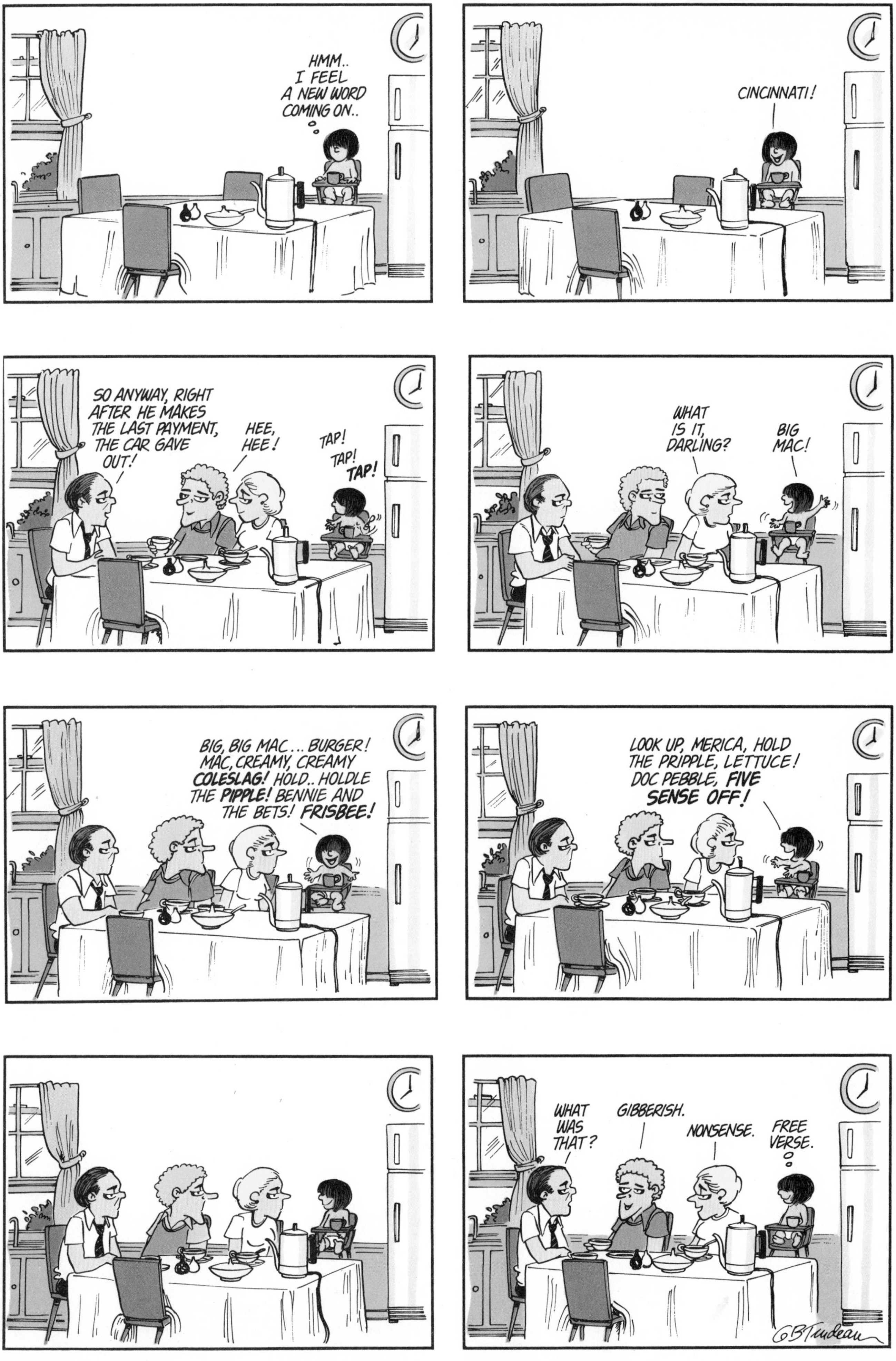
HMM.. I FEEL A NEW WORD COMING ON..
CINCINNATI!
SO ANYWAY, RIGHT AFTER HE MAKES THE LAST PAYMENT, THE CAR GAVE OUT!
HEE, HEE!
TAP! TAP! TAP!
WHAT IS IT, DARLING?
BIG MAC!
BIG, BIG MAC... BURGER! MAC, CREAMY, CREAMY COLESLAG! HOLD.. HOLDLE THE PIPPLE! BENNIE AND THE BETS! FRISBEE!
LOOK UP, MERICA, HOLD THE PRIPPLE, LETTUCE! DOC PEBBLE, FIVE SENSE OFF!
WHAT WAS THAT?
GIBBERISH.
NONSENSE.
FREE VERSE.
G B Trudeau

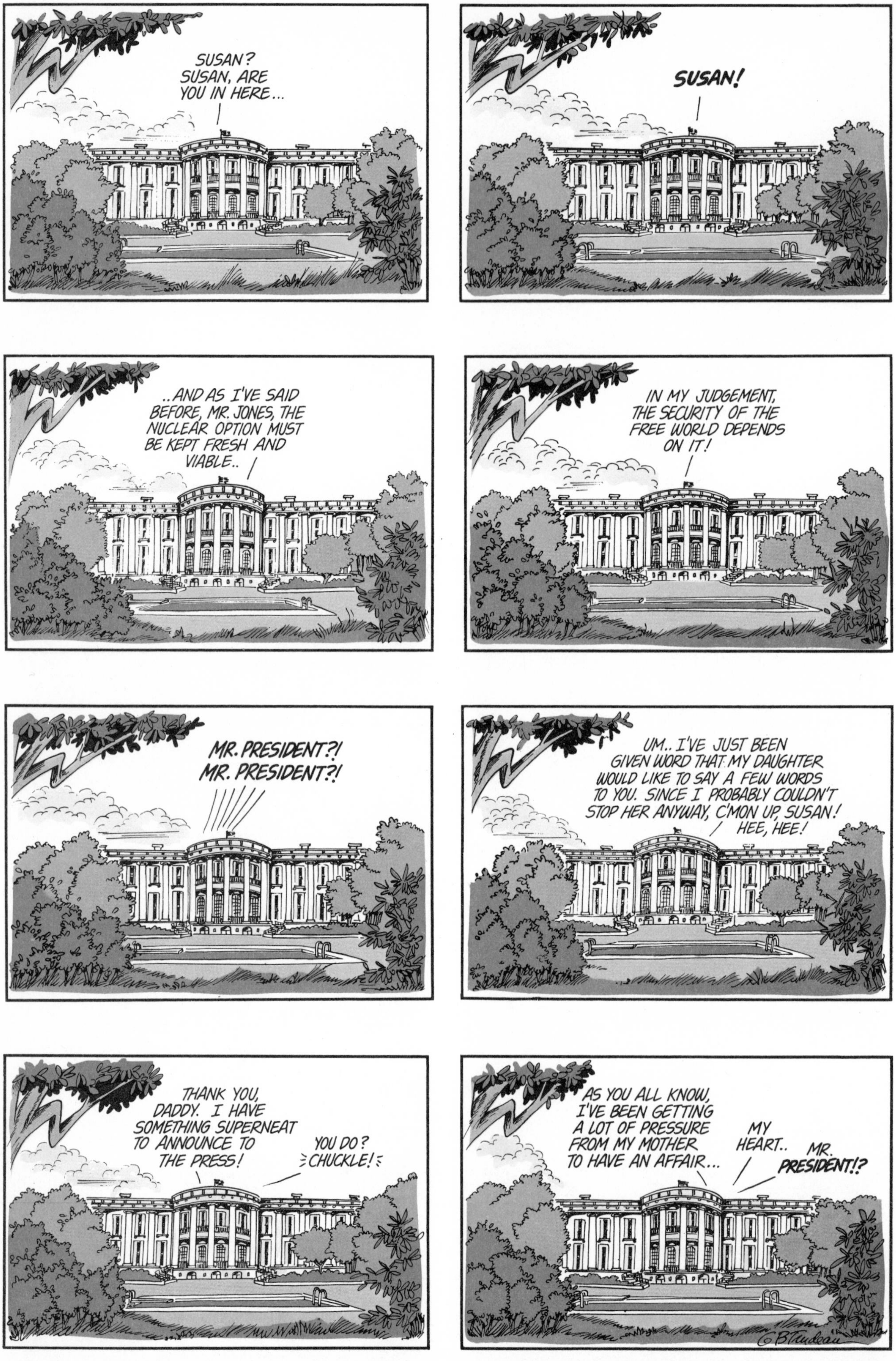
SUSAN? SUSAN, ARE YOU IN HERE...
SUSAN!
..AND AS I'VE SAID BEFORE, MR. JONES, THE NUCLEAR OPTION MUST BE KEPT FRESH AND VIABLE..
IN MY JUDGEMENT, THE SECURITY OF THE FREE WORLD DEPENDS ON IT!
MR. PRESIDENT?! MR. PRESIDENT?!
UM.. I'VE JUST BEEN GIVEN WORD THAT MY DAUGHTER WOULD LIKE TO SAY A FEW WORDS TO YOU. SINCE I PROBABLY COULDN'T STOP HER ANYWAY, C'MON UP, SUSAN!
HEE, HEE!
THANK YOU, DADDY. I HAVE SOMETHING SUPERNEAT TO ANNOUNCE TO THE PRESS!
YOU DO? CHUCKLE!
AS YOU ALL KNOW, I'VE BEEN GETTING A LOT OF PRESSURE FROM MY MOTHER TO HAVE AN AFFAIR...
MY HEART..
MR. PRESIDENT!?
© GBTrudeau

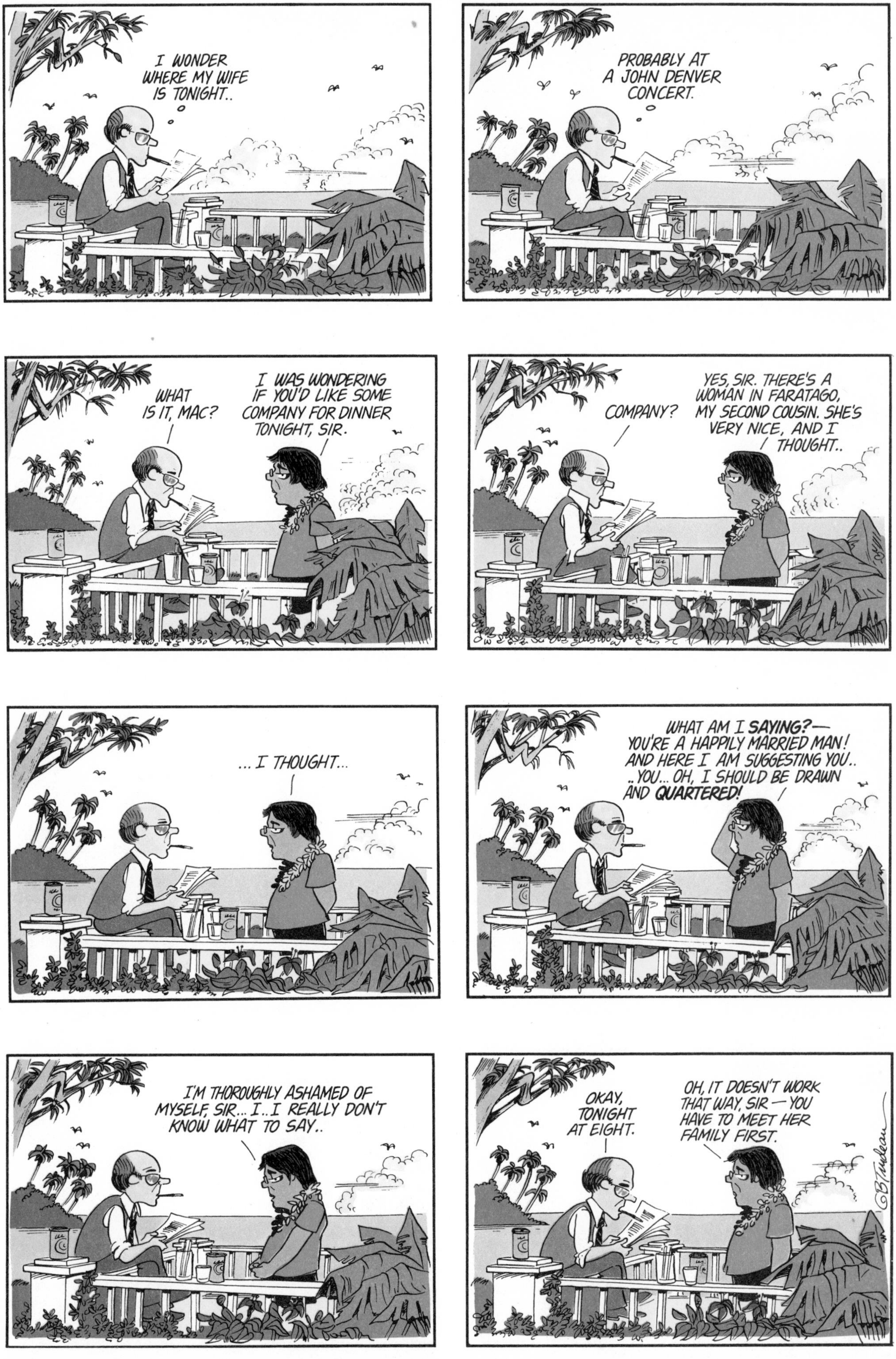
I WONDER WHERE MY WIFE IS TONIGHT..
PROBABLY AT A JOHN DENVER CONCERT.
WHAT IS IT, MAC?
I WAS WONDERING IF YOU'D LIKE SOME COMPANY FOR DINNER TONIGHT, SIR.
COMPANY?
YES, SIR. THERE'S A WOMAN IN FARATAGO, MY SECOND COUSIN. SHE'S VERY NICE, AND I THOUGHT..
... I THOUGHT...
WHAT AM I SAYING?— YOU'RE A HAPPILY MARRIED MAN! AND HERE I AM SUGGESTING YOU.. ..YOU... OH, I SHOULD BE DRAWN AND QUARTERED!
I'M THOROUGHLY ASHAMED OF MYSELF, SIR... I..I REALLY DON'T KNOW WHAT TO SAY..
OKAY, TONIGHT AT EIGHT.
OH, IT DOESN'T WORK THAT WAY, SIR — YOU HAVE TO MEET HER FAMILY FIRST.
©B Trudeau

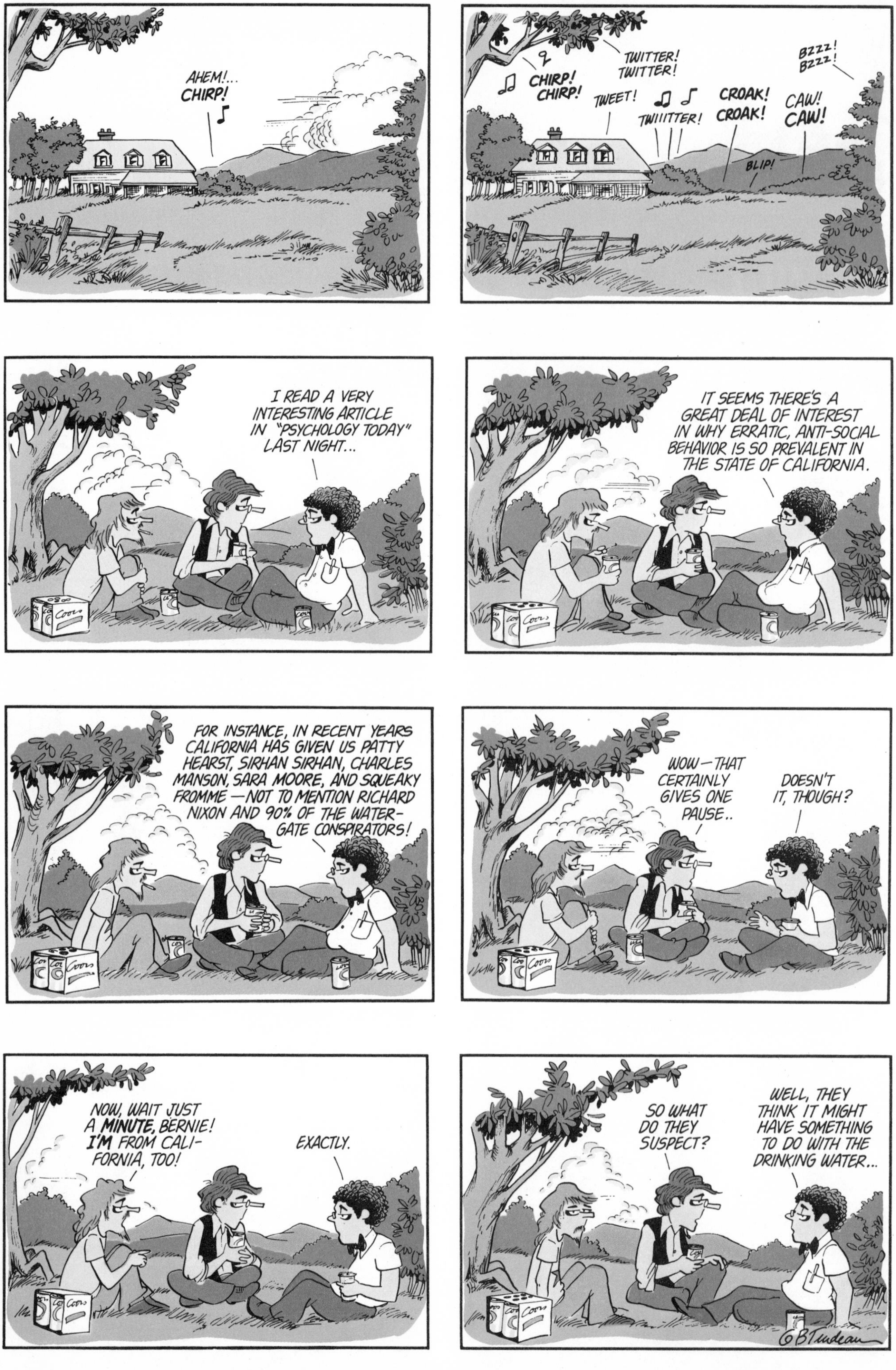
AHEM!... CHIRP!
CHIRP! CHIRP!
TWITTER! TWITTER!
TWEET!
TWIIIITTER!
CROAK! CROAK!
CAW! CAW!
BZZZ! BZZZ!
BLIP!
I READ A VERY INTERESTING ARTICLE IN "PSYCHOLOGY TODAY" LAST NIGHT...
IT SEEMS THERE'S A GREAT DEAL OF INTEREST IN WHY ERRATIC, ANTI-SOCIAL BEHAVIOR IS SO PREVALENT IN THE STATE OF CALIFORNIA.
FOR INSTANCE, IN RECENT YEARS CALIFORNIA HAS GIVEN US PATTY HEARST, SIRHAN SIRHAN, CHARLES MANSON, SARA MOORE, AND SQUEAKY FROMME—NOT TO MENTION RICHARD NIXON AND 90% OF THE WATER-GATE CONSPIRATORS!
WOW—THAT CERTAINLY GIVES ONE PAUSE..
DOESN'T IT, THOUGH?
NOW, WAIT JUST A MINUTE, BERNIE! I'M FROM CALI-FORNIA, TOO!
EXACTLY.
SO WHAT DO THEY SUSPECT?
WELL, THEY THINK IT MIGHT HAVE SOMETHING TO DO WITH THE DRINKING WATER...
GBTrudeau

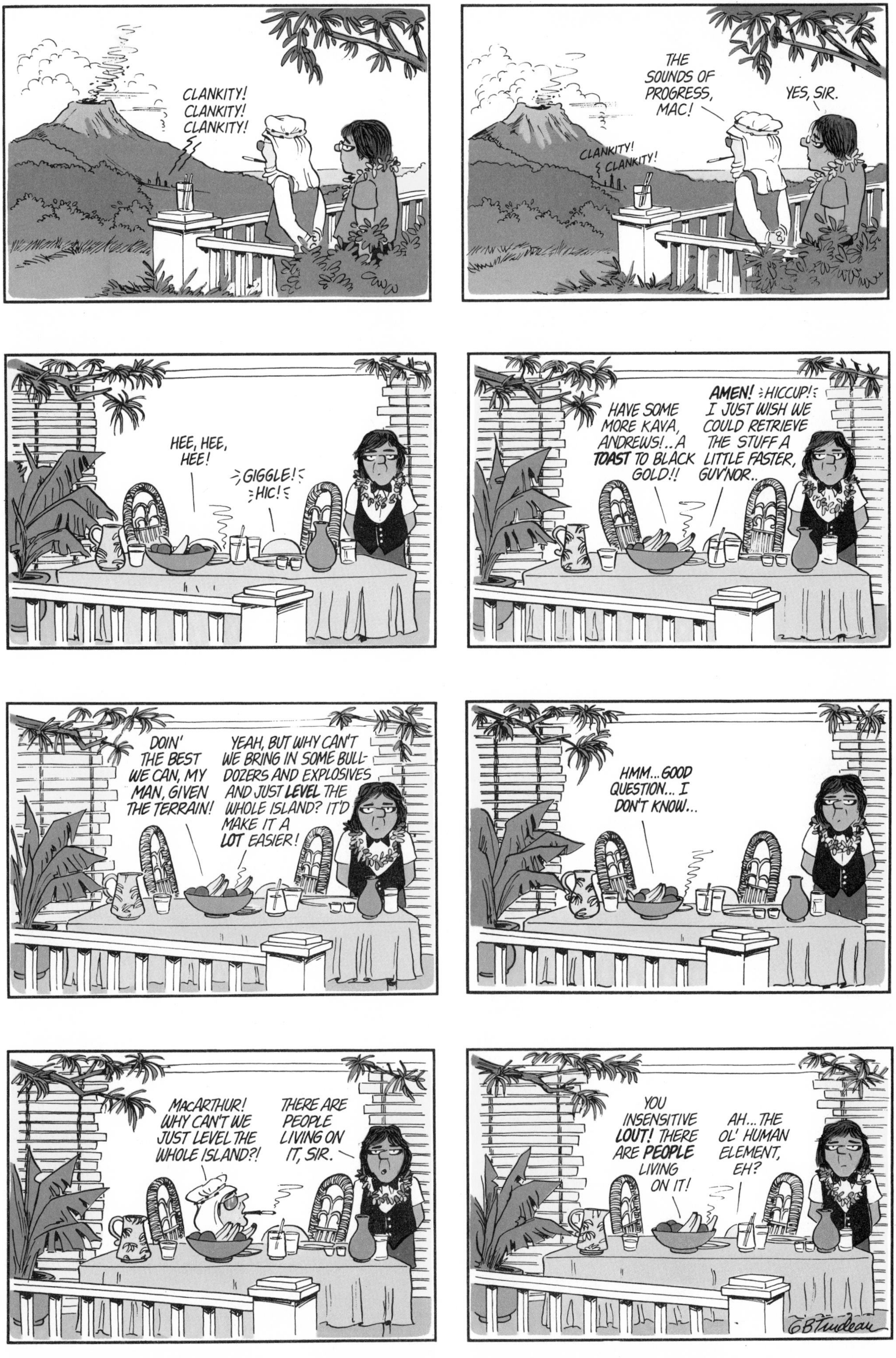
CLANKITY! CLANKITY! CLANKITY!
THE SOUNDS OF PROGRESS, MAC!
YES, SIR.
CLANKITY! CLANKITY!
HEE, HEE, HEE!
GIGGLE! HIC!
HAVE SOME MORE KAVA, ANDREWS!.. A TOAST TO BLACK GOLD!!
AMEN! HICCUP! I JUST WISH WE COULD RETRIEVE THE STUFF A LITTLE FASTER, GUV'NOR..
DOIN' THE BEST WE CAN, MY MAN, GIVEN THE TERRAIN!
YEAH, BUT WHY CAN'T WE BRING IN SOME BULL-DOZERS AND EXPLOSIVES AND JUST LEVEL THE WHOLE ISLAND? IT'D MAKE IT A LOT EASIER!
HMM... GOOD QUESTION... I DON'T KNOW...
MacARTHUR! WHY CAN'T WE JUST LEVEL THE WHOLE ISLAND?!
THERE ARE PEOPLE LIVING ON IT, SIR.
YOU INSENSITIVE LOUT! THERE ARE PEOPLE LIVING ON IT!
AH... THE OL' HUMAN ELEMENT, EH?
GBTrudeau

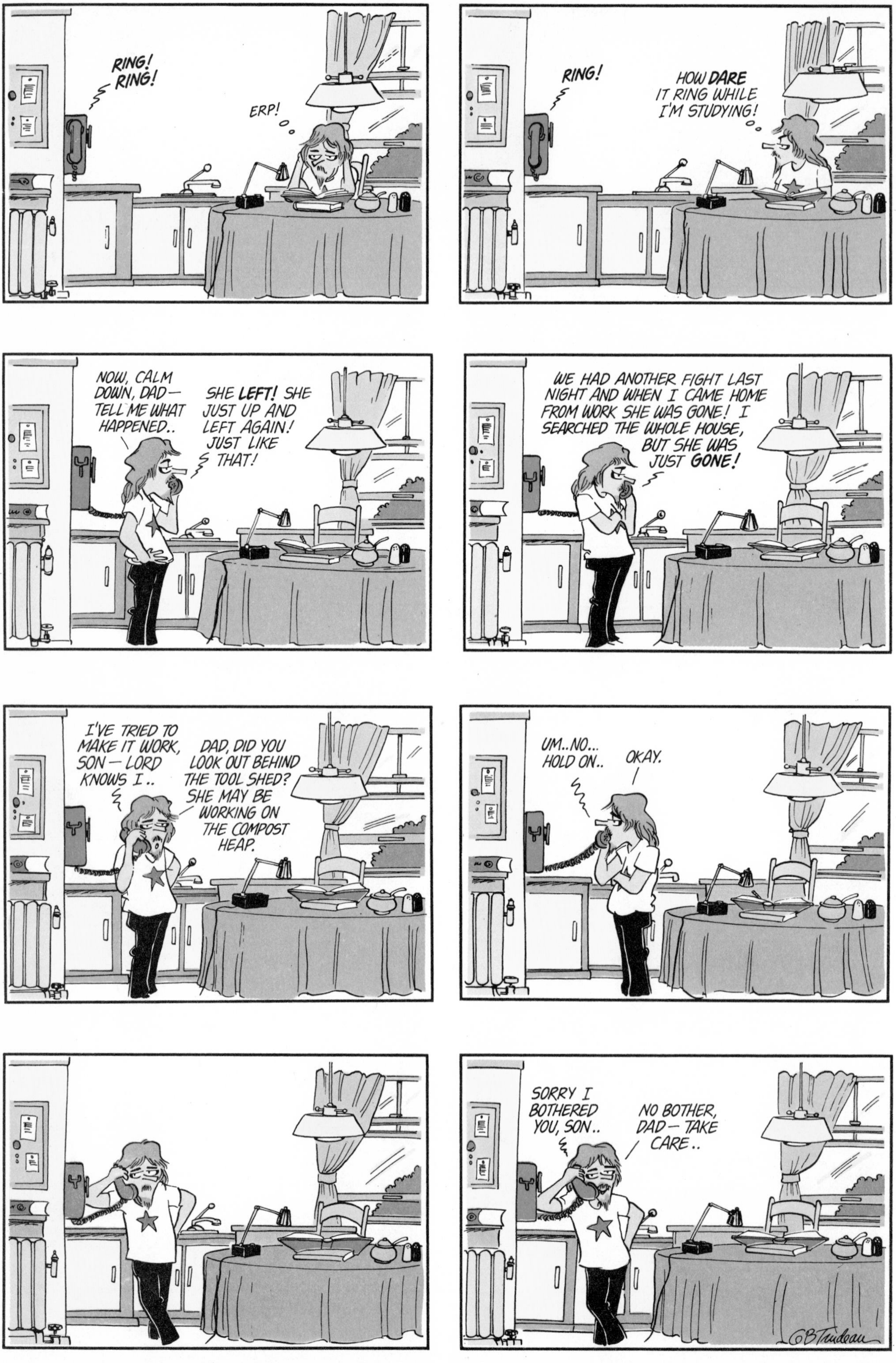
RING! RING!
ERP!
RING!
HOW DARE IT RING WHILE I'M STUDYING!
NOW, CALM DOWN, DAD— TELL ME WHAT HAPPENED..
SHE LEFT! SHE JUST UP AND LEFT AGAIN! JUST LIKE THAT!
WE HAD ANOTHER FIGHT LAST NIGHT AND WHEN I CAME HOME FROM WORK SHE WAS GONE! I SEARCHED THE WHOLE HOUSE, BUT SHE WAS JUST GONE!
I'VE TRIED TO MAKE IT WORK, SON— LORD KNOWS I..
DAD, DID YOU LOOK OUT BEHIND THE TOOL SHED? SHE MAY BE WORKING ON THE COMPOST HEAP.
UM..NO... HOLD ON..
OKAY.
SORRY I BOTHERED YOU, SON..
NO BOTHER, DAD— TAKE CARE..
©GBTrudeau

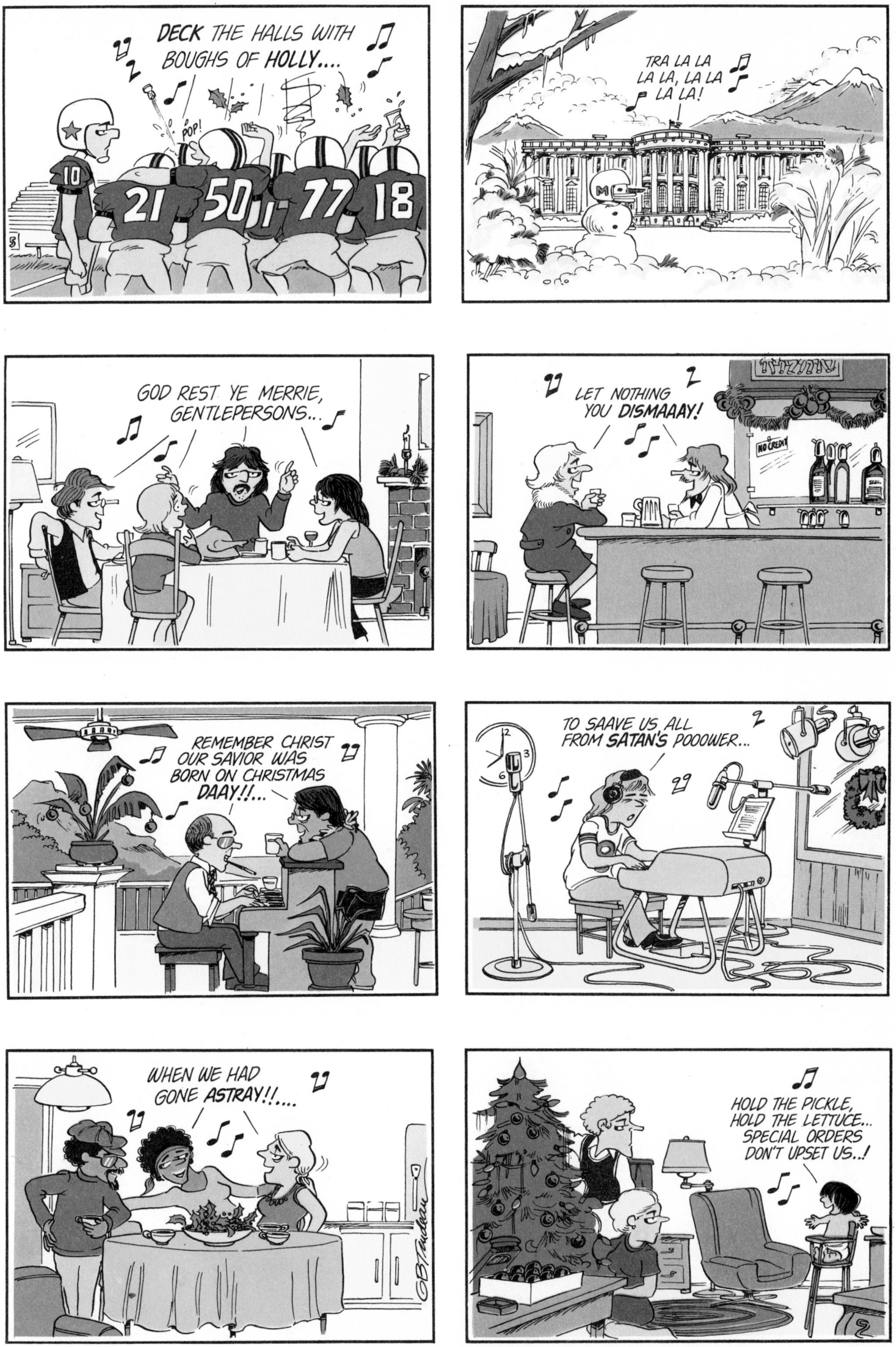
DECK THE HALLS WITH BOUGHS OF HOLLY....
POP!
TRA LA LA LA LA, LA LA LA LA!
GOD REST YE MERRIE, GENTLEPERSONS...
LET NOTHING YOU DISMAAAY!
NO CREDIT
REMEMBER CHRIST OUR SAVIOR WAS BORN ON CHRISTMAS DAAY!!...
TO SAAVE US ALL FROM SATAN'S POOOWER...
WHEN WE HAD GONE ASTRAY!!....
HOLD THE PICKLE, HOLD THE LETTUCE... SPECIAL ORDERS DON'T UPSET US..!

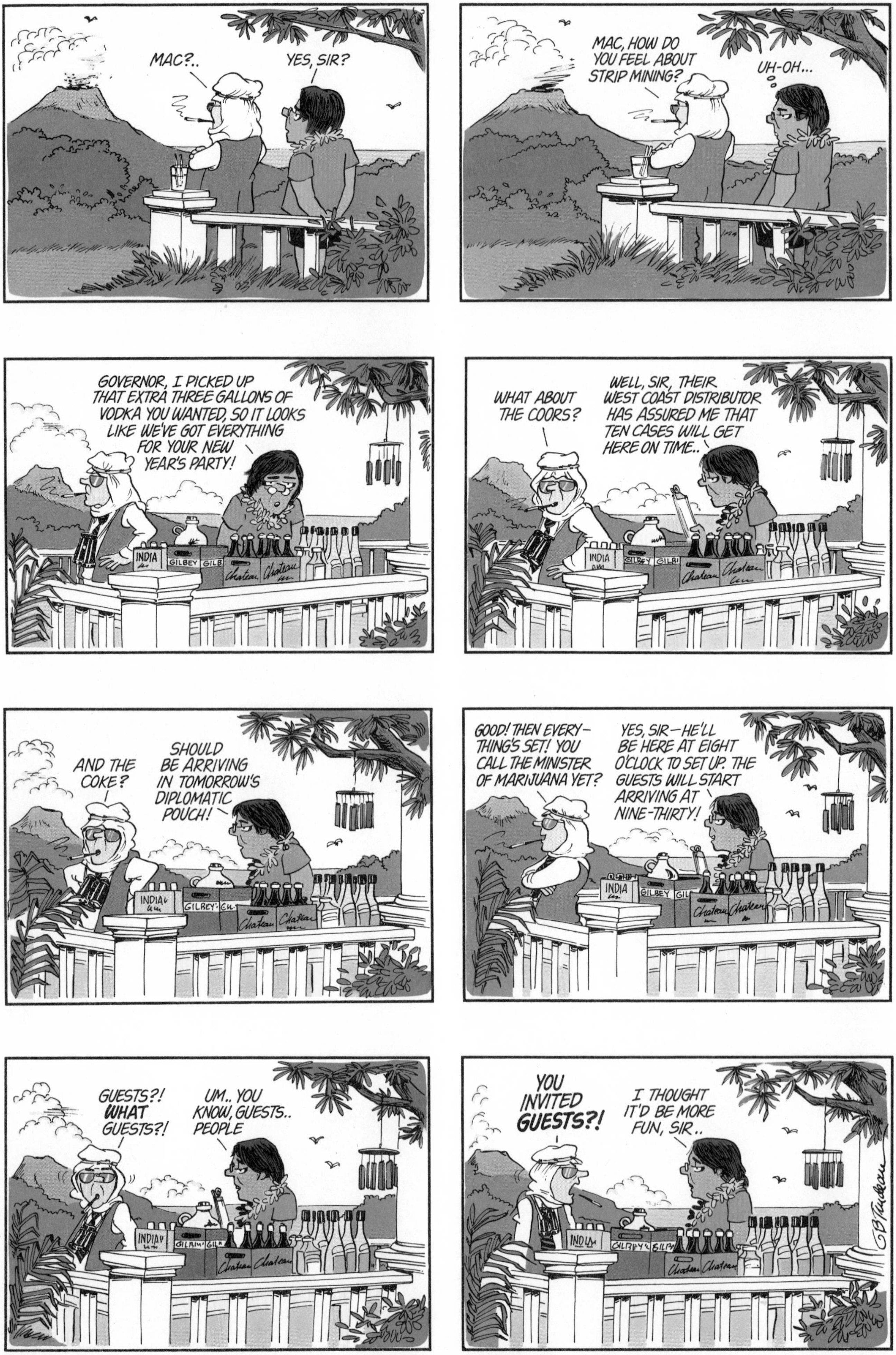
MAC?..
YES, SIR?
MAC, HOW DO YOU FEEL ABOUT STRIP MINING?
UH-OH...
GOVERNOR, I PICKED UP THAT EXTRA THREE GALLONS OF VODKA YOU WANTED, SO IT LOOKS LIKE WE'VE GOT EVERYTHING FOR YOUR NEW YEAR'S PARTY!
WHAT ABOUT THE COORS?
WELL, SIR, THEIR WEST COAST DISTRIBUTOR HAS ASSURED ME THAT TEN CASES WILL GET HERE ON TIME..
AND THE COKE?
SHOULD BE ARRIVING IN TOMORROW'S DIPLOMATIC POUCH!
GOOD! THEN EVERYTHING'S SET! YOU CALL THE MINISTER OF MARIJUANA YET?
YES, SIR—HE'LL BE HERE AT EIGHT O'CLOCK TO SET UP. THE GUESTS WILL START ARRIVING AT NINE-THIRTY!
GUESTS?! WHAT GUESTS?!
UM.. YOU KNOW, GUESTS.. PEOPLE
YOU INVITED GUESTS?!
I THOUGHT IT'D BE MORE FUN, SIR..
GBTrudeau

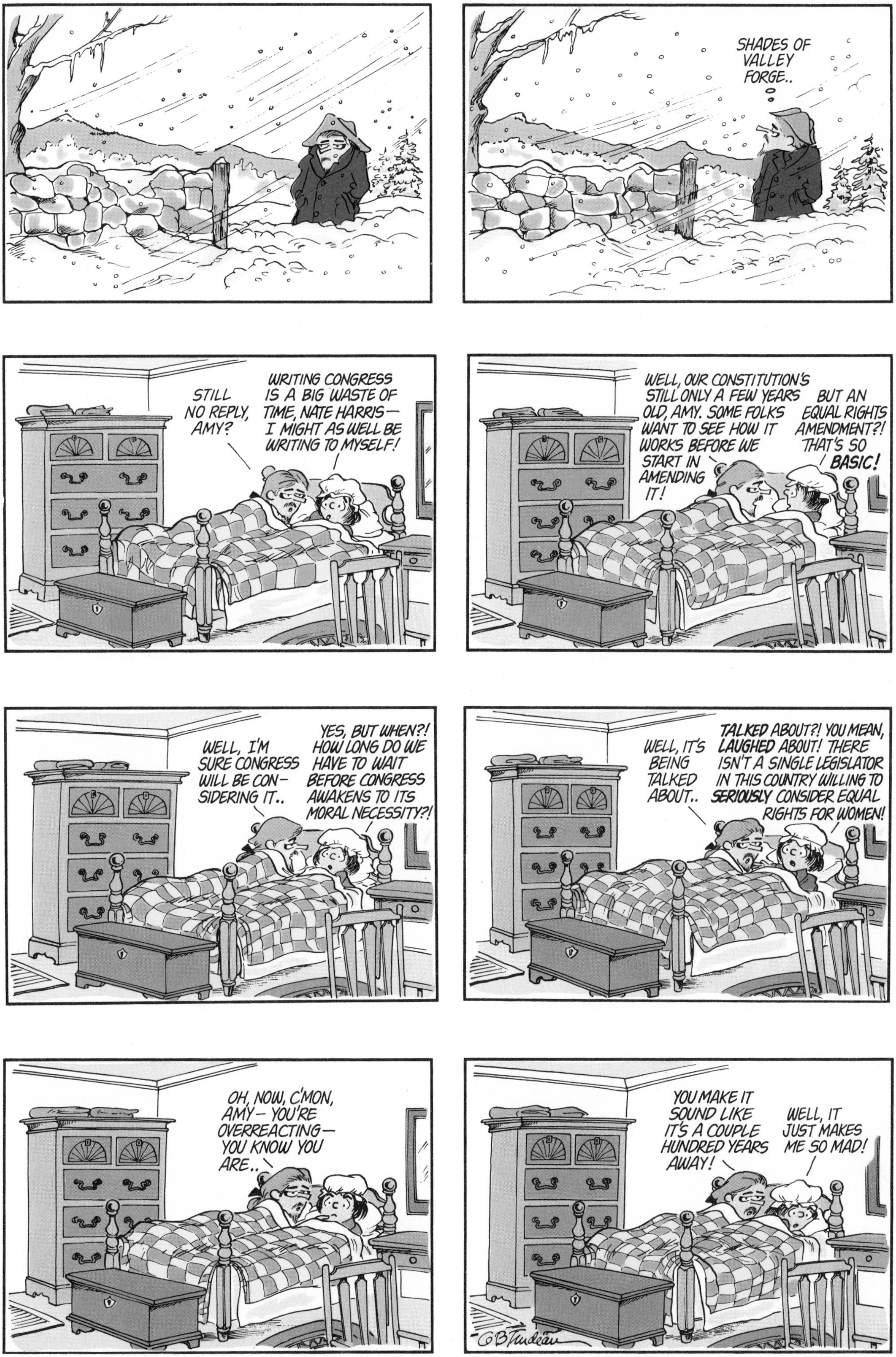
SHADES OF VALLEY FORGE..
STILL NO REPLY, AMY?
WRITING CONGRESS IS A BIG WASTE OF TIME, NATE HARRIS— I MIGHT AS WELL BE WRITING TO MYSELF!
WELL, OUR CONSTITUTION'S STILL ONLY A FEW YEARS OLD, AMY. SOME FOLKS WANT TO SEE HOW IT WORKS BEFORE WE START IN AMENDING IT!
BUT AN EQUAL RIGHTS AMENDMENT?! THAT'S SO **BASIC!**
WELL, I'M SURE CONGRESS WILL BE CON-SIDERING IT..
YES, BUT WHEN?! HOW LONG DO WE HAVE TO WAIT BEFORE CONGRESS AWAKENS TO ITS MORAL NECESSITY?!
WELL, IT'S BEING TALKED ABOUT..
TALKED ABOUT?! YOU MEAN, **LAUGHED** ABOUT! THERE ISN'T A SINGLE LEGISLATOR IN THIS COUNTRY WILLING TO **SERIOUSLY** CONSIDER EQUAL RIGHTS FOR WOMEN!
OH, NOW, C'MON, AMY— YOU'RE OVERREACTING— YOU KNOW YOU ARE..
YOU MAKE IT SOUND LIKE IT'S A COUPLE HUNDRED YEARS AWAY!
WELL, IT JUST MAKES ME SO MAD!

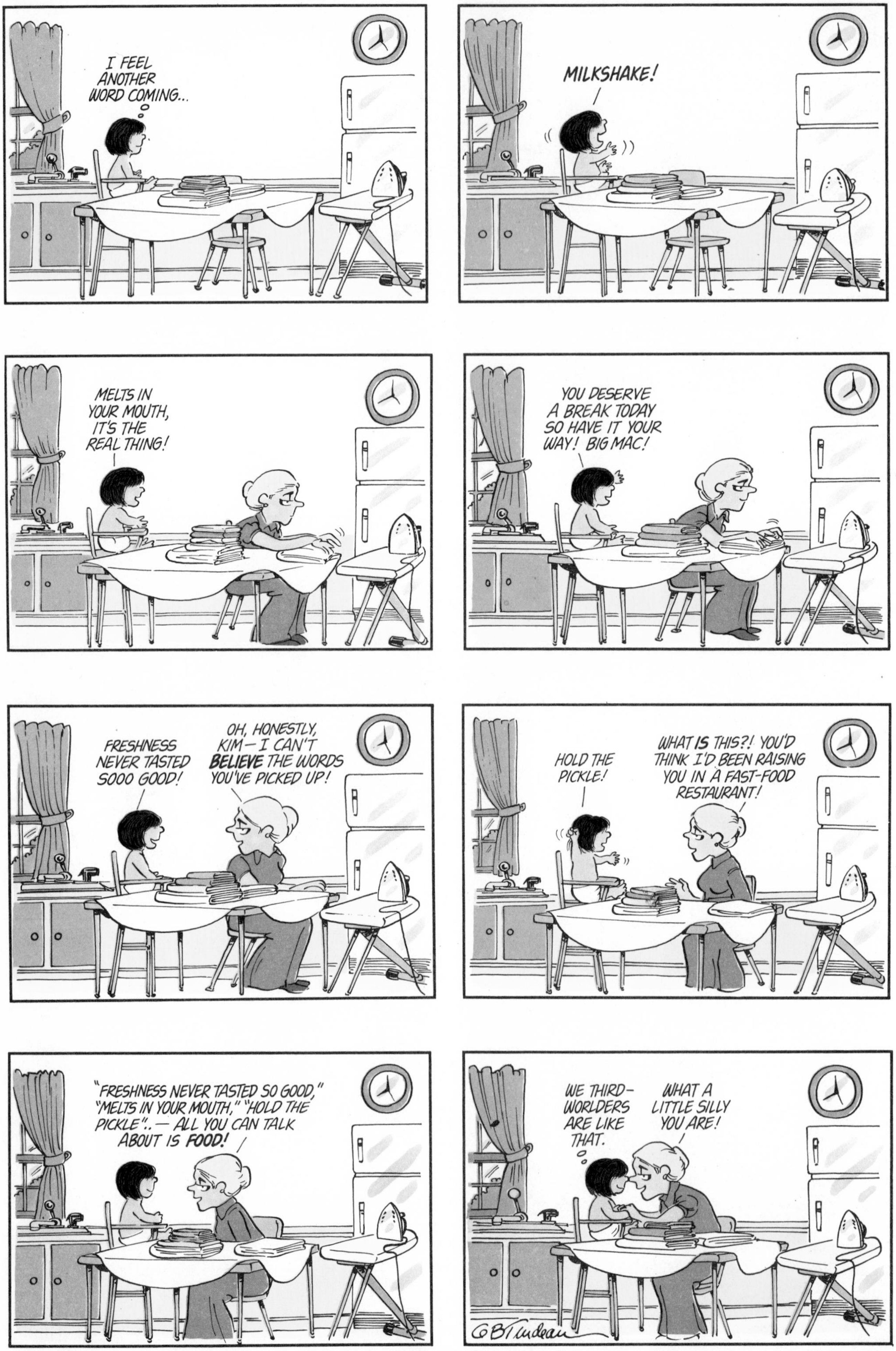
I FEEL ANOTHER WORD COMING...
MILKSHAKE!
MELTS IN YOUR MOUTH, IT'S THE REAL THING!
YOU DESERVE A BREAK TODAY SO HAVE IT YOUR WAY! BIG MAC!
FRESHNESS NEVER TASTED SOOO GOOD!
OH, HONESTLY, KIM— I CAN'T BELIEVE THE WORDS YOU'VE PICKED UP!
HOLD THE PICKLE!
WHAT IS THIS?! YOU'D THINK I'D BEEN RAISING YOU IN A FAST-FOOD RESTAURANT!
"FRESHNESS NEVER TASTED SO GOOD," "MELTS IN YOUR MOUTH," "HOLD THE PICKLE".— ALL YOU CAN TALK ABOUT IS FOOD!
WE THIRD-WORLDERS ARE LIKE THAT.
WHAT A LITTLE SILLY YOU ARE!
© BTrudeau

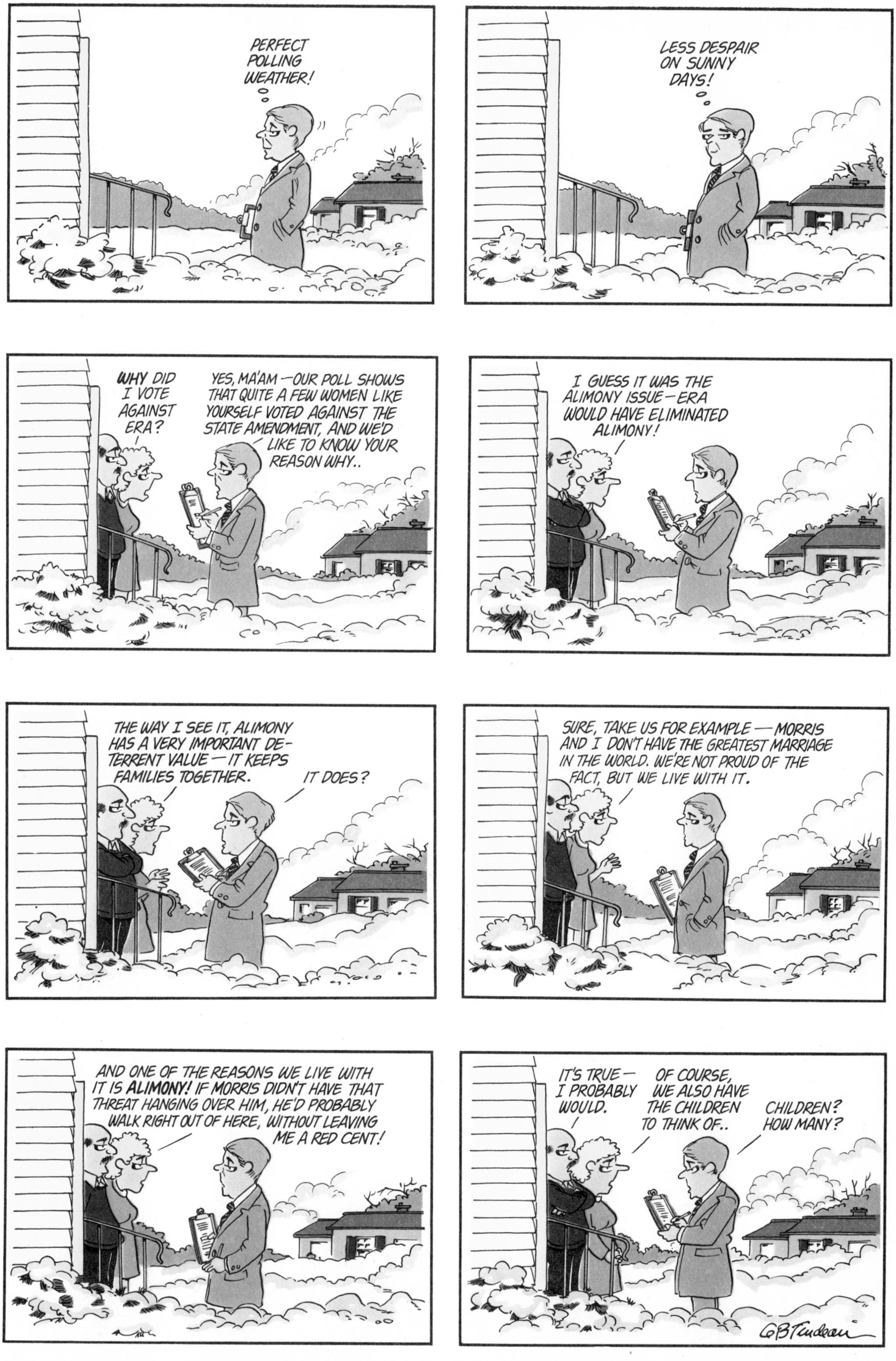

PERFECT POLLING WEATHER!
LESS DESPAIR ON SUNNY DAYS!
WHY DID I VOTE AGAINST ERA?
YES, MA'AM—OUR POLL SHOWS THAT QUITE A FEW WOMEN LIKE YOURSELF VOTED AGAINST THE STATE AMENDMENT, AND WE'D LIKE TO KNOW YOUR REASON WHY..
I GUESS IT WAS THE ALIMONY ISSUE—ERA WOULD HAVE ELIMINATED ALIMONY!
THE WAY I SEE IT, ALIMONY HAS A VERY IMPORTANT DETERRENT VALUE—IT KEEPS FAMILIES TOGETHER.
IT DOES?
SURE, TAKE US FOR EXAMPLE—MORRIS AND I DON'T HAVE THE GREATEST MARRIAGE IN THE WORLD. WE'RE NOT PROUD OF THE FACT, BUT WE LIVE WITH IT.
AND ONE OF THE REASONS WE LIVE WITH IT IS ALIMONY! IF MORRIS DIDN'T HAVE THAT THREAT HANGING OVER HIM, HE'D PROBABLY WALK RIGHT OUT OF HERE, WITHOUT LEAVING ME A RED CENT!
IT'S TRUE—I PROBABLY WOULD.
OF COURSE, WE ALSO HAVE THE CHILDREN TO THINK OF..
CHILDREN? HOW MANY?
GBTrudeau

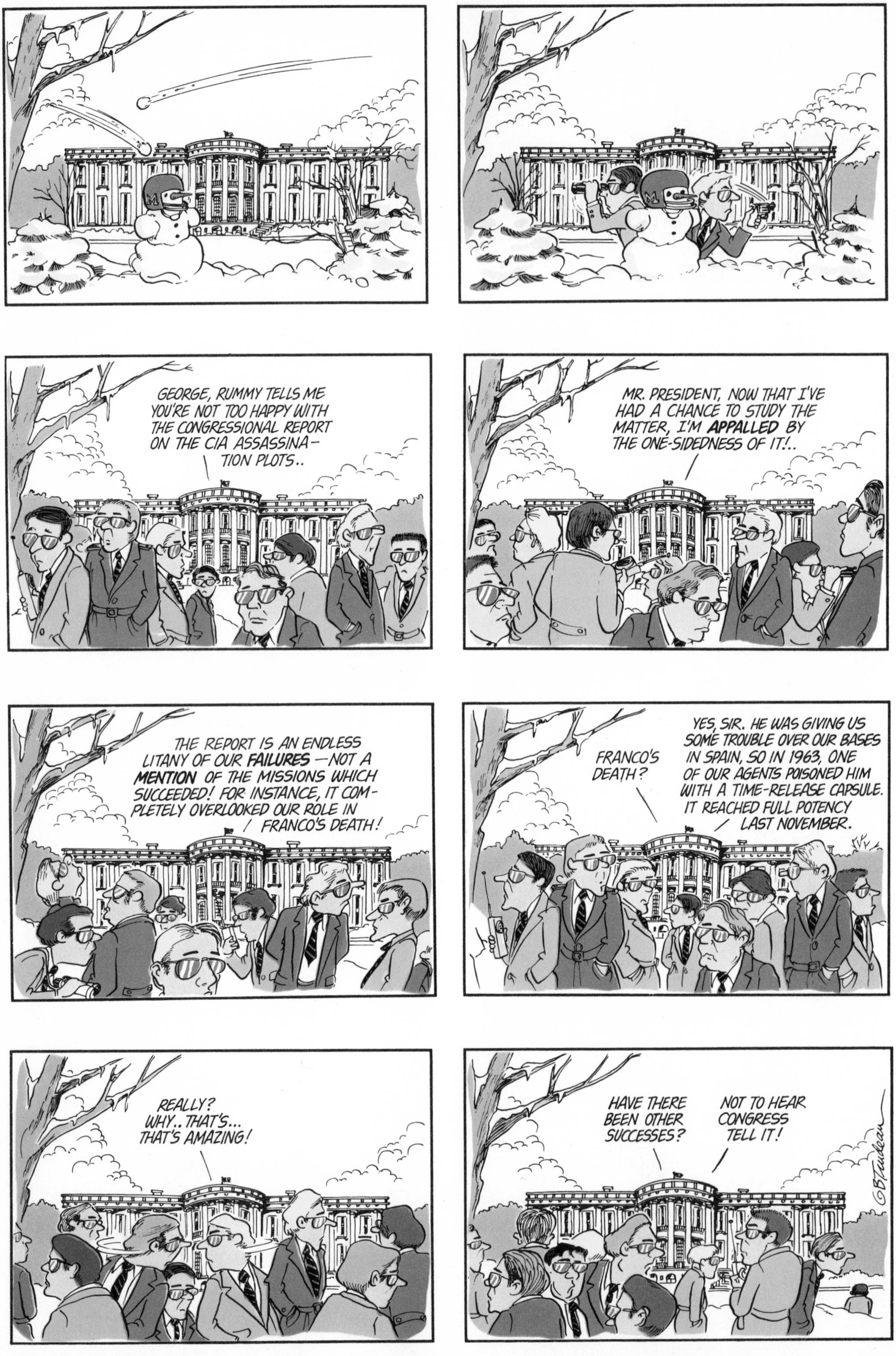
GEORGE, RUMMY TELLS ME YOU'RE NOT TOO HAPPY WITH THE CONGRESSIONAL REPORT ON THE CIA ASSASSINA-TION PLOTS..
MR. PRESIDENT, NOW THAT I'VE HAD A CHANCE TO STUDY THE MATTER, I'M APPALLED BY THE ONE-SIDEDNESS OF IT!..
THE REPORT IS AN ENDLESS LITANY OF OUR FAILURES—NOT A MENTION OF THE MISSIONS WHICH SUCCEEDED! FOR INSTANCE, IT COM-PLETELY OVERLOOKED OUR ROLE IN FRANCO'S DEATH!
FRANCO'S DEATH?
YES, SIR. HE WAS GIVING US SOME TROUBLE OVER OUR BASES IN SPAIN, SO IN 1963, ONE OF OUR AGENTS POISONED HIM WITH A TIME-RELEASE CAPSULE. IT REACHED FULL POTENCY LAST NOVEMBER.
REALLY? WHY.. THAT'S... THAT'S AMAZING!
HAVE THERE BEEN OTHER SUCCESSES?
NOT TO HEAR CONGRESS TELL IT!
©BTrudeau

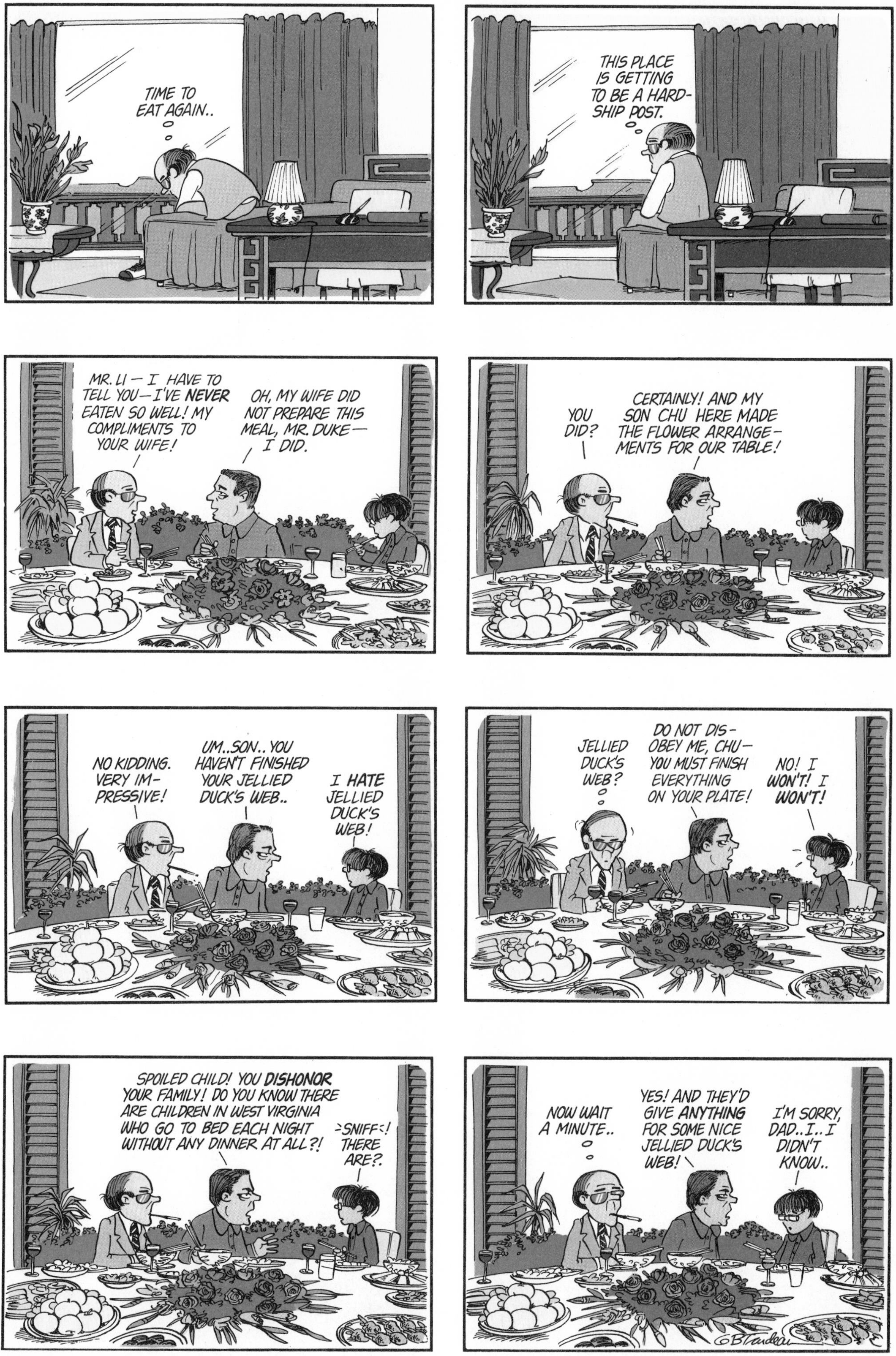
TIME TO EAT AGAIN..
THIS PLACE IS GETTING TO BE A HARD-SHIP POST.
MR. LI — I HAVE TO TELL YOU — I'VE **NEVER** EATEN SO WELL! MY COMPLIMENTS TO YOUR WIFE!
OH, MY WIFE DID NOT PREPARE THIS MEAL, MR. DUKE — I DID.
YOU DID?
CERTAINLY! AND MY SON CHU HERE MADE THE FLOWER ARRANGE-MENTS FOR OUR TABLE!
NO KIDDING. VERY IM-PRESSIVE!
UM..SON..YOU HAVEN'T FINISHED YOUR JELLIED DUCK'S WEB..
I **HATE** JELLIED DUCK'S WEB!
JELLIED DUCK'S WEB?
DO NOT DIS-OBEY ME, CHU — YOU MUST FINISH EVERYTHING ON YOUR PLATE!
NO! I **WON'T!** I **WON'T!**
SPOILED CHILD! YOU **DISHONOR** YOUR FAMILY! DO YOU KNOW THERE ARE CHILDREN IN WEST VIRGINIA WHO GO TO BED EACH NIGHT WITHOUT ANY DINNER AT ALL?!
>SNIFF<! THERE ARE?.
NOW WAIT A MINUTE..
YES! AND THEY'D GIVE **ANYTHING** FOR SOME NICE JELLIED DUCK'S WEB!
I'M SORRY, DAD..I..I DIDN'T KNOW..

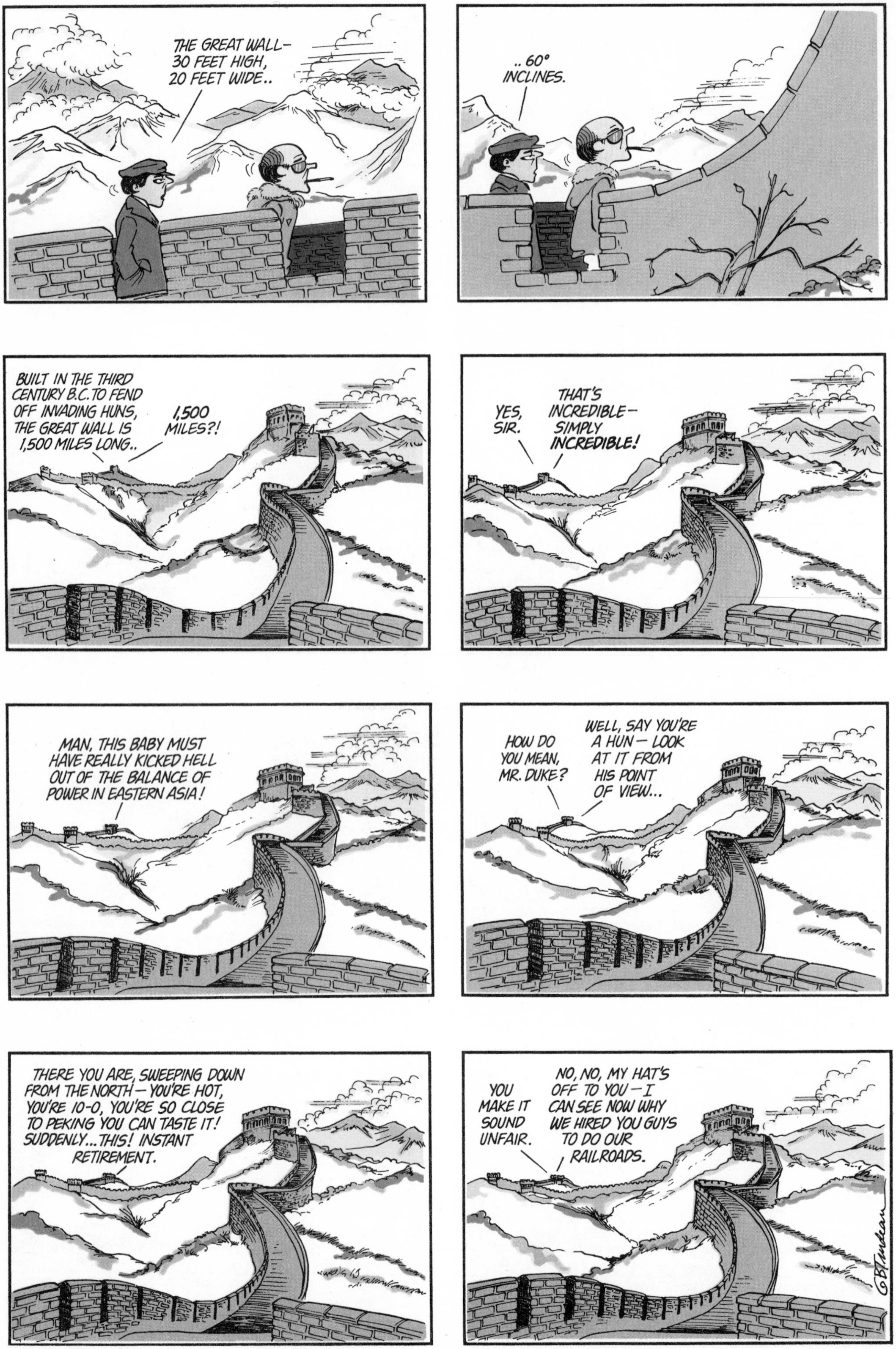
THE GREAT WALL– 30 FEET HIGH, 20 FEET WIDE..
..60° INCLINES.
BUILT IN THE THIRD CENTURY B.C. TO FEND OFF INVADING HUNS, THE GREAT WALL IS 1,500 MILES LONG..
1,500 MILES?!
YES, SIR.
THAT'S INCREDIBLE– SIMPLY **INCREDIBLE!**
MAN, THIS BABY MUST HAVE REALLY KICKED HELL OUT OF THE BALANCE OF POWER IN EASTERN ASIA!
HOW DO YOU MEAN, MR. DUKE?
WELL, SAY YOU'RE A HUN– LOOK AT IT FROM HIS POINT OF VIEW...
THERE YOU ARE, SWEEPING DOWN FROM THE NORTH– YOU'RE HOT, YOU'RE 10-0, YOU'RE SO CLOSE TO PEKING YOU CAN TASTE IT! SUDDENLY...THIS! INSTANT RETIREMENT.
YOU MAKE IT SOUND UNFAIR.
NO, NO, MY HAT'S OFF TO YOU– I CAN SEE NOW WHY WE HIRED YOU GUYS TO DO OUR RAILROADS.
© GBTrudeau

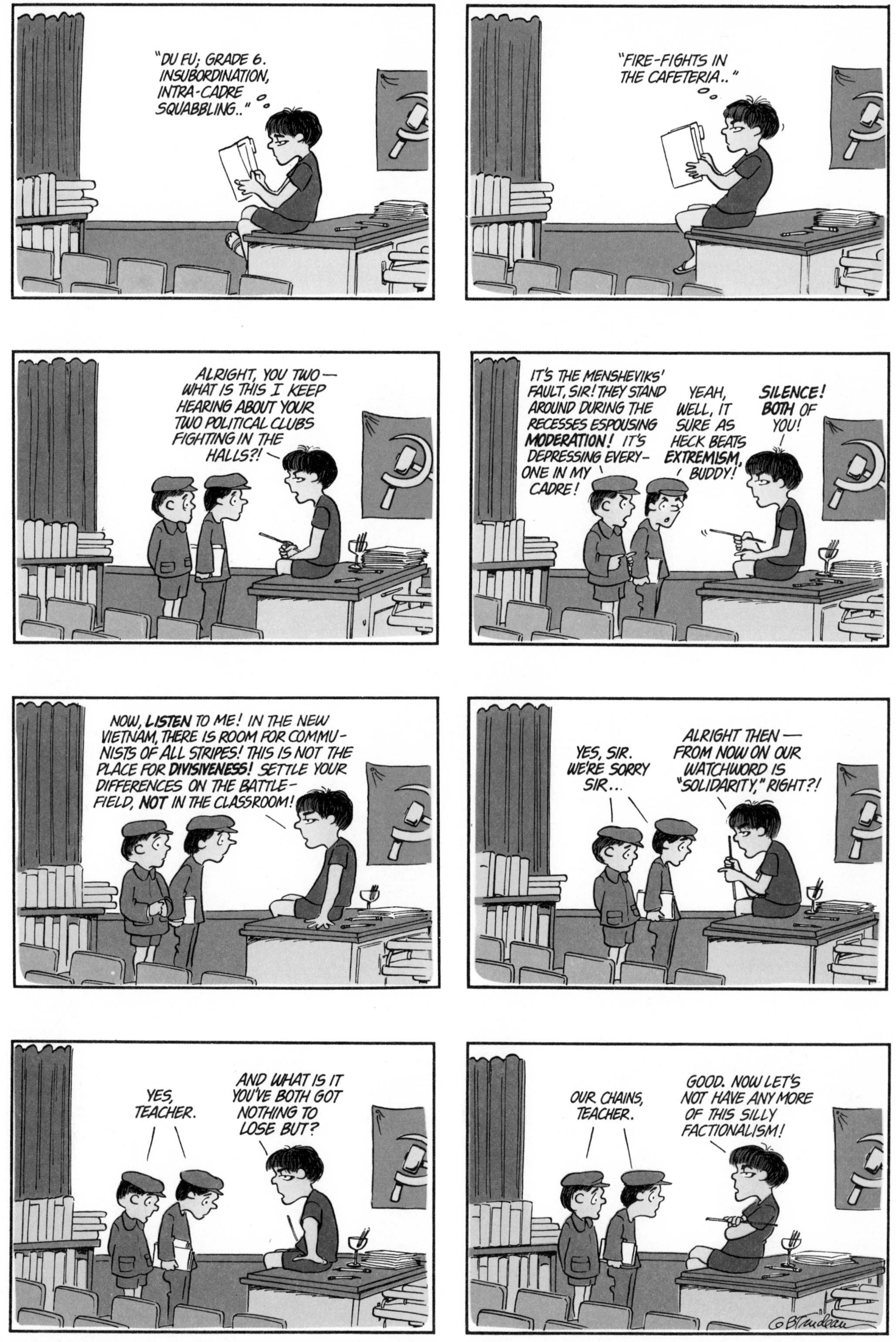
"DU FU; GRADE 6. INSUBORDINATION, INTRA-CADRE SQUABBLING.."
"FIRE-FIGHTS IN THE CAFETERIA.."
ALRIGHT, YOU TWO— WHAT IS THIS I KEEP HEARING ABOUT YOUR TWO POLITICAL CLUBS FIGHTING IN THE HALLS?!
IT'S THE MENSHEVIKS' FAULT, SIR! THEY STAND AROUND DURING THE RECESSES ESPOUSING MODERATION! IT'S DEPRESSING EVERY-ONE IN MY CADRE!
YEAH, WELL, IT SURE AS HECK BEATS EXTREMISM, BUDDY!
SILENCE! BOTH OF YOU!
NOW, LISTEN TO ME! IN THE NEW VIETNAM, THERE IS ROOM FOR COMMU-NISTS OF ALL STRIPES! THIS IS NOT THE PLACE FOR DIVISIVENESS! SETTLE YOUR DIFFERENCES ON THE BATTLE-FIELD, NOT IN THE CLASSROOM!
YES, SIR. WE'RE SORRY SIR...
ALRIGHT THEN— FROM NOW ON OUR WATCHWORD IS "SOLIDARITY," RIGHT?!
YES, TEACHER.
AND WHAT IS IT YOU'VE BOTH GOT NOTHING TO LOSE BUT?
OUR CHAINS, TEACHER.
GOOD. NOW LET'S NOT HAVE ANY MORE OF THIS SILLY FACTIONALISM!

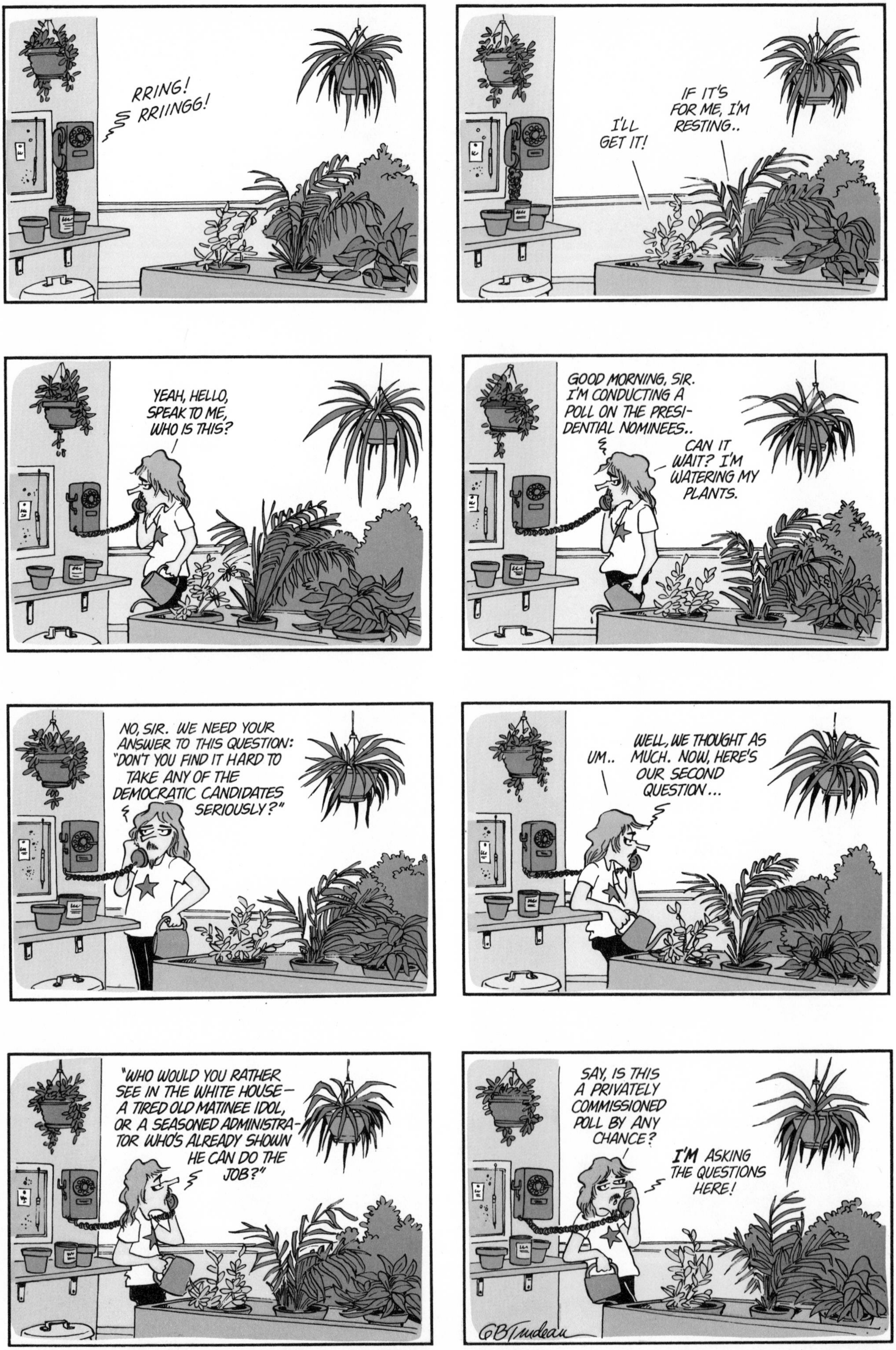
RRING! RRIINGG!
I'LL GET IT!
IF IT'S FOR ME, I'M RESTING..
YEAH, HELLO, SPEAK TO ME, WHO IS THIS?
GOOD MORNING, SIR. I'M CONDUCTING A POLL ON THE PRESIDENTIAL NOMINEES..
CAN IT WAIT? I'M WATERING MY PLANTS.
NO, SIR. WE NEED YOUR ANSWER TO THIS QUESTION: "DON'T YOU FIND IT HARD TO TAKE ANY OF THE DEMOCRATIC CANDIDATES SERIOUSLY?"
UM..
WELL, WE THOUGHT AS MUCH. NOW, HERE'S OUR SECOND QUESTION...
"WHO WOULD YOU RATHER SEE IN THE WHITE HOUSE— A TIRED OLD MATINEE IDOL, OR A SEASONED ADMINISTRATOR WHO'S ALREADY SHOWN HE CAN DO THE JOB?"
SAY, IS THIS A PRIVATELY COMMISSIONED POLL BY ANY CHANCE?
I'M ASKING THE QUESTIONS HERE!
GBTrudeau

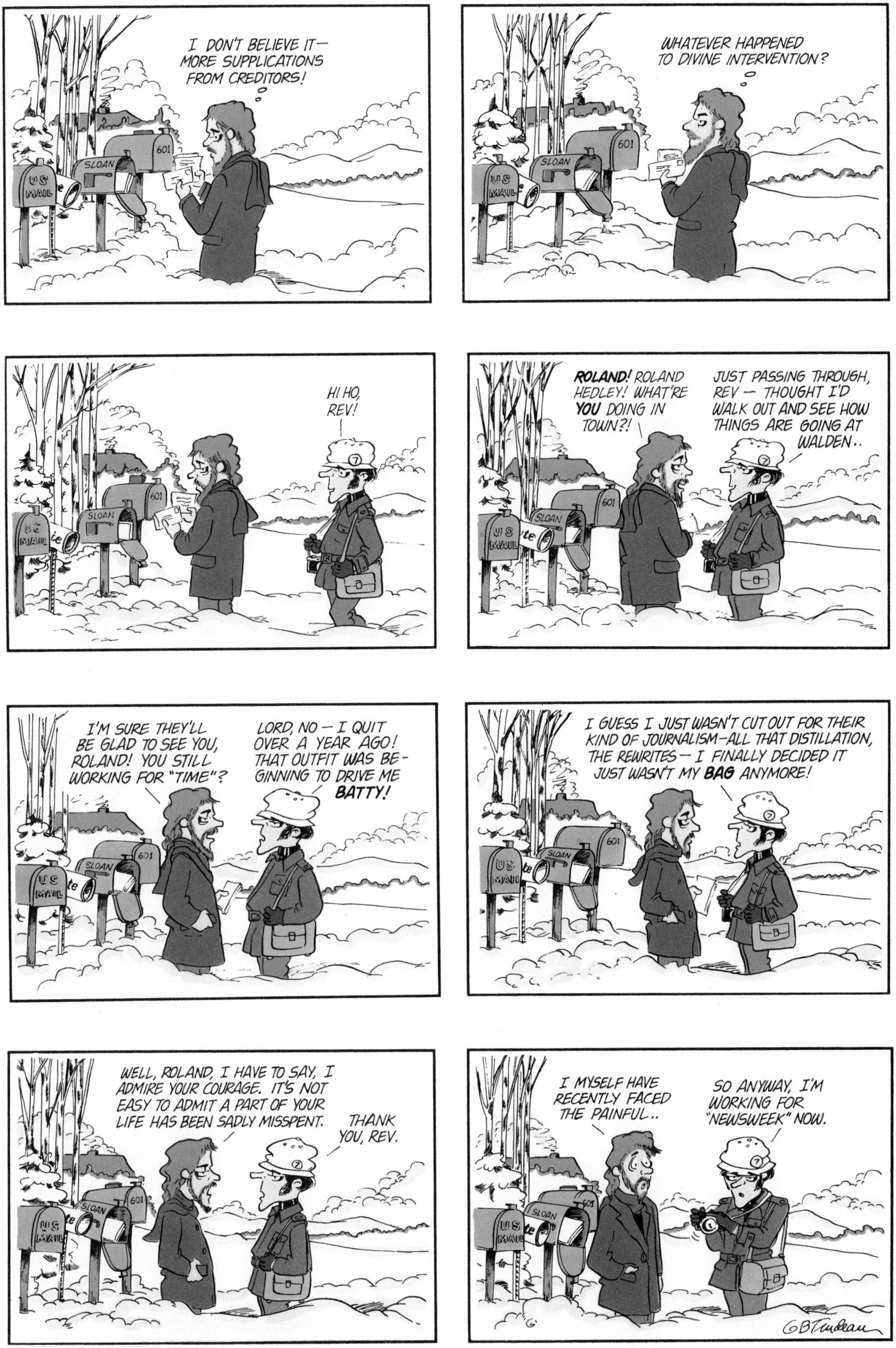

I DON'T BELIEVE IT— MORE SUPPLICATIONS FROM CREDITORS!
WHATEVER HAPPENED TO DIVINE INTERVENTION?
HI HO, REV!
ROLAND! ROLAND HEDLEY! WHAT'RE YOU DOING IN TOWN?!
JUST PASSING THROUGH, REV — THOUGHT I'D WALK OUT AND SEE HOW THINGS ARE GOING AT WALDEN..
I'M SURE THEY'LL BE GLAD TO SEE YOU, ROLAND! YOU STILL WORKING FOR "TIME"?
LORD, NO — I QUIT OVER A YEAR AGO! THAT OUTFIT WAS BE-GINNING TO DRIVE ME BATTY!
I GUESS I JUST WASN'T CUT OUT FOR THEIR KIND OF JOURNALISM—ALL THAT DISTILLATION, THE REWRITES— I FINALLY DECIDED IT JUST WASN'T MY BAG ANYMORE!
WELL, ROLAND, I HAVE TO SAY, I ADMIRE YOUR COURAGE. IT'S NOT EASY TO ADMIT A PART OF YOUR LIFE HAS BEEN SADLY MISSPENT.
THANK YOU, REV.
I MYSELF HAVE RECENTLY FACED THE PAINFUL..
SO ANYWAY, I'M WORKING FOR "NEWSWEEK" NOW.
GBTrudeau

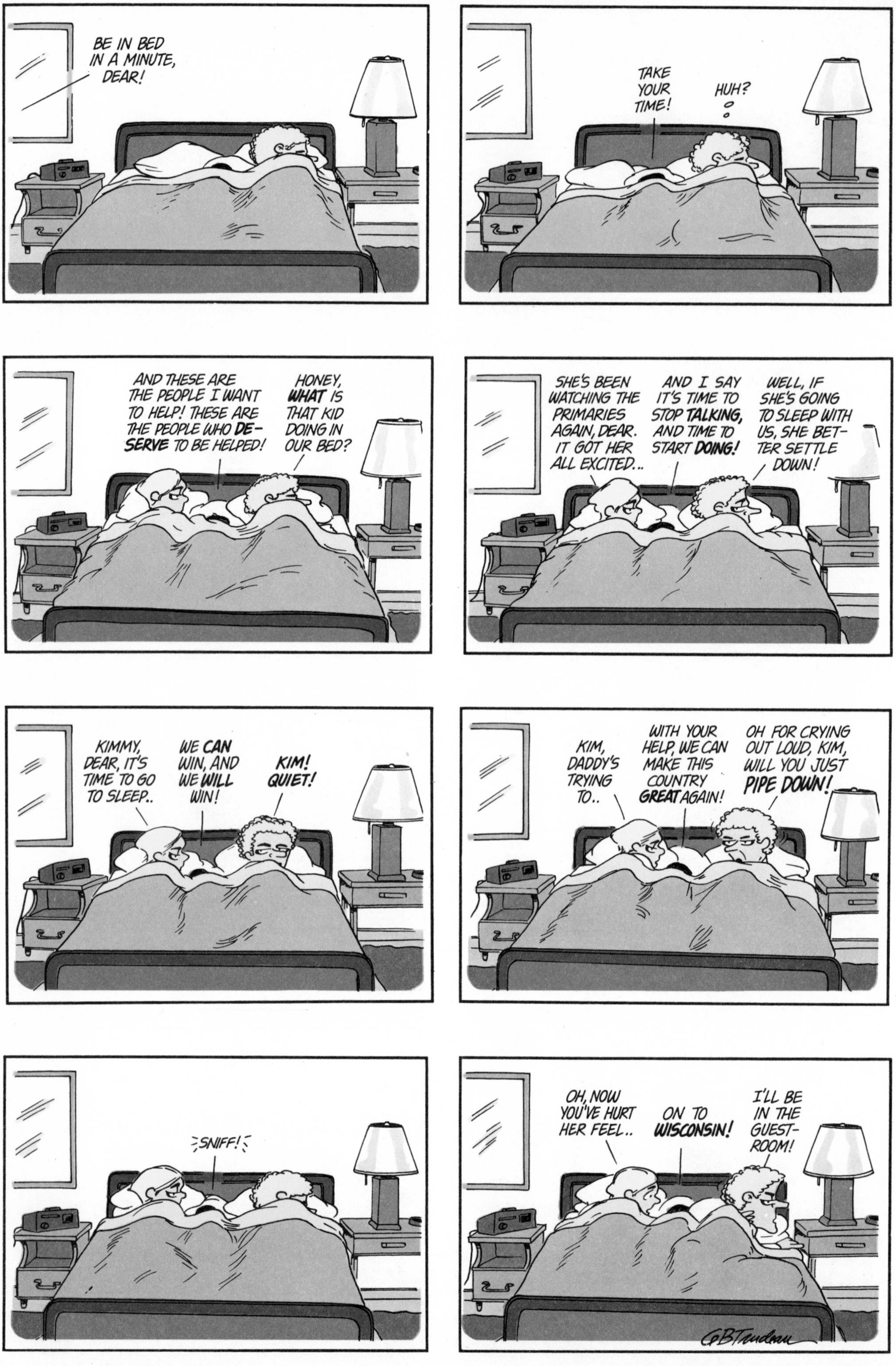
BE IN BED IN A MINUTE, DEAR!
TAKE YOUR TIME!
HUH?
AND THESE ARE THE PEOPLE I WANT TO HELP! THESE ARE THE PEOPLE WHO DE-SERVE TO BE HELPED!
HONEY, WHAT IS THAT KID DOING IN OUR BED?
SHE'S BEEN WATCHING THE PRIMARIES AGAIN, DEAR. IT GOT HER ALL EXCITED...
AND I SAY IT'S TIME TO STOP TALKING, AND TIME TO START DOING!
WELL, IF SHE'S GOING TO SLEEP WITH US, SHE BET-TER SETTLE DOWN!
KIMMY, DEAR, IT'S TIME TO GO TO SLEEP..
WE CAN WIN, AND WE WILL WIN!
KIM! QUIET!
KIM, DADDY'S TRYING TO..
WITH YOUR HELP, WE CAN MAKE THIS COUNTRY GREAT AGAIN!
OH FOR CRYING OUT LOUD, KIM, WILL YOU JUST PIPE DOWN!
SNIFF!
OH, NOW YOU'VE HURT HER FEEL..
ON TO WISCONSIN!
I'LL BE IN THE GUEST-ROOM!
GBTrudeau

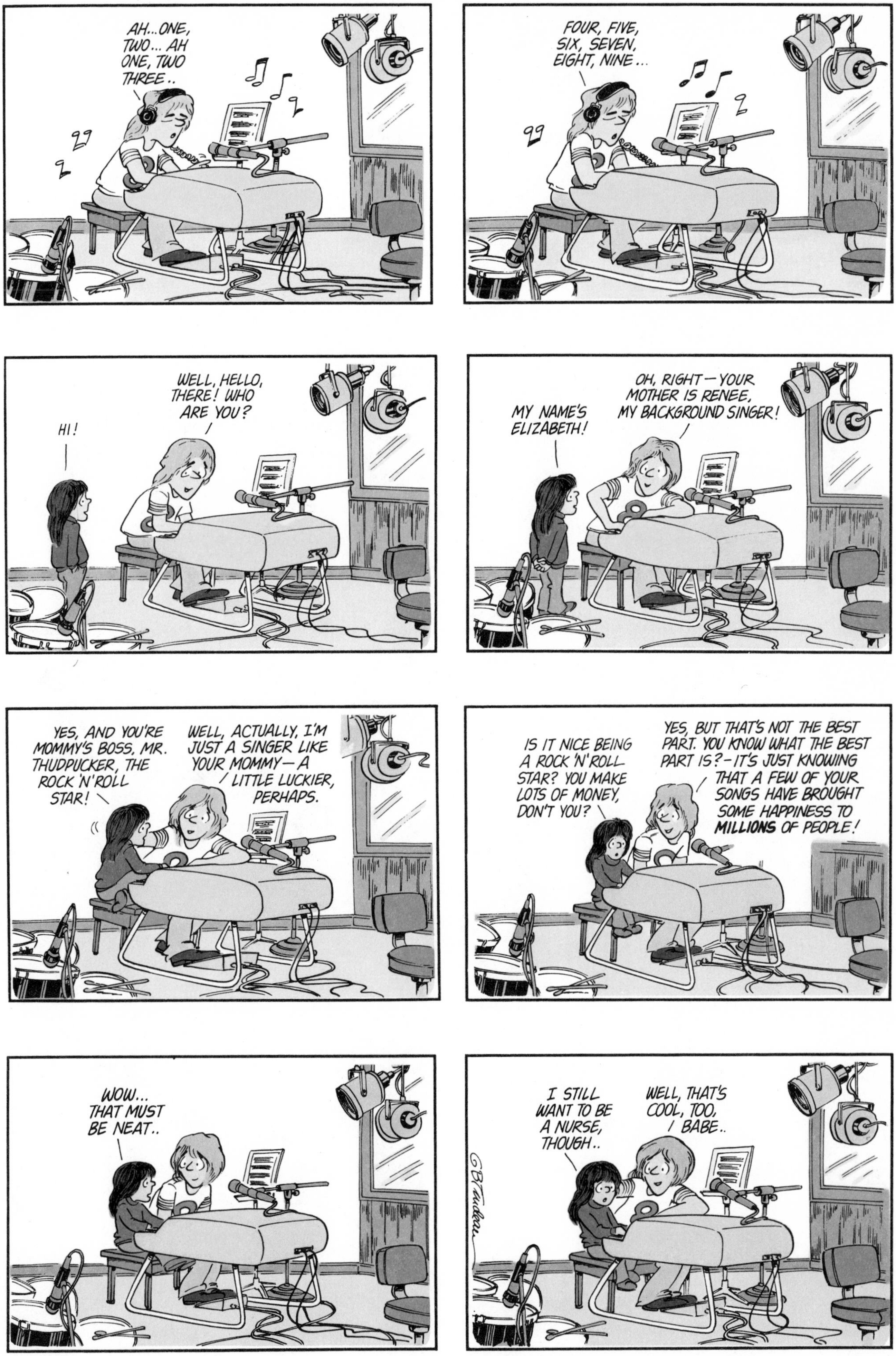
AH...ONE, TWO... AH ONE, TWO THREE..
FOUR, FIVE, SIX, SEVEN, EIGHT, NINE...
HI!
WELL, HELLO, THERE! WHO ARE YOU?
MY NAME'S ELIZABETH!
OH, RIGHT—YOUR MOTHER IS RENEE, MY BACKGROUND SINGER!
YES, AND YOU'RE MOMMY'S BOSS, MR. THUDPUCKER, THE ROCK 'N' ROLL STAR!
WELL, ACTUALLY, I'M JUST A SINGER LIKE YOUR MOMMY—A LITTLE LUCKIER, PERHAPS.
IS IT NICE BEING A ROCK 'N' ROLL STAR? YOU MAKE LOTS OF MONEY, DON'T YOU?
YES, BUT THAT'S NOT THE BEST PART. YOU KNOW WHAT THE BEST PART IS?—IT'S JUST KNOWING THAT A FEW OF YOUR SONGS HAVE BROUGHT SOME HAPPINESS TO **MILLIONS** OF PEOPLE!
WOW... THAT MUST BE NEAT..
I STILL WANT TO BE A NURSE, THOUGH..
WELL, THAT'S COOL, TOO, BABE..
GBTrudeau

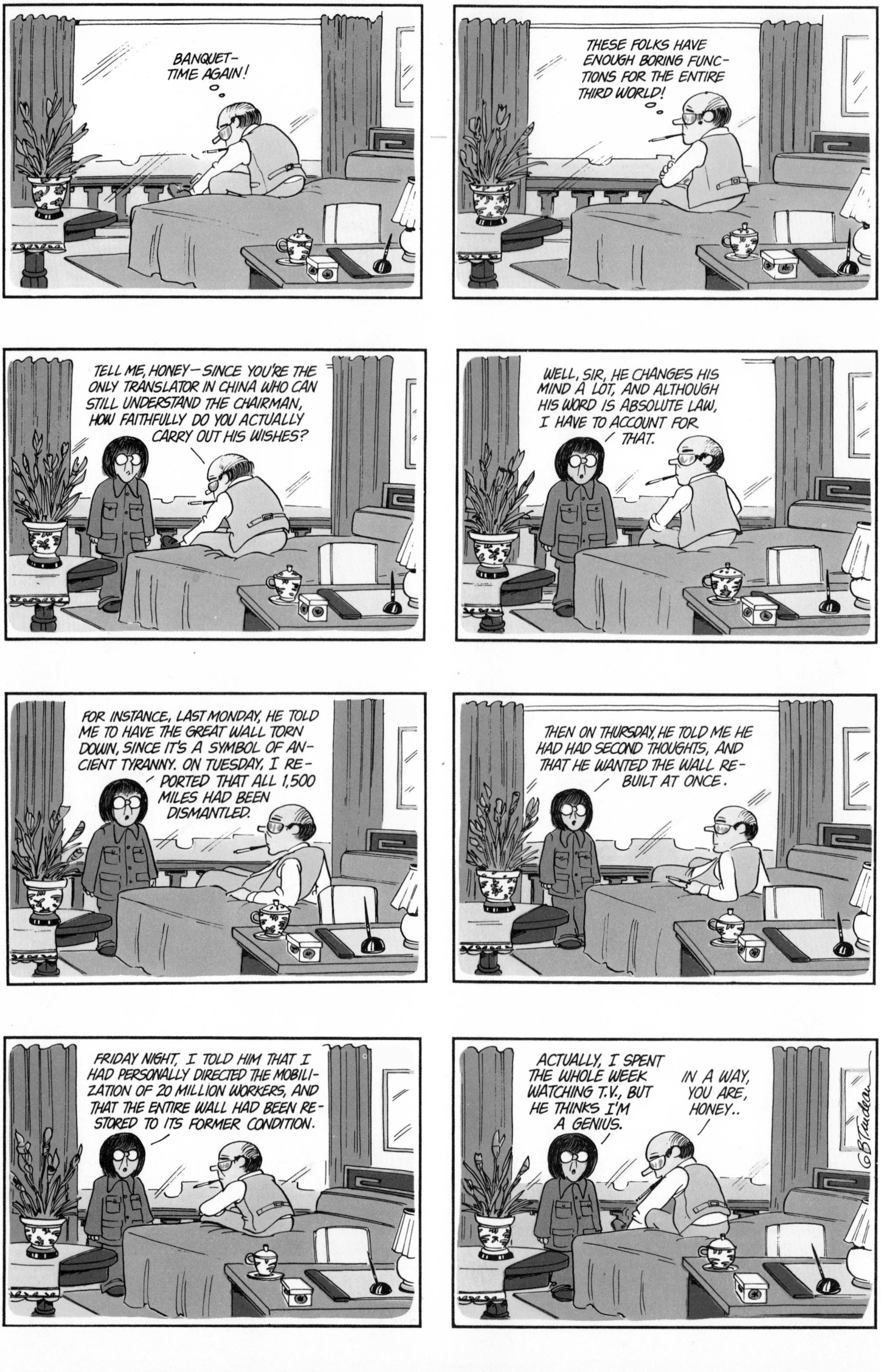
BANQUET-TIME AGAIN!
THESE FOLKS HAVE ENOUGH BORING FUNCTIONS FOR THE ENTIRE THIRD WORLD!
TELL ME, HONEY—SINCE YOU'RE THE ONLY TRANSLATOR IN CHINA WHO CAN STILL UNDERSTAND THE CHAIRMAN, HOW FAITHFULLY DO YOU ACTUALLY CARRY OUT HIS WISHES?
WELL, SIR, HE CHANGES HIS MIND A LOT, AND ALTHOUGH HIS WORD IS ABSOLUTE LAW, I HAVE TO ACCOUNT FOR THAT.
FOR INSTANCE, LAST MONDAY, HE TOLD ME TO HAVE THE GREAT WALL TORN DOWN, SINCE IT'S A SYMBOL OF ANCIENT TYRANNY. ON TUESDAY, I REPORTED THAT ALL 1,500 MILES HAD BEEN DISMANTLED.
THEN ON THURSDAY, HE TOLD ME HE HAD HAD SECOND THOUGHTS, AND THAT HE WANTED THE WALL REBUILT AT ONCE.
FRIDAY NIGHT, I TOLD HIM THAT I HAD PERSONALLY DIRECTED THE MOBILIZATION OF 20 MILLION WORKERS, AND THAT THE ENTIRE WALL HAD BEEN RESTORED TO ITS FORMER CONDITION.
ACTUALLY, I SPENT THE WHOLE WEEK WATCHING T.V., BUT HE THINKS I'M A GENIUS.
IN A WAY, YOU ARE, HONEY..
©BTrudeau

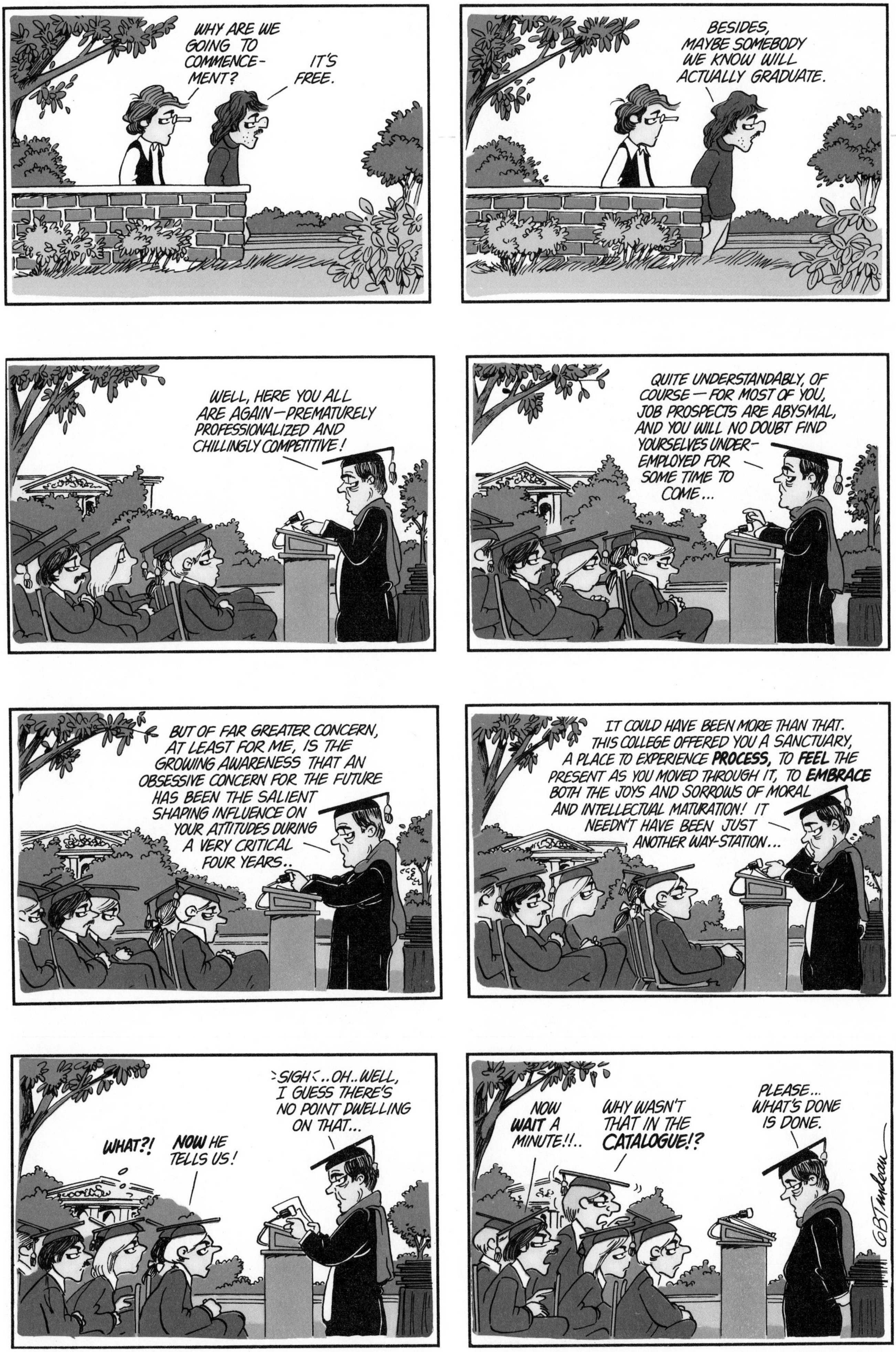
WHY ARE WE GOING TO COMMENCE-MENT?
IT'S FREE.
BESIDES, MAYBE SOMEBODY WE KNOW WILL ACTUALLY GRADUATE.
WELL, HERE YOU ALL ARE AGAIN—PREMATURELY PROFESSIONALIZED AND CHILLINGLY COMPETITIVE!
QUITE UNDERSTANDABLY, OF COURSE—FOR MOST OF YOU, JOB PROSPECTS ARE ABYSMAL, AND YOU WILL NO DOUBT FIND YOURSELVES UNDER-EMPLOYED FOR SOME TIME TO COME...
BUT OF FAR GREATER CONCERN, AT LEAST FOR ME, IS THE GROWING AWARENESS THAT AN OBSESSIVE CONCERN FOR THE FUTURE HAS BEEN THE SALIENT SHAPING INFLUENCE ON YOUR ATTITUDES DURING A VERY CRITICAL FOUR YEARS..
IT COULD HAVE BEEN MORE THAN THAT. THIS COLLEGE OFFERED YOU A SANCTUARY, A PLACE TO EXPERIENCE PROCESS, TO FEEL THE PRESENT AS YOU MOVED THROUGH IT, TO EMBRACE BOTH THE JOYS AND SORROWS OF MORAL AND INTELLECTUAL MATURATION! IT NEEDN'T HAVE BEEN JUST ANOTHER WAY-STATION...
>SIGH<..OH..WELL, I GUESS THERE'S NO POINT DWELLING ON THAT...
WHAT?!
NOW HE TELLS US!
NOW WAIT A MINUTE!!..
WHY WASN'T THAT IN THE CATALOGUE!?
PLEASE... WHAT'S DONE IS DONE.
GBTrudeau

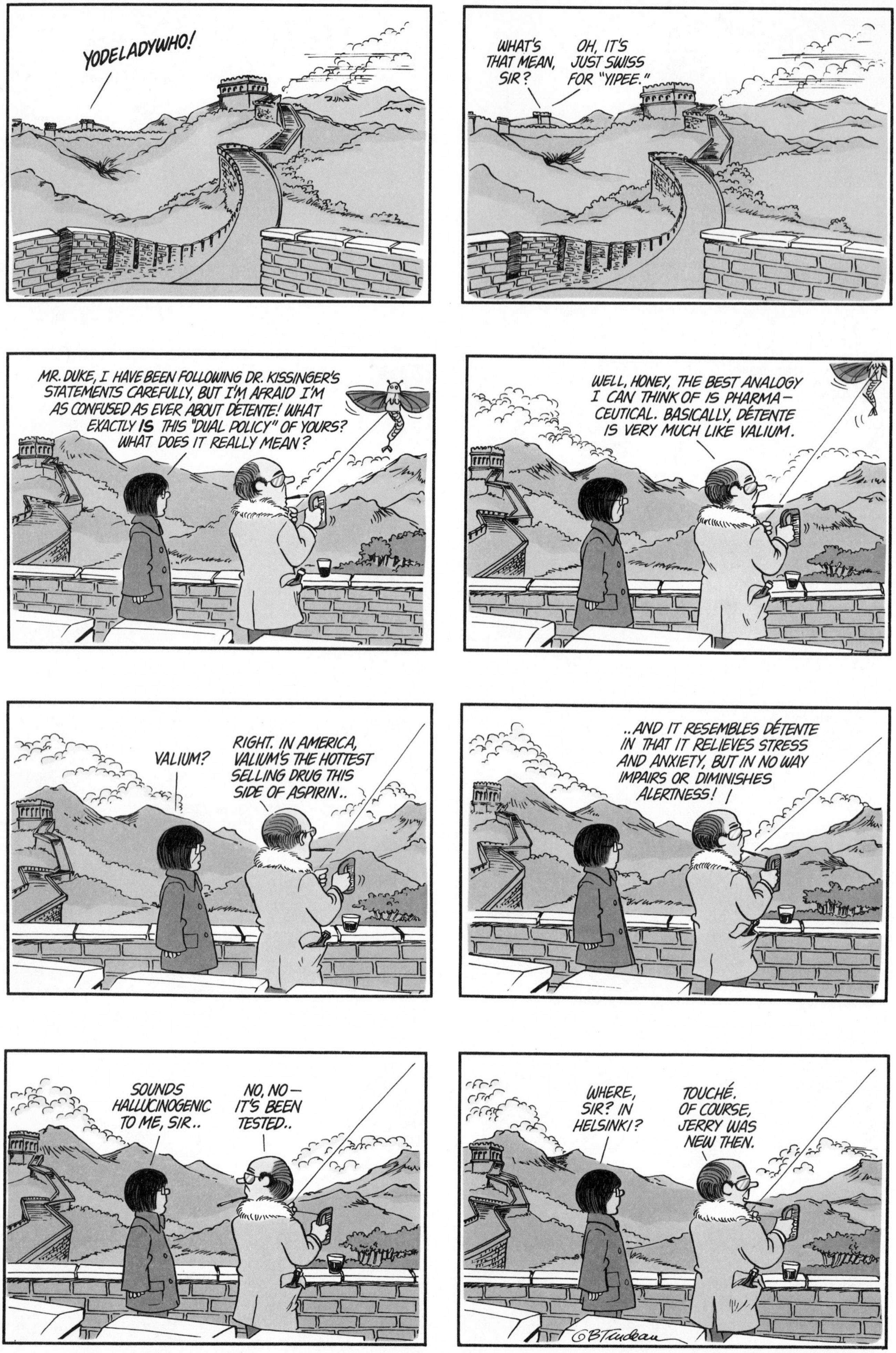

YODELADYWHO!
WHAT'S THAT MEAN, SIR?
OH, IT'S JUST SWISS FOR "YIPEE."
MR. DUKE, I HAVE BEEN FOLLOWING DR. KISSINGER'S STATEMENTS CAREFULLY, BUT I'M AFRAID I'M AS CONFUSED AS EVER ABOUT DÉTENTE! WHAT EXACTLY IS THIS "DUAL POLICY" OF YOURS? WHAT DOES IT REALLY MEAN?
WELL, HONEY, THE BEST ANALOGY I CAN THINK OF IS PHARMA-CEUTICAL. BASICALLY, DÉTENTE IS VERY MUCH LIKE VALIUM.
VALIUM?
RIGHT. IN AMERICA, VALIUM'S THE HOTTEST SELLING DRUG THIS SIDE OF ASPIRIN..
..AND IT RESEMBLES DÉTENTE IN THAT IT RELIEVES STRESS AND ANXIETY, BUT IN NO WAY IMPAIRS OR DIMINISHES ALERTNESS!
SOUNDS HALLUCINOGENIC TO ME, SIR..
NO, NO— IT'S BEEN TESTED..
WHERE, SIR? IN HELSINKI?
TOUCHÉ. OF COURSE, JERRY WAS NEW THEN.
©BTrudeau

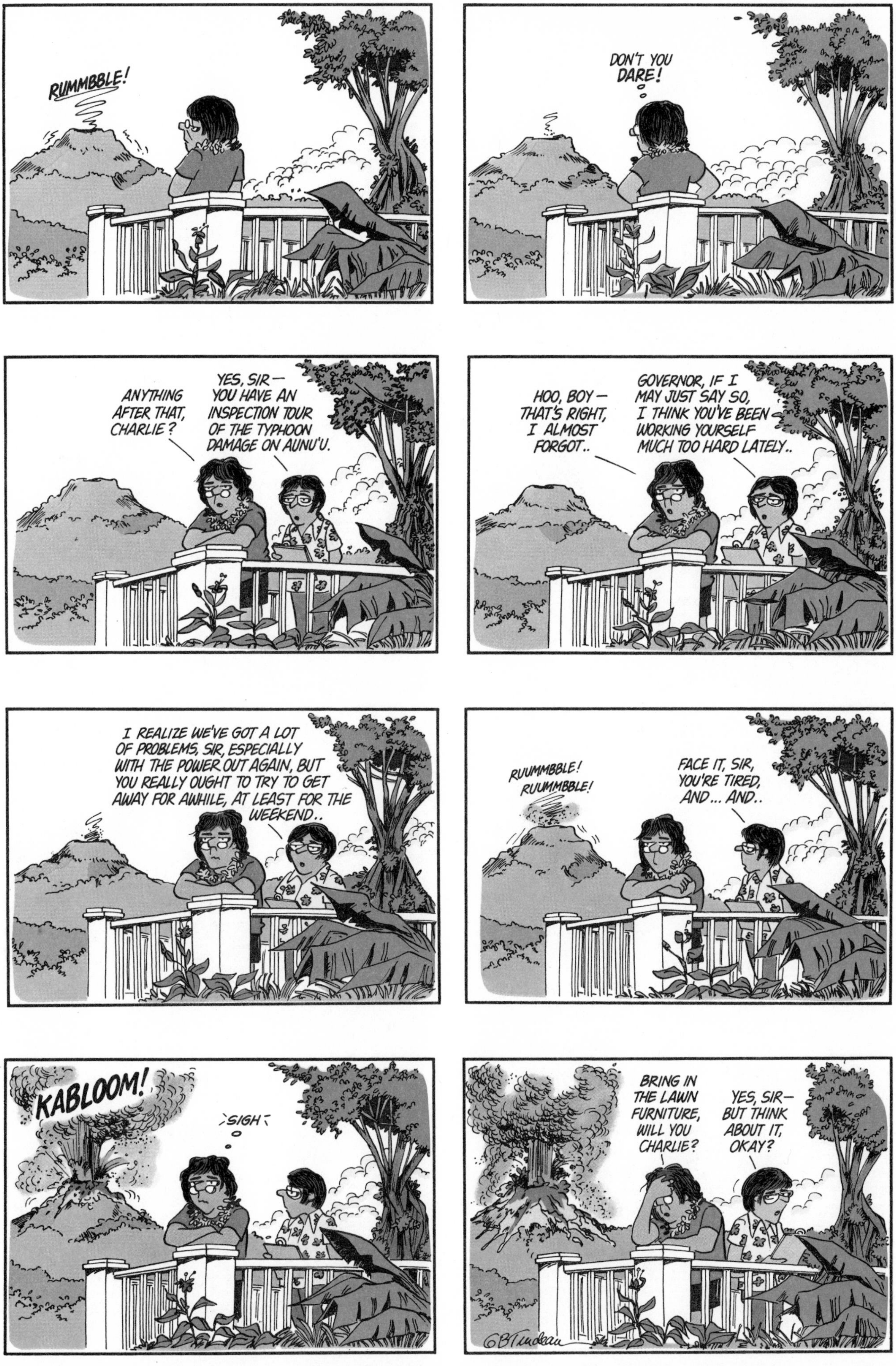
RUMMBBLE!
DON'T YOU DARE!
ANYTHING AFTER THAT, CHARLIE?
YES, SIR— YOU HAVE AN INSPECTION TOUR OF THE TYPHOON DAMAGE ON AUNU'U.
HOO, BOY— THAT'S RIGHT, I ALMOST FORGOT..
GOVERNOR, IF I MAY JUST SAY SO, I THINK YOU'VE BEEN WORKING YOURSELF MUCH TOO HARD LATELY..
I REALIZE WE'VE GOT A LOT OF PROBLEMS, SIR, ESPECIALLY WITH THE POWER OUT AGAIN, BUT YOU REALLY OUGHT TO TRY TO GET AWAY FOR AWHILE, AT LEAST FOR THE WEEKEND..
RUUMMBBLE! RUUMMBBLE!
FACE IT, SIR, YOU'RE TIRED, AND... AND..
KABLOOM!
SIGH
BRING IN THE LAWN FURNITURE, WILL YOU CHARLIE?
YES, SIR— BUT THINK ABOUT IT, OKAY?
GBTrudeau

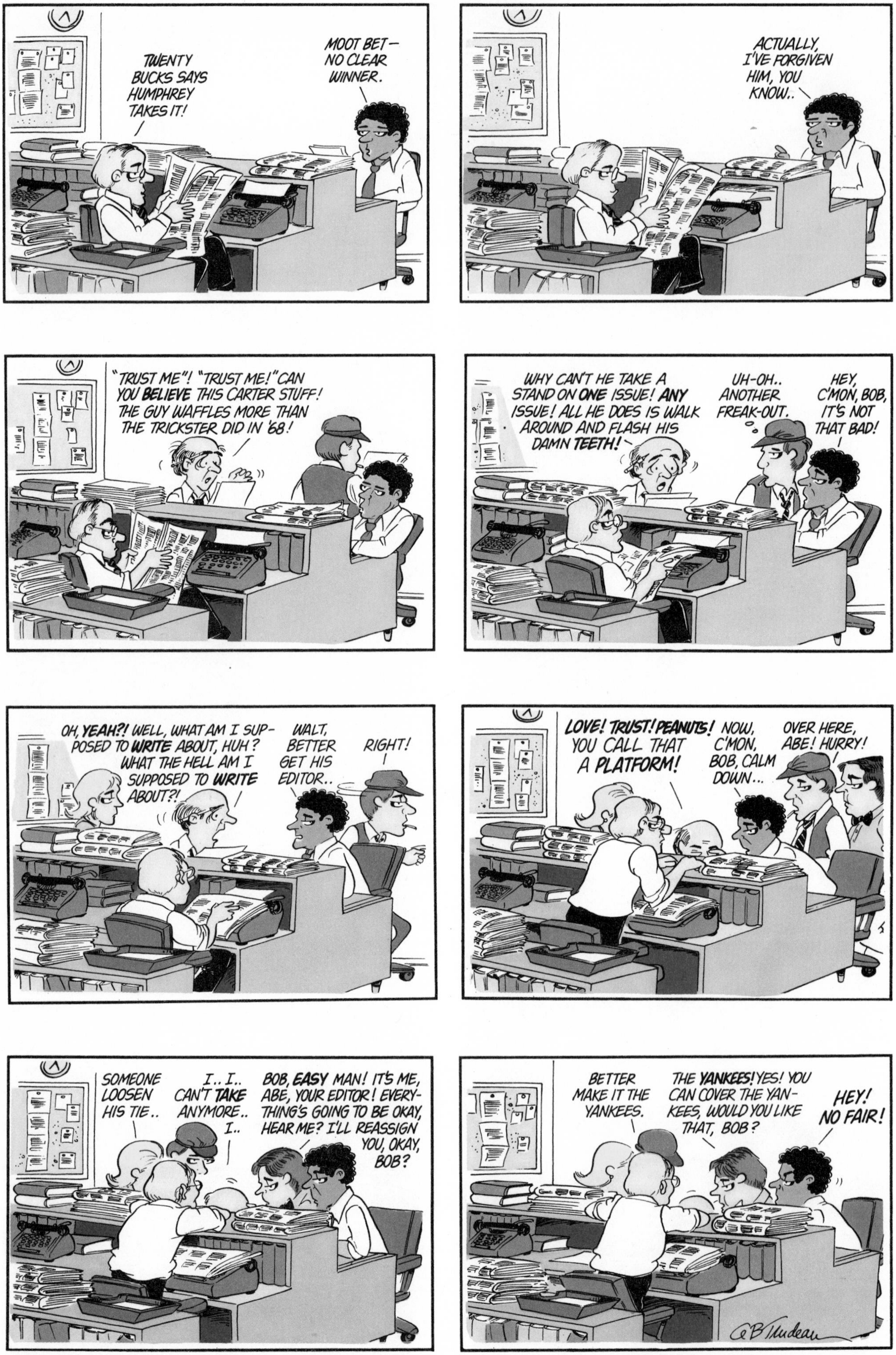
TWENTY BUCKS SAYS HUMPHREY TAKES IT!
MOOT BET— NO CLEAR WINNER.
ACTUALLY, I'VE FORGIVEN HIM, YOU KNOW..
"TRUST ME"! "TRUST ME!" CAN YOU BELIEVE THIS CARTER STUFF! THE GUY WAFFLES MORE THAN THE TRICKSTER DID IN '68!
WHY CAN'T HE TAKE A STAND ON ONE ISSUE! ANY ISSUE! ALL HE DOES IS WALK AROUND AND FLASH HIS DAMN TEETH!
UH-OH.. ANOTHER FREAK-OUT.
HEY, C'MON, BOB, IT'S NOT THAT BAD!
OH, YEAH?! WELL, WHAT AM I SUPPOSED TO WRITE ABOUT, HUH? WHAT THE HELL AM I SUPPOSED TO WRITE ABOUT?!
WALT, BETTER GET HIS EDITOR..
RIGHT!
LOVE! TRUST! PEANUTS! YOU CALL THAT A PLATFORM!
NOW, C'MON, BOB, CALM DOWN...
OVER HERE, ABE! HURRY!
SOMEONE LOOSEN HIS TIE..
I.. I.. CAN'T TAKE ANYMORE.. I..
BOB, EASY MAN! IT'S ME, ABE, YOUR EDITOR! EVERYTHING'S GOING TO BE OKAY, HEAR ME? I'LL REASSIGN YOU, OKAY, BOB?
BETTER MAKE IT THE YANKEES.
THE YANKEES! YES! YOU CAN COVER THE YANKEES, WOULD YOU LIKE THAT, BOB?
HEY! NO FAIR!
GBTrudeau

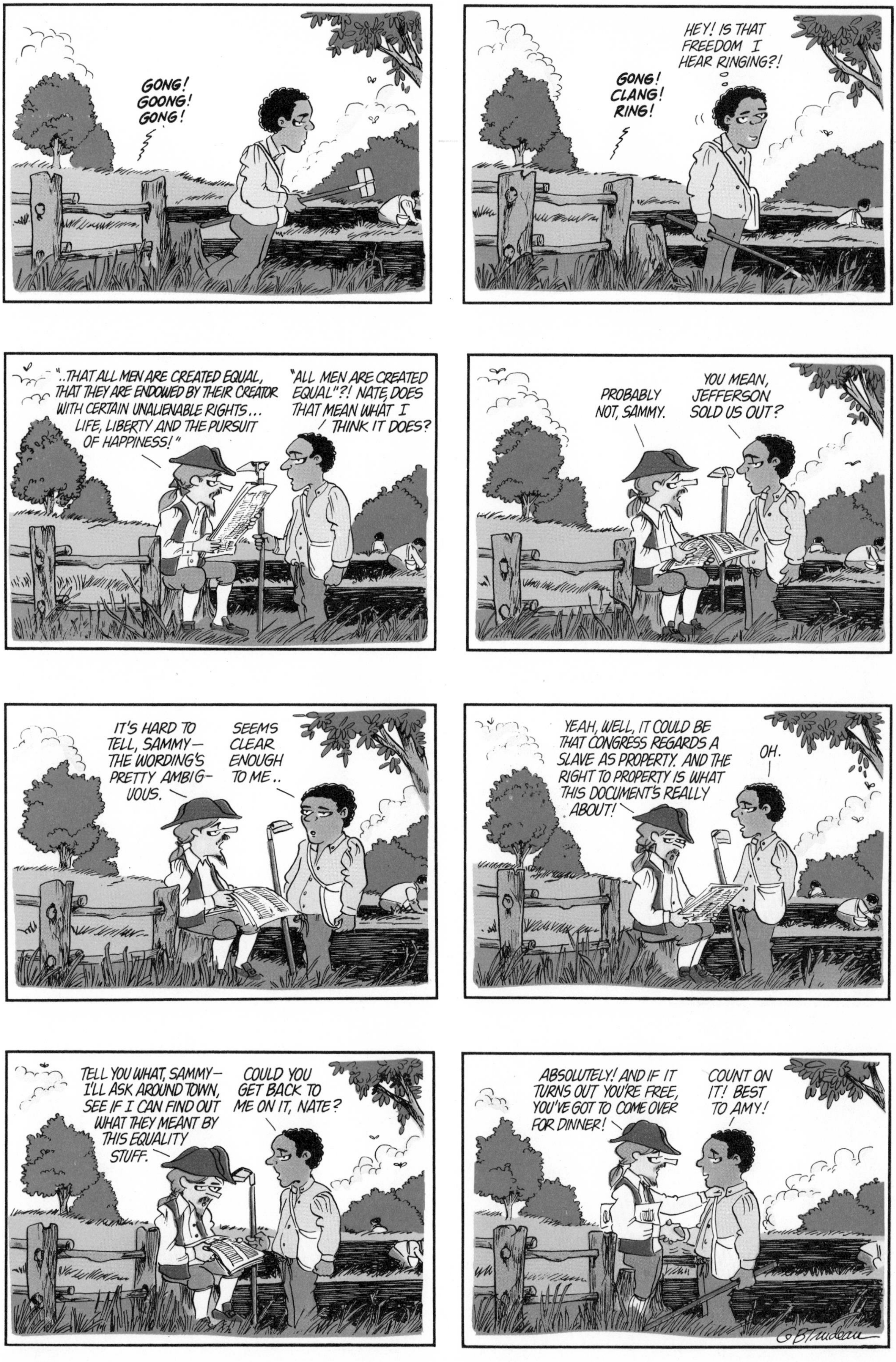
GONG! GOONG! GONG!
GONG! CLANG! RING!
HEY! IS THAT FREEDOM I HEAR RINGING?!
"..THAT ALL MEN ARE CREATED EQUAL, THAT THEY ARE ENDOWED BY THEIR CREATOR WITH CERTAIN UNALIENABLE RIGHTS... LIFE, LIBERTY AND THE PURSUIT OF HAPPINESS!"
"ALL MEN ARE CREATED EQUAL"?! NATE, DOES THAT MEAN WHAT I THINK IT DOES?
PROBABLY NOT, SAMMY.
YOU MEAN, JEFFERSON SOLD US OUT?
IT'S HARD TO TELL, SAMMY— THE WORDING'S PRETTY AMBIG-UOUS.
SEEMS CLEAR ENOUGH TO ME..
YEAH, WELL, IT COULD BE THAT CONGRESS REGARDS A SLAVE AS PROPERTY. AND THE RIGHT TO PROPERTY IS WHAT THIS DOCUMENT'S REALLY ABOUT!
OH.
TELL YOU WHAT, SAMMY— I'LL ASK AROUND TOWN, SEE IF I CAN FIND OUT WHAT THEY MEANT BY THIS EQUALITY STUFF.
COULD YOU GET BACK TO ME ON IT, NATE?
ABSOLUTELY! AND IF IT TURNS OUT YOU'RE FREE, YOU'VE GOT TO COME OVER FOR DINNER!
COUNT ON IT! BEST TO AMY!
GBTrudeau

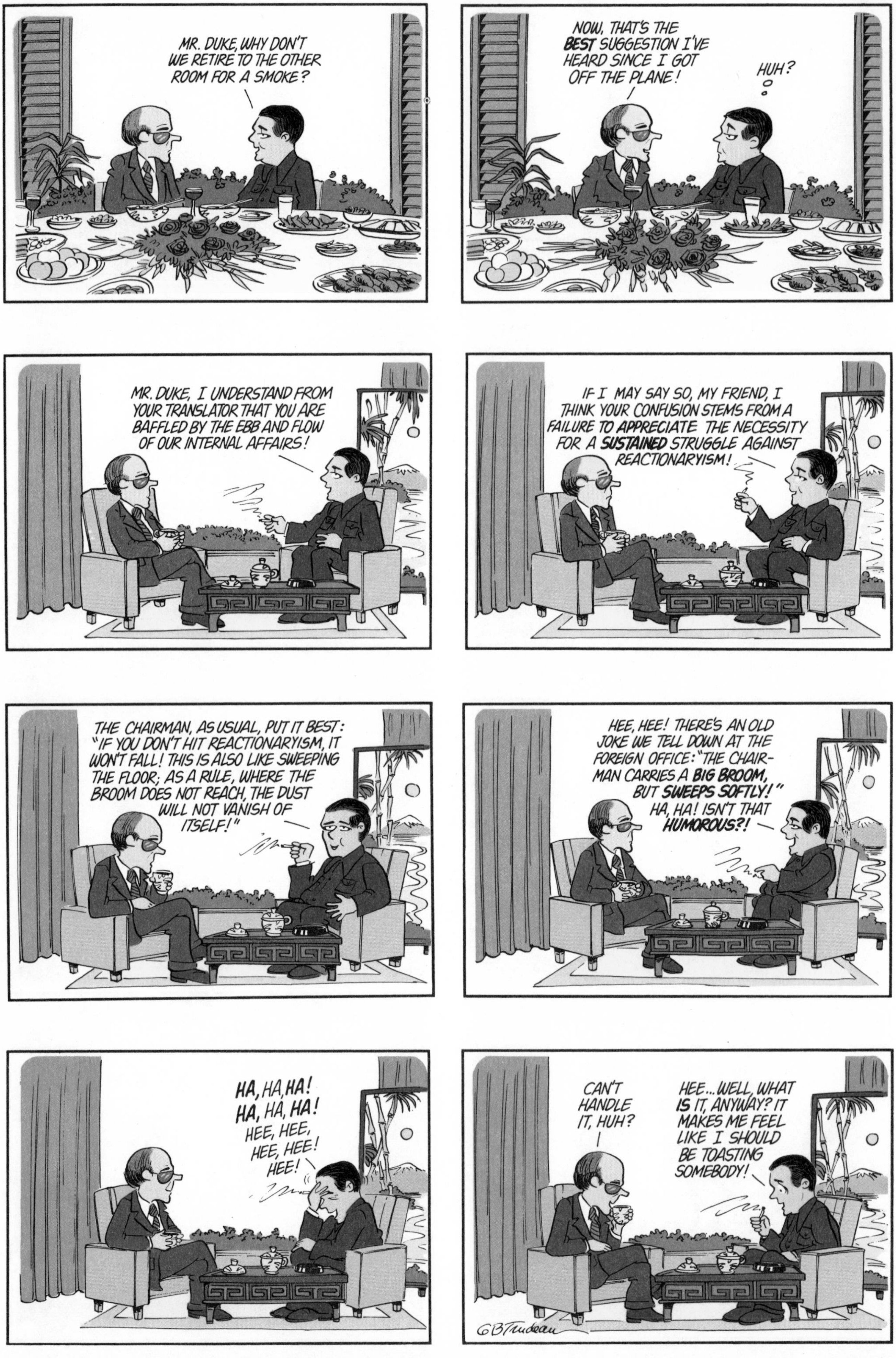
MR. DUKE, WHY DON'T WE RETIRE TO THE OTHER ROOM FOR A SMOKE?
NOW, THAT'S THE **BEST** SUGGESTION I'VE HEARD SINCE I GOT OFF THE PLANE!
HUH?
MR. DUKE, I UNDERSTAND FROM YOUR TRANSLATOR THAT YOU ARE BAFFLED BY THE EBB AND FLOW OF OUR INTERNAL AFFAIRS!
IF I MAY SAY SO, MY FRIEND, I THINK YOUR CONFUSION STEMS FROM A FAILURE TO **APPRECIATE** THE NECESSITY FOR A **SUSTAINED** STRUGGLE AGAINST REACTIONARYISM!
THE CHAIRMAN, AS USUAL, PUT IT BEST: "IF YOU DON'T HIT REACTIONARYISM, IT WON'T FALL! THIS IS ALSO LIKE SWEEPING THE FLOOR; AS A RULE, WHERE THE BROOM DOES NOT REACH, THE DUST WILL NOT VANISH OF ITSELF!"
HEE, HEE! THERE'S AN OLD JOKE WE TELL DOWN AT THE FOREIGN OFFICE: "THE CHAIRMAN CARRIES A **BIG BROOM,** BUT **SWEEPS SOFTLY!**" HA, HA! ISN'T THAT **HUMOROUS?!**
HA, HA, **HA**! **HA**, HA, **HA**! HEE, HEE, HEE, HEE! HEE!
CAN'T HANDLE IT, HUH?
HEE... WELL, WHAT **IS** IT, ANYWAY? IT MAKES ME FEEL LIKE I SHOULD BE TOASTING SOMEBODY!
GBTrudeau

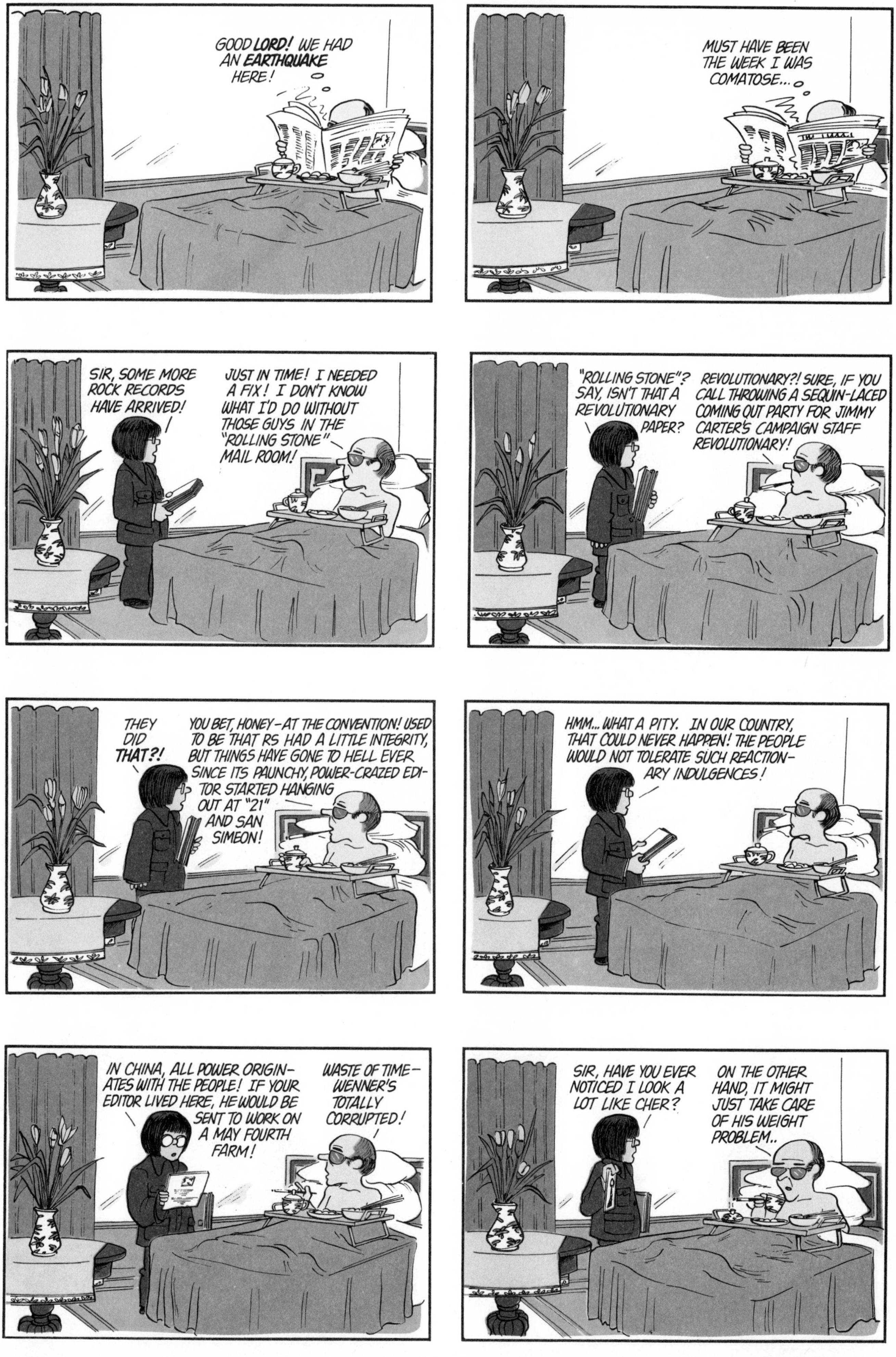
GOOD LORD! WE HAD AN EARTHQUAKE HERE!
MUST HAVE BEEN THE WEEK I WAS COMATOSE...
SIR, SOME MORE ROCK RECORDS HAVE ARRIVED!
JUST IN TIME! I NEEDED A FIX! I DON'T KNOW WHAT I'D DO WITHOUT THOSE GUYS IN THE "ROLLING STONE" MAIL ROOM!
"ROLLING STONE"? SAY, ISN'T THAT A REVOLUTIONARY PAPER?
REVOLUTIONARY?! SURE, IF YOU CALL THROWING A SEQUIN-LACED COMING OUT PARTY FOR JIMMY CARTER'S CAMPAIGN STAFF REVOLUTIONARY!
THEY DID THAT?!
YOU BET, HONEY-AT THE CONVENTION! USED TO BE THAT RS HAD A LITTLE INTEGRITY, BUT THINGS HAVE GONE TO HELL EVER SINCE ITS PAUNCHY, POWER-CRAZED EDITOR STARTED HANGING OUT AT "21" AND SAN SIMEON!
HMM... WHAT A PITY. IN OUR COUNTRY, THAT COULD NEVER HAPPEN! THE PEOPLE WOULD NOT TOLERATE SUCH REACTIONARY INDULGENCES!
IN CHINA, ALL POWER ORIGINATES WITH THE PEOPLE! IF YOUR EDITOR LIVED HERE, HE WOULD BE SENT TO WORK ON A MAY FOURTH FARM!
WASTE OF TIME-WENNER'S TOTALLY CORRUPTED!
SIR, HAVE YOU EVER NOTICED I LOOK A LOT LIKE CHER?
ON THE OTHER HAND, IT MIGHT JUST TAKE CARE OF HIS WEIGHT PROBLEM..

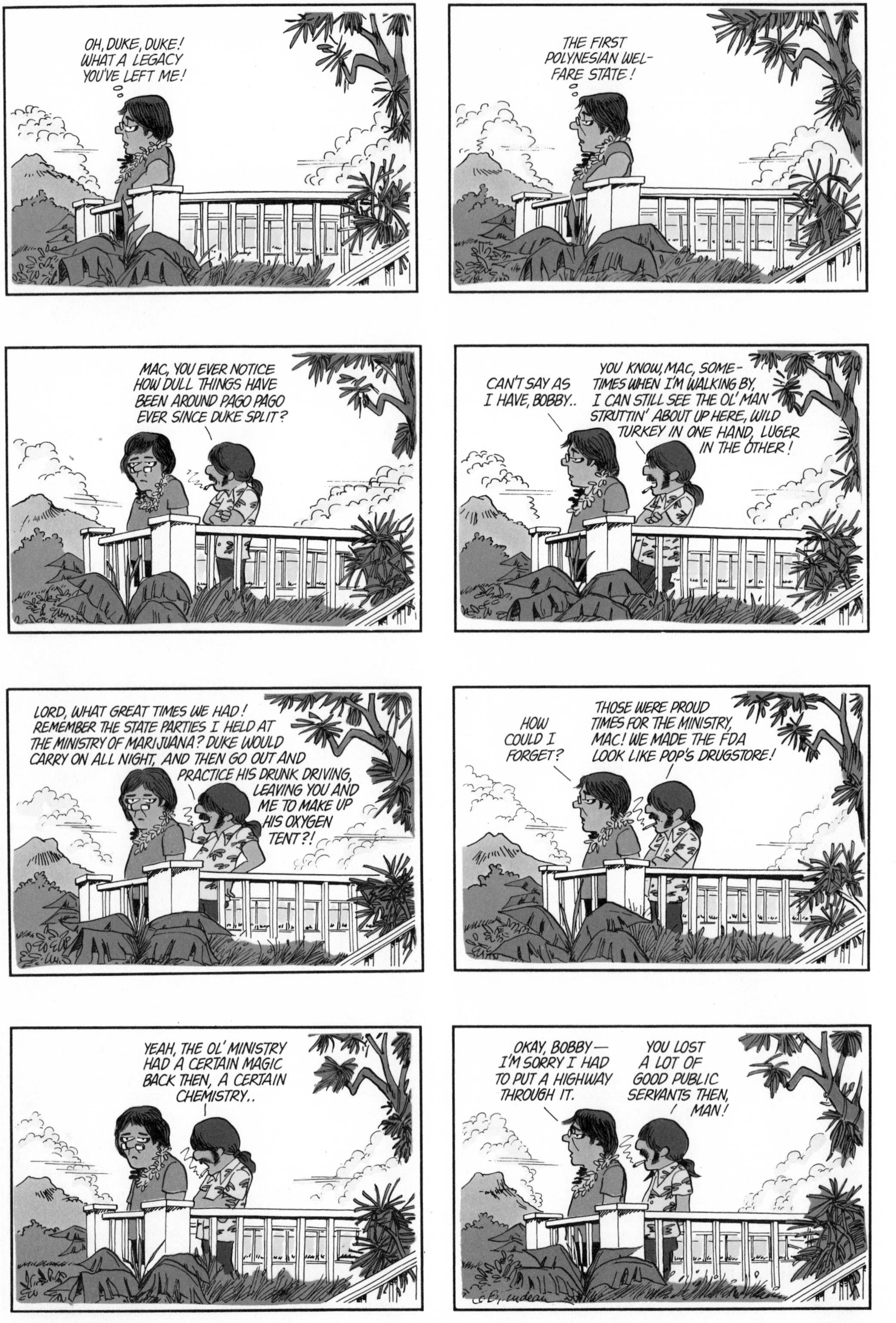
OH, DUKE, DUKE! WHAT A LEGACY YOU'VE LEFT ME!
THE FIRST POLYNESIAN WEL-FARE STATE!
MAC, YOU EVER NOTICE HOW DULL THINGS HAVE BEEN AROUND PAGO PAGO EVER SINCE DUKE SPLIT?
CAN'T SAY AS I HAVE, BOBBY..
YOU KNOW, MAC, SOME-TIMES WHEN I'M WALKING BY, I CAN STILL SEE THE OL' MAN STRUTTIN' ABOUT UP HERE, WILD TURKEY IN ONE HAND, LUGER IN THE OTHER!
LORD, WHAT GREAT TIMES WE HAD! REMEMBER THE STATE PARTIES I HELD AT THE MINISTRY OF MARIJUANA? DUKE WOULD CARRY ON ALL NIGHT, AND THEN GO OUT AND PRACTICE HIS DRUNK DRIVING, LEAVING YOU AND ME TO MAKE UP HIS OXYGEN TENT?!
HOW COULD I FORGET?
THOSE WERE PROUD TIMES FOR THE MINISTRY, MAC! WE MADE THE FDA LOOK LIKE POP'S DRUGSTORE!
YEAH, THE OL' MINISTRY HAD A CERTAIN MAGIC BACK THEN, A CERTAIN CHEMISTRY..
OKAY, BOBBY— I'M SORRY I HAD TO PUT A HIGHWAY THROUGH IT.
YOU LOST A LOT OF GOOD PUBLIC SERVANTS THEN, MAN!

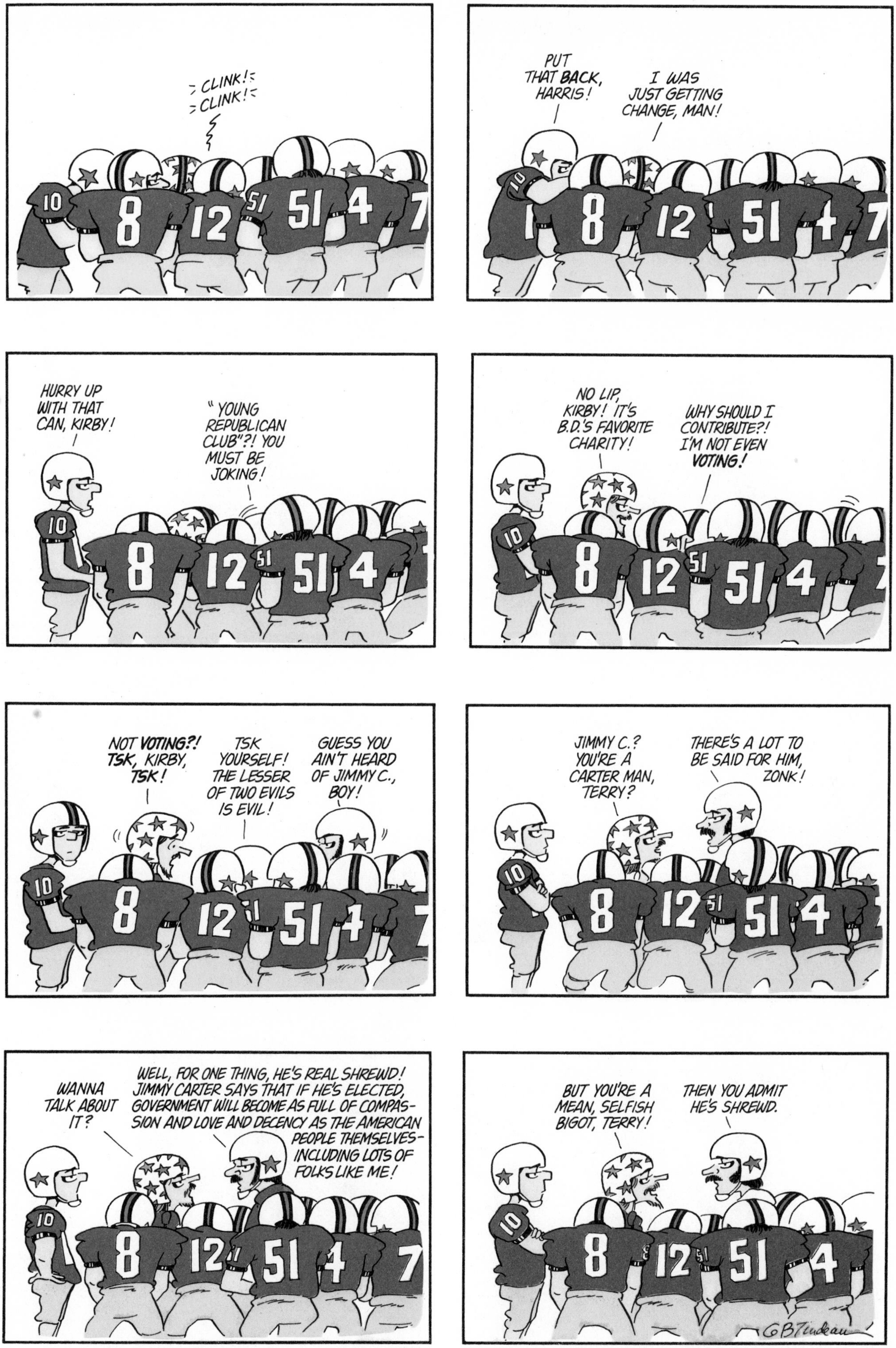
CLINK! CLINK!
PUT THAT BACK, HARRIS!
I WAS JUST GETTING CHANGE, MAN!
HURRY UP WITH THAT CAN, KIRBY!
"YOUNG REPUBLICAN CLUB"?! YOU MUST BE JOKING!
NO LIP, KIRBY! IT'S B.D.'S FAVORITE CHARITY!
WHY SHOULD I CONTRIBUTE?! I'M NOT EVEN VOTING!
NOT VOTING?! TSK, KIRBY, TSK!
TSK YOURSELF! THE LESSER OF TWO EVILS IS EVIL!
GUESS YOU AIN'T HEARD OF JIMMY C., BOY!
JIMMY C.? YOU'RE A CARTER MAN, TERRY?
THERE'S A LOT TO BE SAID FOR HIM, ZONK!
WANNA TALK ABOUT IT?
WELL, FOR ONE THING, HE'S REAL SHREWD! JIMMY CARTER SAYS THAT IF HE'S ELECTED, GOVERNMENT WILL BECOME AS FULL OF COMPASSION AND LOVE AND DECENCY AS THE AMERICAN PEOPLE THEMSELVES— INCLUDING LOTS OF FOLKS LIKE ME!
BUT YOU'RE A MEAN, SELFISH BIGOT, TERRY!
THEN YOU ADMIT HE'S SHREWD.
GBTrudeau

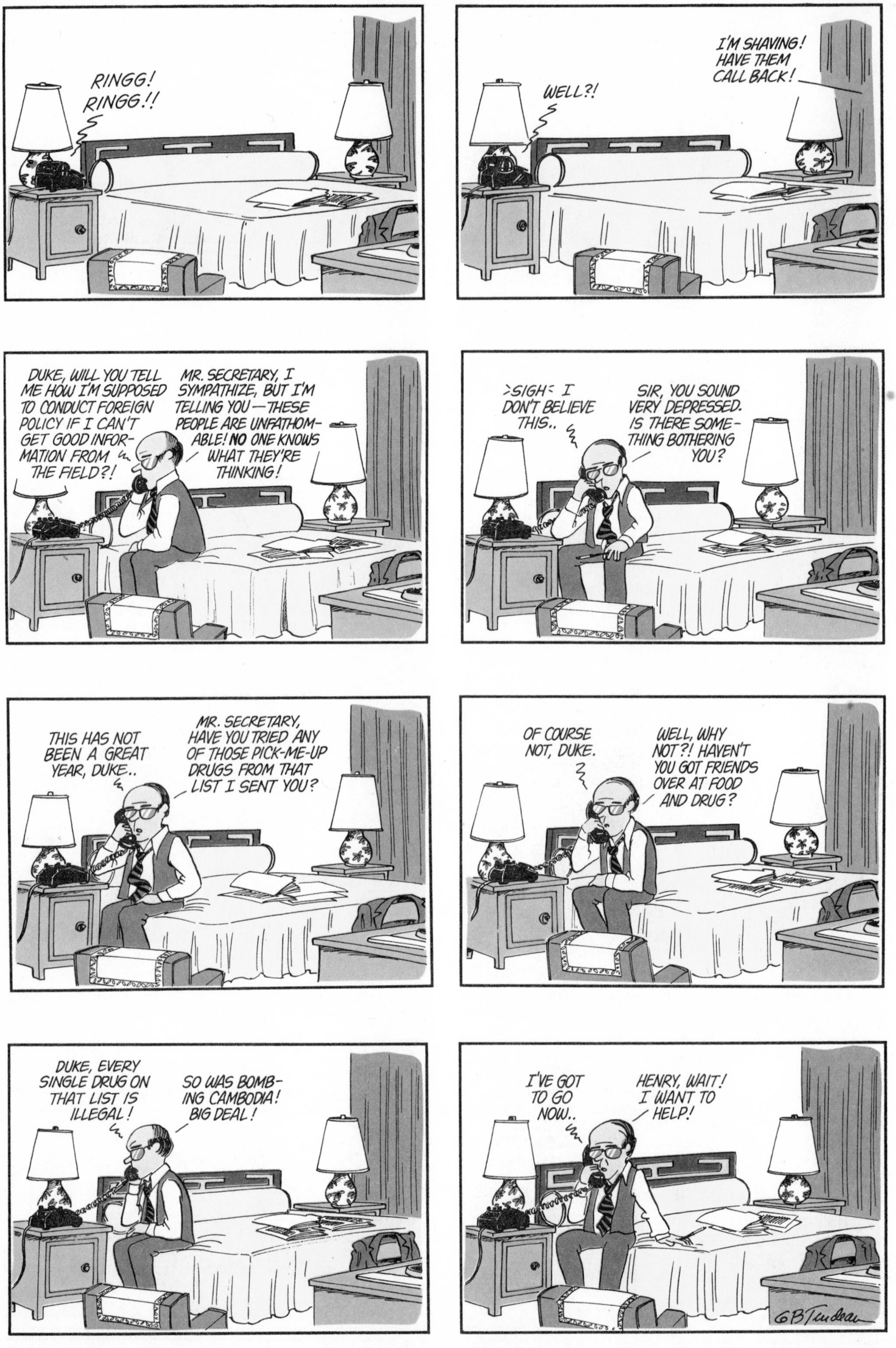
RINGG! RINGG!!
WELL?!
I'M SHAVING! HAVE THEM CALL BACK!
DUKE, WILL YOU TELL ME HOW I'M SUPPOSED TO CONDUCT FOREIGN POLICY IF I CAN'T GET GOOD INFORMATION FROM THE FIELD?!
MR. SECRETARY, I SYMPATHIZE, BUT I'M TELLING YOU — THESE PEOPLE ARE UNFATHOMABLE! NO ONE KNOWS WHAT THEY'RE THINKING!
>SIGH< I DON'T BELIEVE THIS..
SIR, YOU SOUND VERY DEPRESSED. IS THERE SOMETHING BOTHERING YOU?
THIS HAS NOT BEEN A GREAT YEAR, DUKE..
MR. SECRETARY, HAVE YOU TRIED ANY OF THOSE PICK-ME-UP DRUGS FROM THAT LIST I SENT YOU?
OF COURSE NOT, DUKE.
WELL, WHY NOT?! HAVEN'T YOU GOT FRIENDS OVER AT FOOD AND DRUG?
DUKE, EVERY SINGLE DRUG ON THAT LIST IS ILLEGAL!
SO WAS BOMBING CAMBODIA! BIG DEAL!
I'VE GOT TO GO NOW..
HENRY, WAIT! I WANT TO HELP!
GBTrudeau

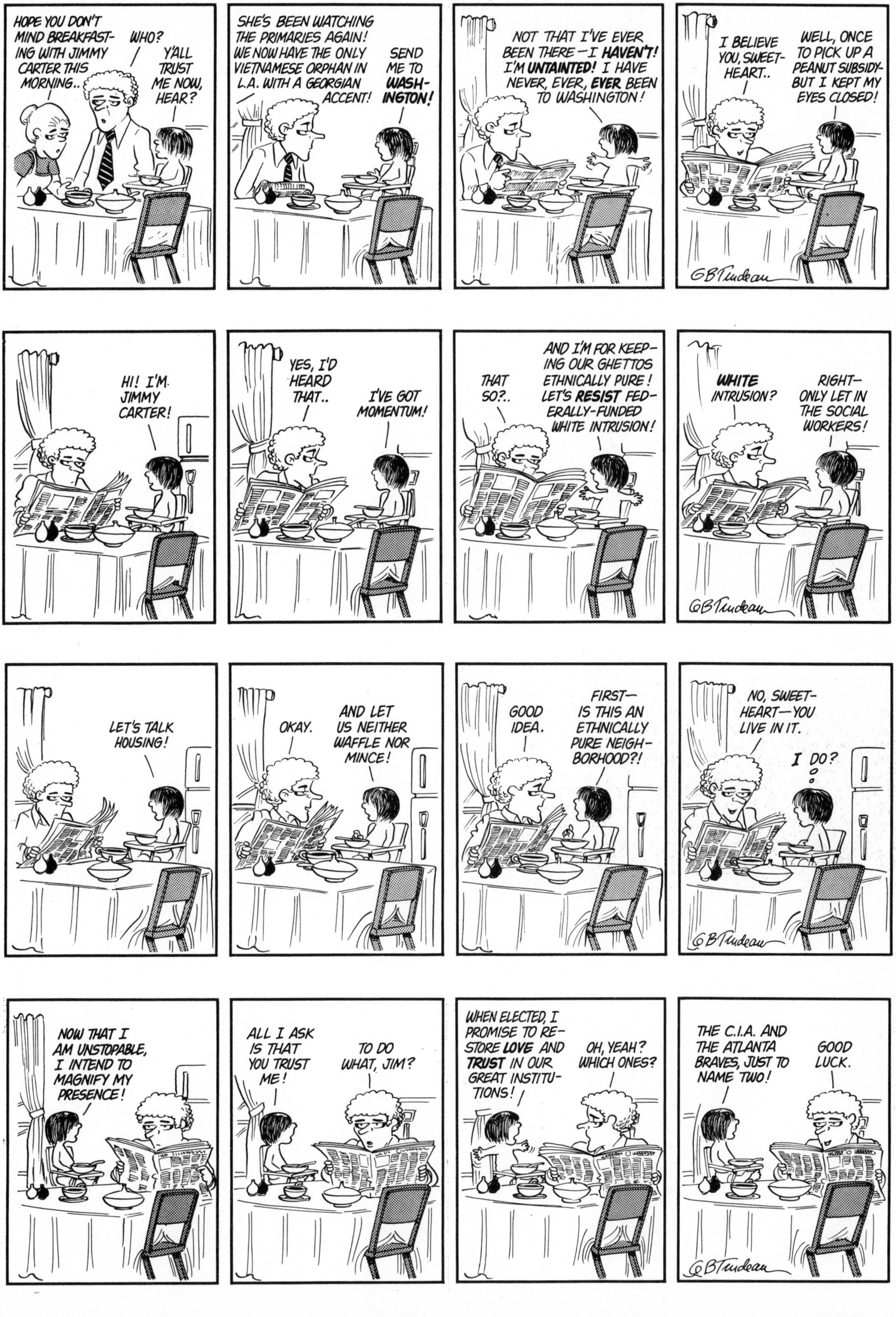
HOPE YOU DON'T MIND BREAKFAST-ING WITH JIMMY CARTER THIS MORNING..
WHO?
Y'ALL TRUST ME NOW, HEAR?
SHE'S BEEN WATCHING THE PRIMARIES AGAIN! WE NOW HAVE THE ONLY VIETNAMESE ORPHAN IN L.A. WITH A GEORGIAN ACCENT!
SEND ME TO WASH-INGTON!
NOT THAT I'VE EVER BEEN THERE—I HAVEN'T! I'M UNTAINTED! I HAVE NEVER, EVER, EVER BEEN TO WASHINGTON!
I BELIEVE YOU, SWEET-HEART..
WELL, ONCE TO PICK UP A PEANUT SUBSIDY-BUT I KEPT MY EYES CLOSED!
GBTrudeau
HI! I'M JIMMY CARTER!
YES, I'D HEARD THAT..
I'VE GOT MOMENTUM!
THAT SO?..
AND I'M FOR KEEP-ING OUR GHETTOS ETHNICALLY PURE! LET'S RESIST FED-ERALLY-FUNDED WHITE INTRUSION!
WHITE INTRUSION?
RIGHT—ONLY LET IN THE SOCIAL WORKERS!
GBTrudeau
LET'S TALK HOUSING!
OKAY.
AND LET US NEITHER WAFFLE NOR MINCE!
GOOD IDEA.
FIRST—IS THIS AN ETHNICALLY PURE NEIGH-BORHOOD?!
NO, SWEET-HEART—YOU LIVE IN IT.
I DO?
GBTrudeau
NOW THAT I AM UNSTOPABLE, I INTEND TO MAGNIFY MY PRESENCE!
ALL I ASK IS THAT YOU TRUST ME!
TO DO WHAT, JIM?
WHEN ELECTED, I PROMISE TO RE-STORE LOVE AND TRUST IN OUR GREAT INSTITU-TIONS!
OH, YEAH? WHICH ONES?
THE C.I.A. AND THE ATLANTA BRAVES, JUST TO NAME TWO!
GOOD LUCK.
GBTrudeau

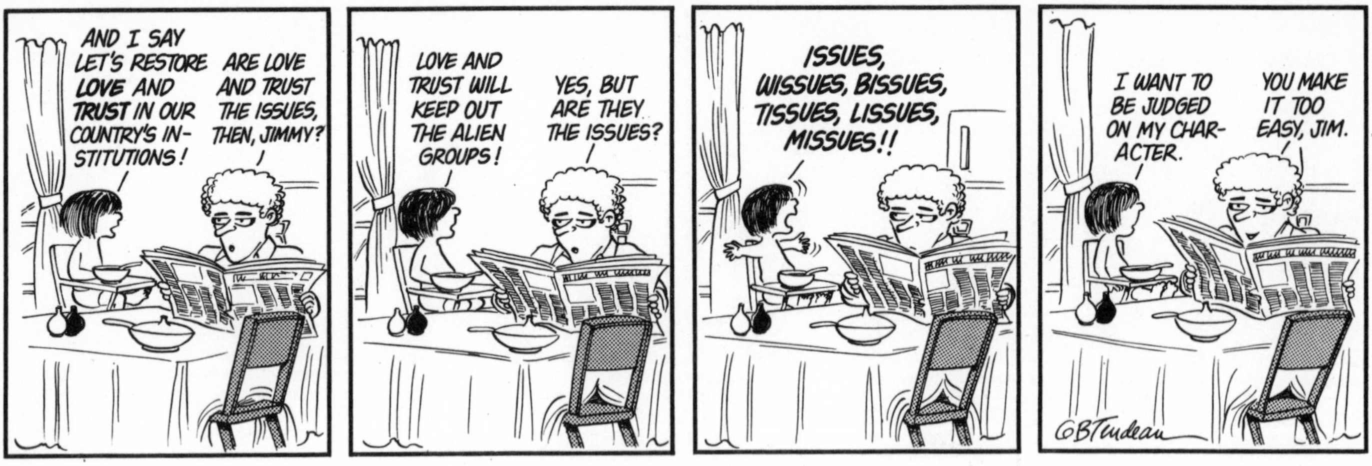
AND I SAY LET'S RESTORE LOVE AND TRUST IN OUR COUNTRY'S INSTITUTIONS!
ARE LOVE AND TRUST THE ISSUES, THEN, JIMMY?
LOVE AND TRUST WILL KEEP OUT THE ALIEN GROUPS!
YES, BUT ARE THEY THE ISSUES?
ISSUES, WISSUES, BISSUES, TISSUES, LISSUES, MISSUES!!
I WANT TO BE JUDGED ON MY CHARACTER.
YOU MAKE IT TOO EASY, JIM.
GBTrudeau

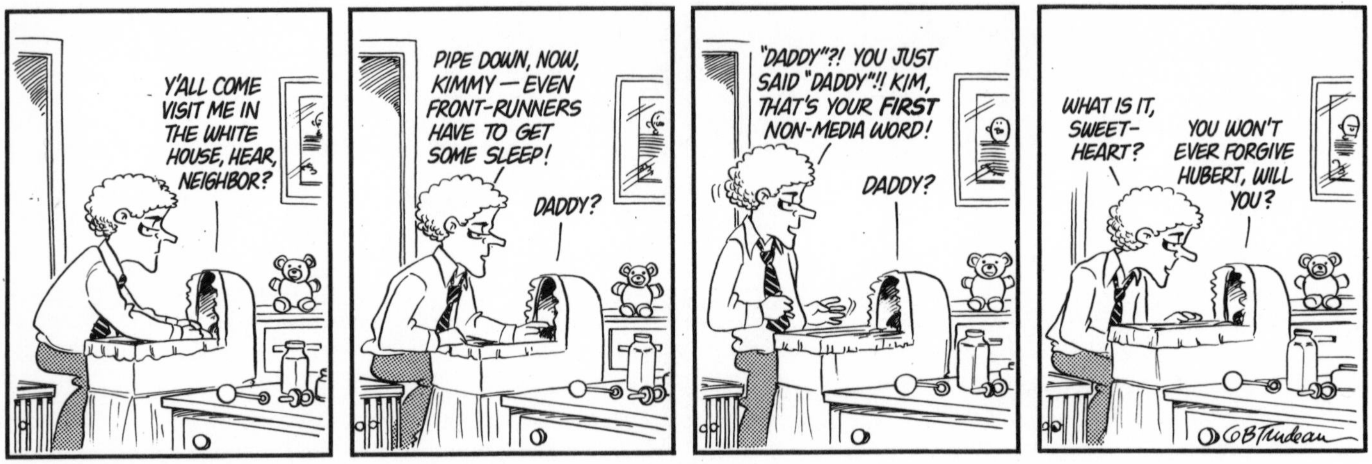
Y'ALL COME VISIT ME IN THE WHITE HOUSE, HEAR, NEIGHBOR?
PIPE DOWN, NOW, KIMMY — EVEN FRONT-RUNNERS HAVE TO GET SOME SLEEP!
DADDY?
"DADDY"?! YOU JUST SAID "DADDY"!! KIM, THAT'S YOUR FIRST NON-MEDIA WORD!
DADDY?
WHAT IS IT, SWEETHEART?
YOU WON'T EVER FORGIVE HUBERT, WILL YOU?
GBTrudeau

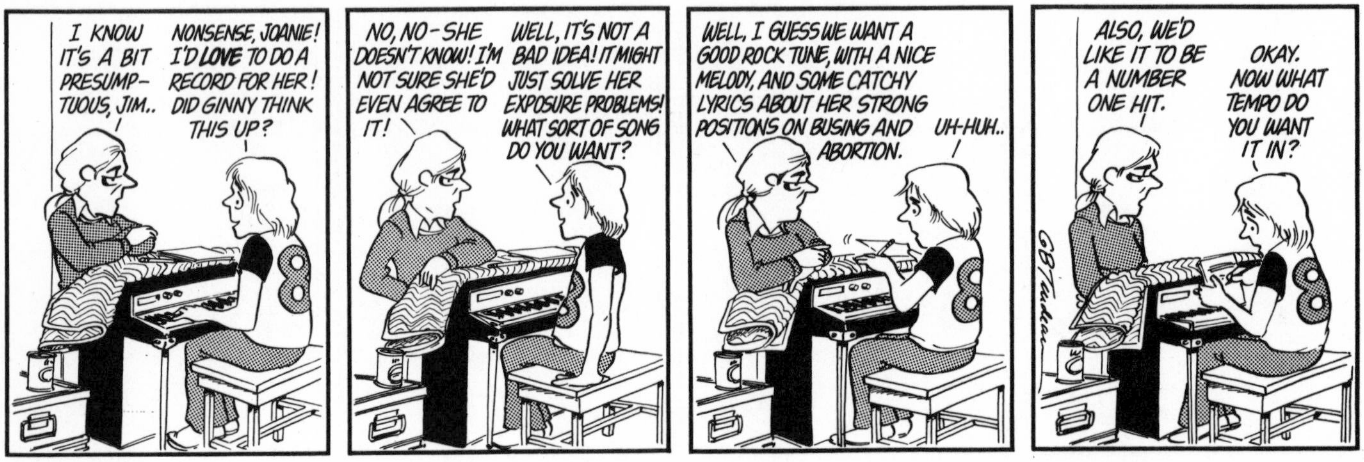
I KNOW IT'S A BIT PRESUMPTUOUS, JIM..
NONSENSE, JOANIE! I'D LOVE TO DO A RECORD FOR HER! DID GINNY THINK THIS UP?
NO, NO - SHE DOESN'T KNOW! I'M NOT SURE SHE'D EVEN AGREE TO IT!
WELL, IT'S NOT A BAD IDEA! IT MIGHT JUST SOLVE HER EXPOSURE PROBLEMS! WHAT SORT OF SONG DO YOU WANT?
WELL, I GUESS WE WANT A GOOD ROCK TUNE, WITH A NICE MELODY, AND SOME CATCHY LYRICS ABOUT HER STRONG POSITIONS ON BUSING AND ABORTION.
UH-HUH..
ALSO, WE'D LIKE IT TO BE A NUMBER ONE HIT.
OKAY. NOW WHAT TEMPO DO YOU WANT IT IN?
GBTrudeau

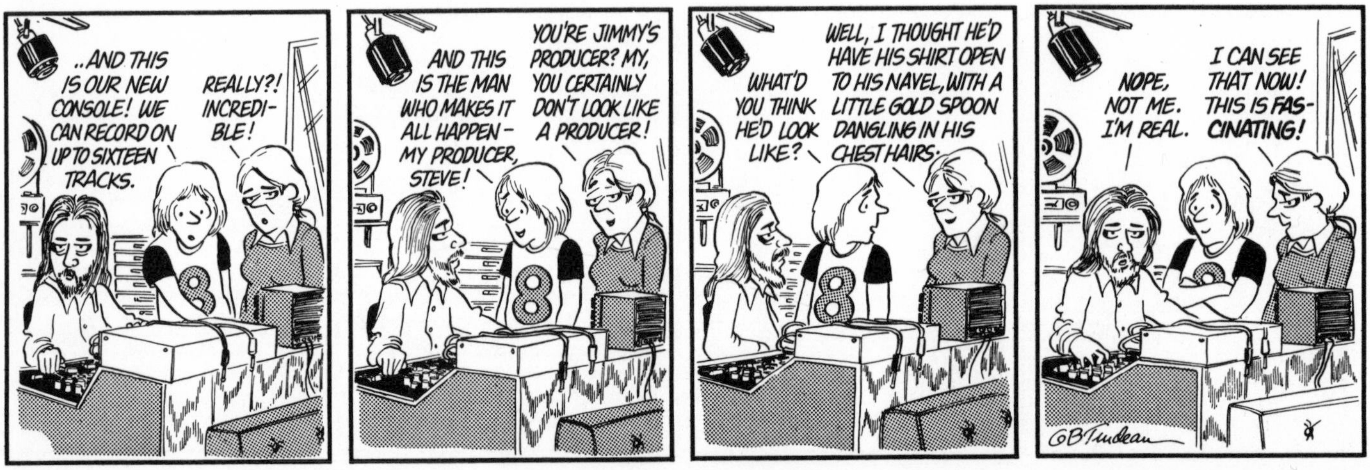
..AND THIS IS OUR NEW CONSOLE! WE CAN RECORD ON UP TO SIXTEEN TRACKS.
REALLY?! INCREDIBLE!
AND THIS IS THE MAN WHO MAKES IT ALL HAPPEN - MY PRODUCER, STEVE!
YOU'RE JIMMY'S PRODUCER? MY, YOU CERTAINLY DON'T LOOK LIKE A PRODUCER!
WHAT'D YOU THINK HE'D LOOK LIKE?
WELL, I THOUGHT HE'D HAVE HIS SHIRT OPEN TO HIS NAVEL, WITH A LITTLE GOLD SPOON DANGLING IN HIS CHEST HAIRS.
NOPE, NOT ME. I'M REAL.
I CAN SEE THAT NOW! THIS IS FASCINATING!
GBTrudeau

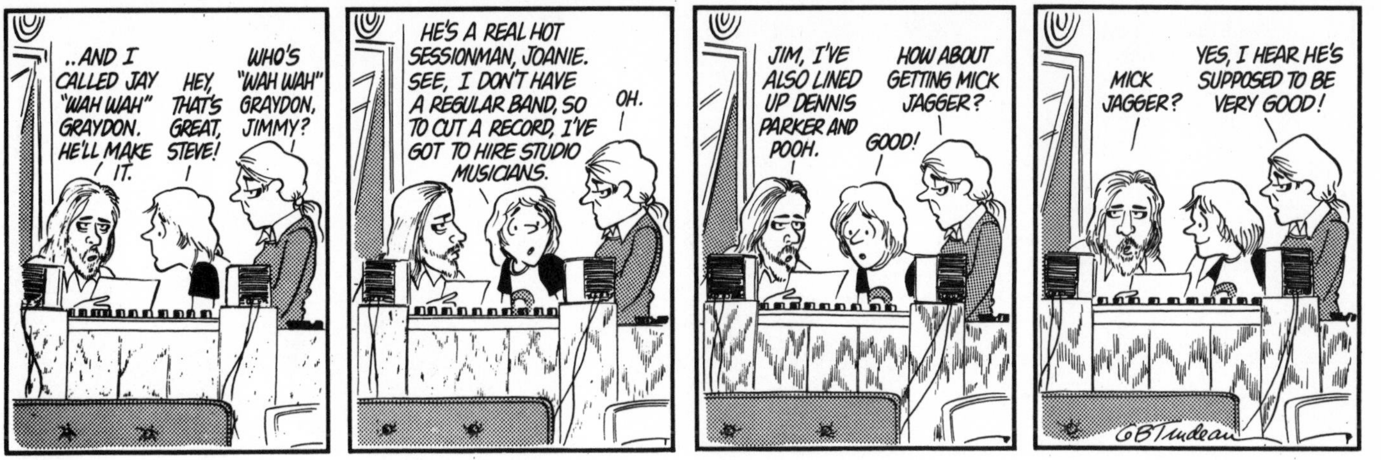
..AND I CALLED JAY "WAH WAH" GRAYDON. HE'LL MAKE IT.
HEY, THAT'S GREAT, STEVE!
WHO'S "WAH WAH" GRAYDON, JIMMY?
HE'S A REAL HOT SESSIONMAN, JOANIE. SEE, I DON'T HAVE A REGULAR BAND, SO TO CUT A RECORD, I'VE GOT TO HIRE STUDIO MUSICIANS.
OH.
JIM, I'VE ALSO LINED UP DENNIS PARKER AND POOH.
GOOD!
HOW ABOUT GETTING MICK JAGGER?
MICK JAGGER?
YES, I HEAR HE'S SUPPOSED TO BE VERY GOOD!
GBTrudeau

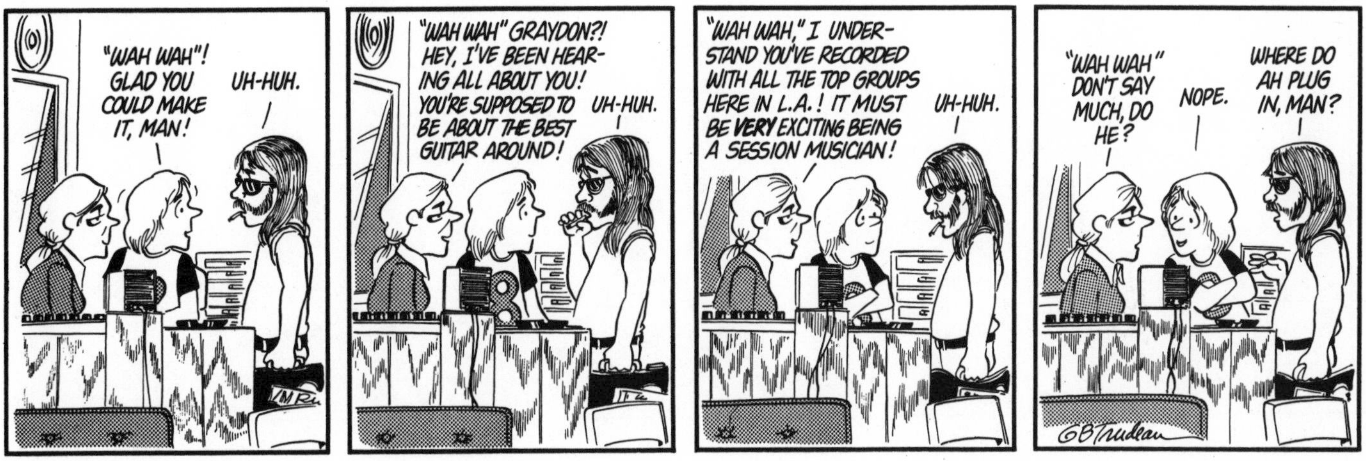
"WAH WAH"! GLAD YOU COULD MAKE IT, MAN!
UH-HUH.
"WAH WAH" GRAYDON?! HEY, I'VE BEEN HEARING ALL ABOUT YOU! YOU'RE SUPPOSED TO BE ABOUT THE BEST GUITAR AROUND!
UH-HUH.
"WAH WAH," I UNDERSTAND YOU'VE RECORDED WITH ALL THE TOP GROUPS HERE IN L.A.! IT MUST BE VERY EXCITING BEING A SESSION MUSICIAN!
UH-HUH.
"WAH WAH" DON'T SAY MUCH, DO HE?
NOPE.
WHERE DO AH PLUG IN, MAN?
GBTrudeau

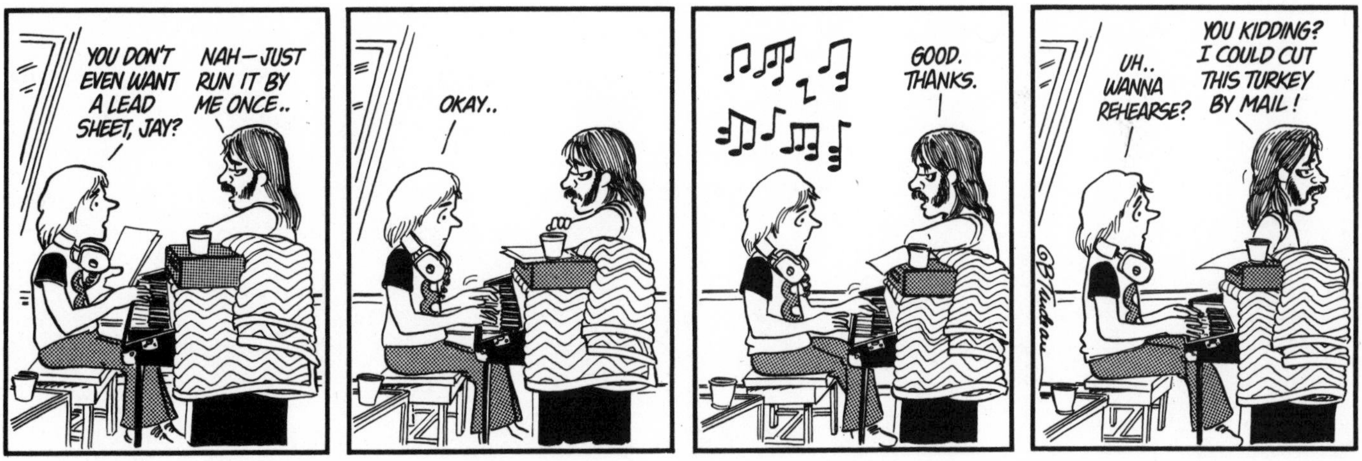
YOU DON'T EVEN WANT A LEAD SHEET, JAY?
NAH—JUST RUN IT BY ME ONCE..
OKAY..
GOOD. THANKS.
UH.. WANNA REHEARSE?
YOU KIDDING? I COULD CUT THIS TURKEY BY MAIL!
GBTrudeau

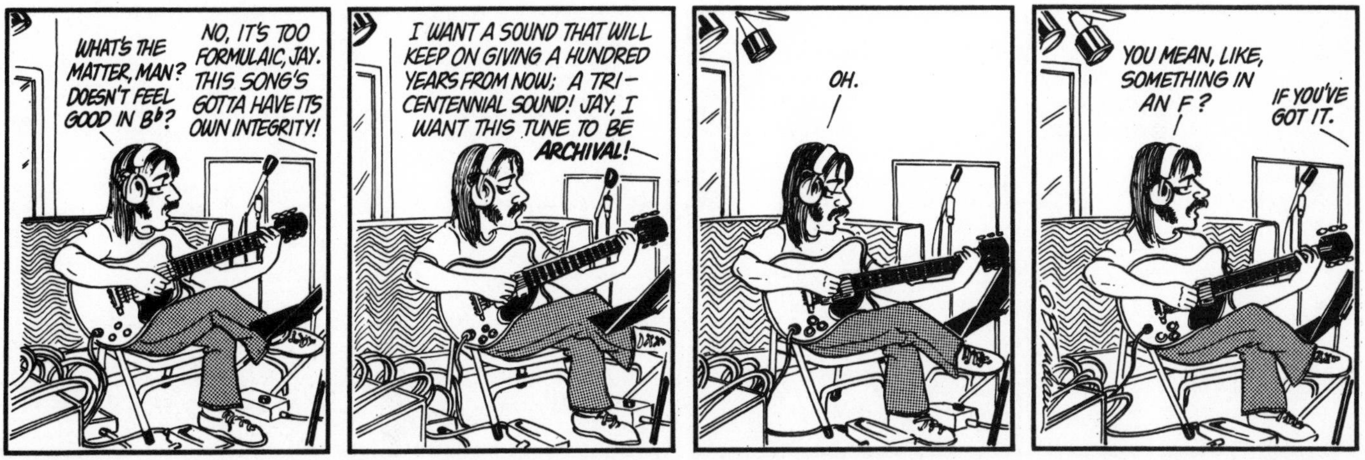
WHAT'S THE MATTER, MAN? DOESN'T FEEL GOOD IN B♭?
NO, IT'S TOO FORMULAIC, JAY. THIS SONG'S GOTTA HAVE ITS OWN INTEGRITY!
I WANT A SOUND THAT WILL KEEP ON GIVING A HUNDRED YEARS FROM NOW; A TRI-CENTENNIAL SOUND! JAY, I WANT THIS TUNE TO BE ARCHIVAL!
OH.
YOU MEAN, LIKE, SOMETHING IN AN F?
IF YOU'VE GOT IT.
GBTrudeau

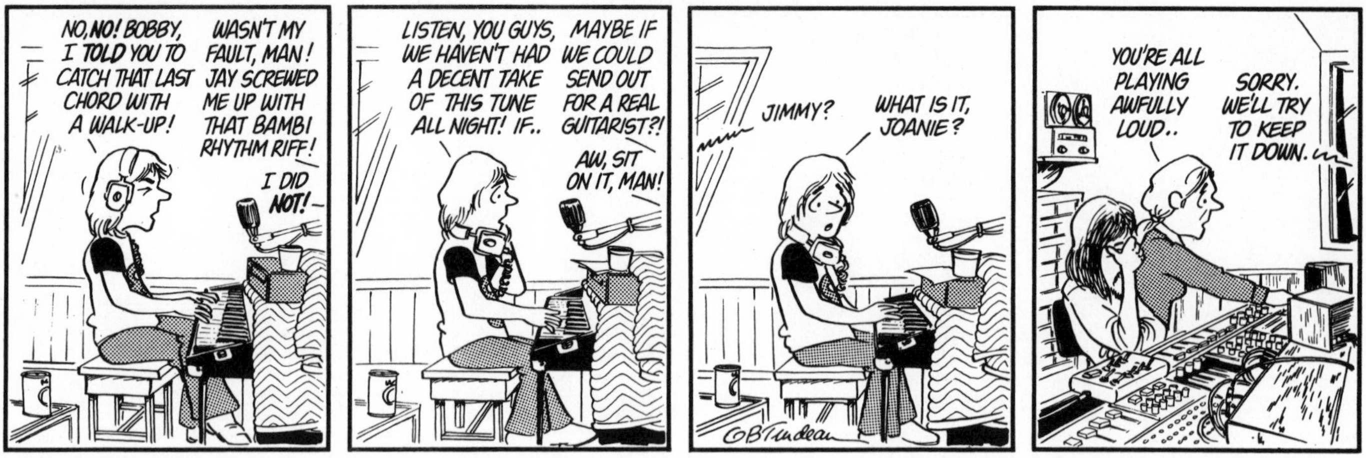
NO, NO! BOBBY, I TOLD YOU TO CATCH THAT LAST CHORD WITH A WALK-UP!
WASN'T MY FAULT, MAN! JAY SCREWED ME UP WITH THAT BAMBI RHYTHM RIFF!
I DID NOT!
LISTEN, YOU GUYS, WE HAVEN'T HAD A DECENT TAKE OF THIS TUNE ALL NIGHT! IF..
MAYBE IF WE COULD SEND OUT FOR A REAL GUITARIST?!
AW, SIT ON IT, MAN!
JIMMY?
WHAT IS IT, JOANIE?
YOU'RE ALL PLAYING AWFULLY LOUD..
SORRY. WE'LL TRY TO KEEP IT DOWN.
GBTrudeau

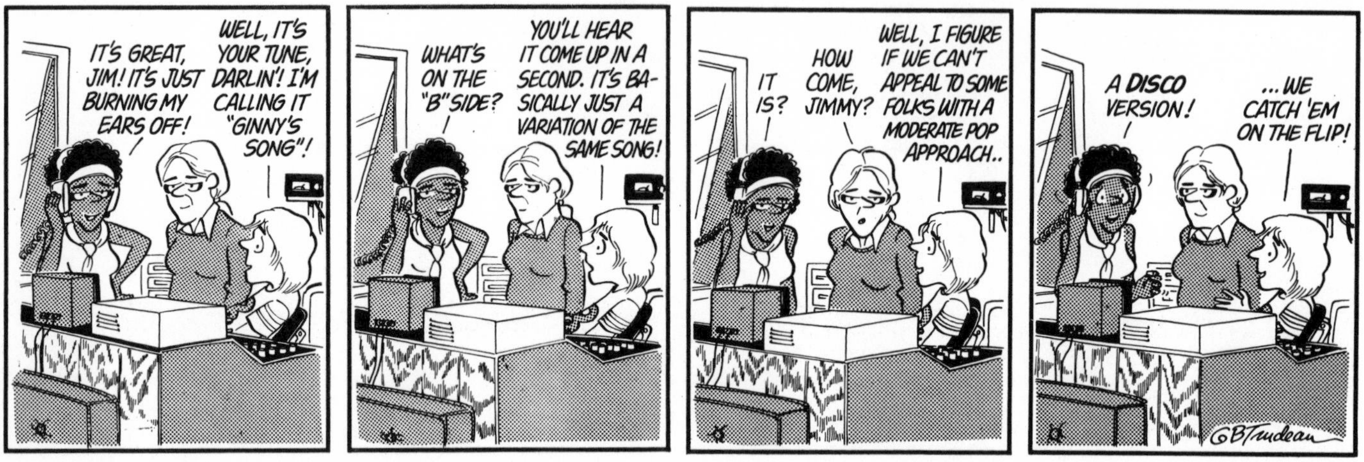
IT'S GREAT, JIM! IT'S JUST BURNING MY EARS OFF!
WELL, IT'S YOUR TUNE, DARLIN'! I'M CALLING IT "GINNY'S SONG"!
WHAT'S ON THE "B" SIDE?
YOU'LL HEAR IT COME UP IN A SECOND. IT'S BASICALLY JUST A VARIATION OF THE SAME SONG!
IT IS?
HOW COME, JIMMY?
WELL, I FIGURE IF WE CAN'T APPEAL TO SOME FOLKS WITH A MODERATE POP APPROACH..
A DISCO VERSION!
... WE CATCH 'EM ON THE FLIP!
GBTrudeau

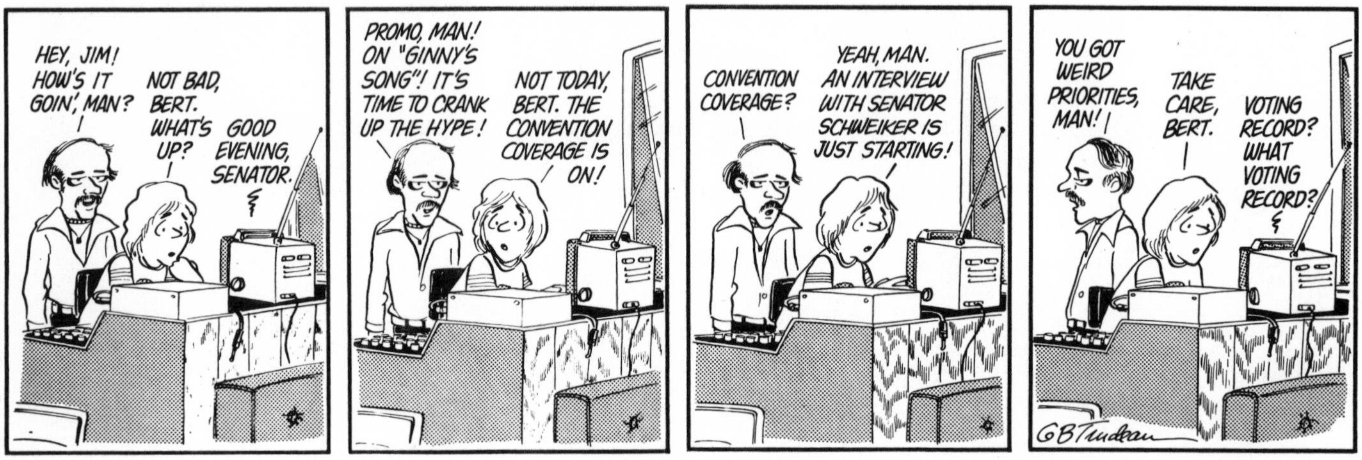
HEY, JIM! HOW'S IT GOIN', MAN?
NOT BAD, BERT. WHAT'S UP?
GOOD EVENING, SENATOR.
PROMO, MAN! ON "GINNY'S SONG"! IT'S TIME TO CRANK UP THE HYPE!
NOT TODAY, BERT. THE CONVENTION COVERAGE IS ON!
CONVENTION COVERAGE?
YEAH, MAN. AN INTERVIEW WITH SENATOR SCHWEIKER IS JUST STARTING!
YOU GOT WEIRD PRIORITIES, MAN!
TAKE CARE, BERT.
VOTING RECORD? WHAT VOTING RECORD?
GBTrudeau

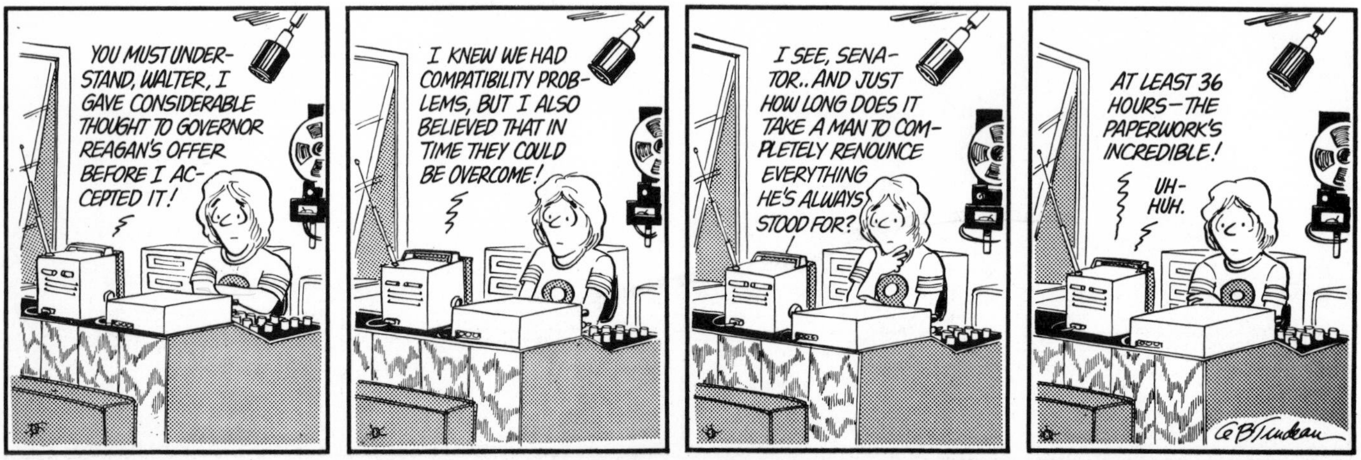
YOU MUST UNDERSTAND, WALTER, I GAVE CONSIDERABLE THOUGHT TO GOVERNOR REAGAN'S OFFER BEFORE I ACCEPTED IT!
I KNEW WE HAD COMPATIBILITY PROBLEMS, BUT I ALSO BELIEVED THAT IN TIME THEY COULD BE OVERCOME!
I SEE, SENATOR.. AND JUST HOW LONG DOES IT TAKE A MAN TO COMPLETELY RENOUNCE EVERYTHING HE'S ALWAYS STOOD FOR?
AT LEAST 36 HOURS—THE PAPERWORK'S INCREDIBLE!
UH-HUH.
GBTrudeau

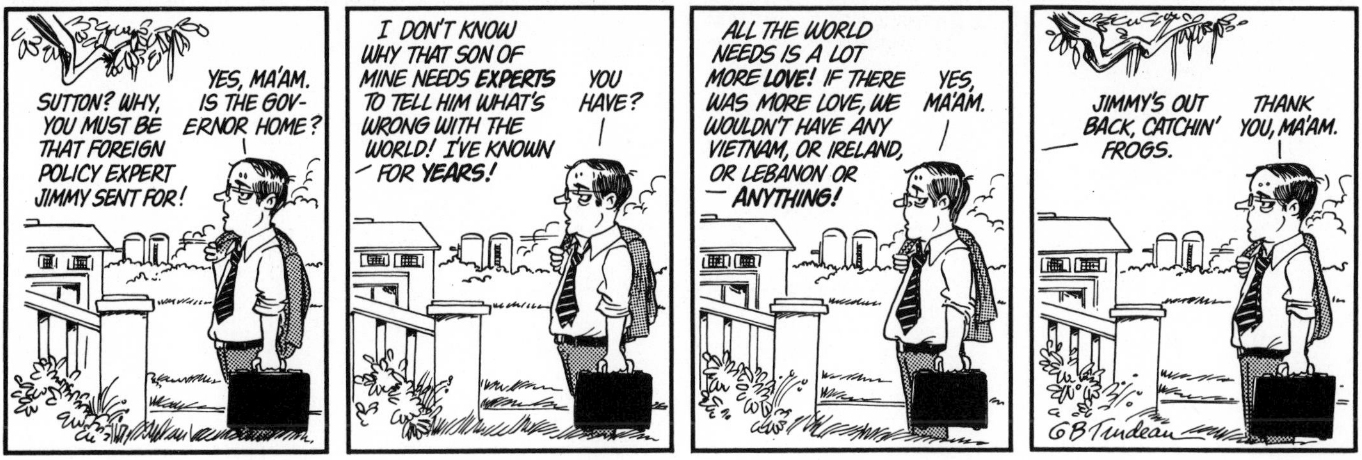
SUTTON? WHY, YOU MUST BE THAT FOREIGN POLICY EXPERT JIMMY SENT FOR!
YES, MA'AM. IS THE GOVERNOR HOME?
I DON'T KNOW WHY THAT SON OF MINE NEEDS **EXPERTS** TO TELL HIM WHAT'S WRONG WITH THE WORLD! I'VE KNOWN FOR **YEARS!**
YOU HAVE?
ALL THE WORLD NEEDS IS A LOT MORE **LOVE!** IF THERE WAS MORE LOVE, WE WOULDN'T HAVE ANY VIETNAM, OR IRELAND, OR LEBANON OR **ANYTHING!**
YES, MA'AM.
JIMMY'S OUT BACK, CATCHIN' FROGS.
THANK YOU, MA'AM.
GBTrudeau

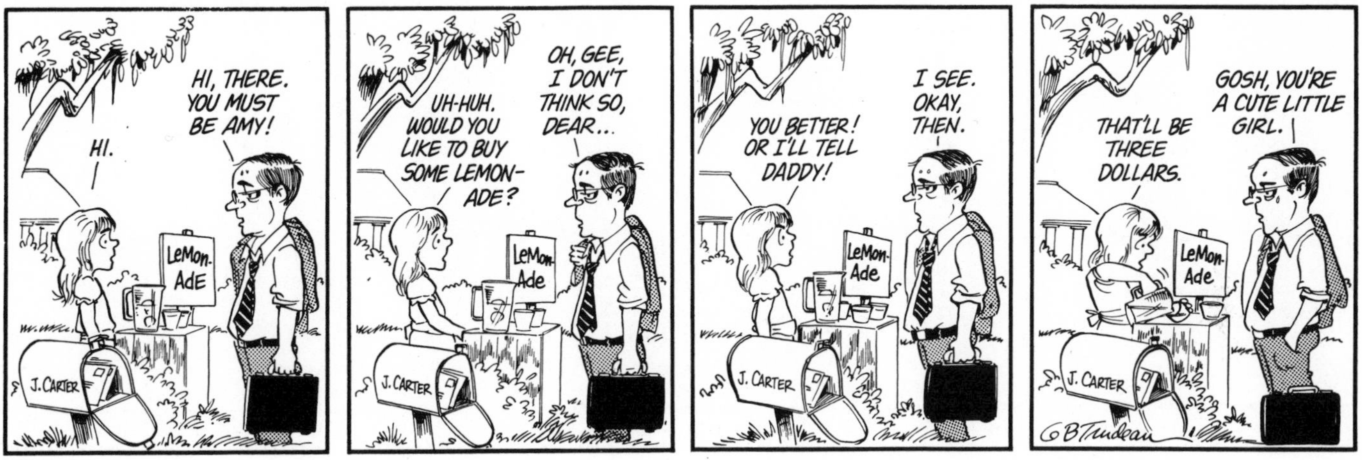
HI.
HI, THERE. YOU MUST BE AMY!
LeMon-AdE
J. CARTER
UH-HUH. WOULD YOU LIKE TO BUY SOME LEMON-ADE?
OH, GEE, I DON'T THINK SO, DEAR...
YOU BETTER! OR I'LL TELL DADDY!
I SEE. OKAY, THEN.
THAT'LL BE THREE DOLLARS.
GOSH, YOU'RE A CUTE LITTLE GIRL.
GBTrudeau

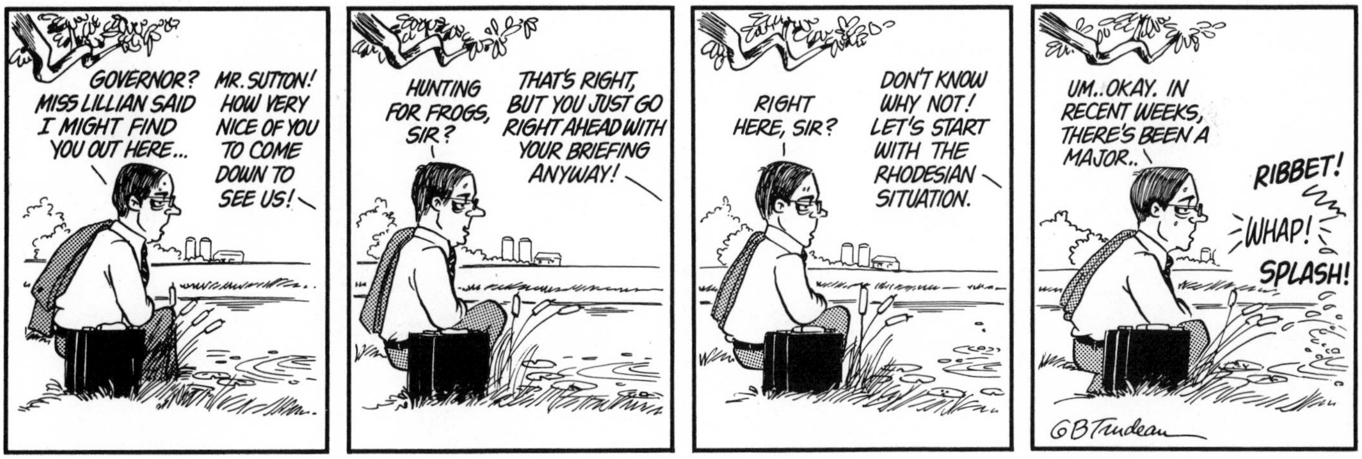
GOVERNOR? MISS LILLIAN SAID I MIGHT FIND YOU OUT HERE...
MR. SUTTON! HOW VERY NICE OF YOU TO COME DOWN TO SEE US!
HUNTING FOR FROGS, SIR?
THAT'S RIGHT, BUT YOU JUST GO RIGHT AHEAD WITH YOUR BRIEFING ANYWAY!
RIGHT HERE, SIR?
DON'T KNOW WHY NOT! LET'S START WITH THE RHODESIAN SITUATION.
UM..OKAY. IN RECENT WEEKS, THERE'S BEEN A MAJOR..
RIBBET!
WHAP!
SPLASH!
GBTrudeau

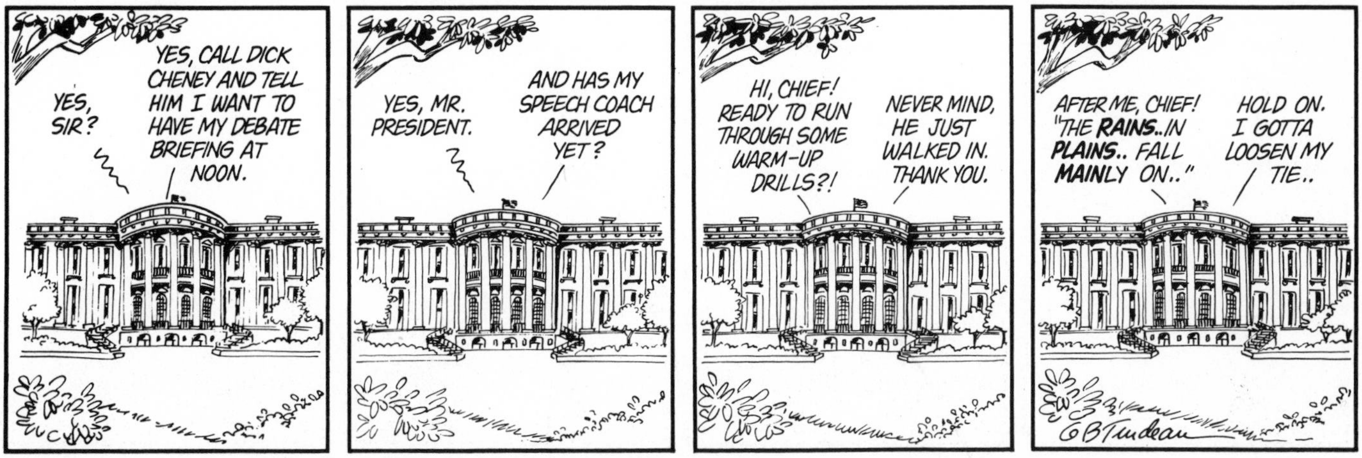
YES, SIR?
YES, CALL DICK CHENEY AND TELL HIM I WANT TO HAVE MY DEBATE BRIEFING AT NOON.
YES, MR. PRESIDENT.
AND HAS MY SPEECH COACH ARRIVED YET?
HI, CHIEF! READY TO RUN THROUGH SOME WARM-UP DRILLS?!
NEVER MIND, HE JUST WALKED IN. THANK YOU.
AFTER ME, CHIEF! "THE **RAINS**..IN **PLAINS**.. FALL **MAIN**LY ON.."
HOLD ON. I GOTTA LOOSEN MY TIE..
GBTrudeau

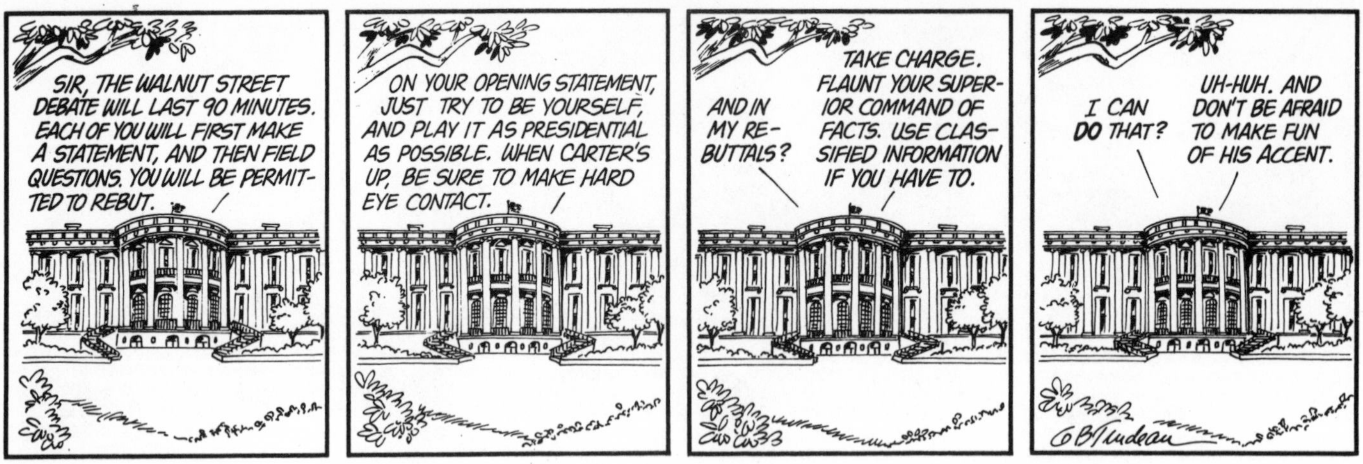
SIR, THE WALNUT STREET DEBATE WILL LAST 90 MINUTES. EACH OF YOU WILL FIRST MAKE A STATEMENT, AND THEN FIELD QUESTIONS. YOU WILL BE PERMITTED TO REBUT.
ON YOUR OPENING STATEMENT, JUST TRY TO BE YOURSELF, AND PLAY IT AS PRESIDENTIAL AS POSSIBLE. WHEN CARTER'S UP, BE SURE TO MAKE HARD EYE CONTACT.
AND IN MY REBUTTALS?
TAKE CHARGE. FLAUNT YOUR SUPERIOR COMMAND OF FACTS. USE CLASSIFIED INFORMATION IF YOU HAVE TO.
I CAN DO THAT?
UH-HUH. AND DON'T BE AFRAID TO MAKE FUN OF HIS ACCENT.
GBTrudeau

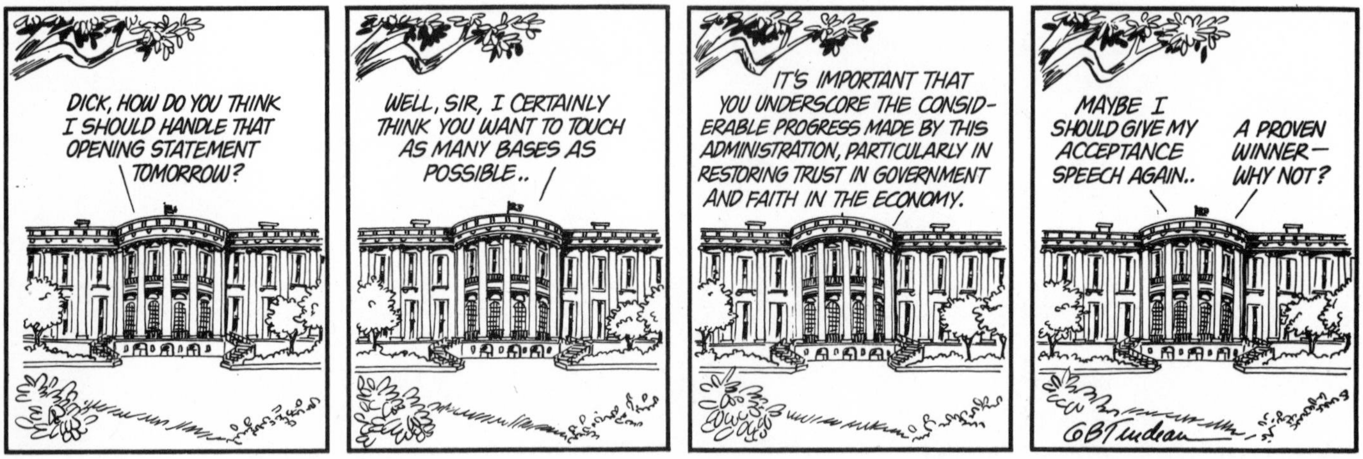
DICK, HOW DO YOU THINK I SHOULD HANDLE THAT OPENING STATEMENT TOMORROW?
WELL, SIR, I CERTAINLY THINK YOU WANT TO TOUCH AS MANY BASES AS POSSIBLE..
IT'S IMPORTANT THAT YOU UNDERSCORE THE CONSIDERABLE PROGRESS MADE BY THIS ADMINISTRATION, PARTICULARLY IN RESTORING TRUST IN GOVERNMENT AND FAITH IN THE ECONOMY.
MAYBE I SHOULD GIVE MY ACCEPTANCE SPEECH AGAIN..
A PROVEN WINNER—WHY NOT?
GBTrudeau

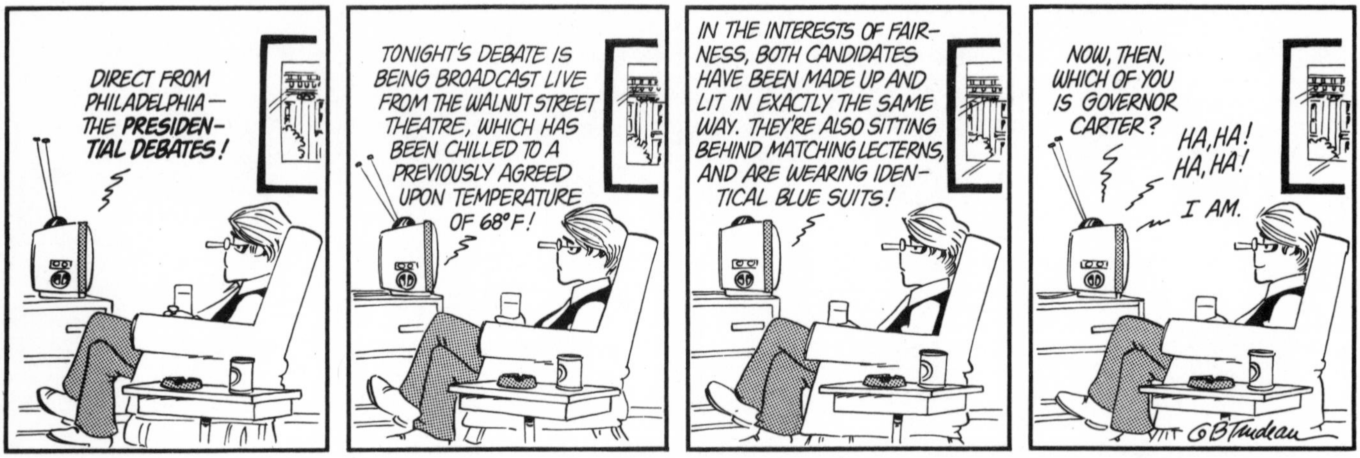
DIRECT FROM PHILADELPHIA—THE PRESIDENTIAL DEBATES!
TONIGHT'S DEBATE IS BEING BROADCAST LIVE FROM THE WALNUT STREET THEATRE, WHICH HAS BEEN CHILLED TO A PREVIOUSLY AGREED UPON TEMPERATURE OF 68° F!
IN THE INTERESTS OF FAIRNESS, BOTH CANDIDATES HAVE BEEN MADE UP AND LIT IN EXACTLY THE SAME WAY. THEY'RE ALSO SITTING BEHIND MATCHING LECTERNS, AND ARE WEARING IDENTICAL BLUE SUITS!
NOW, THEN, WHICH OF YOU IS GOVERNOR CARTER?
HA, HA! HA, HA!
I AM.
GBTrudeau

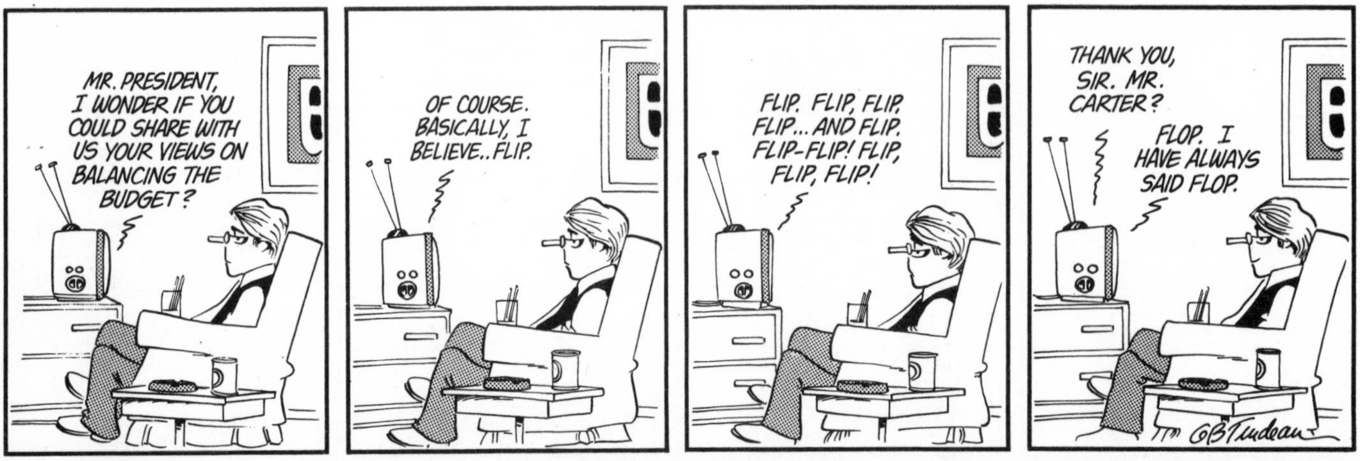
MR. PRESIDENT, I WONDER IF YOU COULD SHARE WITH US YOUR VIEWS ON BALANCING THE BUDGET?
OF COURSE. BASICALLY, I BELIEVE..FLIP.
FLIP. FLIP, FLIP. FLIP... AND FLIP. FLIP-FLIP! FLIP, FLIP, FLIP!
THANK YOU, SIR. MR. CARTER?
FLOP. I HAVE ALWAYS SAID FLOP.
GBTrudeau

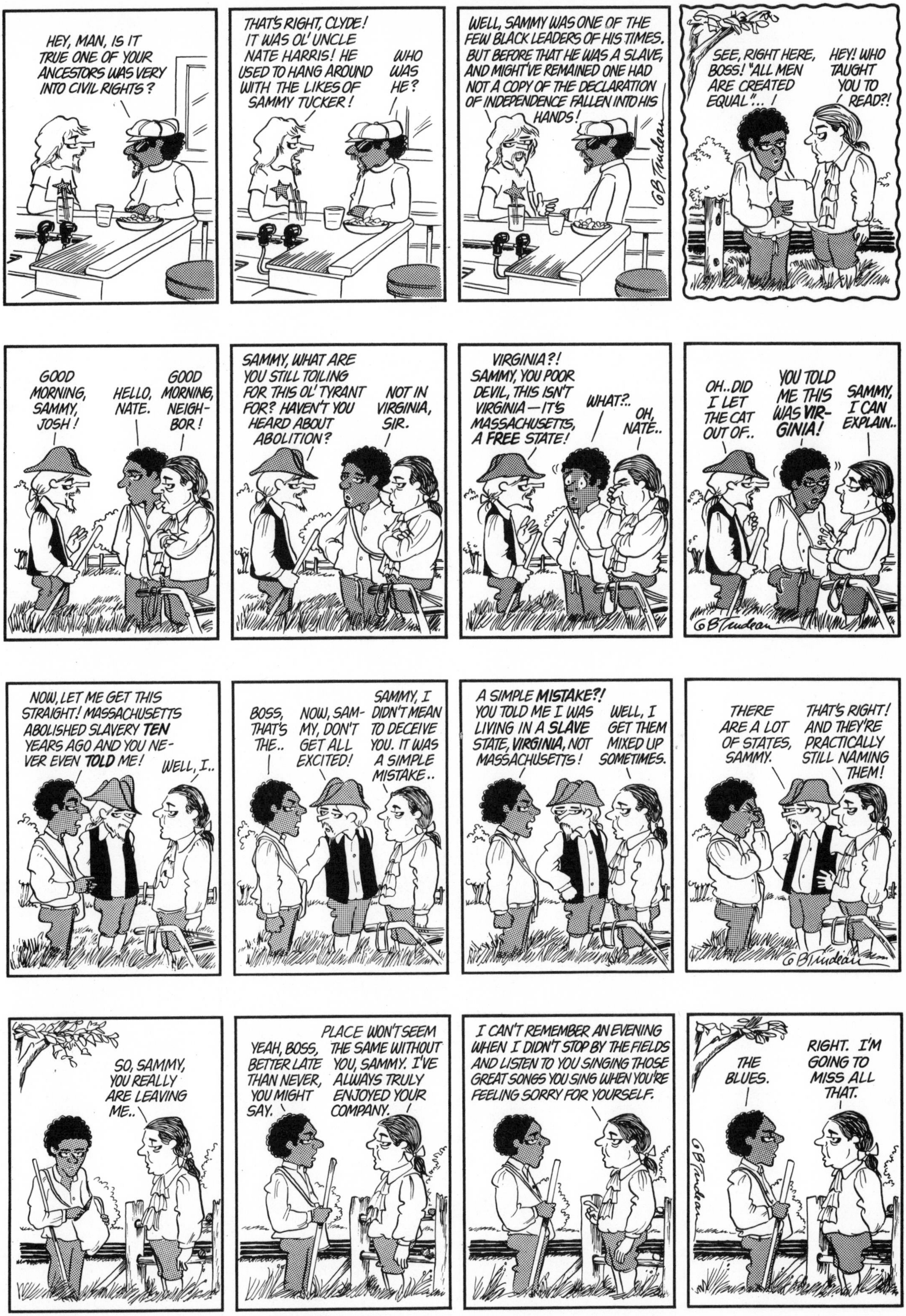
HEY, MAN, IS IT TRUE ONE OF YOUR ANCESTORS WAS VERY INTO CIVIL RIGHTS?
THAT'S RIGHT, CLYDE! IT WAS OL' UNCLE NATE HARRIS! HE USED TO HANG AROUND WITH THE LIKES OF SAMMY TUCKER!
WHO WAS HE?
WELL, SAMMY WAS ONE OF THE FEW BLACK LEADERS OF HIS TIMES. BUT BEFORE THAT HE WAS A SLAVE, AND MIGHT'VE REMAINED ONE HAD NOT A COPY OF THE DECLARATION OF INDEPENDENCE FALLEN INTO HIS HANDS!
SEE, RIGHT HERE, BOSS! "ALL MEN ARE CREATED EQUAL"...!
HEY! WHO TAUGHT YOU TO READ?!
GOOD MORNING, SAMMY, JOSH!
HELLO, NATE.
GOOD MORNING, NEIGHBOR!
SAMMY, WHAT ARE YOU STILL TOILING FOR THIS OL' TYRANT FOR? HAVEN'T YOU HEARD ABOUT ABOLITION?
NOT IN VIRGINIA, SIR.
VIRGINIA?! SAMMY, YOU POOR DEVIL, THIS ISN'T VIRGINIA—IT'S MASSACHUSETTS, A FREE STATE!
WHAT?..
OH, NATE..
OH..DID I LET THE CAT OUT OF..
YOU TOLD ME THIS WAS VIRGINIA!
SAMMY, I CAN EXPLAIN..
NOW, LET ME GET THIS STRAIGHT! MASSACHUSETTS ABOLISHED SLAVERY TEN YEARS AGO AND YOU NEVER EVEN TOLD ME!
WELL, I..
BOSS, THAT'S THE..
NOW, SAMMY, DON'T GET ALL EXCITED!
SAMMY, I DIDN'T MEAN TO DECEIVE YOU. IT WAS A SIMPLE MISTAKE..
A SIMPLE MISTAKE?! YOU TOLD ME I WAS LIVING IN A SLAVE STATE, VIRGINIA, NOT MASSACHUSETTS!
WELL, I GET THEM MIXED UP SOMETIMES.
THERE ARE A LOT OF STATES, SAMMY.
THAT'S RIGHT! AND THEY'RE PRACTICALLY STILL NAMING THEM!
SO, SAMMY, YOU REALLY ARE LEAVING ME..
YEAH, BOSS, BETTER LATE THAN NEVER, YOU MIGHT SAY.
PLACE WON'T SEEM THE SAME WITHOUT YOU, SAMMY. I'VE ALWAYS TRULY ENJOYED YOUR COMPANY.
I CAN'T REMEMBER AN EVENING WHEN I DIDN'T STOP BY THE FIELDS AND LISTEN TO YOU SINGING THOSE GREAT SONGS YOU SING WHEN YOU'RE FEELING SORRY FOR YOURSELF.
THE BLUES.
RIGHT. I'M GOING TO MISS ALL THAT.

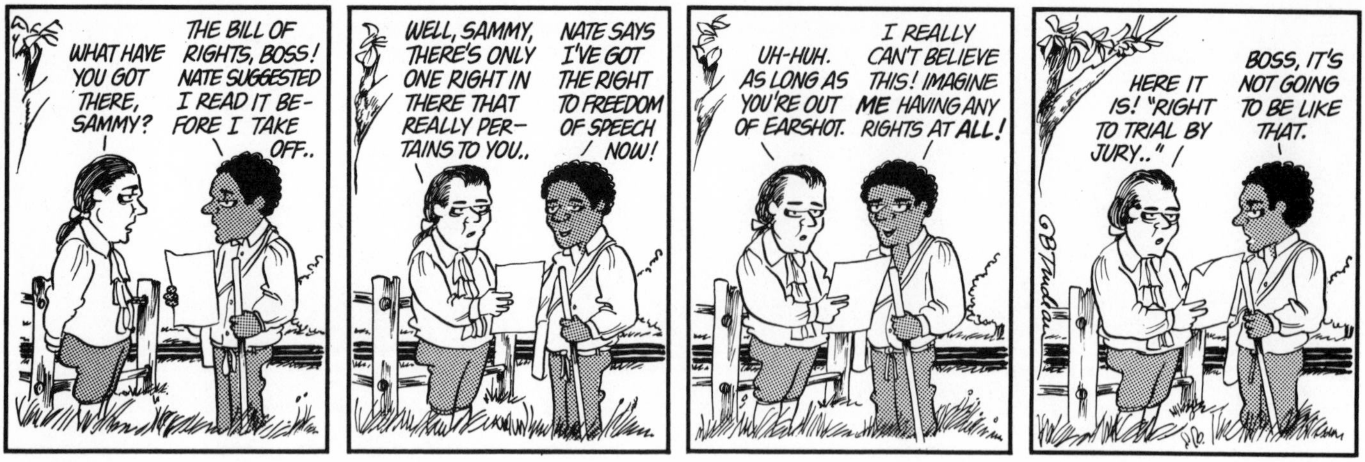
WHAT HAVE YOU GOT THERE, SAMMY?
THE BILL OF RIGHTS, BOSS! NATE SUGGESTED I READ IT BEFORE I TAKE OFF..
WELL, SAMMY, THERE'S ONLY ONE RIGHT IN THERE THAT REALLY PERTAINS TO YOU..
NATE SAYS I'VE GOT THE RIGHT TO FREEDOM OF SPEECH NOW!
UH-HUH. AS LONG AS YOU'RE OUT OF EARSHOT.
I REALLY CAN'T BELIEVE THIS! IMAGINE ME HAVING ANY RIGHTS AT ALL!
HERE IT IS! "RIGHT TO TRIAL BY JURY.."
BOSS, IT'S NOT GOING TO BE LIKE THAT.

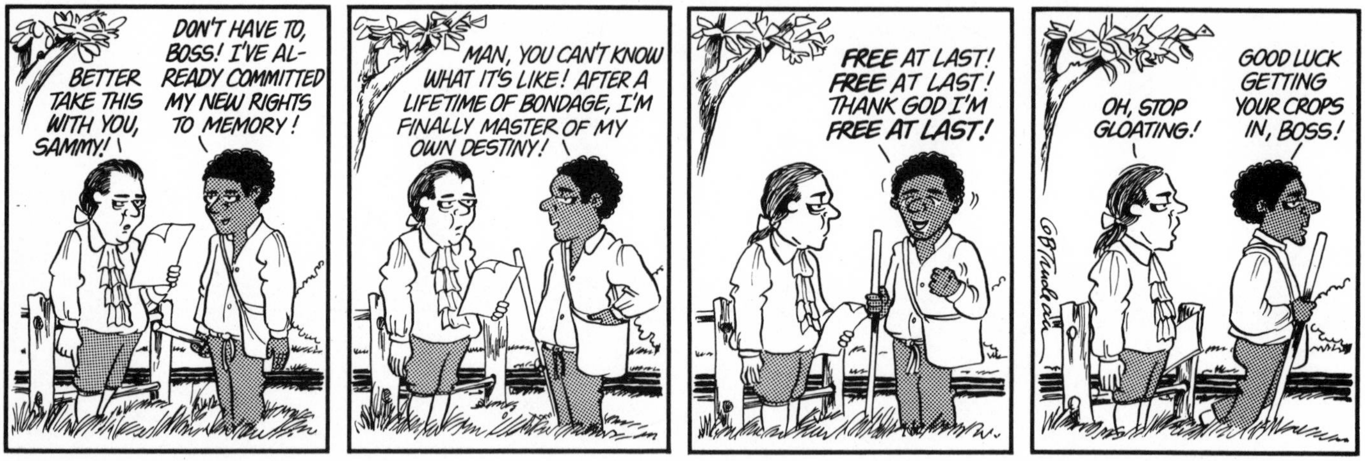
BETTER TAKE THIS WITH YOU, SAMMY!
DON'T HAVE TO, BOSS! I'VE ALREADY COMMITTED MY NEW RIGHTS TO MEMORY!
MAN, YOU CAN'T KNOW WHAT IT'S LIKE! AFTER A LIFETIME OF BONDAGE, I'M FINALLY MASTER OF MY OWN DESTINY!
FREE AT LAST! FREE AT LAST! THANK GOD I'M FREE AT LAST!
OH, STOP GLOATING!
GOOD LUCK GETTING YOUR CROPS IN, BOSS!

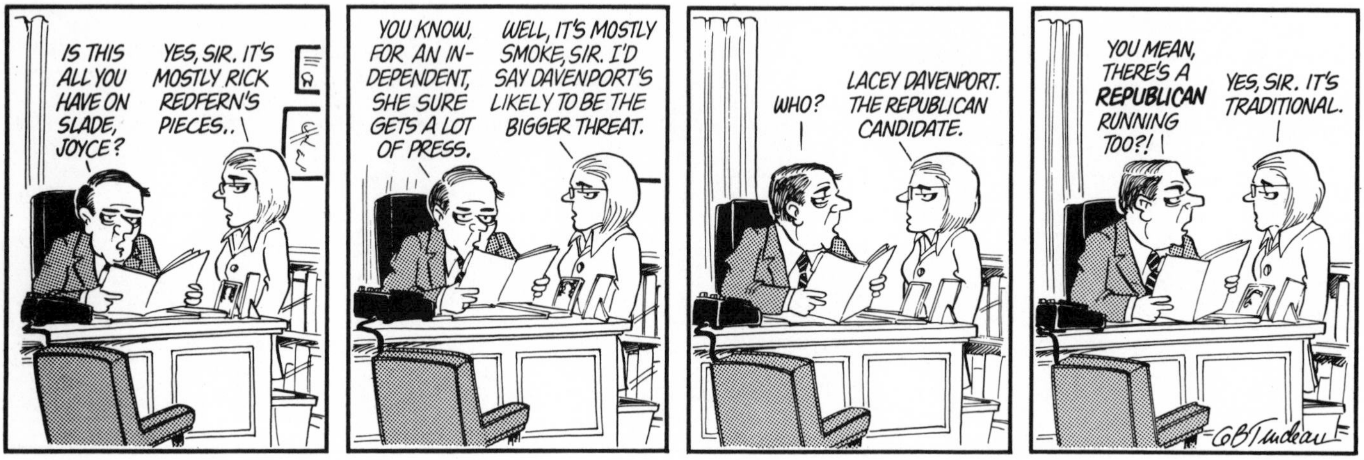
IS THIS ALL YOU HAVE ON SLADE, JOYCE?
YES, SIR. IT'S MOSTLY RICK REDFERN'S PIECES..
YOU KNOW, FOR AN INDEPENDENT, SHE SURE GETS A LOT OF PRESS.
WELL, IT'S MOSTLY SMOKE, SIR. I'D SAY DAVENPORT'S LIKELY TO BE THE BIGGER THREAT.
WHO?
LACEY DAVENPORT. THE REPUBLICAN CANDIDATE.
YOU MEAN, THERE'S A REPUBLICAN RUNNING TOO?!
YES, SIR. IT'S TRADITIONAL.

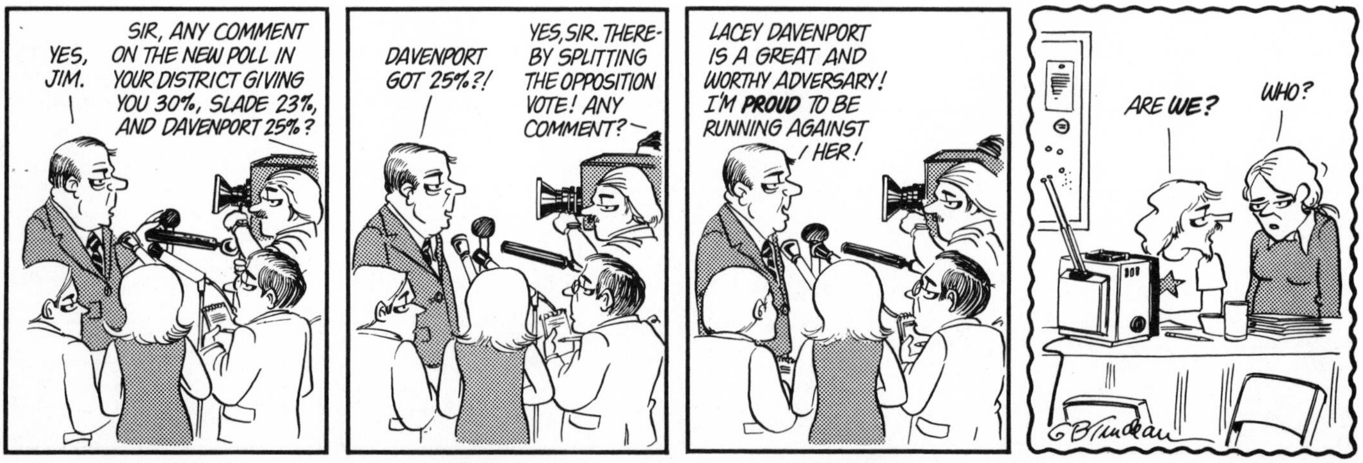
YES, JIM.
SIR, ANY COMMENT ON THE NEW POLL IN YOUR DISTRICT GIVING YOU 30%, SLADE 23%, AND DAVENPORT 25%?
DAVENPORT GOT 25%?!
YES, SIR. THEREBY SPLITTING THE OPPOSITION VOTE! ANY COMMENT?
LACEY DAVENPORT IS A GREAT AND WORTHY ADVERSARY! I'M PROUD TO BE RUNNING AGAINST HER!
ARE WE?
WHO?

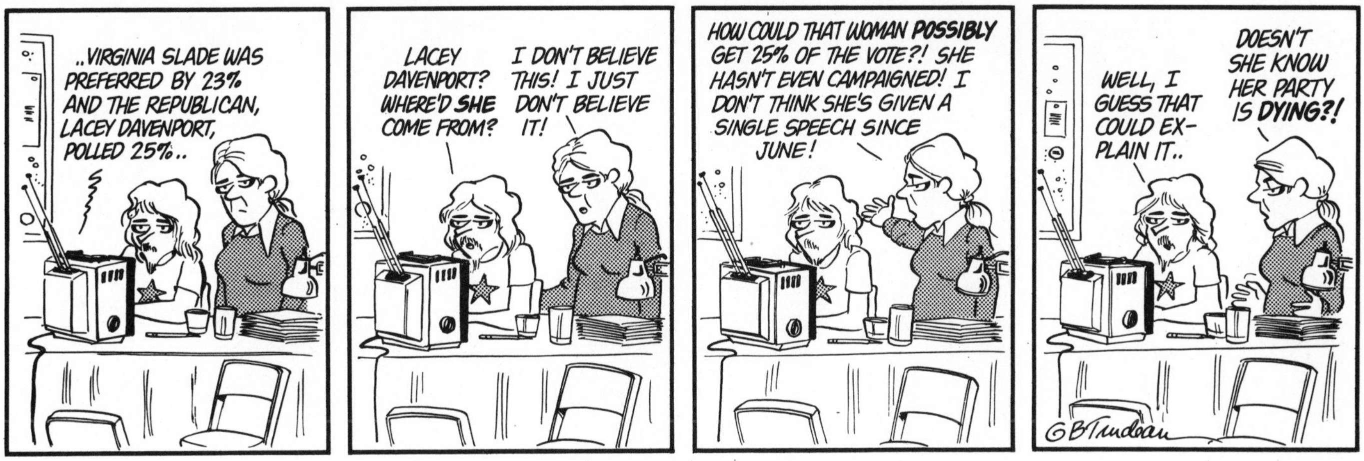
..VIRGINIA SLADE WAS PREFERRED BY 23% AND THE REPUBLICAN, LACEY DAVENPORT, POLLED 25%..
LACEY DAVENPORT? WHERE'D **SHE** COME FROM?
I DON'T BELIEVE THIS! I JUST DON'T BELIEVE IT!
HOW COULD THAT WOMAN **POSSIBLY** GET 25% OF THE VOTE?! SHE HASN'T EVEN CAMPAIGNED! I DON'T THINK SHE'S GIVEN A SINGLE SPEECH SINCE JUNE!
WELL, I GUESS THAT COULD EXPLAIN IT..
DOESN'T SHE KNOW HER PARTY IS **DYING?!**
GBTrudeau

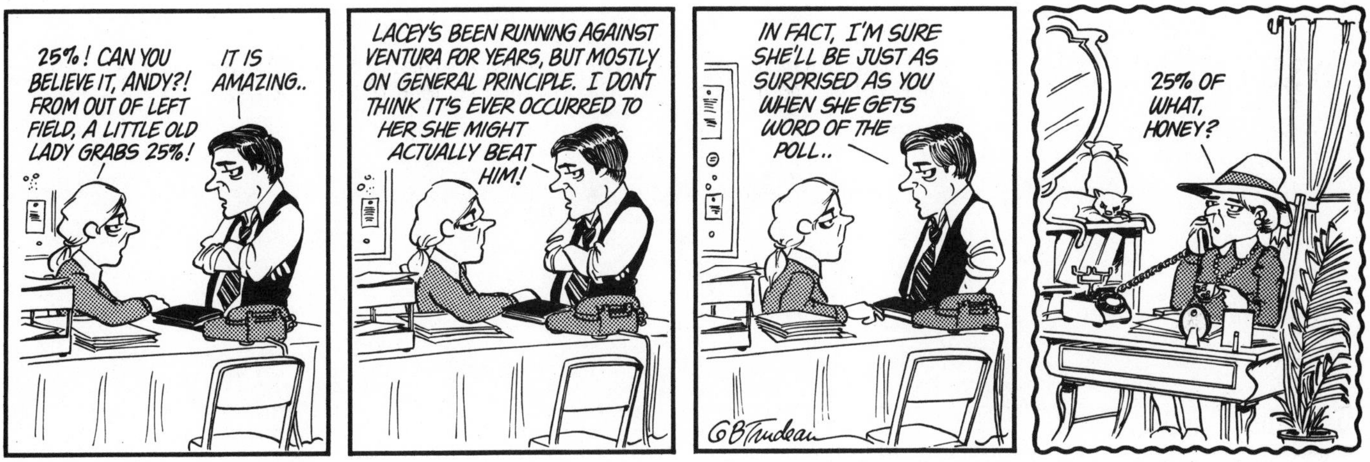
25%! CAN YOU BELIEVE IT, ANDY?! FROM OUT OF LEFT FIELD, A LITTLE OLD LADY GRABS 25%!
IT IS AMAZING..
LACEY'S BEEN RUNNING AGAINST VENTURA FOR YEARS, BUT MOSTLY ON GENERAL PRINCIPLE. I DONT THINK IT'S EVER OCCURRED TO HER SHE MIGHT ACTUALLY BEAT HIM!
IN FACT, I'M SURE SHE'LL BE JUST AS SURPRISED AS YOU WHEN SHE GETS WORD OF THE POLL..
GBTrudeau
25% OF WHAT, HONEY?

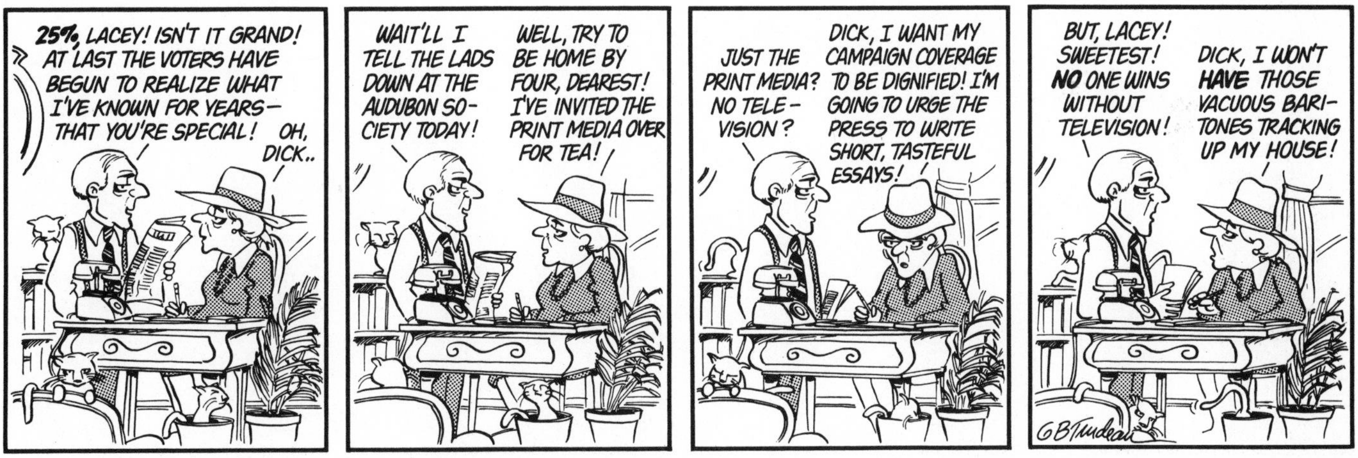
25%, LACEY! ISN'T IT GRAND! AT LAST THE VOTERS HAVE BEGUN TO REALIZE WHAT I'VE KNOWN FOR YEARS— THAT YOU'RE SPECIAL!
OH, DICK..
WAIT'LL I TELL THE LADS DOWN AT THE AUDUBON SOCIETY TODAY!
WELL, TRY TO BE HOME BY FOUR, DEAREST! I'VE INVITED THE PRINT MEDIA OVER FOR TEA!
JUST THE PRINT MEDIA? NO TELEVISION?
DICK, I WANT MY CAMPAIGN COVERAGE TO BE DIGNIFIED! I'M GOING TO URGE THE PRESS TO WRITE SHORT, TASTEFUL ESSAYS!
BUT, LACEY! SWEETEST! **NO** ONE WINS WITHOUT TELEVISION!
DICK, I WON'T **HAVE** THOSE VACUOUS BARITONES TRACKING UP MY HOUSE!
GBTrudeau

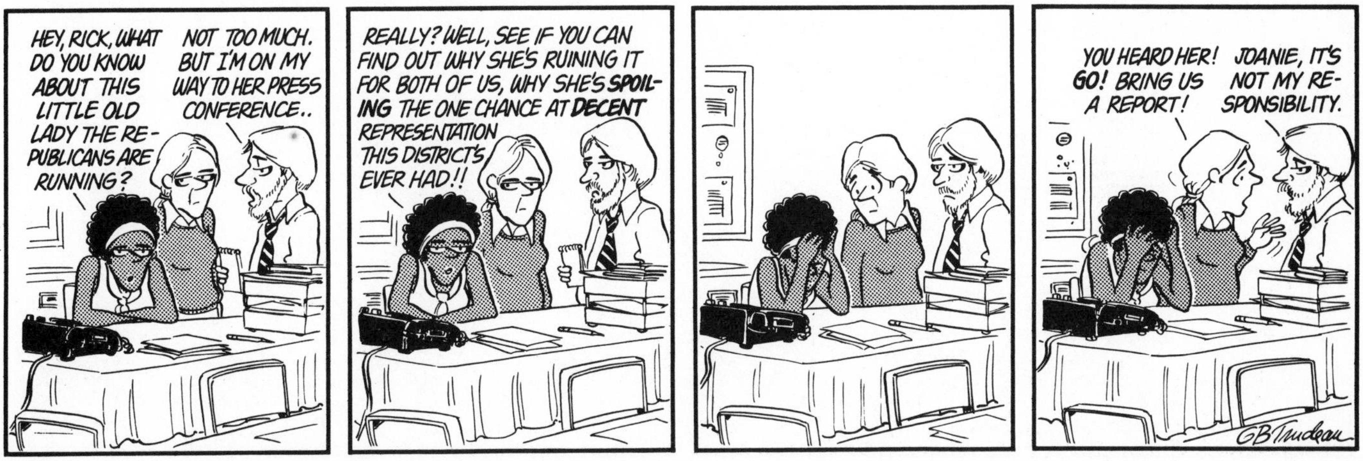
HEY, RICK, WHAT DO YOU KNOW ABOUT THIS LITTLE OLD LADY THE REPUBLICANS ARE RUNNING?
NOT TOO MUCH. BUT I'M ON MY WAY TO HER PRESS CONFERENCE..
REALLY? WELL, SEE IF YOU CAN FIND OUT WHY SHE'S RUINING IT FOR BOTH OF US, WHY SHE'S **SPOILING** THE ONE CHANCE AT **DECENT** REPRESENTATION THIS DISTRICT'S EVER HAD!!
YOU HEARD HER! **GO!** BRING US A REPORT!
JOANIE, IT'S NOT MY RESPONSIBILITY.
GBTrudeau

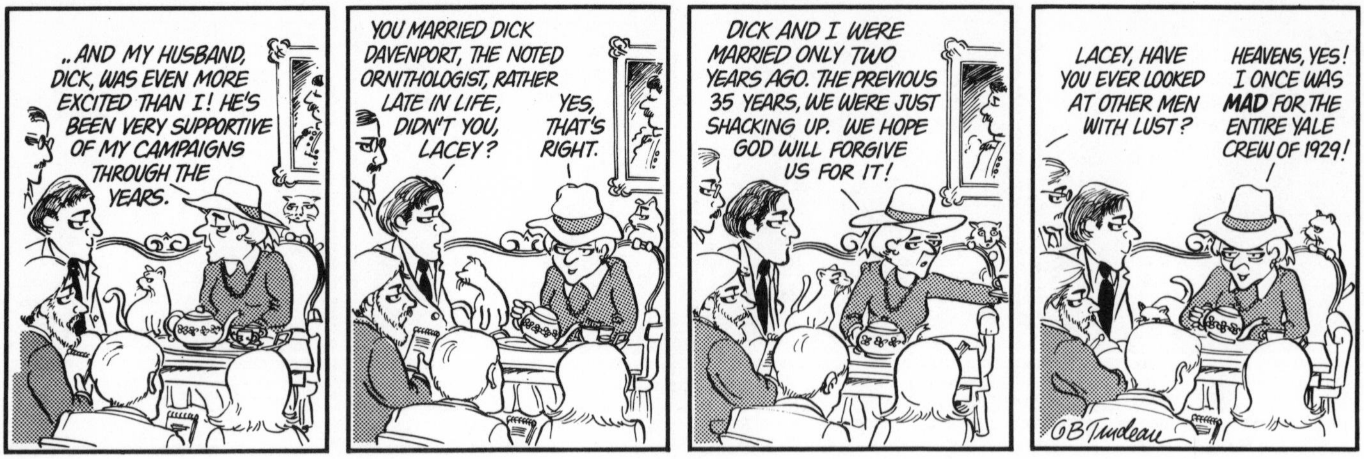
..AND MY HUSBAND, DICK, WAS EVEN MORE EXCITED THAN I! HE'S BEEN VERY SUPPORTIVE OF MY CAMPAIGNS THROUGH THE YEARS.
YOU MARRIED DICK DAVENPORT, THE NOTED ORNITHOLOGIST, RATHER LATE IN LIFE, DIDN'T YOU, LACEY?
YES, THAT'S RIGHT.
DICK AND I WERE MARRIED ONLY TWO YEARS AGO. THE PREVIOUS 35 YEARS, WE WERE JUST SHACKING UP. WE HOPE GOD WILL FORGIVE US FOR IT!
LACEY, HAVE YOU EVER LOOKED AT OTHER MEN WITH LUST?
HEAVENS, YES! I ONCE WAS MAD FOR THE ENTIRE YALE CREW OF 1929!

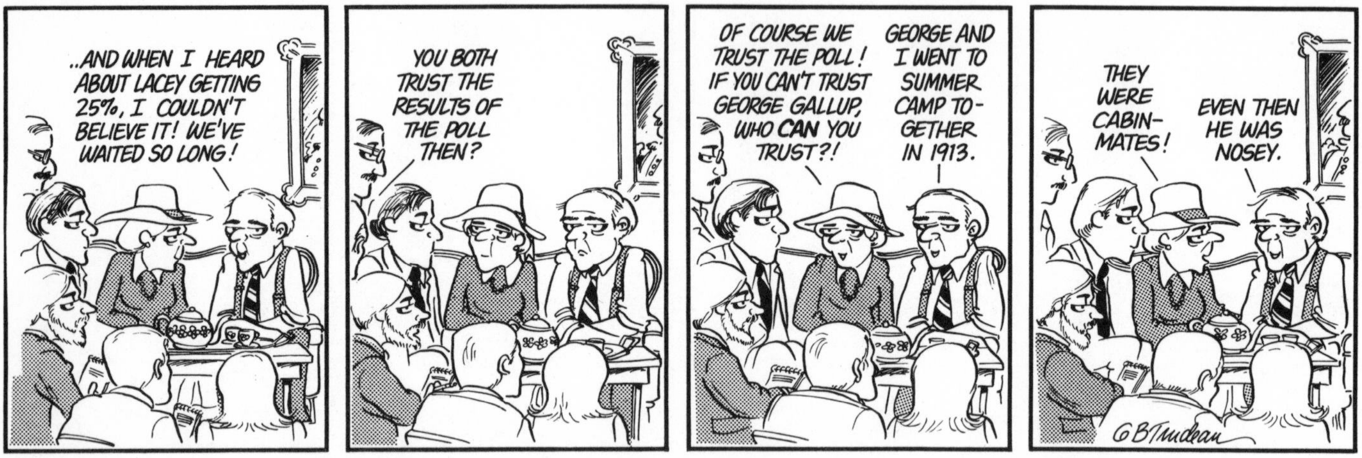
..AND WHEN I HEARD ABOUT LACEY GETTING 25%, I COULDN'T BELIEVE IT! WE'VE WAITED SO LONG!
YOU BOTH TRUST THE RESULTS OF THE POLL THEN?
OF COURSE WE TRUST THE POLL! IF YOU CAN'T TRUST GEORGE GALLUP, WHO CAN YOU TRUST?!
GEORGE AND I WENT TO SUMMER CAMP TOGETHER IN 1913.
THEY WERE CABINMATES!
EVEN THEN HE WAS NOSEY.

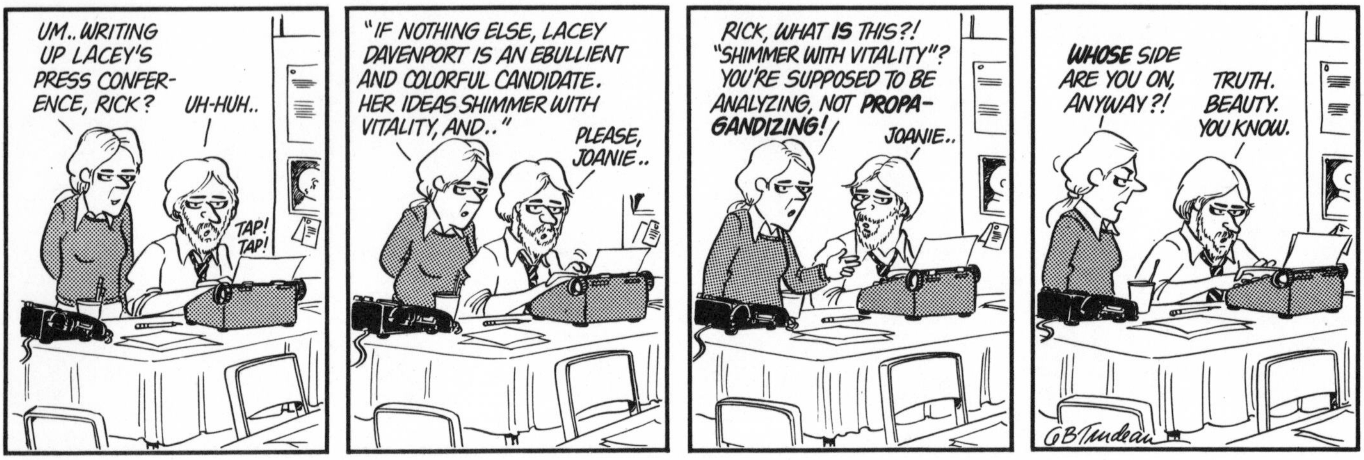
UM.. WRITING UP LACEY'S PRESS CONFERENCE, RICK?
UH-HUH..
TAP! TAP!
"IF NOTHING ELSE, LACEY DAVENPORT IS AN EBULLIENT AND COLORFUL CANDIDATE. HER IDEAS SHIMMER WITH VITALITY, AND.."
PLEASE, JOANIE..
RICK, WHAT IS THIS?! "SHIMMER WITH VITALITY"? YOU'RE SUPPOSED TO BE ANALYZING, NOT PROPAGANDIZING!
JOANIE..
WHOSE SIDE ARE YOU ON, ANYWAY?!
TRUTH. BEAUTY. YOU KNOW.

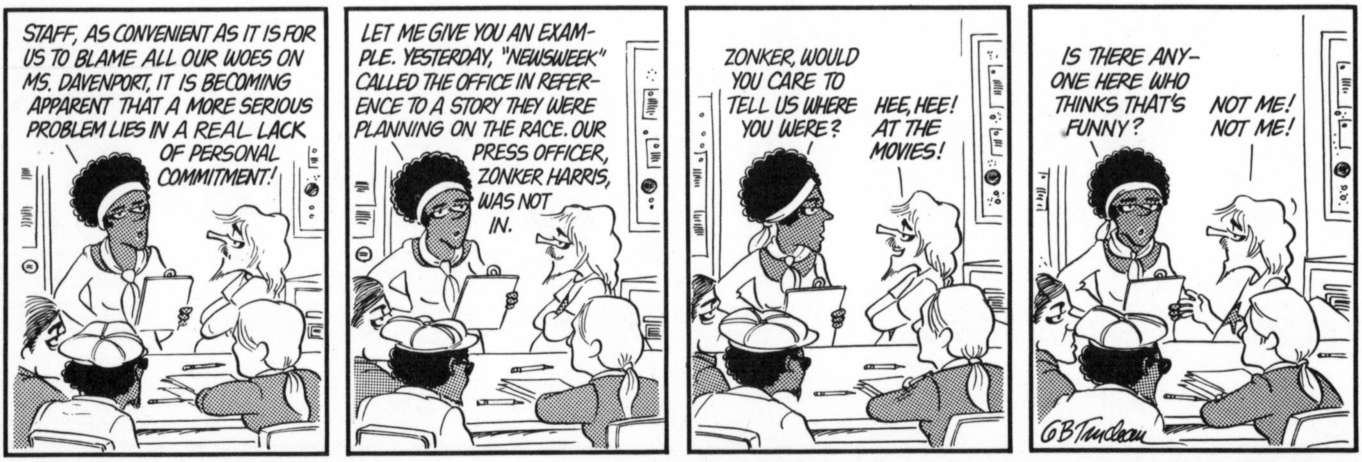
STAFF, AS CONVENIENT AS IT IS FOR US TO BLAME ALL OUR WOES ON MS. DAVENPORT, IT IS BECOMING APPARENT THAT A MORE SERIOUS PROBLEM LIES IN A REAL LACK OF PERSONAL COMMITMENT!
LET ME GIVE YOU AN EXAMPLE. YESTERDAY, "NEWSWEEK" CALLED THE OFFICE IN REFERENCE TO A STORY THEY WERE PLANNING ON THE RACE. OUR PRESS OFFICER, ZONKER HARRIS, WAS NOT IN.
ZONKER, WOULD YOU CARE TO TELL US WHERE YOU WERE?
HEE, HEE! AT THE MOVIES!
IS THERE ANYONE HERE WHO THINKS THAT'S FUNNY?
NOT ME! NOT ME!

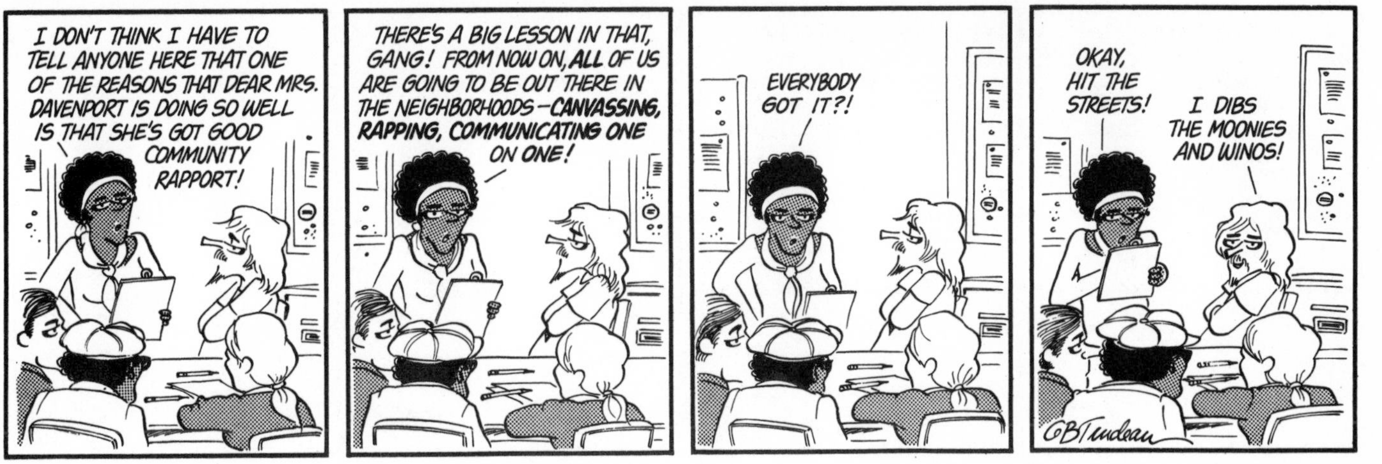
I DON'T THINK I HAVE TO TELL ANYONE HERE THAT ONE OF THE REASONS THAT DEAR MRS. DAVENPORT IS DOING SO WELL IS THAT SHE'S GOT GOOD COMMUNITY RAPPORT!
THERE'S A BIG LESSON IN THAT, GANG! FROM NOW ON, ALL OF US ARE GOING TO BE OUT THERE IN THE NEIGHBORHOODS—CANVASSING, RAPPING, COMMUNICATING ONE ON ONE!
EVERYBODY GOT IT?!
OKAY, HIT THE STREETS!
I DIBS THE MOONIES AND WINOS!

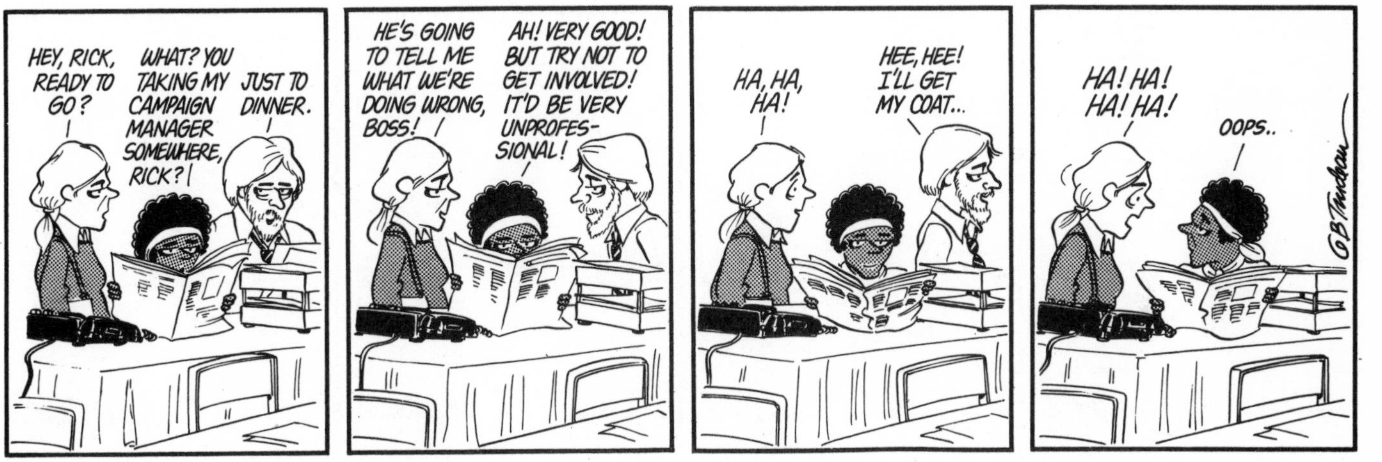
HEY, RICK, READY TO GO?
WHAT? YOU TAKING MY CAMPAIGN MANAGER SOMEWHERE, RICK?
JUST TO DINNER.
HE'S GOING TO TELL ME WHAT WE'RE DOING WRONG, BOSS!
AH! VERY GOOD! BUT TRY NOT TO GET INVOLVED! IT'D BE VERY UNPROFESSIONAL!
HA, HA, HA!
HEE, HEE! I'LL GET MY COAT...
HA! HA! HA! HA!
OOPS..

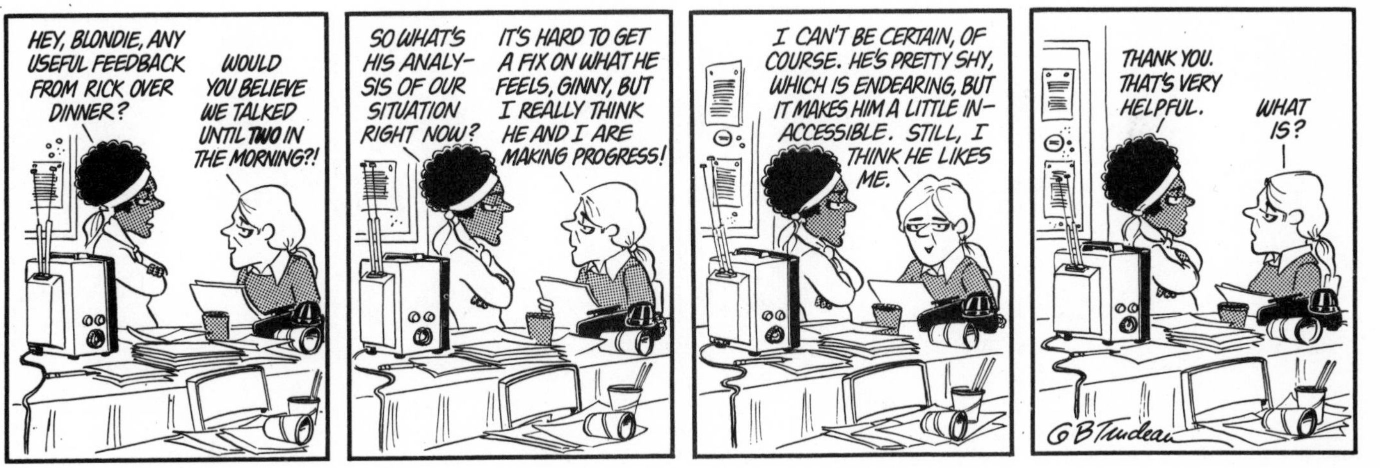
HEY, BLONDIE, ANY USEFUL FEEDBACK FROM RICK OVER DINNER?
WOULD YOU BELIEVE WE TALKED UNTIL TWO IN THE MORNING?!
SO WHAT'S HIS ANALYSIS OF OUR SITUATION RIGHT NOW?
IT'S HARD TO GET A FIX ON WHAT HE FEELS, GINNY, BUT I REALLY THINK HE AND I ARE MAKING PROGRESS!
I CAN'T BE CERTAIN, OF COURSE. HE'S PRETTY SHY, WHICH IS ENDEARING, BUT IT MAKES HIM A LITTLE INACCESSIBLE. STILL, I THINK HE LIKES ME.
THANK YOU. THAT'S VERY HELPFUL.
WHAT IS?

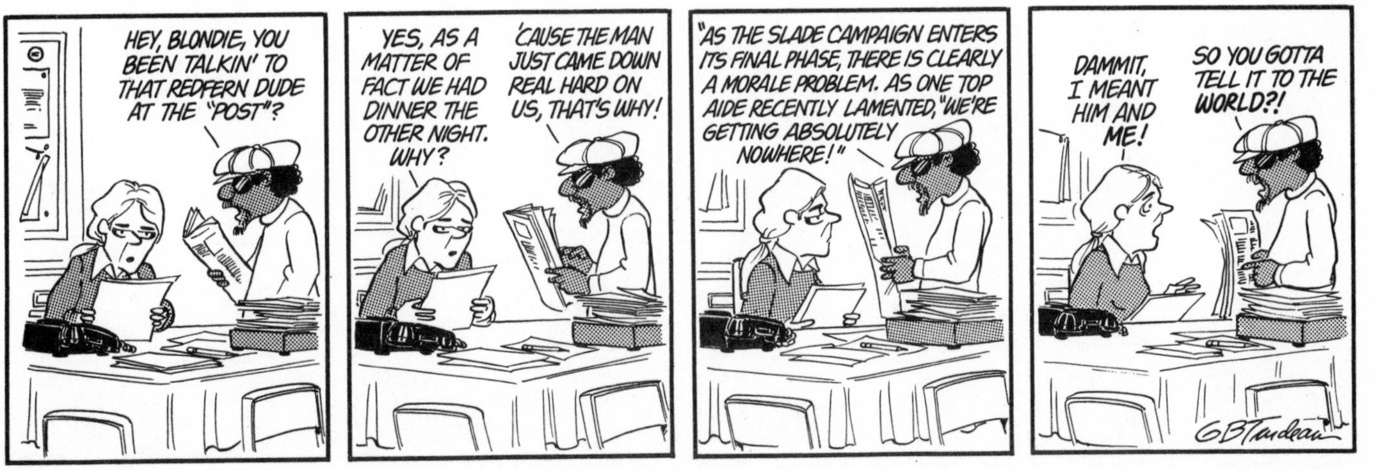
HEY, BLONDIE, YOU BEEN TALKIN' TO THAT REDFERN DUDE AT THE "POST"?
YES, AS A MATTER OF FACT WE HAD DINNER THE OTHER NIGHT. WHY?
'CAUSE THE MAN JUST CAME DOWN REAL HARD ON US, THAT'S WHY!
"AS THE SLADE CAMPAIGN ENTERS ITS FINAL PHASE, THERE IS CLEARLY A MORALE PROBLEM. AS ONE TOP AIDE RECENTLY LAMENTED, 'WE'RE GETTING ABSOLUTELY NOWHERE!'"
DAMMIT, I MEANT HIM AND ME!
SO YOU GOTTA TELL IT TO THE WORLD?!

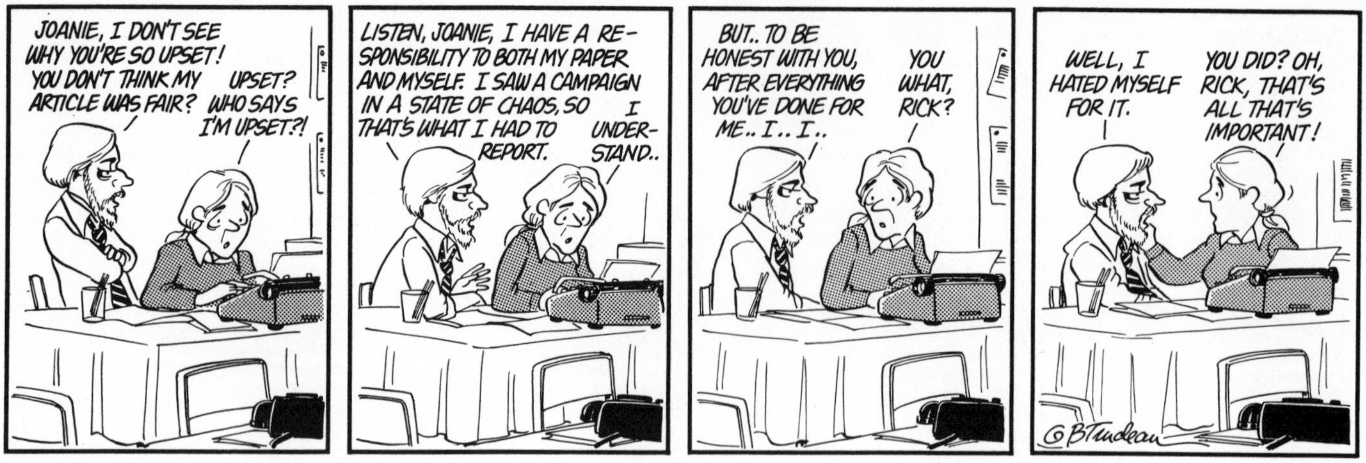
JOANIE, I DON'T SEE WHY YOU'RE SO UPSET! YOU DON'T THINK MY ARTICLE WAS FAIR?
UPSET? WHO SAYS I'M UPSET?!
LISTEN, JOANIE, I HAVE A RESPONSIBILITY TO BOTH MY PAPER AND MYSELF. I SAW A CAMPAIGN IN A STATE OF CHAOS, SO THAT'S WHAT I HAD TO REPORT.
I UNDERSTAND..
BUT.. TO BE HONEST WITH YOU, AFTER EVERYTHING YOU'VE DONE FOR ME.. I.. I..
YOU WHAT, RICK?
WELL, I HATED MYSELF FOR IT.
YOU DID? OH, RICK, THAT'S ALL THAT'S IMPORTANT!
© B Trudeau

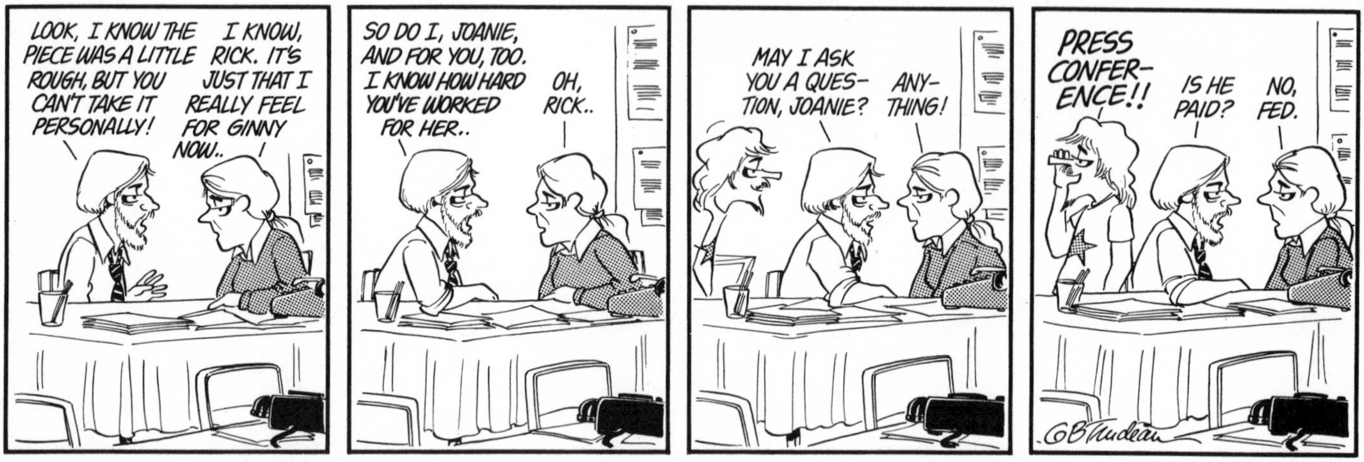
LOOK, I KNOW THE PIECE WAS A LITTLE ROUGH, BUT YOU CAN'T TAKE IT PERSONALLY!
I KNOW, RICK. IT'S JUST THAT I REALLY FEEL FOR GINNY NOW..
SO DO I, JOANIE, AND FOR YOU, TOO. I KNOW HOW HARD YOU'VE WORKED FOR HER..
OH, RICK..
MAY I ASK YOU A QUESTION, JOANIE?
ANYTHING!
PRESS CONFERENCE!!
IS HE PAID?
NO, FED.
© B Trudeau

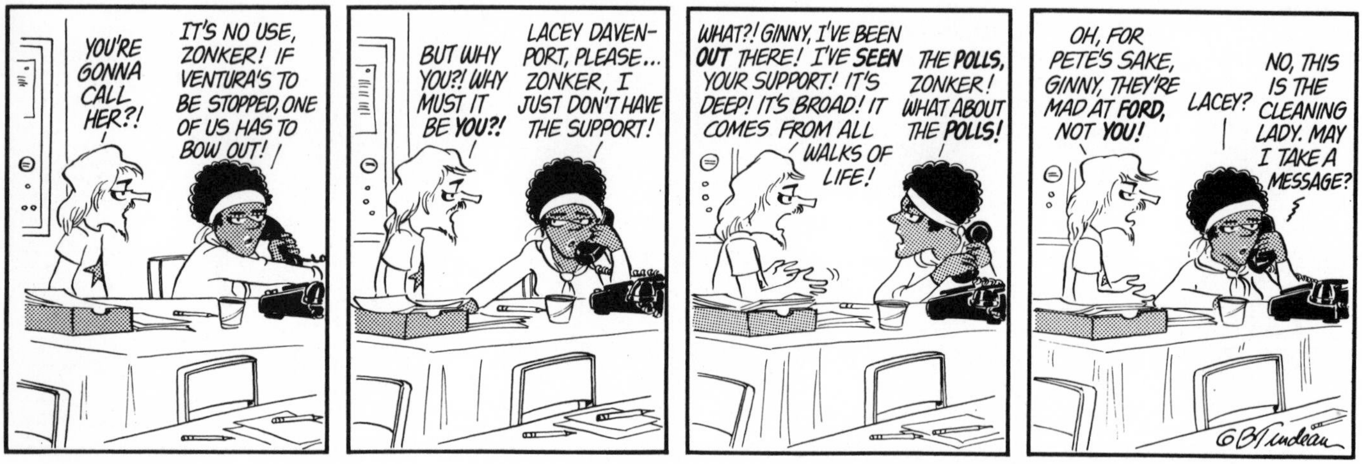
YOU'RE GONNA CALL HER?!
IT'S NO USE, ZONKER! IF VENTURA'S TO BE STOPPED, ONE OF US HAS TO BOW OUT!
BUT WHY YOU?! WHY MUST IT BE YOU?!
LACEY DAVENPORT, PLEASE... ZONKER, I JUST DON'T HAVE THE SUPPORT!
WHAT?! GINNY, I'VE BEEN OUT THERE! I'VE SEEN YOUR SUPPORT! IT'S DEEP! IT'S BROAD! IT COMES FROM ALL WALKS OF LIFE!
THE POLLS, ZONKER! WHAT ABOUT THE POLLS!
OH, FOR PETE'S SAKE, GINNY, THEY'RE MAD AT FORD, NOT YOU!
LACEY?
NO, THIS IS THE CLEANING LADY. MAY I TAKE A MESSAGE?
© B Trudeau

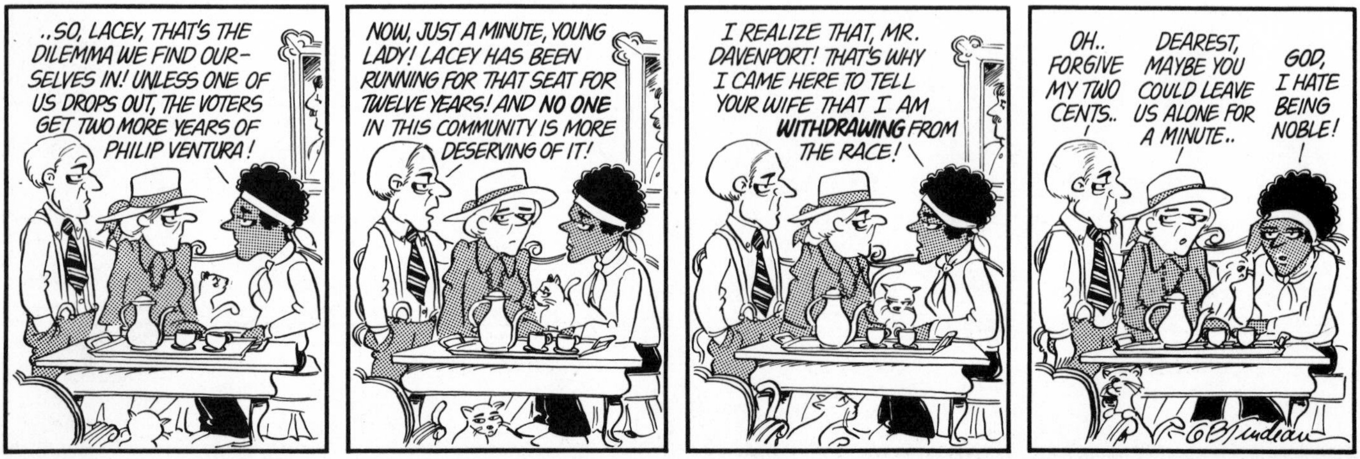
..SO, LACEY, THAT'S THE DILEMMA WE FIND OURSELVES IN! UNLESS ONE OF US DROPS OUT, THE VOTERS GET TWO MORE YEARS OF PHILIP VENTURA!
NOW, JUST A MINUTE, YOUNG LADY! LACEY HAS BEEN RUNNING FOR THAT SEAT FOR TWELVE YEARS! AND NO ONE IN THIS COMMUNITY IS MORE DESERVING OF IT!
I REALIZE THAT, MR. DAVENPORT! THAT'S WHY I CAME HERE TO TELL YOUR WIFE THAT I AM WITHDRAWING FROM THE RACE!
OH.. FORGIVE MY TWO CENTS..
DEAREST, MAYBE YOU COULD LEAVE US ALONE FOR A MINUTE..
GOD, I HATE BEING NOBLE!
© B Trudeau

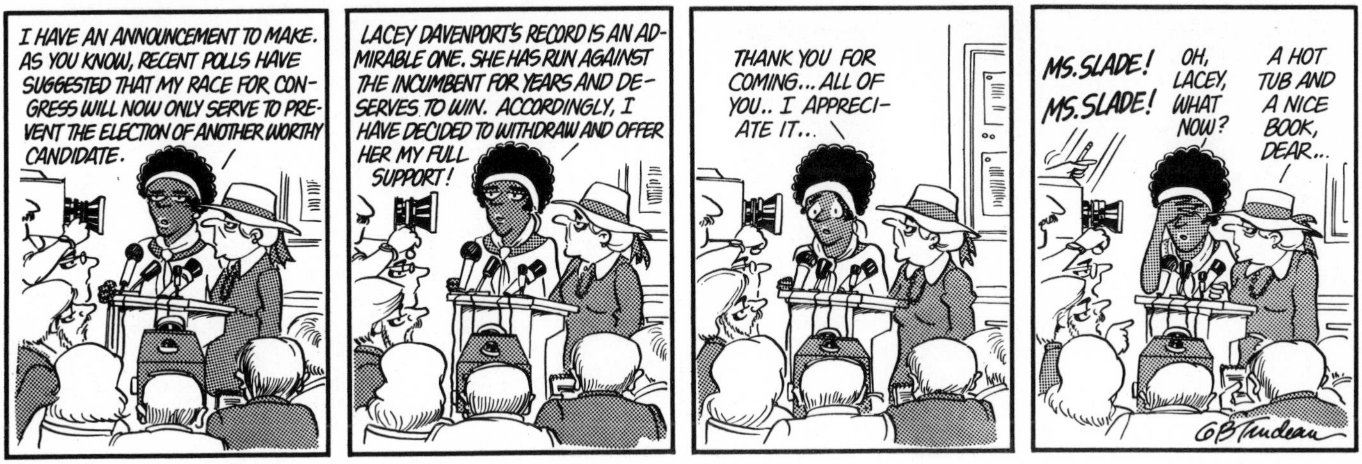
I HAVE AN ANNOUNCEMENT TO MAKE. AS YOU KNOW, RECENT POLLS HAVE SUGGESTED THAT MY RACE FOR CONGRESS WILL NOW ONLY SERVE TO PREVENT THE ELECTION OF ANOTHER WORTHY CANDIDATE.
LACEY DAVENPORT'S RECORD IS AN ADMIRABLE ONE. SHE HAS RUN AGAINST THE INCUMBENT FOR YEARS AND DESERVES TO WIN. ACCORDINGLY, I HAVE DECIDED TO WITHDRAW AND OFFER HER MY FULL SUPPORT!
THANK YOU FOR COMING... ALL OF YOU.. I APPRECIATE IT...
MS. SLADE! MS. SLADE!
OH, LACEY, WHAT NOW?
A HOT TUB AND A NICE BOOK, DEAR...
GBTrudeau

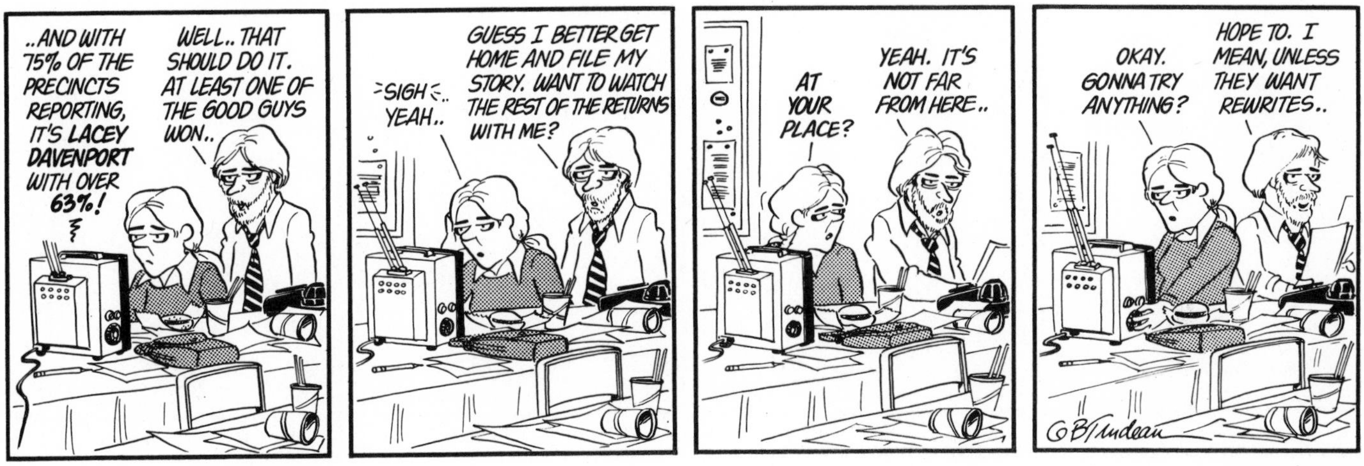
..AND WITH 75% OF THE PRECINCTS REPORTING, IT'S LACEY DAVENPORT WITH OVER 63%!
WELL.. THAT SHOULD DO IT. AT LEAST ONE OF THE GOOD GUYS WON..
SIGH YEAH..
GUESS I BETTER GET HOME AND FILE MY STORY. WANT TO WATCH THE REST OF THE RETURNS WITH ME?
AT YOUR PLACE?
YEAH. IT'S NOT FAR FROM HERE..
OKAY. GONNA TRY ANYTHING?
HOPE TO. I MEAN, UNLESS THEY WANT REWRITES..
GBTrudeau

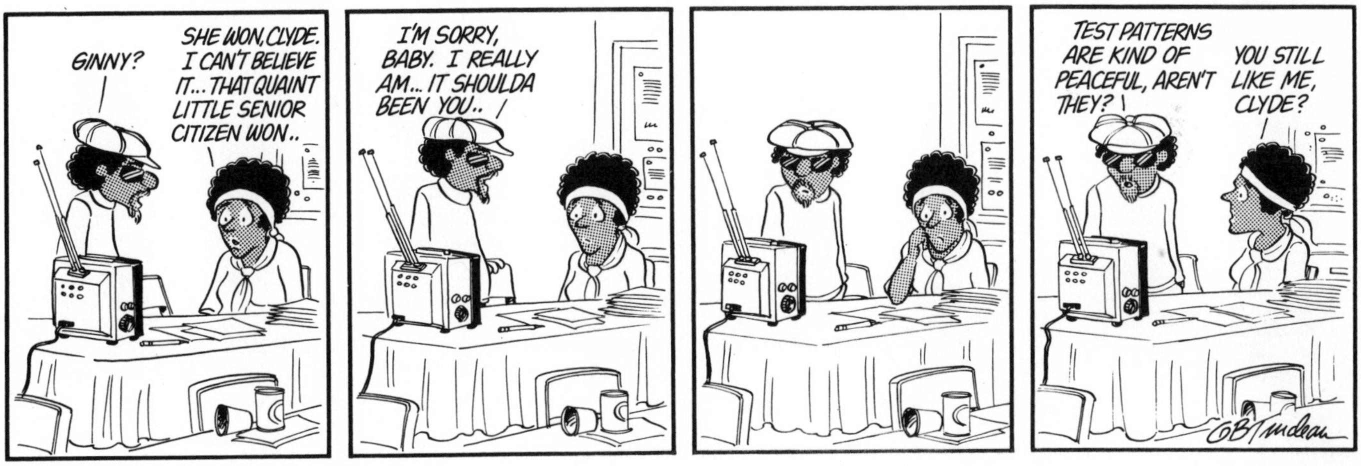
GINNY?
SHE WON, CLYDE. I CAN'T BELIEVE IT... THAT QUAINT LITTLE SENIOR CITIZEN WON..
I'M SORRY, BABY. I REALLY AM... IT SHOULDA BEEN YOU..
TEST PATTERNS ARE KIND OF PEACEFUL, AREN'T THEY?
YOU STILL LIKE ME, CLYDE?
GBTrudeau

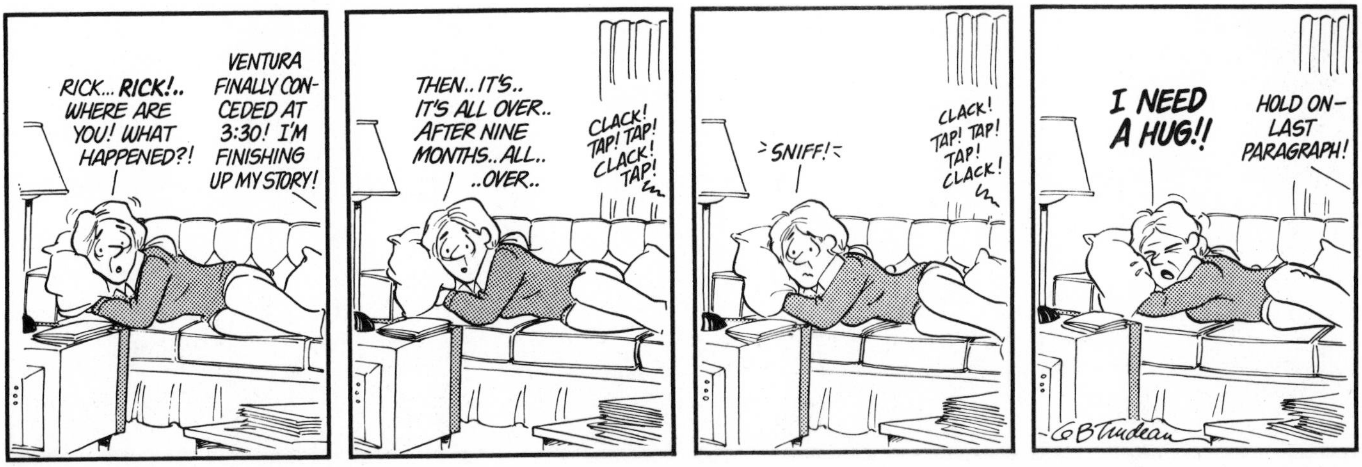
RICK... RICK!.. WHERE ARE YOU! WHAT HAPPENED?!
VENTURA FINALLY CONCEDED AT 3:30! I'M FINISHING UP MY STORY!
THEN.. IT'S.. IT'S ALL OVER.. AFTER NINE MONTHS.. ALL.. ..OVER..
CLACK! TAP! TAP! CLACK! TAP!
SNIFF!
CLACK! TAP! TAP! TAP! CLACK!
I NEED A HUG!!
HOLD ON– LAST PARAGRAPH!
GBTrudeau

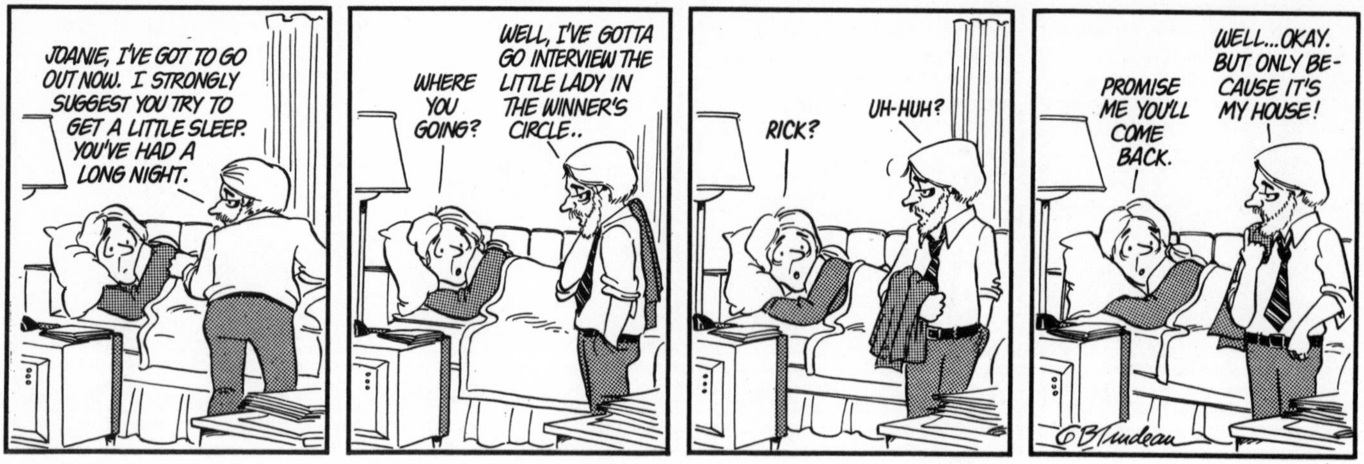
JOANIE, I'VE GOT TO GO OUT NOW. I STRONGLY SUGGEST YOU TRY TO GET A LITTLE SLEEP. YOU'VE HAD A LONG NIGHT.
WHERE YOU GOING?
WELL, I'VE GOTTA GO INTERVIEW THE LITTLE LADY IN THE WINNER'S CIRCLE..
RICK?
UH-HUH?
PROMISE ME YOU'LL COME BACK.
WELL...OKAY. BUT ONLY BECAUSE IT'S MY HOUSE!
GBTrudeau

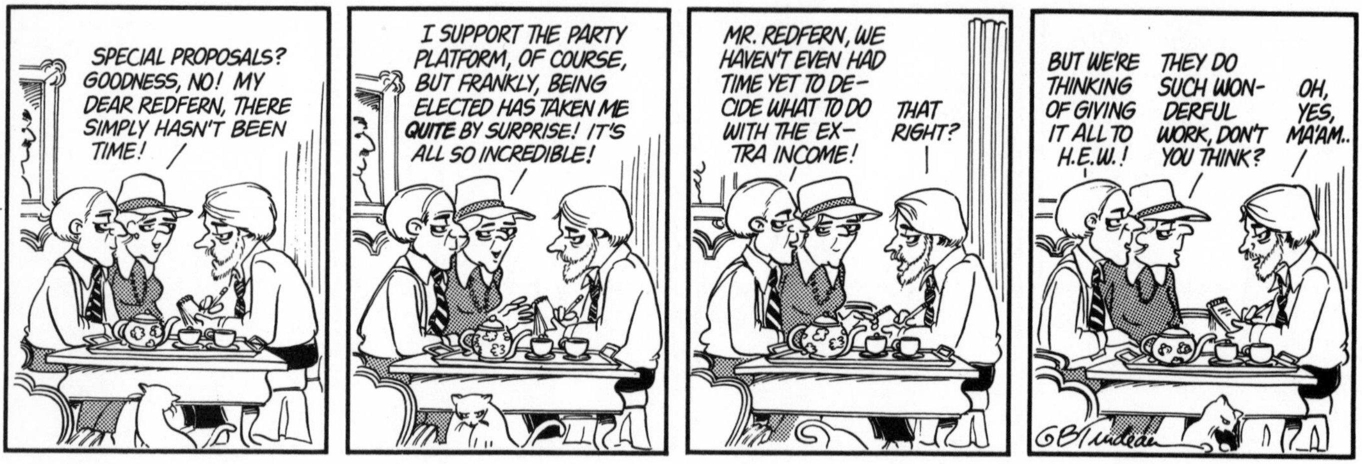
SPECIAL PROPOSALS? GOODNESS, NO! MY DEAR REDFERN, THERE SIMPLY HASN'T BEEN TIME!
I SUPPORT THE PARTY PLATFORM, OF COURSE, BUT FRANKLY, BEING ELECTED HAS TAKEN ME QUITE BY SURPRISE! IT'S ALL SO INCREDIBLE!
MR. REDFERN, WE HAVEN'T EVEN HAD TIME YET TO DECIDE WHAT TO DO WITH THE EXTRA INCOME!
THAT RIGHT?
BUT WE'RE THINKING OF GIVING IT ALL TO H.E.W.!
THEY DO SUCH WONDERFUL WORK, DON'T YOU THINK?
OH, YES, MA'AM..
GBTrudeau

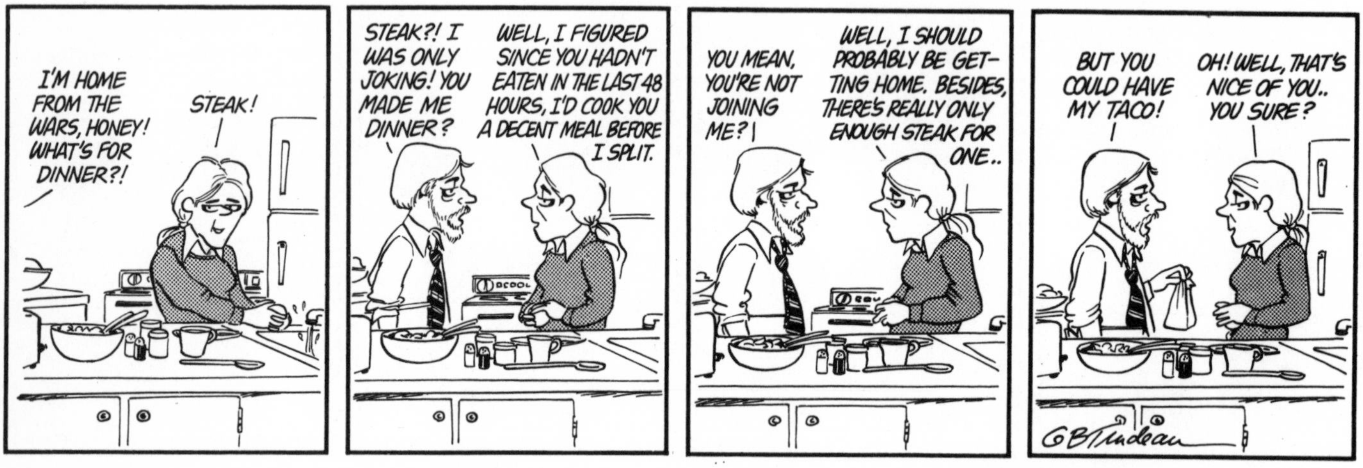
I'M HOME FROM THE WARS, HONEY! WHAT'S FOR DINNER?!
STEAK!
STEAK?! I WAS ONLY JOKING! YOU MADE ME DINNER?
WELL, I FIGURED SINCE YOU HADN'T EATEN IN THE LAST 48 HOURS, I'D COOK YOU A DECENT MEAL BEFORE I SPLIT.
YOU MEAN, YOU'RE NOT JOINING ME?
WELL, I SHOULD PROBABLY BE GETTING HOME. BESIDES, THERE'S REALLY ONLY ENOUGH STEAK FOR ONE..
BUT YOU COULD HAVE MY TACO!
OH! WELL, THAT'S NICE OF YOU.. YOU SURE?
GBTrudeau

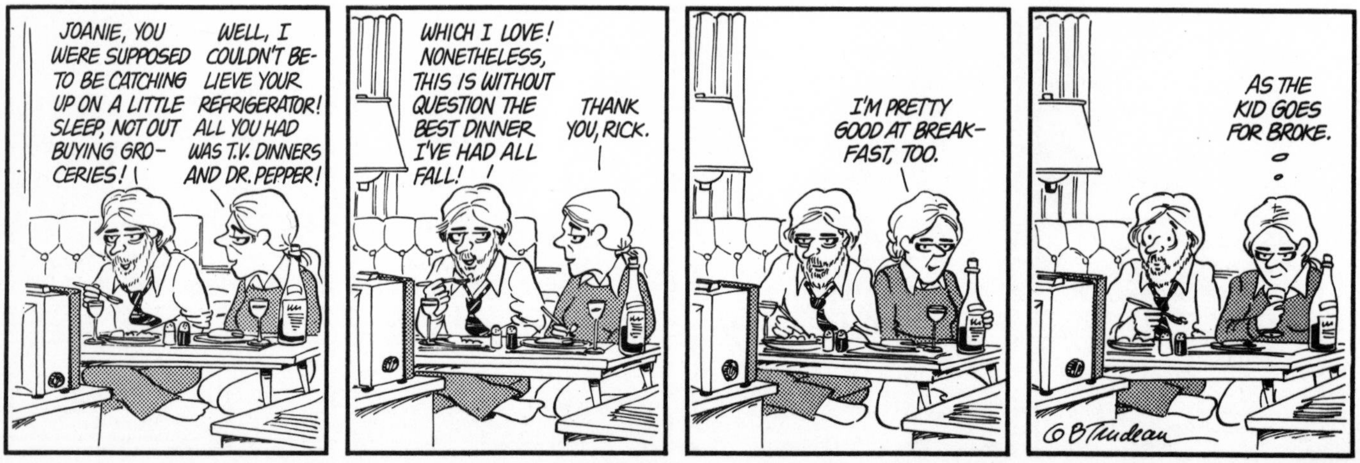
JOANIE, YOU WERE SUPPOSED TO BE CATCHING UP ON A LITTLE SLEEP, NOT OUT BUYING GROCERIES!
WELL, I COULDN'T BELIEVE YOUR REFRIGERATOR! ALL YOU HAD WAS T.V. DINNERS AND DR. PEPPER!
WHICH I LOVE! NONETHELESS, THIS IS WITHOUT QUESTION THE BEST DINNER I'VE HAD ALL FALL!
THANK YOU, RICK.
I'M PRETTY GOOD AT BREAKFAST, TOO.
AS THE KID GOES FOR BROKE.
GBTrudeau

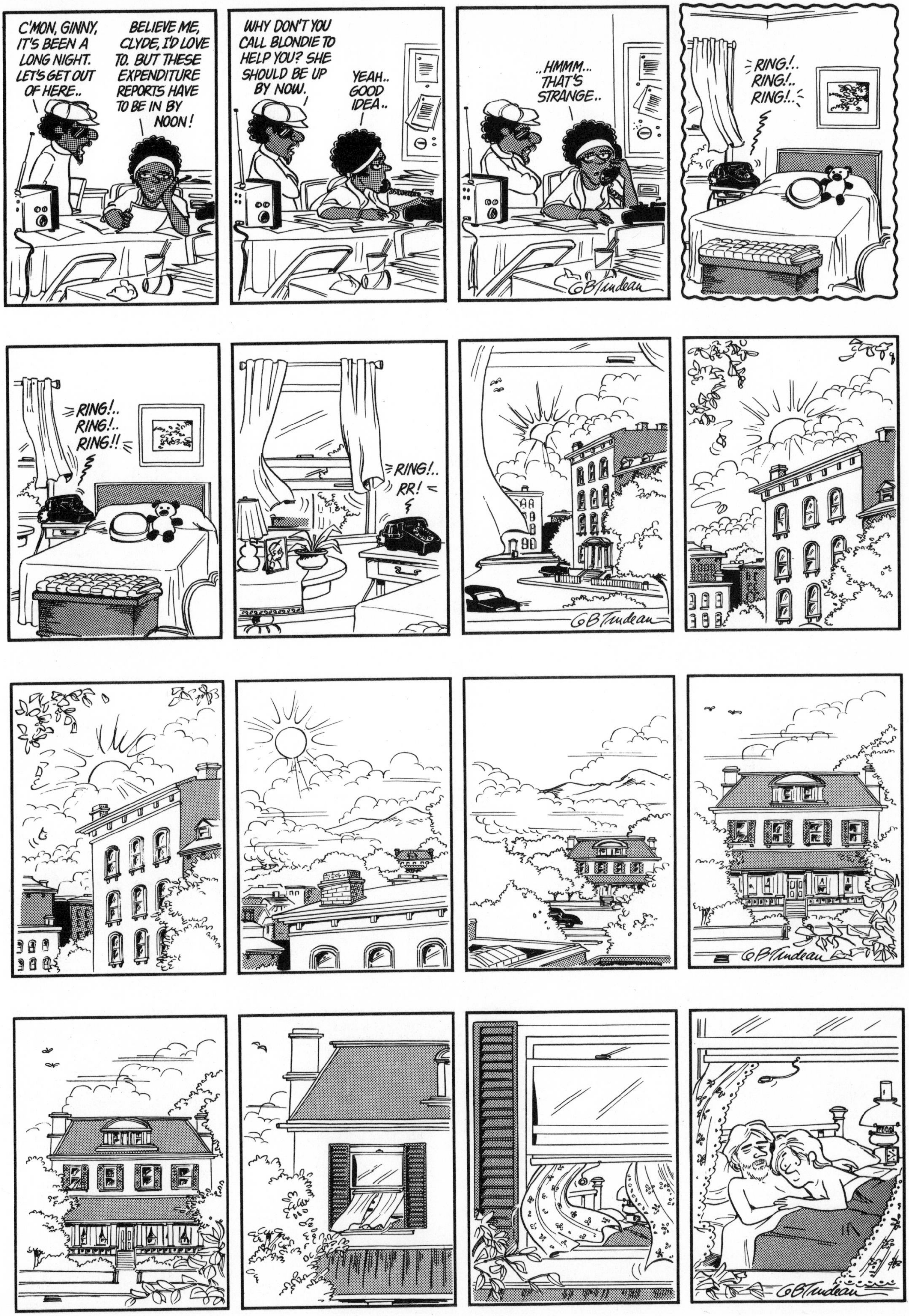
C'MON, GINNY, IT'S BEEN A LONG NIGHT. LET'S GET OUT OF HERE..
BELIEVE ME, CLYDE, I'D LOVE TO. BUT THESE EXPENDITURE REPORTS HAVE TO BE IN BY NOON!
WHY DON'T YOU CALL BLONDIE TO HELP YOU? SHE SHOULD BE UP BY NOW.
YEAH.. GOOD IDEA..
..HMMM... THAT'S STRANGE..
GBTrudeau
RING!.. RING!.. RING!..
RING!.. RING!.. RING!!
RING!.. RR!
GBTrudeau
GBTrudeau
GBTrudeau

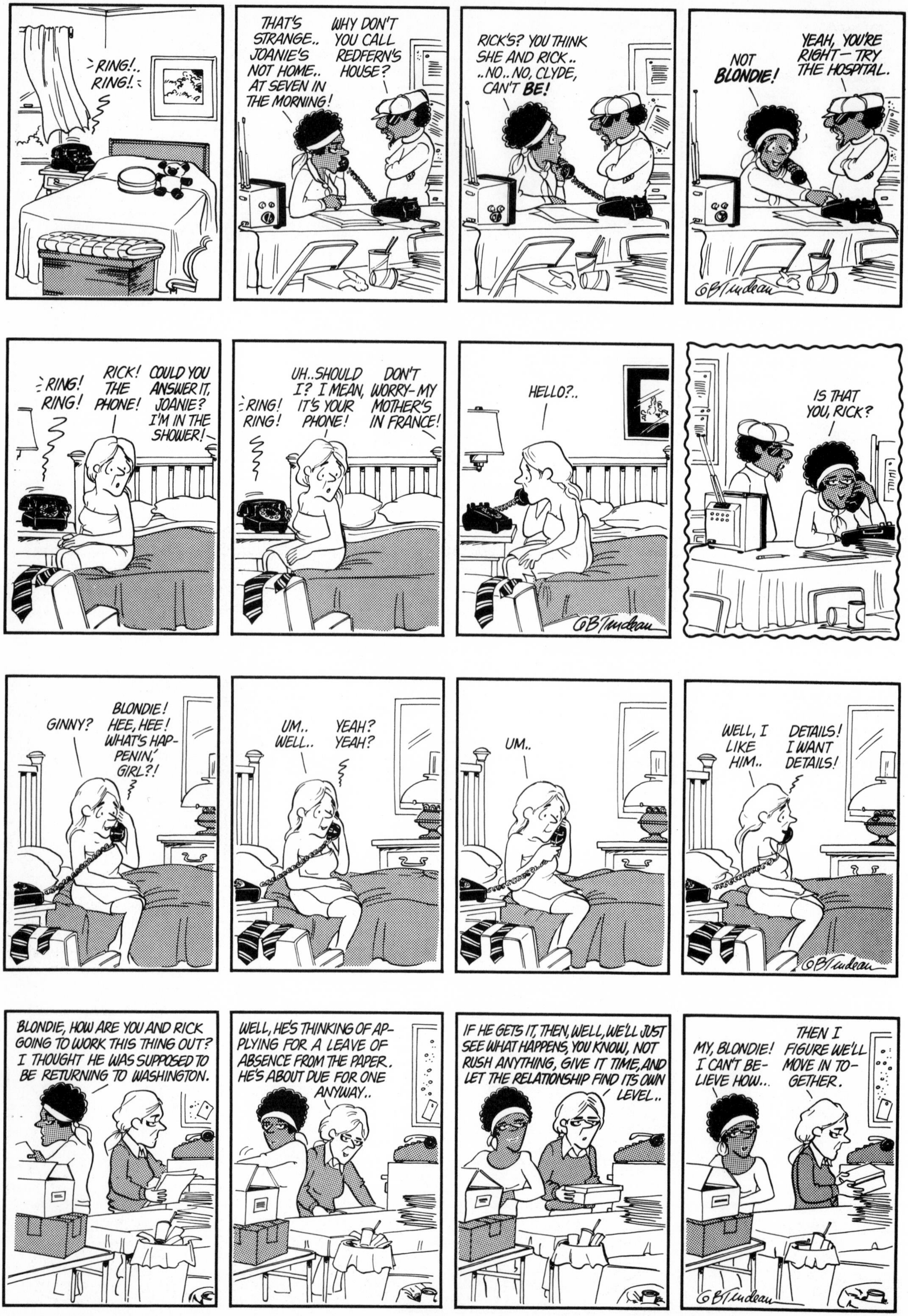
RING!.. RING!..
THAT'S STRANGE.. JOANIE'S NOT HOME.. AT SEVEN IN THE MORNING!
WHY DON'T YOU CALL REDFERN'S HOUSE?
RICK'S? YOU THINK SHE AND RICK.. ..NO.. NO, CLYDE, CAN'T BE!
NOT BLONDIE!
YEAH, YOU'RE RIGHT — TRY THE HOSPITAL.
©BTrudeau
RING! RING!
RICK! THE PHONE!
COULD YOU ANSWER IT, JOANIE? I'M IN THE SHOWER!
RING! RING!
UH.. SHOULD I? I MEAN, IT'S YOUR PHONE!
DON'T WORRY- MY MOTHER'S IN FRANCE!
HELLO?..
©BTrudeau
IS THAT YOU, RICK?
GINNY?
BLONDIE! HEE, HEE! WHAT'S HAPPENIN,' GIRL?!
UM.. WELL..
YEAH? YEAH?
UM..
WELL, I LIKE HIM..
DETAILS! I WANT DETAILS!
©BTrudeau
BLONDIE, HOW ARE YOU AND RICK GOING TO WORK THIS THING OUT? I THOUGHT HE WAS SUPPOSED TO BE RETURNING TO WASHINGTON.
WELL, HE'S THINKING OF APPLYING FOR A LEAVE OF ABSENCE FROM THE PAPER. HE'S ABOUT DUE FOR ONE ANYWAY..
IF HE GETS IT, THEN, WELL, WE'LL JUST SEE WHAT HAPPENS, YOU KNOW, NOT RUSH ANYTHING, GIVE IT TIME, AND LET THE RELATIONSHIP FIND ITS OWN LEVEL..
MY, BLONDIE! I CAN'T BELIEVE HOW...
THEN I FIGURE WE'LL MOVE IN TOGETHER.
©BTrudeau

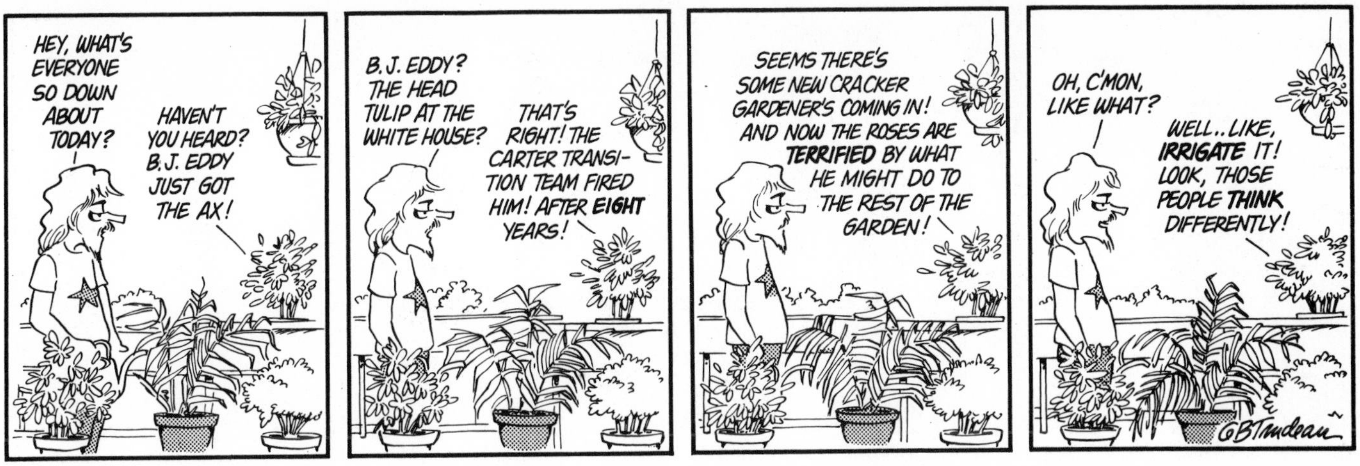
HEY, WHAT'S EVERYONE SO DOWN ABOUT TODAY?
HAVEN'T YOU HEARD? B.J. EDDY JUST GOT THE AX!
B.J. EDDY? THE HEAD TULIP AT THE WHITE HOUSE?
THAT'S RIGHT! THE CARTER TRANSITION TEAM FIRED HIM! AFTER **EIGHT** YEARS!
SEEMS THERE'S SOME NEW CRACKER GARDENER'S COMING IN! AND NOW THE ROSES ARE **TERRIFIED** BY WHAT HE MIGHT DO TO THE REST OF THE GARDEN!
OH, C'MON, LIKE WHAT?
WELL.. LIKE, **IRRIGATE** IT! LOOK, THOSE PEOPLE **THINK** DIFFERENTLY!

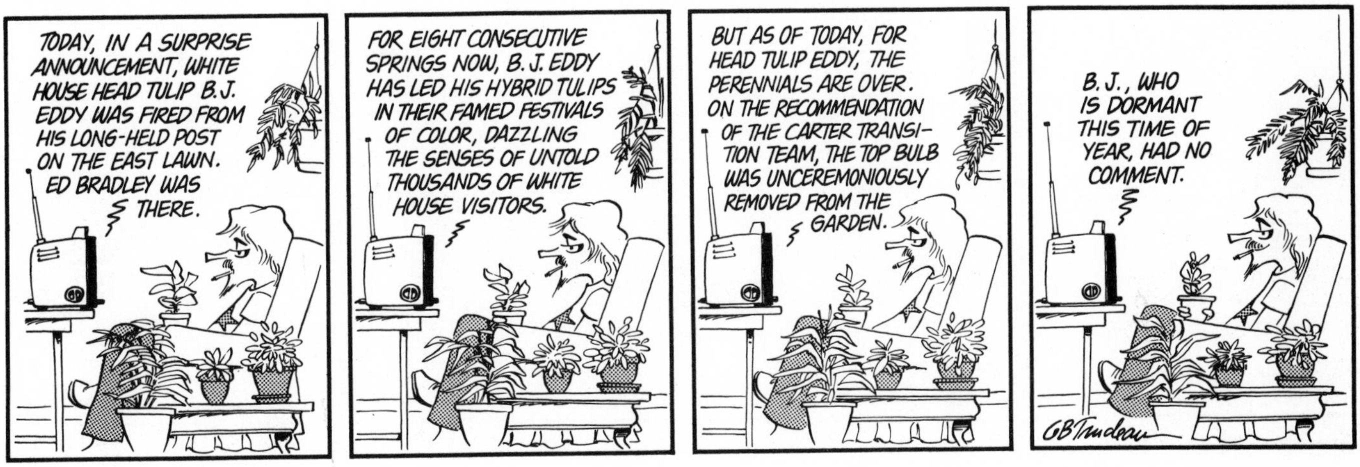
TODAY, IN A SURPRISE ANNOUNCEMENT, WHITE HOUSE HEAD TULIP B.J. EDDY WAS FIRED FROM HIS LONG-HELD POST ON THE EAST LAWN. ED BRADLEY WAS THERE.
FOR EIGHT CONSECUTIVE SPRINGS NOW, B.J. EDDY HAS LED HIS HYBRID TULIPS IN THEIR FAMED FESTIVALS OF COLOR, DAZZLING THE SENSES OF UNTOLD THOUSANDS OF WHITE HOUSE VISITORS.
BUT AS OF TODAY, FOR HEAD TULIP EDDY, THE PERENNIALS ARE OVER. ON THE RECOMMENDATION OF THE CARTER TRANSITION TEAM, THE TOP BULB WAS UNCEREMONIOUSLY REMOVED FROM THE GARDEN.
B.J., WHO IS DORMANT THIS TIME OF YEAR, HAD NO COMMENT.

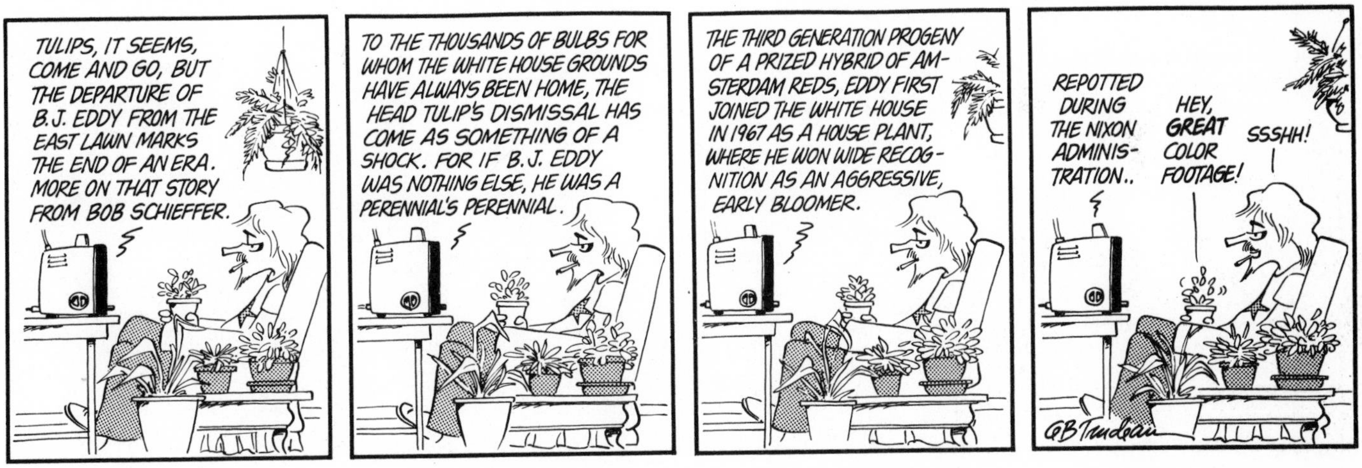
TULIPS, IT SEEMS, COME AND GO, BUT THE DEPARTURE OF B.J. EDDY FROM THE EAST LAWN MARKS THE END OF AN ERA. MORE ON THAT STORY FROM BOB SCHIEFFER.
TO THE THOUSANDS OF BULBS FOR WHOM THE WHITE HOUSE GROUNDS HAVE ALWAYS BEEN HOME, THE HEAD TULIP'S DISMISSAL HAS COME AS SOMETHING OF A SHOCK. FOR IF B.J. EDDY WAS NOTHING ELSE, HE WAS A PERENNIAL'S PERENNIAL.
THE THIRD GENERATION PROGENY OF A PRIZED HYBRID OF AMSTERDAM REDS, EDDY FIRST JOINED THE WHITE HOUSE IN 1967 AS A HOUSE PLANT, WHERE HE WON WIDE RECOGNITION AS AN AGGRESSIVE, EARLY BLOOMER.
REPOTTED DURING THE NIXON ADMINISTRATION..
HEY, **GREAT** COLOR FOOTAGE!
SSSHH!

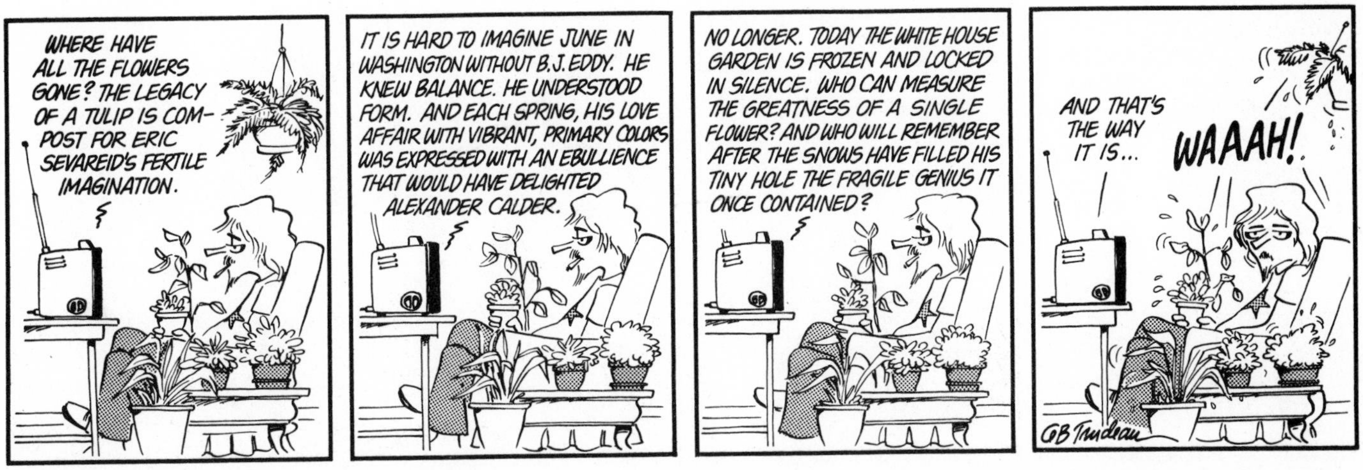
WHERE HAVE ALL THE FLOWERS GONE? THE LEGACY OF A TULIP IS COMPOST FOR ERIC SEVAREID'S FERTILE IMAGINATION.
IT IS HARD TO IMAGINE JUNE IN WASHINGTON WITHOUT B.J. EDDY. HE KNEW BALANCE. HE UNDERSTOOD FORM. AND EACH SPRING, HIS LOVE AFFAIR WITH VIBRANT, PRIMARY COLORS WAS EXPRESSED WITH AN EBULLIENCE THAT WOULD HAVE DELIGHTED ALEXANDER CALDER.
NO LONGER. TODAY THE WHITE HOUSE GARDEN IS FROZEN AND LOCKED IN SILENCE. WHO CAN MEASURE THE GREATNESS OF A SINGLE FLOWER? AND WHO WILL REMEMBER AFTER THE SNOWS HAVE FILLED HIS TINY HOLE THE FRAGILE GENIUS IT ONCE CONTAINED?
AND THAT'S THE WAY IT IS...
WAAAH!

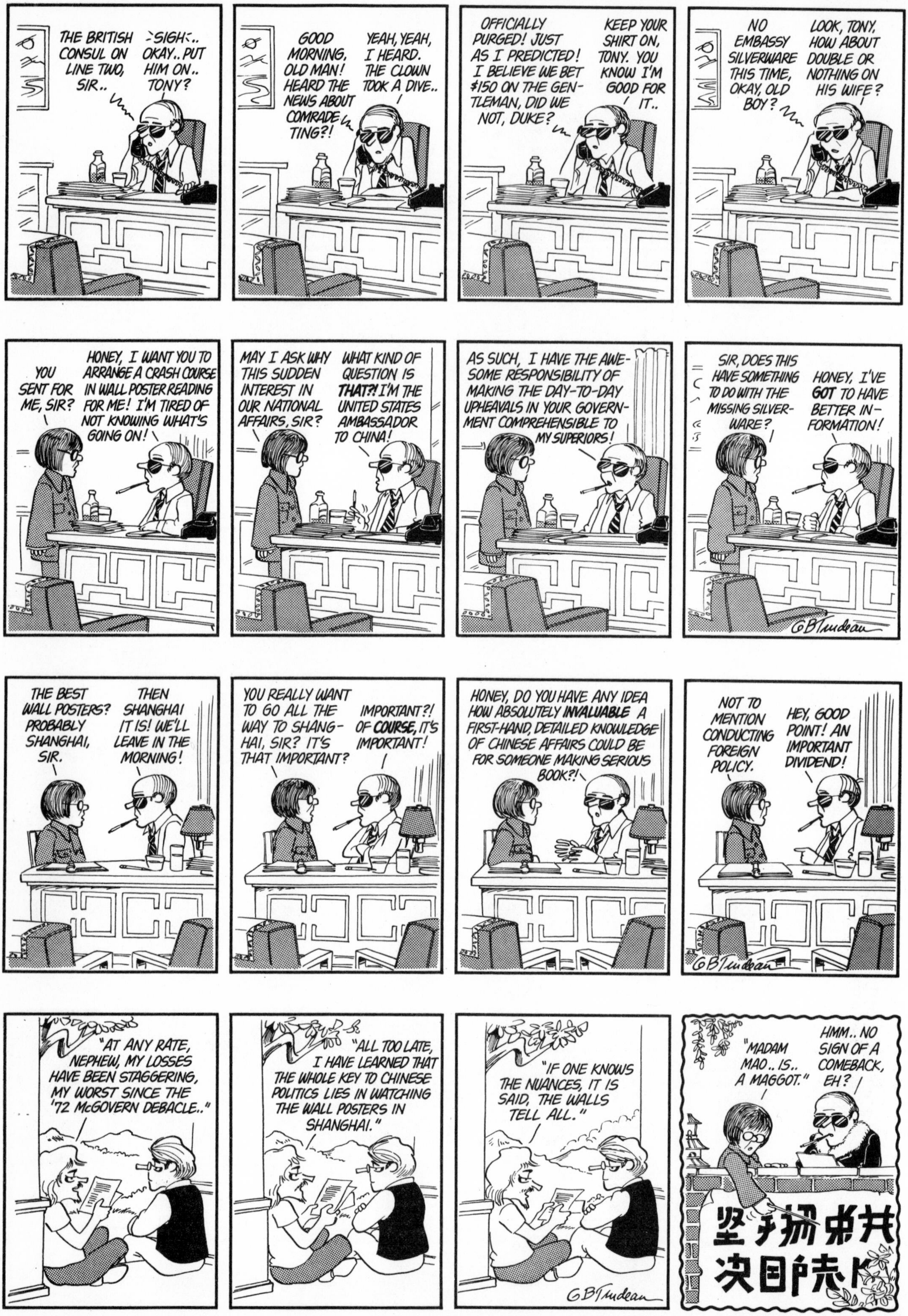
THE BRITISH CONSUL ON LINE TWO, SIR..
>SIGH<.. OKAY.. PUT HIM ON.. TONY?
GOOD MORNING, OLD MAN! HEARD THE NEWS ABOUT COMRADE TING?!
YEAH, YEAH, I HEARD. THE CLOWN TOOK A DIVE..
OFFICIALLY PURGED! JUST AS I PREDICTED! I BELIEVE WE BET $150 ON THE GENTLEMAN, DID WE NOT, DUKE?
KEEP YOUR SHIRT ON, TONY. YOU KNOW I'M GOOD FOR IT..
NO EMBASSY SILVERWARE THIS TIME, OKAY, OLD BOY?
LOOK, TONY, HOW ABOUT DOUBLE OR NOTHING ON HIS WIFE?
YOU SENT FOR ME, SIR?
HONEY, I WANT YOU TO ARRANGE A CRASH COURSE IN WALL POSTER READING FOR ME! I'M TIRED OF NOT KNOWING WHAT'S GOING ON!
MAY I ASK WHY THIS SUDDEN INTEREST IN OUR NATIONAL AFFAIRS, SIR?
WHAT KIND OF QUESTION IS THAT?! I'M THE UNITED STATES AMBASSADOR TO CHINA!
AS SUCH, I HAVE THE AWESOME RESPONSIBILITY OF MAKING THE DAY-TO-DAY UPHEAVALS IN YOUR GOVERNMENT COMPREHENSIBLE TO MY SUPERIORS!
SIR, DOES THIS HAVE SOMETHING TO DO WITH THE MISSING SILVERWARE?
HONEY, I'VE GOT TO HAVE BETTER INFORMATION!
G B Trudeau
THE BEST WALL POSTERS? PROBABLY SHANGHAI, SIR.
THEN SHANGHAI IT IS! WE'LL LEAVE IN THE MORNING!
YOU REALLY WANT TO GO ALL THE WAY TO SHANGHAI, SIR? IT'S THAT IMPORTANT?
IMPORTANT?! OF COURSE, IT'S IMPORTANT!
HONEY, DO YOU HAVE ANY IDEA HOW ABSOLUTELY INVALUABLE A FIRST-HAND, DETAILED KNOWLEDGE OF CHINESE AFFAIRS COULD BE FOR SOMEONE MAKING SERIOUS BOOK?!
NOT TO MENTION CONDUCTING FOREIGN POLICY.
HEY, GOOD POINT! AN IMPORTANT DIVIDEND!
G B Trudeau
"AT ANY RATE, NEPHEW, MY LOSSES HAVE BEEN STAGGERING, MY WORST SINCE THE '72 McGOVERN DEBACLE.."
"ALL TOO LATE, I HAVE LEARNED THAT THE WHOLE KEY TO CHINESE POLITICS LIES IN WATCHING THE WALL POSTERS IN SHANGHAI."
"IF ONE KNOWS THE NUANCES, IT IS SAID, THE WALLS TELL ALL."
G B Trudeau
"MADAM MAO.. IS.. A MAGGOT."
HMM.. NO SIGN OF A COMEBACK, EH?

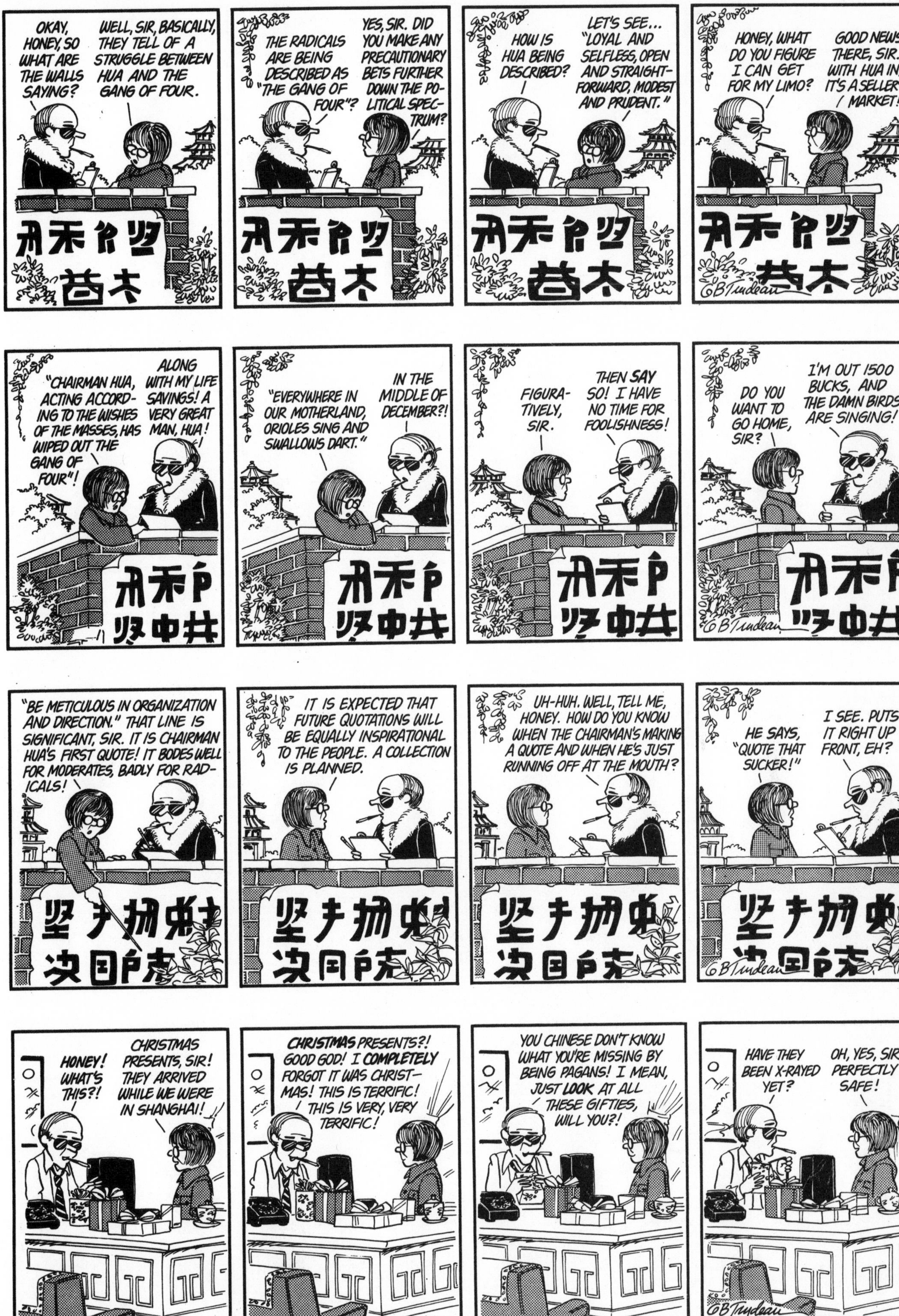
OKAY, HONEY, SO WHAT ARE THE WALLS SAYING?
WELL, SIR, BASICALLY, THEY TELL OF A STRUGGLE BETWEEN HUA AND THE GANG OF FOUR.
THE RADICALS ARE BEING DESCRIBED AS "THE GANG OF FOUR"?
YES, SIR. DID YOU MAKE ANY PRECAUTIONARY BETS FURTHER DOWN THE POLITICAL SPECTRUM?
HOW IS HUA BEING DESCRIBED?
LET'S SEE... "LOYAL AND SELFLESS, OPEN AND STRAIGHTFORWARD, MODEST AND PRUDENT."
HONEY, WHAT DO YOU FIGURE I CAN GET FOR MY LIMO?
GOOD NEWS THERE, SIR. WITH HUA IN, IT'S A SELLER'S MARKET!
©B Trudeau
"CHAIRMAN HUA, ACTING ACCORDING TO THE WISHES OF THE MASSES, HAS WIPED OUT THE GANG OF FOUR"!
ALONG WITH MY LIFE SAVINGS! A VERY GREAT MAN, HUA!
"EVERYWHERE IN OUR MOTHERLAND, ORIOLES SING AND SWALLOWS DART."
IN THE MIDDLE OF DECEMBER?!
FIGURATIVELY, SIR.
THEN SAY SO! I HAVE NO TIME FOR FOOLISHNESS!
DO YOU WANT TO GO HOME, SIR?
I'M OUT 1500 BUCKS, AND THE DAMN BIRDS ARE SINGING!
©B Trudeau
"BE METICULOUS IN ORGANIZATION AND DIRECTION." THAT LINE IS SIGNIFICANT, SIR. IT IS CHAIRMAN HUA'S FIRST QUOTE! IT BODES WELL FOR MODERATES, BADLY FOR RADICALS!
IT IS EXPECTED THAT FUTURE QUOTATIONS WILL BE EQUALLY INSPIRATIONAL TO THE PEOPLE. A COLLECTION IS PLANNED.
UH-HUH. WELL, TELL ME, HONEY. HOW DO YOU KNOW WHEN THE CHAIRMAN'S MAKING A QUOTE AND WHEN HE'S JUST RUNNING OFF AT THE MOUTH?
HE SAYS, "QUOTE THAT SUCKER!"
I SEE. PUTS IT RIGHT UP FRONT, EH?
©B Trudeau
HONEY! WHAT'S THIS?!
CHRISTMAS PRESENTS, SIR! THEY ARRIVED WHILE WE WERE IN SHANGHAI!
CHRISTMAS PRESENTS?! GOOD GOD! I COMPLETELY FORGOT IT WAS CHRISTMAS! THIS IS TERRIFIC! THIS IS VERY, VERY TERRIFIC!
YOU CHINESE DON'T KNOW WHAT YOU'RE MISSING BY BEING PAGANS! I MEAN, JUST LOOK AT ALL THESE GIFTIES, WILL YOU?!
HAVE THEY BEEN X-RAYED YET?
OH, YES, SIR! PERFECTLY SAFE!
©B Trudeau

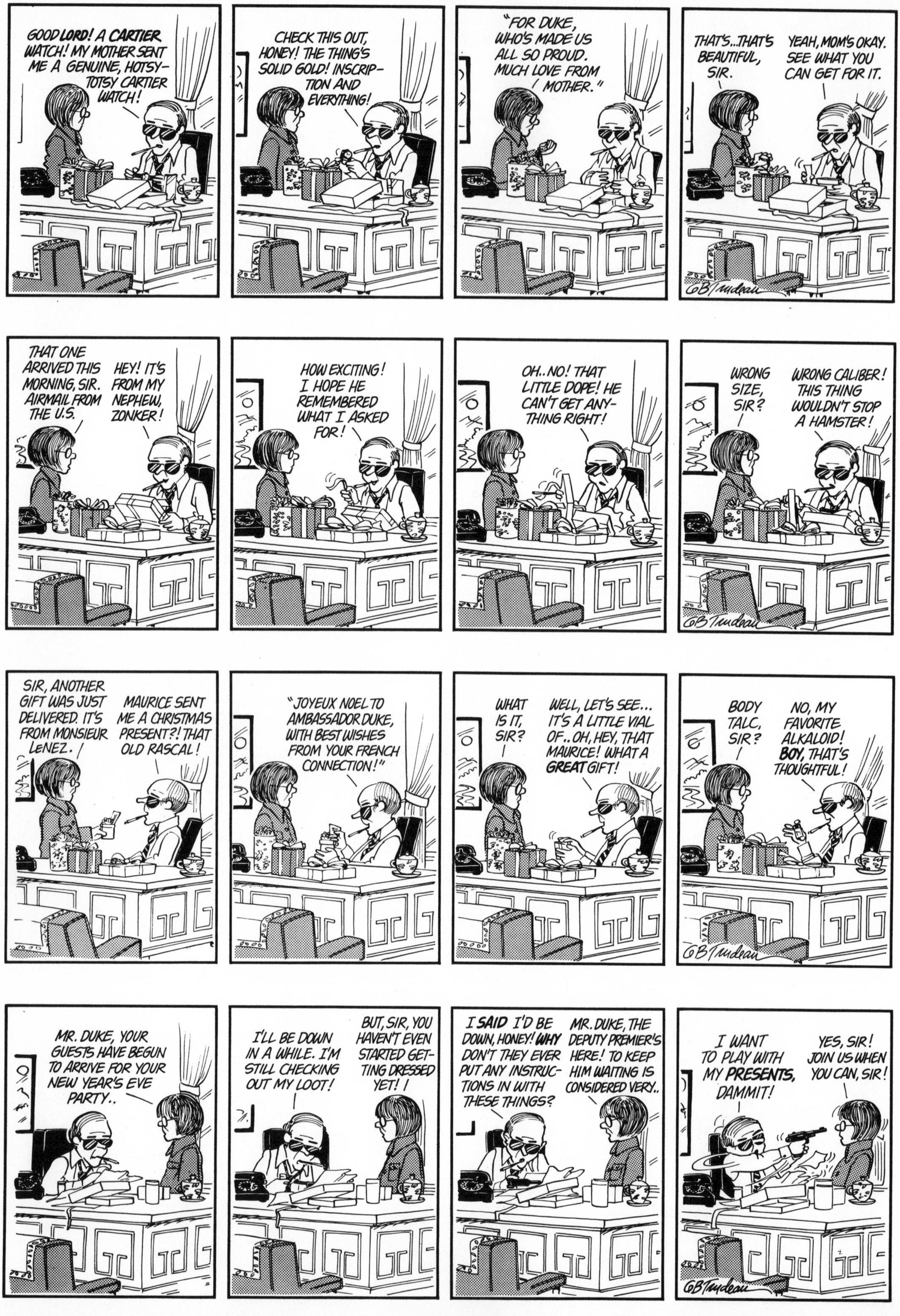
GOOD LORD! A CARTIER WATCH! MY MOTHER SENT ME A GENUINE, HOTSY-TOTSY CARTIER WATCH!
CHECK THIS OUT, HONEY! THE THING'S SOLID GOLD! INSCRIPTION AND EVERYTHING!
"FOR DUKE, WHO'S MADE US ALL SO PROUD. MUCH LOVE FROM MOTHER."
THAT'S...THAT'S BEAUTIFUL, SIR.
YEAH, MOM'S OKAY. SEE WHAT YOU CAN GET FOR IT.
GBTrudeau
THAT ONE ARRIVED THIS MORNING, SIR. AIRMAIL FROM THE U.S.
HEY! IT'S FROM MY NEPHEW, ZONKER!
HOW EXCITING! I HOPE HE REMEMBERED WHAT I ASKED FOR!
OH.. NO! THAT LITTLE DOPE! HE CAN'T GET ANYTHING RIGHT!
WRONG SIZE, SIR?
WRONG CALIBER! THIS THING WOULDN'T STOP A HAMSTER!
GBTrudeau
SIR, ANOTHER GIFT WAS JUST DELIVERED. IT'S FROM MONSIEUR LENEZ.
MAURICE SENT ME A CHRISTMAS PRESENT?! THAT OLD RASCAL!
"JOYEUX NOEL TO AMBASSADOR DUKE, WITH BEST WISHES FROM YOUR FRENCH CONNECTION!"
WHAT IS IT, SIR?
WELL, LET'S SEE... IT'S A LITTLE VIAL OF.. OH, HEY, THAT MAURICE! WHAT A GREAT GIFT!
BODY TALC, SIR?
NO, MY FAVORITE ALKALOID! BOY, THAT'S THOUGHTFUL!
GBTrudeau
MR. DUKE, YOUR GUESTS HAVE BEGUN TO ARRIVE FOR YOUR NEW YEAR'S EVE PARTY..
I'LL BE DOWN IN A WHILE. I'M STILL CHECKING OUT MY LOOT!
BUT, SIR, YOU HAVEN'T EVEN STARTED GETTING DRESSED YET!
I SAID I'D BE DOWN, HONEY! WHY DON'T THEY EVER PUT ANY INSTRUCTIONS IN WITH THESE THINGS?
MR. DUKE, THE DEPUTY PREMIER'S HERE! TO KEEP HIM WAITING IS CONSIDERED VERY..
I WANT TO PLAY WITH MY PRESENTS, DAMMIT!
YES, SIR! JOIN US WHEN YOU CAN, SIR!
GBTrudeau

ACT THREE

Time: 1977 (Early Disco)

Selected Scenes:

"People Who Hype People" . . . . Rick, Brenda
"The Braxton-Hicks Backbeat" . . . . Jimmy, Jenny,
Feedback
"Something From Gandhi" . . . . Duane Delacourt
"Ta Da!" (Mortarboard Reverie) . . . . Joanie
"Why Woodcock?" (Duke's Lament) . . . . Duke, Honey
"Stalking the Perfect Tan" . . . . Zonker, Cornell
"The Koreagate Rag" . . . . Joanie, Lacey,
U.S. Congress
"Original Panama Follies" . . . . Zonker, B.D.,
Kirby
"Back to You, Barbara" . . . . Roland Burton
Hedley, Jr.,
Marvelous Mark
"Sixties Revival Party" (coda) . . . . Ensemble

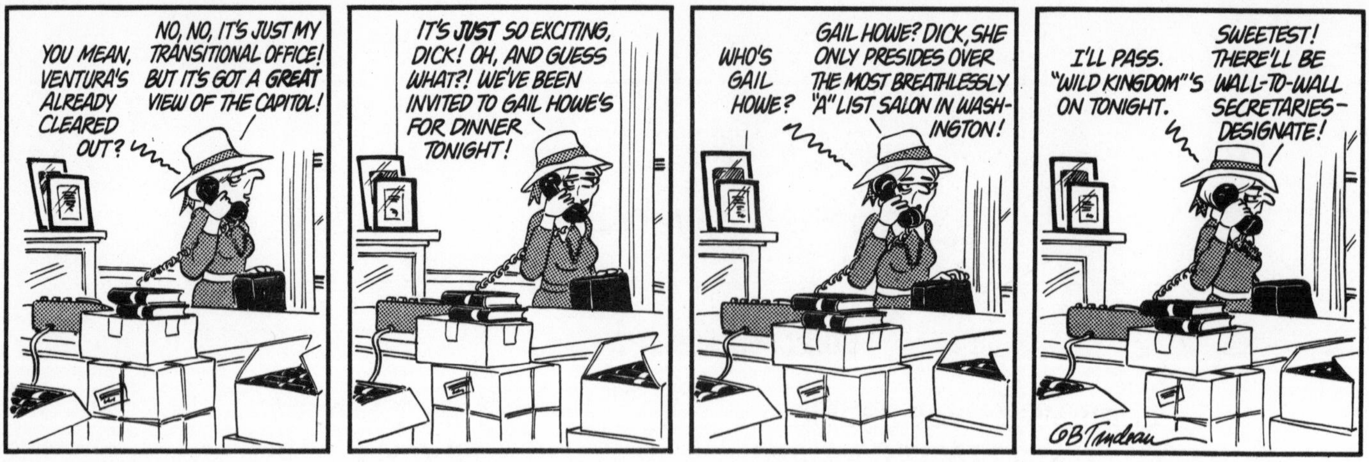
YOU MEAN, VENTURA'S ALREADY CLEARED OUT?
NO, NO, IT'S JUST MY TRANSITIONAL OFFICE! BUT IT'S GOT A GREAT VIEW OF THE CAPITOL!
IT'S JUST SO EXCITING, DICK! OH, AND GUESS WHAT?! WE'VE BEEN INVITED TO GAIL HOWE'S FOR DINNER TONIGHT!
WHO'S GAIL HOWE?
GAIL HOWE? DICK, SHE ONLY PRESIDES OVER THE MOST BREATHLESSLY "A" LIST SALON IN WASHINGTON!
I'LL PASS. "WILD KINGDOM"'S ON TONIGHT.
SWEETEST! THERE'LL BE WALL-TO-WALL SECRETARIES-DESIGNATE!
GBTrudeau

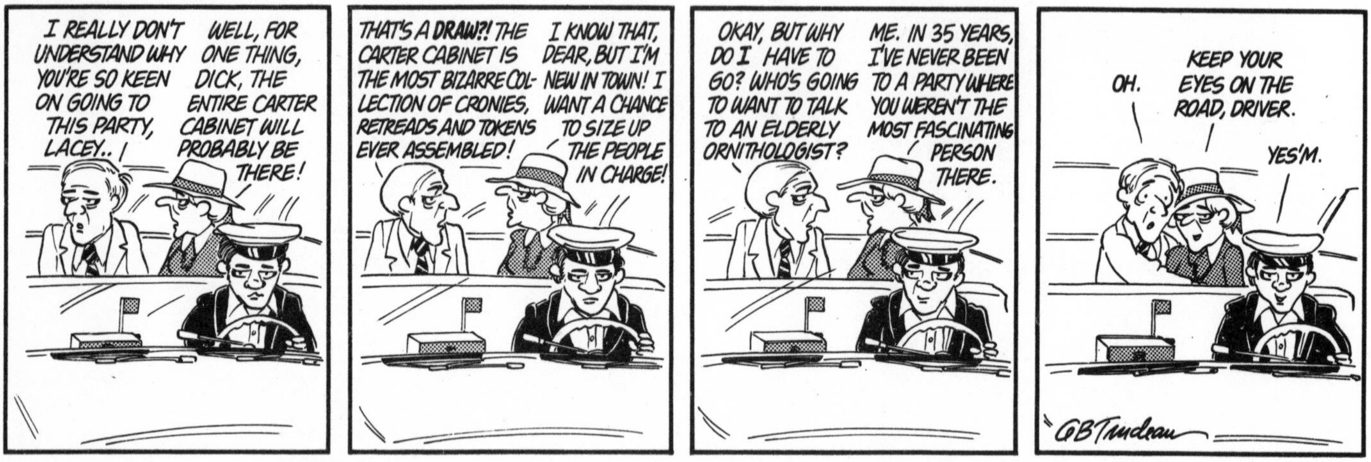
I REALLY DON'T UNDERSTAND WHY YOU'RE SO KEEN ON GOING TO THIS PARTY, LACEY..
WELL, FOR ONE THING, DICK, THE ENTIRE CARTER CABINET WILL PROBABLY BE THERE!
THAT'S A DRAW?! THE CARTER CABINET IS THE MOST BIZARRE COLLECTION OF CRONIES, RETREADS AND TOKENS EVER ASSEMBLED!
I KNOW THAT, DEAR, BUT I'M NEW IN TOWN! I WANT A CHANCE TO SIZE UP THE PEOPLE IN CHARGE!
OKAY, BUT WHY DO I HAVE TO GO? WHO'S GOING TO WANT TO TALK TO AN ELDERLY ORNITHOLOGIST?
ME. IN 35 YEARS, I'VE NEVER BEEN TO A PARTY WHERE YOU WEREN'T THE MOST FASCINATING PERSON THERE.
OH.
KEEP YOUR EYES ON THE ROAD, DRIVER.
YES'M.
GBTrudeau

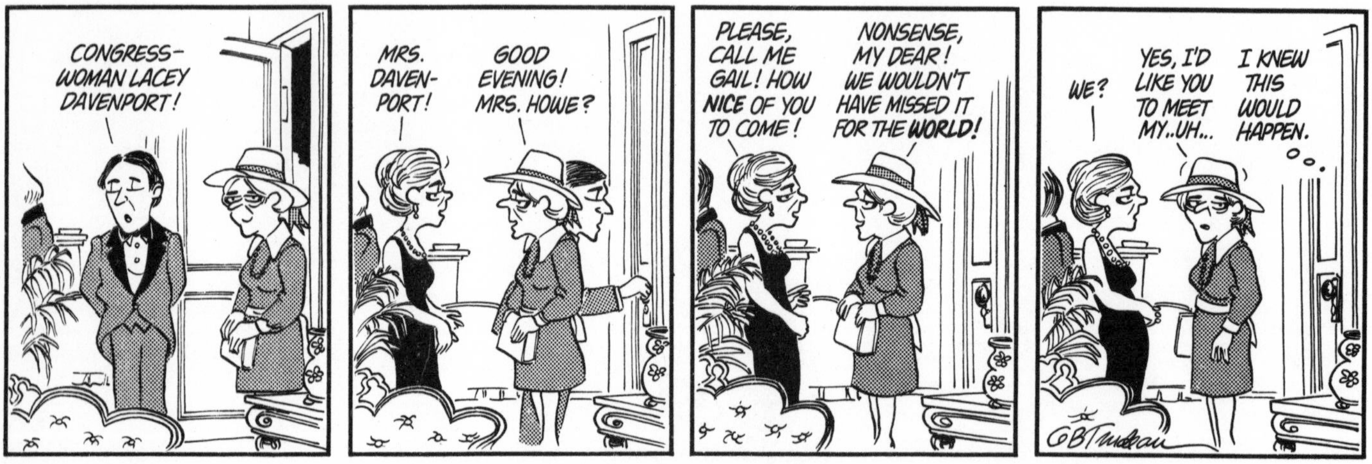
CONGRESSWOMAN LACEY DAVENPORT!
MRS. DAVENPORT!
GOOD EVENING! MRS. HOWE?
PLEASE, CALL ME GAIL! HOW NICE OF YOU TO COME!
NONSENSE, MY DEAR! WE WOULDN'T HAVE MISSED IT FOR THE WORLD!
WE?
YES, I'D LIKE YOU TO MEET MY..UH...
I KNEW THIS WOULD HAPPEN.
GBTrudeau

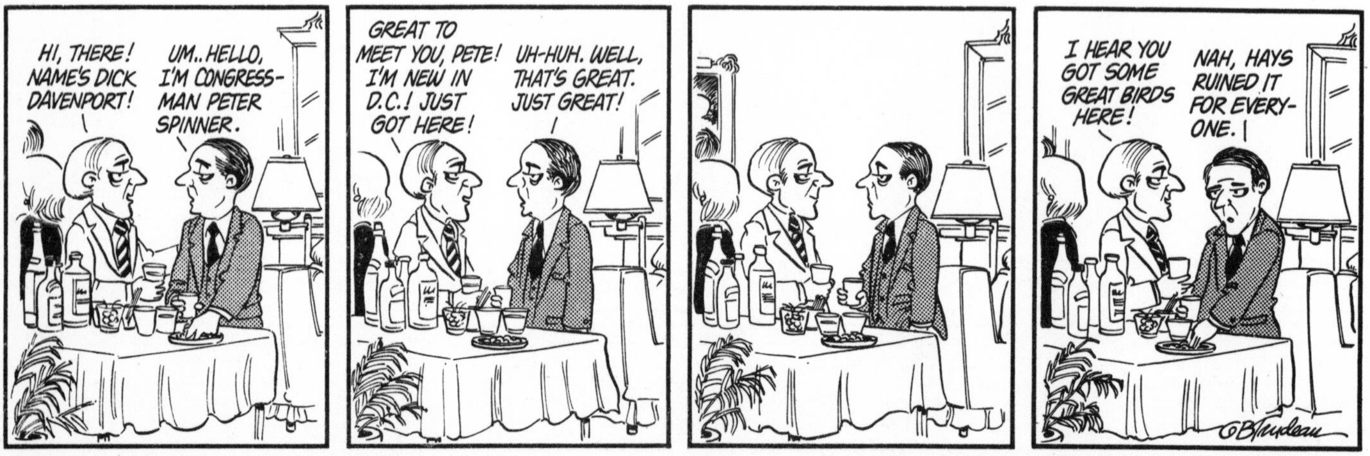
HI, THERE! NAME'S DICK DAVENPORT!
UM..HELLO, I'M CONGRESSMAN PETER SPINNER.
GREAT TO MEET YOU, PETE! I'M NEW IN D.C.! JUST GOT HERE!
UH-HUH. WELL, THAT'S GREAT. JUST GREAT!
I HEAR YOU GOT SOME GREAT BIRDS HERE!
NAH, HAYS RUINED IT FOR EVERYONE.
GBTrudeau

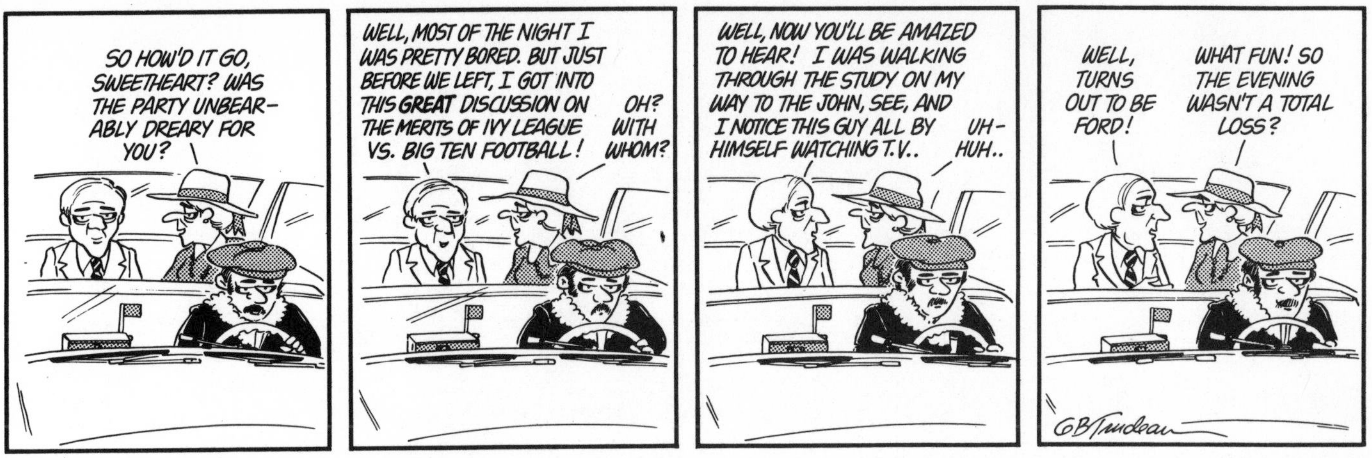
SO HOW'D IT GO, SWEETHEART? WAS THE PARTY UNBEARABLY DREARY FOR YOU?
WELL, MOST OF THE NIGHT I WAS PRETTY BORED. BUT JUST BEFORE WE LEFT, I GOT INTO THIS GREAT DISCUSSION ON THE MERITS OF IVY LEAGUE VS. BIG TEN FOOTBALL!
OH? WITH WHOM?
WELL, NOW YOU'LL BE AMAZED TO HEAR! I WAS WALKING THROUGH THE STUDY ON MY WAY TO THE JOHN, SEE, AND I NOTICE THIS GUY ALL BY HIMSELF WATCHING T.V..
UH-HUH..
WELL, TURNS OUT TO BE FORD!
WHAT FUN! SO THE EVENING WASN'T A TOTAL LOSS?
GBTrudeau

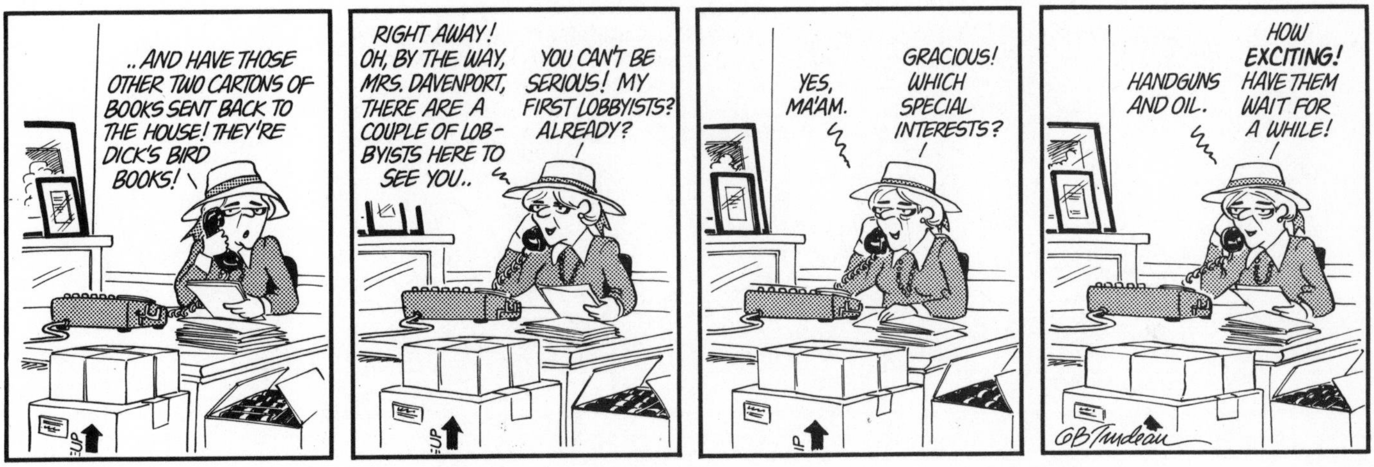
..AND HAVE THOSE OTHER TWO CARTONS OF BOOKS SENT BACK TO THE HOUSE! THEY'RE DICK'S BIRD BOOKS!
RIGHT AWAY! OH, BY THE WAY, MRS. DAVENPORT, THERE ARE A COUPLE OF LOBBYISTS HERE TO SEE YOU..
YOU CAN'T BE SERIOUS! MY FIRST LOBBYISTS? ALREADY?
YES, MA'AM.
GRACIOUS! WHICH SPECIAL INTERESTS?
HANDGUNS AND OIL.
HOW EXCITING! HAVE THEM WAIT FOR A WHILE!
GBTrudeau

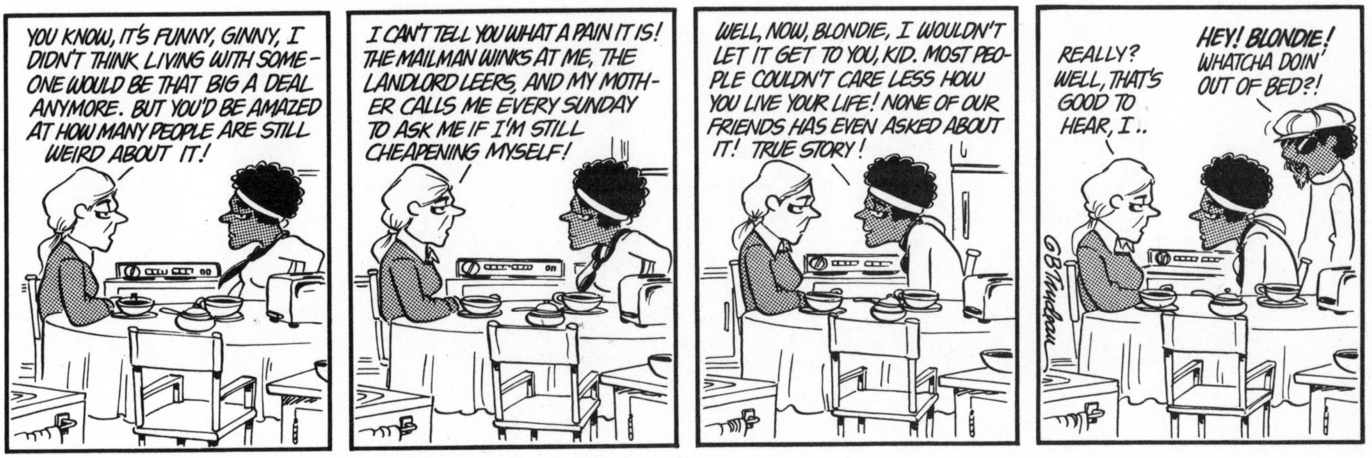
YOU KNOW, IT'S FUNNY, GINNY, I DIDN'T THINK LIVING WITH SOMEONE WOULD BE THAT BIG A DEAL ANYMORE. BUT YOU'D BE AMAZED AT HOW MANY PEOPLE ARE STILL WEIRD ABOUT IT!
I CAN'T TELL YOU WHAT A PAIN IT IS! THE MAILMAN WINKS AT ME, THE LANDLORD LEERS, AND MY MOTHER CALLS ME EVERY SUNDAY TO ASK ME IF I'M STILL CHEAPENING MYSELF!
WELL, NOW, BLONDIE, I WOULDN'T LET IT GET TO YOU, KID. MOST PEOPLE COULDN'T CARE LESS HOW YOU LIVE YOUR LIFE! NONE OF OUR FRIENDS HAS EVEN ASKED ABOUT IT! TRUE STORY!
GBTrudeau
REALLY? WELL, THAT'S GOOD TO HEAR, I..
HEY! BLONDIE! WHATCHA DOIN' OUT OF BED?!

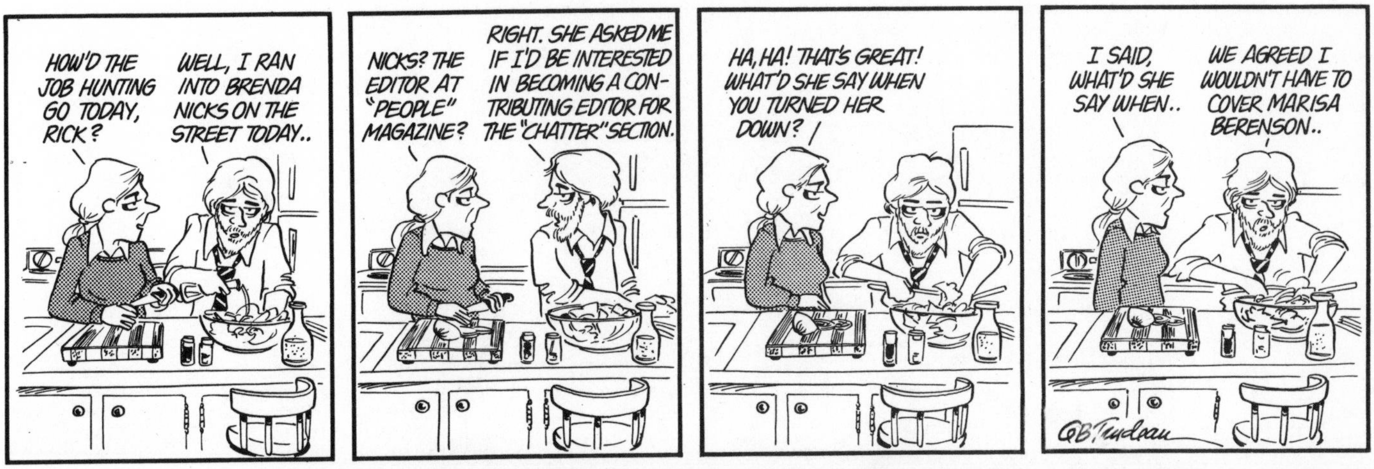
HOW'D THE JOB HUNTING GO TODAY, RICK?
WELL, I RAN INTO BRENDA NICKS ON THE STREET TODAY..
NICKS? THE EDITOR AT "PEOPLE" MAGAZINE?
RIGHT. SHE ASKED ME IF I'D BE INTERESTED IN BECOMING A CONTRIBUTING EDITOR FOR THE "CHATTER" SECTION.
HA, HA! THAT'S GREAT! WHAT'D SHE SAY WHEN YOU TURNED HER DOWN?
I SAID, WHAT'D SHE SAY WHEN..
WE AGREED I WOULDN'T HAVE TO COVER MARISA BERENSON..
GBTrudeau

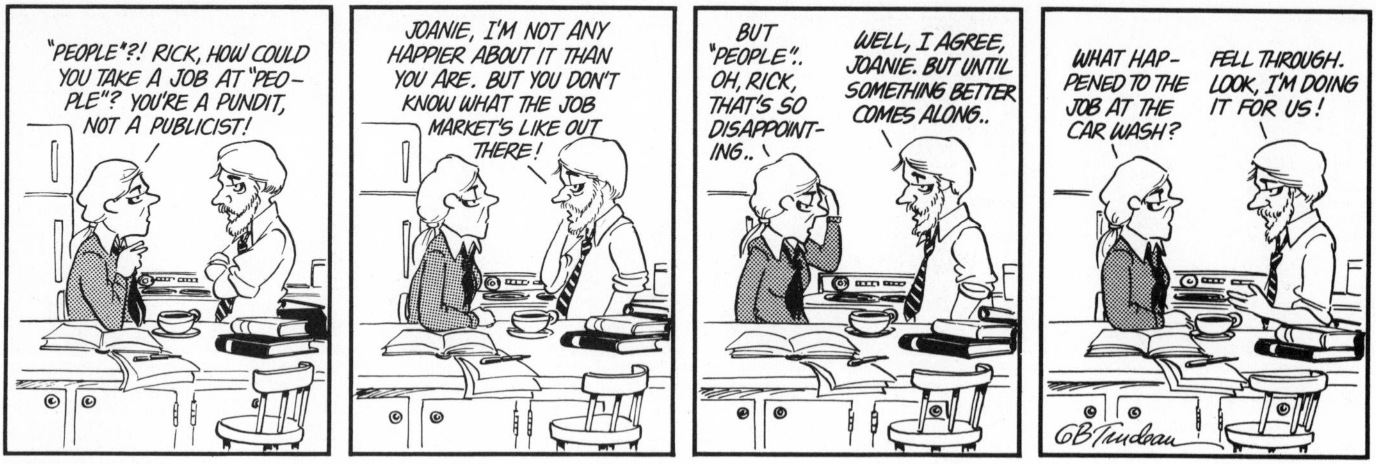
"PEOPLE"?! RICK, HOW COULD YOU TAKE A JOB AT "PEOPLE"? YOU'RE A PUNDIT, NOT A PUBLICIST!
JOANIE, I'M NOT ANY HAPPIER ABOUT IT THAN YOU ARE. BUT YOU DON'T KNOW WHAT THE JOB MARKET'S LIKE OUT THERE!
BUT "PEOPLE".. OH, RICK, THAT'S SO DISAPPOINTING..
WELL, I AGREE, JOANIE. BUT UNTIL SOMETHING BETTER COMES ALONG..
WHAT HAPPENED TO THE JOB AT THE CAR WASH?
FELL THROUGH. LOOK, I'M DOING IT FOR US!

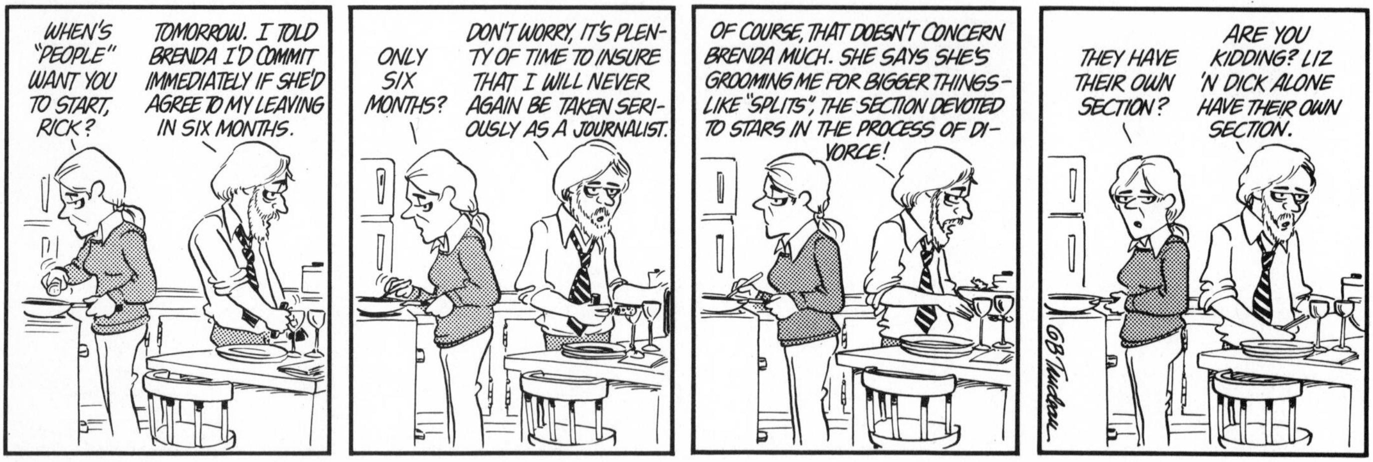
WHEN'S "PEOPLE" WANT YOU TO START, RICK?
TOMORROW. I TOLD BRENDA I'D COMMIT IMMEDIATELY IF SHE'D AGREE TO MY LEAVING IN SIX MONTHS.
ONLY SIX MONTHS?
DON'T WORRY, IT'S PLENTY OF TIME TO INSURE THAT I WILL NEVER AGAIN BE TAKEN SERIOUSLY AS A JOURNALIST.
OF COURSE, THAT DOESN'T CONCERN BRENDA MUCH. SHE SAYS SHE'S GROOMING ME FOR BIGGER THINGS-LIKE "SPLITS", THE SECTION DEVOTED TO STARS IN THE PROCESS OF DIVORCE!
THEY HAVE THEIR OWN SECTION?
ARE YOU KIDDING? LIZ 'N DICK ALONE HAVE THEIR OWN SECTION.

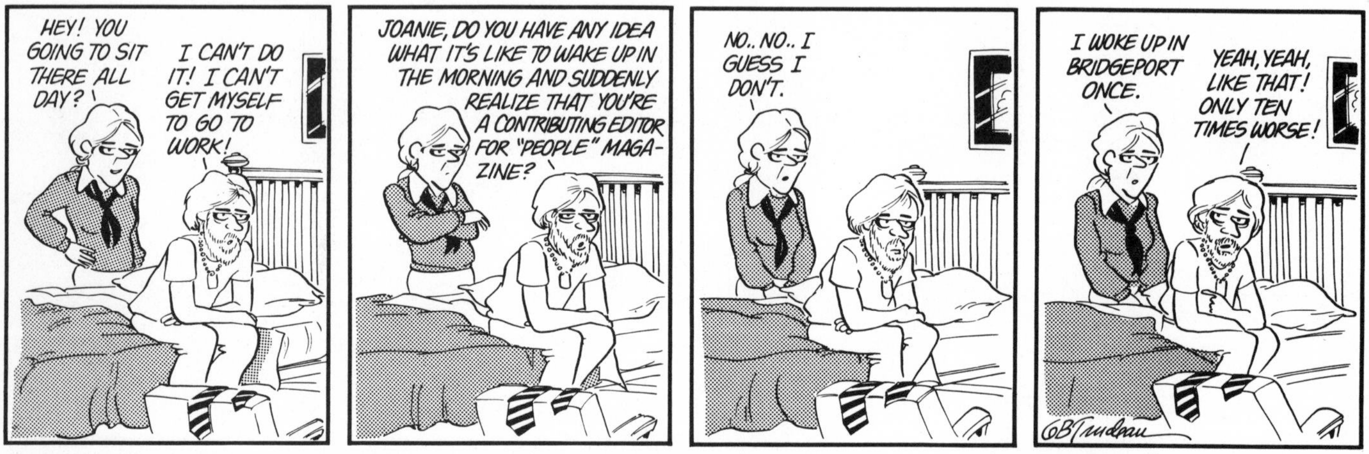
HEY! YOU GOING TO SIT THERE ALL DAY?
I CAN'T DO IT! I CAN'T GET MYSELF TO GO TO WORK!
JOANIE, DO YOU HAVE ANY IDEA WHAT IT'S LIKE TO WAKE UP IN THE MORNING AND SUDDENLY REALIZE THAT YOU'RE A CONTRIBUTING EDITOR FOR "PEOPLE" MAGAZINE?
NO.. NO.. I GUESS I DON'T.
I WOKE UP IN BRIDGEPORT ONCE.
YEAH, YEAH, LIKE THAT! ONLY TEN TIMES WORSE!

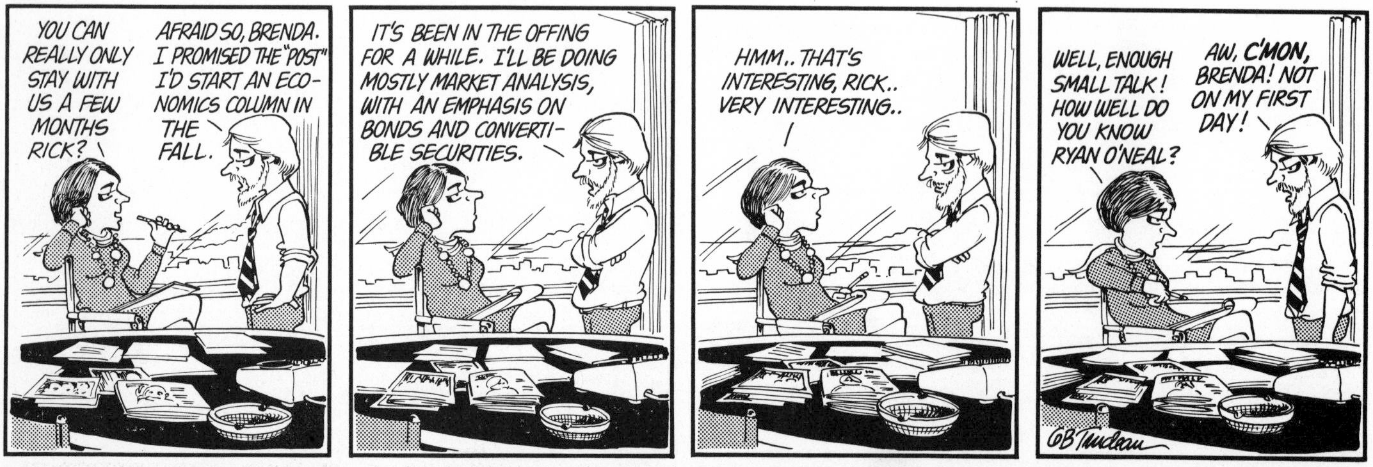
YOU CAN REALLY ONLY STAY WITH US A FEW MONTHS RICK?
AFRAID SO, BRENDA. I PROMISED THE "POST" I'D START AN ECONOMICS COLUMN IN THE FALL.
IT'S BEEN IN THE OFFING FOR A WHILE. I'LL BE DOING MOSTLY MARKET ANALYSIS, WITH AN EMPHASIS ON BONDS AND CONVERTIBLE SECURITIES.
HMM.. THAT'S INTERESTING, RICK.. VERY INTERESTING..
WELL, ENOUGH SMALL TALK! HOW WELL DO YOU KNOW RYAN O'NEAL?
AW, C'MON, BRENDA! NOT ON MY FIRST DAY!

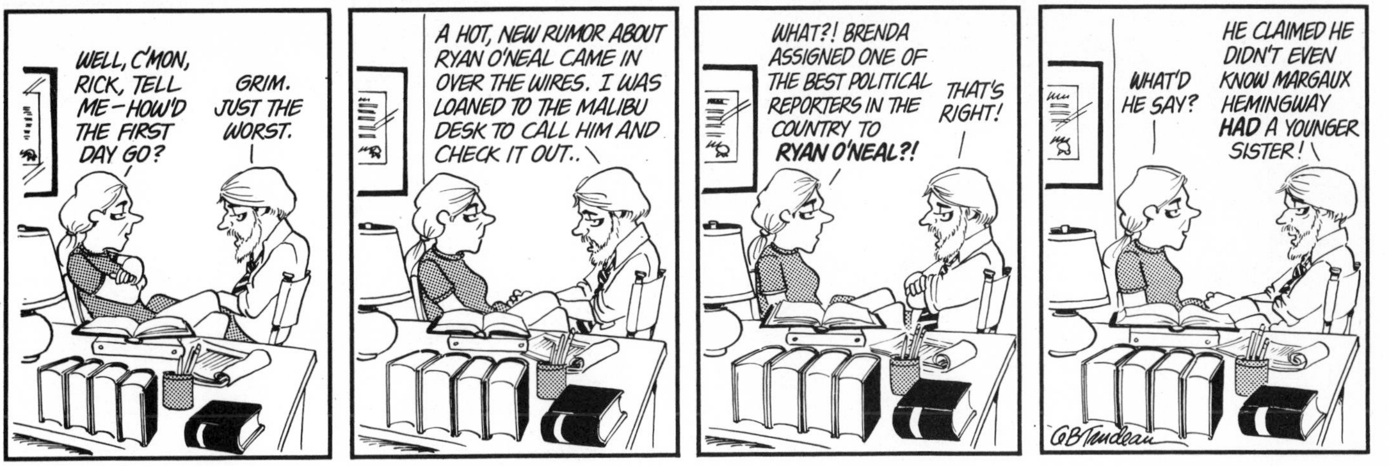
WELL, C'MON, RICK, TELL ME—HOW'D THE FIRST DAY GO?
GRIM. JUST THE WORST.
A HOT, NEW RUMOR ABOUT RYAN O'NEAL CAME IN OVER THE WIRES. I WAS LOANED TO THE MALIBU DESK TO CALL HIM AND CHECK IT OUT..
WHAT?! BRENDA ASSIGNED ONE OF THE BEST POLITICAL REPORTERS IN THE COUNTRY TO **RYAN O'NEAL?!**
THAT'S RIGHT!
WHAT'D HE SAY?
HE CLAIMED HE DIDN'T EVEN KNOW MARGAUX HEMINGWAY **HAD** A YOUNGER SISTER!
GBTrudeau

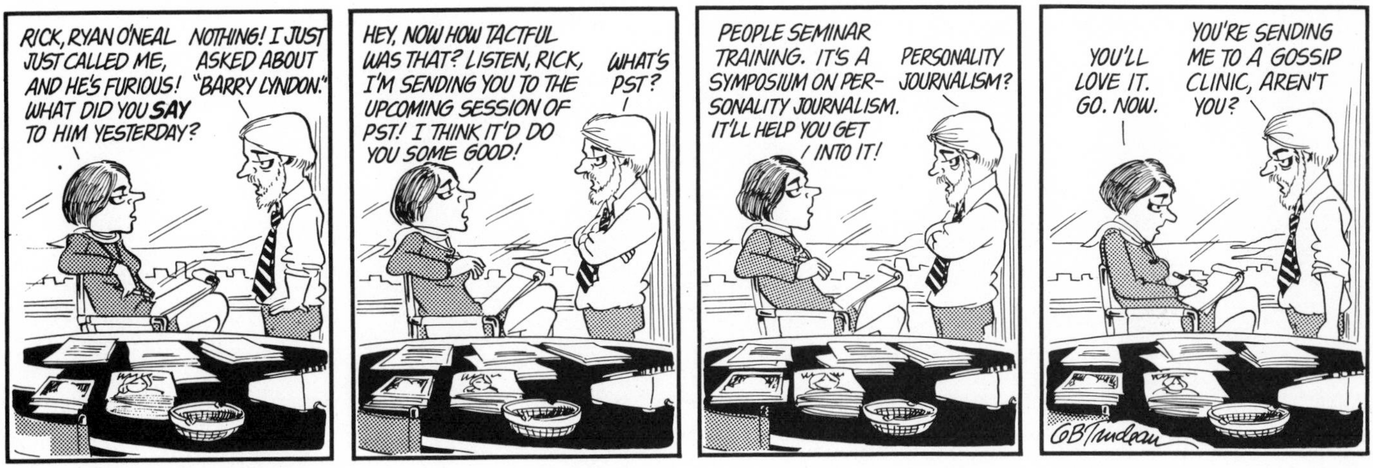
RICK, RYAN O'NEAL JUST CALLED ME, AND HE'S FURIOUS! WHAT DID YOU **SAY** TO HIM YESTERDAY?
NOTHING! I JUST ASKED ABOUT "BARRY LYNDON."
HEY, NOW HOW TACTFUL WAS THAT? LISTEN, RICK, I'M SENDING YOU TO THE UPCOMING SESSION OF PST! I THINK IT'D DO YOU SOME GOOD!
WHAT'S PST?
PEOPLE SEMINAR TRAINING. IT'S A SYMPOSIUM ON PERSONALITY JOURNALISM. IT'LL HELP YOU GET INTO IT!
PERSONALITY JOURNALISM?
YOU'LL LOVE IT. GO. NOW.
YOU'RE SENDING ME TO A GOSSIP CLINIC, AREN'T YOU?
GBTrudeau

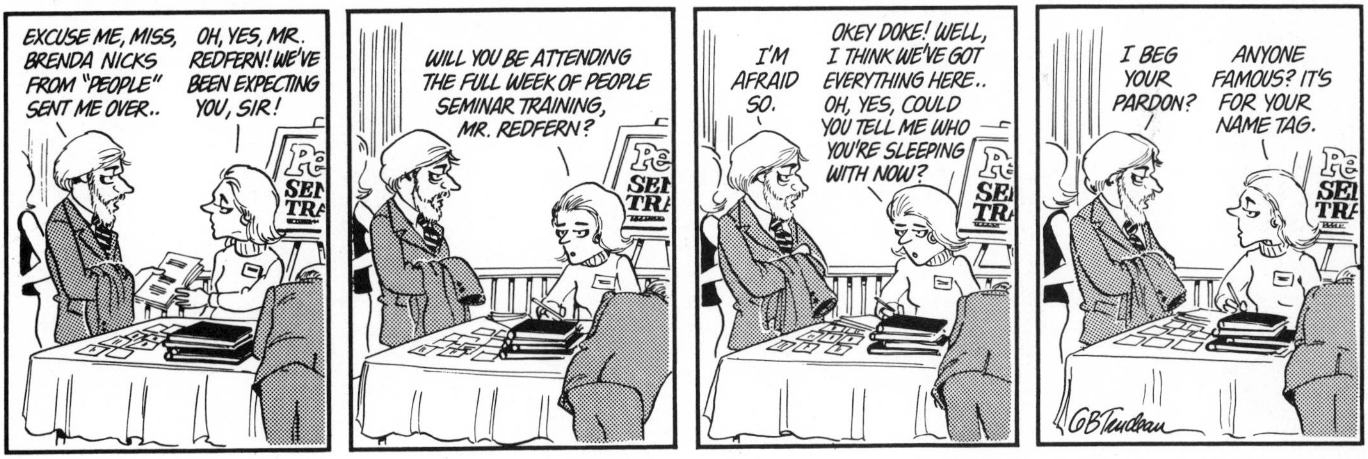
EXCUSE ME, MISS, BRENDA NICKS FROM "PEOPLE" SENT ME OVER..
OH, YES, MR. REDFERN! WE'VE BEEN EXPECTING YOU, SIR!
WILL YOU BE ATTENDING THE FULL WEEK OF PEOPLE SEMINAR TRAINING, MR. REDFERN?
I'M AFRAID SO.
OKEY DOKE! WELL, I THINK WE'VE GOT EVERYTHING HERE.. OH, YES, COULD YOU TELL ME WHO YOU'RE SLEEPING WITH NOW?
I BEG YOUR PARDON?
ANYONE FAMOUS? IT'S FOR YOUR NAME TAG.
GBTrudeau

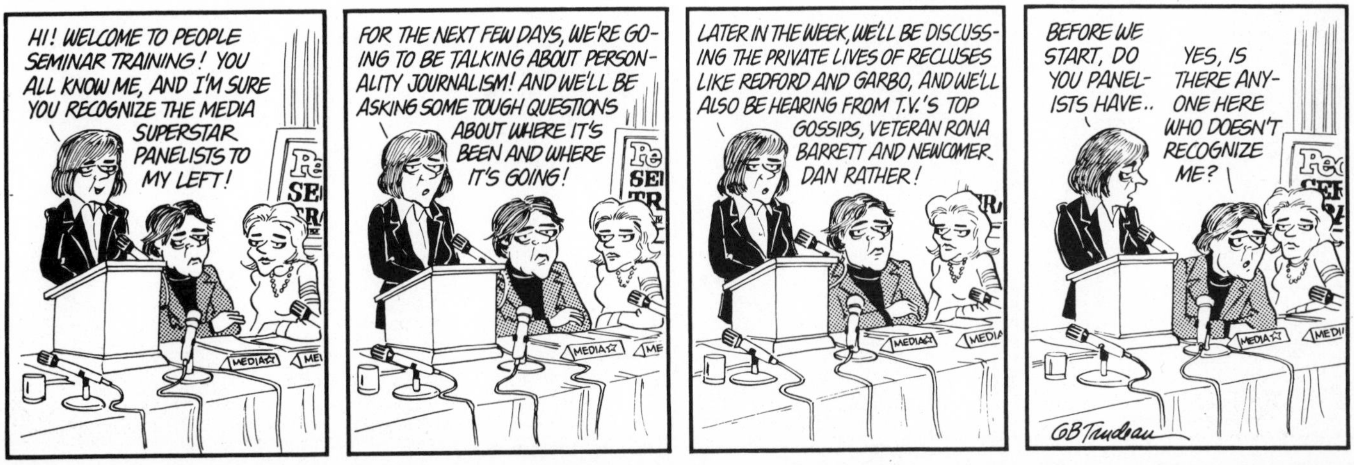
HI! WELCOME TO PEOPLE SEMINAR TRAINING! YOU ALL KNOW ME, AND I'M SURE YOU RECOGNIZE THE MEDIA SUPERSTAR PANELISTS TO MY LEFT!
FOR THE NEXT FEW DAYS, WE'RE GOING TO BE TALKING ABOUT PERSONALITY JOURNALISM! AND WE'LL BE ASKING SOME TOUGH QUESTIONS ABOUT WHERE IT'S BEEN AND WHERE IT'S GOING!
LATER IN THE WEEK, WE'LL BE DISCUSSING THE PRIVATE LIVES OF RECLUSES LIKE REDFORD AND GARBO, AND WE'LL ALSO BE HEARING FROM T.V.'S TOP GOSSIPS, VETERAN RONA BARRETT AND NEWCOMER DAN RATHER!
BEFORE WE START, DO YOU PANELISTS HAVE..
YES, IS THERE ANYONE HERE WHO DOESN'T RECOGNIZE ME?
GBTrudeau

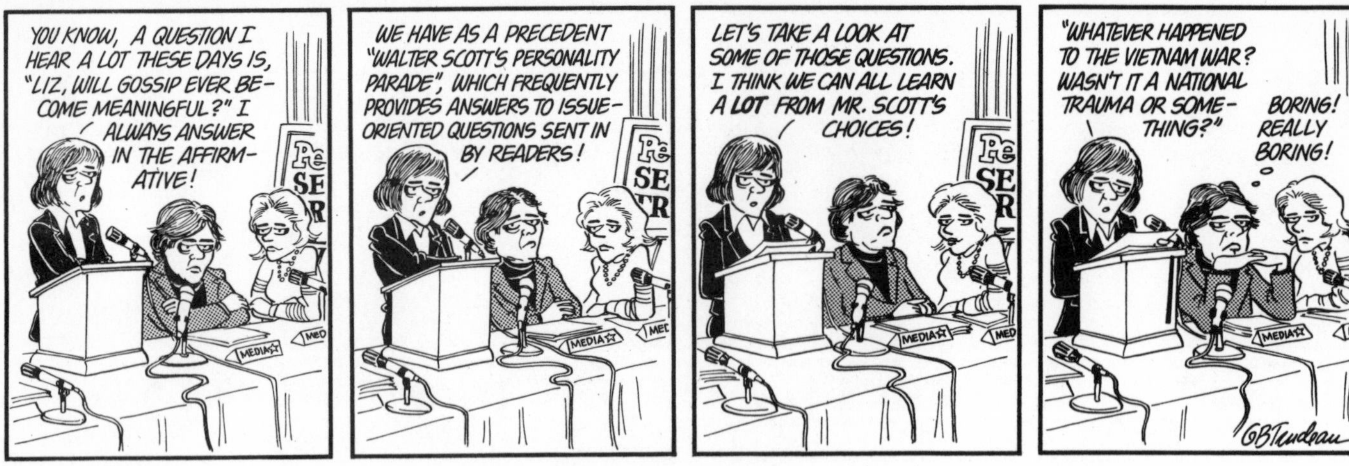
YOU KNOW, A QUESTION I HEAR A LOT THESE DAYS IS, "LIZ, WILL GOSSIP EVER BECOME MEANINGFUL?" I ALWAYS ANSWER IN THE AFFIRMATIVE!
WE HAVE AS A PRECEDENT "WALTER SCOTT'S PERSONALITY PARADE", WHICH FREQUENTLY PROVIDES ANSWERS TO ISSUE-ORIENTED QUESTIONS SENT IN BY READERS!
LET'S TAKE A LOOK AT SOME OF THOSE QUESTIONS. I THINK WE CAN ALL LEARN A LOT FROM MR. SCOTT'S CHOICES!
"WHATEVER HAPPENED TO THE VIETNAM WAR? WASN'T IT A NATIONAL TRAUMA OR SOMETHING?"
BORING! REALLY BORING!
GBTrudeau

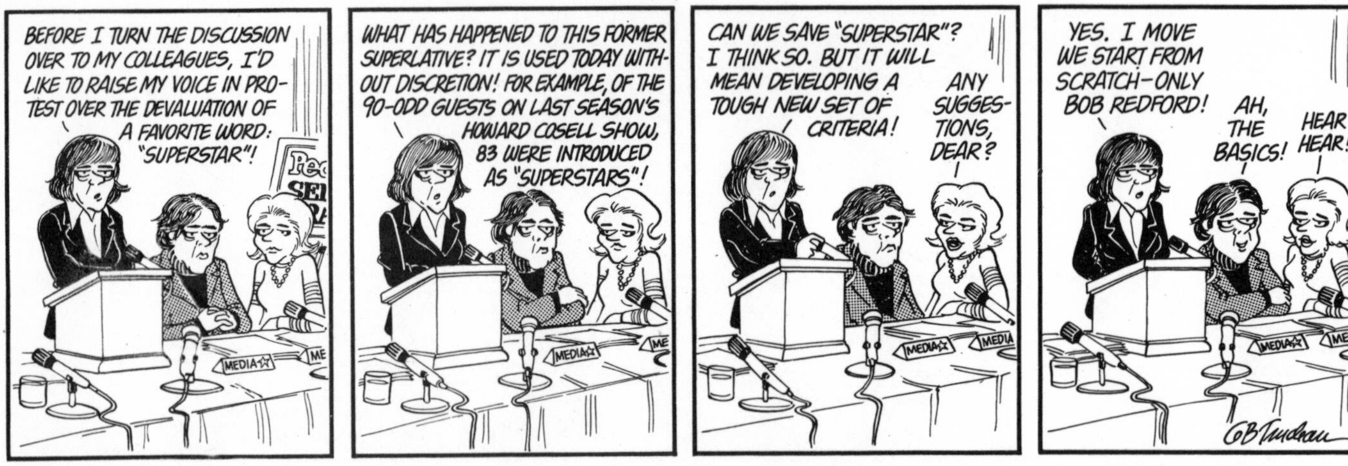
BEFORE I TURN THE DISCUSSION OVER TO MY COLLEAGUES, I'D LIKE TO RAISE MY VOICE IN PROTEST OVER THE DEVALUATION OF A FAVORITE WORD: "SUPERSTAR"!
WHAT HAS HAPPENED TO THIS FORMER SUPERLATIVE? IT IS USED TODAY WITHOUT DISCRETION! FOR EXAMPLE, OF THE 90-ODD GUESTS ON LAST SEASON'S HOWARD COSELL SHOW, 83 WERE INTRODUCED AS "SUPERSTARS"!
CAN WE SAVE "SUPERSTAR"? I THINK SO. BUT IT WILL MEAN DEVELOPING A TOUGH NEW SET OF CRITERIA!
ANY SUGGESTIONS, DEAR?
YES. I MOVE WE START FROM SCRATCH—ONLY BOB REDFORD!
AH, THE BASICS!
HEAR! HEAR!
GBTrudeau

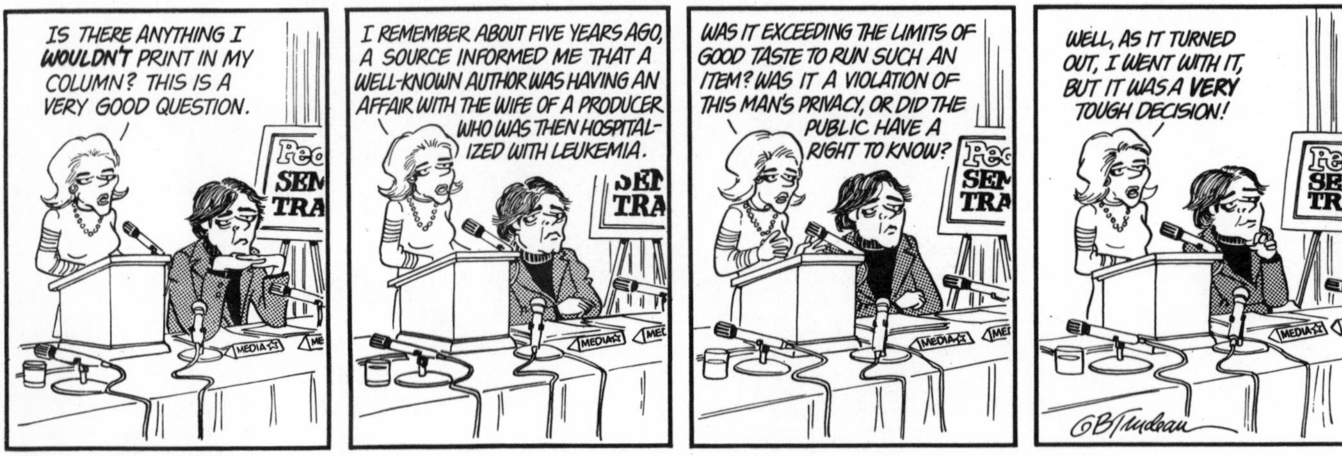
IS THERE ANYTHING I WOULDN'T PRINT IN MY COLUMN? THIS IS A VERY GOOD QUESTION.
I REMEMBER ABOUT FIVE YEARS AGO, A SOURCE INFORMED ME THAT A WELL-KNOWN AUTHOR WAS HAVING AN AFFAIR WITH THE WIFE OF A PRODUCER WHO WAS THEN HOSPITALIZED WITH LEUKEMIA.
WAS IT EXCEEDING THE LIMITS OF GOOD TASTE TO RUN SUCH AN ITEM? WAS IT A VIOLATION OF THIS MAN'S PRIVACY, OR DID THE PUBLIC HAVE A RIGHT TO KNOW?
WELL, AS IT TURNED OUT, I WENT WITH IT, BUT IT WAS A VERY TOUGH DECISION!
GBTrudeau

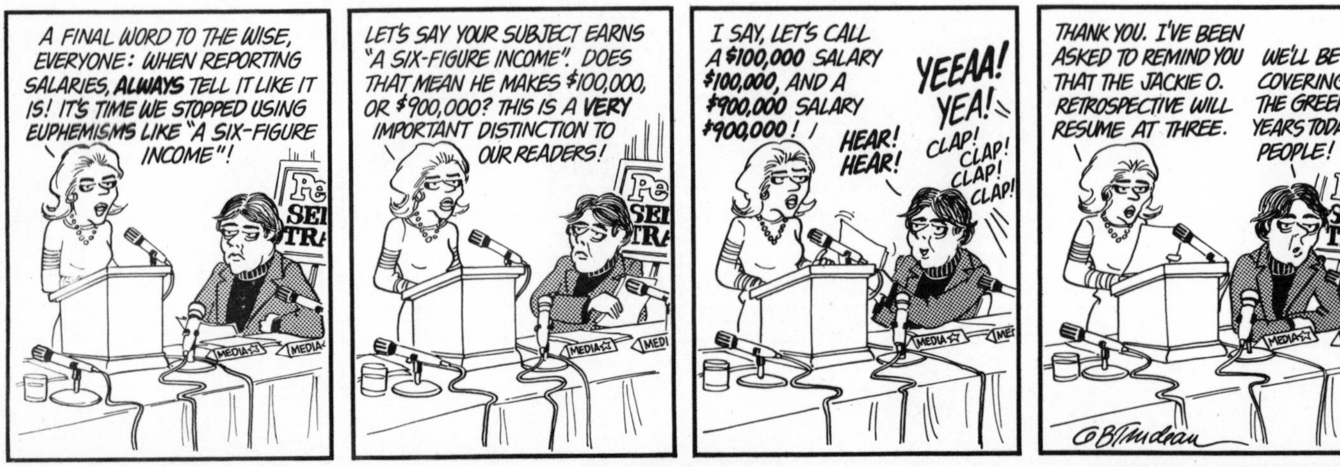
A FINAL WORD TO THE WISE, EVERYONE: WHEN REPORTING SALARIES, ALWAYS TELL IT LIKE IT IS! IT'S TIME WE STOPPED USING EUPHEMISMS LIKE "A SIX-FIGURE INCOME"!
LET'S SAY YOUR SUBJECT EARNS "A SIX-FIGURE INCOME". DOES THAT MEAN HE MAKES $100,000, OR $900,000? THIS IS A VERY IMPORTANT DISTINCTION TO OUR READERS!
I SAY, LET'S CALL A $100,000 SALARY $100,000, AND A $900,000 SALARY $900,000!
YEEAA! YEA!
HEAR! HEAR!
CLAP! CLAP! CLAP! CLAP!
THANK YOU. I'VE BEEN ASKED TO REMIND YOU THAT THE JACKIE O. RETROSPECTIVE WILL RESUME AT THREE.
WE'LL BE COVERING THE GREEK YEARS TODAY, PEOPLE!
GBTrudeau

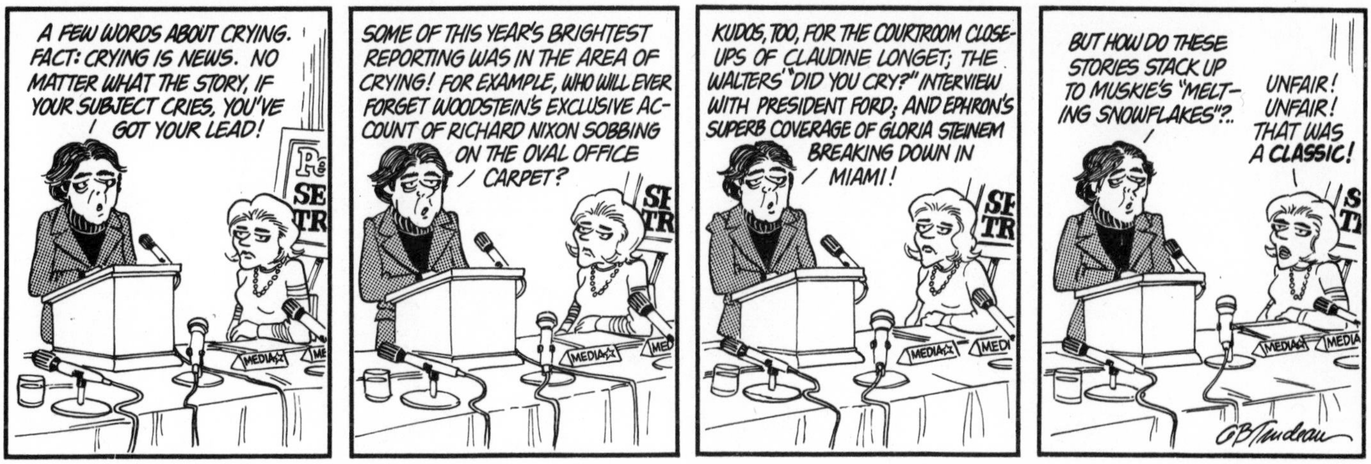
A FEW WORDS ABOUT CRYING. FACT: CRYING IS NEWS. NO MATTER WHAT THE STORY, IF YOUR SUBJECT CRIES, YOU'VE GOT YOUR LEAD!
SOME OF THIS YEAR'S BRIGHTEST REPORTING WAS IN THE AREA OF CRYING! FOR EXAMPLE, WHO WILL EVER FORGET WOODSTEIN'S EXCLUSIVE ACCOUNT OF RICHARD NIXON SOBBING ON THE OVAL OFFICE CARPET?
KUDOS, TOO, FOR THE COURTROOM CLOSE-UPS OF CLAUDINE LONGET; THE WALTERS' "DID YOU CRY?" INTERVIEW WITH PRESIDENT FORD; AND EPHRON'S SUPERB COVERAGE OF GLORIA STEINEM BREAKING DOWN IN MIAMI!
BUT HOW DO THESE STORIES STACK UP TO MUSKIE'S "MELTING SNOWFLAKES"?..
UNFAIR! UNFAIR! THAT WAS A CLASSIC!
MEDIA☆
GBTrudeau

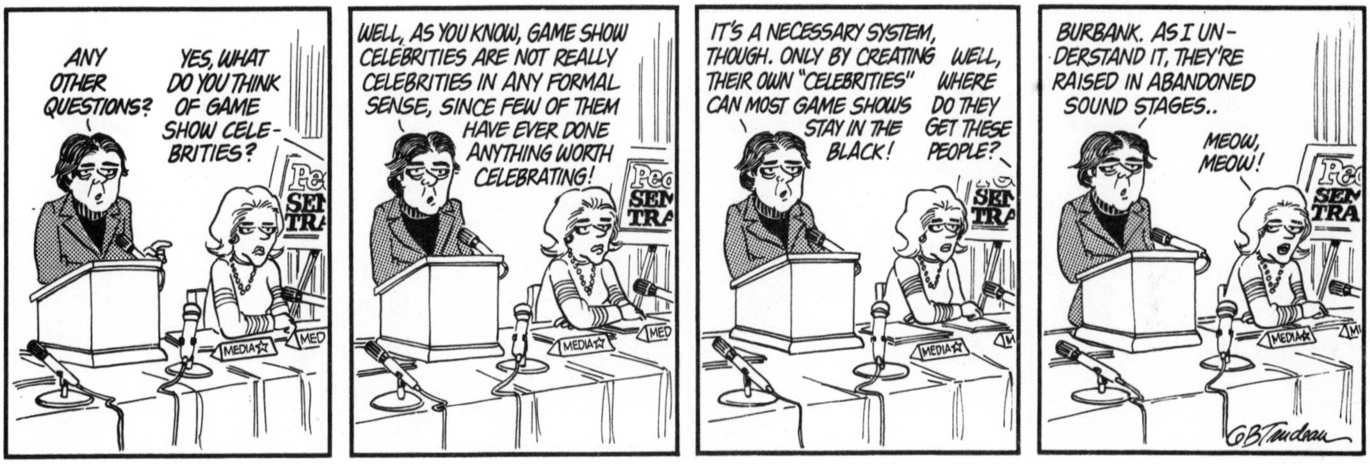
ANY OTHER QUESTIONS?
YES, WHAT DO YOU THINK OF GAME SHOW CELEBRITIES?
WELL, AS YOU KNOW, GAME SHOW CELEBRITIES ARE NOT REALLY CELEBRITIES IN ANY FORMAL SENSE, SINCE FEW OF THEM HAVE EVER DONE ANYTHING WORTH CELEBRATING!
IT'S A NECESSARY SYSTEM, THOUGH. ONLY BY CREATING THEIR OWN "CELEBRITIES" CAN MOST GAME SHOWS STAY IN THE BLACK!
WELL, WHERE DO THEY GET THESE PEOPLE?
BURBANK. AS I UNDERSTAND IT, THEY'RE RAISED IN ABANDONED SOUND STAGES..
MEOW, MEOW!
MEDIA☆
GBTrudeau

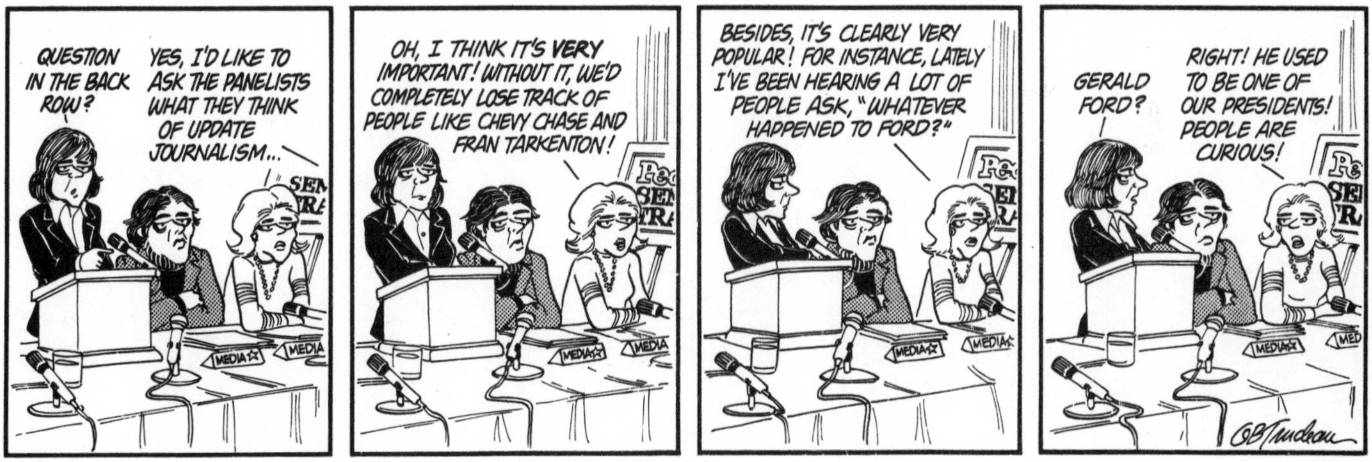
QUESTION IN THE BACK ROW?
YES, I'D LIKE TO ASK THE PANELISTS WHAT THEY THINK OF UPDATE JOURNALISM...
OH, I THINK IT'S VERY IMPORTANT! WITHOUT IT, WE'D COMPLETELY LOSE TRACK OF PEOPLE LIKE CHEVY CHASE AND FRAN TARKENTON!
BESIDES, IT'S CLEARLY VERY POPULAR! FOR INSTANCE, LATELY I'VE BEEN HEARING A LOT OF PEOPLE ASK, "WHATEVER HAPPENED TO FORD?"
GERALD FORD?
RIGHT! HE USED TO BE ONE OF OUR PRESIDENTS! PEOPLE ARE CURIOUS!
MEDIA☆
GBTrudeau

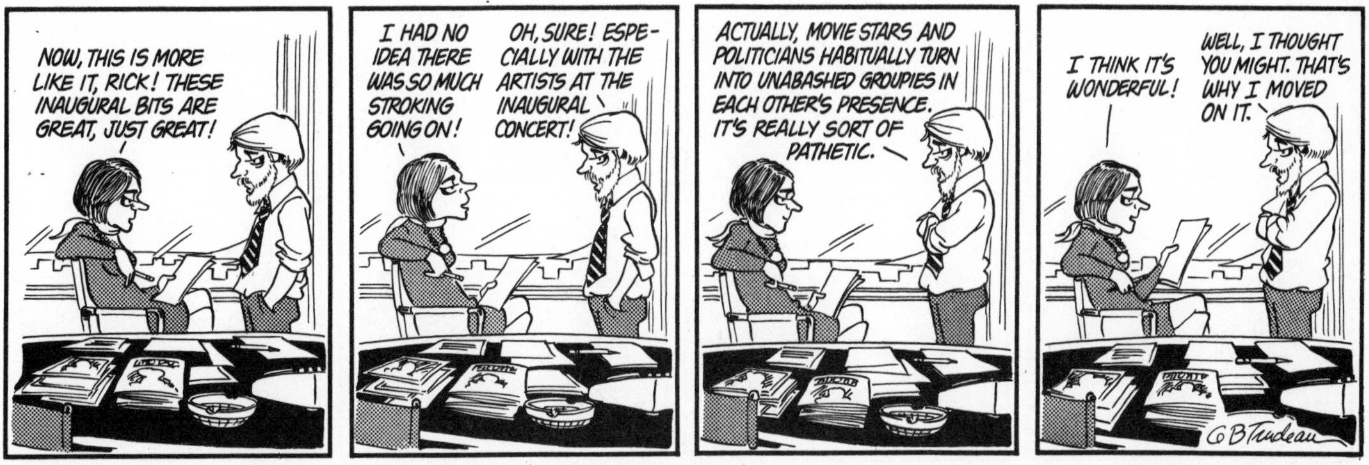
NOW, THIS IS MORE LIKE IT, RICK! THESE INAUGURAL BITS ARE GREAT, JUST GREAT!
I HAD NO IDEA THERE WAS SO MUCH STROKING GOING ON!
OH, SURE! ESPECIALLY WITH THE ARTISTS AT THE INAUGURAL CONCERT!
ACTUALLY, MOVIE STARS AND POLITICIANS HABITUALLY TURN INTO UNABASHED GROUPIES IN EACH OTHER'S PRESENCE. IT'S REALLY SORT OF PATHETIC.
I THINK IT'S WONDERFUL!
WELL, I THOUGHT YOU MIGHT. THAT'S WHY I MOVED ON IT.
GBTrudeau

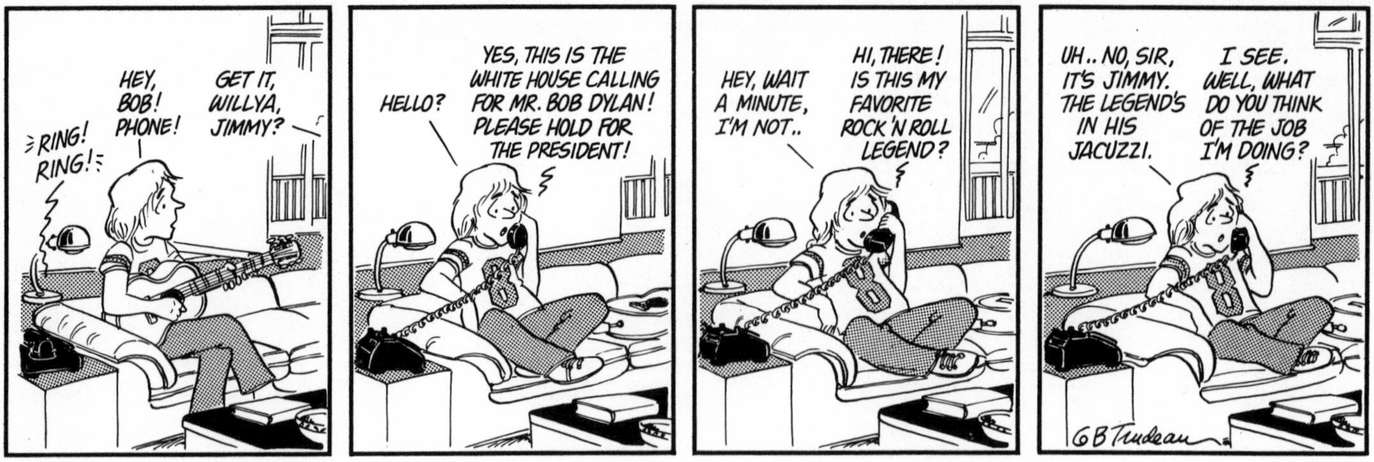
RING! RING!
HEY, BOB! PHONE!
GET IT, WILLYA, JIMMY?
HELLO?
YES, THIS IS THE WHITE HOUSE CALLING FOR MR. BOB DYLAN! PLEASE HOLD FOR THE PRESIDENT!
HEY, WAIT A MINUTE, I'M NOT..
HI, THERE! IS THIS MY FAVORITE ROCK 'N ROLL LEGEND?
UH.. NO, SIR, IT'S JIMMY. THE LEGEND'S IN HIS JACUZZI.
I SEE. WELL, WHAT DO YOU THINK OF THE JOB I'M DOING?

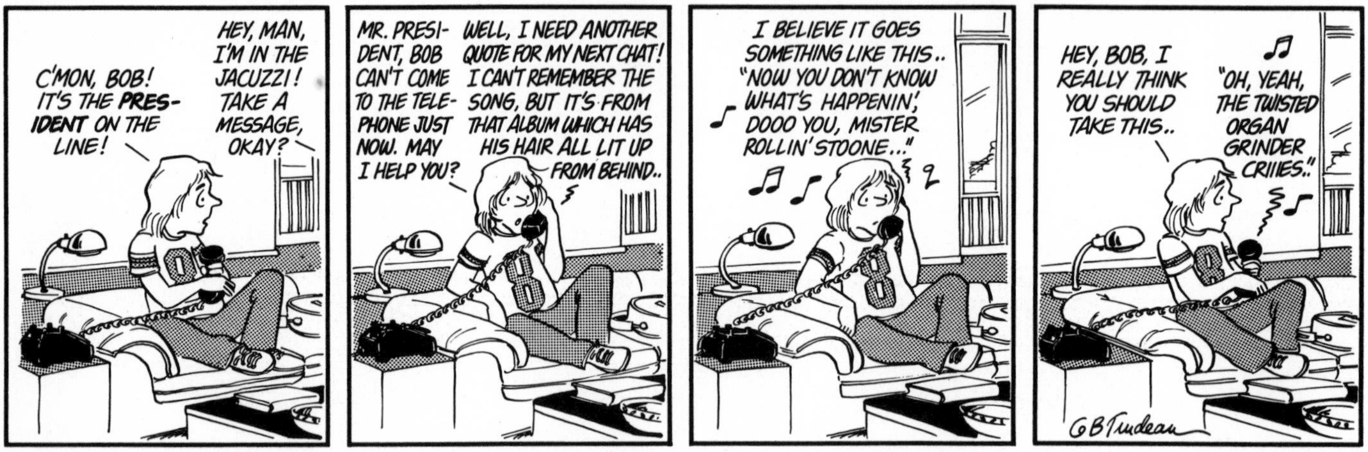
C'MON, BOB! IT'S THE PRESIDENT ON THE LINE!
HEY, MAN, I'M IN THE JACUZZI! TAKE A MESSAGE, OKAY?
MR. PRESIDENT, BOB CAN'T COME TO THE TELEPHONE JUST NOW. MAY I HELP YOU?
WELL, I NEED ANOTHER QUOTE FOR MY NEXT CHAT! I CAN'T REMEMBER THE SONG, BUT IT'S FROM THAT ALBUM WHICH HAS HIS HAIR ALL LIT UP FROM BEHIND..
I BELIEVE IT GOES SOMETHING LIKE THIS.. "NOW YOU DON'T KNOW WHAT'S HAPPENIN', DOOO YOU, MISTER ROLLIN' STOONE..."
HEY, BOB, I REALLY THINK YOU SHOULD TAKE THIS..
"OH, YEAH, THE TWISTED ORGAN GRINDER CRIIES.."

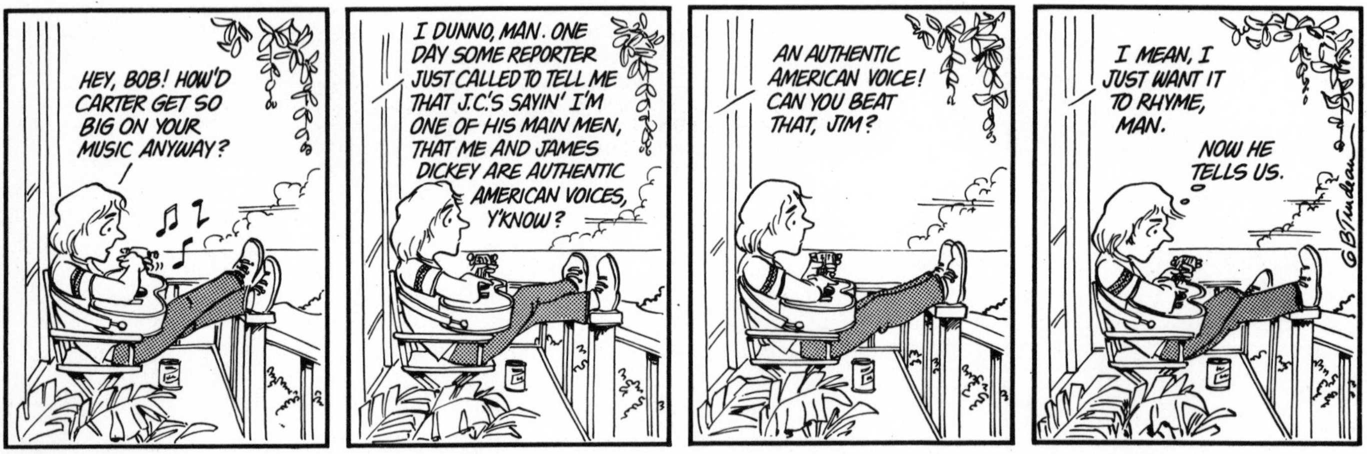
HEY, BOB! HOW'D CARTER GET SO BIG ON YOUR MUSIC ANYWAY?
I DUNNO, MAN. ONE DAY SOME REPORTER JUST CALLED TO TELL ME THAT J.C.'S SAYIN' I'M ONE OF HIS MAIN MEN, THAT ME AND JAMES DICKEY ARE AUTHENTIC AMERICAN VOICES, Y'KNOW?
AN AUTHENTIC AMERICAN VOICE! CAN YOU BEAT THAT, JIM?
I MEAN, I JUST WANT IT TO RHYME, MAN.
NOW HE TELLS US.

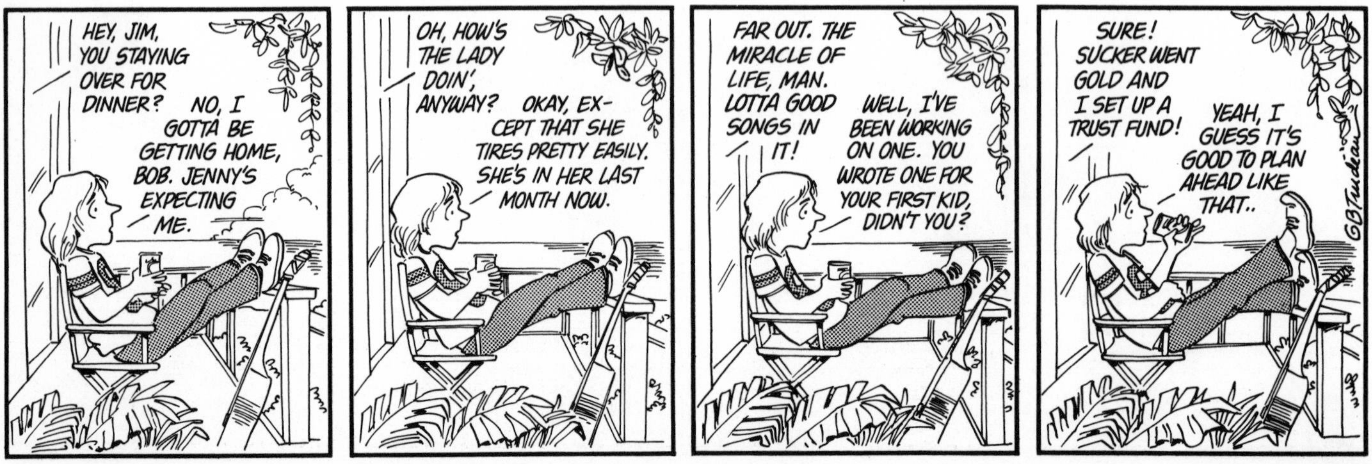
HEY, JIM, YOU STAYING OVER FOR DINNER?
NO, I GOTTA BE GETTING HOME, BOB. JENNY'S EXPECTING ME.
OH, HOW'S THE LADY DOIN', ANYWAY?
OKAY, EXCEPT THAT SHE TIRES PRETTY EASILY. SHE'S IN HER LAST MONTH NOW.
FAR OUT. THE MIRACLE OF LIFE, MAN. LOTTA GOOD SONGS IN IT!
WELL, I'VE BEEN WORKING ON ONE. YOU WROTE ONE FOR YOUR FIRST KID, DIDN'T YOU?
SURE! SUCKER WENT GOLD AND I SET UP A TRUST FUND!
YEAH, I GUESS IT'S GOOD TO PLAN AHEAD LIKE THAT..

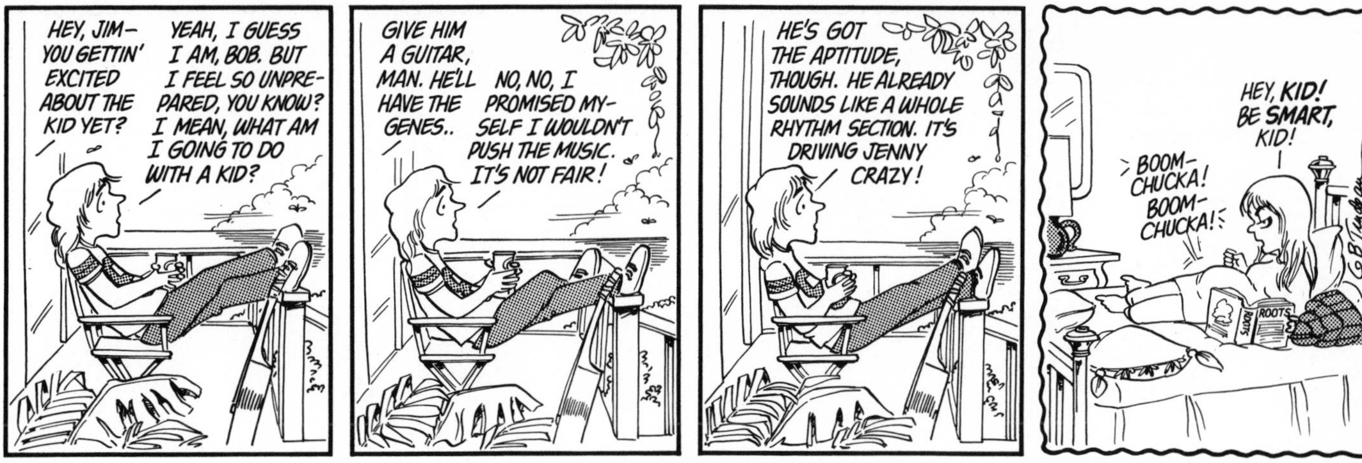
HEY, JIM– YOU GETTIN' EXCITED ABOUT THE KID YET?
YEAH, I GUESS I AM, BOB. BUT I FEEL SO UNPREPARED, YOU KNOW? I MEAN, WHAT AM I GOING TO DO WITH A KID?
GIVE HIM A GUITAR, MAN. HE'LL HAVE THE GENES..
NO, NO, I PROMISED MYSELF I WOULDN'T PUSH THE MUSIC. IT'S NOT FAIR!
HE'S GOT THE APTITUDE, THOUGH. HE ALREADY SOUNDS LIKE A WHOLE RHYTHM SECTION. IT'S DRIVING JENNY CRAZY!
BOOM-CHUCKA! BOOM-CHUCKA!
HEY, KID! BE SMART, KID!
ROOTS
GBTrudeau

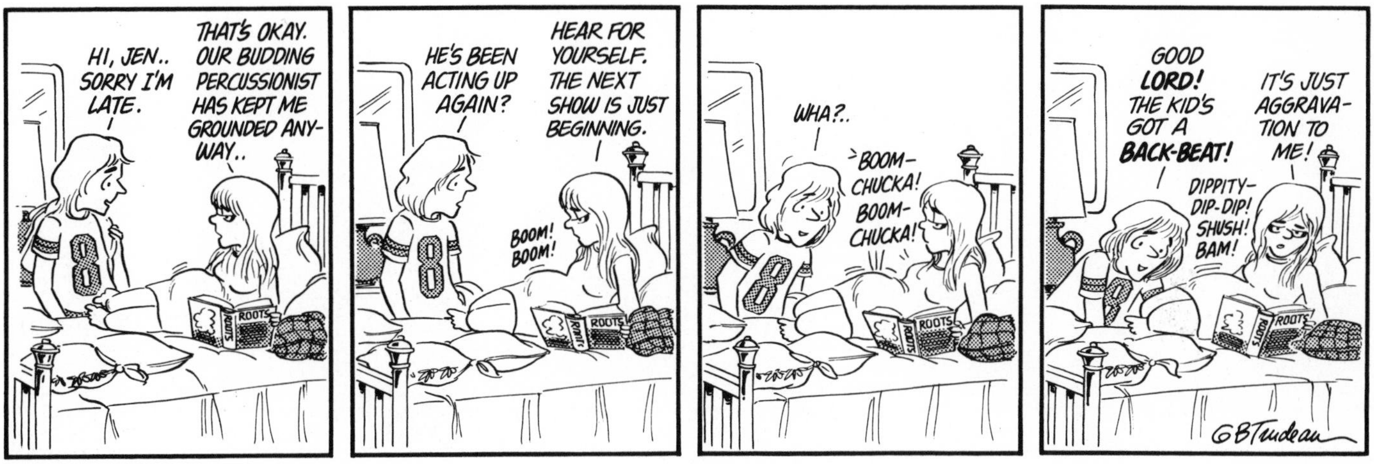
HI, JEN.. SORRY I'M LATE.
THAT'S OKAY. OUR BUDDING PERCUSSIONIST HAS KEPT ME GROUNDED ANYWAY..
ROOTS
HE'S BEEN ACTING UP AGAIN?
HEAR FOR YOURSELF. THE NEXT SHOW IS JUST BEGINNING.
BOOM! BOOM!
ROOTS
WHA?..
BOOM-CHUCKA! BOOM-CHUCKA!
ROOTS
GOOD LORD! THE KID'S GOT A BACK-BEAT!
IT'S JUST AGGRAVATION TO ME!
DIPPITY-DIP-DIP! SHUSH! BAM!
ROOTS
GBTrudeau

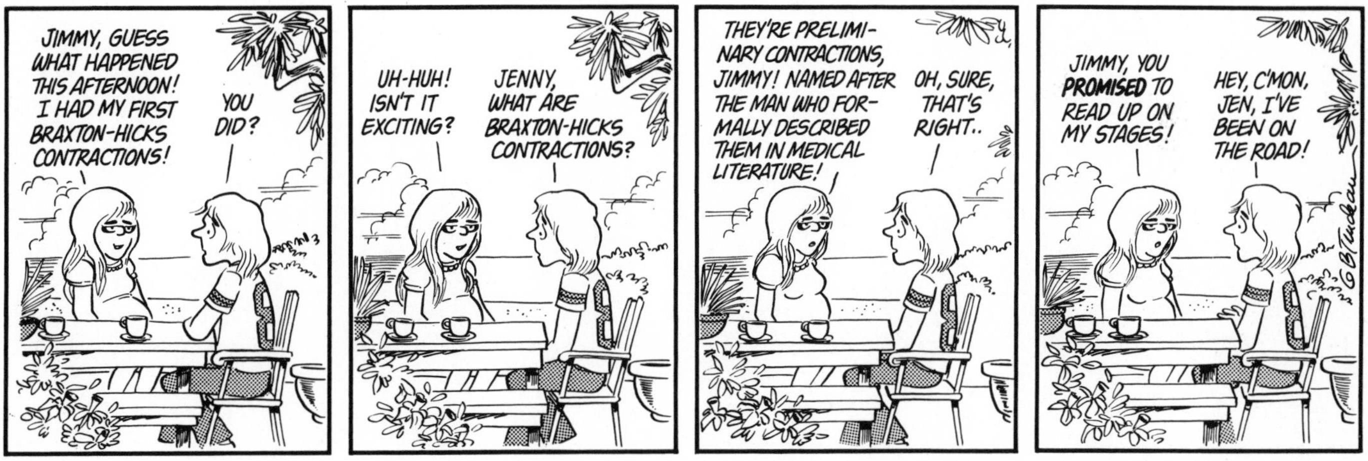
JIMMY, GUESS WHAT HAPPENED THIS AFTERNOON! I HAD MY FIRST BRAXTON-HICKS CONTRACTIONS!
YOU DID?
UH-HUH! ISN'T IT EXCITING?
JENNY, WHAT ARE BRAXTON-HICKS CONTRACTIONS?
THEY'RE PRELIMINARY CONTRACTIONS, JIMMY! NAMED AFTER THE MAN WHO FORMALLY DESCRIBED THEM IN MEDICAL LITERATURE!
OH, SURE, THAT'S RIGHT..
JIMMY, YOU PROMISED TO READ UP ON MY STAGES!
HEY, C'MON, JEN, I'VE BEEN ON THE ROAD!
GBTrudeau

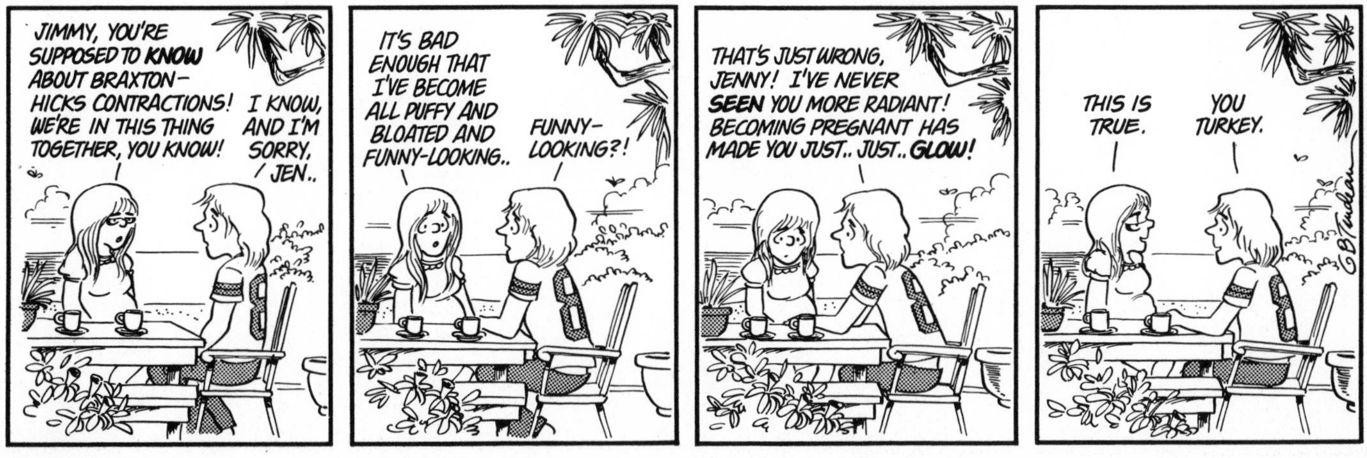
JIMMY, YOU'RE SUPPOSED TO KNOW ABOUT BRAXTON-HICKS CONTRACTIONS! WE'RE IN THIS THING TOGETHER, YOU KNOW!
I KNOW, AND I'M SORRY, JEN..
IT'S BAD ENOUGH THAT I'VE BECOME ALL PUFFY AND BLOATED AND FUNNY-LOOKING..
FUNNY-LOOKING?!
THAT'S JUST WRONG, JENNY! I'VE NEVER SEEN YOU MORE RADIANT! BECOMING PREGNANT HAS MADE YOU JUST.. JUST.. GLOW!
THIS IS TRUE.
YOU TURKEY.
GBTrudeau

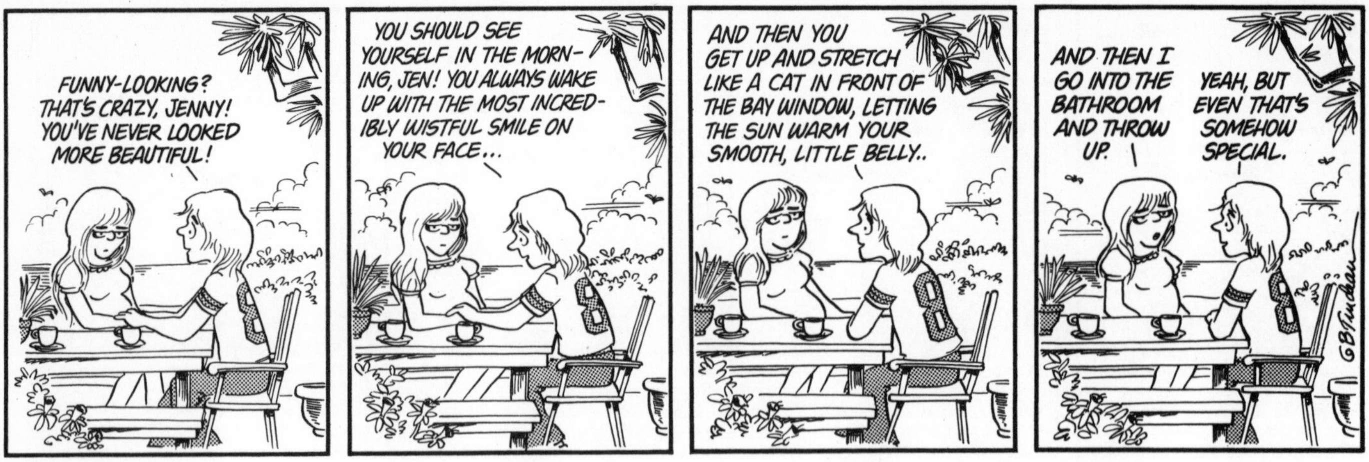
FUNNY-LOOKING? THAT'S CRAZY, JENNY! YOU'VE NEVER LOOKED MORE BEAUTIFUL!
YOU SHOULD SEE YOURSELF IN THE MORNING, JEN! YOU ALWAYS WAKE UP WITH THE MOST INCREDIBLY WISTFUL SMILE ON YOUR FACE...
AND THEN YOU GET UP AND STRETCH LIKE A CAT IN FRONT OF THE BAY WINDOW, LETTING THE SUN WARM YOUR SMOOTH, LITTLE BELLY..
AND THEN I GO INTO THE BATHROOM AND THROW UP.
YEAH, BUT EVEN THAT'S SOMEHOW SPECIAL.

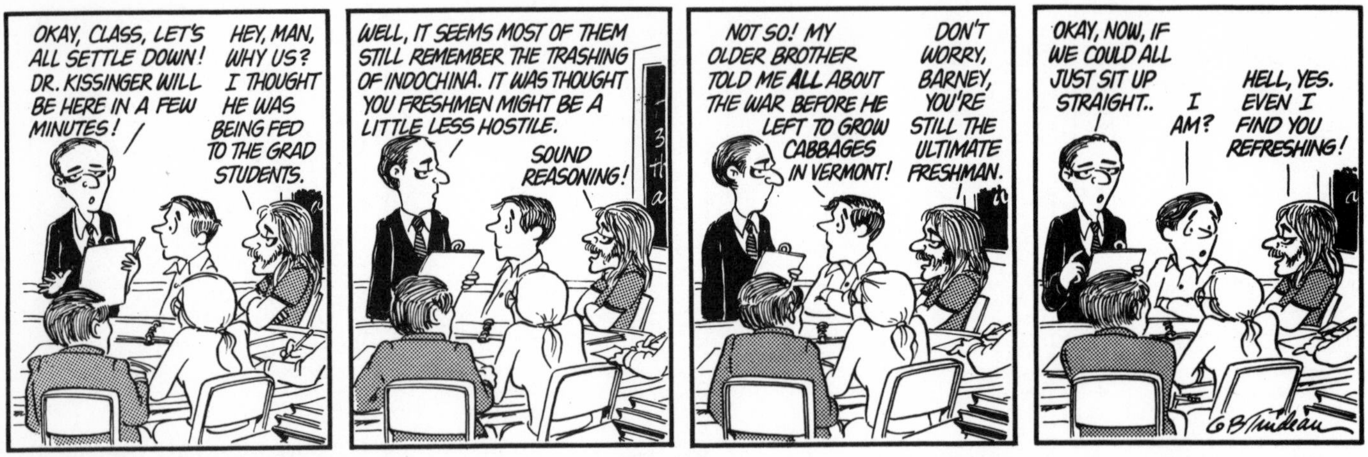
OKAY, CLASS, LET'S ALL SETTLE DOWN! DR. KISSINGER WILL BE HERE IN A FEW MINUTES!
HEY, MAN, WHY US? I THOUGHT HE WAS BEING FED TO THE GRAD STUDENTS.
WELL, IT SEEMS MOST OF THEM STILL REMEMBER THE TRASHING OF INDOCHINA. IT WAS THOUGHT YOU FRESHMEN MIGHT BE A LITTLE LESS HOSTILE.
SOUND REASONING!
NOT SO! MY OLDER BROTHER TOLD ME ALL ABOUT THE WAR BEFORE HE LEFT TO GROW CABBAGES IN VERMONT!
DON'T WORRY, BARNEY, YOU'RE STILL THE ULTIMATE FRESHMAN.
OKAY, NOW, IF WE COULD ALL JUST SIT UP STRAIGHT..
I AM?
HELL, YES. EVEN I FIND YOU REFRESHING!

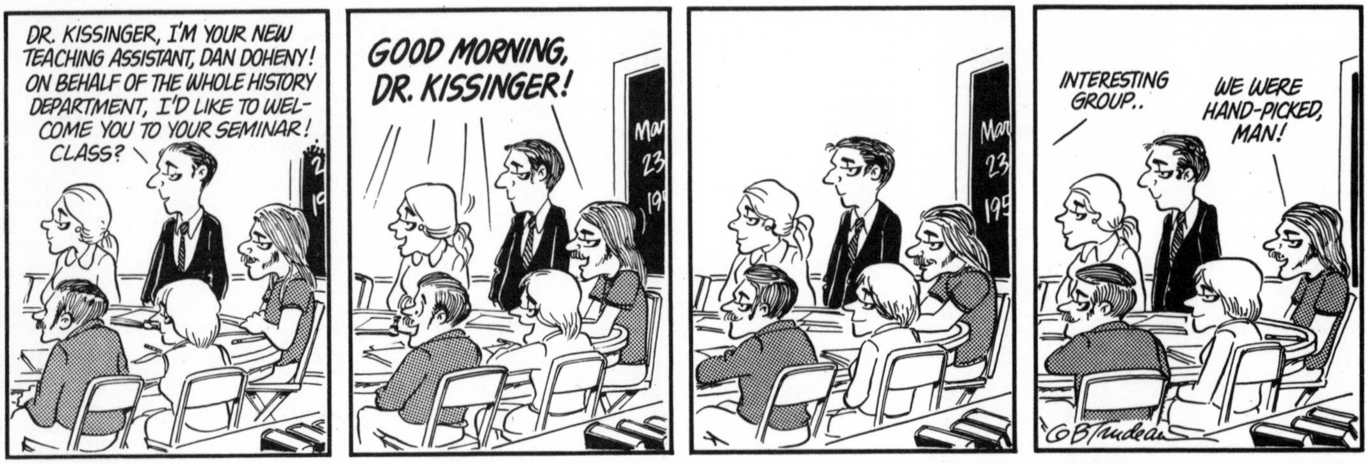
DR. KISSINGER, I'M YOUR NEW TEACHING ASSISTANT, DAN DOHENY! ON BEHALF OF THE WHOLE HISTORY DEPARTMENT, I'D LIKE TO WELCOME YOU TO YOUR SEMINAR! CLASS?
GOOD MORNING, DR. KISSINGER!
INTERESTING GROUP..
WE WERE HAND-PICKED, MAN!

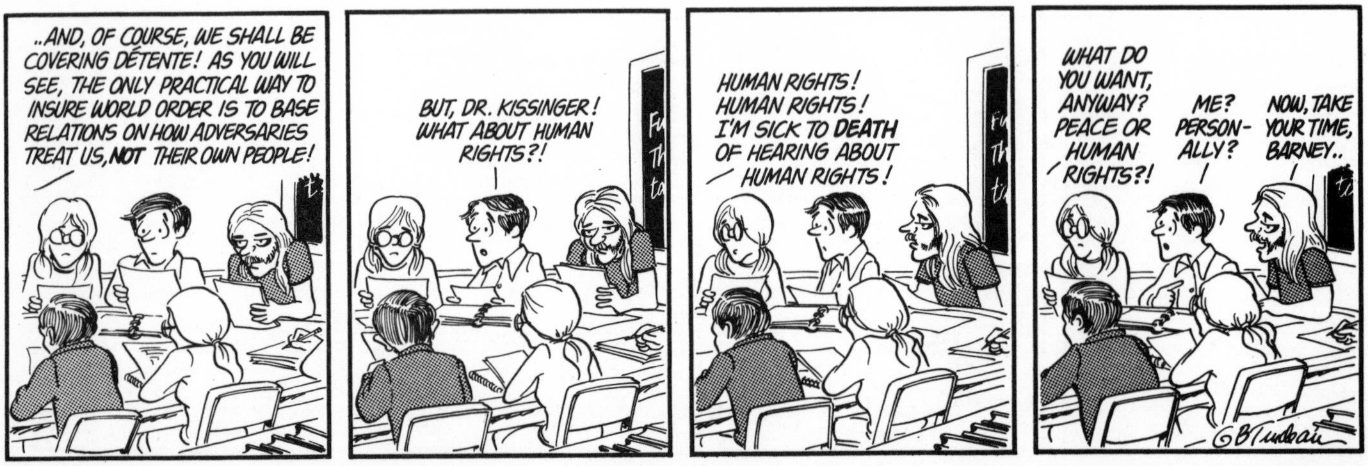
..AND, OF COURSE, WE SHALL BE COVERING DÉTENTE! AS YOU WILL SEE, THE ONLY PRACTICAL WAY TO INSURE WORLD ORDER IS TO BASE RELATIONS ON HOW ADVERSARIES TREAT US, NOT THEIR OWN PEOPLE!
BUT, DR. KISSINGER! WHAT ABOUT HUMAN RIGHTS?!
HUMAN RIGHTS! HUMAN RIGHTS! I'M SICK TO DEATH OF HEARING ABOUT HUMAN RIGHTS!
WHAT DO YOU WANT, ANYWAY? PEACE OR HUMAN RIGHTS?!
ME? PERSONALLY?
NOW, TAKE YOUR TIME, BARNEY..

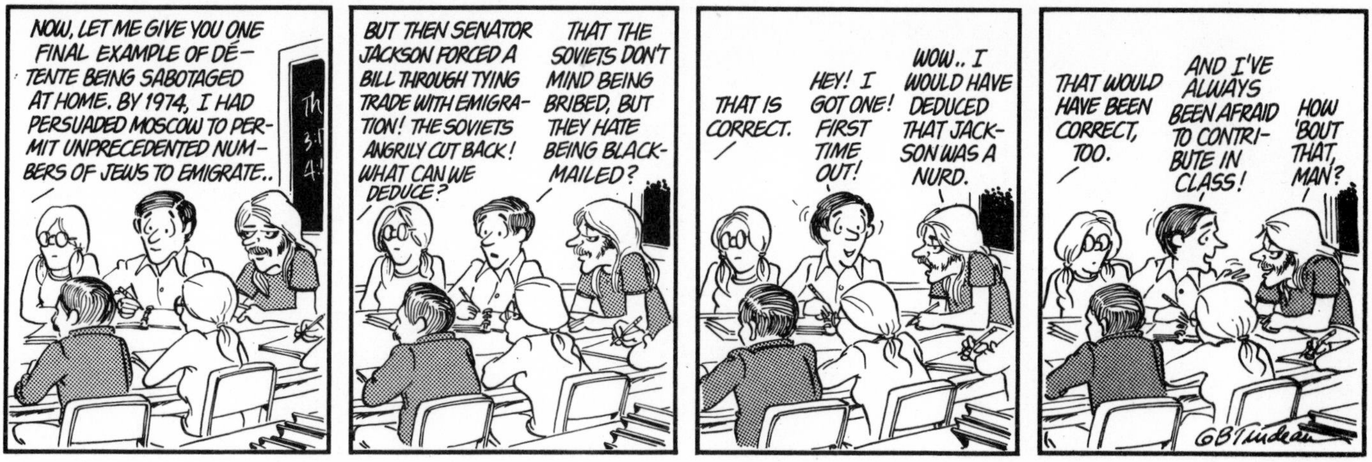
NOW, LET ME GIVE YOU ONE FINAL EXAMPLE OF DÉTENTE BEING SABOTAGED AT HOME. BY 1974, I HAD PERSUADED MOSCOW TO PERMIT UNPRECEDENTED NUMBERS OF JEWS TO EMIGRATE..
BUT THEN SENATOR JACKSON FORCED A BILL THROUGH TYING TRADE WITH EMIGRATION! THE SOVIETS ANGRILY CUT BACK! WHAT CAN WE DEDUCE?
THAT THE SOVIETS DON'T MIND BEING BRIBED, BUT THEY HATE BEING BLACKMAILED?
THAT IS CORRECT.
HEY! I GOT ONE! FIRST TIME OUT!
WOW.. I WOULD HAVE DEDUCED THAT JACKSON WAS A NURD.
THAT WOULD HAVE BEEN CORRECT, TOO.
AND I'VE ALWAYS BEEN AFRAID TO CONTRIBUTE IN CLASS!
HOW 'BOUT THAT, MAN?
GBTrudeau

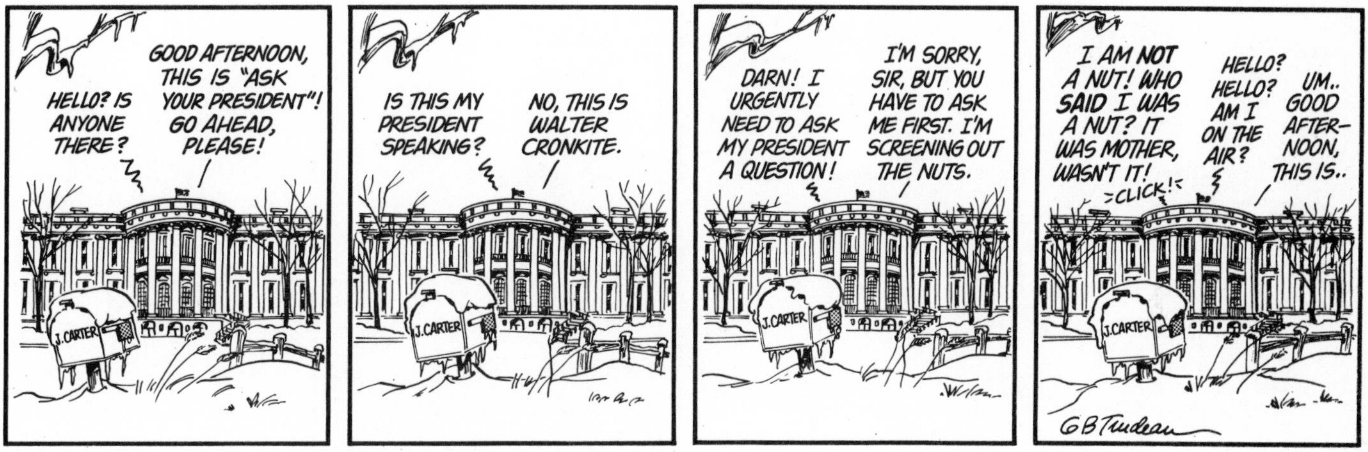
HELLO? IS ANYONE THERE?
GOOD AFTERNOON, THIS IS "ASK YOUR PRESIDENT"! GO AHEAD, PLEASE!
J. CARTER
IS THIS MY PRESIDENT SPEAKING?
NO, THIS IS WALTER CRONKITE.
J. CARTER
DARN! I URGENTLY NEED TO ASK MY PRESIDENT A QUESTION!
I'M SORRY, SIR, BUT YOU HAVE TO ASK ME FIRST. I'M SCREENING OUT THE NUTS.
J. CARTER
I AM **NOT** A NUT! WHO **SAID** I WAS A NUT? IT WAS MOTHER, WASN'T IT!
CLICK!
HELLO? HELLO? AM I ON THE AIR?
UM.. GOOD AFTERNOON, THIS IS..
J. CARTER
GBTrudeau

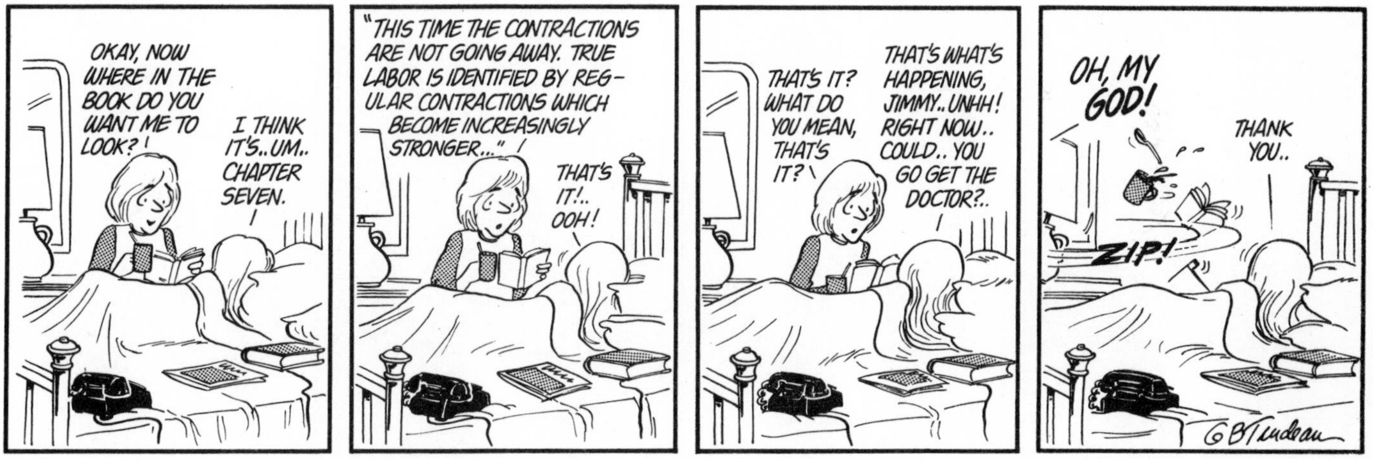
OKAY, NOW WHERE IN THE BOOK DO YOU WANT ME TO LOOK?
I THINK IT'S..UM.. CHAPTER SEVEN.
"THIS TIME THE CONTRACTIONS ARE NOT GOING AWAY. TRUE LABOR IS IDENTIFIED BY REGULAR CONTRACTIONS WHICH BECOME INCREASINGLY STRONGER..."
THAT'S IT!.. OOH!
THAT'S IT? WHAT DO YOU MEAN, THAT'S IT?
THAT'S WHAT'S HAPPENING, JIMMY.. UNHH! RIGHT NOW.. COULD.. YOU GO GET THE DOCTOR?..
OH, MY **GOD!**
THANK YOU..
ZIP!
GBTrudeau

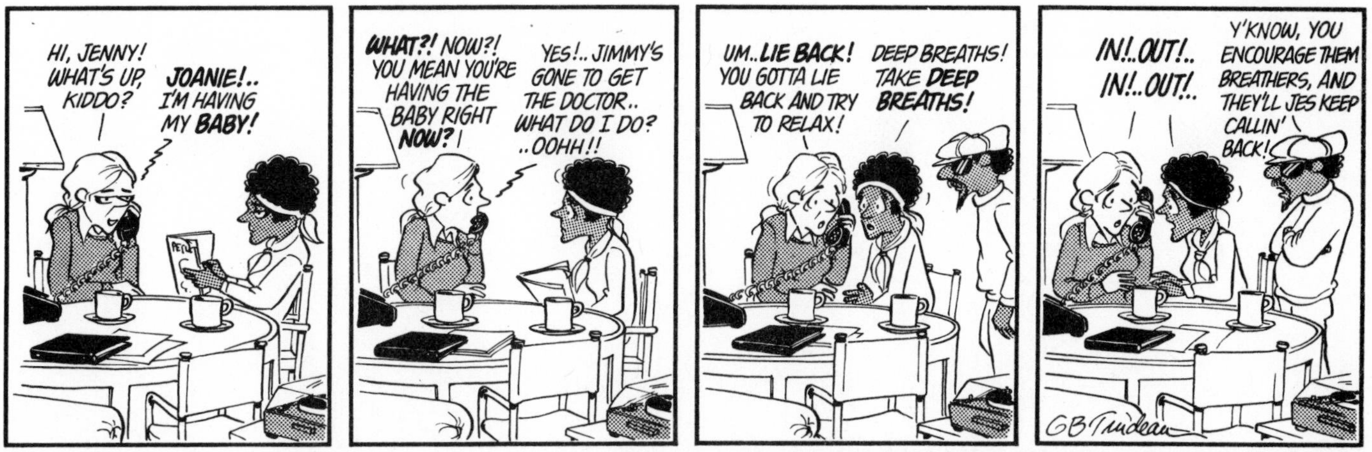
HI, JENNY! WHAT'S UP, KIDDO?
JOANIE!.. I'M HAVING MY **BABY!**
WHAT?! NOW?! YOU MEAN YOU'RE HAVING THE BABY RIGHT **NOW?**
YES!.. JIMMY'S GONE TO GET THE DOCTOR.. WHAT DO I DO? ..OOHH!!
UM.. **LIE BACK!** YOU GOTTA LIE BACK AND TRY TO RELAX!
DEEP BREATHS! TAKE **DEEP BREATHS!**
IN!..OUT!.. IN!..OUT!..
Y'KNOW, YOU ENCOURAGE THEM BREATHERS, AND THEY'LL JES KEEP CALLIN' BACK!
GBTrudeau

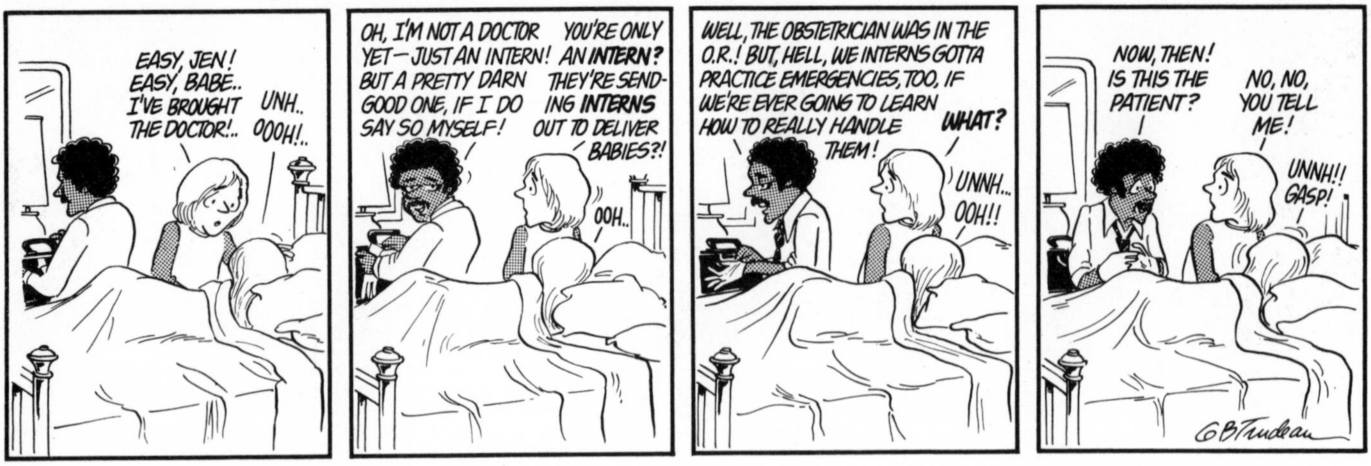
EASY, JEN! EASY, BABE.. I'VE BROUGHT THE DOCTOR!..
UNH.. OOOH!..
OH, I'M NOT A DOCTOR YET—JUST AN INTERN! BUT A PRETTY DARN GOOD ONE, IF I DO SAY SO MYSELF!
YOU'RE ONLY AN INTERN? THEY'RE SENDING INTERNS OUT TO DELIVER BABIES?!
OOH..
WELL, THE OBSTETRICIAN WAS IN THE O.R.! BUT, HELL, WE INTERNS GOTTA PRACTICE EMERGENCIES, TOO, IF WE'RE EVER GOING TO LEARN HOW TO REALLY HANDLE THEM!
WHAT?
UNNH... OOH!!
NOW, THEN! IS THIS THE PATIENT?
NO, NO, YOU TELL ME!
UNNH!! GASP!
GBTrudeau

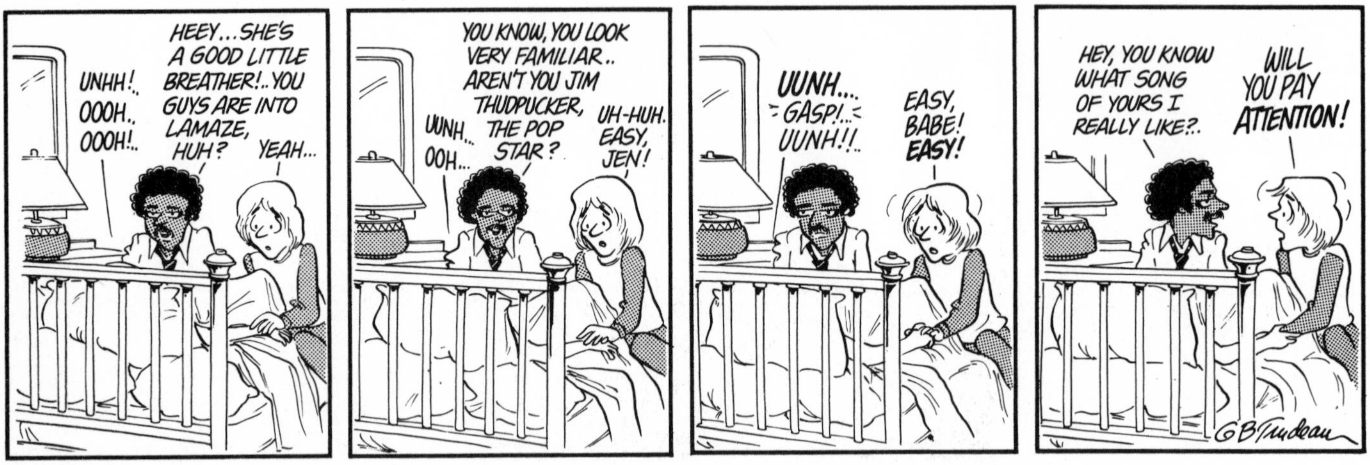
UNHH!.. OOOH.. OOOH!..
HEEY... SHE'S A GOOD LITTLE BREATHER!.. YOU GUYS ARE INTO LAMAZE, HUH?
YEAH...
YOU KNOW, YOU LOOK VERY FAMILIAR.. AREN'T YOU JIM THUDPUCKER, THE POP STAR?
UNNH.. OOH...
UH-HUH. EASY, JEN!
UUNH.... GASP!.. UUNH!!..
EASY, BABE! EASY!
HEY, YOU KNOW WHAT SONG OF YOURS I REALLY LIKE?..
WILL YOU PAY ATTENTION!
GBTrudeau

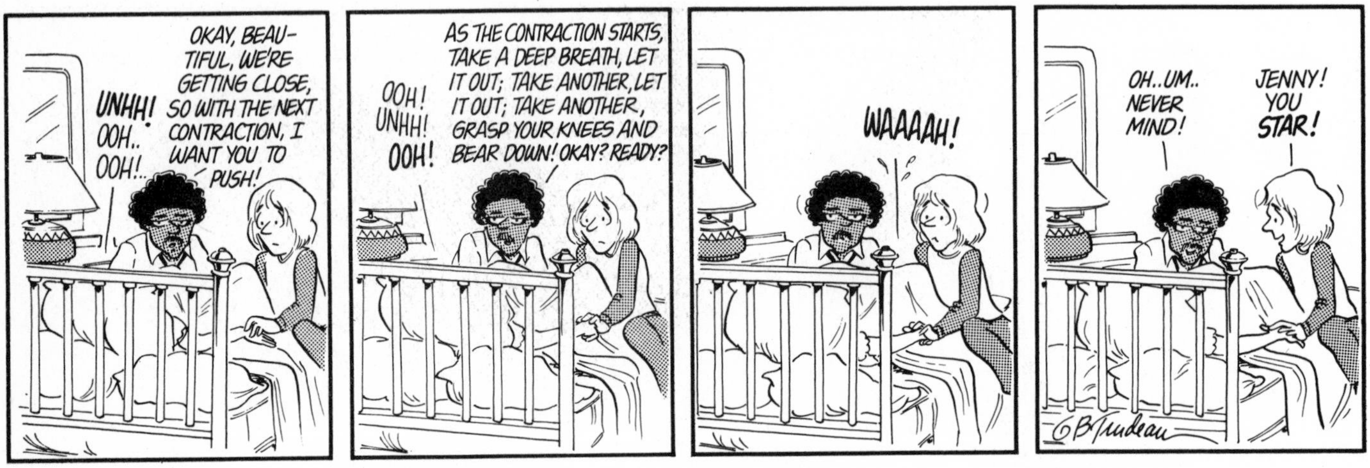
UNHH! OOH.. OOH!..
OKAY, BEAUTIFUL, WE'RE GETTING CLOSE, SO WITH THE NEXT CONTRACTION, I WANT YOU TO PUSH!
OOH! UNHH! OOH!
AS THE CONTRACTION STARTS, TAKE A DEEP BREATH, LET IT OUT; TAKE ANOTHER, LET IT OUT; TAKE ANOTHER, GRASP YOUR KNEES AND BEAR DOWN! OKAY? READY?
WAAAAH!
OH..UM.. NEVER MIND!
JENNY! YOU STAR!
GBTrudeau

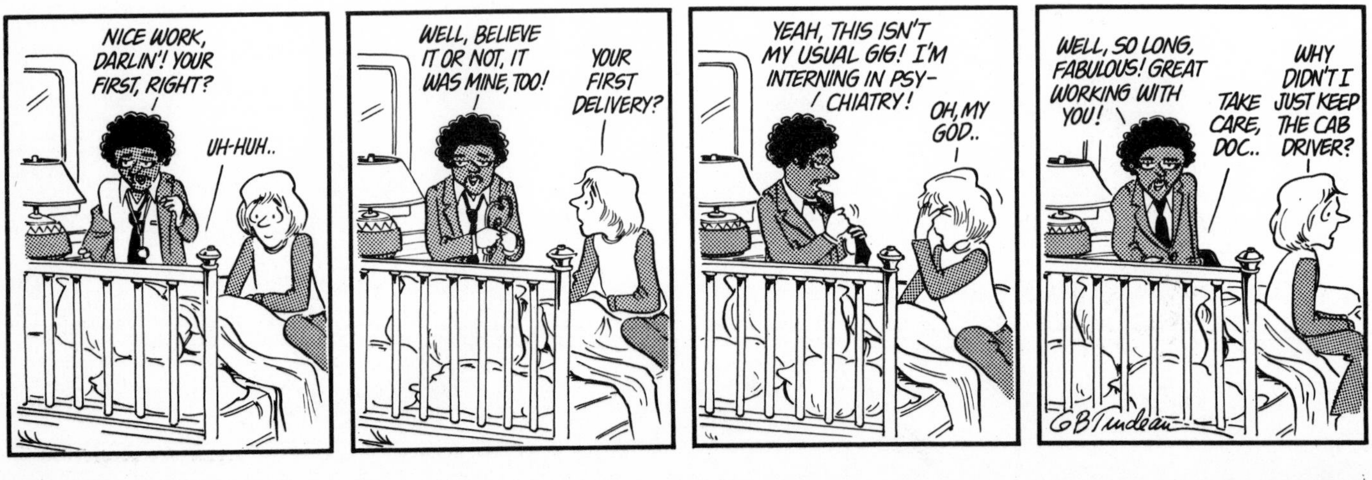
NICE WORK, DARLIN'! YOUR FIRST, RIGHT?
UH-HUH..
WELL, BELIEVE IT OR NOT, IT WAS MINE, TOO!
YOUR FIRST DELIVERY?
YEAH, THIS ISN'T MY USUAL GIG! I'M INTERNING IN PSYCHIATRY!
OH, MY GOD..
WELL, SO LONG, FABULOUS! GREAT WORKING WITH YOU!
TAKE CARE, DOC..
WHY DIDN'T I JUST KEEP THE CAB DRIVER?
GBTrudeau

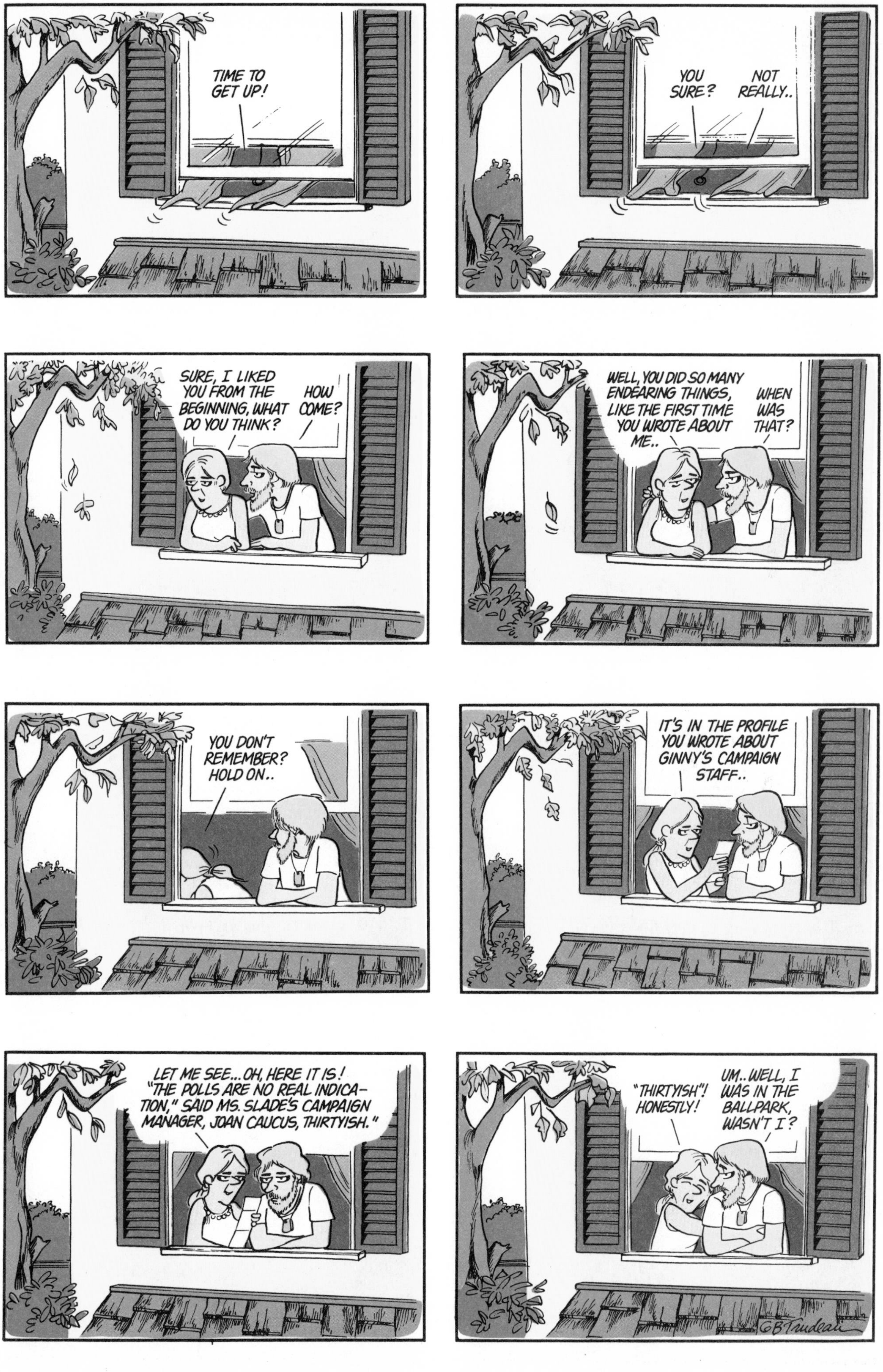
TIME TO GET UP!
YOU SURE?
NOT REALLY..
SURE, I LIKED YOU FROM THE BEGINNING, WHAT DO YOU THINK?
HOW COME?
WELL, YOU DID SO MANY ENDEARING THINGS, LIKE THE FIRST TIME YOU WROTE ABOUT ME..
WHEN WAS THAT?
YOU DON'T REMEMBER? HOLD ON..
IT'S IN THE PROFILE YOU WROTE ABOUT GINNY'S CAMPAIGN STAFF..
LET ME SEE...OH, HERE IT IS! "THE POLLS ARE NO REAL INDICA-TION," SAID MS. SLADE'S CAMPAIGN MANAGER, JOAN CAUCUS, THIRTYISH."
"THIRTYISH"! HONESTLY!
UM.. WELL, I WAS IN THE BALLPARK, WASN'T I?
GB Trudeau

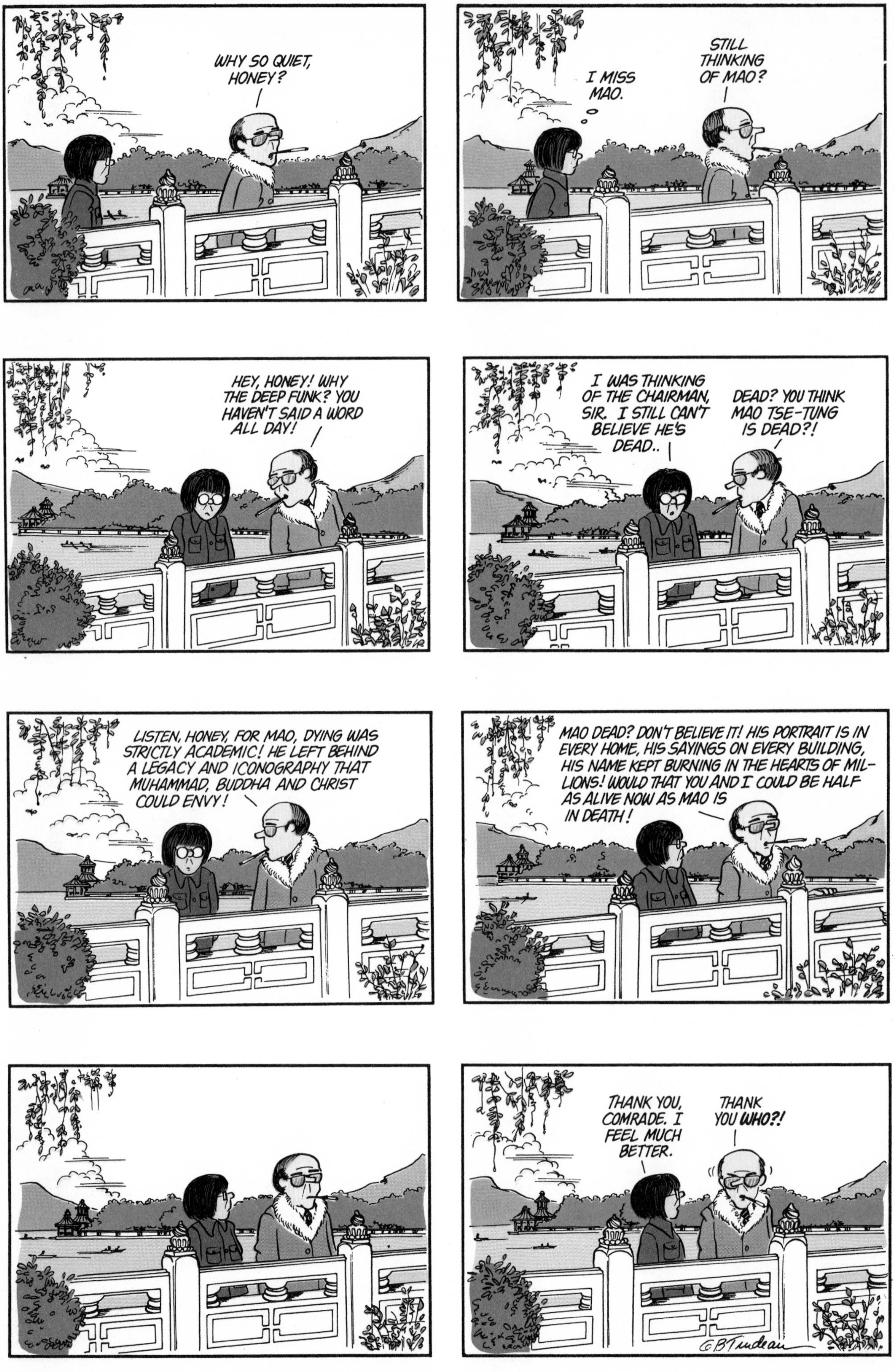
WHY SO QUIET, HONEY?
I MISS MAO.
STILL THINKING OF MAO?
HEY, HONEY! WHY THE DEEP FUNK? YOU HAVEN'T SAID A WORD ALL DAY!
I WAS THINKING OF THE CHAIRMAN, SIR. I STILL CAN'T BELIEVE HE'S DEAD..
DEAD? YOU THINK MAO TSE-TUNG IS DEAD?!
LISTEN, HONEY. FOR MAO, DYING WAS STRICTLY ACADEMIC! HE LEFT BEHIND A LEGACY AND ICONOGRAPHY THAT MUHAMMAD, BUDDHA AND CHRIST COULD ENVY!
MAO DEAD? DON'T BELIEVE IT! HIS PORTRAIT IS IN EVERY HOME, HIS SAYINGS ON EVERY BUILDING, HIS NAME KEPT BURNING IN THE HEARTS OF MILLIONS! WOULD THAT YOU AND I COULD BE HALF AS ALIVE NOW AS MAO IS IN DEATH!
THANK YOU, COMRADE. I FEEL MUCH BETTER.
THANK YOU **WHO?!**
©GBTrudeau

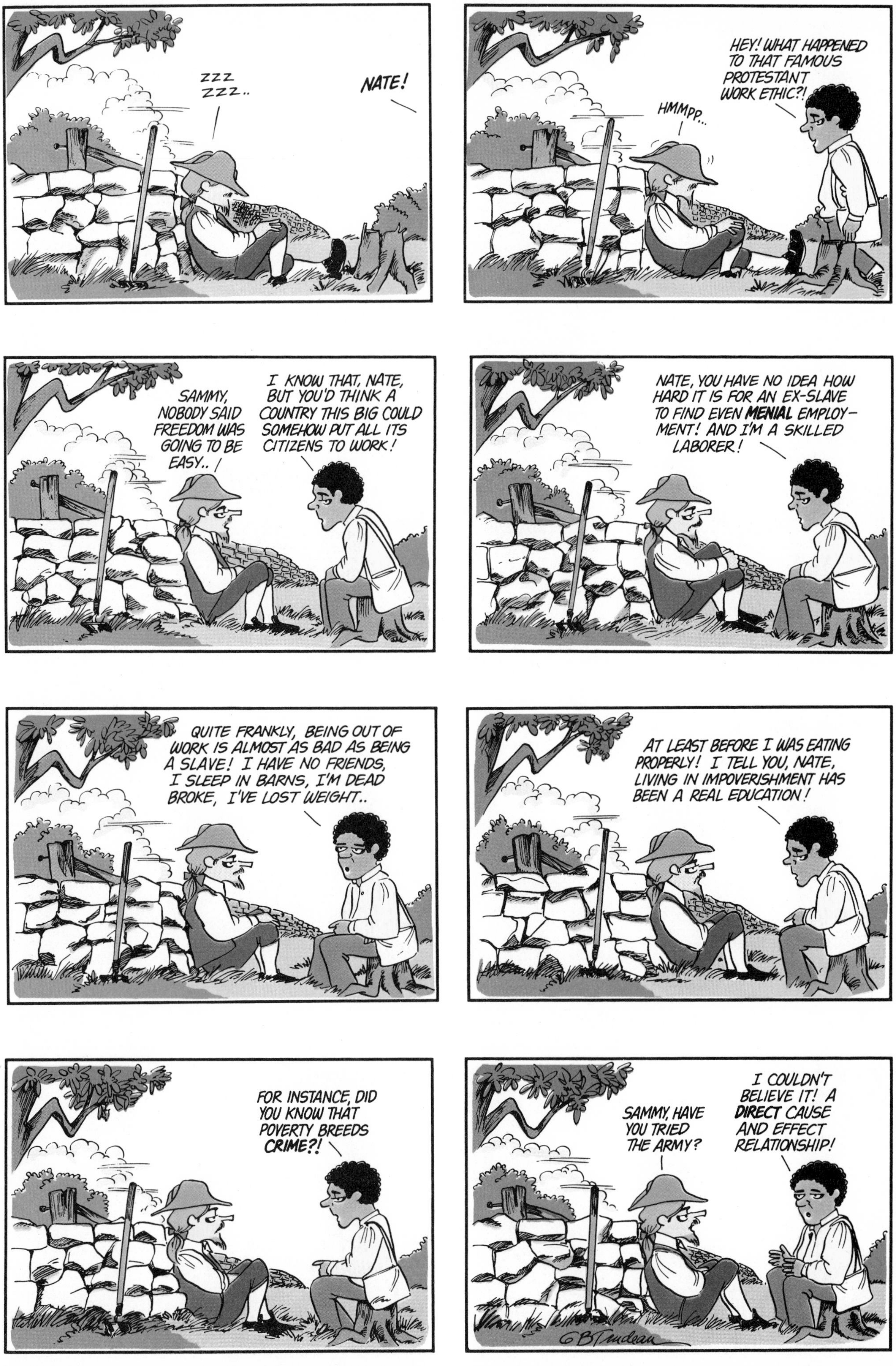
ZZZ
ZZZ..
NATE!
HMMPP..
HEY! WHAT HAPPENED TO THAT FAMOUS PROTESTANT WORK ETHIC?!
SAMMY, NOBODY SAID FREEDOM WAS GOING TO BE EASY..
I KNOW THAT, NATE, BUT YOU'D THINK A COUNTRY THIS BIG COULD SOMEHOW PUT ALL ITS CITIZENS TO WORK!
NATE, YOU HAVE NO IDEA HOW HARD IT IS FOR AN EX-SLAVE TO FIND EVEN **MENIAL** EMPLOYMENT! AND I'M A SKILLED LABORER!
QUITE FRANKLY, BEING OUT OF WORK IS ALMOST AS BAD AS BEING A SLAVE! I HAVE NO FRIENDS, I SLEEP IN BARNS, I'M DEAD BROKE, I'VE LOST WEIGHT..
AT LEAST BEFORE I WAS EATING PROPERLY! I TELL YOU, NATE, LIVING IN IMPOVERISHMENT HAS BEEN A REAL EDUCATION!
FOR INSTANCE, DID YOU KNOW THAT POVERTY BREEDS **CRIME?!**
SAMMY, HAVE YOU TRIED THE ARMY?
I COULDN'T BELIEVE IT! A **DIRECT** CAUSE AND EFFECT RELATIONSHIP!
GBTrudeau

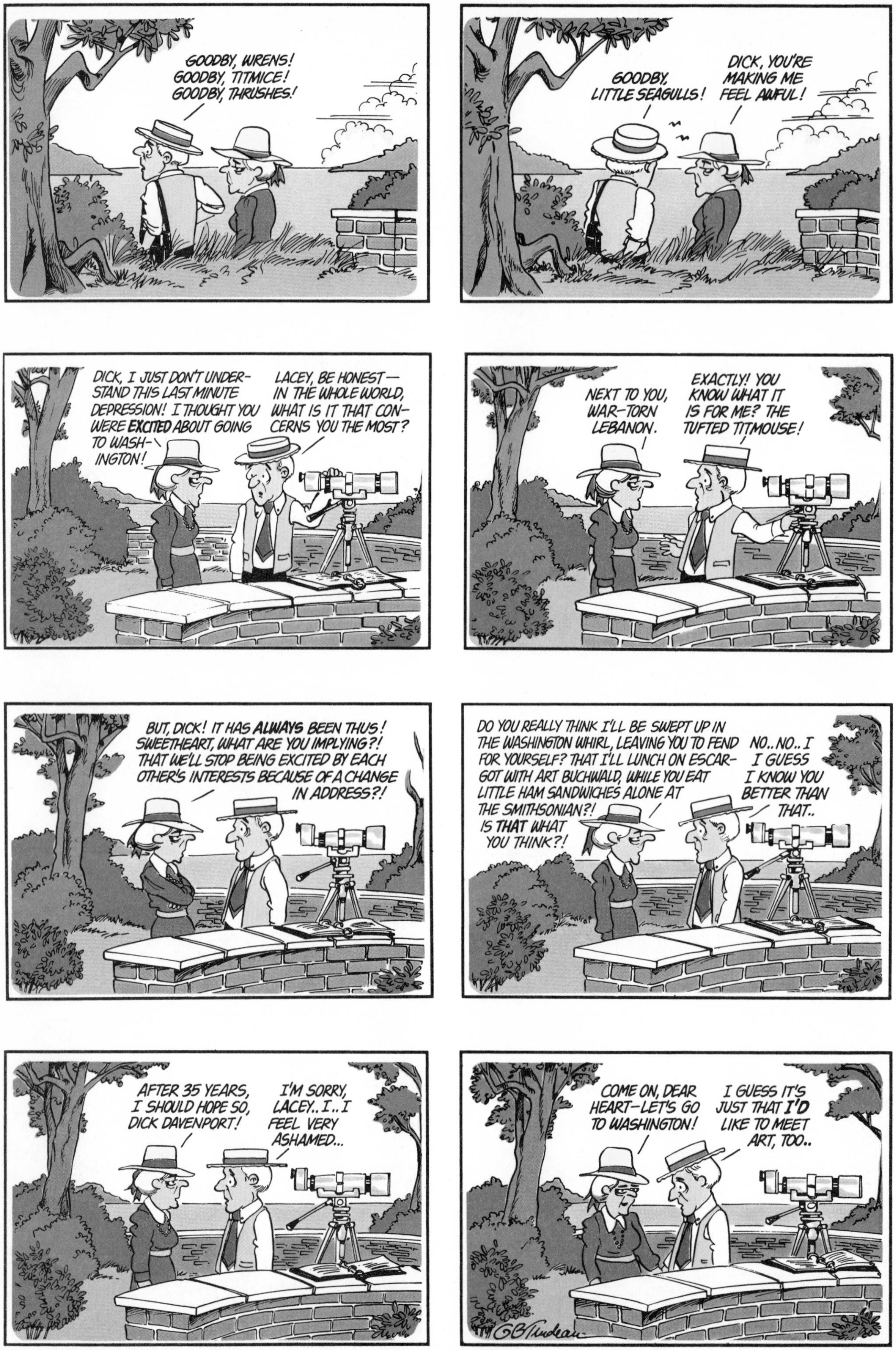
GOODBY, WRENS! GOODBY, TITMICE! GOODBY, THRUSHES!
GOODBY, LITTLE SEAGULLS!
DICK, YOU'RE MAKING ME FEEL AWFUL!
DICK, I JUST DON'T UNDERSTAND THIS LAST MINUTE DEPRESSION! I THOUGHT YOU WERE EXCITED ABOUT GOING TO WASHINGTON!
LACEY, BE HONEST— IN THE WHOLE WORLD, WHAT IS IT THAT CONCERNS YOU THE MOST?
NEXT TO YOU, WAR-TORN LEBANON.
EXACTLY! YOU KNOW WHAT IT IS FOR ME? THE TUFTED TITMOUSE!
BUT, DICK! IT HAS ALWAYS BEEN THUS! SWEETHEART, WHAT ARE YOU IMPLYING?! THAT WE'LL STOP BEING EXCITED BY EACH OTHER'S INTERESTS BECAUSE OF A CHANGE IN ADDRESS?!
DO YOU REALLY THINK I'LL BE SWEPT UP IN THE WASHINGTON WHIRL, LEAVING YOU TO FEND FOR YOURSELF? THAT I'LL LUNCH ON ESCARGOT WITH ART BUCHWALD, WHILE YOU EAT LITTLE HAM SANDWICHES ALONE AT THE SMITHSONIAN?! IS THAT WHAT YOU THINK?!
NO.. NO.. I I GUESS I KNOW YOU BETTER THAN THAT..
AFTER 35 YEARS, I SHOULD HOPE SO, DICK DAVENPORT!
I'M SORRY, LACEY.. I.. I FEEL VERY ASHAMED...
COME ON, DEAR HEART—LET'S GO TO WASHINGTON!
I GUESS IT'S JUST THAT I'D LIKE TO MEET ART, TOO..
GBTrudeau

EVERYBODY READY?!
TEN-FOUR!
YUP!
WAIT A MINUTE! MY HAIR'S A MESS!
LET'S DO IT!
READY HERE!
O.K.!
WE WISH YOU A MERRY CHRISTMAS!
WEEE WISH YOU..
..A MERRY CHRISTMAS!..
WEEE WISH YOU...
..A MERRY CHRISTMAS...
AND A HAPPPY NEW YEARR!!
..OF THE DRAGON!
SLAM!
SINGIN' IN THE RAAIN!
GBTrudeau

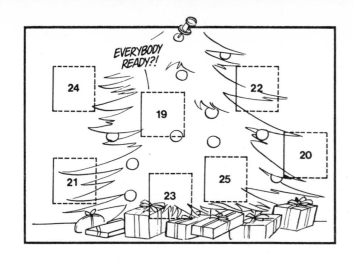

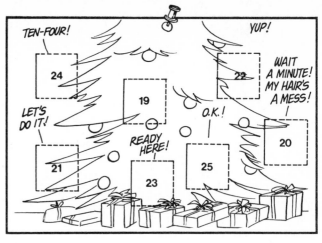

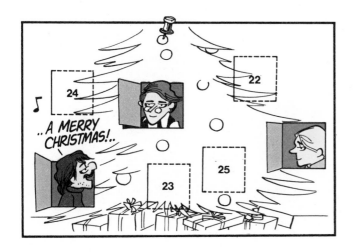

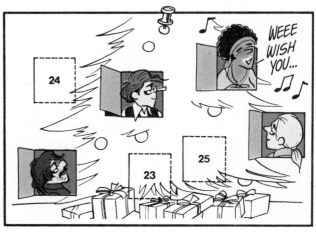

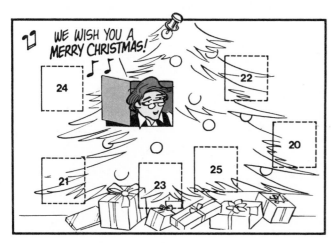

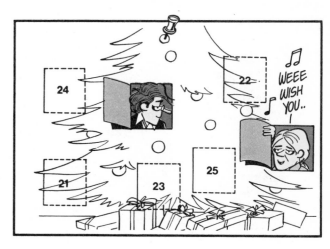

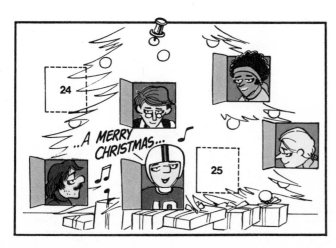

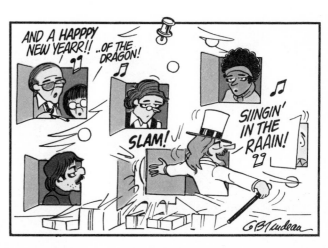

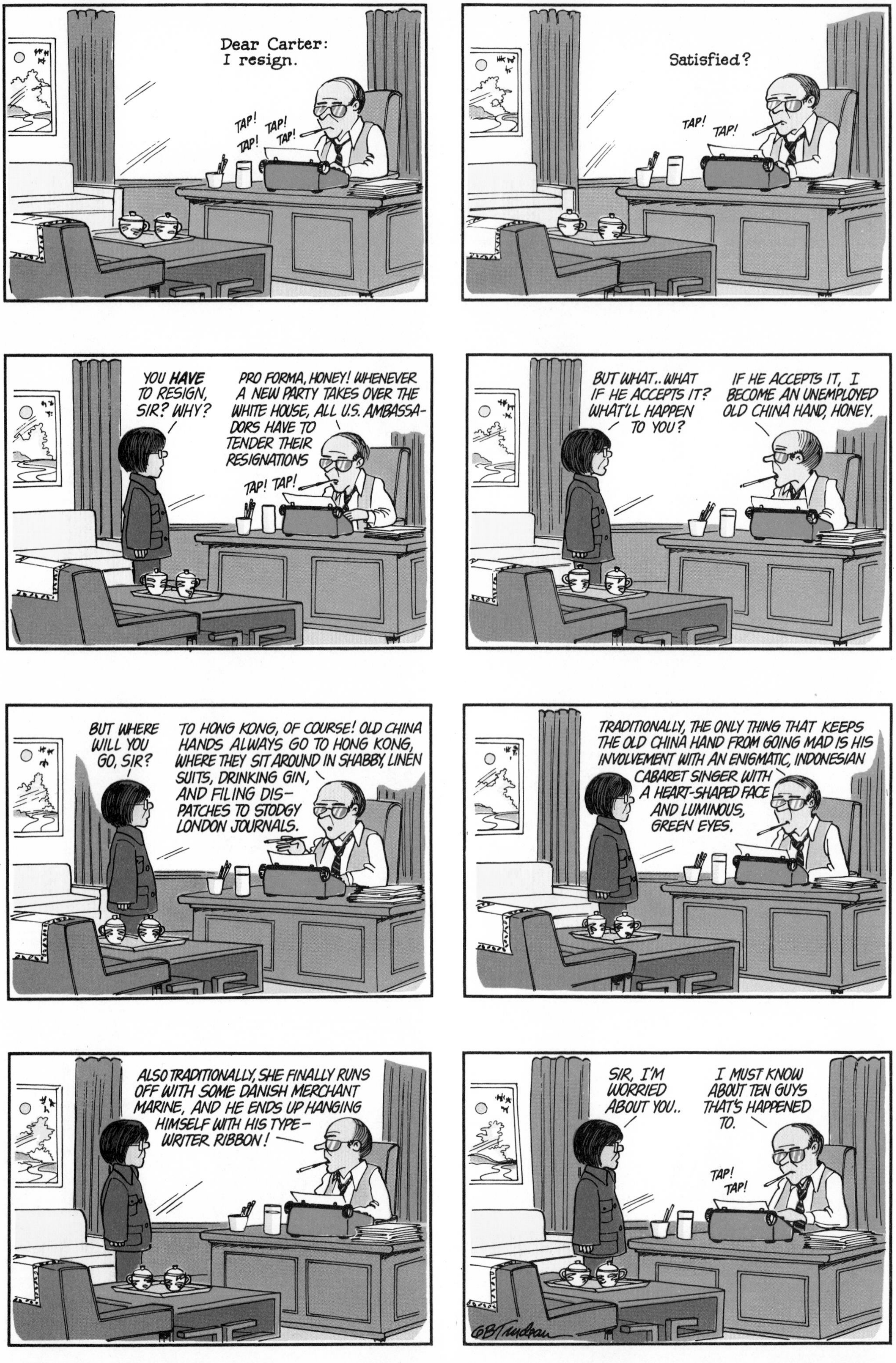
Dear Carter:
I resign.
TAP! TAP! TAP! TAP!
Satisfied?
TAP! TAP!
YOU HAVE TO RESIGN, SIR? WHY?
PRO FORMA, HONEY! WHENEVER A NEW PARTY TAKES OVER THE WHITE HOUSE, ALL U.S. AMBASSADORS HAVE TO TENDER THEIR RESIGNATIONS
TAP! TAP!
BUT WHAT.. WHAT IF HE ACCEPTS IT? WHAT'LL HAPPEN TO YOU?
IF HE ACCEPTS IT, I BECOME AN UNEMPLOYED OLD CHINA HAND, HONEY.
BUT WHERE WILL YOU GO, SIR?
TO HONG KONG, OF COURSE! OLD CHINA HANDS ALWAYS GO TO HONG KONG, WHERE THEY SIT AROUND IN SHABBY, LINEN SUITS, DRINKING GIN, AND FILING DISPATCHES TO STODGY LONDON JOURNALS.
TRADITIONALLY, THE ONLY THING THAT KEEPS THE OLD CHINA HAND FROM GOING MAD IS HIS INVOLVEMENT WITH AN ENIGMATIC, INDONESIAN CABARET SINGER WITH A HEART-SHAPED FACE AND LUMINOUS, GREEN EYES.
ALSO TRADITIONALLY, SHE FINALLY RUNS OFF WITH SOME DANISH MERCHANT MARINE, AND HE ENDS UP HANGING HIMSELF WITH HIS TYPEWRITER RIBBON!
SIR, I'M WORRIED ABOUT YOU..
I MUST KNOW ABOUT TEN GUYS THAT'S HAPPENED TO.
TAP! TAP!
GBTrudeau

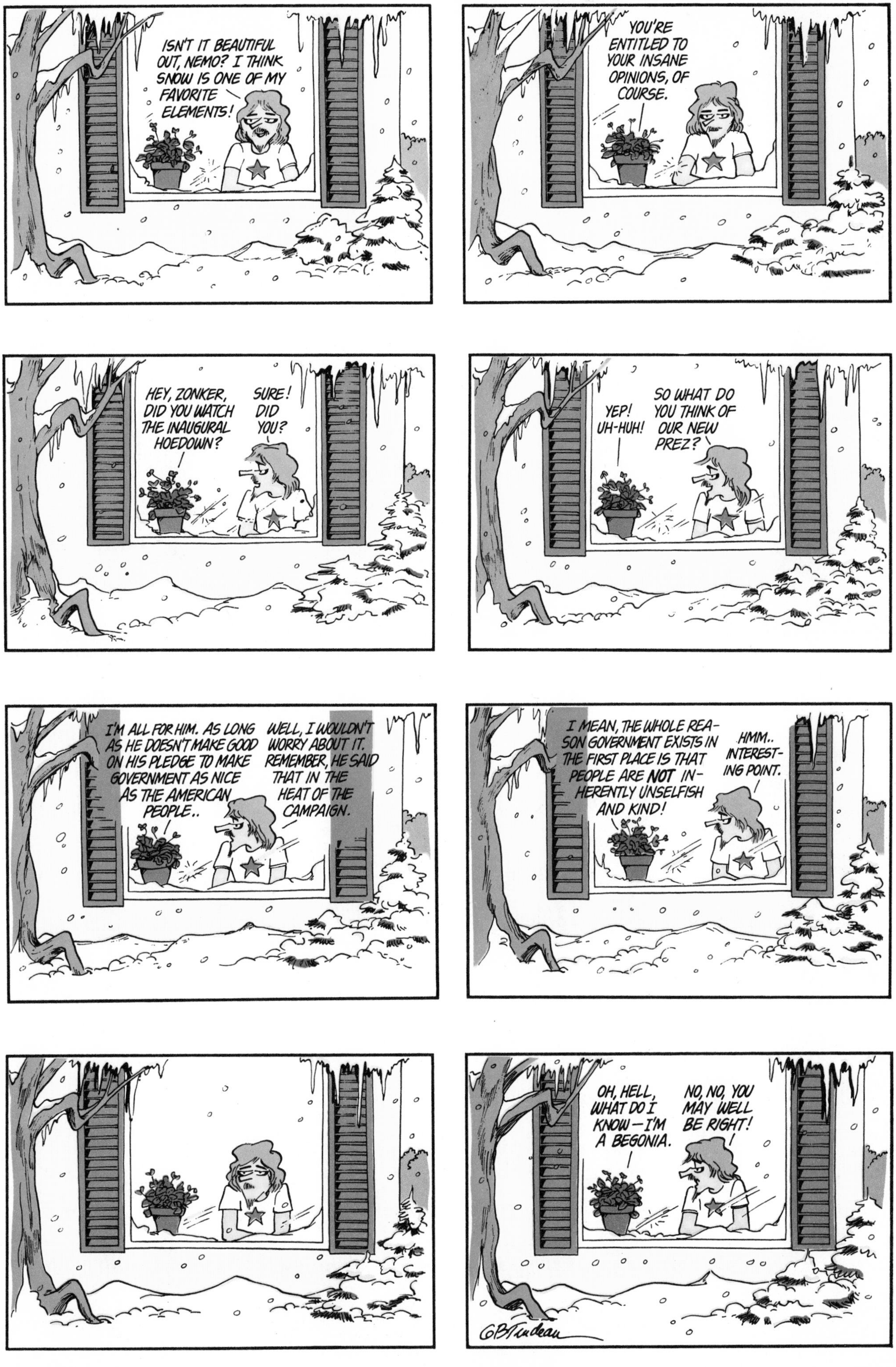
ISN'T IT BEAUTIFUL OUT, NEMO? I THINK SNOW IS ONE OF MY FAVORITE ELEMENTS!
YOU'RE ENTITLED TO YOUR INSANE OPINIONS, OF COURSE.
HEY, ZONKER, DID YOU WATCH THE INAUGURAL HOEDOWN?
SURE! DID YOU?
YEP! UH-HUH!
SO WHAT DO YOU THINK OF OUR NEW PREZ?
I'M ALL FOR HIM. AS LONG AS HE DOESN'T MAKE GOOD ON HIS PLEDGE TO MAKE GOVERNMENT AS NICE AS THE AMERICAN PEOPLE..
WELL, I WOULDN'T WORRY ABOUT IT. REMEMBER, HE SAID THAT IN THE HEAT OF THE CAMPAIGN.
I MEAN, THE WHOLE REASON GOVERNMENT EXISTS IN THE FIRST PLACE IS THAT PEOPLE ARE NOT INHERENTLY UNSELFISH AND KIND!
HMM.. INTERESTING POINT.
OH, HELL, WHAT DO I KNOW—I'M A BEGONIA.
NO, NO, YOU MAY WELL BE RIGHT!
GBTrudeau

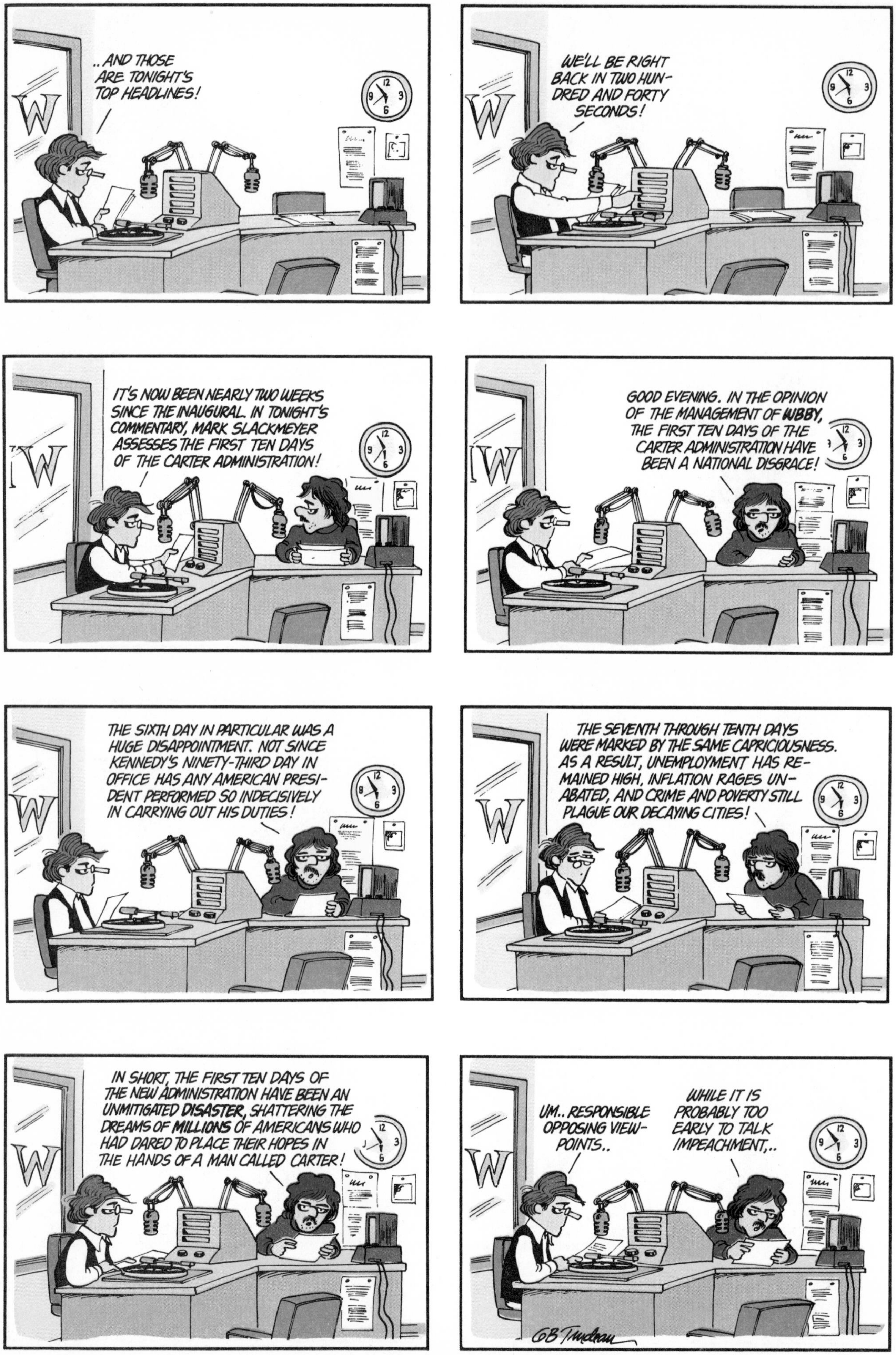
..AND THOSE ARE TONIGHT'S TOP HEADLINES!
WE'LL BE RIGHT BACK IN TWO HUNDRED AND FORTY SECONDS!
W
IT'S NOW BEEN NEARLY TWO WEEKS SINCE THE INAUGURAL. IN TONIGHT'S COMMENTARY, MARK SLACKMEYER ASSESSES THE FIRST TEN DAYS OF THE CARTER ADMINISTRATION!
GOOD EVENING. IN THE OPINION OF THE MANAGEMENT OF WBBY, THE FIRST TEN DAYS OF THE CARTER ADMINISTRATION HAVE BEEN A NATIONAL DISGRACE!
THE SIXTH DAY IN PARTICULAR WAS A HUGE DISAPPOINTMENT. NOT SINCE KENNEDY'S NINETY-THIRD DAY IN OFFICE HAS ANY AMERICAN PRESIDENT PERFORMED SO INDECISIVELY IN CARRYING OUT HIS DUTIES!
THE SEVENTH THROUGH TENTH DAYS WERE MARKED BY THE SAME CAPRICIOUSNESS. AS A RESULT, UNEMPLOYMENT HAS REMAINED HIGH, INFLATION RAGES UNABATED, AND CRIME AND POVERTY STILL PLAGUE OUR DECAYING CITIES!
IN SHORT, THE FIRST TEN DAYS OF THE NEW ADMINISTRATION HAVE BEEN AN UNMITIGATED DISASTER, SHATTERING THE DREAMS OF MILLIONS OF AMERICANS WHO HAD DARED TO PLACE THEIR HOPES IN THE HANDS OF A MAN CALLED CARTER!
UM.. RESPONSIBLE OPPOSING VIEWPOINTS..
WHILE IT IS PROBABLY TOO EARLY TO TALK IMPEACHMENT,..
GB Trudeau

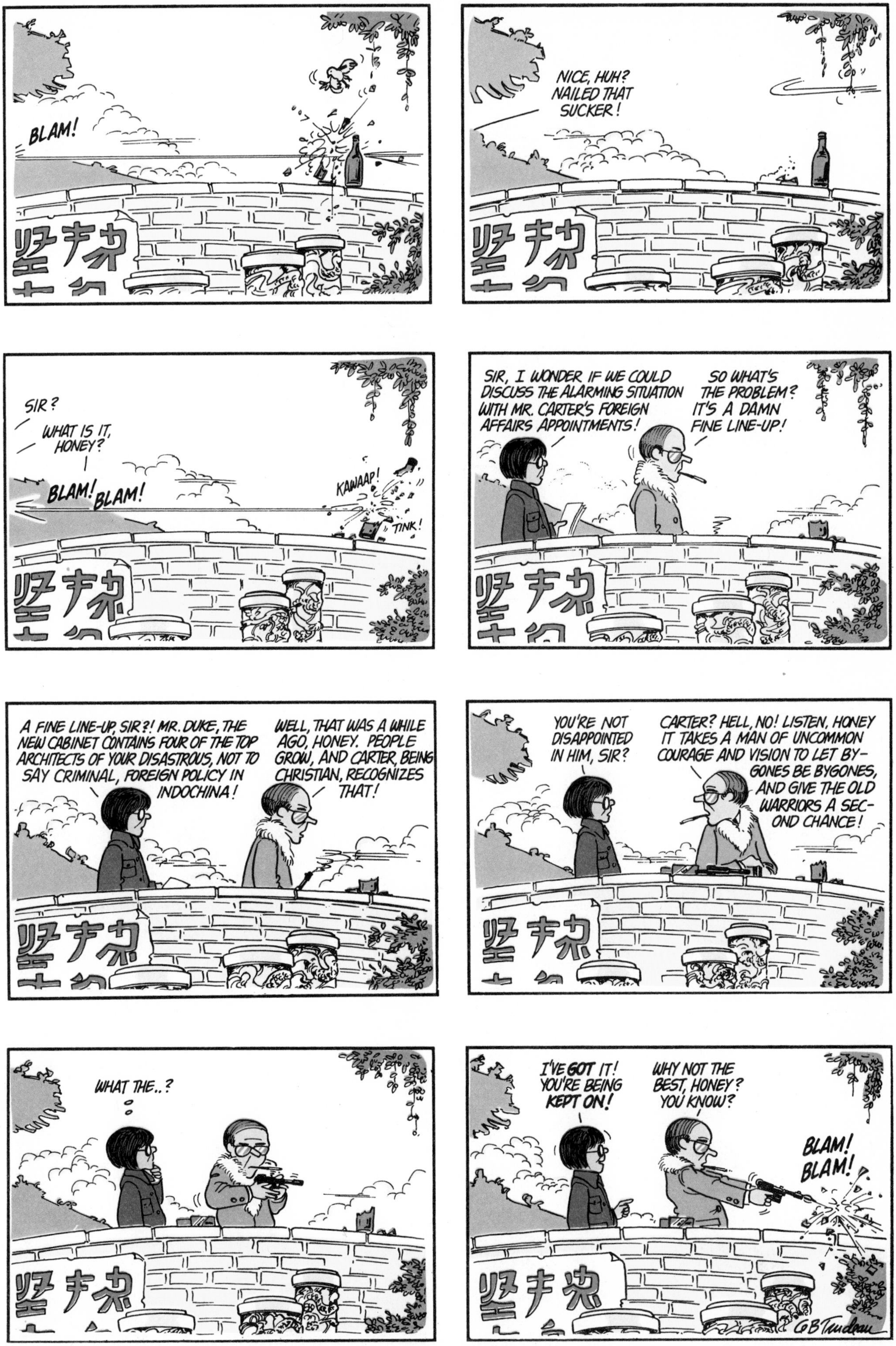
BLAM!
NICE, HUH? NAILED THAT SUCKER!
SIR?
WHAT IS IT, HONEY?
BLAM! BLAM!
KAWAAP!
TINK!
SIR, I WONDER IF WE COULD DISCUSS THE ALARMING SITUATION WITH MR. CARTER'S FOREIGN AFFAIRS APPOINTMENTS!
SO WHAT'S THE PROBLEM? IT'S A DAMN FINE LINE-UP!
A FINE LINE-UP, SIR?! MR. DUKE, THE NEW CABINET CONTAINS FOUR OF THE TOP ARCHITECTS OF YOUR DISASTROUS, NOT TO SAY CRIMINAL, FOREIGN POLICY IN INDOCHINA!
WELL, THAT WAS A WHILE AGO, HONEY. PEOPLE GROW, AND CARTER, BEING CHRISTIAN, RECOGNIZES THAT!
YOU'RE NOT DISAPPOINTED IN HIM, SIR?
CARTER? HELL, NO! LISTEN, HONEY IT TAKES A MAN OF UNCOMMON COURAGE AND VISION TO LET BY-GONES BE BYGONES, AND GIVE THE OLD WARRIORS A SEC-OND CHANCE!
WHAT THE..?
I'VE GOT IT! YOU'RE BEING KEPT ON!
WHY NOT THE BEST, HONEY? YOU KNOW?
BLAM! BLAM!
GBTrudeau

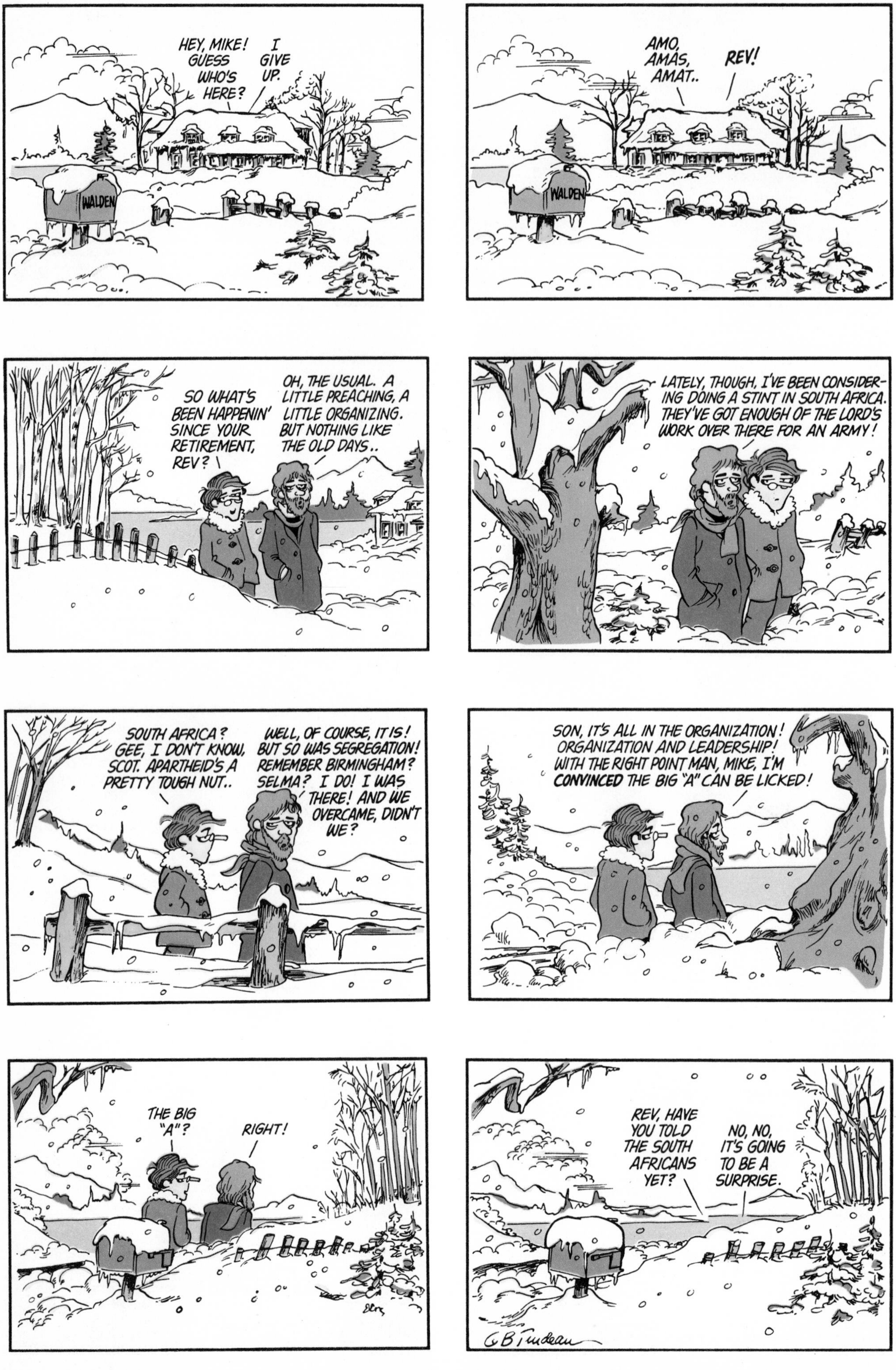
HEY, MIKE! GUESS WHO'S HERE?
I GIVE UP.
WALDEN
AMO, AMÁS, AMAT..
REV!
WALDEN
SO WHAT'S BEEN HAPPENIN' SINCE YOUR RETIREMENT, REV?
OH, THE USUAL. A LITTLE PREACHING, A LITTLE ORGANIZING. BUT NOTHING LIKE THE OLD DAYS..
LATELY, THOUGH, I'VE BEEN CONSIDERING DOING A STINT IN SOUTH AFRICA. THEY'VE GOT ENOUGH OF THE LORD'S WORK OVER THERE FOR AN ARMY!
SOUTH AFRICA? GEE, I DON'T KNOW, SCOT. APARTHEID'S A PRETTY TOUGH NUT..
WELL, OF COURSE, IT IS! BUT SO WAS SEGREGATION! REMEMBER BIRMINGHAM? SELMA? I DO! I WAS THERE! AND WE OVERCAME, DIDN'T WE?
SON, IT'S ALL IN THE ORGANIZATION! ORGANIZATION AND LEADERSHIP! WITH THE RIGHT POINT MAN, MIKE, I'M CONVINCED THE BIG "A" CAN BE LICKED!
THE BIG "A"?
RIGHT!
REV, HAVE YOU TOLD THE SOUTH AFRICANS YET?
NO, NO, IT'S GOING TO BE A SURPRISE.
G B Trudeau

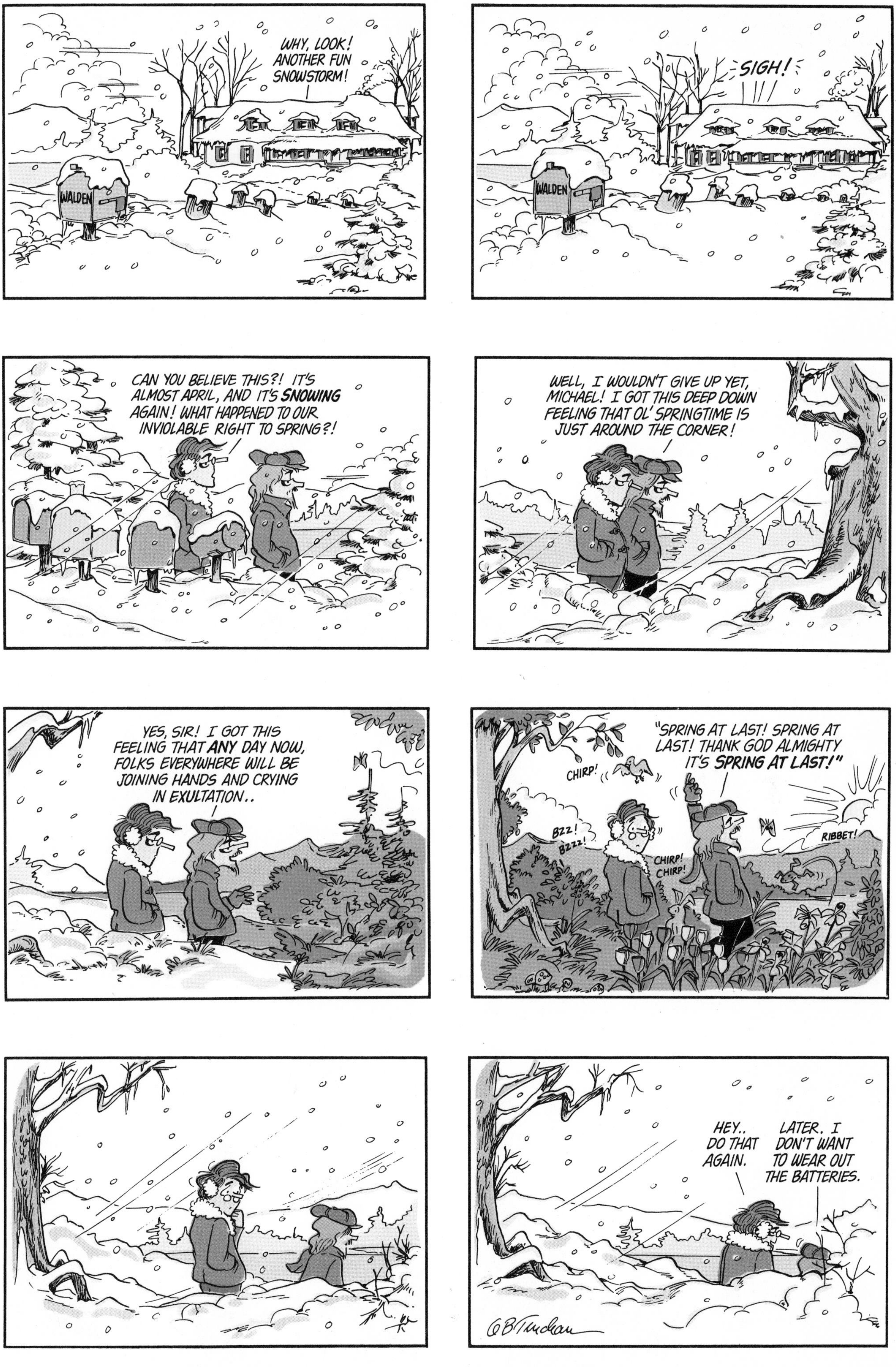
WHY, LOOK! ANOTHER FUN SNOWSTORM!
WALDEN
SIGH!
WALDEN
CAN YOU BELIEVE THIS?! IT'S ALMOST APRIL, AND IT'S **SNOWING** AGAIN! WHAT HAPPENED TO OUR INVIOLABLE RIGHT TO SPRING?!
WELL, I WOULDN'T GIVE UP YET, MICHAEL! I GOT THIS DEEP DOWN FEELING THAT OL' SPRINGTIME IS JUST AROUND THE CORNER!
YES, SIR! I GOT THIS FEELING THAT **ANY** DAY NOW, FOLKS EVERYWHERE WILL BE JOINING HANDS AND CRYING IN EXULTATION..
"SPRING AT LAST! SPRING AT LAST! THANK GOD ALMIGHTY IT'S **SPRING AT LAST!**"
CHIRP!
BZZ! BZZZ!
CHIRP! CHIRP!
RIBBET!
HEY.. DO THAT AGAIN.
LATER. I DON'T WANT TO WEAR OUT THE BATTERIES.

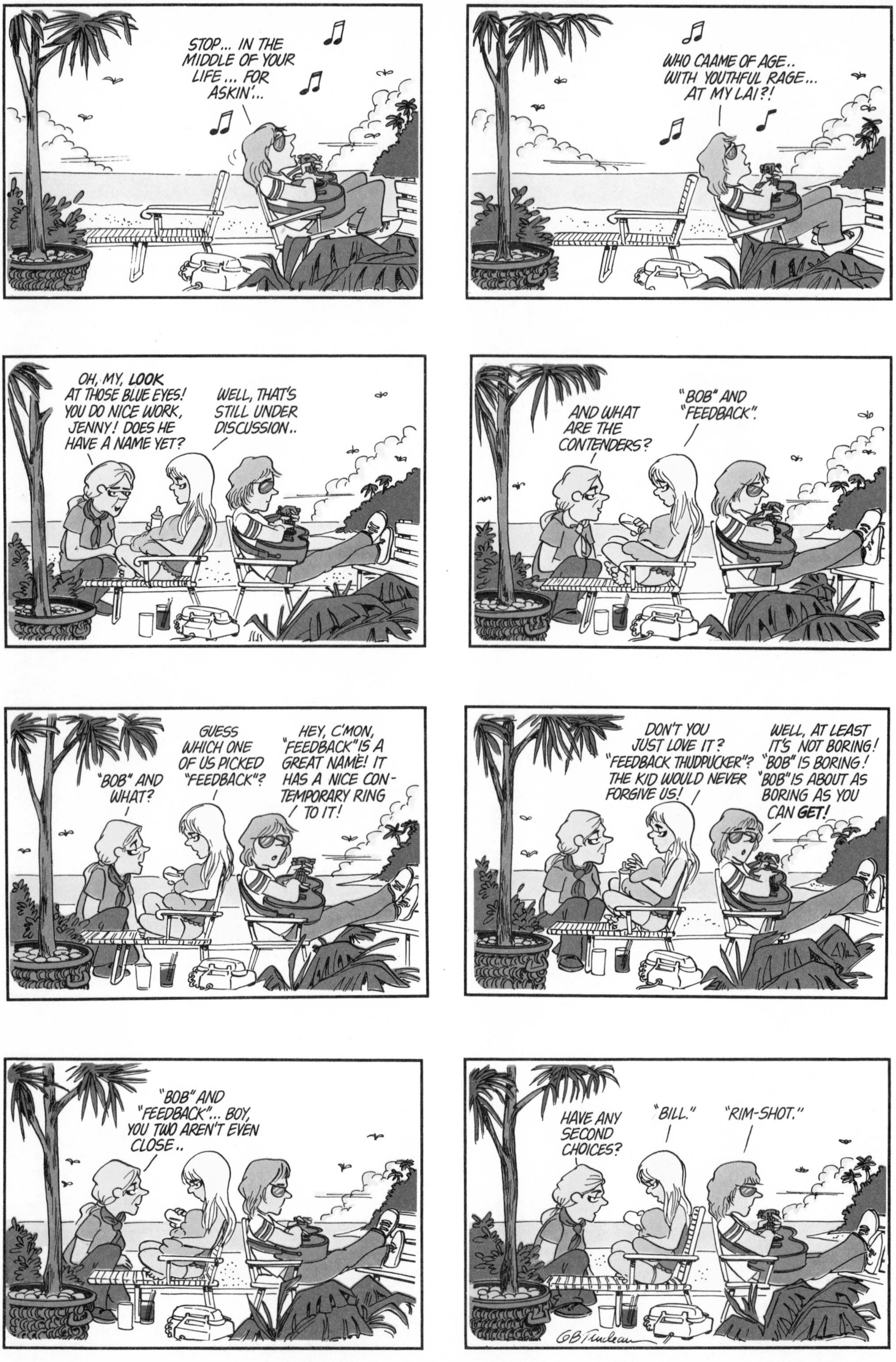
STOP... IN THE MIDDLE OF YOUR LIFE... FOR ASKIN'..
WHO CAAME OF AGE.. WITH YOUTHFUL RAGE... AT MY LAI?!
OH, MY, **LOOK** AT THOSE BLUE EYES! YOU DO NICE WORK, JENNY! DOES HE HAVE A NAME YET?
WELL, THAT'S STILL UNDER DISCUSSION..
AND WHAT ARE THE CONTENDERS?
"BOB" AND "FEEDBACK".
"BOB" AND WHAT?
GUESS WHICH ONE OF US PICKED "FEEDBACK"?
HEY, C'MON, "FEEDBACK" IS A GREAT NAME! IT HAS A NICE CONTEMPORARY RING TO IT!
DON'T YOU JUST LOVE IT? "FEEDBACK THUDPUCKER"? THE KID WOULD NEVER FORGIVE US!
WELL, AT LEAST IT'S NOT BORING! "BOB" IS BORING! "BOB" IS ABOUT AS BORING AS YOU CAN **GET!**
"BOB" AND "FEEDBACK"... BOY, YOU TWO AREN'T EVEN CLOSE..
HAVE ANY SECOND CHOICES?
"BILL."
"RIM-SHOT."
GBTrudeau

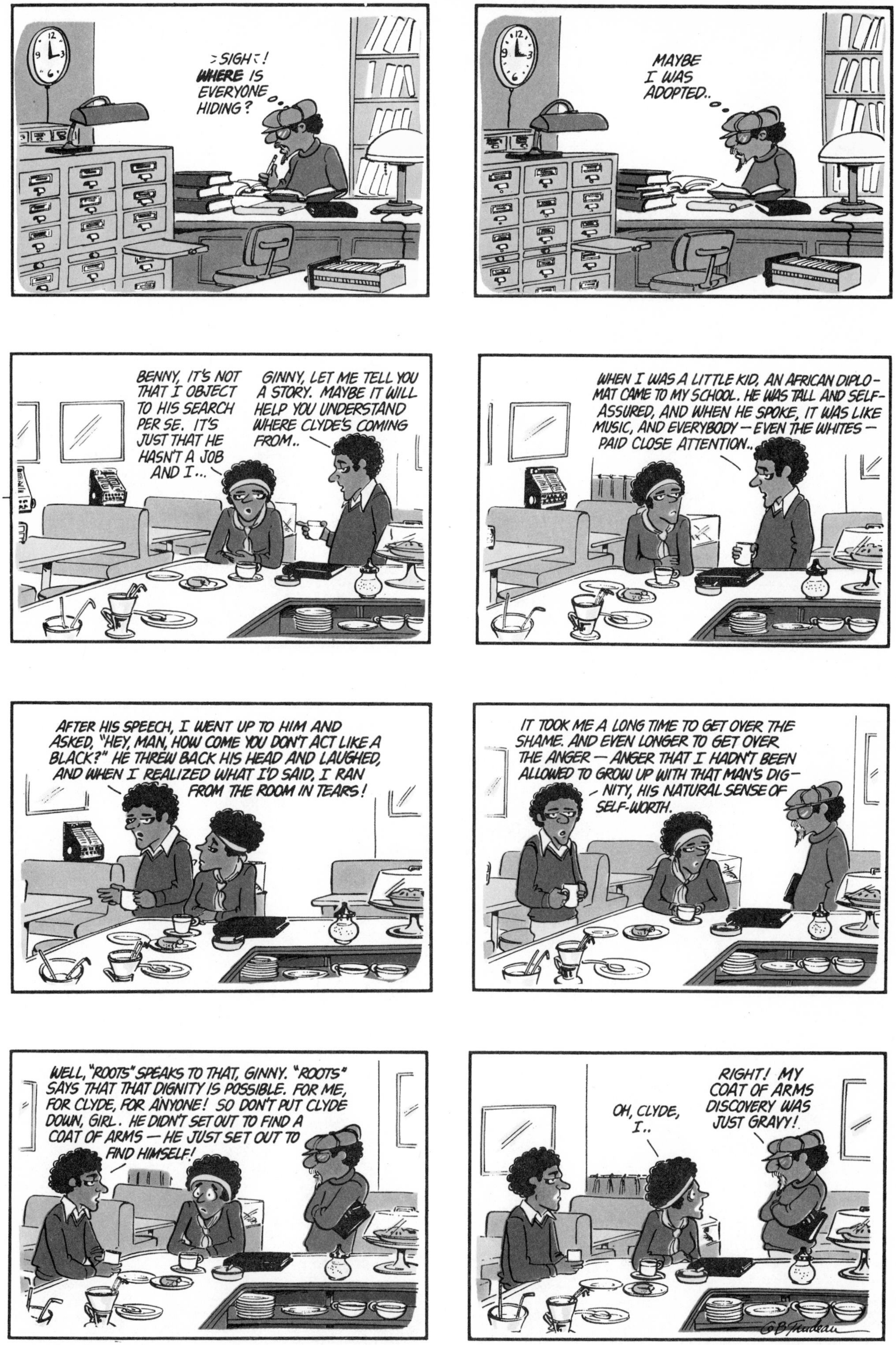
SIGH! WHERE IS EVERYONE HIDING?
MAYBE I WAS ADOPTED..
BENNY, IT'S NOT THAT I OBJECT TO HIS SEARCH PER SE. IT'S JUST THAT HE HASN'T A JOB AND I...
GINNY, LET ME TELL YOU A STORY. MAYBE IT WILL HELP YOU UNDERSTAND WHERE CLYDE'S COMING FROM..
WHEN I WAS A LITTLE KID, AN AFRICAN DIPLOMAT CAME TO MY SCHOOL. HE WAS TALL AND SELF-ASSURED, AND WHEN HE SPOKE, IT WAS LIKE MUSIC, AND EVERYBODY — EVEN THE WHITES — PAID CLOSE ATTENTION..
AFTER HIS SPEECH, I WENT UP TO HIM AND ASKED, "HEY, MAN, HOW COME YOU DON'T ACT LIKE A BLACK?" HE THREW BACK HIS HEAD AND LAUGHED, AND WHEN I REALIZED WHAT I'D SAID, I RAN FROM THE ROOM IN TEARS!
IT TOOK ME A LONG TIME TO GET OVER THE SHAME. AND EVEN LONGER TO GET OVER THE ANGER — ANGER THAT I HADN'T BEEN ALLOWED TO GROW UP WITH THAT MAN'S DIGNITY, HIS NATURAL SENSE OF SELF-WORTH.
WELL, "ROOTS" SPEAKS TO THAT, GINNY. "ROOTS" SAYS THAT THAT DIGNITY IS POSSIBLE. FOR ME, FOR CLYDE, FOR ANYONE! SO DON'T PUT CLYDE DOWN, GIRL. HE DIDN'T SET OUT TO FIND A COAT OF ARMS — HE JUST SET OUT TO FIND HIMSELF!
OH, CLYDE, I..
RIGHT! MY COAT OF ARMS DISCOVERY WAS JUST GRAVY!
G.B. Trudeau

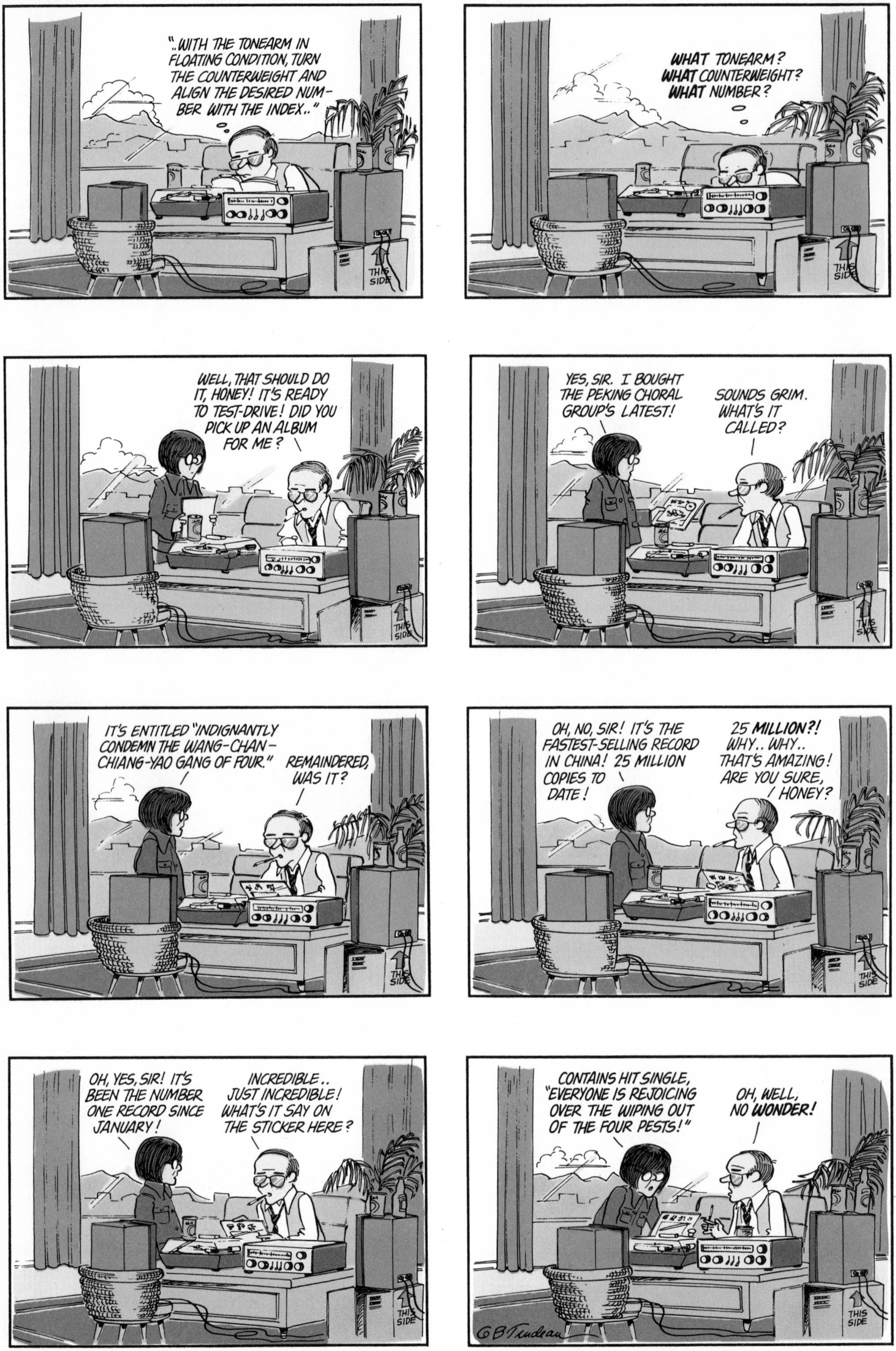
"..WITH THE TONEARM IN FLOATING CONDITION, TURN THE COUNTERWEIGHT AND ALIGN THE DESIRED NUMBER WITH THE INDEX.."
WHAT TONEARM? WHAT COUNTERWEIGHT? WHAT NUMBER?
WELL, THAT SHOULD DO IT, HONEY! IT'S READY TO TEST-DRIVE! DID YOU PICK UP AN ALBUM FOR ME?
YES, SIR. I BOUGHT THE PEKING CHORAL GROUP'S LATEST!
SOUNDS GRIM. WHAT'S IT CALLED?
IT'S ENTITLED "INDIGNANTLY CONDEMN THE WANG-CHAN-CHIANG-YAO GANG OF FOUR."
REMAINDERED, WAS IT?
OH, NO, SIR! IT'S THE FASTEST-SELLING RECORD IN CHINA! 25 MILLION COPIES TO DATE!
25 MILLION?! WHY.. WHY.. THAT'S AMAZING! ARE YOU SURE, HONEY?
OH, YES, SIR! IT'S BEEN THE NUMBER ONE RECORD SINCE JANUARY!
INCREDIBLE.. JUST INCREDIBLE! WHAT'S IT SAY ON THE STICKER HERE?
CONTAINS HIT SINGLE, "EVERYONE IS REJOICING OVER THE WIPING OUT OF THE FOUR PESTS!"
OH, WELL, NO WONDER!
THIS SIDE
GBTrudeau

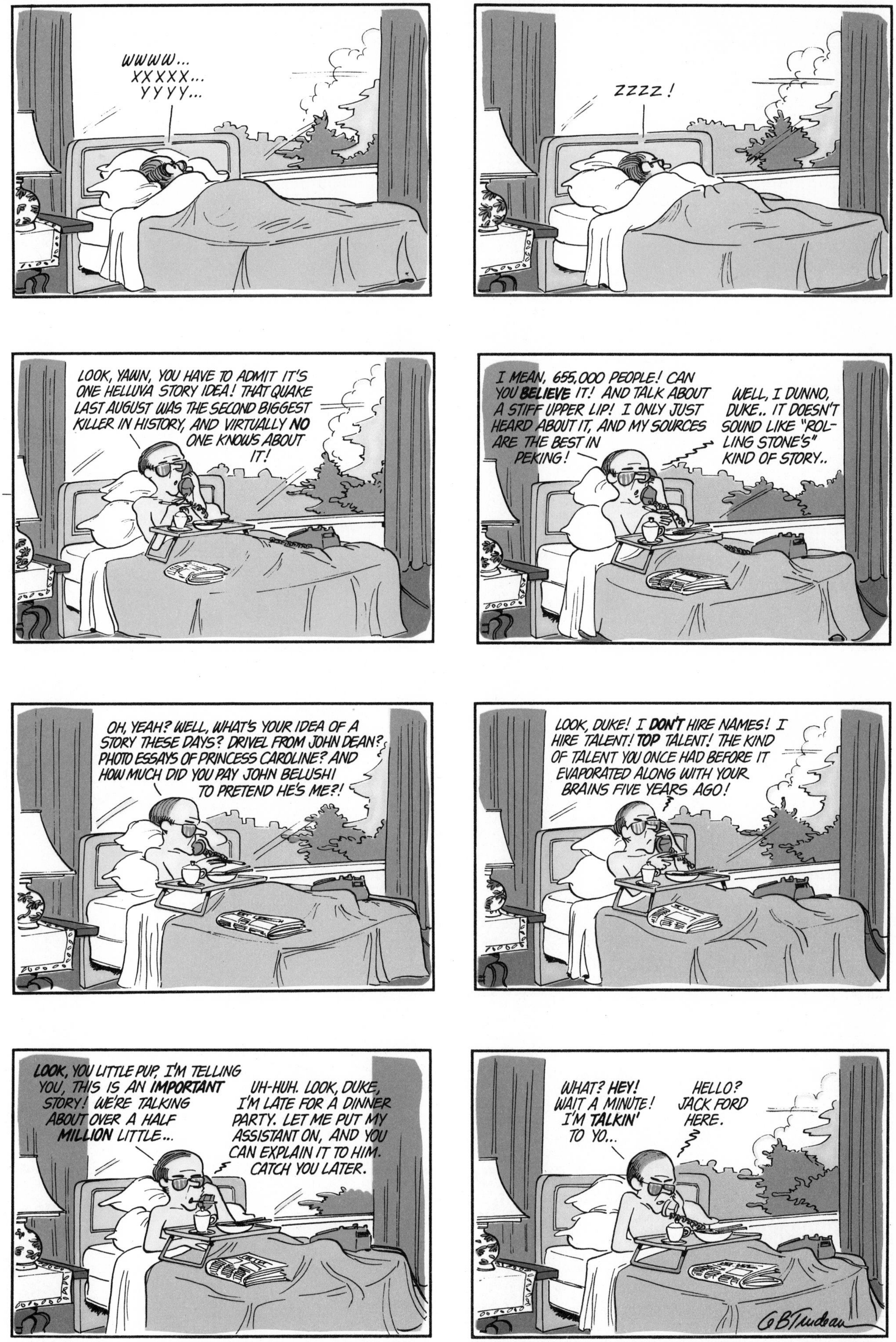
WWWW...
XXXXX...
YYYY...
ZZZZ!
LOOK, YAWN, YOU HAVE TO ADMIT IT'S ONE HELLUVA STORY IDEA! THAT QUAKE LAST AUGUST WAS THE SECOND BIGGEST KILLER IN HISTORY, AND VIRTUALLY NO ONE KNOWS ABOUT IT!
I MEAN, 655,000 PEOPLE! CAN YOU BELIEVE IT! AND TALK ABOUT A STIFF UPPER LIP! I ONLY JUST HEARD ABOUT IT, AND MY SOURCES ARE THE BEST IN PEKING!
WELL, I DUNNO, DUKE.. IT DOESN'T SOUND LIKE "ROL-LING STONE'S" KIND OF STORY..
OH, YEAH? WELL, WHAT'S YOUR IDEA OF A STORY THESE DAYS? DRIVEL FROM JOHN DEAN? PHOTO ESSAYS OF PRINCESS CAROLINE? AND HOW MUCH DID YOU PAY JOHN BELUSHI TO PRETEND HE'S ME?!
LOOK, DUKE! I DON'T HIRE NAMES! I HIRE TALENT! TOP TALENT! THE KIND OF TALENT YOU ONCE HAD BEFORE IT EVAPORATED ALONG WITH YOUR BRAINS FIVE YEARS AGO!
LOOK, YOU LITTLE PUP, I'M TELLING YOU, THIS IS AN IMPORTANT STORY! WE'RE TALKING ABOUT OVER A HALF MILLION LITTLE...
UH-HUH. LOOK, DUKE, I'M LATE FOR A DINNER PARTY. LET ME PUT MY ASSISTANT ON, AND YOU CAN EXPLAIN IT TO HIM. CATCH YOU LATER.
WHAT? HEY! WAIT A MINUTE! I'M TALKIN' TO YO...
HELLO? JACK FORD HERE.
GBTrudeau

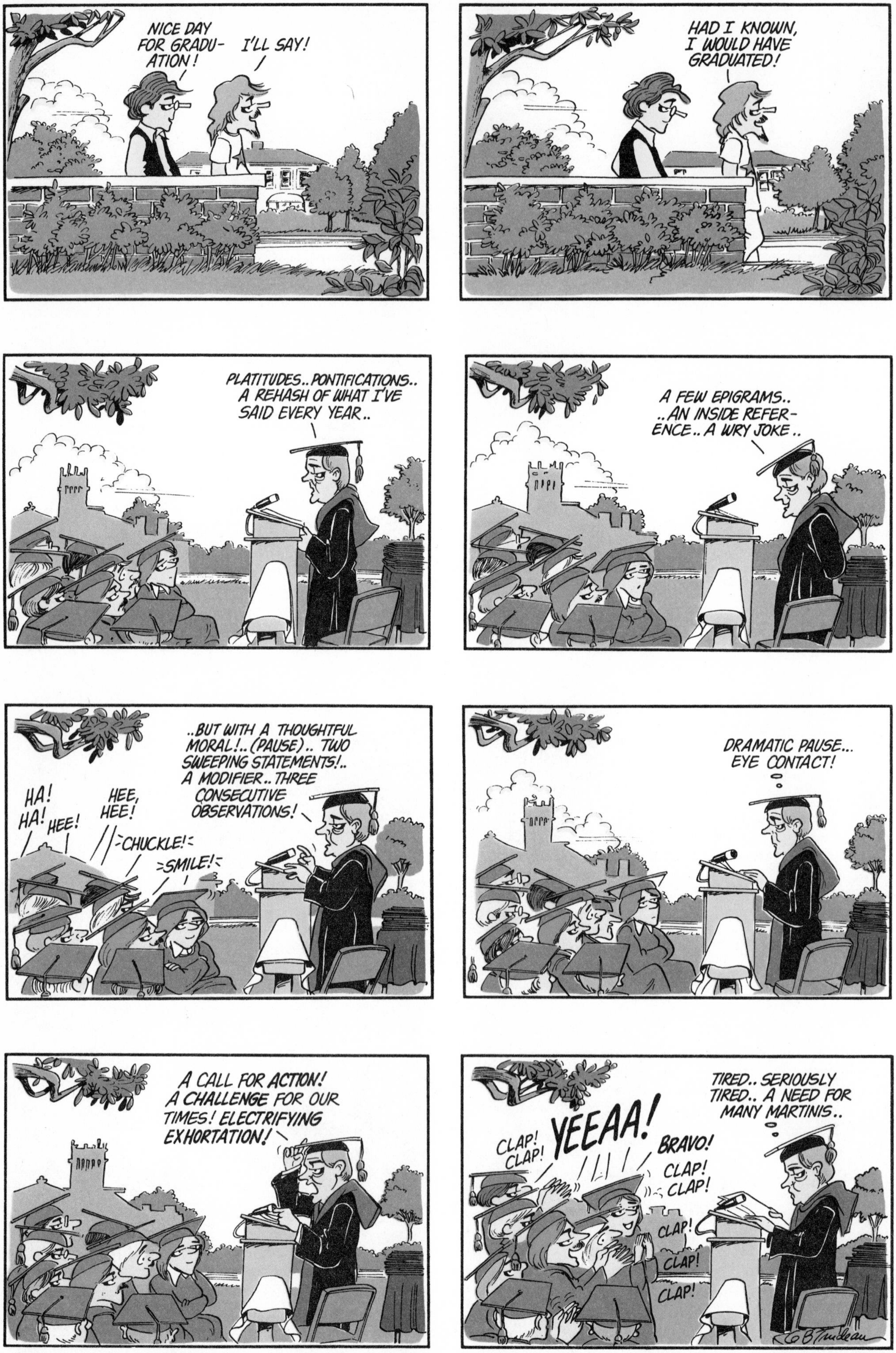
NICE DAY FOR GRADU-ATION!
I'LL SAY!
HAD I KNOWN, I WOULD HAVE GRADUATED!
PLATITUDES.. PONTIFICATIONS.. A REHASH OF WHAT I'VE SAID EVERY YEAR..
A FEW EPIGRAMS.. ..AN INSIDE REFER-ENCE.. A WRY JOKE..
..BUT WITH A THOUGHTFUL MORAL!.. (PAUSE).. TWO SWEEPING STATEMENTS!.. A MODIFIER.. THREE CONSECUTIVE OBSERVATIONS!
HA! HA!
HEE!
HEE, HEE!
CHUCKLE!
SMILE!
DRAMATIC PAUSE... EYE CONTACT!
A CALL FOR ACTION! A CHALLENGE FOR OUR TIMES! ELECTRIFYING EXHORTATION!
CLAP! CLAP!
YEEAA!
BRAVO!
CLAP! CLAP!
CLAP!
CLAP!
CLAP!
TIRED.. SERIOUSLY TIRED.. A NEED FOR MANY MARTINIS..
G B Trudeau

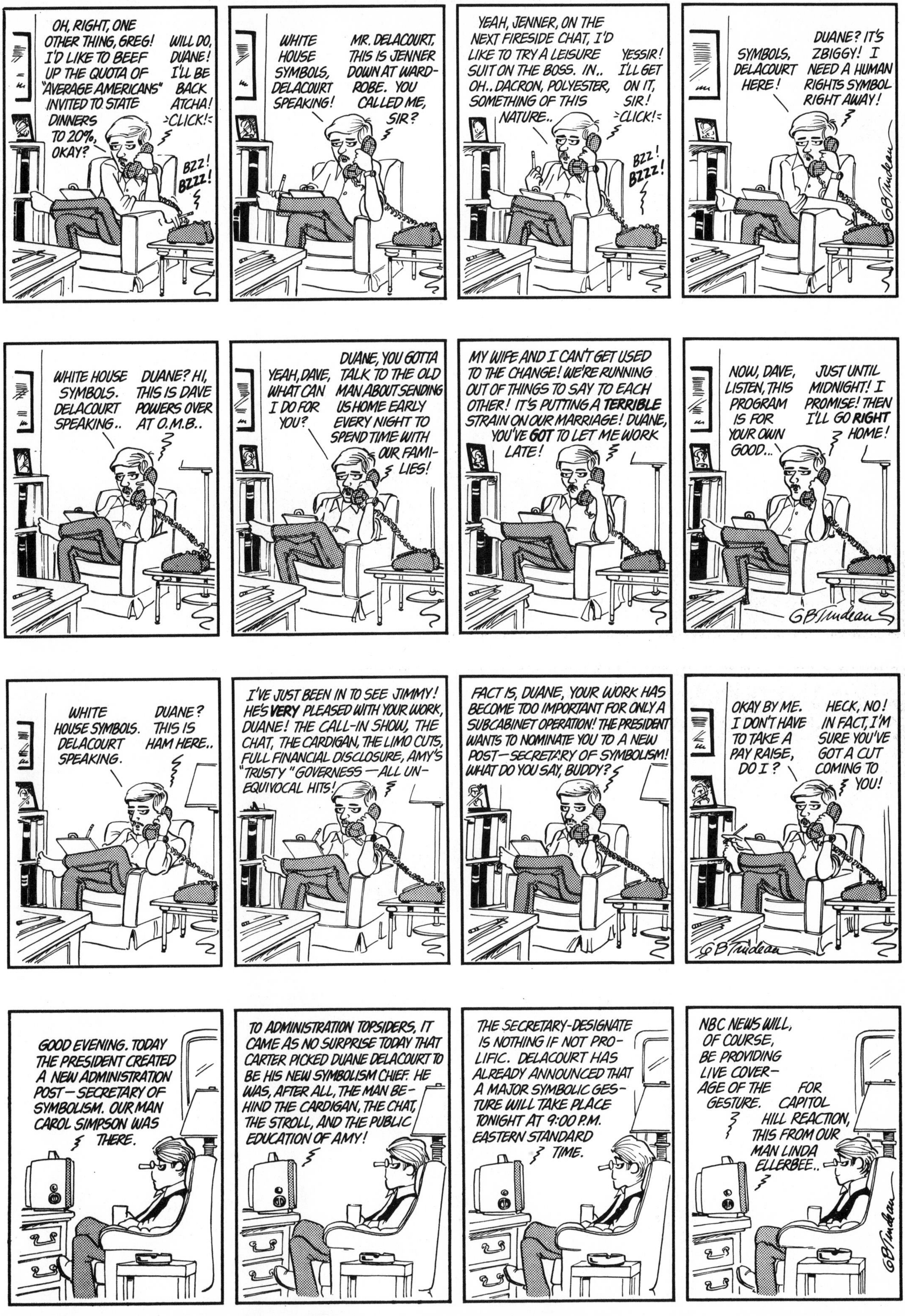
OH, RIGHT, ONE OTHER THING, GREG! I'D LIKE TO BEEF UP THE QUOTA OF "AVERAGE AMERICANS" INVITED TO STATE DINNERS TO 20%, OKAY?
WILL DO, DUANE! I'LL BE BACK ATCHA! CLICK!
BZZ! BZZZ!
WHITE HOUSE SYMBOLS, DELACOURT SPEAKING!
MR. DELACOURT, THIS IS JENNER DOWN AT WARDROBE. YOU CALLED ME, SIR?
YEAH, JENNER, ON THE NEXT FIRESIDE CHAT, I'D LIKE TO TRY A LEISURE SUIT ON THE BOSS. IN.. OH.. DACRON, POLYESTER, SOMETHING OF THIS NATURE..
YESSIR! I'LL GET ON IT, SIR! CLICK!
BZZ! BZZZ!
SYMBOLS, DELACOURT HERE!
DUANE? IT'S ZBIGGY! I NEED A HUMAN RIGHTS SYMBOL RIGHT AWAY!
G B Trudeau
WHITE HOUSE SYMBOLS. DELACOURT SPEAKING..
DUANE? HI, THIS IS DAVE POWERS OVER AT O.M.B..
YEAH, DAVE, WHAT CAN I DO FOR YOU?
DUANE, YOU GOTTA TALK TO THE OLD MAN ABOUT SENDING US HOME EARLY EVERY NIGHT TO SPEND TIME WITH OUR FAMILIES!
MY WIFE AND I CAN'T GET USED TO THE CHANGE! WE'RE RUNNING OUT OF THINGS TO SAY TO EACH OTHER! IT'S PUTTING A TERRIBLE STRAIN ON OUR MARRIAGE! DUANE, YOU'VE GOT TO LET ME WORK LATE!
NOW, DAVE, LISTEN, THIS PROGRAM IS FOR YOUR OWN GOOD...
JUST UNTIL MIDNIGHT! I PROMISE! THEN I'LL GO RIGHT HOME!
G B Trudeau
WHITE HOUSE SYMBOLS. DELACOURT SPEAKING.
DUANE? THIS IS HAM HERE..
I'VE JUST BEEN IN TO SEE JIMMY! HE'S VERY PLEASED WITH YOUR WORK, DUANE! THE CALL-IN SHOW, THE CHAT, THE CARDIGAN, THE LIMO CUTS, FULL FINANCIAL DISCLOSURE, AMY'S "TRUSTY" GOVERNESS — ALL UNEQUIVOCAL HITS!
FACT IS, DUANE, YOUR WORK HAS BECOME TOO IMPORTANT FOR ONLY A SUBCABINET OPERATION! THE PRESIDENT WANTS TO NOMINATE YOU TO A NEW POST—SECRETARY OF SYMBOLISM! WHAT DO YOU SAY, BUDDY?
OKAY BY ME. I DON'T HAVE TO TAKE A PAY RAISE, DO I?
HECK, NO! IN FACT, I'M SURE YOU'VE GOT A CUT COMING TO YOU!
G B Trudeau
GOOD EVENING. TODAY THE PRESIDENT CREATED A NEW ADMINISTRATION POST—SECRETARY OF SYMBOLISM. OUR MAN CAROL SIMPSON WAS THERE.
TO ADMINISTRATION TOPSIDERS, IT CAME AS NO SURPRISE TODAY THAT CARTER PICKED DUANE DELACOURT TO BE HIS NEW SYMBOLISM CHIEF. HE WAS, AFTER ALL, THE MAN BEHIND THE CARDIGAN, THE CHAT, THE STROLL, AND THE PUBLIC EDUCATION OF AMY!
THE SECRETARY-DESIGNATE IS NOTHING IF NOT PROLIFIC. DELACOURT HAS ALREADY ANNOUNCED THAT A MAJOR SYMBOLIC GESTURE WILL TAKE PLACE TONIGHT AT 9:00 P.M. EASTERN STANDARD TIME.
NBC NEWS WILL, OF COURSE, BE PROVIDING LIVE COVERAGE OF THE GESTURE.
FOR CAPITOL HILL REACTION, THIS FROM OUR MAN LINDA ELLERBEE..
G B Trudeau

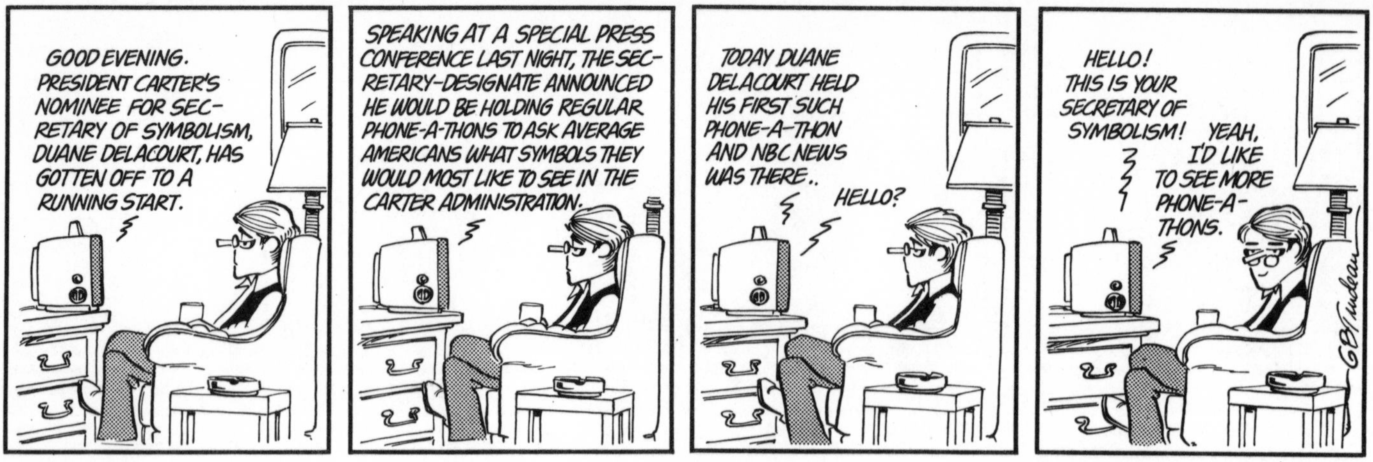
GOOD EVENING. PRESIDENT CARTER'S NOMINEE FOR SECRETARY OF SYMBOLISM, DUANE DELACOURT, HAS GOTTEN OFF TO A RUNNING START.
SPEAKING AT A SPECIAL PRESS CONFERENCE LAST NIGHT, THE SECRETARY-DESIGNATE ANNOUNCED HE WOULD BE HOLDING REGULAR PHONE-A-THONS TO ASK AVERAGE AMERICANS WHAT SYMBOLS THEY WOULD MOST LIKE TO SEE IN THE CARTER ADMINISTRATION.
TODAY DUANE DELACOURT HELD HIS FIRST SUCH PHONE-A-THON AND NBC NEWS WAS THERE..
HELLO?
HELLO! THIS IS YOUR SECRETARY OF SYMBOLISM!
YEAH, I'D LIKE TO SEE MORE PHONE-A-THONS.
GBTrudeau

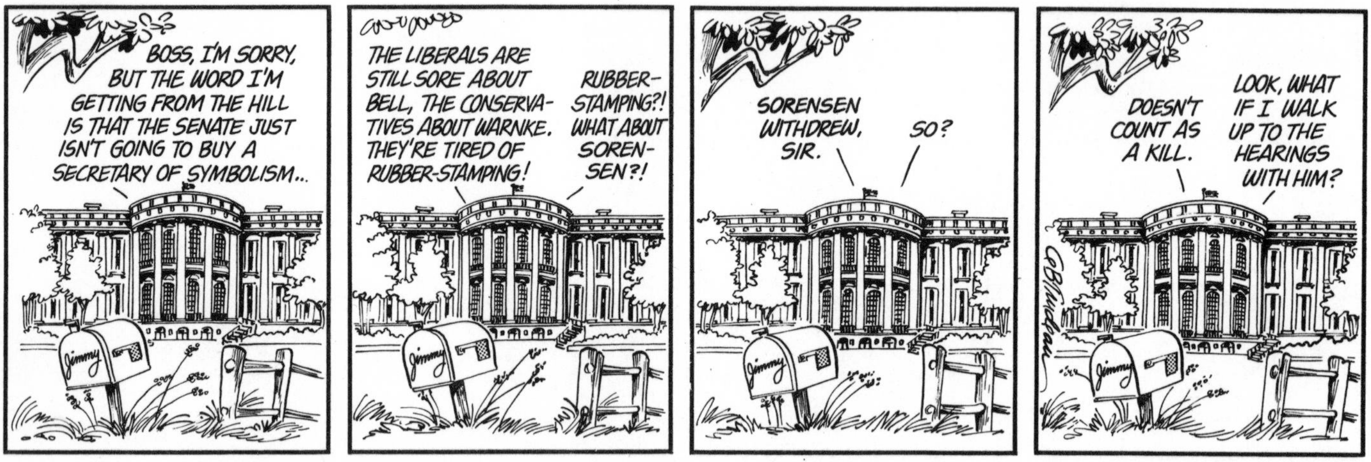
BOSS, I'M SORRY, BUT THE WORD I'M GETTING FROM THE HILL IS THAT THE SENATE JUST ISN'T GOING TO BUY A SECRETARY OF SYMBOLISM...
jimmy
THE LIBERALS ARE STILL SORE ABOUT BELL, THE CONSERVATIVES ABOUT WARNKE. THEY'RE TIRED OF RUBBER-STAMPING!
RUBBER-STAMPING?! WHAT ABOUT SORENSEN?!
SORENSEN WITHDREW, SIR.
SO?
DOESN'T COUNT AS A KILL.
LOOK, WHAT IF I WALK UP TO THE HEARINGS WITH HIM?
GBTrudeau

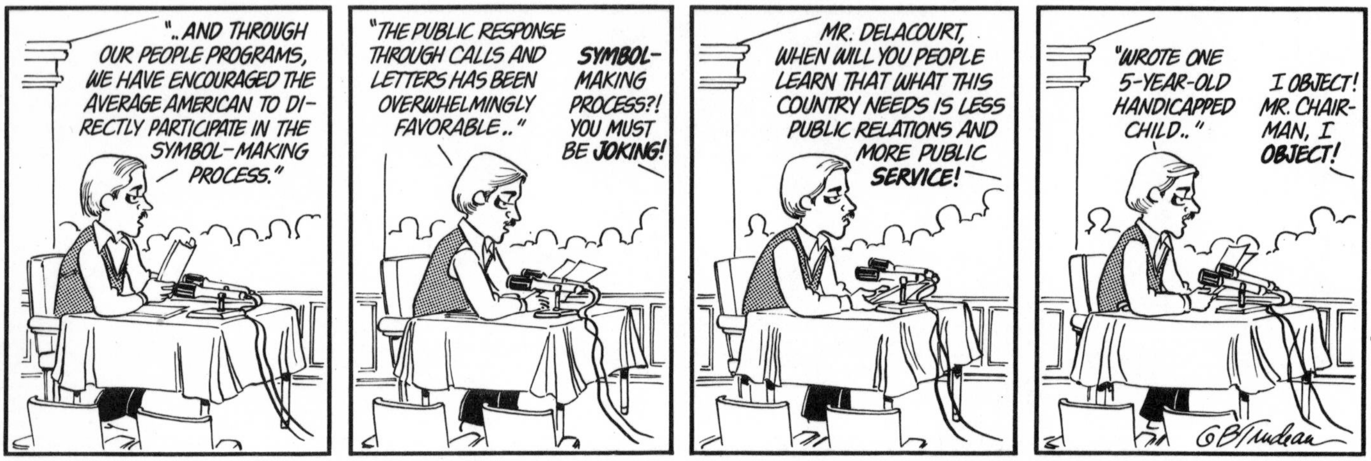
"..AND THROUGH OUR PEOPLE PROGRAMS, WE HAVE ENCOURAGED THE AVERAGE AMERICAN TO DIRECTLY PARTICIPATE IN THE SYMBOL-MAKING PROCESS."
"THE PUBLIC RESPONSE THROUGH CALLS AND LETTERS HAS BEEN OVERWHELMINGLY FAVORABLE.."
SYMBOL-MAKING PROCESS?! YOU MUST BE JOKING!
MR. DELACOURT, WHEN WILL YOU PEOPLE LEARN THAT WHAT THIS COUNTRY NEEDS IS LESS PUBLIC RELATIONS AND MORE PUBLIC SERVICE!
"WROTE ONE 5-YEAR-OLD HANDICAPPED CHILD.."
I OBJECT! MR. CHAIRMAN, I OBJECT!
GBTrudeau

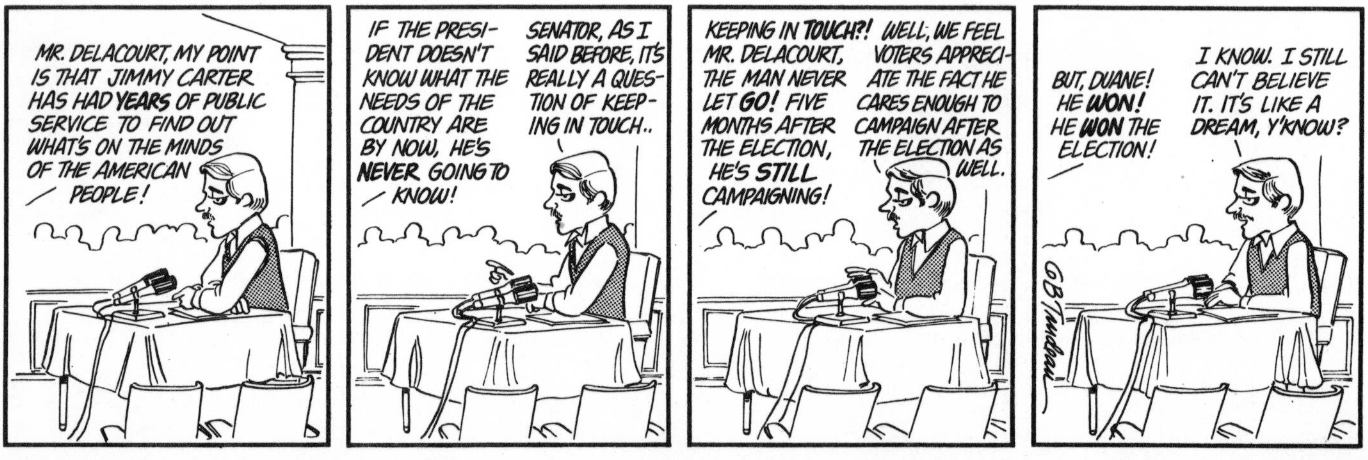
MR. DELACOURT, MY POINT IS THAT JIMMY CARTER HAS HAD YEARS OF PUBLIC SERVICE TO FIND OUT WHAT'S ON THE MINDS OF THE AMERICAN PEOPLE!
IF THE PRESIDENT DOESN'T KNOW WHAT THE NEEDS OF THE COUNTRY ARE BY NOW, HE'S NEVER GOING TO KNOW!
SENATOR, AS I SAID BEFORE, IT'S REALLY A QUESTION OF KEEPING IN TOUCH..
KEEPING IN TOUCH?! MR. DELACOURT, THE MAN NEVER LET GO! FIVE MONTHS AFTER THE ELECTION, HE'S STILL CAMPAIGNING!
WELL, WE FEEL VOTERS APPRECIATE THE FACT HE CARES ENOUGH TO CAMPAIGN AFTER THE ELECTION AS WELL.
BUT, DUANE! HE WON! HE WON THE ELECTION!
I KNOW. I STILL CAN'T BELIEVE IT. IT'S LIKE A DREAM, Y'KNOW?
GBTrudeau

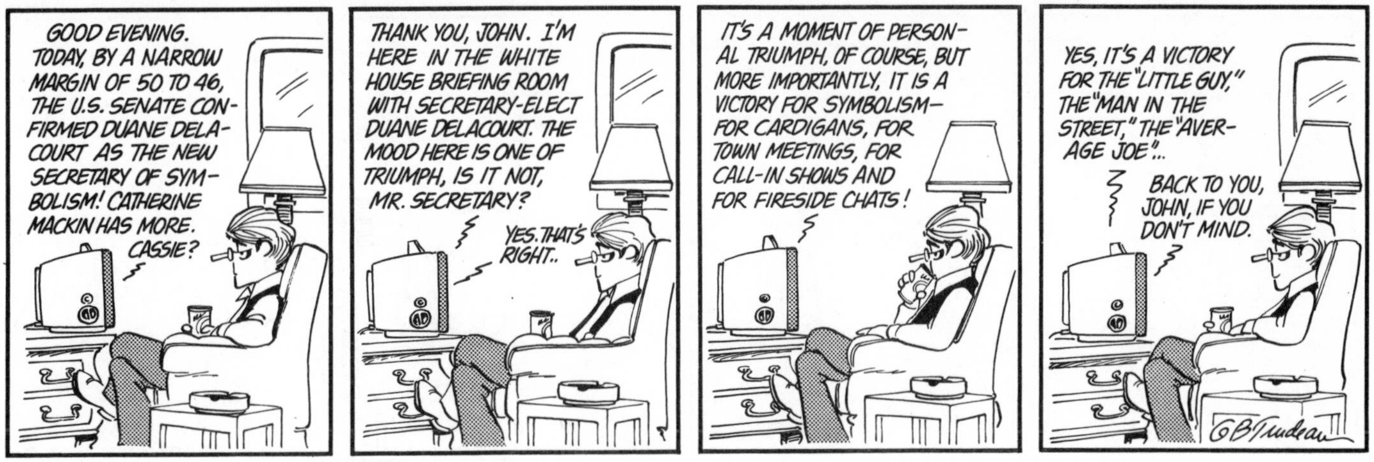
GOOD EVENING. TODAY, BY A NARROW MARGIN OF 50 TO 46, THE U.S. SENATE CONFIRMED DUANE DELACOURT AS THE NEW SECRETARY OF SYMBOLISM! CATHERINE MACKIN HAS MORE. CASSIE?
THANK YOU, JOHN. I'M HERE IN THE WHITE HOUSE BRIEFING ROOM WITH SECRETARY-ELECT DUANE DELACOURT. THE MOOD HERE IS ONE OF TRIUMPH, IS IT NOT, MR. SECRETARY?
YES. THAT'S RIGHT..
IT'S A MOMENT OF PERSONAL TRIUMPH, OF COURSE, BUT MORE IMPORTANTLY, IT IS A VICTORY FOR SYMBOLISM— FOR CARDIGANS, FOR TOWN MEETINGS, FOR CALL-IN SHOWS AND FOR FIRESIDE CHATS!
YES, IT'S A VICTORY FOR THE "LITTLE GUY," THE "MAN IN THE STREET," THE "AVERAGE JOE"..
BACK TO YOU, JOHN, IF YOU DON'T MIND.
GBTrudeau

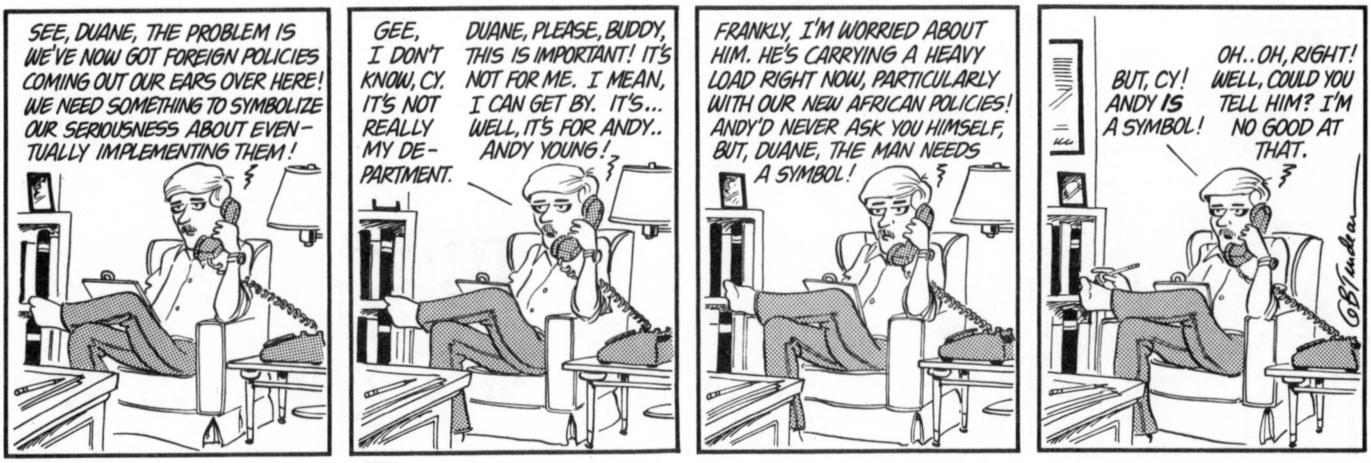
SEE, DUANE, THE PROBLEM IS WE'VE NOW GOT FOREIGN POLICIES COMING OUT OUR EARS OVER HERE! WE NEED SOMETHING TO SYMBOLIZE OUR SERIOUSNESS ABOUT EVENTUALLY IMPLEMENTING THEM!
GEE, I DON'T KNOW, CY. IT'S NOT REALLY MY DEPARTMENT.
DUANE, PLEASE, BUDDY, THIS IS IMPORTANT! IT'S NOT FOR ME. I MEAN, I CAN GET BY. IT'S... WELL, IT'S FOR ANDY.. ANDY YOUNG!
FRANKLY, I'M WORRIED ABOUT HIM. HE'S CARRYING A HEAVY LOAD RIGHT NOW, PARTICULARLY WITH OUR NEW AFRICAN POLICIES! ANDY'D NEVER ASK YOU HIMSELF, BUT, DUANE, THE MAN NEEDS A SYMBOL!
BUT, CY! ANDY IS A SYMBOL!
OH.. OH, RIGHT! WELL, COULD YOU TELL HIM? I'M NO GOOD AT THAT.
GBTrudeau

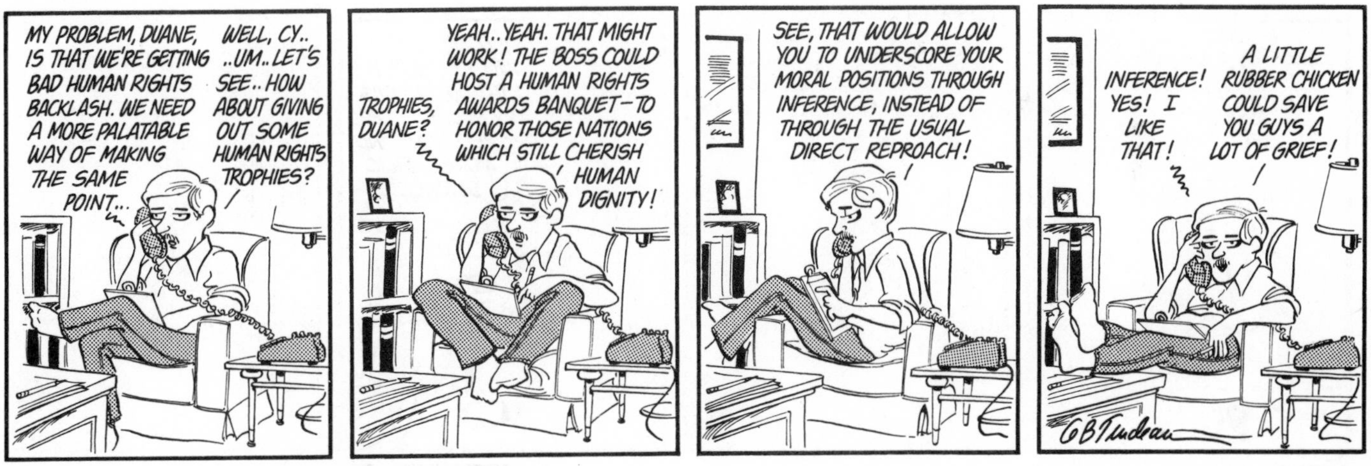
MY PROBLEM, DUANE, IS THAT WE'RE GETTING BAD HUMAN RIGHTS BACKLASH. WE NEED A MORE PALATABLE WAY OF MAKING THE SAME POINT...
WELL, CY.. ..UM.. LET'S SEE.. HOW ABOUT GIVING OUT SOME HUMAN RIGHTS TROPHIES?
TROPHIES, DUANE?
YEAH.. YEAH. THAT MIGHT WORK! THE BOSS COULD HOST A HUMAN RIGHTS AWARDS BANQUET—TO HONOR THOSE NATIONS WHICH STILL CHERISH HUMAN DIGNITY!
SEE, THAT WOULD ALLOW YOU TO UNDERSCORE YOUR MORAL POSITIONS THROUGH INFERENCE, INSTEAD OF THROUGH THE USUAL DIRECT REPROACH!
INFERENCE! YES! I LIKE THAT!
A LITTLE RUBBER CHICKEN COULD SAVE YOU GUYS A LOT OF GRIEF!
GBTrudeau

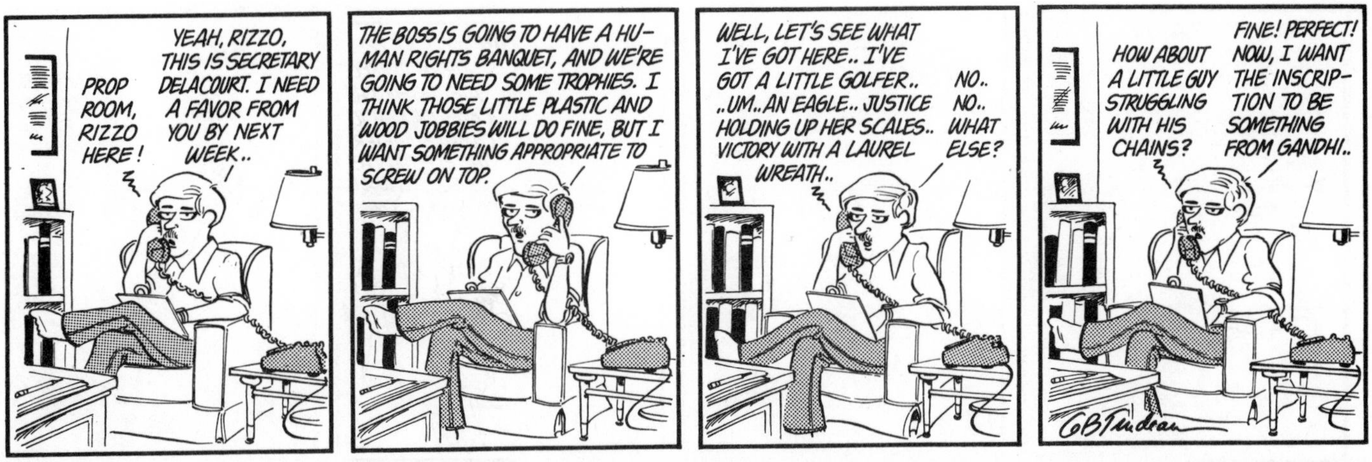
PROP ROOM, RIZZO HERE!
YEAH, RIZZO, THIS IS SECRETARY DELACOURT. I NEED A FAVOR FROM YOU BY NEXT WEEK..
THE BOSS IS GOING TO HAVE A HUMAN RIGHTS BANQUET, AND WE'RE GOING TO NEED SOME TROPHIES. I THINK THOSE LITTLE PLASTIC AND WOOD JOBBIES WILL DO FINE, BUT I WANT SOMETHING APPROPRIATE TO SCREW ON TOP.
WELL, LET'S SEE WHAT I'VE GOT HERE.. I'VE GOT A LITTLE GOLFER.. ..UM.. AN EAGLE.. JUSTICE HOLDING UP HER SCALES.. VICTORY WITH A LAUREL WREATH..
NO.. NO.. WHAT ELSE?
HOW ABOUT A LITTLE GUY STRUGGLING WITH HIS CHAINS?
FINE! PERFECT! NOW, I WANT THE INSCRIPTION TO BE SOMETHING FROM GANDHI..
GBTrudeau

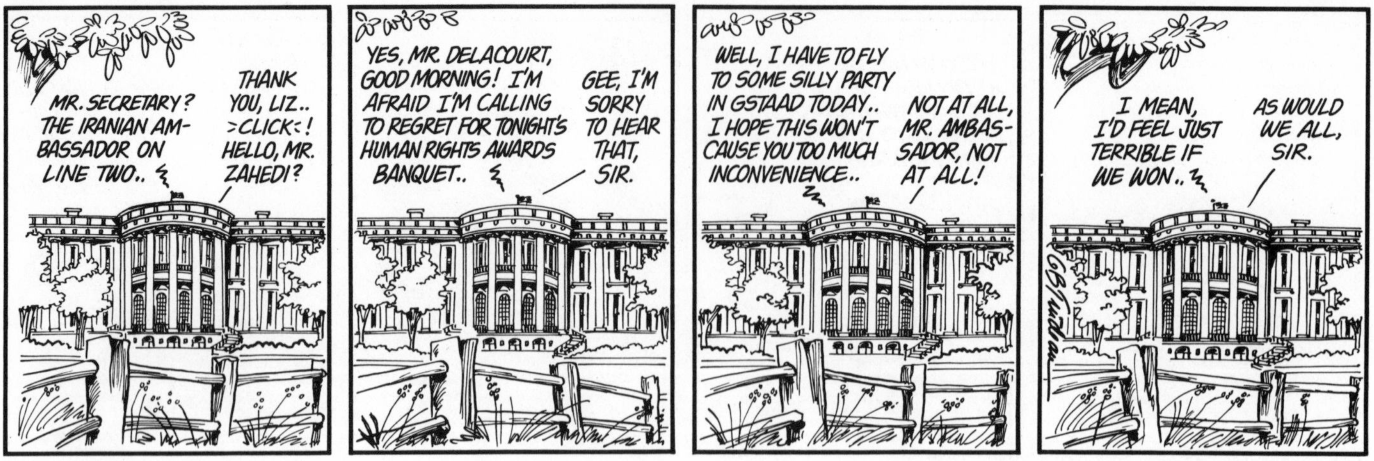
MR. SECRETARY? THE IRANIAN AMBASSADOR ON LINE TWO..
THANK YOU, LIZ.. >CLICK<! HELLO, MR. ZAHEDI?
YES, MR. DELACOURT, GOOD MORNING! I'M AFRAID I'M CALLING TO REGRET FOR TONIGHT'S HUMAN RIGHTS AWARDS BANQUET..
GEE, I'M SORRY TO HEAR THAT, SIR.
WELL, I HAVE TO FLY TO SOME SILLY PARTY IN GSTAAD TODAY.. I HOPE THIS WON'T CAUSE YOU TOO MUCH INCONVENIENCE..
NOT AT ALL, MR. AMBASSADOR, NOT AT ALL!
I MEAN, I'D FEEL JUST TERRIBLE IF WE WON..
AS WOULD WE ALL, SIR.
GBTrudeau

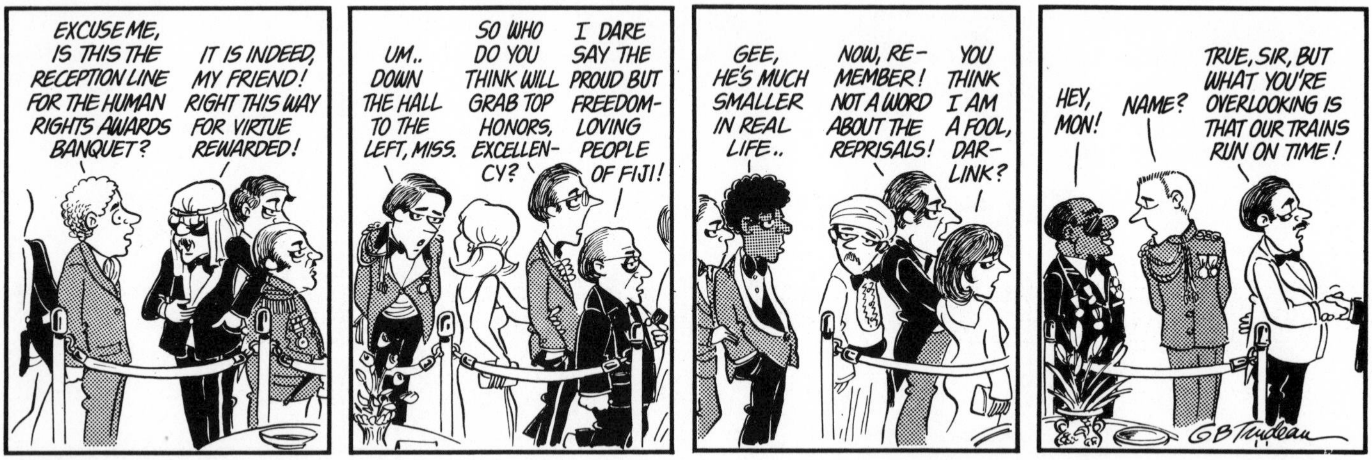
EXCUSE ME, IS THIS THE RECEPTION LINE FOR THE HUMAN RIGHTS AWARDS BANQUET?
IT IS INDEED, MY FRIEND! RIGHT THIS WAY FOR VIRTUE REWARDED!
UM.. DOWN THE HALL TO THE LEFT, MISS.
SO WHO DO YOU THINK WILL GRAB TOP HONORS, EXCELLENCY?
I DARE SAY THE PROUD BUT FREEDOM-LOVING PEOPLE OF FIJI!
GEE, HE'S MUCH SMALLER IN REAL LIFE..
NOW, REMEMBER! NOT A WORD ABOUT THE REPRISALS!
YOU THINK I AM A FOOL, DARLINK?
HEY, MON!
NAME?
TRUE, SIR, BUT WHAT YOU'RE OVERLOOKING IS THAT OUR TRAINS RUN ON TIME!
GBTrudeau

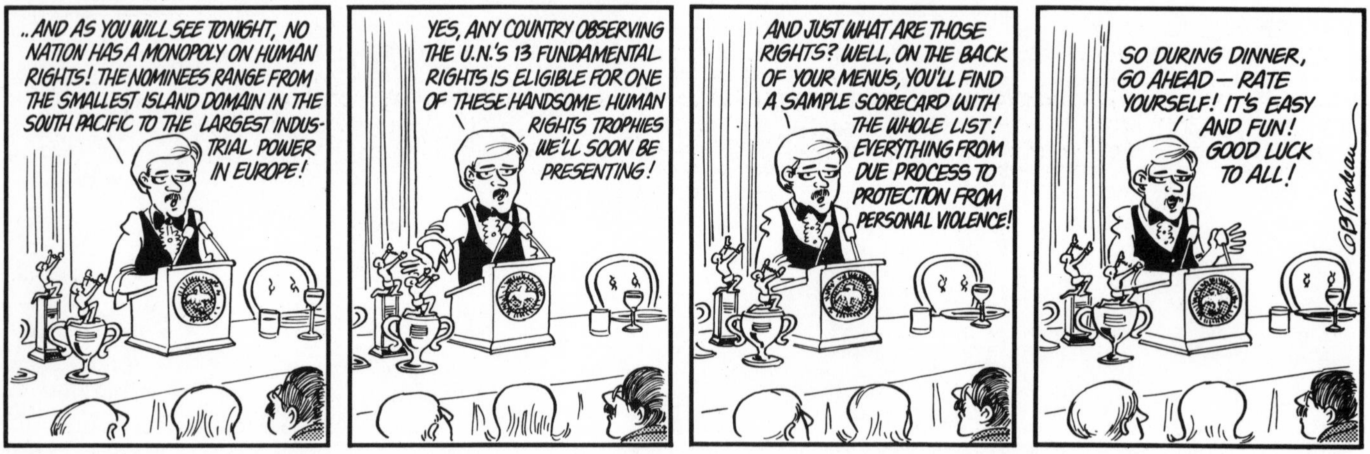
..AND AS YOU WILL SEE TONIGHT, NO NATION HAS A MONOPOLY ON HUMAN RIGHTS! THE NOMINEES RANGE FROM THE SMALLEST ISLAND DOMAIN IN THE SOUTH PACIFIC TO THE LARGEST INDUSTRIAL POWER IN EUROPE!
YES, ANY COUNTRY OBSERVING THE U.N.'S 13 FUNDAMENTAL RIGHTS IS ELIGIBLE FOR ONE OF THESE HANDSOME HUMAN RIGHTS TROPHIES WE'LL SOON BE PRESENTING!
AND JUST WHAT ARE THOSE RIGHTS? WELL, ON THE BACK OF YOUR MENUS, YOU'LL FIND A SAMPLE SCORECARD WITH THE WHOLE LIST! EVERYTHING FROM DUE PROCESS TO PROTECTION FROM PERSONAL VIOLENCE!
SO DURING DINNER, GO AHEAD — RATE YOURSELF! IT'S EASY AND FUN! GOOD LUCK TO ALL!
GBTrudeau

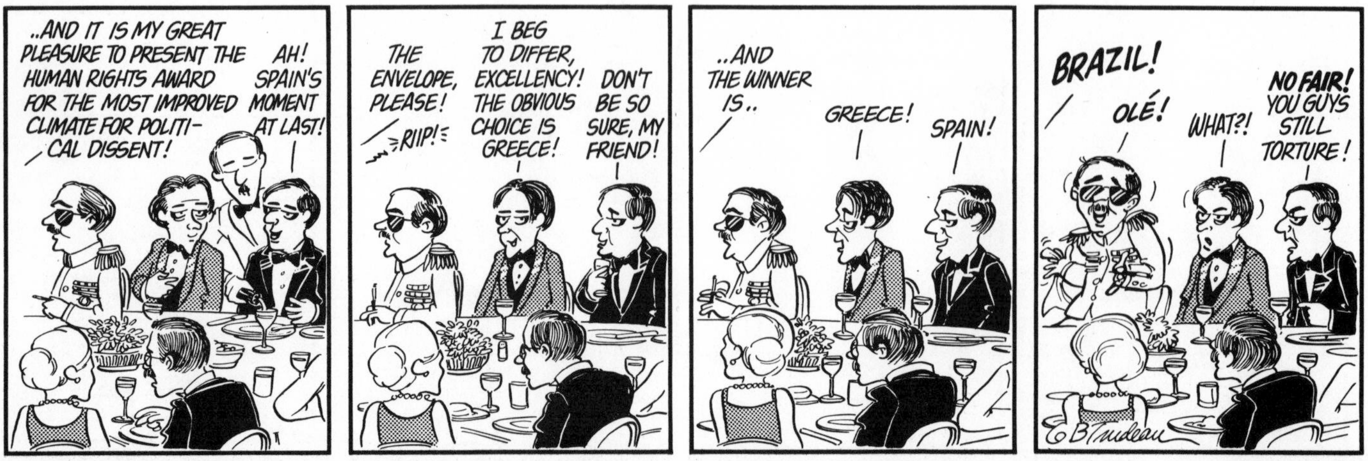
..AND IT IS MY GREAT PLEASURE TO PRESENT THE HUMAN RIGHTS AWARD FOR THE MOST IMPROVED CLIMATE FOR POLITICAL DISSENT!
AH! SPAIN'S MOMENT AT LAST!
THE ENVELOPE, PLEASE!
RIIP!
I BEG TO DIFFER, EXCELLENCY! THE OBVIOUS CHOICE IS GREECE!
DON'T BE SO SURE, MY FRIEND!
..AND THE WINNER IS..
GREECE!
SPAIN!
BRAZIL!
OLÉ!
WHAT?!
NO FAIR! YOU GUYS STILL TORTURE!
GBTrudeau

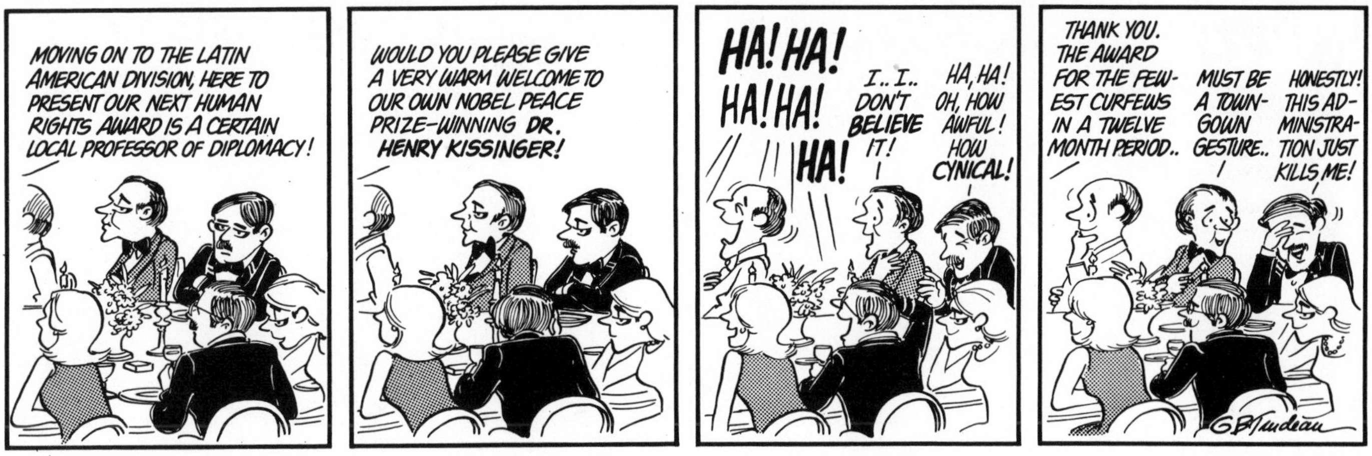
MOVING ON TO THE LATIN AMERICAN DIVISION, HERE TO PRESENT OUR NEXT HUMAN RIGHTS AWARD IS A CERTAIN LOCAL PROFESSOR OF DIPLOMACY!
WOULD YOU PLEASE GIVE A VERY WARM WELCOME TO OUR OWN NOBEL PEACE PRIZE-WINNING DR. HENRY KISSINGER!
HA! HA! HA! HA! HA!
I.. I.. DON'T BELIEVE IT!
HA, HA! OH, HOW AWFUL! HOW CYNICAL!
THANK YOU. THE AWARD FOR THE FEWEST CURFEWS IN A TWELVE MONTH PERIOD..
MUST BE A TOWN-GOWN GESTURE..
HONESTLY! THIS ADMINISTRATION JUST KILLS ME!
G B Trudeau

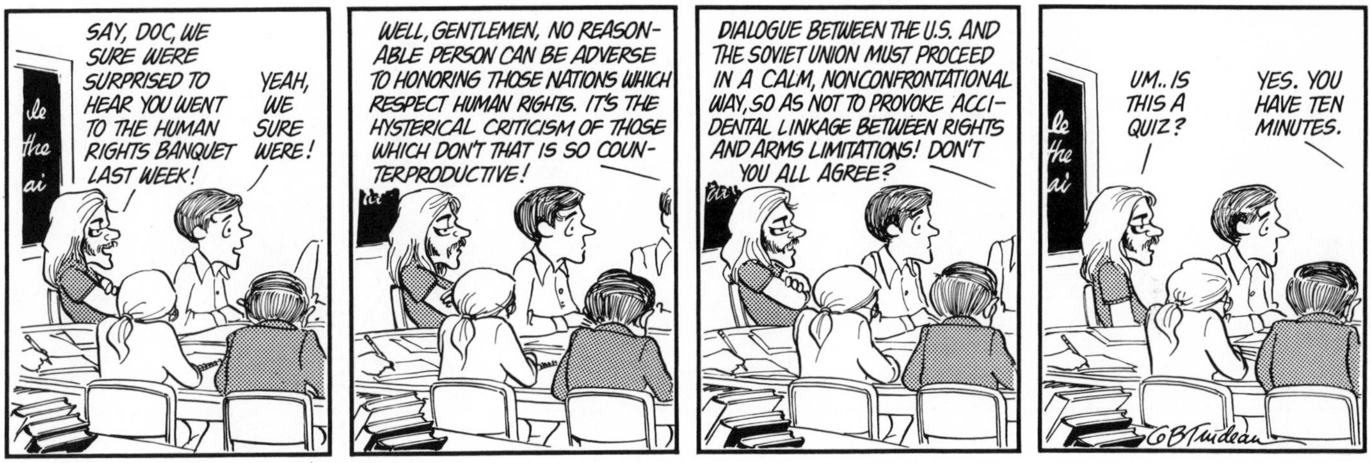
SAY, DOC, WE SURE WERE SURPRISED TO HEAR YOU WENT TO THE HUMAN RIGHTS BANQUET LAST WEEK!
YEAH, WE SURE WERE!
WELL, GENTLEMEN, NO REASONABLE PERSON CAN BE ADVERSE TO HONORING THOSE NATIONS WHICH RESPECT HUMAN RIGHTS. IT'S THE HYSTERICAL CRITICISM OF THOSE WHICH DON'T THAT IS SO COUNTERPRODUCTIVE!
DIALOGUE BETWEEN THE U.S. AND THE SOVIET UNION MUST PROCEED IN A CALM, NONCONFRONTATIONAL WAY, SO AS NOT TO PROVOKE ACCIDENTAL LINKAGE BETWEEN RIGHTS AND ARMS LIMITATIONS! DON'T YOU ALL AGREE?
UM.. IS THIS A QUIZ?
YES. YOU HAVE TEN MINUTES.
G B Trudeau

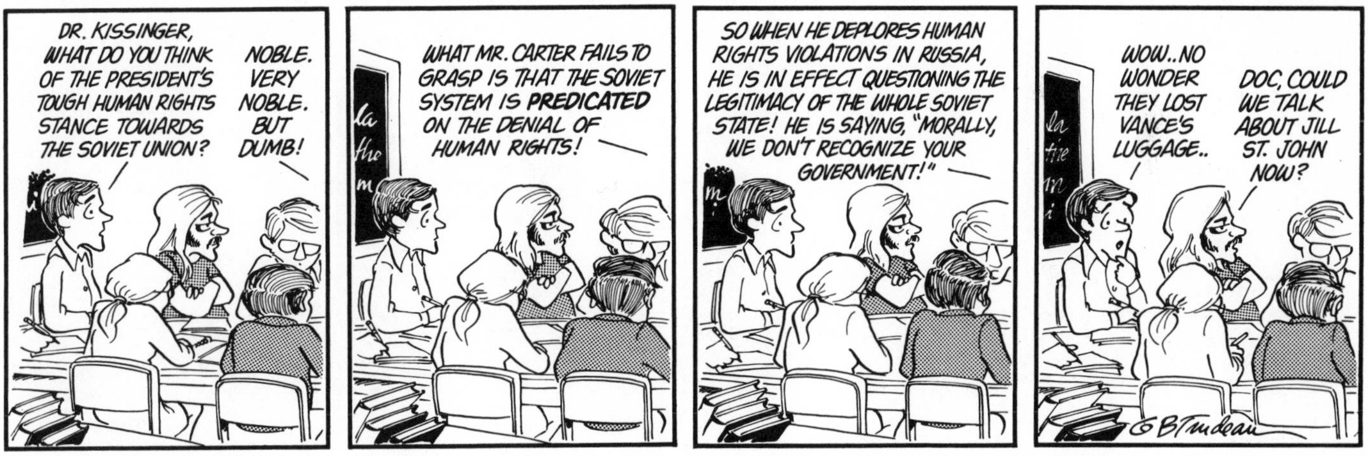
DR. KISSINGER, WHAT DO YOU THINK OF THE PRESIDENT'S TOUGH HUMAN RIGHTS STANCE TOWARDS THE SOVIET UNION?
NOBLE. VERY NOBLE. BUT DUMB!
WHAT MR. CARTER FAILS TO GRASP IS THAT THE SOVIET SYSTEM IS PREDICATED ON THE DENIAL OF HUMAN RIGHTS!
SO WHEN HE DEPLORES HUMAN RIGHTS VIOLATIONS IN RUSSIA, HE IS IN EFFECT QUESTIONING THE LEGITIMACY OF THE WHOLE SOVIET STATE! HE IS SAYING, "MORALLY, WE DON'T RECOGNIZE YOUR GOVERNMENT!"
WOW.. NO WONDER THEY LOST VANCE'S LUGGAGE..
DOC, COULD WE TALK ABOUT JILL ST. JOHN NOW?
G B Trudeau

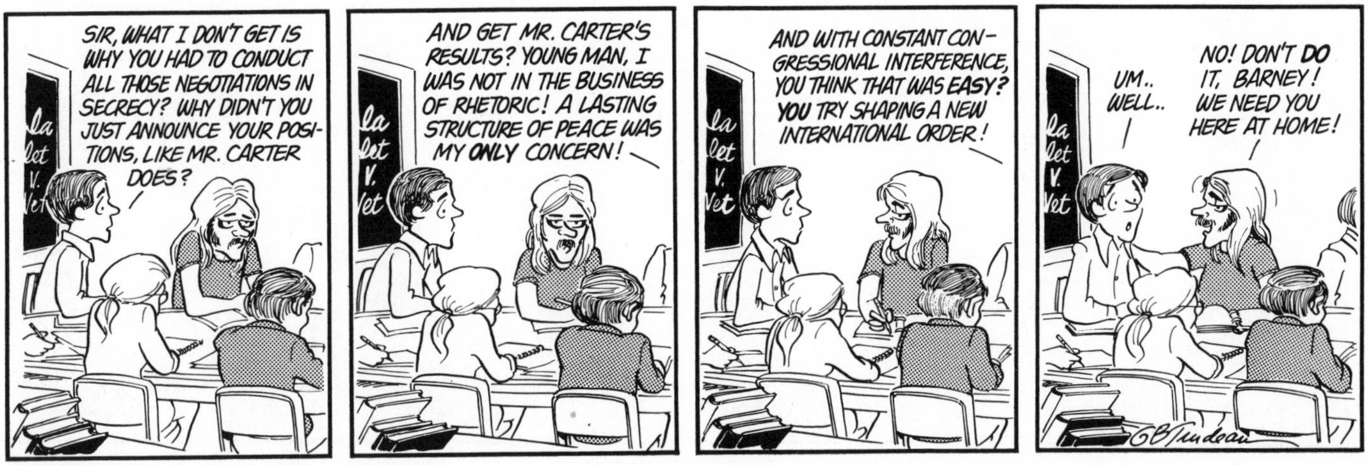
SIR, WHAT I DON'T GET IS WHY YOU HAD TO CONDUCT ALL THOSE NEGOTIATIONS IN SECRECY? WHY DIDN'T YOU JUST ANNOUNCE YOUR POSITIONS, LIKE MR. CARTER DOES?
AND GET MR. CARTER'S RESULTS? YOUNG MAN, I WAS NOT IN THE BUSINESS OF RHETORIC! A LASTING STRUCTURE OF PEACE WAS MY ONLY CONCERN!
AND WITH CONSTANT CONGRESSIONAL INTERFERENCE, YOU THINK THAT WAS EASY? YOU TRY SHAPING A NEW INTERNATIONAL ORDER!
UM.. WELL..
NO! DON'T DO IT, BARNEY! WE NEED YOU HERE AT HOME!
G B Trudeau

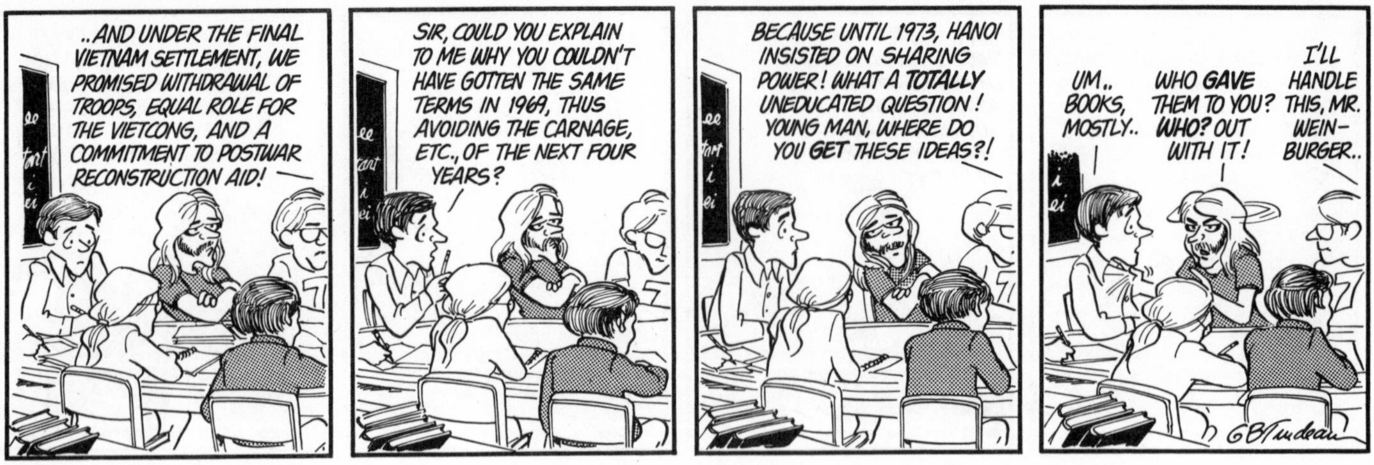
..AND UNDER THE FINAL VIETNAM SETTLEMENT, WE PROMISED WITHDRAWAL OF TROOPS, EQUAL ROLE FOR THE VIETCONG, AND A COMMITMENT TO POSTWAR RECONSTRUCTION AID!
SIR, COULD YOU EXPLAIN TO ME WHY YOU COULDN'T HAVE GOTTEN THE SAME TERMS IN 1969, THUS AVOIDING THE CARNAGE, ETC., OF THE NEXT FOUR YEARS?
BECAUSE UNTIL 1973, HANOI INSISTED ON SHARING POWER! WHAT A TOTALLY UNEDUCATED QUESTION! YOUNG MAN, WHERE DO YOU GET THESE IDEAS?!
UM.. BOOKS, MOSTLY..
WHO GAVE THEM TO YOU? WHO? OUT WITH IT!
I'LL HANDLE THIS, MR. WEIN-BURGER..
G B Trudeau

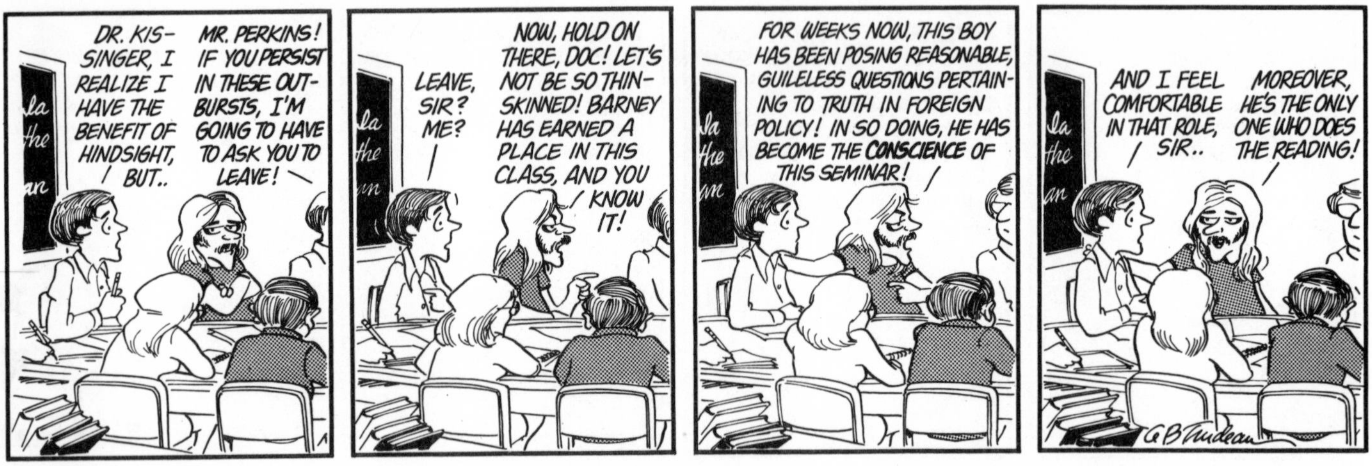
DR. KIS-SINGER, I REALIZE I HAVE THE BENEFIT OF HINDSIGHT, BUT..
MR. PERKINS! IF YOU PERSIST IN THESE OUT-BURSTS, I'M GOING TO HAVE TO ASK YOU TO LEAVE!
LEAVE, SIR? ME?
NOW, HOLD ON THERE, DOC! LET'S NOT BE SO THIN-SKINNED! BARNEY HAS EARNED A PLACE IN THIS CLASS, AND YOU KNOW IT!
FOR WEEKS NOW, THIS BOY HAS BEEN POSING REASONABLE, GUILELESS QUESTIONS PERTAINING TO TRUTH IN FOREIGN POLICY! IN SO DOING, HE HAS BECOME THE CONSCIENCE OF THIS SEMINAR!
AND I FEEL COMFORTABLE IN THAT ROLE, SIR..
MOREOVER, HE'S THE ONLY ONE WHO DOES THE READING!
G B Trudeau

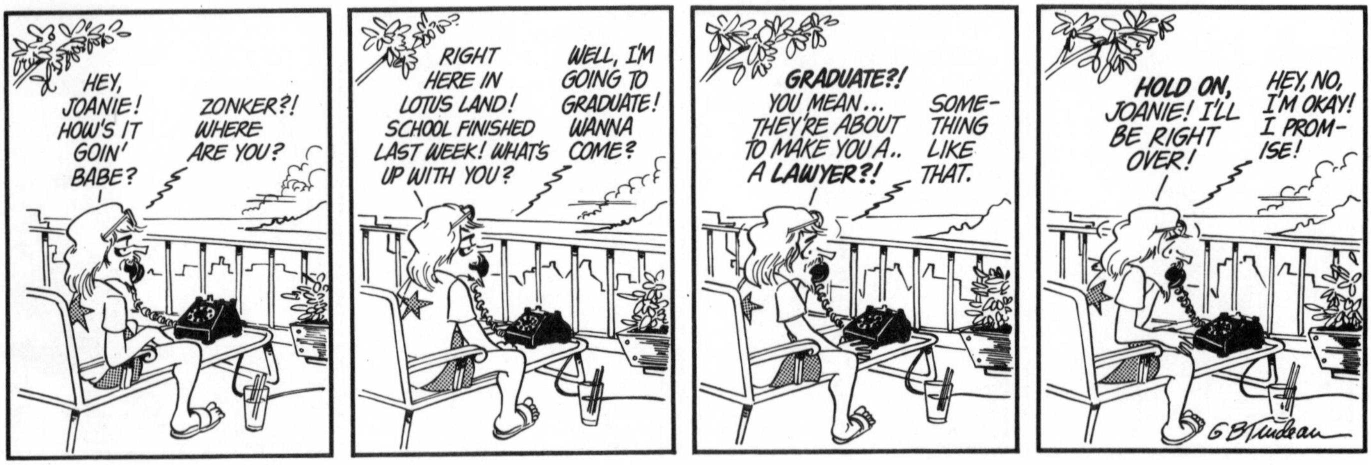
HEY, JOANIE! HOW'S IT GOIN' BABE?
ZONKER?! WHERE ARE YOU?
RIGHT HERE IN LOTUS LAND! SCHOOL FINISHED LAST WEEK! WHAT'S UP WITH YOU?
WELL, I'M GOING TO GRADUATE! WANNA COME?
GRADUATE?! YOU MEAN... THEY'RE ABOUT TO MAKE YOU A.. A LAWYER?!
SOME-THING LIKE THAT.
HOLD ON, JOANIE! I'LL BE RIGHT OVER!
HEY, NO, I'M OKAY! I PROM-ISE!
G B Trudeau

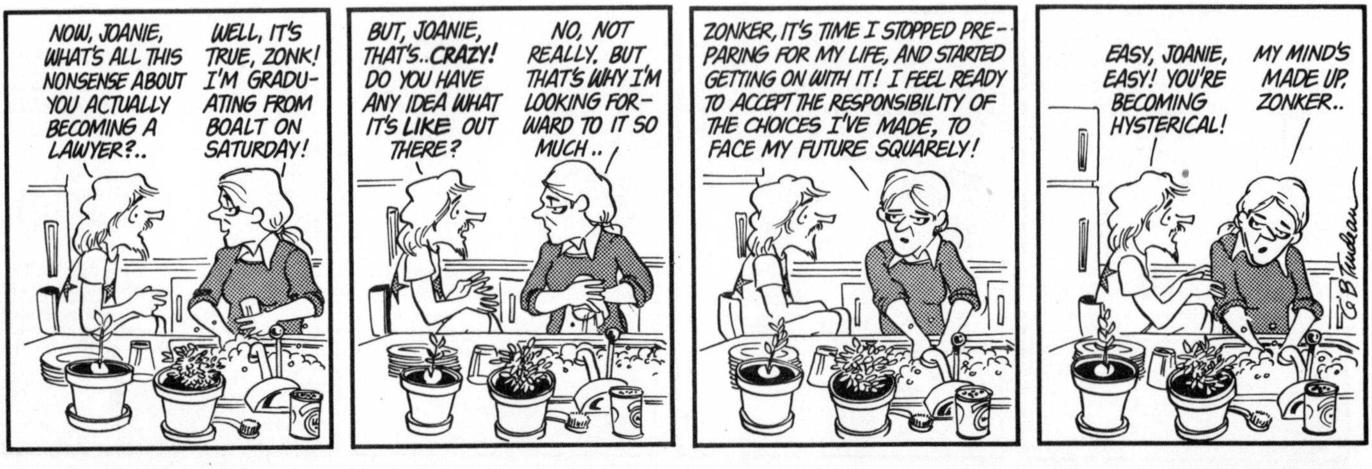
NOW, JOANIE, WHAT'S ALL THIS NONSENSE ABOUT YOU ACTUALLY BECOMING A LAWYER?..
WELL, IT'S TRUE, ZONK! I'M GRADU-ATING FROM BOALT ON SATURDAY!
BUT, JOANIE, THAT'S..CRAZY! DO YOU HAVE ANY IDEA WHAT IT'S LIKE OUT THERE?
NO, NOT REALLY. BUT THAT'S WHY I'M LOOKING FOR-WARD TO IT SO MUCH..
ZONKER, IT'S TIME I STOPPED PRE-PARING FOR MY LIFE, AND STARTED GETTING ON WITH IT! I FEEL READY TO ACCEPT THE RESPONSIBILITY OF THE CHOICES I'VE MADE, TO FACE MY FUTURE SQUARELY!
EASY, JOANIE, EASY! YOU'RE BECOMING HYSTERICAL!
MY MIND'S MADE UP, ZONKER..
G B Trudeau

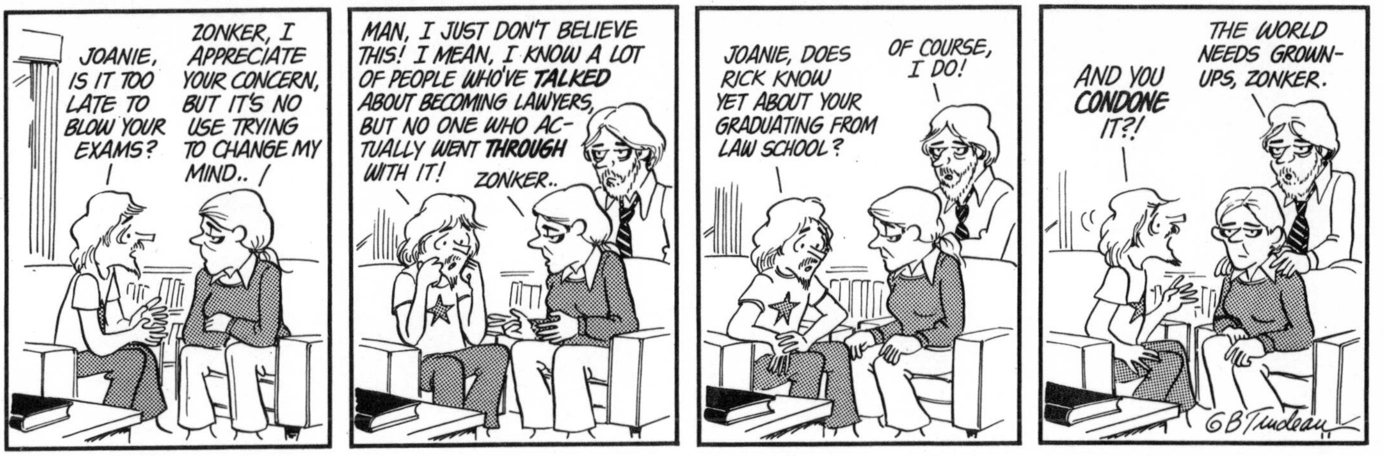
JOANIE, IS IT TOO LATE TO BLOW YOUR EXAMS?
ZONKER, I APPRECIATE YOUR CONCERN, BUT IT'S NO USE TRYING TO CHANGE MY MIND..
MAN, I JUST DON'T BELIEVE THIS! I MEAN, I KNOW A LOT OF PEOPLE WHO'VE TALKED ABOUT BECOMING LAWYERS, BUT NO ONE WHO ACTUALLY WENT THROUGH WITH IT!
ZONKER..
JOANIE, DOES RICK KNOW YET ABOUT YOUR GRADUATING FROM LAW SCHOOL?
OF COURSE, I DO!
AND YOU CONDONE IT?!
THE WORLD NEEDS GROWN-UPS, ZONKER.
GBTrudeau

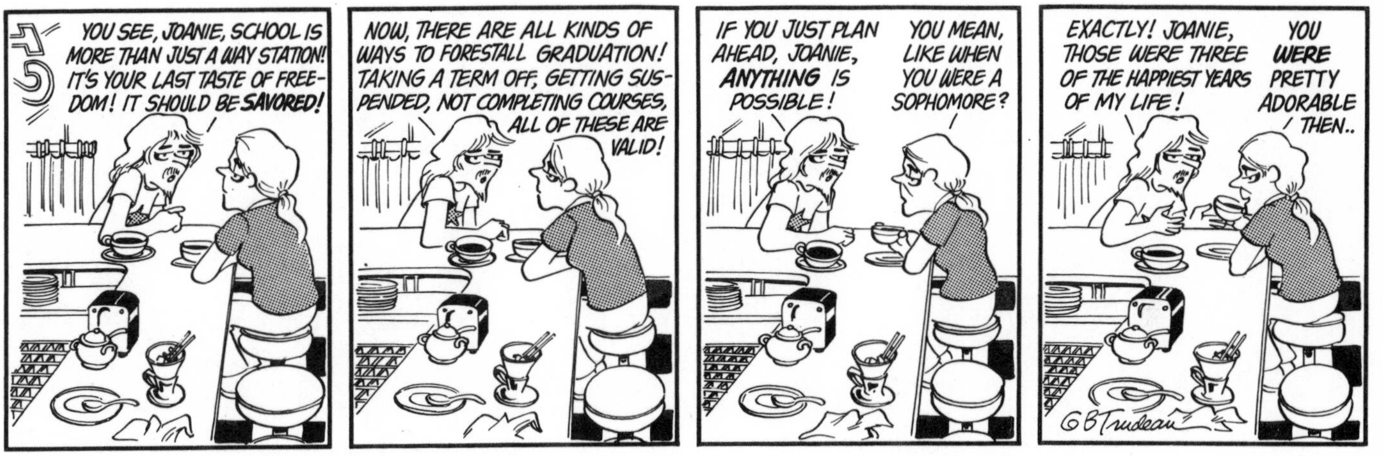
YOU SEE, JOANIE, SCHOOL IS MORE THAN JUST A WAY STATION! IT'S YOUR LAST TASTE OF FREEDOM! IT SHOULD BE SAVORED!
NOW, THERE ARE ALL KINDS OF WAYS TO FORESTALL GRADUATION! TAKING A TERM OFF, GETTING SUSPENDED, NOT COMPLETING COURSES, ALL OF THESE ARE VALID!
IF YOU JUST PLAN AHEAD, JOANIE, ANYTHING IS POSSIBLE!
YOU MEAN, LIKE WHEN YOU WERE A SOPHOMORE?
EXACTLY! JOANIE, THOSE WERE THREE OF THE HAPPIEST YEARS OF MY LIFE!
YOU WERE PRETTY ADORABLE THEN..
GBTrudeau

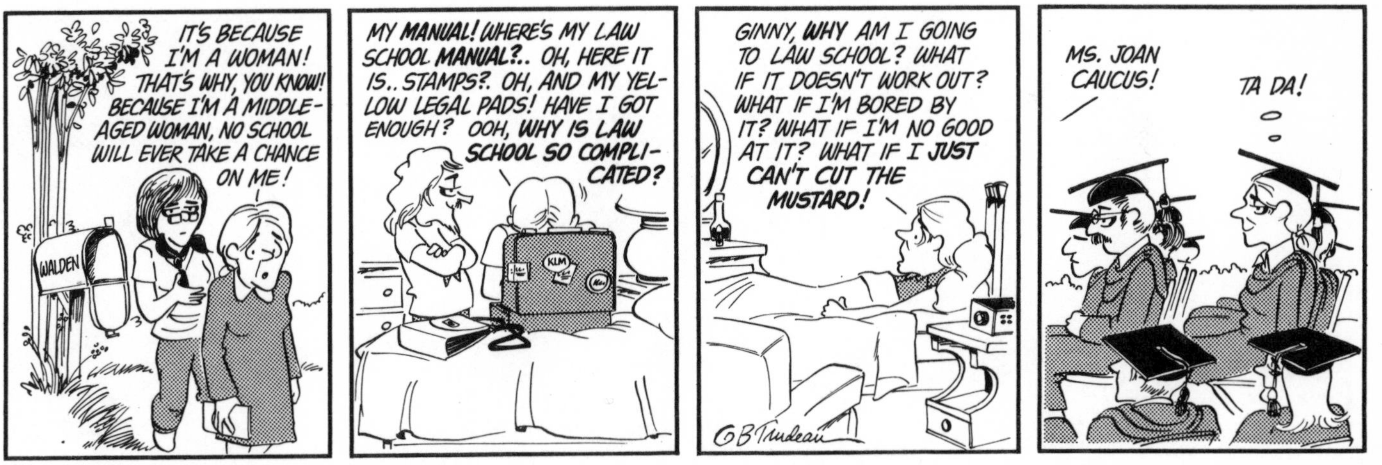
IT'S BECAUSE I'M A WOMAN! THAT'S WHY, YOU KNOW! BECAUSE I'M A MIDDLE-AGED WOMAN, NO SCHOOL WILL EVER TAKE A CHANCE ON ME!
WALDEN
MY MANUAL! WHERE'S MY LAW SCHOOL MANUAL?.. OH, HERE IT IS.. STAMPS?. OH, AND MY YELLOW LEGAL PADS! HAVE I GOT ENOUGH? OOH, WHY IS LAW SCHOOL SO COMPLICATED?
KLM
GINNY, WHY AM I GOING TO LAW SCHOOL? WHAT IF IT DOESN'T WORK OUT? WHAT IF I'M BORED BY IT? WHAT IF I'M NO GOOD AT IT? WHAT IF I JUST CAN'T CUT THE MUSTARD!
GBTrudeau
MS. JOAN CAUCUS!
TA DA!

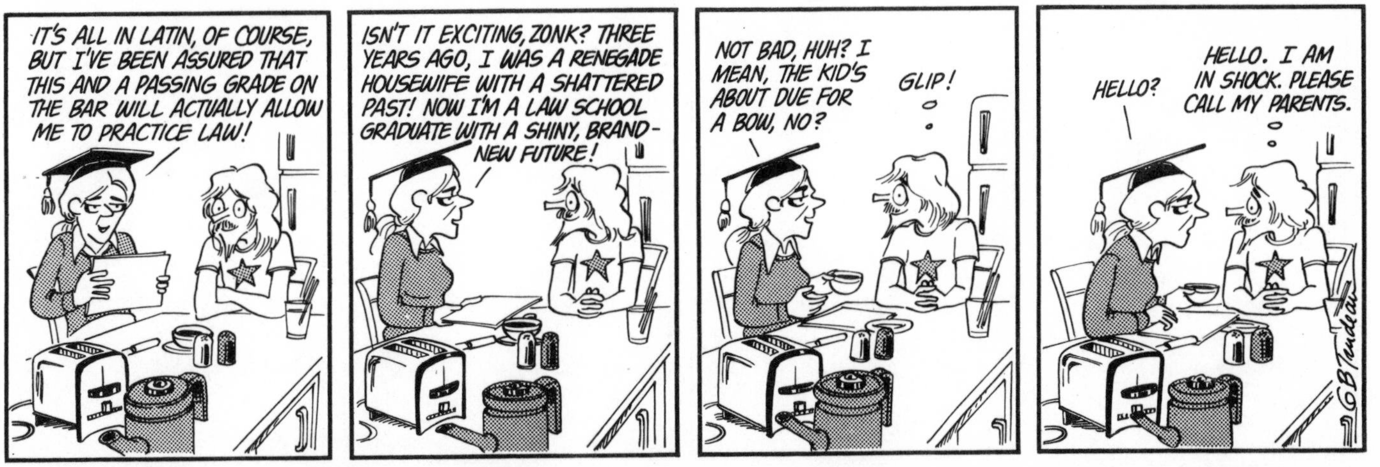
IT'S ALL IN LATIN, OF COURSE, BUT I'VE BEEN ASSURED THAT THIS AND A PASSING GRADE ON THE BAR WILL ACTUALLY ALLOW ME TO PRACTICE LAW!
ISN'T IT EXCITING, ZONK? THREE YEARS AGO, I WAS A RENEGADE HOUSEWIFE WITH A SHATTERED PAST! NOW I'M A LAW SCHOOL GRADUATE WITH A SHINY, BRAND-NEW FUTURE!
NOT BAD, HUH? I MEAN, THE KID'S ABOUT DUE FOR A BOW, NO?
GLIP!
HELLO?
HELLO. I AM IN SHOCK. PLEASE CALL MY PARENTS.
©GBTrudeau

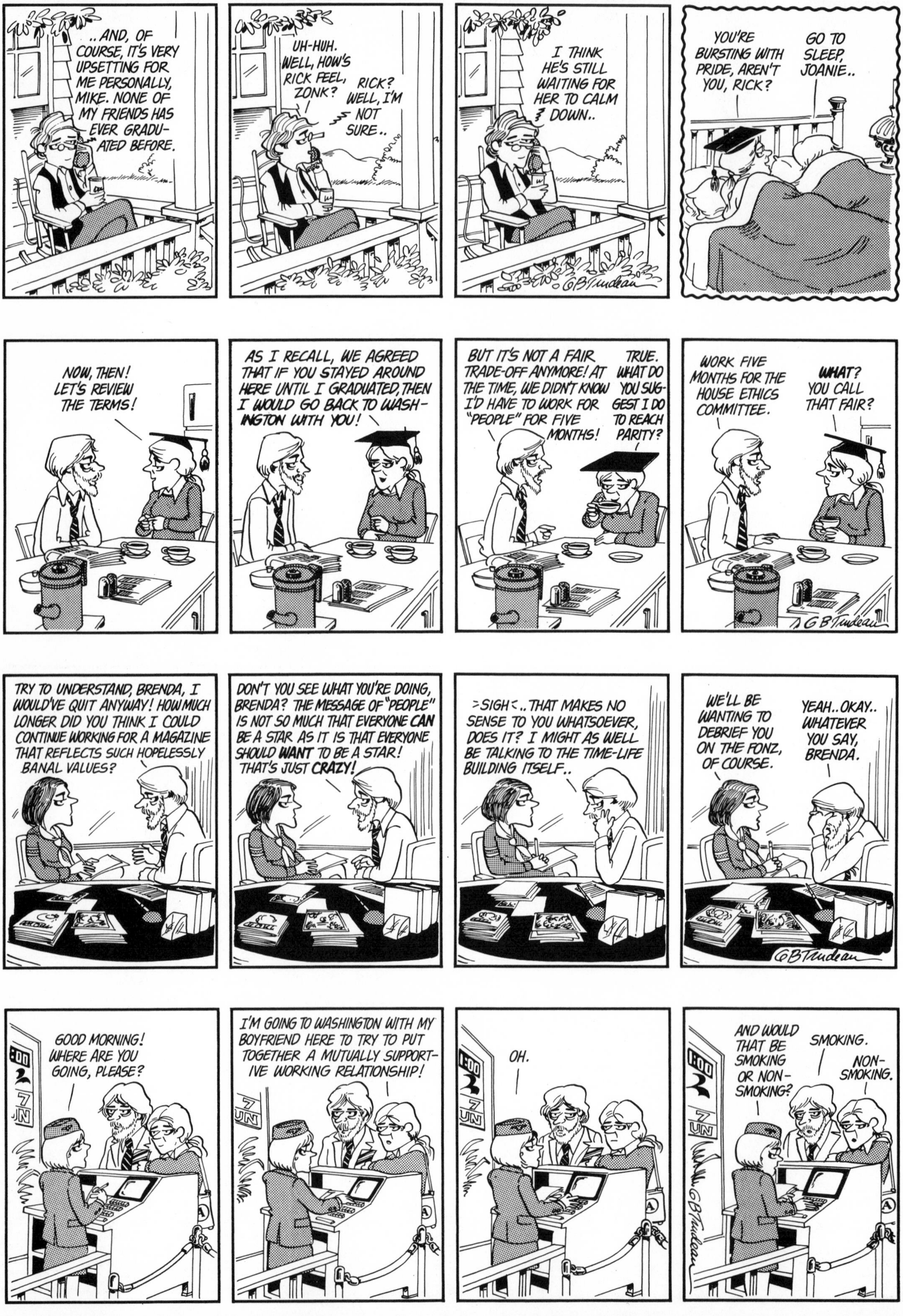
..AND, OF COURSE, IT'S VERY UPSETTING FOR ME PERSONALLY, MIKE. NONE OF MY FRIENDS HAS EVER GRADUATED BEFORE.
UH-HUH. WELL, HOW'S RICK FEEL, ZONK?
RICK? WELL, I'M NOT SURE..
I THINK HE'S STILL WAITING FOR HER TO CALM DOWN..
G B Trudeau
YOU'RE BURSTING WITH PRIDE, AREN'T YOU, RICK?
GO TO SLEEP, JOANIE..
NOW, THEN! LET'S REVIEW THE TERMS!
AS I RECALL, WE AGREED THAT IF YOU STAYED AROUND HERE UNTIL I GRADUATED, THEN I WOULD GO BACK TO WASHINGTON WITH YOU!
BUT IT'S NOT A FAIR TRADE-OFF ANYMORE! AT THE TIME, WE DIDN'T KNOW I'D HAVE TO WORK FOR "PEOPLE" FOR FIVE MONTHS!
TRUE. WHAT DO YOU SUGGEST I DO TO REACH PARITY?
WORK FIVE MONTHS FOR THE HOUSE ETHICS COMMITTEE.
WHAT? YOU CALL THAT FAIR?
G B Trudeau
TRY TO UNDERSTAND, BRENDA, I WOULD'VE QUIT ANYWAY! HOW MUCH LONGER DID YOU THINK I COULD CONTINUE WORKING FOR A MAGAZINE THAT REFLECTS SUCH HOPELESSLY BANAL VALUES?
DON'T YOU SEE WHAT YOU'RE DOING, BRENDA? THE MESSAGE OF "PEOPLE" IS NOT SO MUCH THAT EVERYONE CAN BE A STAR AS IT IS THAT EVERYONE SHOULD WANT TO BE A STAR! THAT'S JUST CRAZY!
>SIGH<..THAT MAKES NO SENSE TO YOU WHATSOEVER, DOES IT? I MIGHT AS WELL BE TALKING TO THE TIME-LIFE BUILDING ITSELF..
WE'LL BE WANTING TO DEBRIEF YOU ON THE FONZ, OF COURSE.
YEAH..OKAY.. WHATEVER YOU SAY, BRENDA.
G B Trudeau
GOOD MORNING! WHERE ARE YOU GOING, PLEASE?
I'M GOING TO WASHINGTON WITH MY BOYFRIEND HERE TO TRY TO PUT TOGETHER A MUTUALLY SUPPORTIVE WORKING RELATIONSHIP!
OH.
AND WOULD THAT BE SMOKING OR NON-SMOKING?
SMOKING.
NON-SMOKING.
G B Trudeau

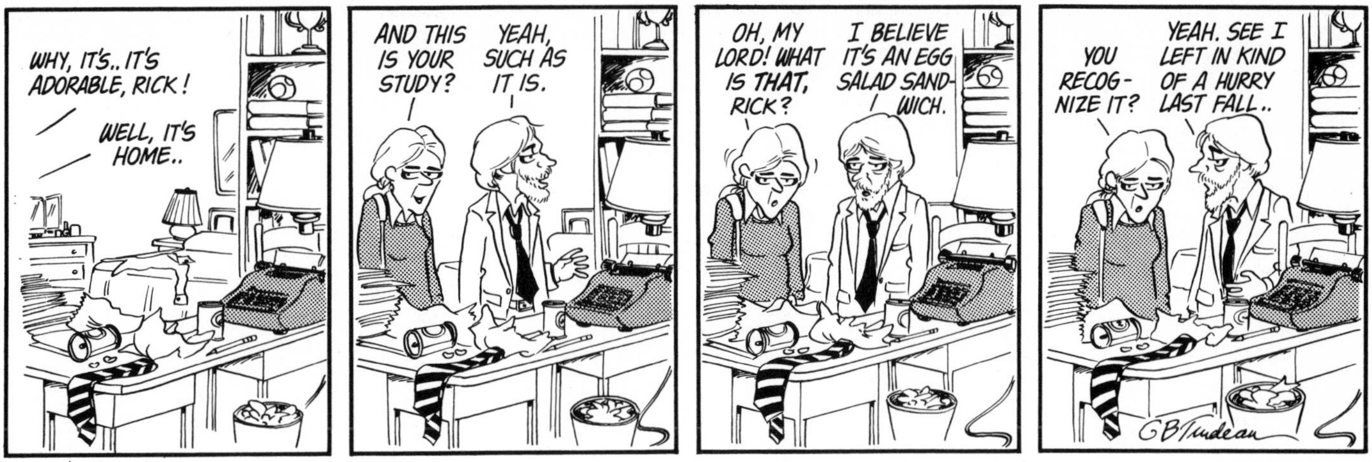
WHY, IT'S.. IT'S ADORABLE, RICK!
WELL, IT'S HOME..
AND THIS IS YOUR STUDY?
YEAH, SUCH AS IT IS.
OH, MY LORD! WHAT IS THAT, RICK?
I BELIEVE IT'S AN EGG SALAD SANDWICH.
YOU RECOGNIZE IT?
YEAH. SEE I LEFT IN KIND OF A HURRY LAST FALL..
GBTrudeau

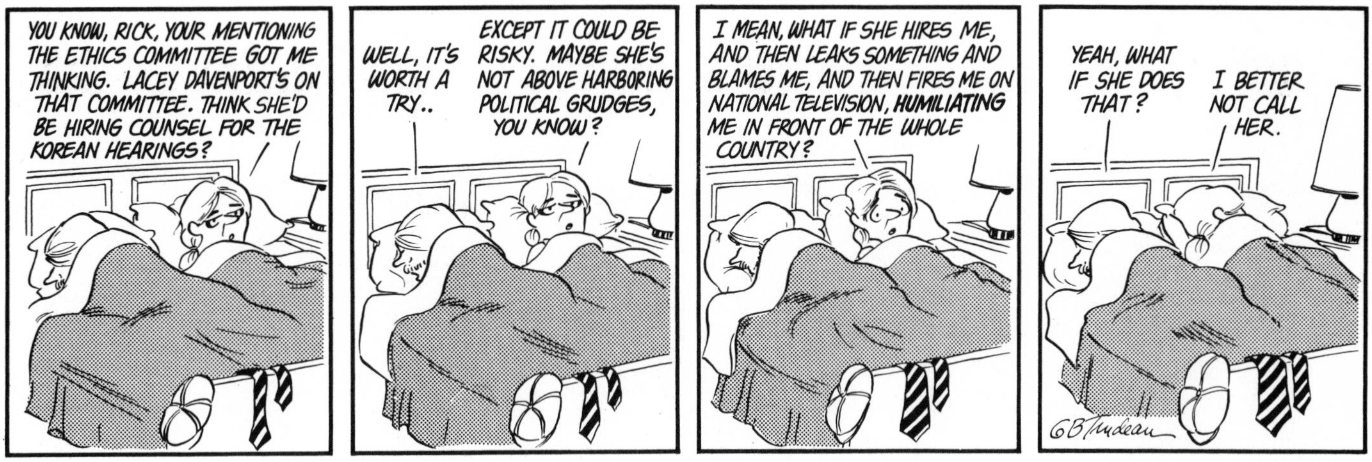
YOU KNOW, RICK, YOUR MENTIONING THE ETHICS COMMITTEE GOT ME THINKING. LACEY DAVENPORT'S ON THAT COMMITTEE. THINK SHE'D BE HIRING COUNSEL FOR THE KOREAN HEARINGS?
WELL, IT'S WORTH A TRY..
EXCEPT IT COULD BE RISKY. MAYBE SHE'S NOT ABOVE HARBORING POLITICAL GRUDGES, YOU KNOW?
I MEAN, WHAT IF SHE HIRES ME, AND THEN LEAKS SOMETHING AND BLAMES ME, AND THEN FIRES ME ON NATIONAL TELEVISION, HUMILIATING ME IN FRONT OF THE WHOLE COUNTRY?
YEAH, WHAT IF SHE DOES THAT?
I BETTER NOT CALL HER.
GBTrudeau

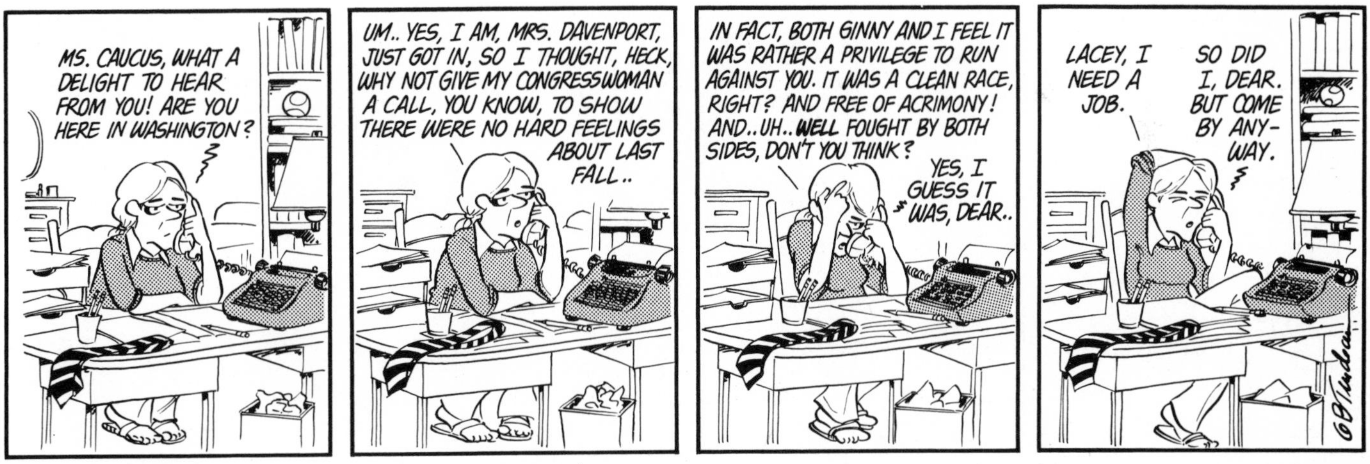
MS. CAUCUS, WHAT A DELIGHT TO HEAR FROM YOU! ARE YOU HERE IN WASHINGTON?
UM.. YES, I AM, MRS. DAVENPORT, JUST GOT IN, SO I THOUGHT, HECK, WHY NOT GIVE MY CONGRESSWOMAN A CALL, YOU KNOW, TO SHOW THERE WERE NO HARD FEELINGS ABOUT LAST FALL..
IN FACT, BOTH GINNY AND I FEEL IT WAS RATHER A PRIVILEGE TO RUN AGAINST YOU. IT WAS A CLEAN RACE, RIGHT? AND FREE OF ACRIMONY! AND..UH.. WELL FOUGHT BY BOTH SIDES, DON'T YOU THINK?
YES, I GUESS IT WAS, DEAR..
LACEY, I NEED A JOB.
SO DID I, DEAR. BUT COME BY ANYWAY.
GBTrudeau

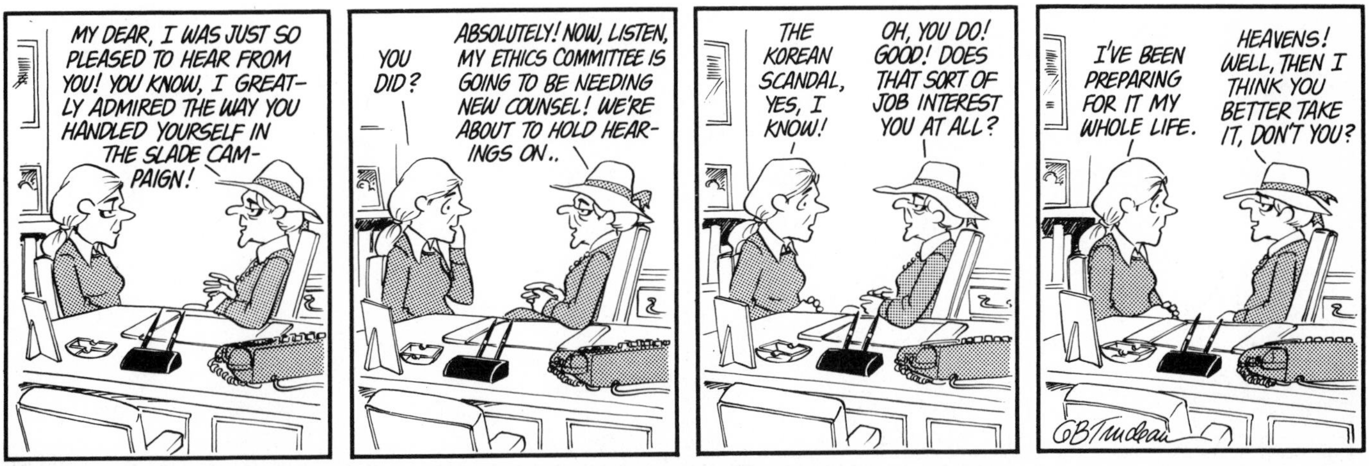
MY DEAR, I WAS JUST SO PLEASED TO HEAR FROM YOU! YOU KNOW, I GREATLY ADMIRED THE WAY YOU HANDLED YOURSELF IN THE SLADE CAMPAIGN!
YOU DID?
ABSOLUTELY! NOW, LISTEN, MY ETHICS COMMITTEE IS GOING TO BE NEEDING NEW COUNSEL! WE'RE ABOUT TO HOLD HEARINGS ON..
THE KOREAN SCANDAL, YES, I KNOW!
OH, YOU DO! GOOD! DOES THAT SORT OF JOB INTEREST YOU AT ALL?
I'VE BEEN PREPARING FOR IT MY WHOLE LIFE.
HEAVENS! WELL, THEN I THINK YOU BETTER TAKE IT, DON'T YOU?
GBTrudeau

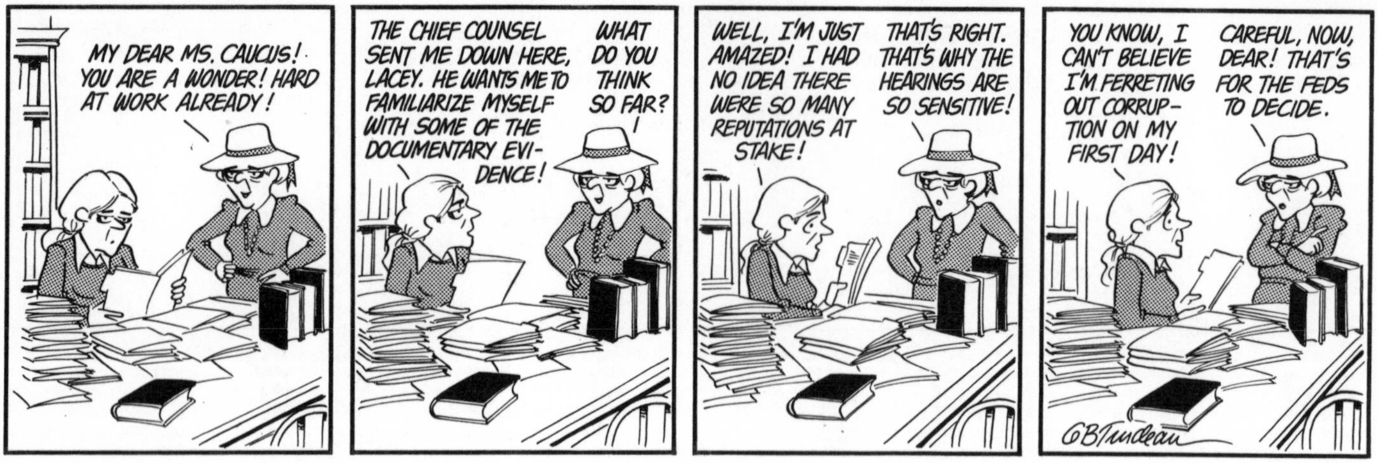
MY DEAR MS. CAUCUS! YOU ARE A WONDER! HARD AT WORK ALREADY!
THE CHIEF COUNSEL SENT ME DOWN HERE, LACEY. HE WANTS ME TO FAMILIARIZE MYSELF WITH SOME OF THE DOCUMENTARY EVI-DENCE!
WHAT DO YOU THINK SO FAR?
WELL, I'M JUST AMAZED! I HAD NO IDEA THERE WERE SO MANY REPUTATIONS AT STAKE!
THAT'S RIGHT. THAT'S WHY THE HEARINGS ARE SO SENSITIVE!
YOU KNOW, I CAN'T BELIEVE I'M FERRETING OUT CORRUP-TION ON MY FIRST DAY!
CAREFUL, NOW, DEAR! THAT'S FOR THE FEDS TO DECIDE.

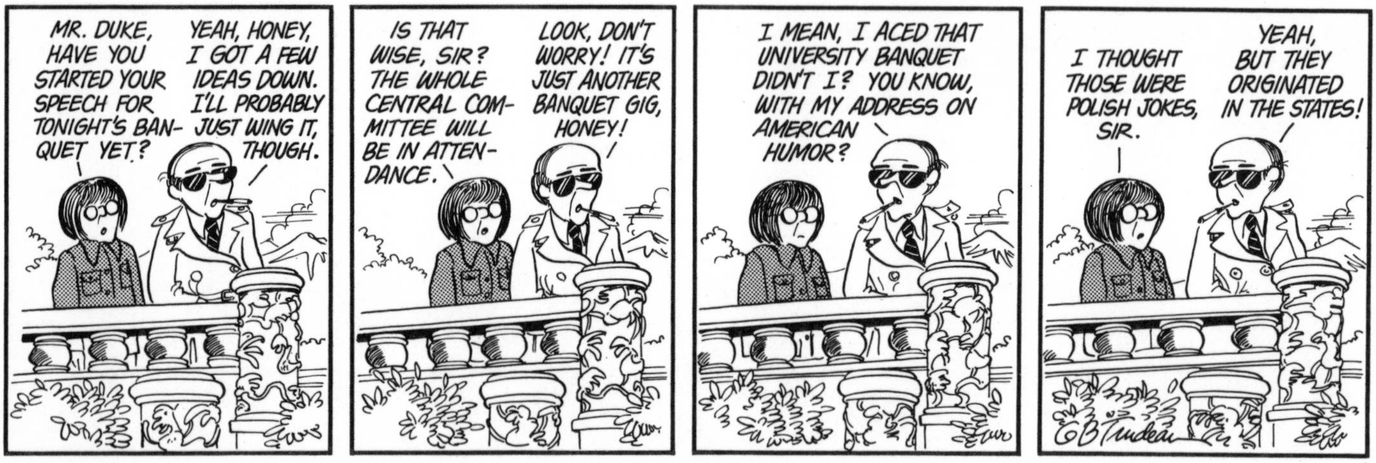
MR. DUKE, HAVE YOU STARTED YOUR SPEECH FOR TONIGHT'S BAN-QUET YET?
YEAH, HONEY, I GOT A FEW IDEAS DOWN. I'LL PROBABLY JUST WING IT, THOUGH.
IS THAT WISE, SIR? THE WHOLE CENTRAL COM-MITTEE WILL BE IN ATTEN-DANCE.
LOOK, DON'T WORRY! IT'S JUST ANOTHER BANQUET GIG, HONEY!
I MEAN, I ACED THAT UNIVERSITY BANQUET DIDN'T I? YOU KNOW, WITH MY ADDRESS ON AMERICAN HUMOR?
I THOUGHT THOSE WERE POLISH JOKES, SIR.
YEAH, BUT THEY ORIGINATED IN THE STATES!

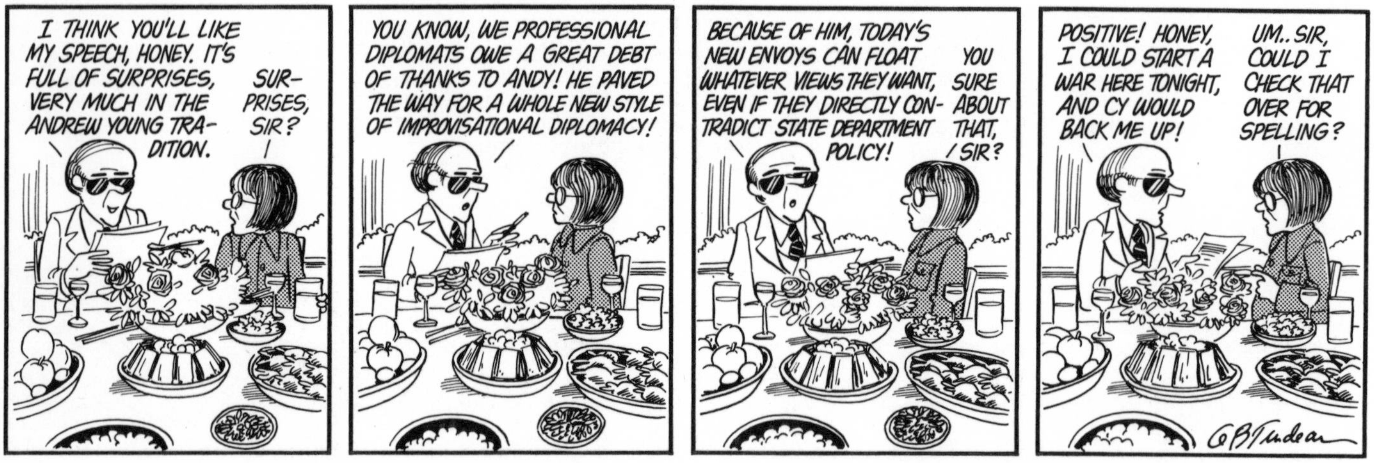
I THINK YOU'LL LIKE MY SPEECH, HONEY. IT'S FULL OF SURPRISES, VERY MUCH IN THE ANDREW YOUNG TRA-DITION.
SUR-PRISES, SIR?
YOU KNOW, WE PROFESSIONAL DIPLOMATS OWE A GREAT DEBT OF THANKS TO ANDY! HE PAVED THE WAY FOR A WHOLE NEW STYLE OF IMPROVISATIONAL DIPLOMACY!
BECAUSE OF HIM, TODAY'S NEW ENVOYS CAN FLOAT WHATEVER VIEWS THEY WANT, EVEN IF THEY DIRECTLY CON-TRADICT STATE DEPARTMENT POLICY!
YOU SURE ABOUT THAT, SIR?
POSITIVE! HONEY, I COULD START A WAR HERE TONIGHT, AND CY WOULD BACK ME UP!
UM.. SIR, COULD I CHECK THAT OVER FOR SPELLING?

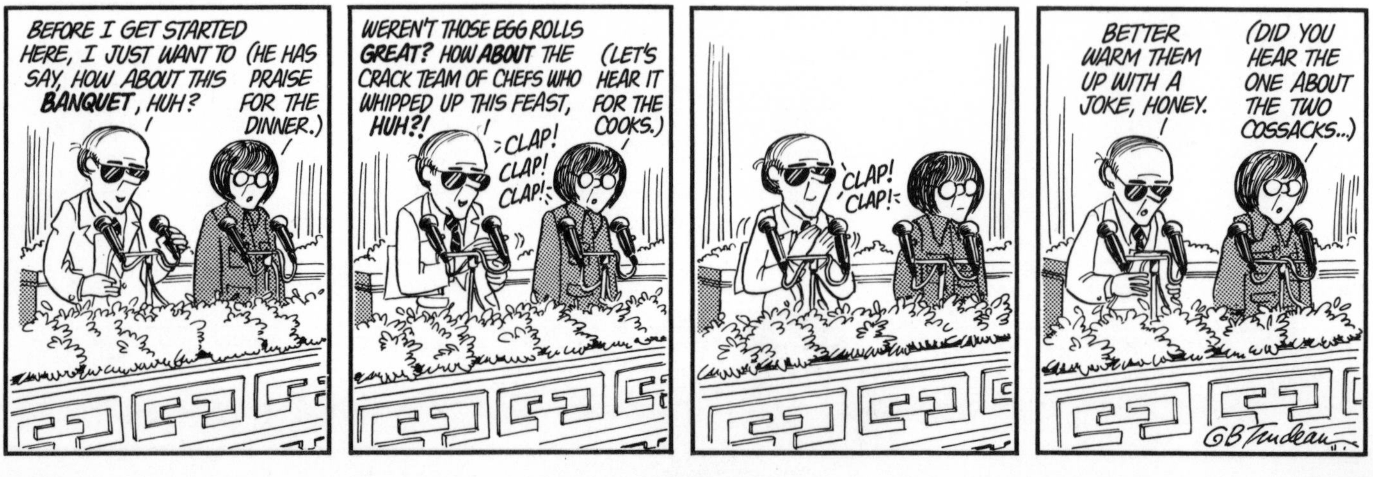
BEFORE I GET STARTED HERE, I JUST WANT TO SAY, HOW ABOUT THIS BANQUET, HUH?
(HE HAS PRAISE FOR THE DINNER.)
WEREN'T THOSE EGG ROLLS GREAT? HOW ABOUT THE CRACK TEAM OF CHEFS WHO WHIPPED UP THIS FEAST, HUH?!
(LET'S HEAR IT FOR THE COOKS.)
CLAP! CLAP! CLAP!
CLAP! CLAP!
BETTER WARM THEM UP WITH A JOKE, HONEY.
(DID YOU HEAR THE ONE ABOUT THE TWO COSSACKS...)

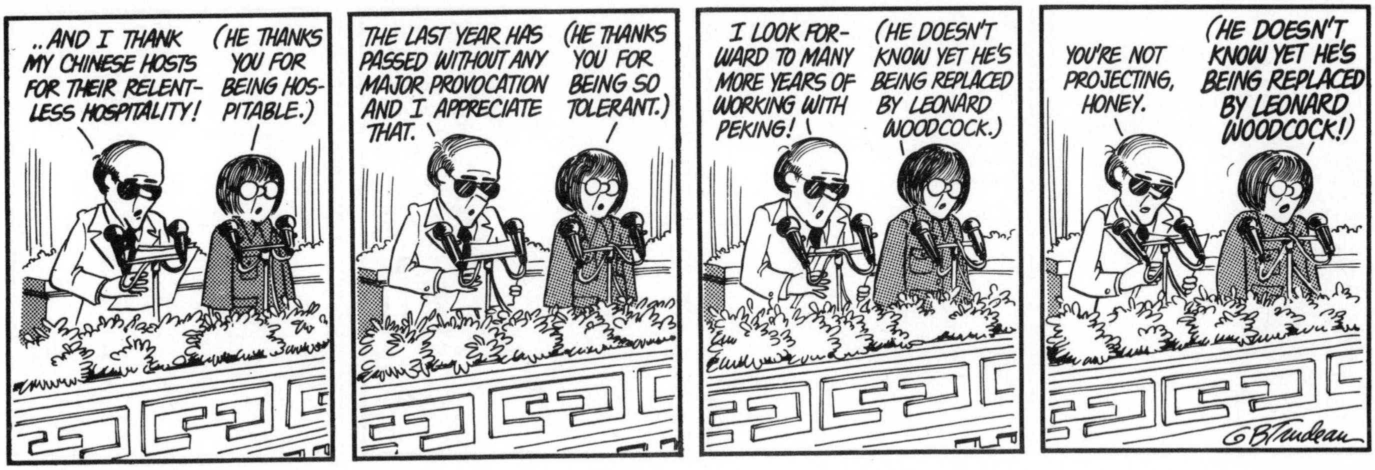
..AND I THANK MY CHINESE HOSTS FOR THEIR RELENTLESS HOSPITALITY!
(HE THANKS YOU FOR BEING HOSPITABLE.)
THE LAST YEAR HAS PASSED WITHOUT ANY MAJOR PROVOCATION AND I APPRECIATE THAT.
(HE THANKS YOU FOR BEING SO TOLERANT.)
I LOOK FORWARD TO MANY MORE YEARS OF WORKING WITH PEKING!
(HE DOESN'T KNOW YET HE'S BEING REPLACED BY LEONARD WOODCOCK.)
YOU'RE NOT PROJECTING, HONEY.
(HE DOESN'T KNOW YET HE'S BEING REPLACED BY LEONARD WOODCOCK!)
G.B. Trudeau

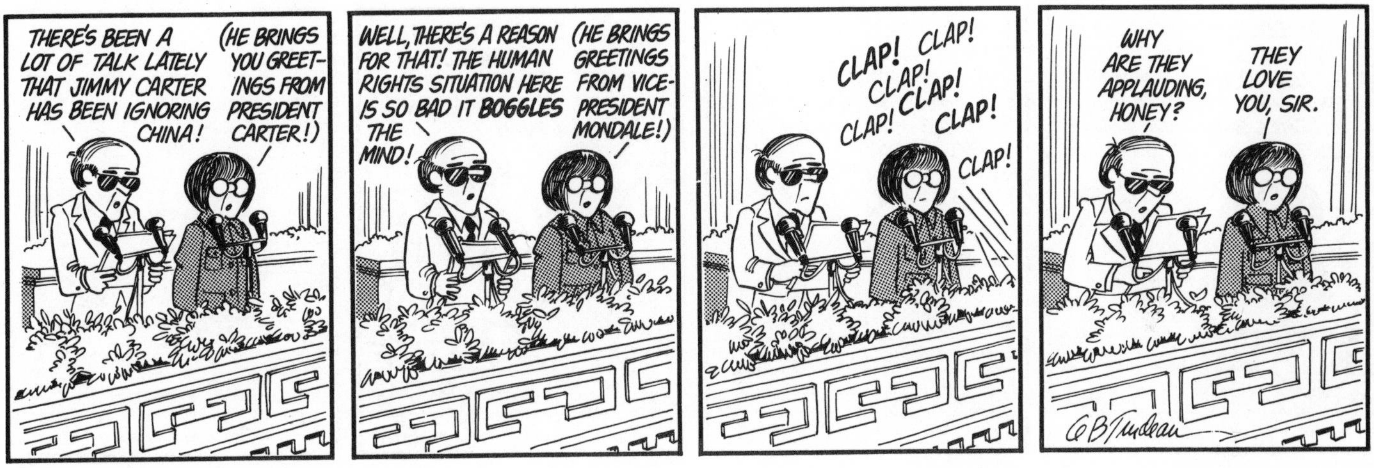
THERE'S BEEN A LOT OF TALK LATELY THAT JIMMY CARTER HAS BEEN IGNORING CHINA!
(HE BRINGS YOU GREETINGS FROM PRESIDENT CARTER!)
WELL, THERE'S A REASON FOR THAT! THE HUMAN RIGHTS SITUATION HERE IS SO BAD IT BOGGLES THE MIND!
(HE BRINGS GREETINGS FROM VICE-PRESIDENT MONDALE!)
CLAP! CLAP! CLAP! CLAP! CLAP! CLAP! CLAP!
WHY ARE THEY APPLAUDING, HONEY?
THEY LOVE YOU, SIR.
G.B. Trudeau

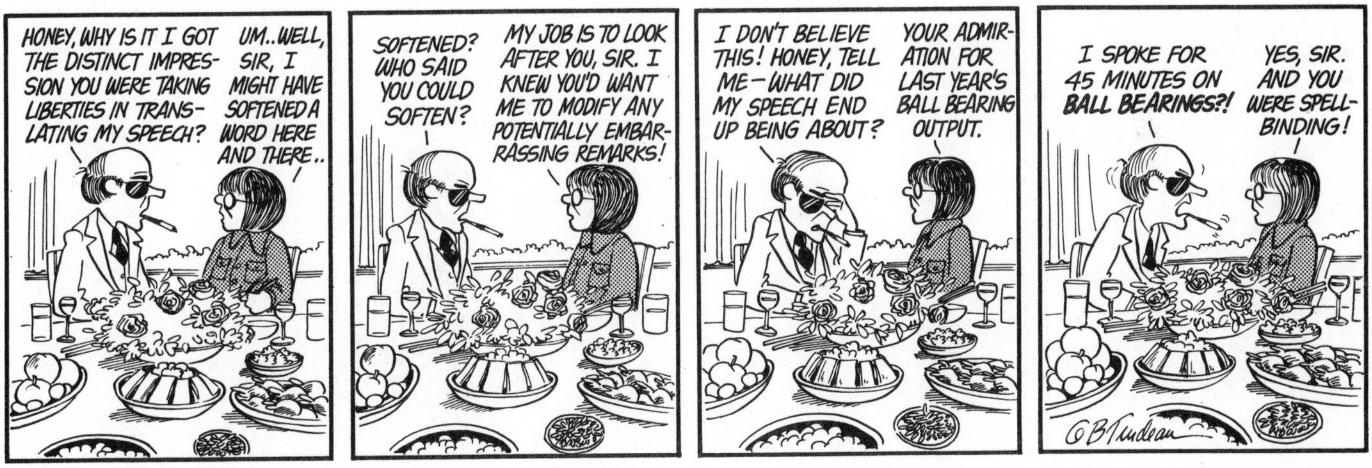
HONEY, WHY IS IT I GOT THE DISTINCT IMPRESSION YOU WERE TAKING LIBERTIES IN TRANSLATING MY SPEECH?
UM..WELL, SIR, I MIGHT HAVE SOFTENED A WORD HERE AND THERE..
SOFTENED? WHO SAID YOU COULD SOFTEN?
MY JOB IS TO LOOK AFTER YOU, SIR. I KNEW YOU'D WANT ME TO MODIFY ANY POTENTIALLY EMBARRASSING REMARKS!
I DON'T BELIEVE THIS! HONEY, TELL ME—WHAT DID MY SPEECH END UP BEING ABOUT?
YOUR ADMIRATION FOR LAST YEAR'S BALL BEARING OUTPUT.
I SPOKE FOR 45 MINUTES ON BALL BEARINGS?!
YES, SIR. AND YOU WERE SPELLBINDING!
G.B. Trudeau

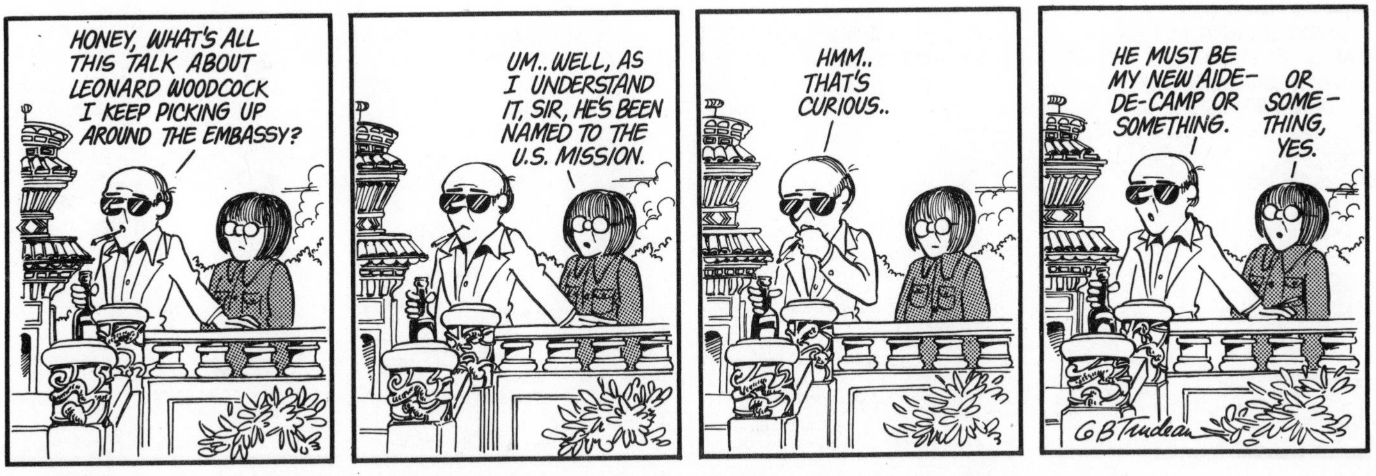
HONEY, WHAT'S ALL THIS TALK ABOUT LEONARD WOODCOCK I KEEP PICKING UP AROUND THE EMBASSY?
UM..WELL, AS I UNDERSTAND IT, SIR, HE'S BEEN NAMED TO THE U.S. MISSION.
HMM.. THAT'S CURIOUS..
HE MUST BE MY NEW AIDE-DE-CAMP OR SOMETHING.
OR SOMETHING, YES.
G.B. Trudeau

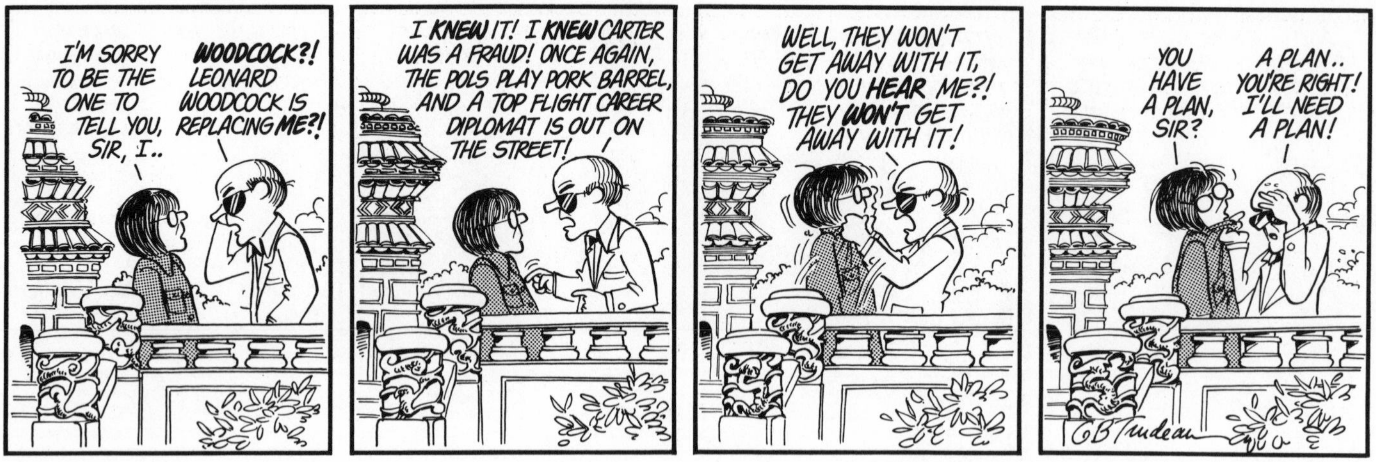
I'M SORRY TO BE THE ONE TO TELL YOU, SIR, I..
WOODCOCK?! LEONARD WOODCOCK IS REPLACING ME?!
I KNEW IT! I KNEW CARTER WAS A FRAUD! ONCE AGAIN, THE POLS PLAY PORK BARREL, AND A TOP FLIGHT CAREER DIPLOMAT IS OUT ON THE STREET!
WELL, THEY WON'T GET AWAY WITH IT, DO YOU HEAR ME?! THEY WON'T GET AWAY WITH IT!
YOU HAVE A PLAN, SIR?
A PLAN.. YOU'RE RIGHT! I'LL NEED A PLAN!
GBTrudeau

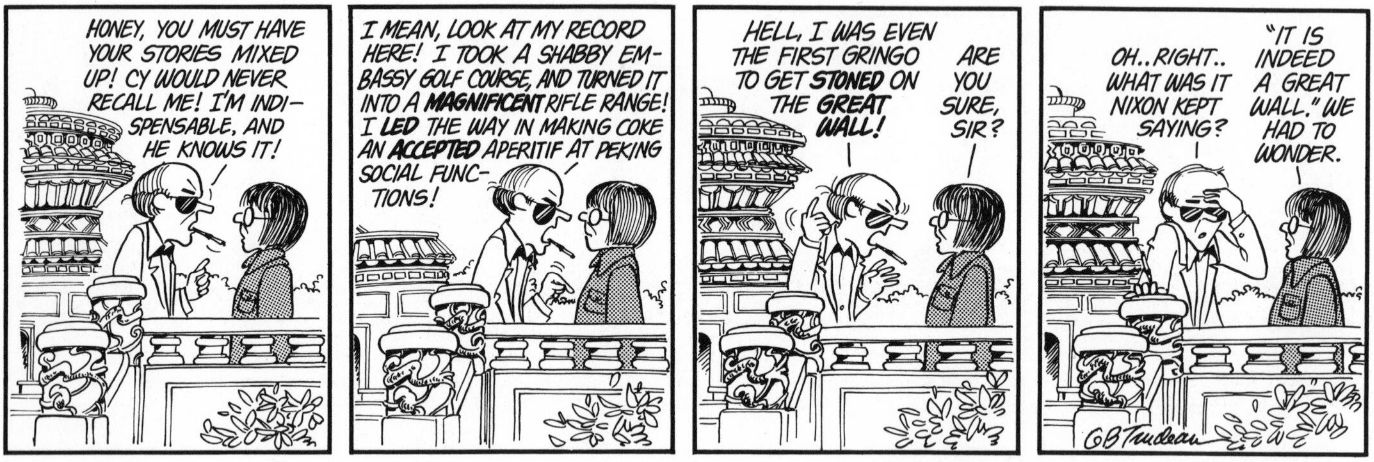
HONEY, YOU MUST HAVE YOUR STORIES MIXED UP! CY WOULD NEVER RECALL ME! I'M INDISPENSABLE, AND HE KNOWS IT!
I MEAN, LOOK AT MY RECORD HERE! I TOOK A SHABBY EMBASSY GOLF COURSE, AND TURNED IT INTO A MAGNIFICENT RIFLE RANGE! I LED THE WAY IN MAKING COKE AN ACCEPTED APERITIF AT PEKING SOCIAL FUNCTIONS!
HELL, I WAS EVEN THE FIRST GRINGO TO GET STONED ON THE GREAT WALL!
ARE YOU SURE, SIR?
OH.. RIGHT.. WHAT WAS IT NIXON KEPT SAYING?
"IT IS INDEED A GREAT WALL." WE HAD TO WONDER.
GBTrudeau

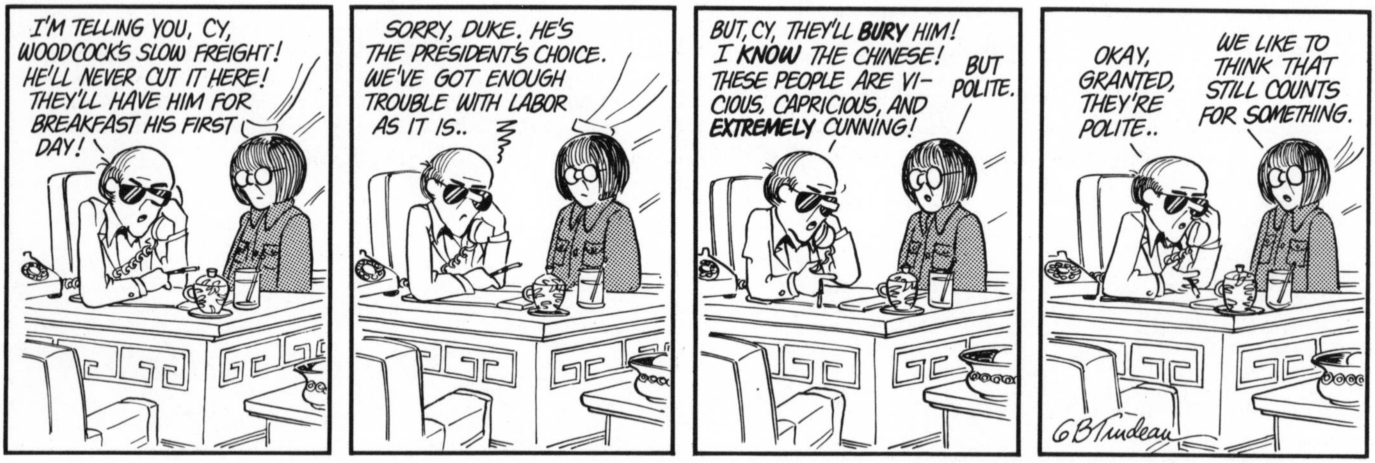
I'M TELLING YOU, CY, WOODCOCK'S SLOW FREIGHT! HE'LL NEVER CUT IT HERE! THEY'LL HAVE HIM FOR BREAKFAST HIS FIRST DAY!
SORRY, DUKE. HE'S THE PRESIDENT'S CHOICE. WE'VE GOT ENOUGH TROUBLE WITH LABOR AS IT IS..
BUT, CY, THEY'LL BURY HIM! I KNOW THE CHINESE! THESE PEOPLE ARE VICIOUS, CAPRICIOUS, AND EXTREMELY CUNNING!
BUT POLITE.
OKAY, GRANTED, THEY'RE POLITE..
WE LIKE TO THINK THAT STILL COUNTS FOR SOMETHING.
GBTrudeau

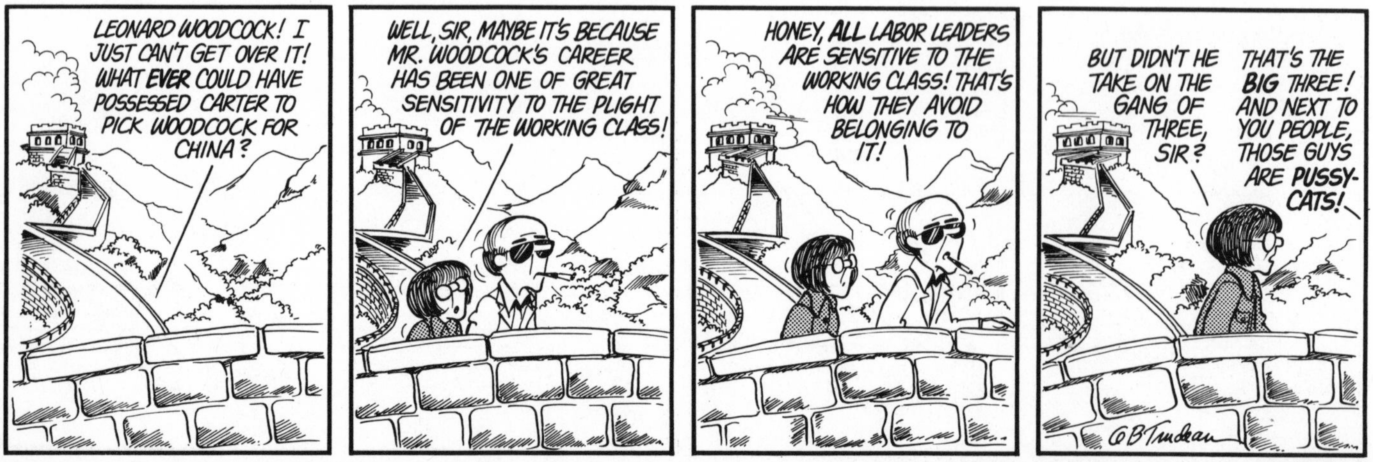
LEONARD WOODCOCK! I JUST CAN'T GET OVER IT! WHAT EVER COULD HAVE POSSESSED CARTER TO PICK WOODCOCK FOR CHINA?
WELL, SIR, MAYBE IT'S BECAUSE MR. WOODCOCK'S CAREER HAS BEEN ONE OF GREAT SENSITIVITY TO THE PLIGHT OF THE WORKING CLASS!
HONEY, ALL LABOR LEADERS ARE SENSITIVE TO THE WORKING CLASS! THAT'S HOW THEY AVOID BELONGING TO IT!
BUT DIDN'T HE TAKE ON THE GANG OF THREE, SIR?
THAT'S THE BIG THREE! AND NEXT TO YOU PEOPLE, THOSE GUYS ARE PUSSY-CATS!
GBTrudeau

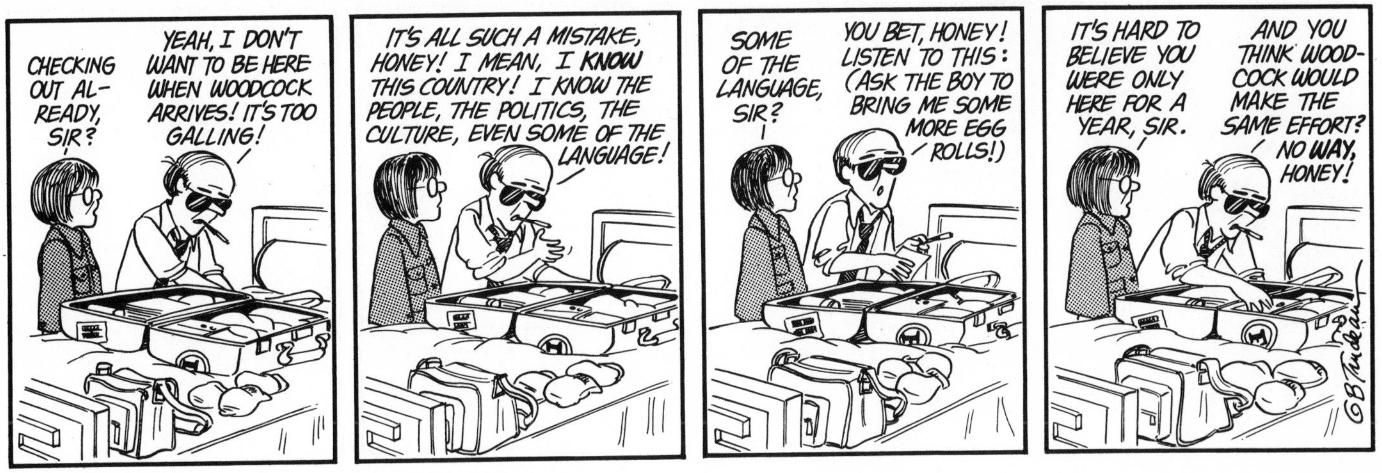
CHECKING OUT AL-READY, SIR?
YEAH, I DON'T WANT TO BE HERE WHEN WOODCOCK ARRIVES! IT'S TOO GALLING!
IT'S ALL SUCH A MISTAKE, HONEY! I MEAN, I KNOW THIS COUNTRY! I KNOW THE PEOPLE, THE POLITICS, THE CULTURE, EVEN SOME OF THE LANGUAGE!
SOME OF THE LANGUAGE, SIR?
YOU BET, HONEY! LISTEN TO THIS: (ASK THE BOY TO BRING ME SOME MORE EGG ROLLS!)
IT'S HARD TO BELIEVE YOU WERE ONLY HERE FOR A YEAR, SIR.
AND YOU THINK WOOD-COCK WOULD MAKE THE SAME EFFORT? NO WAY, HONEY!
GB Trudeau

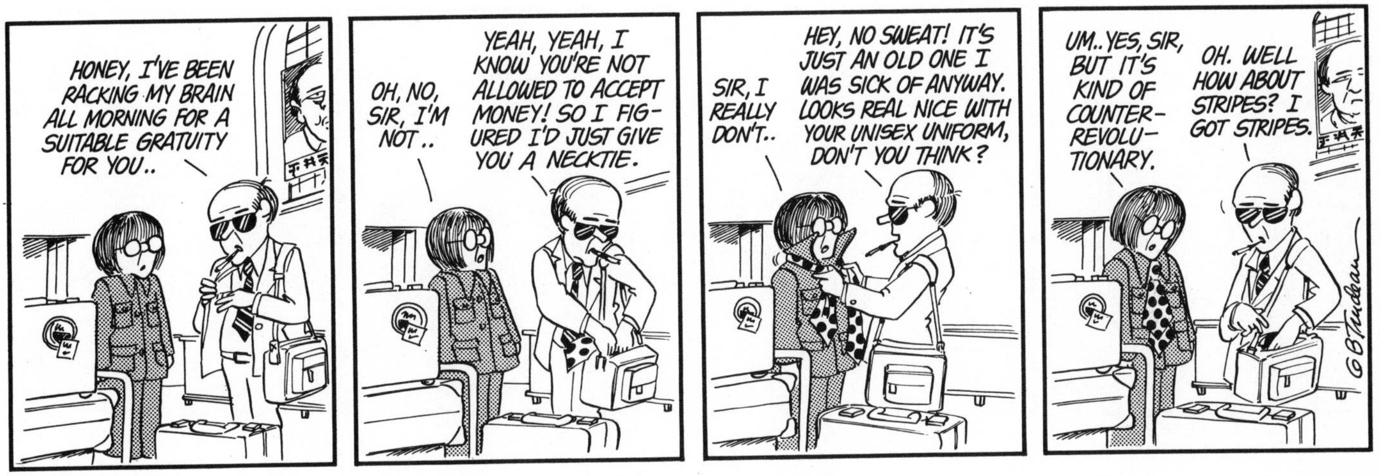
HONEY, I'VE BEEN RACKING MY BRAIN ALL MORNING FOR A SUITABLE GRATUITY FOR YOU..
OH, NO, SIR, I'M NOT..
YEAH, YEAH, I KNOW YOU'RE NOT ALLOWED TO ACCEPT MONEY! SO I FIG-URED I'D JUST GIVE YOU A NECKTIE.
SIR, I REALLY DON'T..
HEY, NO SWEAT! IT'S JUST AN OLD ONE I WAS SICK OF ANYWAY. LOOKS REAL NICE WITH YOUR UNISEX UNIFORM, DON'T YOU THINK?
UM.. YES, SIR, BUT IT'S KIND OF COUNTER-REVOLU-TIONARY.
OH. WELL HOW ABOUT STRIPES? I GOT STRIPES.
GB Trudeau

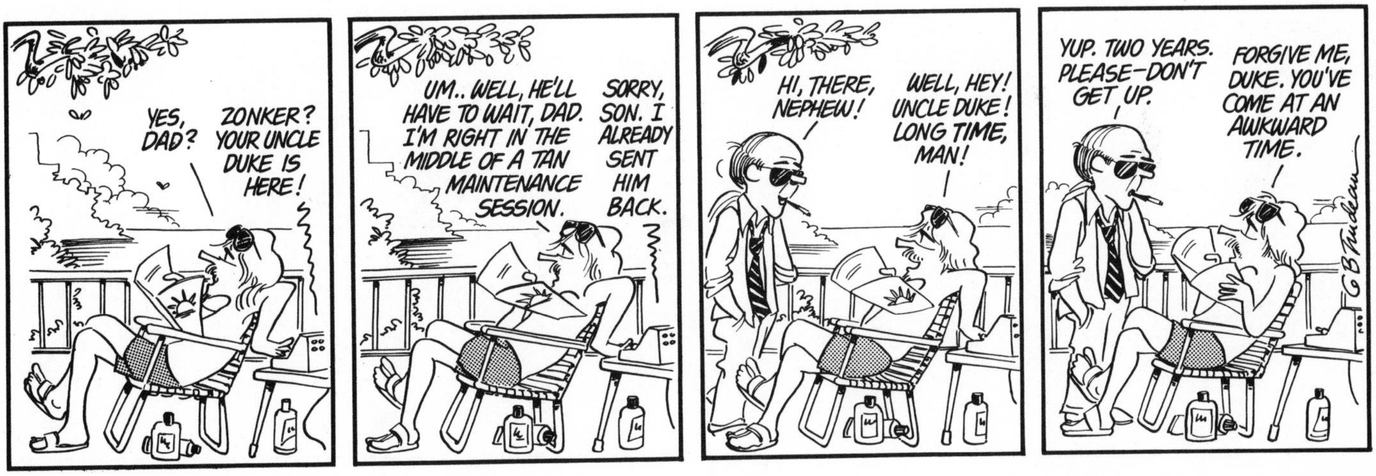
YES, DAD?
ZONKER? YOUR UNCLE DUKE IS HERE!
UM.. WELL, HE'LL HAVE TO WAIT, DAD. I'M RIGHT IN THE MIDDLE OF A TAN MAINTENANCE SESSION.
SORRY, SON. I ALREADY SENT HIM BACK.
HI, THERE, NEPHEW!
WELL, HEY! UNCLE DUKE! LONG TIME, MAN!
YUP. TWO YEARS. PLEASE—DON'T GET UP.
FORGIVE ME, DUKE. YOU'VE COME AT AN AWKWARD TIME.
GB Trudeau

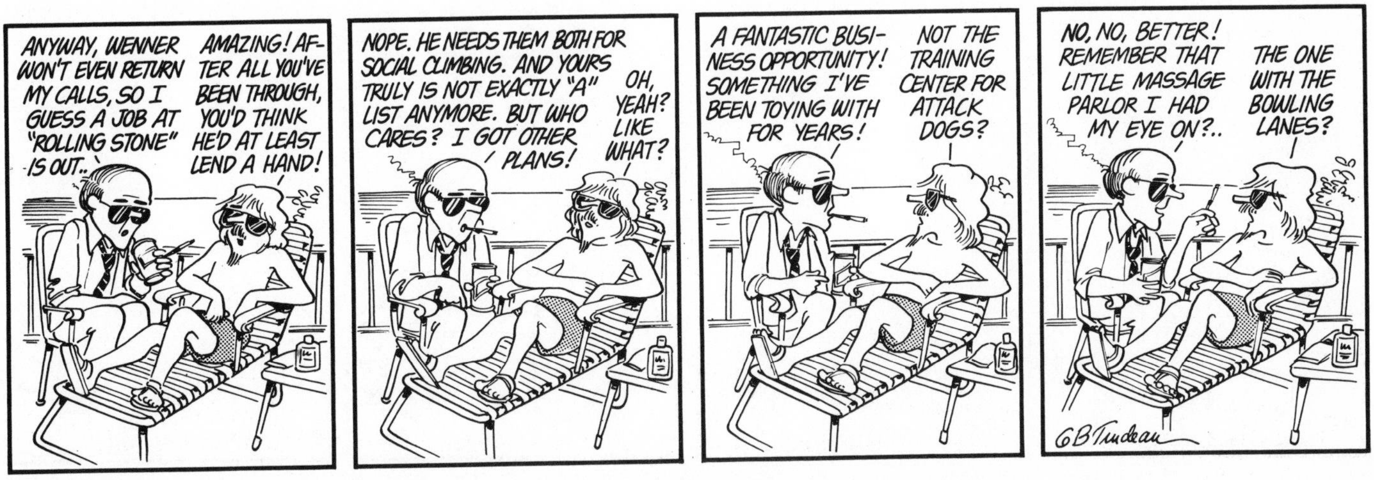
ANYWAY, WENNER WON'T EVEN RETURN MY CALLS, SO I GUESS A JOB AT "ROLLING STONE" IS OUT..
AMAZING! AF-TER ALL YOU'VE BEEN THROUGH, YOU'D THINK HE'D AT LEAST LEND A HAND!
NOPE. HE NEEDS THEM BOTH FOR SOCIAL CLIMBING. AND YOURS TRULY IS NOT EXACTLY "A" LIST ANYMORE. BUT WHO CARES? I GOT OTHER PLANS!
OH, YEAH? LIKE WHAT?
A FANTASTIC BUSI-NESS OPPORTUNITY! SOMETHING I'VE BEEN TOYING WITH FOR YEARS!
NOT THE TRAINING CENTER FOR ATTACK DOGS?
NO, NO, BETTER! REMEMBER THAT LITTLE MASSAGE PARLOR I HAD MY EYE ON?..
THE ONE WITH THE BOWLING LANES?
GB Trudeau

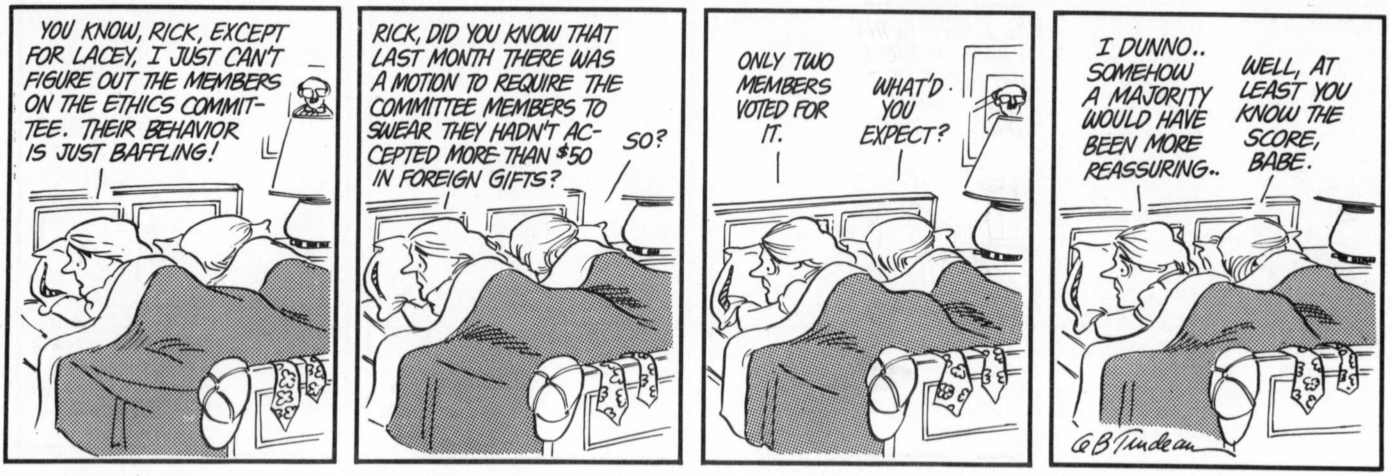
YOU KNOW, RICK, EXCEPT FOR LACEY, I JUST CAN'T FIGURE OUT THE MEMBERS ON THE ETHICS COMMITTEE. THEIR BEHAVIOR IS JUST BAFFLING!
RICK, DID YOU KNOW THAT LAST MONTH THERE WAS A MOTION TO REQUIRE THE COMMITTEE MEMBERS TO SWEAR THEY HADN'T ACCEPTED MORE THAN $50 IN FOREIGN GIFTS?
SO?
ONLY TWO MEMBERS VOTED FOR IT.
WHAT'D YOU EXPECT?
I DUNNO.. SOMEHOW A MAJORITY WOULD HAVE BEEN MORE REASSURING..
WELL, AT LEAST YOU KNOW THE SCORE, BABE.
GBTrudeau

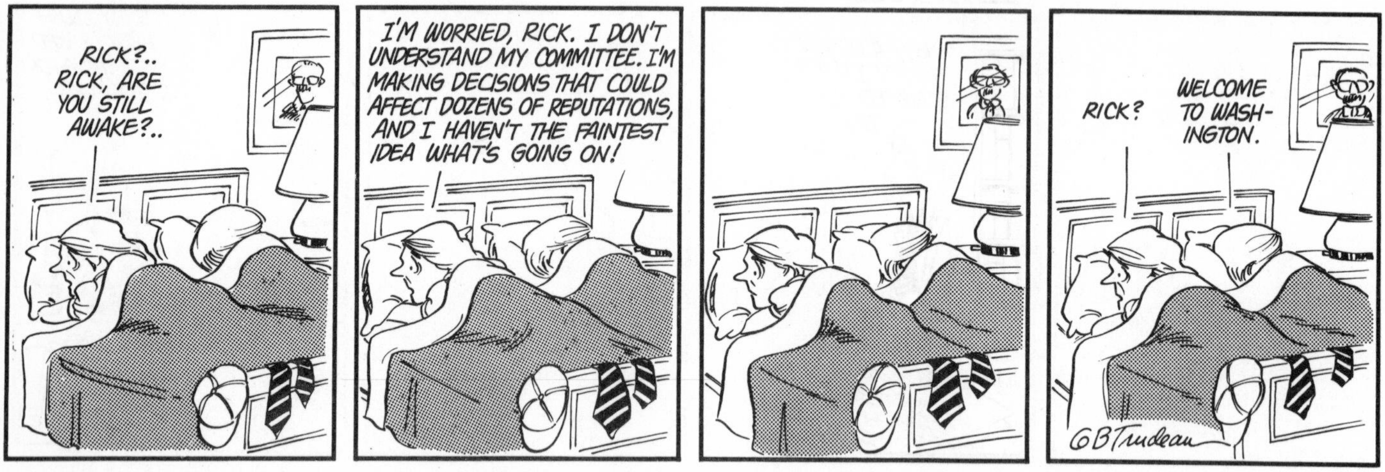
RICK?.. RICK, ARE YOU STILL AWAKE?..
I'M WORRIED, RICK. I DON'T UNDERSTAND MY COMMITTEE. I'M MAKING DECISIONS THAT COULD AFFECT DOZENS OF REPUTATIONS, AND I HAVEN'T THE FAINTEST IDEA WHAT'S GOING ON!
RICK?
WELCOME TO WASHINGTON.
GBTrudeau

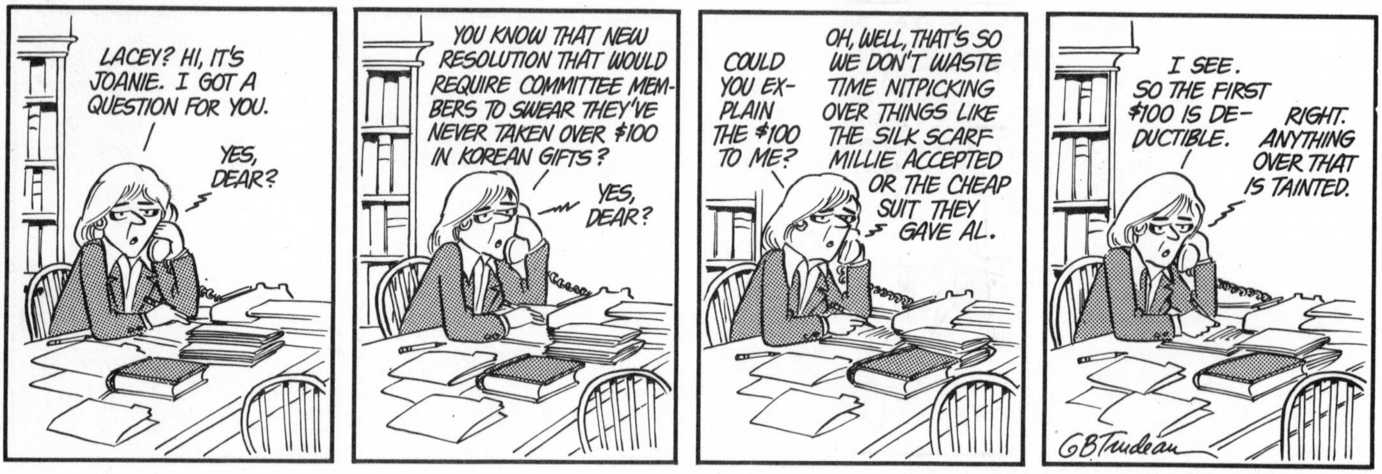
LACEY? HI, IT'S JOANIE. I GOT A QUESTION FOR YOU.
YES, DEAR?
YOU KNOW THAT NEW RESOLUTION THAT WOULD REQUIRE COMMITTEE MEMBERS TO SWEAR THEY'VE NEVER TAKEN OVER $100 IN KOREAN GIFTS?
YES, DEAR?
COULD YOU EXPLAIN THE $100 TO ME?
OH, WELL, THAT'S SO WE DON'T WASTE TIME NITPICKING OVER THINGS LIKE THE SILK SCARF MILLIE ACCEPTED OR THE CHEAP SUIT THEY GAVE AL.
I SEE. SO THE FIRST $100 IS DEDUCTIBLE.
RIGHT. ANYTHING OVER THAT IS TAINTED.
GBTrudeau

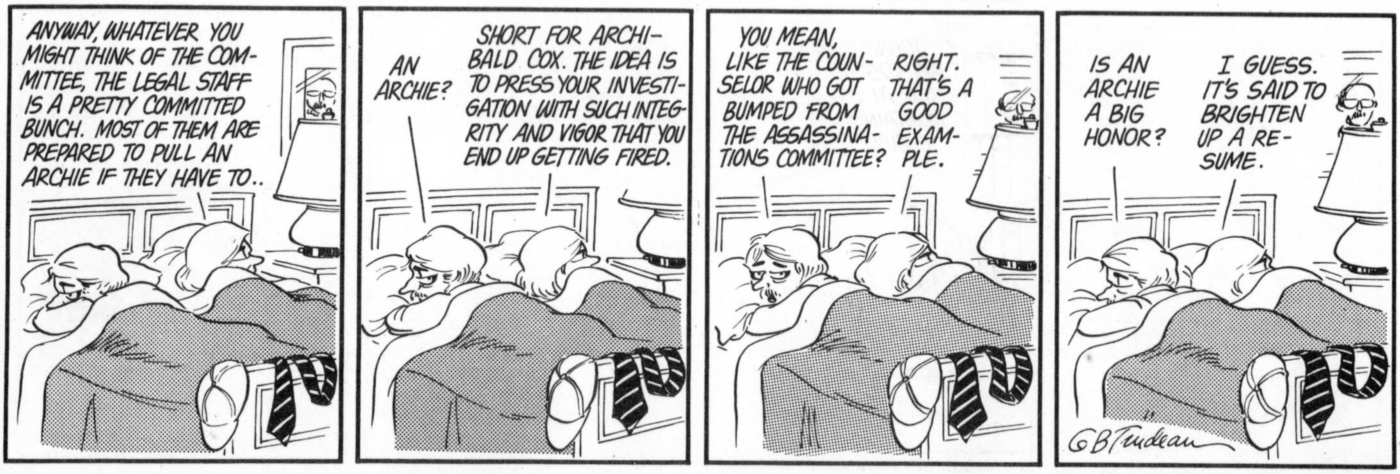
ANYWAY, WHATEVER YOU MIGHT THINK OF THE COMMITTEE, THE LEGAL STAFF IS A PRETTY COMMITTED BUNCH. MOST OF THEM ARE PREPARED TO PULL AN ARCHIE IF THEY HAVE TO..
AN ARCHIE?
SHORT FOR ARCHIBALD COX. THE IDEA IS TO PRESS YOUR INVESTIGATION WITH SUCH INTEGRITY AND VIGOR THAT YOU END UP GETTING FIRED.
YOU MEAN, LIKE THE COUNSELOR WHO GOT BUMPED FROM THE ASSASSINATIONS COMMITTEE?
RIGHT. THAT'S A GOOD EXAMPLE.
IS AN ARCHIE A BIG HONOR?
I GUESS. IT'S SAID TO BRIGHTEN UP A RESUME.
GBTrudeau

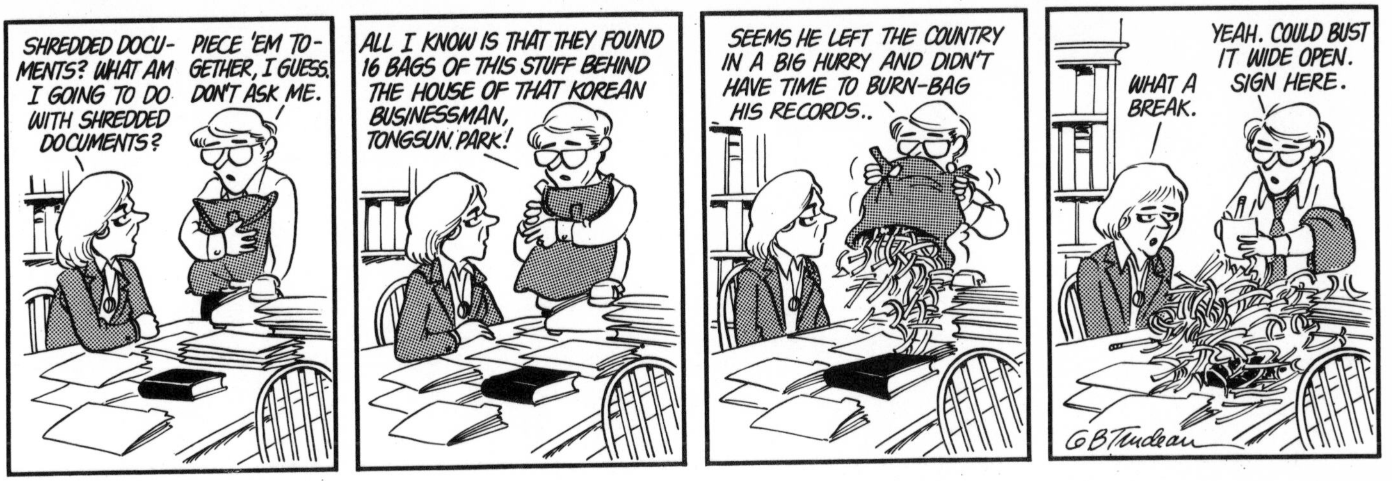
SHREDDED DOCUMENTS? WHAT AM I GOING TO DO WITH SHREDDED DOCUMENTS?
PIECE 'EM TOGETHER, I GUESS. DON'T ASK ME.
ALL I KNOW IS THAT THEY FOUND 16 BAGS OF THIS STUFF BEHIND THE HOUSE OF THAT KOREAN BUSINESSMAN, TONGSUN PARK!
SEEMS HE LEFT THE COUNTRY IN A BIG HURRY AND DIDN'T HAVE TIME TO BURN-BAG HIS RECORDS..
WHAT A BREAK.
YEAH. COULD BUST IT WIDE OPEN. SIGN HERE.
GBTrudeau

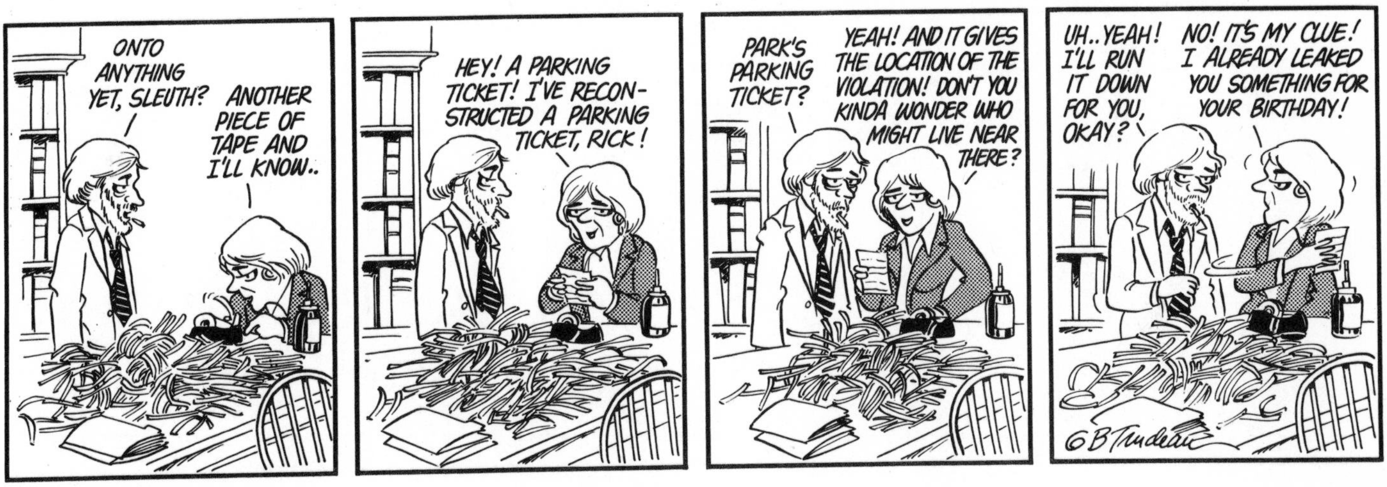
ONTO ANYTHING YET, SLEUTH?
ANOTHER PIECE OF TAPE AND I'LL KNOW..
HEY! A PARKING TICKET! I'VE RECONSTRUCTED A PARKING TICKET, RICK!
PARK'S PARKING TICKET?
YEAH! AND IT GIVES THE LOCATION OF THE VIOLATION! DON'T YOU KINDA WONDER WHO MIGHT LIVE NEAR THERE?
UH.. YEAH! I'LL RUN IT DOWN FOR YOU, OKAY?
NO! IT'S MY CLUE! I ALREADY LEAKED YOU SOMETHING FOR YOUR BIRTHDAY!
GBTrudeau

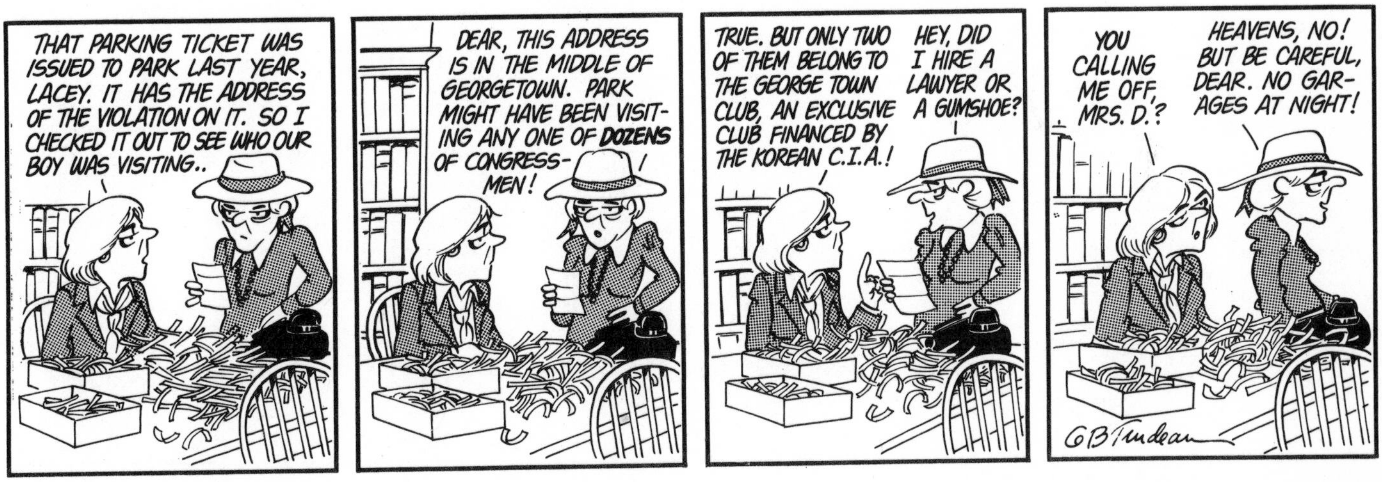
THAT PARKING TICKET WAS ISSUED TO PARK LAST YEAR, LACEY. IT HAS THE ADDRESS OF THE VIOLATION ON IT. SO I CHECKED IT OUT TO SEE WHO OUR BOY WAS VISITING..
DEAR, THIS ADDRESS IS IN THE MIDDLE OF GEORGETOWN. PARK MIGHT HAVE BEEN VISITING ANY ONE OF DOZENS OF CONGRESSMEN!
TRUE. BUT ONLY TWO OF THEM BELONG TO THE GEORGE TOWN CLUB, AN EXCLUSIVE CLUB FINANCED BY THE KOREAN C.I.A.!
HEY, DID I HIRE A LAWYER OR A GUMSHOE?
YOU CALLING ME OFF, MRS. D.?
HEAVENS, NO! BUT BE CAREFUL, DEAR. NO GARAGES AT NIGHT!
GBTrudeau

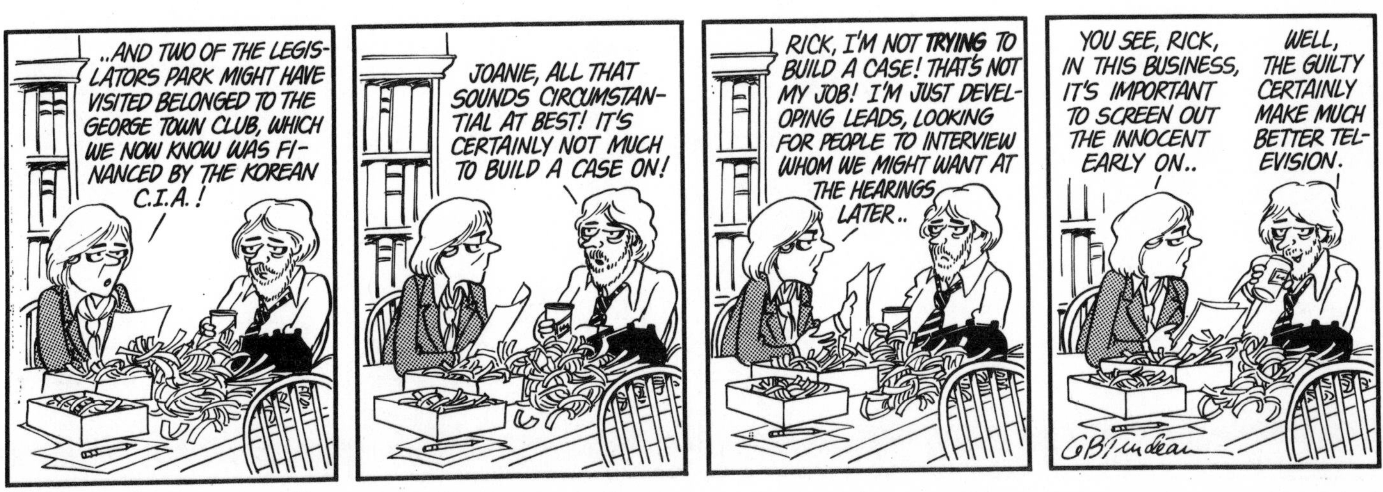
..AND TWO OF THE LEGISLATORS PARK MIGHT HAVE VISITED BELONGED TO THE GEORGE TOWN CLUB, WHICH WE NOW KNOW WAS FINANCED BY THE KOREAN C.I.A.!
JOANIE, ALL THAT SOUNDS CIRCUMSTANTIAL AT BEST! IT'S CERTAINLY NOT MUCH TO BUILD A CASE ON!
RICK, I'M NOT TRYING TO BUILD A CASE! THAT'S NOT MY JOB! I'M JUST DEVELOPING LEADS, LOOKING FOR PEOPLE TO INTERVIEW WHOM WE MIGHT WANT AT THE HEARINGS LATER..
YOU SEE, RICK, IN THIS BUSINESS, IT'S IMPORTANT TO SCREEN OUT THE INNOCENT EARLY ON..
WELL, THE GUILTY CERTAINLY MAKE MUCH BETTER TELEVISION.
GBTrudeau

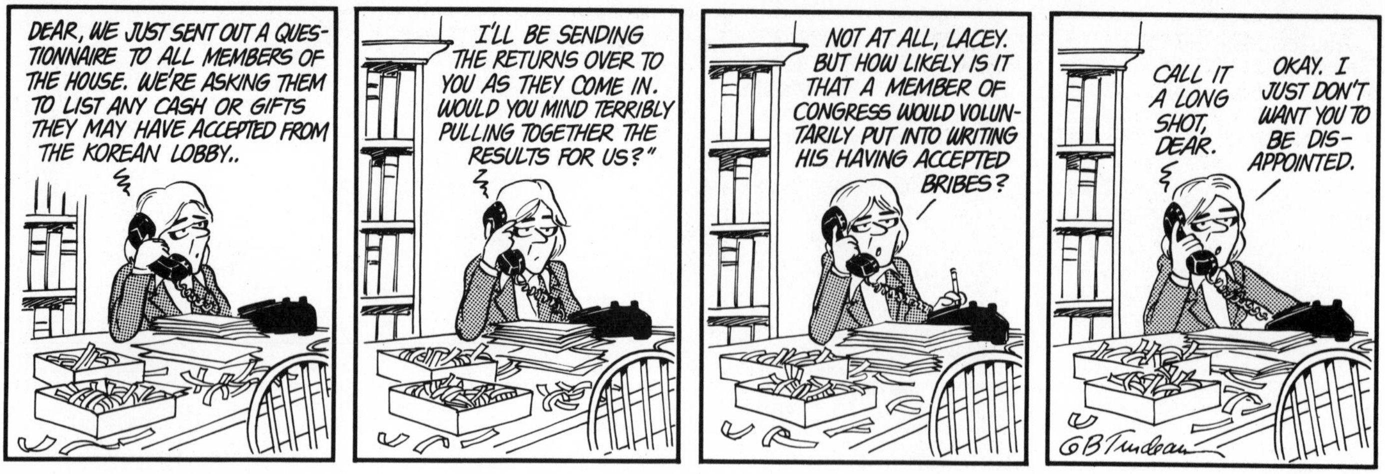
DEAR, WE JUST SENT OUT A QUESTIONNAIRE TO ALL MEMBERS OF THE HOUSE. WE'RE ASKING THEM TO LIST ANY CASH OR GIFTS THEY MAY HAVE ACCEPTED FROM THE KOREAN LOBBY..
I'LL BE SENDING THE RETURNS OVER TO YOU AS THEY COME IN. WOULD YOU MIND TERRIBLY PULLING TOGETHER THE RESULTS FOR US?"
NOT AT ALL, LACEY. BUT HOW LIKELY IS IT THAT A MEMBER OF CONGRESS WOULD VOLUNTARILY PUT INTO WRITING HIS HAVING ACCEPTED BRIBES?
CALL IT A LONG SHOT, DEAR.
OKAY. I JUST DON'T WANT YOU TO BE DISAPPOINTED.
GBTrudeau

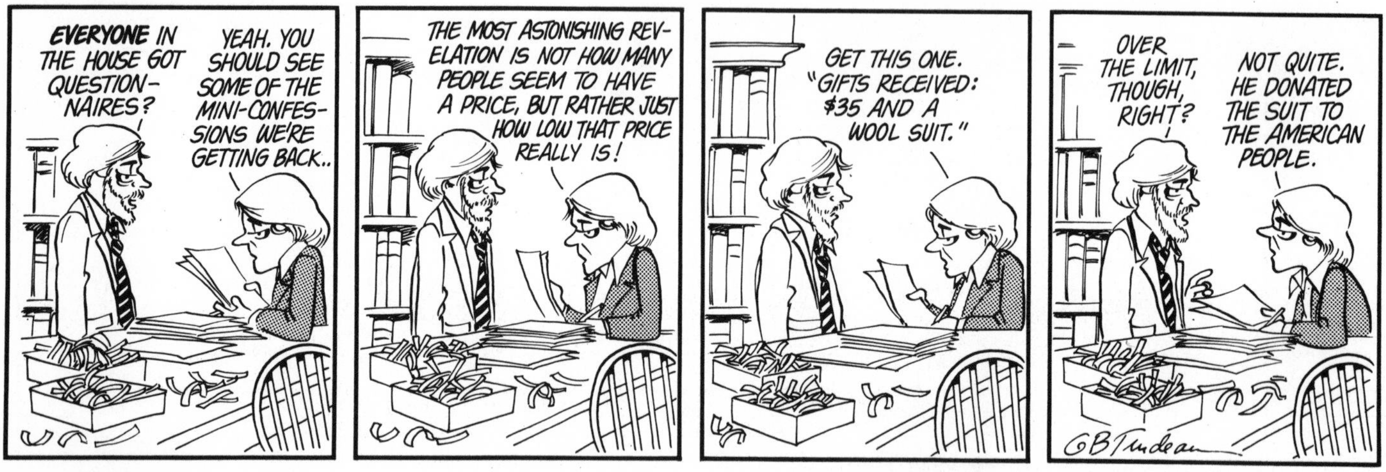
EVERYONE IN THE HOUSE GOT QUESTIONNAIRES?
YEAH. YOU SHOULD SEE SOME OF THE MINI-CONFESSIONS WE'RE GETTING BACK..
THE MOST ASTONISHING REVELATION IS NOT HOW MANY PEOPLE SEEM TO HAVE A PRICE, BUT RATHER JUST HOW LOW THAT PRICE REALLY IS!
GET THIS ONE. "GIFTS RECEIVED: $35 AND A WOOL SUIT."
OVER THE LIMIT, THOUGH, RIGHT?
NOT QUITE. HE DONATED THE SUIT TO THE AMERICAN PEOPLE.
GBTrudeau

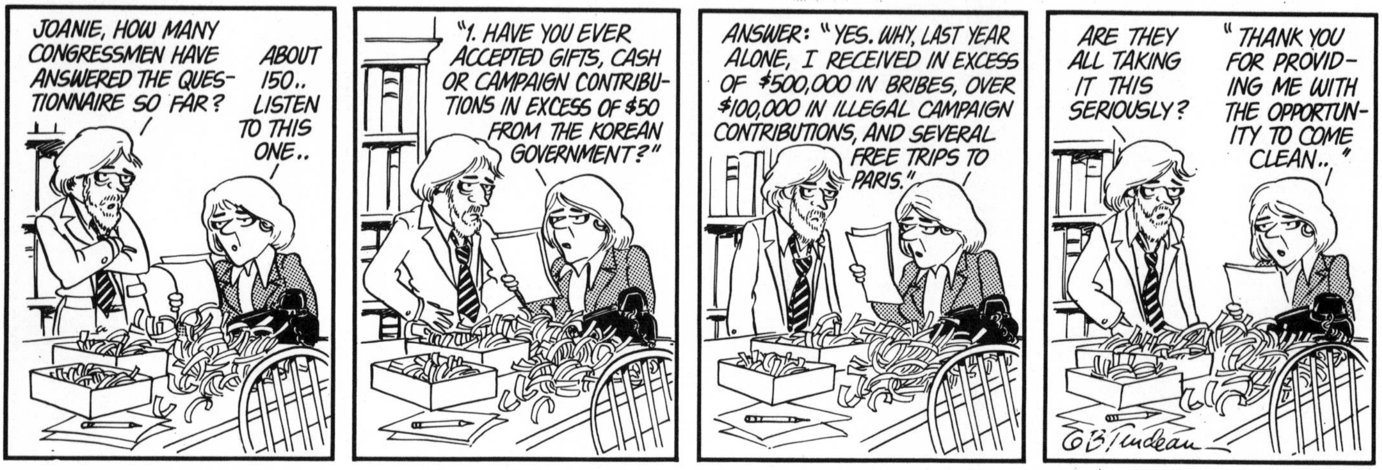
JOANIE, HOW MANY CONGRESSMEN HAVE ANSWERED THE QUESTIONNAIRE SO FAR?
ABOUT 150.. LISTEN TO THIS ONE..
"1. HAVE YOU EVER ACCEPTED GIFTS, CASH OR CAMPAIGN CONTRIBUTIONS IN EXCESS OF $50 FROM THE KOREAN GOVERNMENT?"
ANSWER: "YES. WHY, LAST YEAR ALONE, I RECEIVED IN EXCESS OF $500,000 IN BRIBES, OVER $100,000 IN ILLEGAL CAMPAIGN CONTRIBUTIONS, AND SEVERAL FREE TRIPS TO PARIS."
ARE THEY ALL TAKING IT THIS SERIOUSLY?
"THANK YOU FOR PROVIDING ME WITH THE OPPORTUNITY TO COME CLEAN.."
GBTrudeau

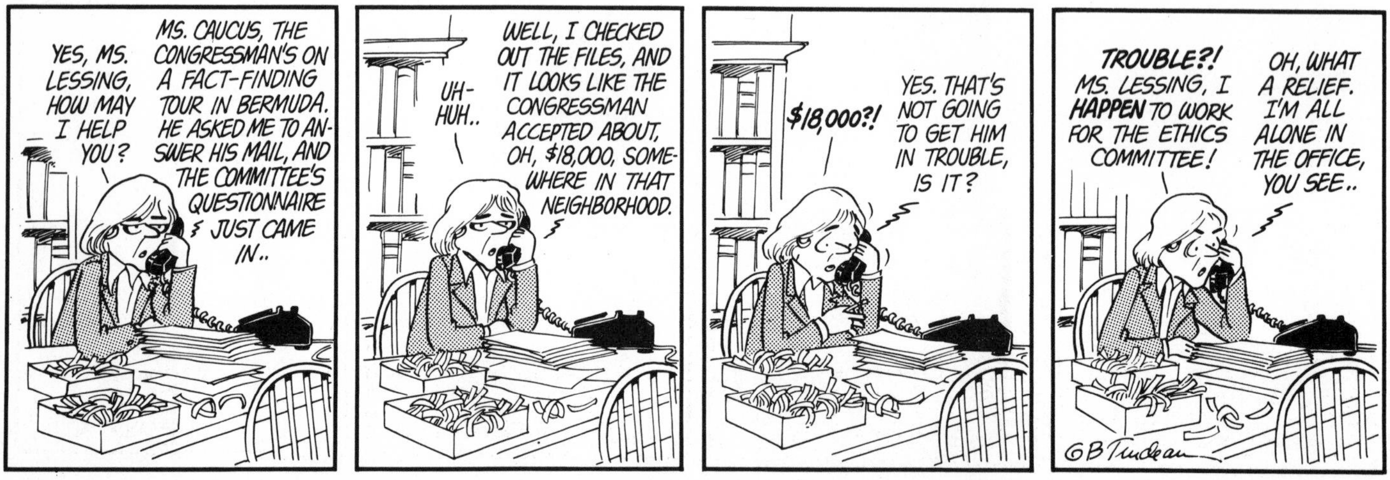
YES, MS. LESSING, HOW MAY I HELP YOU?
MS. CAUCUS, THE CONGRESSMAN'S ON A FACT-FINDING TOUR IN BERMUDA. HE ASKED ME TO ANSWER HIS MAIL, AND THE COMMITTEE'S QUESTIONNAIRE JUST CAME IN..
UH-HUH..
WELL, I CHECKED OUT THE FILES, AND IT LOOKS LIKE THE CONGRESSMAN ACCEPTED ABOUT, OH, $18,000, SOMEWHERE IN THAT NEIGHBORHOOD.
$18,000?!
YES. THAT'S NOT GOING TO GET HIM IN TROUBLE, IS IT?
TROUBLE?! MS. LESSING, I HAPPEN TO WORK FOR THE ETHICS COMMITTEE!
OH, WHAT A RELIEF. I'M ALL ALONE IN THE OFFICE, YOU SEE..
GBTrudeau

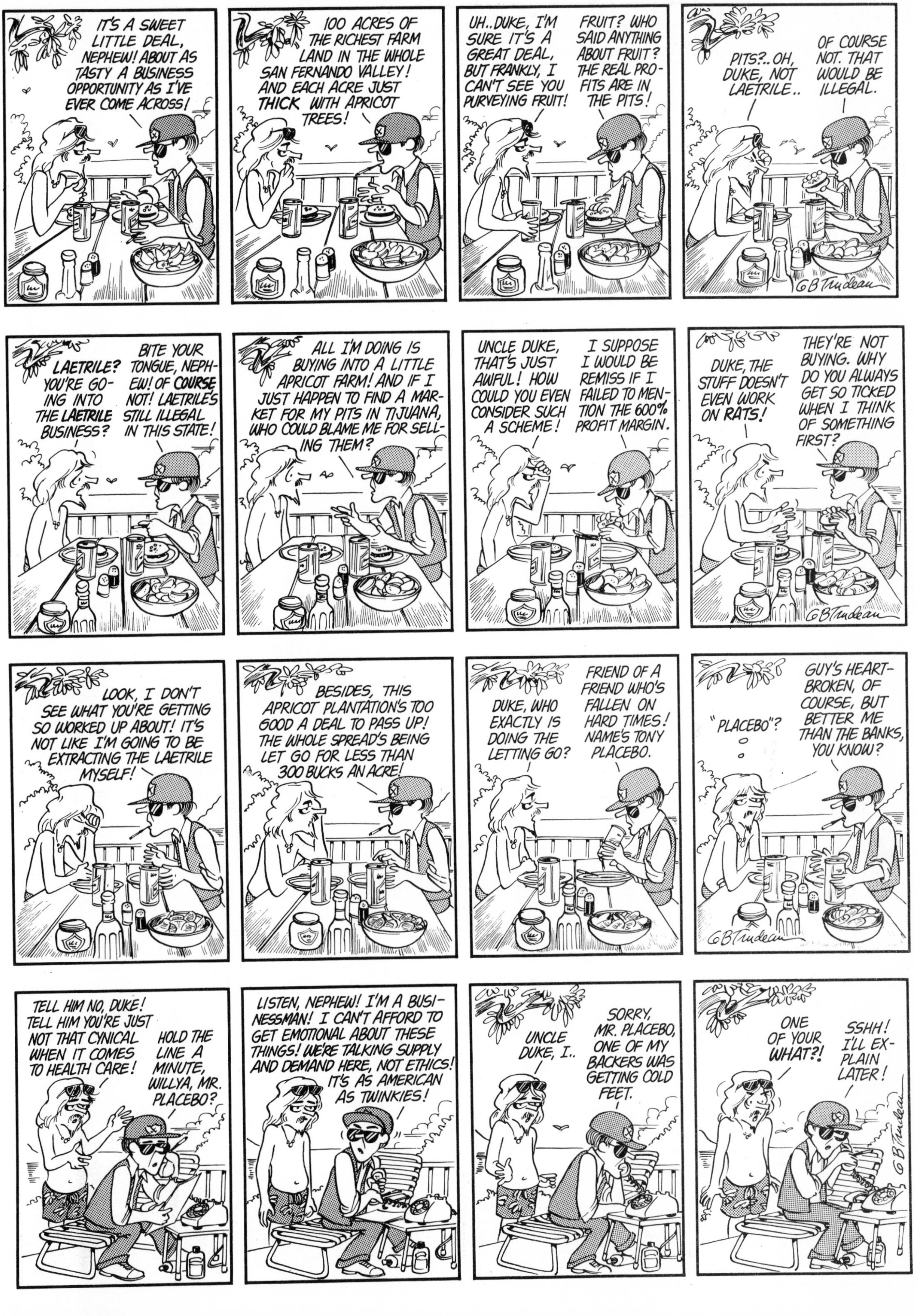
IT'S A SWEET LITTLE DEAL, NEPHEW! ABOUT AS TASTY A BUSINESS OPPORTUNITY AS I'VE EVER COME ACROSS!
100 ACRES OF THE RICHEST FARM LAND IN THE WHOLE SAN FERNANDO VALLEY! AND EACH ACRE JUST THICK WITH APRICOT TREES!
UH..DUKE, I'M SURE IT'S A GREAT DEAL, BUT FRANKLY, I CAN'T SEE YOU PURVEYING FRUIT!
FRUIT? WHO SAID ANYTHING ABOUT FRUIT? THE REAL PROFITS ARE IN THE PITS!
PITS?..OH, DUKE, NOT LAETRILE..
OF COURSE NOT. THAT WOULD BE ILLEGAL.
GBTrudeau
LAETRILE? YOU'RE GOING INTO THE LAETRILE BUSINESS?
BITE YOUR TONGUE, NEPHEW! OF COURSE NOT! LAETRILE'S STILL ILLEGAL IN THIS STATE!
ALL I'M DOING IS BUYING INTO A LITTLE APRICOT FARM! AND IF I JUST HAPPEN TO FIND A MARKET FOR MY PITS IN TIJUANA, WHO COULD BLAME ME FOR SELLING THEM?
UNCLE DUKE, THAT'S JUST AWFUL! HOW COULD YOU EVEN CONSIDER SUCH A SCHEME!
I SUPPOSE I WOULD BE REMISS IF I FAILED TO MENTION THE 600% PROFIT MARGIN.
DUKE, THE STUFF DOESN'T EVEN WORK ON RATS!
THEY'RE NOT BUYING. WHY DO YOU ALWAYS GET SO TICKED WHEN I THINK OF SOMETHING FIRST?
GBTrudeau
LOOK, I DON'T SEE WHAT YOU'RE GETTING SO WORKED UP ABOUT! IT'S NOT LIKE I'M GOING TO BE EXTRACTING THE LAETRILE MYSELF!
BESIDES, THIS APRICOT PLANTATION'S TOO GOOD A DEAL TO PASS UP! THE WHOLE SPREAD'S BEING LET GO FOR LESS THAN 300 BUCKS AN ACRE!
DUKE, WHO EXACTLY IS DOING THE LETTING GO?
FRIEND OF A FRIEND WHO'S FALLEN ON HARD TIMES! NAME'S TONY PLACEBO.
"PLACEBO"?
GUY'S HEARTBROKEN, OF COURSE, BUT BETTER ME THAN THE BANKS, YOU KNOW?
GBTrudeau
TELL HIM NO, DUKE! TELL HIM YOU'RE JUST NOT THAT CYNICAL WHEN IT COMES TO HEALTH CARE!
HOLD THE LINE A MINUTE, WILLYA, MR. PLACEBO?
LISTEN, NEPHEW! I'M A BUSINESSMAN! I CAN'T AFFORD TO GET EMOTIONAL ABOUT THESE THINGS! WE'RE TALKING SUPPLY AND DEMAND HERE, NOT ETHICS! IT'S AS AMERICAN AS TWINKIES!
UNCLE DUKE, I..
SORRY, MR. PLACEBO, ONE OF MY BACKERS WAS GETTING COLD FEET.
ONE OF YOUR WHAT?!
SSHH! I'LL EXPLAIN LATER!
GBTrudeau

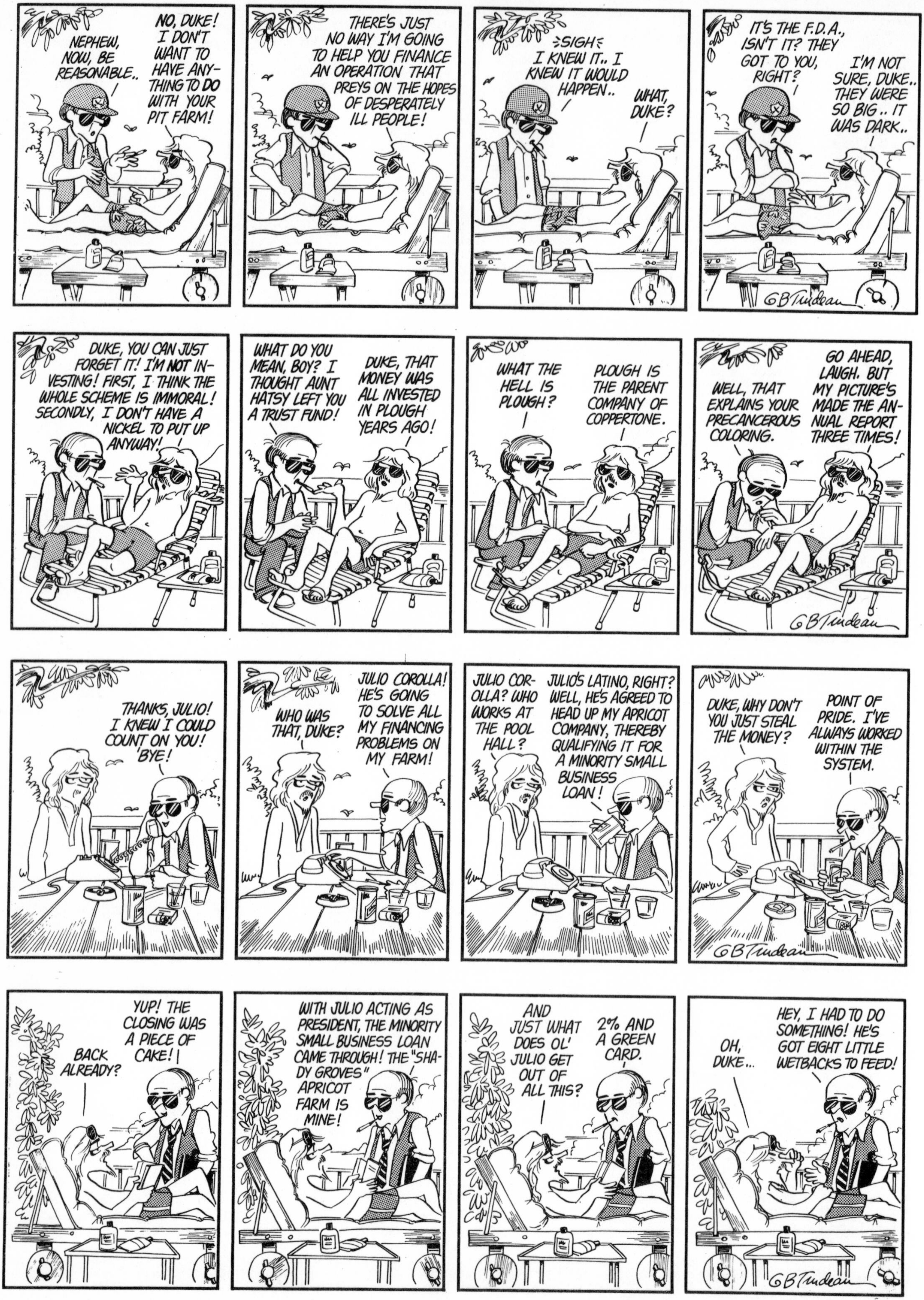
NEPHEW, NOW, BE REASONABLE..
NO, DUKE! I DON'T WANT TO HAVE ANYTHING TO DO WITH YOUR PIT FARM!
THERE'S JUST NO WAY I'M GOING TO HELP YOU FINANCE AN OPERATION THAT PREYS ON THE HOPES OF DESPERATELY ILL PEOPLE!
SIGH
I KNEW IT.. I KNEW IT WOULD HAPPEN..
WHAT, DUKE?
IT'S THE F.D.A., ISN'T IT? THEY GOT TO YOU, RIGHT?
I'M NOT SURE, DUKE.. THEY WERE SO BIG.. IT WAS DARK..
GBTrudeau
DUKE, YOU CAN JUST FORGET IT! I'M NOT INVESTING! FIRST, I THINK THE WHOLE SCHEME IS IMMORAL! SECONDLY, I DON'T HAVE A NICKEL TO PUT UP ANYWAY!
WHAT DO YOU MEAN, BOY? I THOUGHT AUNT HATSY LEFT YOU A TRUST FUND!
DUKE, THAT MONEY WAS ALL INVESTED IN PLOUGH YEARS AGO!
WHAT THE HELL IS PLOUGH?
PLOUGH IS THE PARENT COMPANY OF COPPERTONE.
WELL, THAT EXPLAINS YOUR PRECANCEROUS COLORING.
GO AHEAD, LAUGH. BUT MY PICTURE'S MADE THE ANNUAL REPORT THREE TIMES!
GBTrudeau
THANKS, JULIO! I KNEW I COULD COUNT ON YOU! 'BYE!
WHO WAS THAT, DUKE?
JULIO COROLLA! HE'S GOING TO SOLVE ALL MY FINANCING PROBLEMS ON MY FARM!
JULIO COROLLA? WHO WORKS AT THE POOL HALL?
JULIO'S LATINO, RIGHT? WELL, HE'S AGREED TO HEAD UP MY APRICOT COMPANY, THEREBY QUALIFYING IT FOR A MINORITY SMALL BUSINESS LOAN!
DUKE, WHY DON'T YOU JUST STEAL THE MONEY?
POINT OF PRIDE. I'VE ALWAYS WORKED WITHIN THE SYSTEM.
GBTrudeau
BACK ALREADY?
YUP! THE CLOSING WAS A PIECE OF CAKE!
WITH JULIO ACTING AS PRESIDENT, THE MINORITY SMALL BUSINESS LOAN CAME THROUGH! THE "SHADY GROVES" APRICOT FARM IS MINE!
AND JUST WHAT DOES OL' JULIO GET OUT OF ALL THIS?
2% AND A GREEN CARD.
OH, DUKE...
HEY, I HAD TO DO SOMETHING! HE'S GOT EIGHT LITTLE WETBACKS TO FEED!
GBTrudeau

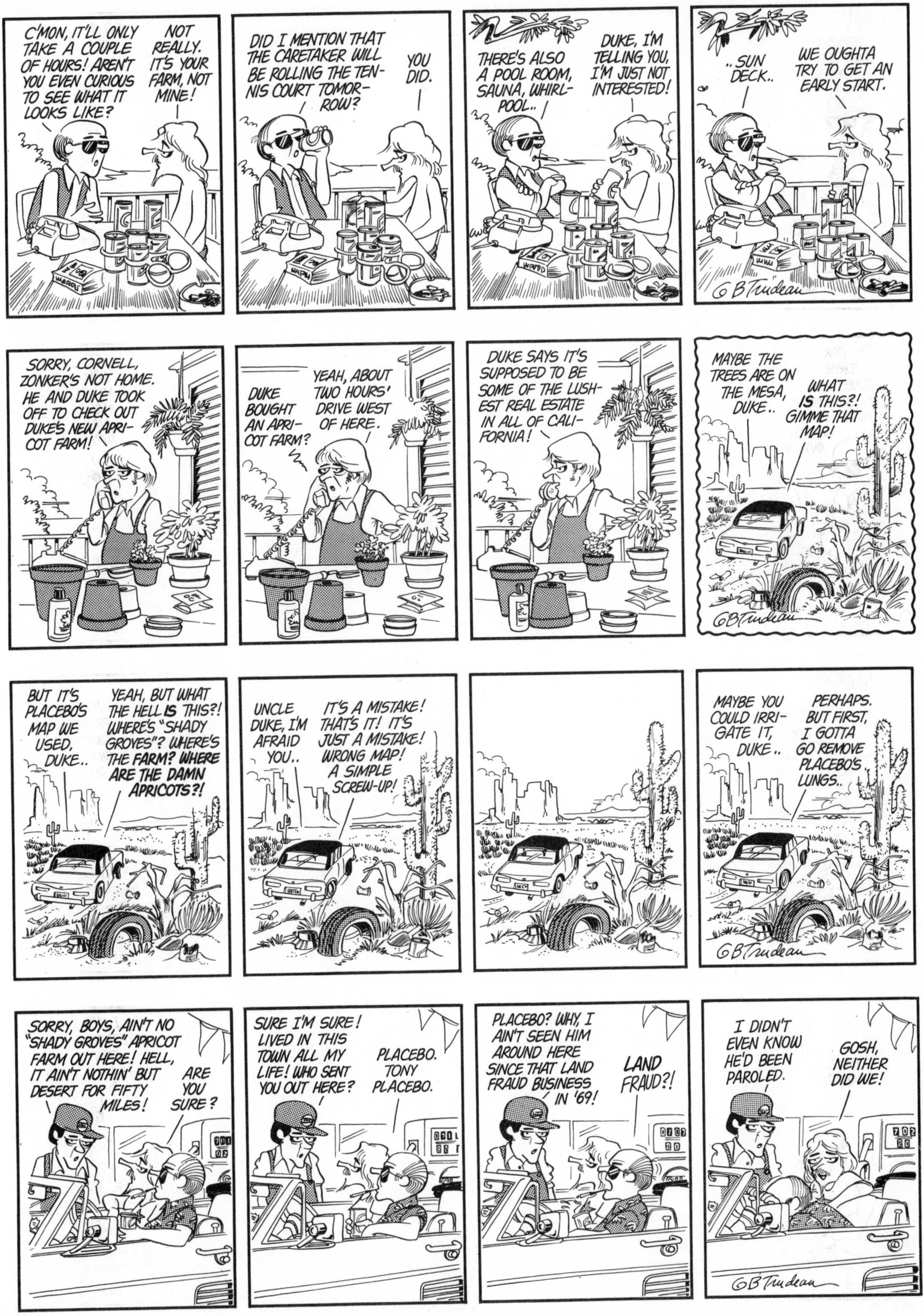
C'MON, IT'LL ONLY TAKE A COUPLE OF HOURS! AREN'T YOU EVEN CURIOUS TO SEE WHAT IT LOOKS LIKE?
NOT REALLY. IT'S YOUR FARM, NOT MINE!
DID I MENTION THAT THE CARETAKER WILL BE ROLLING THE TEN-NIS COURT TOMOR-ROW?
YOU DID.
THERE'S ALSO A POOL ROOM, SAUNA, WHIRL-POOL..
DUKE, I'M TELLING YOU, I'M JUST NOT INTERESTED!
..SUN DECK..
WE OUGHTA TRY TO GET AN EARLY START.
GBTrudeau
SORRY, CORNELL, ZONKER'S NOT HOME. HE AND DUKE TOOK OFF TO CHECK OUT DUKE'S NEW APRI-COT FARM!
DUKE BOUGHT AN APRI-COT FARM?
YEAH, ABOUT TWO HOURS' DRIVE WEST OF HERE.
DUKE SAYS IT'S SUPPOSED TO BE SOME OF THE LUSH-EST REAL ESTATE IN ALL OF CALI-FORNIA!
MAYBE THE TREES ARE ON THE MESA, DUKE..
WHAT IS THIS?! GIMME THAT MAP!
GBTrudeau
BUT IT'S PLACEBO'S MAP WE USED, DUKE..
YEAH, BUT WHAT THE HELL IS THIS?! WHERE'S "SHADY GROVES"? WHERE'S THE FARM? WHERE ARE THE DAMN APRICOTS?!
UNCLE DUKE, I'M AFRAID YOU..
IT'S A MISTAKE! THAT'S IT! IT'S JUST A MISTAKE! WRONG MAP! A SIMPLE SCREW-UP!
MAYBE YOU COULD IRRI-GATE IT, DUKE..
PERHAPS. BUT FIRST, I GOTTA GO REMOVE PLACEBO'S LUNGS..
GBTrudeau
SORRY, BOYS, AIN'T NO "SHADY GROVES" APRICOT FARM OUT HERE! HELL, IT AIN'T NOTHIN' BUT DESERT FOR FIFTY MILES!
ARE YOU SURE?
SURE I'M SURE! LIVED IN THIS TOWN ALL MY LIFE! WHO SENT YOU OUT HERE?
PLACEBO. TONY PLACEBO.
PLACEBO? WHY, I AIN'T SEEN HIM AROUND HERE SINCE THAT LAND FRAUD BUSINESS IN '69!
LAND FRAUD?!
I DIDN'T EVEN KNOW HE'D BEEN PAROLED.
GOSH, NEITHER DID WE!
GBTrudeau

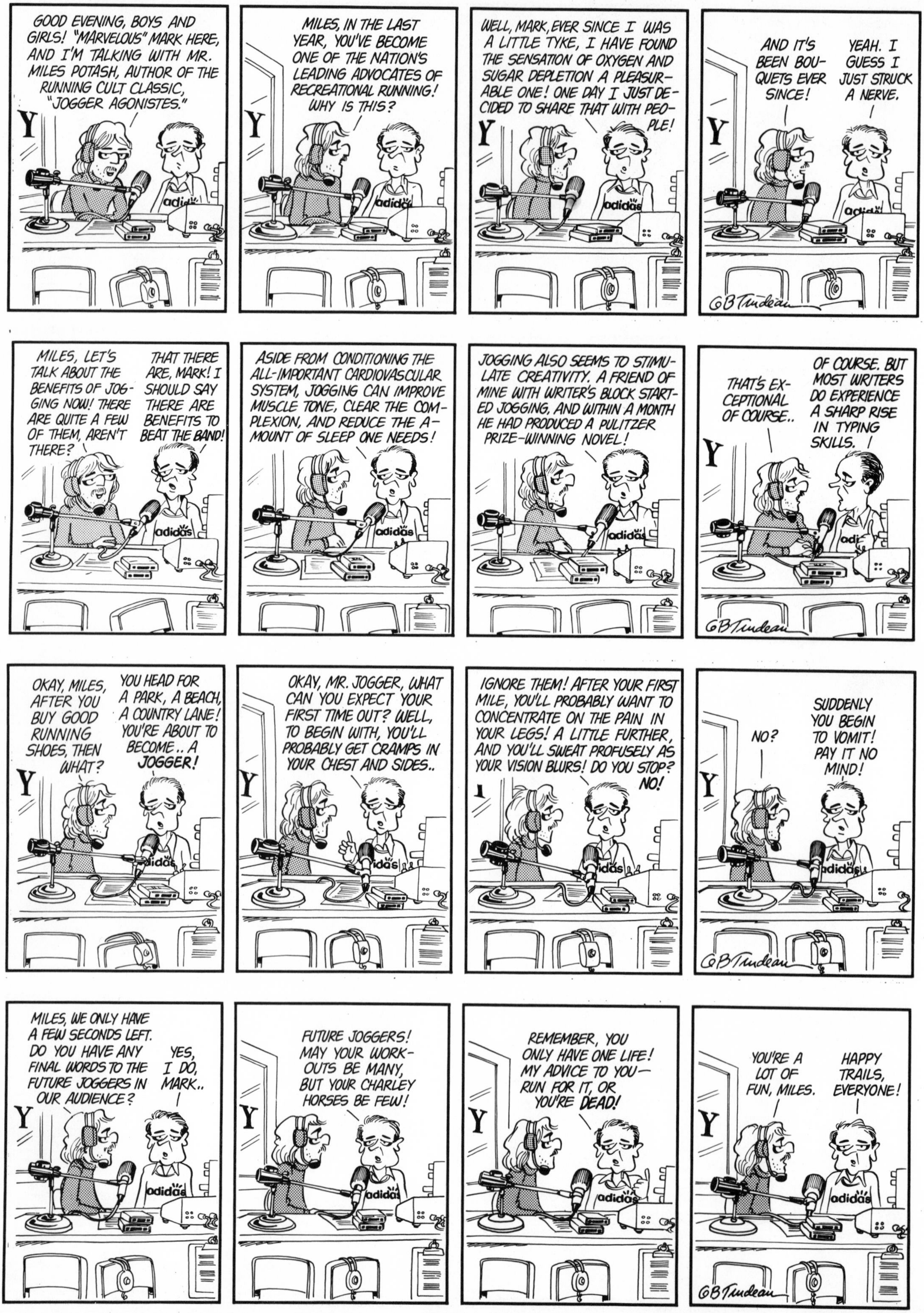
GOOD EVENING, BOYS AND GIRLS! "MARVELOUS" MARK HERE, AND I'M TALKING WITH MR. MILES POTASH, AUTHOR OF THE RUNNING CULT CLASSIC, "JOGGER AGONISTES."
adidas
MILES, IN THE LAST YEAR, YOU'VE BECOME ONE OF THE NATION'S LEADING ADVOCATES OF RECREATIONAL RUNNING! WHY IS THIS?
adidas
WELL, MARK, EVER SINCE I WAS A LITTLE TYKE, I HAVE FOUND THE SENSATION OF OXYGEN AND SUGAR DEPLETION A PLEASURABLE ONE! ONE DAY I JUST DECIDED TO SHARE THAT WITH PEOPLE!
adidas
AND IT'S BEEN BOUQUETS EVER SINCE!
YEAH. I GUESS I JUST STRUCK A NERVE.
G.B. Trudeau
MILES, LET'S TALK ABOUT THE BENEFITS OF JOGGING NOW! THERE ARE QUITE A FEW OF THEM, AREN'T THERE?
THAT THERE ARE, MARK! I SHOULD SAY THERE ARE BENEFITS TO BEAT THE BAND!
adidas
ASIDE FROM CONDITIONING THE ALL-IMPORTANT CARDIOVASCULAR SYSTEM, JOGGING CAN IMPROVE MUSCLE TONE, CLEAR THE COMPLEXION, AND REDUCE THE AMOUNT OF SLEEP ONE NEEDS!
adidas
JOGGING ALSO SEEMS TO STIMULATE CREATIVITY. A FRIEND OF MINE WITH WRITER'S BLOCK STARTED JOGGING, AND WITHIN A MONTH HE HAD PRODUCED A PULITZER PRIZE-WINNING NOVEL!
adidas
THAT'S EXCEPTIONAL OF COURSE..
OF COURSE. BUT MOST WRITERS DO EXPERIENCE A SHARP RISE IN TYPING SKILLS.
G.B. Trudeau
OKAY, MILES, AFTER YOU BUY GOOD RUNNING SHOES, THEN WHAT?
YOU HEAD FOR A PARK, A BEACH, A COUNTRY LANE! YOU'RE ABOUT TO BECOME.. A JOGGER!
OKAY, MR. JOGGER, WHAT CAN YOU EXPECT YOUR FIRST TIME OUT? WELL, TO BEGIN WITH, YOU'LL PROBABLY GET CRAMPS IN YOUR CHEST AND SIDES..
IGNORE THEM! AFTER YOUR FIRST MILE, YOU'LL PROBABLY WANT TO CONCENTRATE ON THE PAIN IN YOUR LEGS! A LITTLE FURTHER, AND YOU'LL SWEAT PROFUSELY AS YOUR VISION BLURS! DO YOU STOP? NO!
NO?
SUDDENLY YOU BEGIN TO VOMIT! PAY IT NO MIND!
adidas
G.B. Trudeau
MILES, WE ONLY HAVE A FEW SECONDS LEFT. DO YOU HAVE ANY FINAL WORDS TO THE FUTURE JOGGERS IN OUR AUDIENCE?
YES, I DO, MARK..
adidas
FUTURE JOGGERS! MAY YOUR WORKOUTS BE MANY, BUT YOUR CHARLEY HORSES BE FEW!
adidas
REMEMBER, YOU ONLY HAVE ONE LIFE! MY ADVICE TO YOU— RUN FOR IT, OR YOU'RE DEAD!
adidas
YOU'RE A LOT OF FUN, MILES.
HAPPY TRAILS, EVERYONE!
adidas
G.B. Trudeau

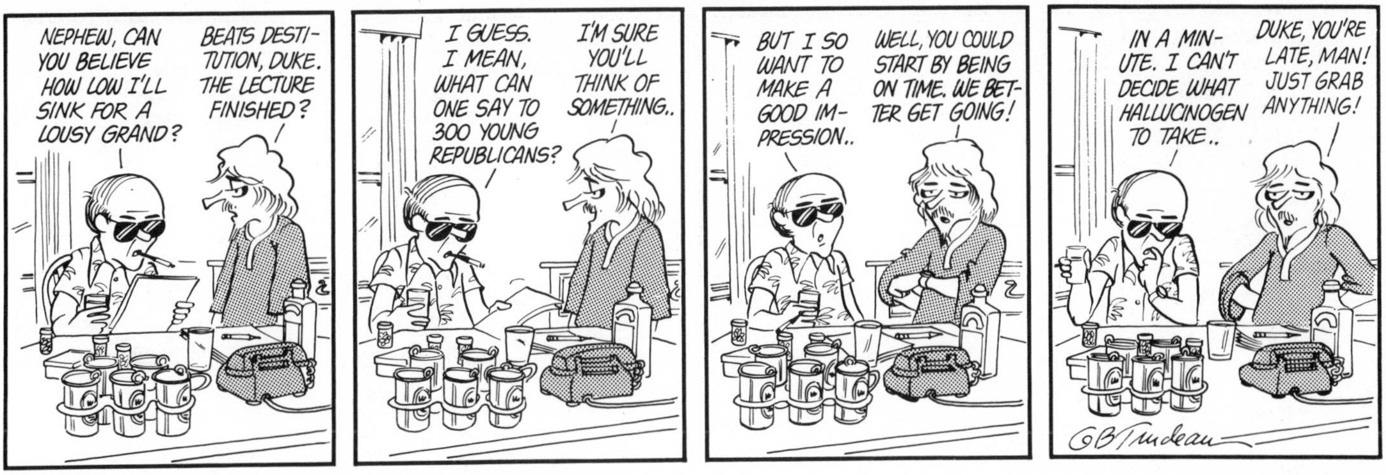
NEPHEW, CAN YOU BELIEVE HOW LOW I'LL SINK FOR A LOUSY GRAND?
BEATS DESTITUTION, DUKE. THE LECTURE FINISHED?
I GUESS. I MEAN, WHAT CAN ONE SAY TO 300 YOUNG REPUBLICANS?
I'M SURE YOU'LL THINK OF SOMETHING..
BUT I SO WANT TO MAKE A GOOD IMPRESSION..
WELL, YOU COULD START BY BEING ON TIME. WE BETTER GET GOING!
IN A MINUTE. I CAN'T DECIDE WHAT HALLUCINOGEN TO TAKE..
DUKE, YOU'RE LATE, MAN! JUST GRAB ANYTHING!
GB Trudeau

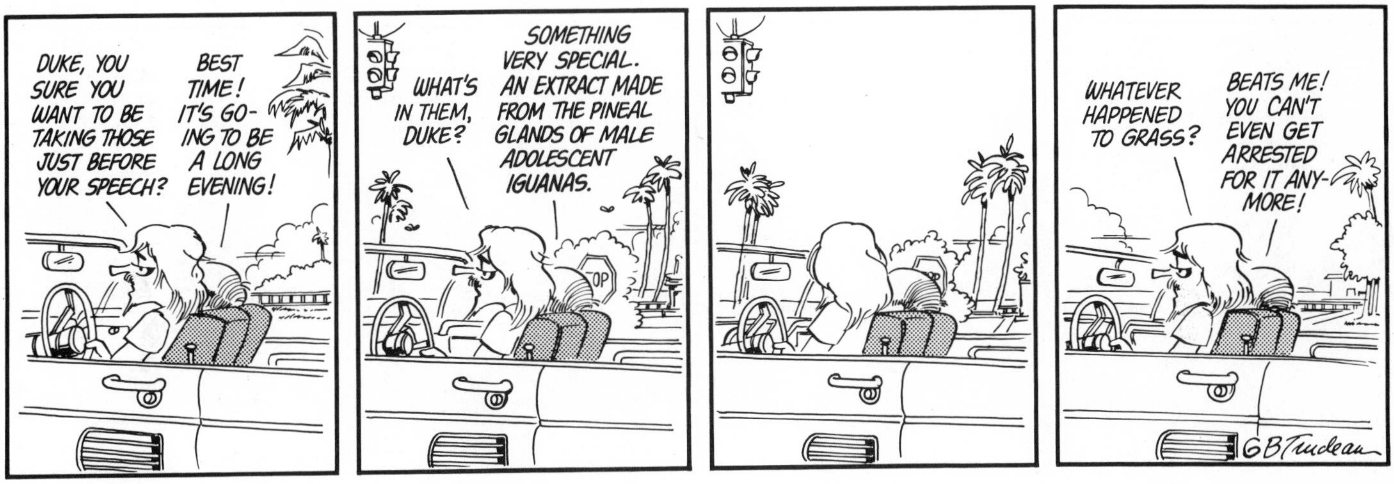
DUKE, YOU SURE YOU WANT TO BE TAKING THOSE JUST BEFORE YOUR SPEECH?
BEST TIME! IT'S GOING TO BE A LONG EVENING!
WHAT'S IN THEM, DUKE?
SOMETHING VERY SPECIAL. AN EXTRACT MADE FROM THE PINEAL GLANDS OF MALE ADOLESCENT IGUANAS.
WHATEVER HAPPENED TO GRASS?
BEATS ME! YOU CAN'T EVEN GET ARRESTED FOR IT ANYMORE!
GB Trudeau

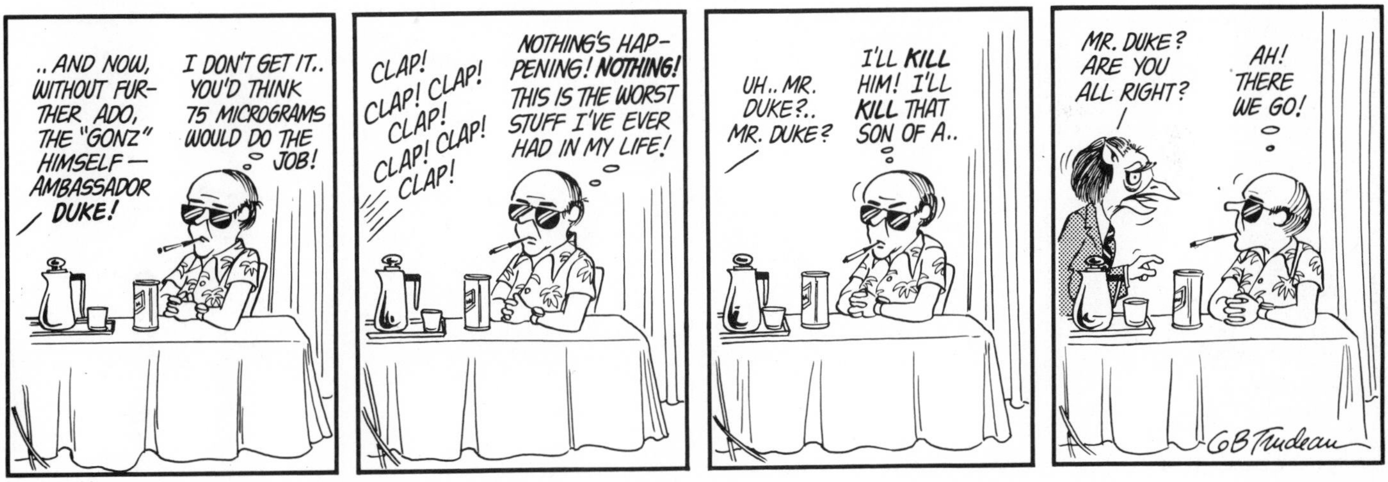
..AND NOW, WITHOUT FURTHER ADO, THE "GONZ" HIMSELF— AMBASSADOR DUKE!
I DON'T GET IT.. YOU'D THINK 75 MICROGRAMS WOULD DO THE JOB!
CLAP! CLAP! CLAP! CLAP! CLAP! CLAP! CLAP!
NOTHING'S HAPPENING! NOTHING! THIS IS THE WORST STUFF I'VE EVER HAD IN MY LIFE!
UH.. MR. DUKE?.. MR. DUKE?
I'LL KILL HIM! I'LL KILL THAT SON OF A..
MR. DUKE? ARE YOU ALL RIGHT?
AH! THERE WE GO!
GB Trudeau

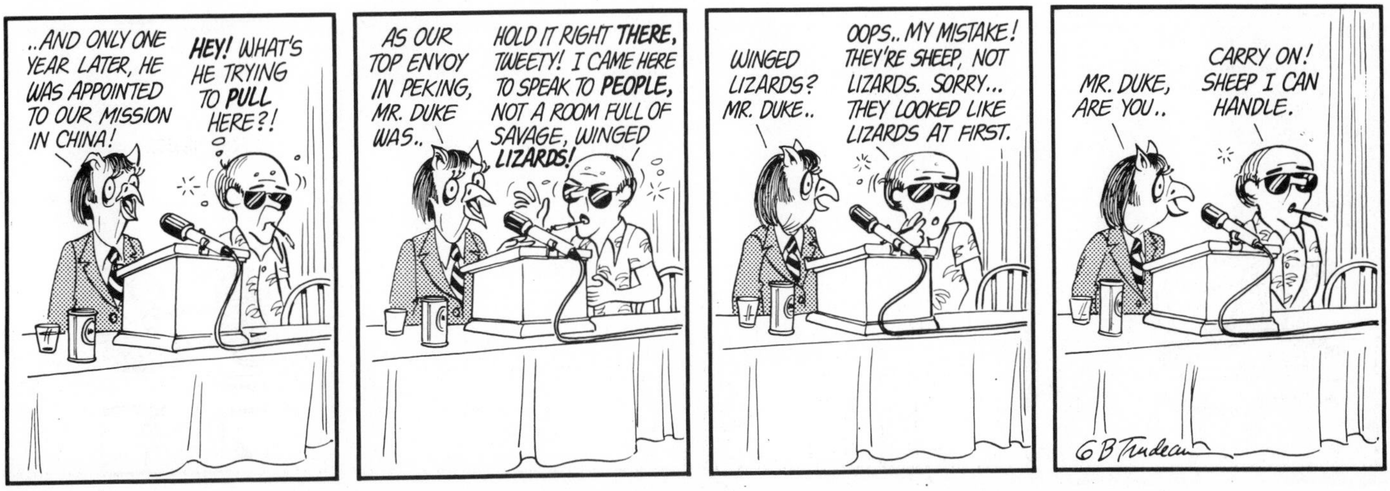
..AND ONLY ONE YEAR LATER, HE WAS APPOINTED TO OUR MISSION IN CHINA!
HEY! WHAT'S HE TRYING TO PULL HERE?!
AS OUR TOP ENVOY IN PEKING, MR. DUKE WAS..
HOLD IT RIGHT THERE, TWEETY! I CAME HERE TO SPEAK TO PEOPLE, NOT A ROOM FULL OF SAVAGE, WINGED LIZARDS!
WINGED LIZARDS? MR. DUKE..
OOPS.. MY MISTAKE! THEY'RE SHEEP, NOT LIZARDS. SORRY... THEY LOOKED LIKE LIZARDS AT FIRST.
MR. DUKE, ARE YOU..
CARRY ON! SHEEP I CAN HANDLE.
GB Trudeau

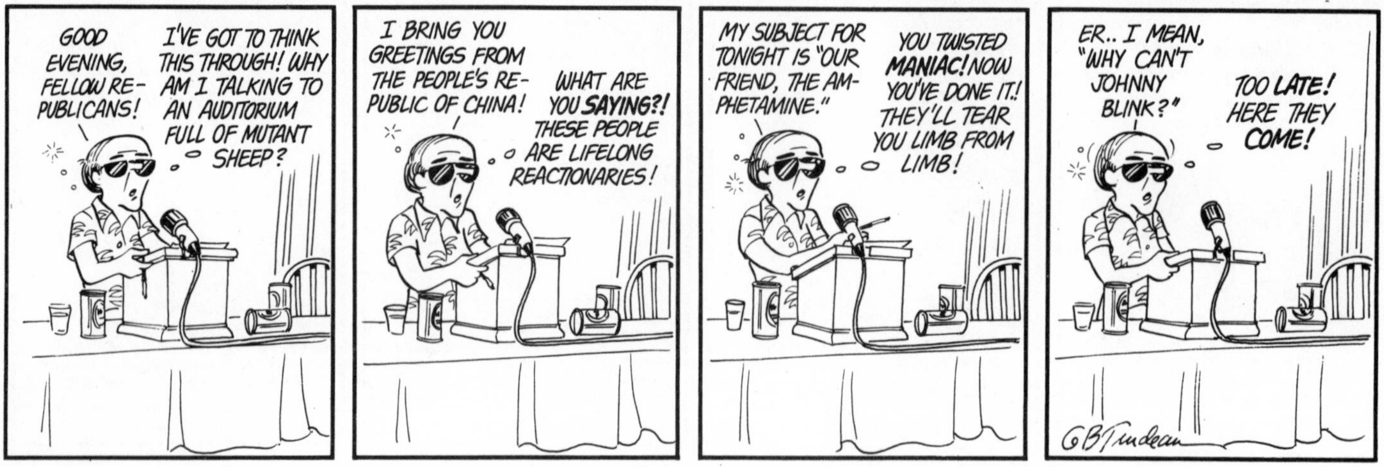
GOOD EVENING, FELLOW RE-PUBLICANS!
I'VE GOT TO THINK THIS THROUGH! WHY AM I TALKING TO AN AUDITORIUM FULL OF MUTANT SHEEP?
I BRING YOU GREETINGS FROM THE PEOPLE'S RE-PUBLIC OF CHINA!
WHAT ARE YOU SAYING?! THESE PEOPLE ARE LIFELONG REACTIONARIES!
MY SUBJECT FOR TONIGHT IS "OUR FRIEND, THE AM-PHETAMINE."
YOU TWISTED MANIAC! NOW YOU'VE DONE IT.! THEY'LL TEAR YOU LIMB FROM LIMB!
ER.. I MEAN, "WHY CAN'T JOHNNY BLINK?"
TOO LATE! HERE THEY COME!
GBTrudeau

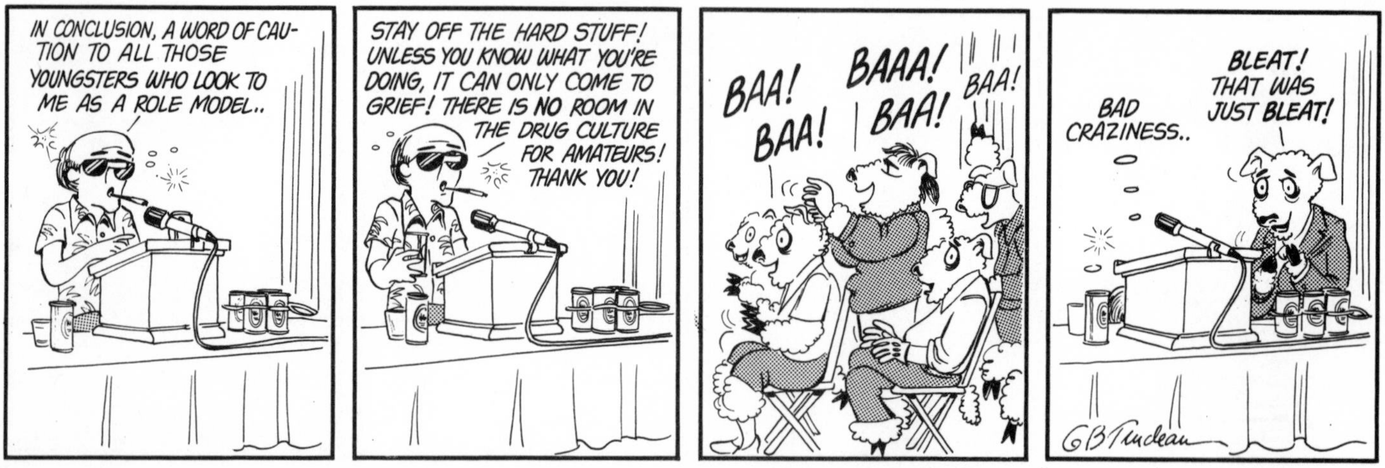
IN CONCLUSION, A WORD OF CAU-TION TO ALL THOSE YOUNGSTERS WHO LOOK TO ME AS A ROLE MODEL..
STAY OFF THE HARD STUFF! UNLESS YOU KNOW WHAT YOU'RE DOING, IT CAN ONLY COME TO GRIEF! THERE IS NO ROOM IN THE DRUG CULTURE FOR AMATEURS! THANK YOU!
BAA! BAA!
BAAA! BAA!
BAA!
BAD CRAZINESS..
BLEAT! THAT WAS JUST BLEAT!
GBTrudeau

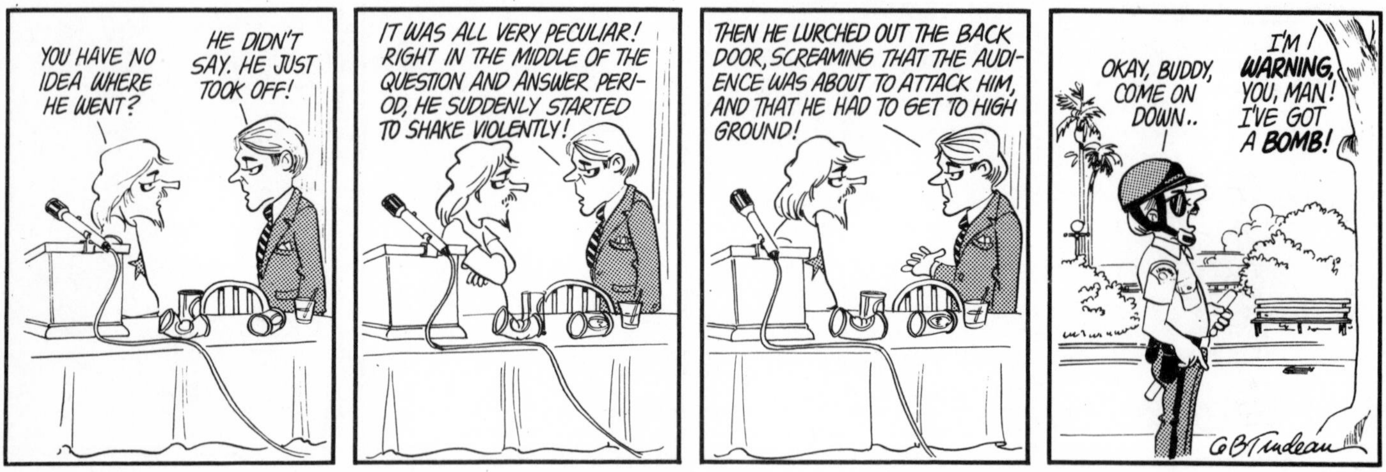
YOU HAVE NO IDEA WHERE HE WENT?
HE DIDN'T SAY. HE JUST TOOK OFF!
IT WAS ALL VERY PECULIAR! RIGHT IN THE MIDDLE OF THE QUESTION AND ANSWER PERI-OD, HE SUDDENLY STARTED TO SHAKE VIOLENTLY!
THEN HE LURCHED OUT THE BACK DOOR, SCREAMING THAT THE AUDI-ENCE WAS ABOUT TO ATTACK HIM, AND THAT HE HAD TO GET TO HIGH GROUND!
OKAY, BUDDY, COME ON DOWN..
I'M WARNING, YOU, MAN! I'VE GOT A BOMB!
GBTrudeau

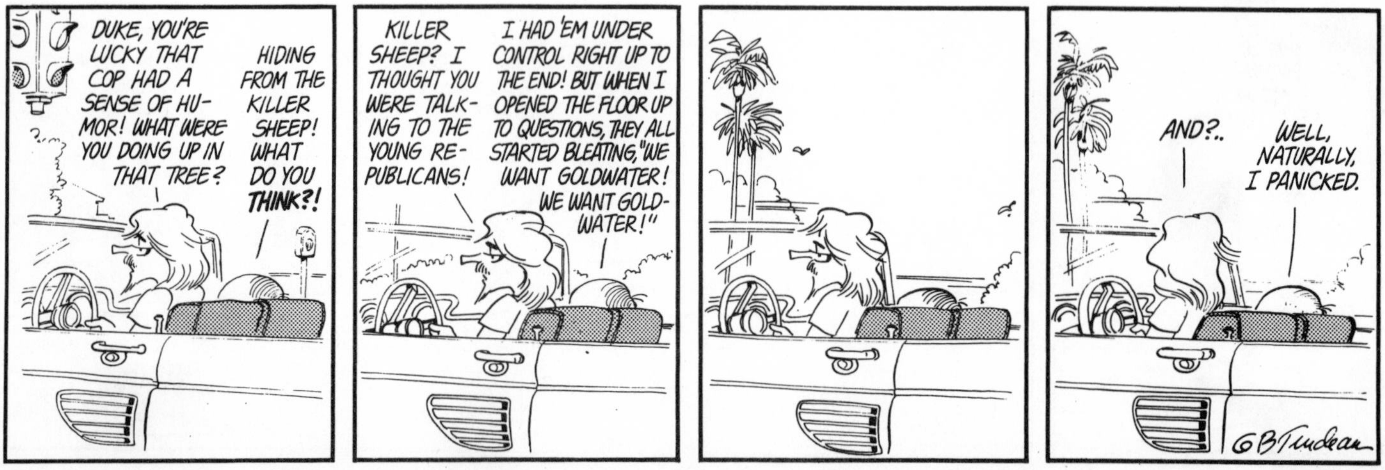
DUKE, YOU'RE LUCKY THAT COP HAD A SENSE OF HU-MOR! WHAT WERE YOU DOING UP IN THAT TREE?
HIDING FROM THE KILLER SHEEP! WHAT DO YOU THINK?!
KILLER SHEEP? I THOUGHT YOU WERE TALK-ING TO THE YOUNG RE-PUBLICANS!
I HAD 'EM UNDER CONTROL RIGHT UP TO THE END! BUT WHEN I OPENED THE FLOOR UP TO QUESTIONS, THEY ALL STARTED BLEATING, "WE WANT GOLDWATER! WE WANT GOLD-WATER!"
AND?..
WELL, NATURALLY, I PANICKED.
GBTrudeau

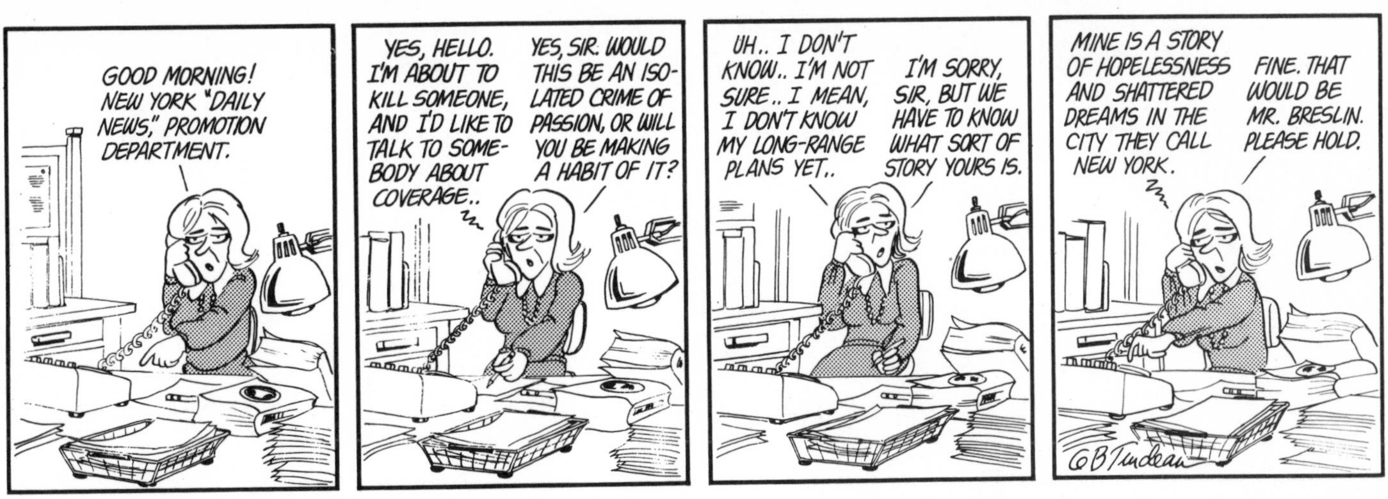
GOOD MORNING! NEW YORK "DAILY NEWS," PROMOTION DEPARTMENT.
YES, HELLO. I'M ABOUT TO KILL SOMEONE, AND I'D LIKE TO TALK TO SOMEBODY ABOUT COVERAGE..
YES, SIR. WOULD THIS BE AN ISOLATED CRIME OF PASSION, OR WILL YOU BE MAKING A HABIT OF IT?
UH.. I DON'T KNOW.. I'M NOT SURE.. I MEAN, I DON'T KNOW MY LONG-RANGE PLANS YET..
I'M SORRY, SIR, BUT WE HAVE TO KNOW WHAT SORT OF STORY YOURS IS.
MINE IS A STORY OF HOPELESSNESS AND SHATTERED DREAMS IN THE CITY THEY CALL NEW YORK.
FINE. THAT WOULD BE MR. BRESLIN. PLEASE HOLD.

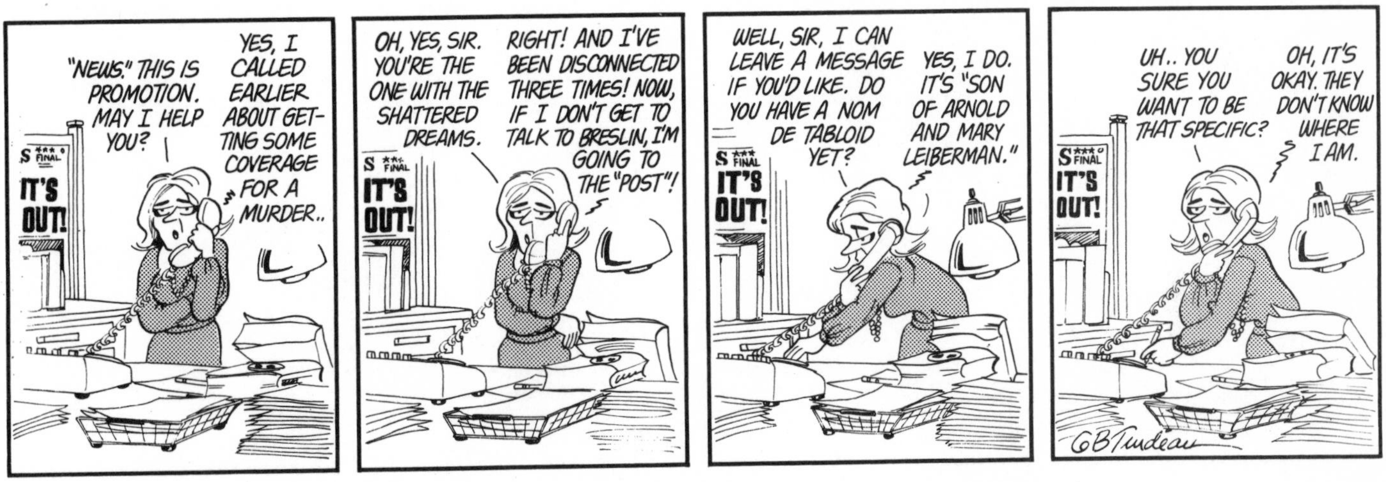
"NEWS." THIS IS PROMOTION. MAY I HELP YOU?
YES, I CALLED EARLIER ABOUT GETTING SOME COVERAGE FOR A MURDER..
OH, YES, SIR. YOU'RE THE ONE WITH THE SHATTERED DREAMS.
RIGHT! AND I'VE BEEN DISCONNECTED THREE TIMES! NOW, IF I DON'T GET TO TALK TO BRESLIN, I'M GOING TO THE "POST"!
WELL, SIR, I CAN LEAVE A MESSAGE IF YOU'D LIKE. DO YOU HAVE A NOM DE TABLOID YET?
YES, I DO. IT'S "SON OF ARNOLD AND MARY LEIBERMAN."
UH.. YOU SURE YOU WANT TO BE THAT SPECIFIC?
OH, IT'S OKAY. THEY DON'T KNOW WHERE I AM.

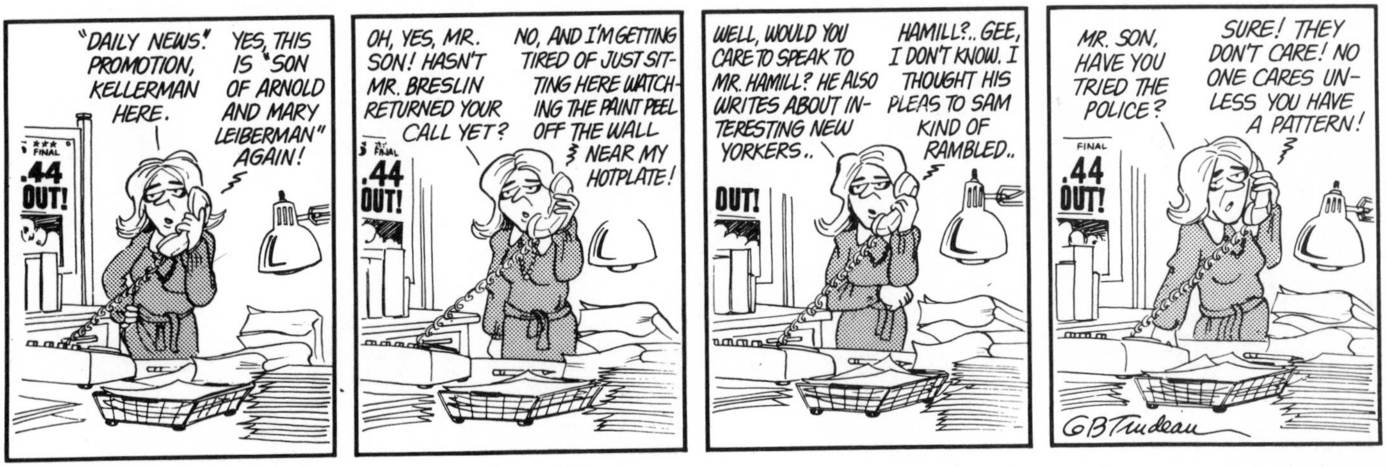
"DAILY NEWS." PROMOTION, KELLERMAN HERE.
YES, THIS IS "SON OF ARNOLD AND MARY LEIBERMAN" AGAIN!
OH, YES, MR. SON! HASN'T MR. BRESLIN RETURNED YOUR CALL YET?
NO, AND I'M GETTING TIRED OF JUST SITTING HERE WATCHING THE PAINT PEEL OFF THE WALL NEAR MY HOTPLATE!
WELL, WOULD YOU CARE TO SPEAK TO MR. HAMILL? HE ALSO WRITES ABOUT INTERESTING NEW YORKERS..
HAMILL?.. GEE, I DON'T KNOW. I THOUGHT HIS PLEAS TO SAM KIND OF RAMBLED..
MR. SON, HAVE YOU TRIED THE POLICE?
SURE! THEY DON'T CARE! NO ONE CARES UNLESS YOU HAVE A PATTERN!

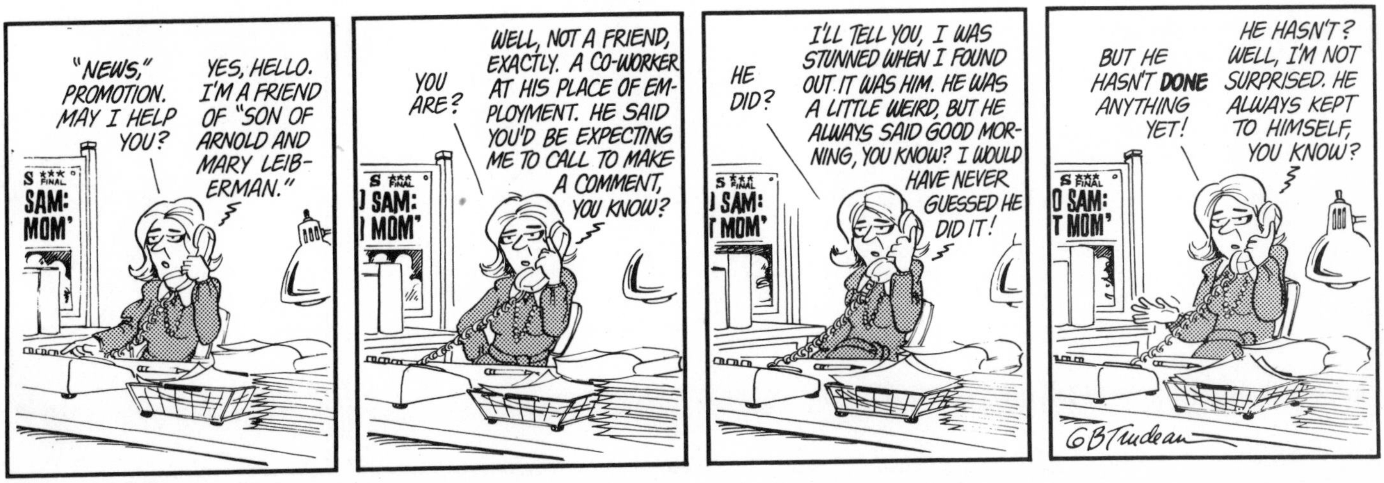
"NEWS," PROMOTION. MAY I HELP YOU?
YES, HELLO. I'M A FRIEND OF "SON OF ARNOLD AND MARY LEIBERMAN."
YOU ARE?
WELL, NOT A FRIEND, EXACTLY. A CO-WORKER AT HIS PLACE OF EMPLOYMENT. HE SAID YOU'D BE EXPECTING ME TO CALL TO MAKE A COMMENT, YOU KNOW?
HE DID?
I'LL TELL YOU, I WAS STUNNED WHEN I FOUND OUT IT WAS HIM. HE WAS A LITTLE WEIRD, BUT HE ALWAYS SAID GOOD MORNING, YOU KNOW? I WOULD HAVE NEVER GUESSED HE DID IT!
BUT HE HASN'T DONE ANYTHING YET!
HE HASN'T? WELL, I'M NOT SURPRISED. HE ALWAYS KEPT TO HIMSELF, YOU KNOW?

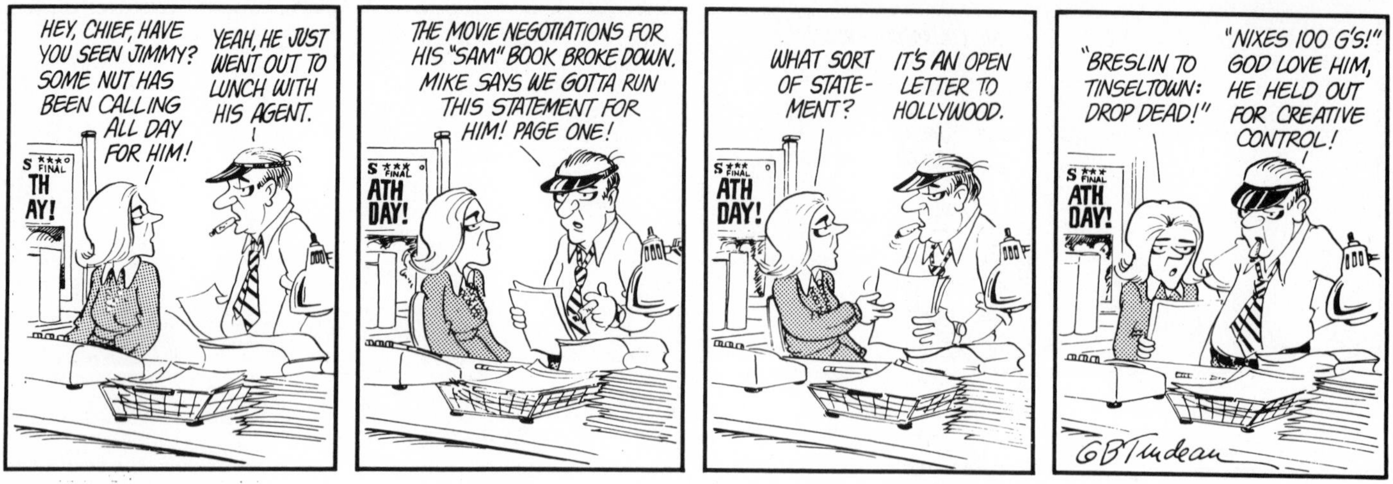
HEY, CHIEF, HAVE YOU SEEN JIMMY? SOME NUT HAS BEEN CALLING ALL DAY FOR HIM!
YEAH, HE JUST WENT OUT TO LUNCH WITH HIS AGENT.
THE MOVIE NEGOTIATIONS FOR HIS "SAM" BOOK BROKE DOWN. MIKE SAYS WE GOTTA RUN THIS STATEMENT FOR HIM! PAGE ONE!
WHAT SORT OF STATEMENT?
IT'S AN OPEN LETTER TO HOLLYWOOD.
"BRESLIN TO TINSELTOWN: DROP DEAD!"
"NIXES 100 G'S!" GOD LOVE HIM, HE HELD OUT FOR CREATIVE CONTROL!
GBTrudeau

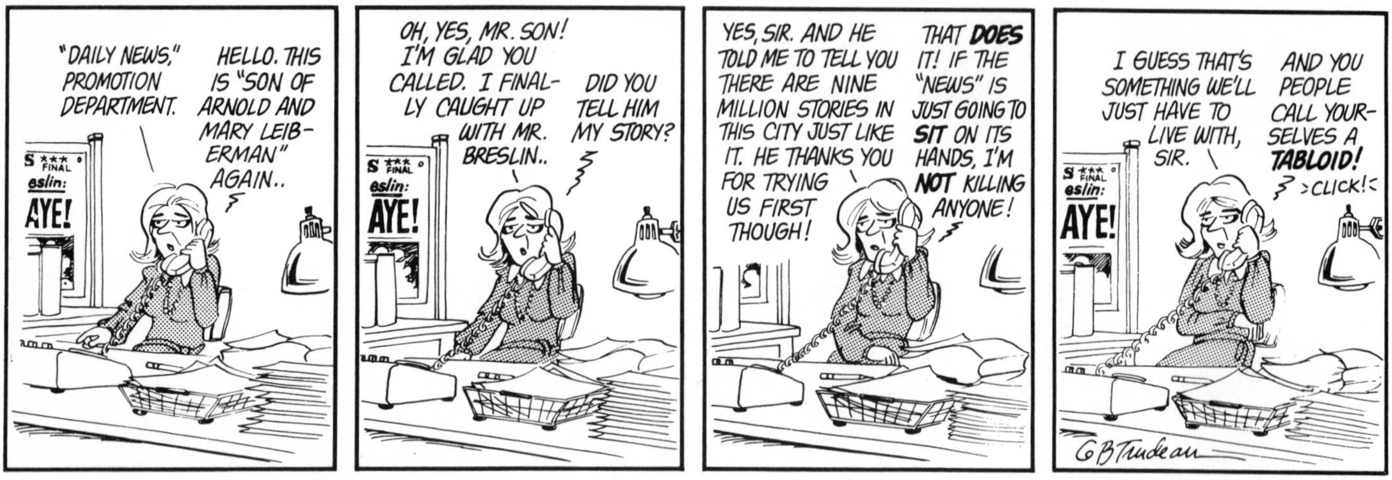
"DAILY NEWS," PROMOTION DEPARTMENT.
HELLO. THIS IS "SON OF ARNOLD AND MARY LEIBERMAN" AGAIN..
OH, YES, MR. SON! I'M GLAD YOU CALLED. I FINALLY CAUGHT UP WITH MR. BRESLIN..
DID YOU TELL HIM MY STORY?
YES, SIR. AND HE TOLD ME TO TELL YOU THERE ARE NINE MILLION STORIES IN THIS CITY JUST LIKE IT. HE THANKS YOU FOR TRYING US FIRST THOUGH!
THAT DOES IT! IF THE "NEWS" IS JUST GOING TO SIT ON ITS HANDS, I'M NOT KILLING ANYONE!
I GUESS THAT'S SOMETHING WE'LL JUST HAVE TO LIVE WITH, SIR.
AND YOU PEOPLE CALL YOURSELVES A TABLOID!
>CLICK!<
GBTrudeau

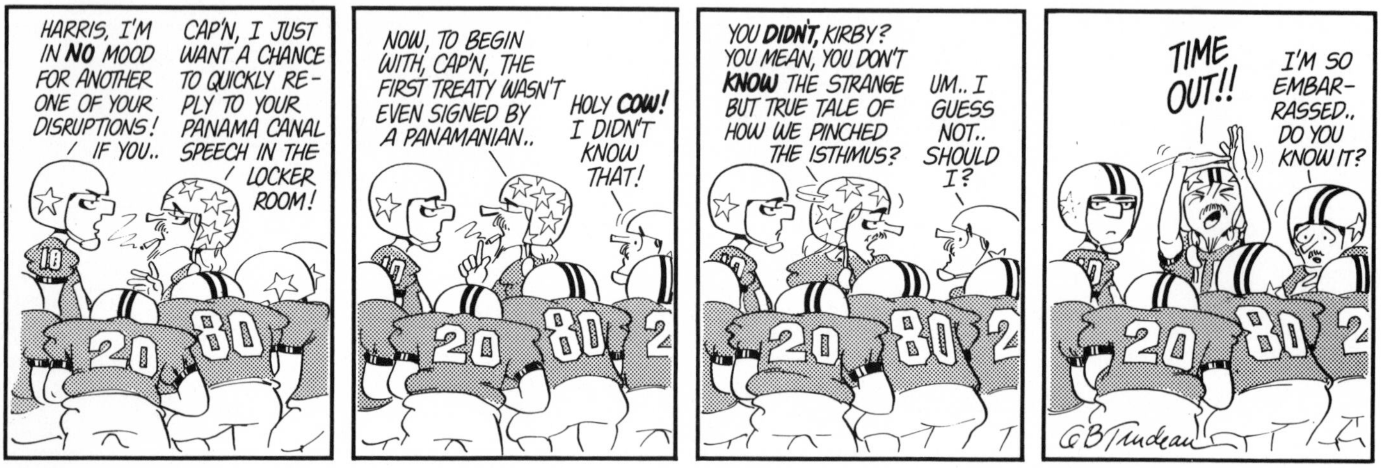
HARRIS, I'M IN NO MOOD FOR ANOTHER ONE OF YOUR DISRUPTIONS! IF YOU..
CAP'N, I JUST WANT A CHANCE TO QUICKLY REPLY TO YOUR PANAMA CANAL SPEECH IN THE LOCKER ROOM!
NOW, TO BEGIN WITH, CAP'N, THE FIRST TREATY WASN'T EVEN SIGNED BY A PANAMANIAN..
HOLY COW! I DIDN'T KNOW THAT!
YOU DIDN'T, KIRBY? YOU MEAN, YOU DON'T KNOW THE STRANGE BUT TRUE TALE OF HOW WE PINCHED THE ISTHMUS?
UM.. I GUESS NOT.. SHOULD I?
TIME OUT!!
I'M SO EMBARRASSED.. DO YOU KNOW IT?
GBTrudeau

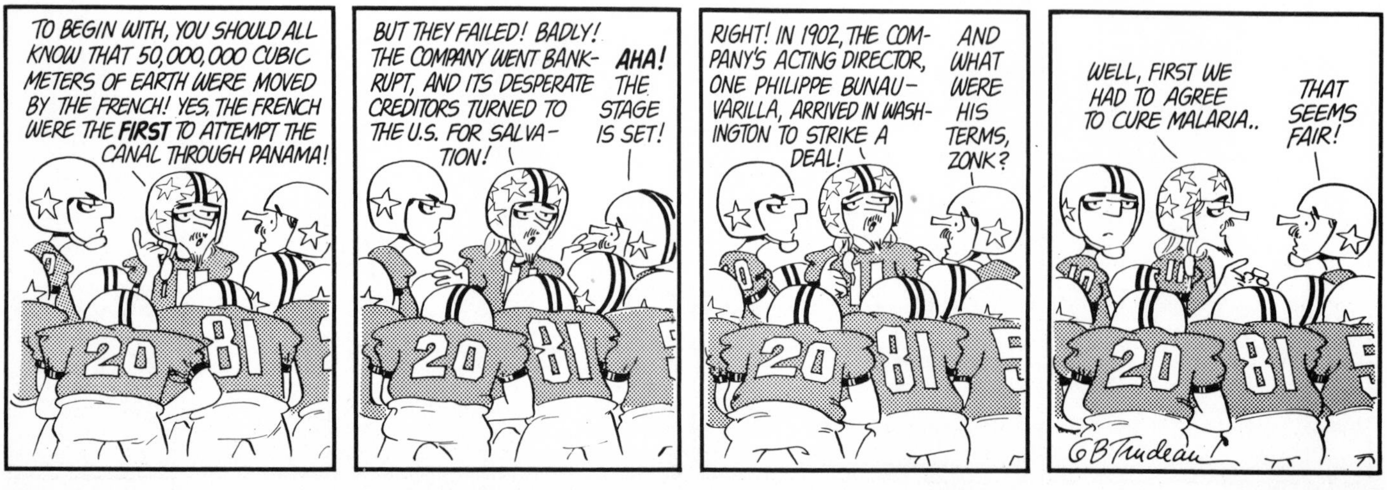
TO BEGIN WITH, YOU SHOULD ALL KNOW THAT 50,000,000 CUBIC METERS OF EARTH WERE MOVED BY THE FRENCH! YES, THE FRENCH WERE THE FIRST TO ATTEMPT THE CANAL THROUGH PANAMA!
BUT THEY FAILED! BADLY! THE COMPANY WENT BANKRUPT, AND ITS DESPERATE CREDITORS TURNED TO THE U.S. FOR SALVATION!
AHA! THE STAGE IS SET!
RIGHT! IN 1902, THE COMPANY'S ACTING DIRECTOR, ONE PHILIPPE BUNAU-VARILLA, ARRIVED IN WASHINGTON TO STRIKE A DEAL!
AND WHAT WERE HIS TERMS, ZONK?
WELL, FIRST WE HAD TO AGREE TO CURE MALARIA..
THAT SEEMS FAIR!
GBTrudeau

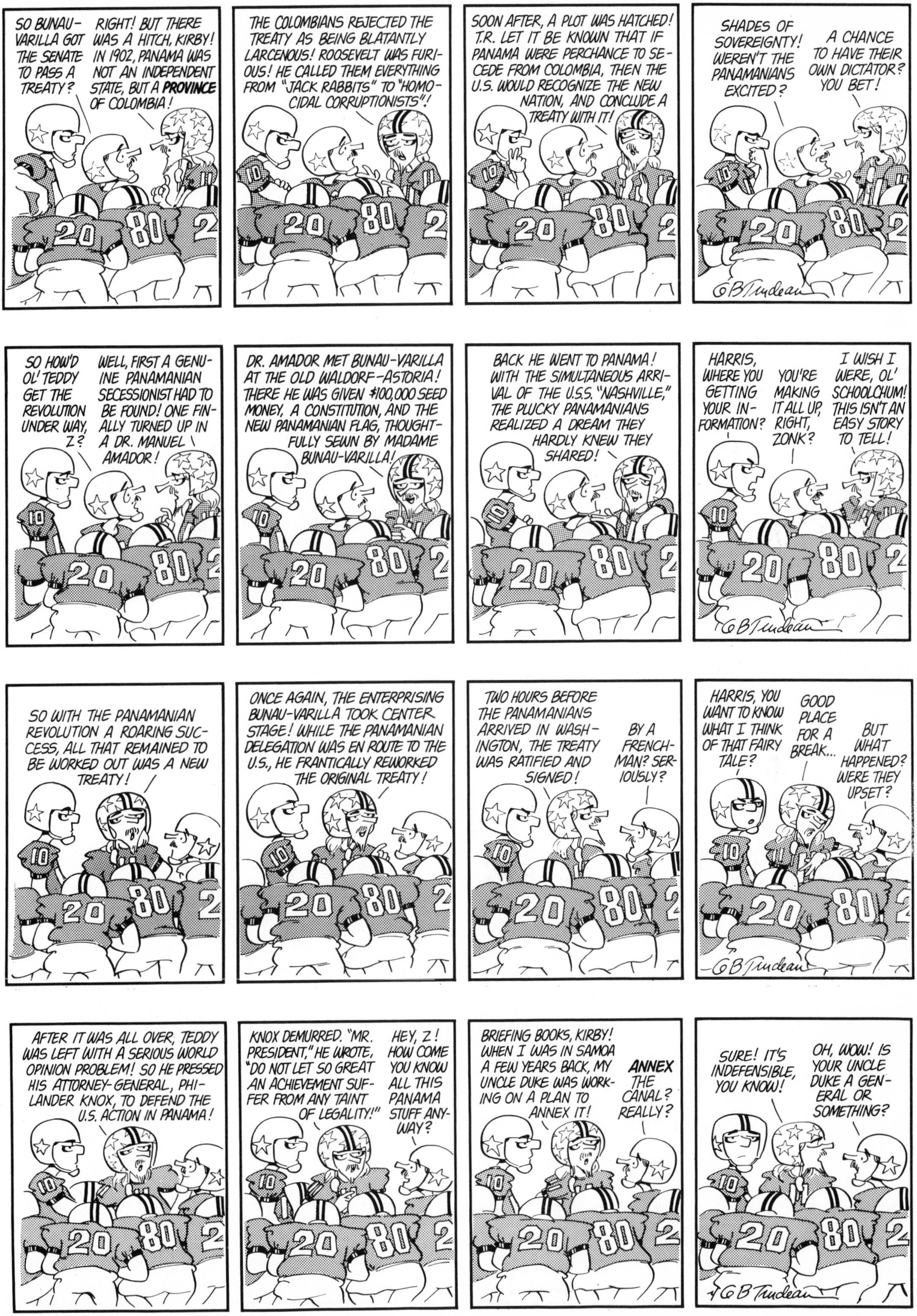
SO BUNAU-VARILLA GOT THE SENATE TO PASS A TREATY?
RIGHT! BUT THERE WAS A HITCH, KIRBY! IN 1902, PANAMA WAS NOT AN INDEPENDENT STATE, BUT A **PROVINCE** OF COLOMBIA!
THE COLOMBIANS REJECTED THE TREATY AS BEING BLATANTLY LARCENOUS! ROOSEVELT WAS FURIOUS! HE CALLED THEM EVERYTHING FROM "JACK RABBITS" TO "HOMOCIDAL CORRUPTIONISTS"!
SOON AFTER, A PLOT WAS HATCHED! T.R. LET IT BE KNOWN THAT IF PANAMA WERE PERCHANCE TO SECEDE FROM COLOMBIA, THEN THE U.S. WOULD RECOGNIZE THE NEW NATION, AND CONCLUDE A TREATY WITH IT!
SHADES OF SOVEREIGNTY! WEREN'T THE PANAMANIANS EXCITED?
A CHANCE TO HAVE THEIR OWN DICTATOR? YOU BET!
GBTrudeau
SO HOW'D OL' TEDDY GET THE REVOLUTION UNDER WAY, Z?
WELL, FIRST A GENUINE PANAMANIAN SECESSIONIST HAD TO BE FOUND! ONE FINALLY TURNED UP IN A DR. MANUEL AMADOR!
DR. AMADOR MET BUNAU-VARILLA AT THE OLD WALDORF-ASTORIA! THERE HE WAS GIVEN $100,000 SEED MONEY, A CONSTITUTION, AND THE NEW PANAMANIAN FLAG, THOUGHTFULLY SEWN BY MADAME BUNAU-VARILLA!
BACK HE WENT TO PANAMA! WITH THE SIMULTANEOUS ARRIVAL OF THE U.S.S. "NASHVILLE," THE PLUCKY PANAMANIANS REALIZED A DREAM THEY HARDLY KNEW THEY SHARED!
HARRIS, WHERE YOU GETTING YOUR INFORMATION?
YOU'RE MAKING IT ALL UP, RIGHT, ZONK?
I WISH I WERE, OL' SCHOOLCHUM! THIS ISN'T AN EASY STORY TO TELL!
GBTrudeau
SO WITH THE PANAMANIAN REVOLUTION A ROARING SUCCESS, ALL THAT REMAINED TO BE WORKED OUT WAS A NEW TREATY!
ONCE AGAIN, THE ENTERPRISING BUNAU-VARILLA TOOK CENTER STAGE! WHILE THE PANAMANIAN DELEGATION WAS EN ROUTE TO THE U.S., HE FRANTICALLY REWORKED THE ORIGINAL TREATY!
TWO HOURS BEFORE THE PANAMANIANS ARRIVED IN WASHINGTON, THE TREATY WAS RATIFIED AND SIGNED!
BY A FRENCHMAN? SERIOUSLY?
HARRIS, YOU WANT TO KNOW WHAT I THINK OF THAT FAIRY TALE?
GOOD PLACE FOR A BREAK...
BUT WHAT HAPPENED? WERE THEY UPSET?
GBTrudeau
AFTER IT WAS ALL OVER, TEDDY WAS LEFT WITH A SERIOUS WORLD OPINION PROBLEM! SO HE PRESSED HIS ATTORNEY-GENERAL, PHILANDER KNOX, TO DEFEND THE U.S. ACTION IN PANAMA!
KNOX DEMURRED. "MR. PRESIDENT," HE WROTE, "DO NOT LET SO GREAT AN ACHIEVEMENT SUFFER FROM ANY TAINT OF LEGALITY!"
HEY, Z! HOW COME YOU KNOW ALL THIS PANAMA STUFF ANYWAY?
BRIEFING BOOKS, KIRBY! WHEN I WAS IN SAMOA A FEW YEARS BACK, MY UNCLE DUKE WAS WORKING ON A PLAN TO ANNEX IT!
ANNEX THE CANAL? REALLY?
SURE! IT'S INDEFENSIBLE, YOU KNOW!
OH, WOW! IS YOUR UNCLE DUKE A GENERAL OR SOMETHING?
GBTrudeau

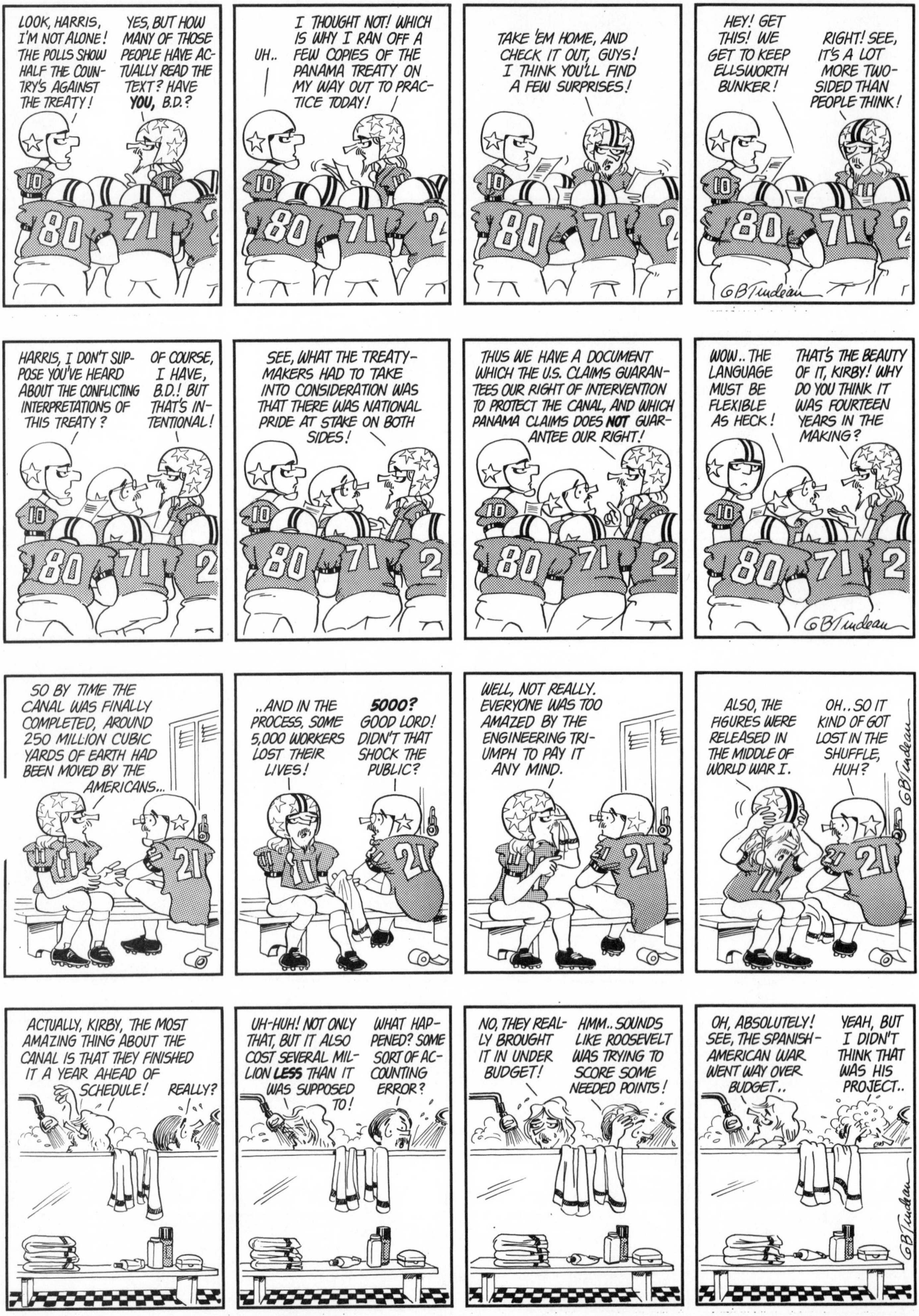
LOOK, HARRIS, I'M NOT ALONE! THE POLLS SHOW HALF THE COUNTRY'S AGAINST THE TREATY!
YES, BUT HOW MANY OF THOSE PEOPLE HAVE ACTUALLY READ THE TEXT? HAVE **YOU,** B.D.?
UH..
I THOUGHT NOT! WHICH IS WHY I RAN OFF A FEW COPIES OF THE PANAMA TREATY ON MY WAY OUT TO PRACTICE TODAY!
TAKE 'EM HOME, AND CHECK IT OUT, GUYS! I THINK YOU'LL FIND A FEW SURPRISES!
HEY! GET THIS! WE GET TO KEEP ELLSWORTH BUNKER!
RIGHT! SEE, IT'S A LOT MORE TWO-SIDED THAN PEOPLE THINK!
© B Trudeau
HARRIS, I DON'T SUPPOSE YOU'VE HEARD ABOUT THE CONFLICTING INTERPRETATIONS OF THIS TREATY?
OF COURSE, I HAVE, B.D.! BUT THAT'S INTENTIONAL!
SEE, WHAT THE TREATY-MAKERS HAD TO TAKE INTO CONSIDERATION WAS THAT THERE WAS NATIONAL PRIDE AT STAKE ON BOTH SIDES!
THUS WE HAVE A DOCUMENT WHICH THE U.S. CLAIMS GUARANTEES OUR RIGHT OF INTERVENTION TO PROTECT THE CANAL, AND WHICH PANAMA CLAIMS DOES **NOT** GUARANTEE OUR RIGHT!
WOW.. THE LANGUAGE MUST BE FLEXIBLE AS HECK!
THAT'S THE BEAUTY OF IT, KIRBY! WHY DO YOU THINK IT WAS FOURTEEN YEARS IN THE MAKING?
© B Trudeau
SO BY TIME THE CANAL WAS FINALLY COMPLETED, AROUND 250 MILLION CUBIC YARDS OF EARTH HAD BEEN MOVED BY THE AMERICANS...
..AND IN THE PROCESS, SOME 5,000 WORKERS LOST THEIR LIVES!
5000? GOOD LORD! DIDN'T THAT SHOCK THE PUBLIC?
WELL, NOT REALLY. EVERYONE WAS TOO AMAZED BY THE ENGINEERING TRIUMPH TO PAY IT ANY MIND.
ALSO, THE FIGURES WERE RELEASED IN THE MIDDLE OF WORLD WAR I.
OH.. SO IT KIND OF GOT LOST IN THE SHUFFLE, HUH?
© B Trudeau
ACTUALLY, KIRBY, THE MOST AMAZING THING ABOUT THE CANAL IS THAT THEY FINISHED IT A YEAR AHEAD OF SCHEDULE!
REALLY?
UH-HUH! NOT ONLY THAT, BUT IT ALSO COST SEVERAL MILLION **LESS** THAN IT WAS SUPPOSED TO!
WHAT HAPPENED? SOME SORT OF ACCOUNTING ERROR?
NO, THEY REALLY BROUGHT IT IN UNDER BUDGET!
HMM.. SOUNDS LIKE ROOSEVELT WAS TRYING TO SCORE SOME NEEDED POINTS!
OH, ABSOLUTELY! SEE, THE SPANISH-AMERICAN WAR WENT WAY OVER BUDGET..
YEAH, BUT I DIDN'T THINK THAT WAS HIS PROJECT..
© B Trudeau

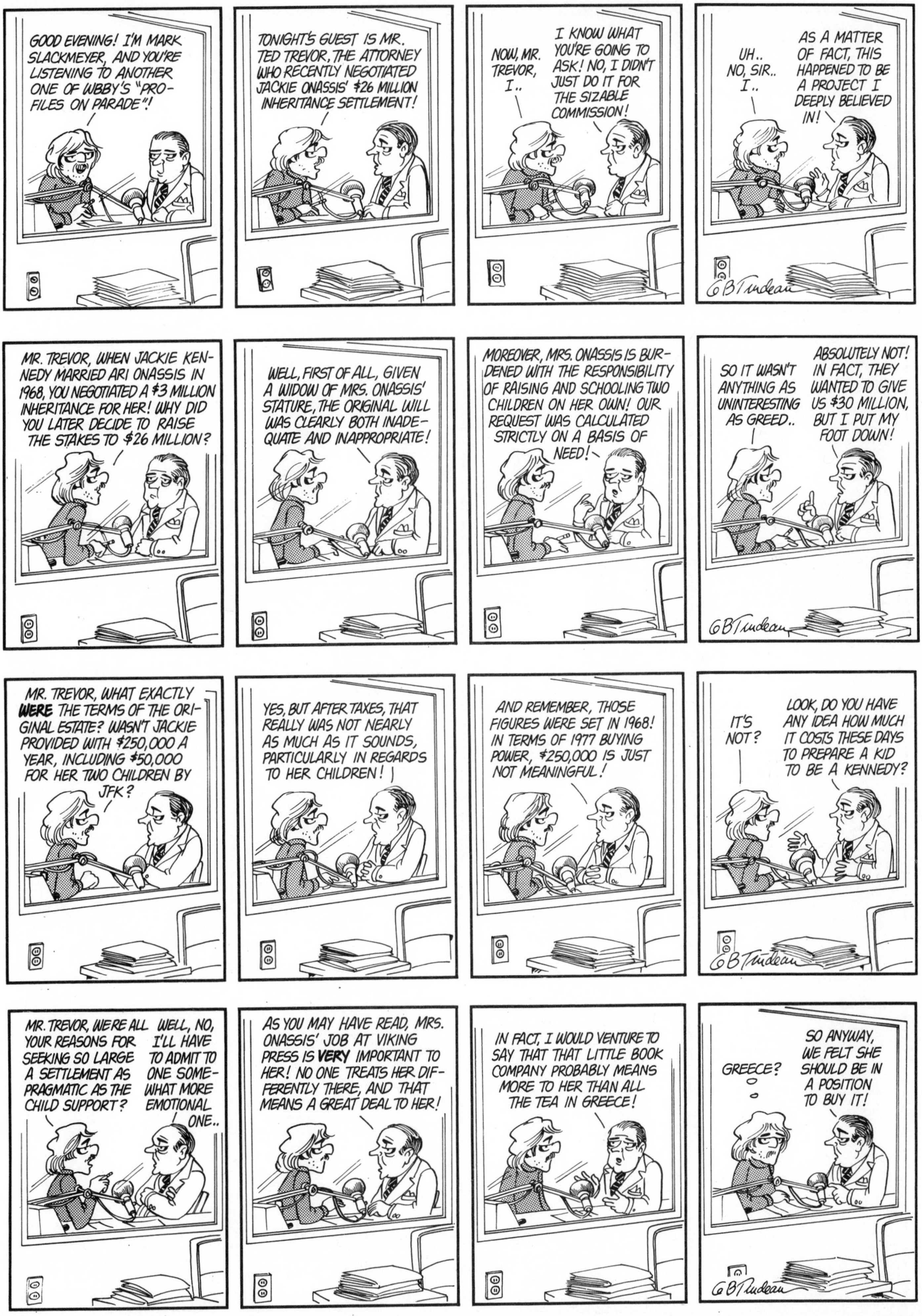
GOOD EVENING! I'M MARK SLACKMEYER, AND YOU'RE LISTENING TO ANOTHER ONE OF WBBY'S "PROFILES ON PARADE"!
TONIGHT'S GUEST IS MR. TED TREVOR, THE ATTORNEY WHO RECENTLY NEGOTIATED JACKIE ONASSIS' $26 MILLION INHERITANCE SETTLEMENT!
NOW, MR. TREVOR, I..
I KNOW WHAT YOU'RE GOING TO ASK! NO, I DIDN'T JUST DO IT FOR THE SIZABLE COMMISSION!
UH.. NO, SIR.. I..
AS A MATTER OF FACT, THIS HAPPENED TO BE A PROJECT I DEEPLY BELIEVED IN!
GBTrudeau
MR. TREVOR, WHEN JACKIE KENNEDY MARRIED ARI ONASSIS IN 1968, YOU NEGOTIATED A $3 MILLION INHERITANCE FOR HER! WHY DID YOU LATER DECIDE TO RAISE THE STAKES TO $26 MILLION?
WELL, FIRST OF ALL, GIVEN A WIDOW OF MRS. ONASSIS' STATURE, THE ORIGINAL WILL WAS CLEARLY BOTH INADEQUATE AND INAPPROPRIATE!
MOREOVER, MRS. ONASSIS IS BURDENED WITH THE RESPONSIBILITY OF RAISING AND SCHOOLING TWO CHILDREN ON HER OWN! OUR REQUEST WAS CALCULATED STRICTLY ON A BASIS OF NEED!
SO IT WASN'T ANYTHING AS UNINTERESTING AS GREED..
ABSOLUTELY NOT! IN FACT, THEY WANTED TO GIVE US $30 MILLION, BUT I PUT MY FOOT DOWN!
GBTrudeau
MR. TREVOR, WHAT EXACTLY WERE THE TERMS OF THE ORIGINAL ESTATE? WASN'T JACKIE PROVIDED WITH $250,000 A YEAR, INCLUDING $50,000 FOR HER TWO CHILDREN BY JFK?
YES, BUT AFTER TAXES, THAT REALLY WAS NOT NEARLY AS MUCH AS IT SOUNDS, PARTICULARLY IN REGARDS TO HER CHILDREN!
AND REMEMBER, THOSE FIGURES WERE SET IN 1968! IN TERMS OF 1977 BUYING POWER, $250,000 IS JUST NOT MEANINGFUL!
IT'S NOT?
LOOK, DO YOU HAVE ANY IDEA HOW MUCH IT COSTS THESE DAYS TO PREPARE A KID TO BE A KENNEDY?
GBTrudeau
MR. TREVOR, WERE ALL YOUR REASONS FOR SEEKING SO LARGE A SETTLEMENT AS PRAGMATIC AS THE CHILD SUPPORT?
WELL, NO, I'LL HAVE TO ADMIT TO ONE SOMEWHAT MORE EMOTIONAL ONE..
AS YOU MAY HAVE READ, MRS. ONASSIS' JOB AT VIKING PRESS IS VERY IMPORTANT TO HER! NO ONE TREATS HER DIFFERENTLY THERE, AND THAT MEANS A GREAT DEAL TO HER!
IN FACT, I WOULD VENTURE TO SAY THAT THAT LITTLE BOOK COMPANY PROBABLY MEANS MORE TO HER THAN ALL THE TEA IN GREECE!
GREECE?
SO ANYWAY, WE FELT SHE SHOULD BE IN A POSITION TO BUY IT!
GBTrudeau

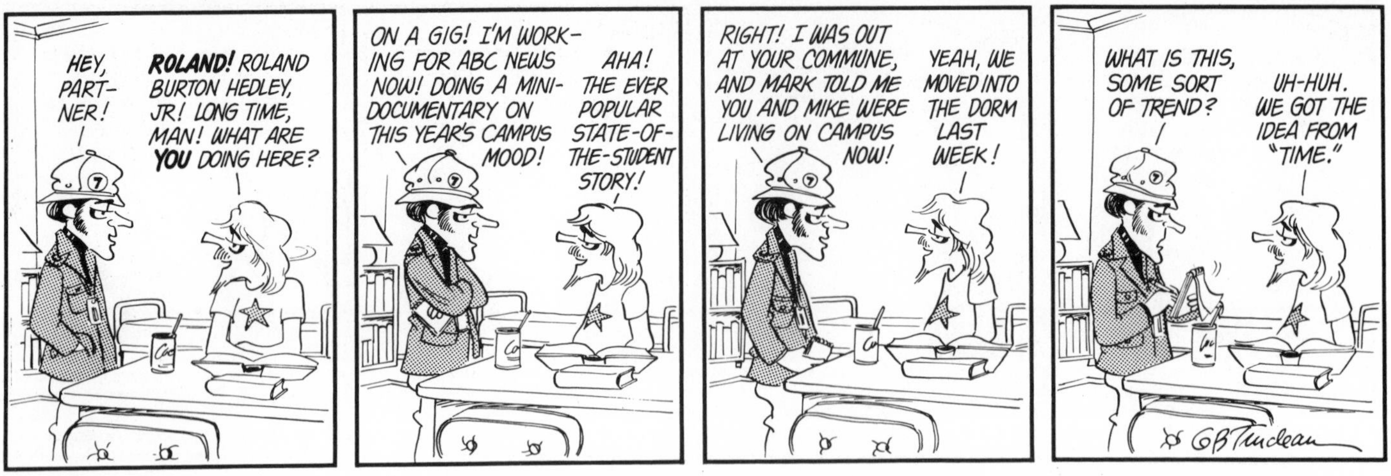
HEY, PARTNER!
ROLAND! ROLAND BURTON HEDLEY, JR! LONG TIME, MAN! WHAT ARE YOU DOING HERE?
ON A GIG! I'M WORKING FOR ABC NEWS NOW! DOING A MINI-DOCUMENTARY ON THIS YEAR'S CAMPUS MOOD!
AHA! THE EVER POPULAR STATE-OF-THE-STUDENT STORY!
RIGHT! I WAS OUT AT YOUR COMMUNE, AND MARK TOLD ME YOU AND MIKE WERE LIVING ON CAMPUS NOW!
YEAH, WE MOVED INTO THE DORM LAST WEEK!
WHAT IS THIS, SOME SORT OF TREND?
UH-HUH. WE GOT THE IDEA FROM "TIME."
GBTrudeau

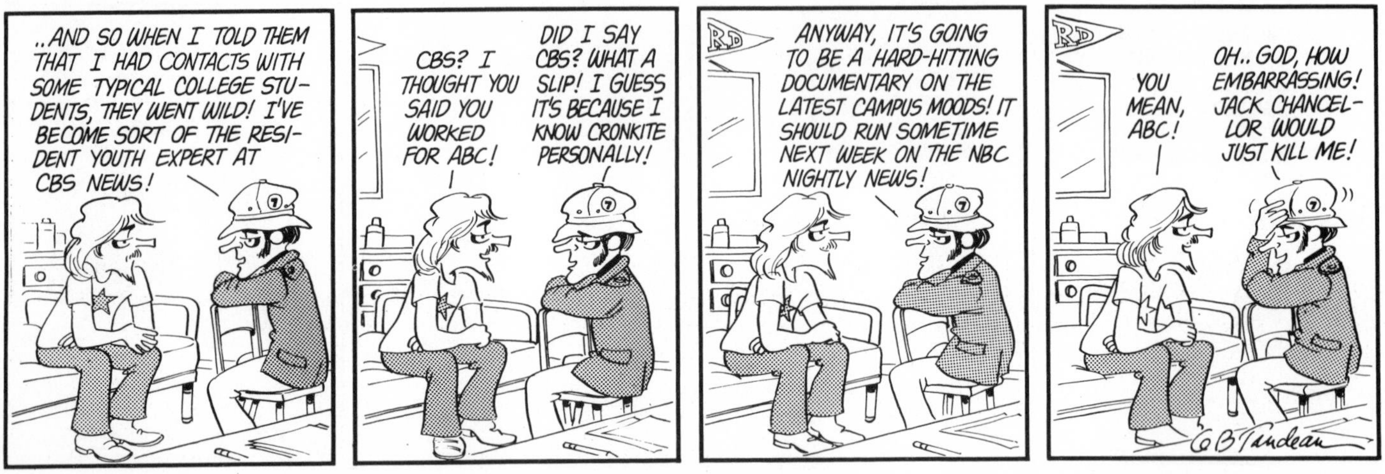
..AND SO WHEN I TOLD THEM THAT I HAD CONTACTS WITH SOME TYPICAL COLLEGE STUDENTS, THEY WENT WILD! I'VE BECOME SORT OF THE RESIDENT YOUTH EXPERT AT CBS NEWS!
CBS? I THOUGHT YOU SAID YOU WORKED FOR ABC!
DID I SAY CBS? WHAT A SLIP! I GUESS IT'S BECAUSE I KNOW CRONKITE PERSONALLY!
ANYWAY, IT'S GOING TO BE A HARD-HITTING DOCUMENTARY ON THE LATEST CAMPUS MOODS! IT SHOULD RUN SOMETIME NEXT WEEK ON THE NBC NIGHTLY NEWS!
YOU MEAN, ABC!
OH.. GOD, HOW EMBARRASSING! JACK CHANCELLOR WOULD JUST KILL ME!
GBTrudeau

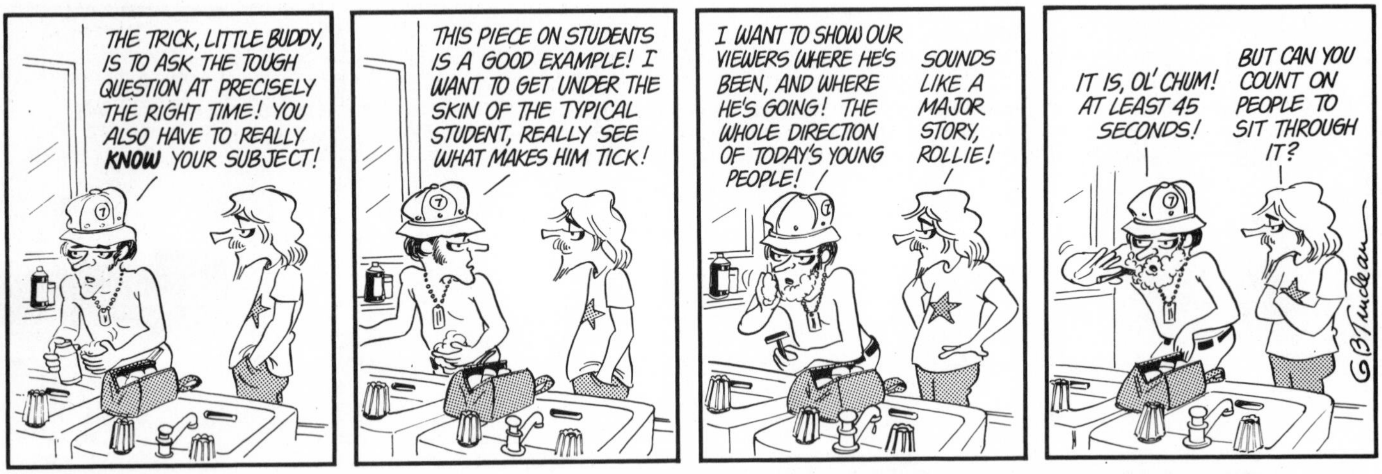
THE TRICK, LITTLE BUDDY, IS TO ASK THE TOUGH QUESTION AT PRECISELY THE RIGHT TIME! YOU ALSO HAVE TO REALLY KNOW YOUR SUBJECT!
THIS PIECE ON STUDENTS IS A GOOD EXAMPLE! I WANT TO GET UNDER THE SKIN OF THE TYPICAL STUDENT, REALLY SEE WHAT MAKES HIM TICK!
I WANT TO SHOW OUR VIEWERS WHERE HE'S BEEN, AND WHERE HE'S GOING! THE WHOLE DIRECTION OF TODAY'S YOUNG PEOPLE!
SOUNDS LIKE A MAJOR STORY, ROLLIE!
IT IS, OL' CHUM! AT LEAST 45 SECONDS!
BUT CAN YOU COUNT ON PEOPLE TO SIT THROUGH IT?
GBTrudeau

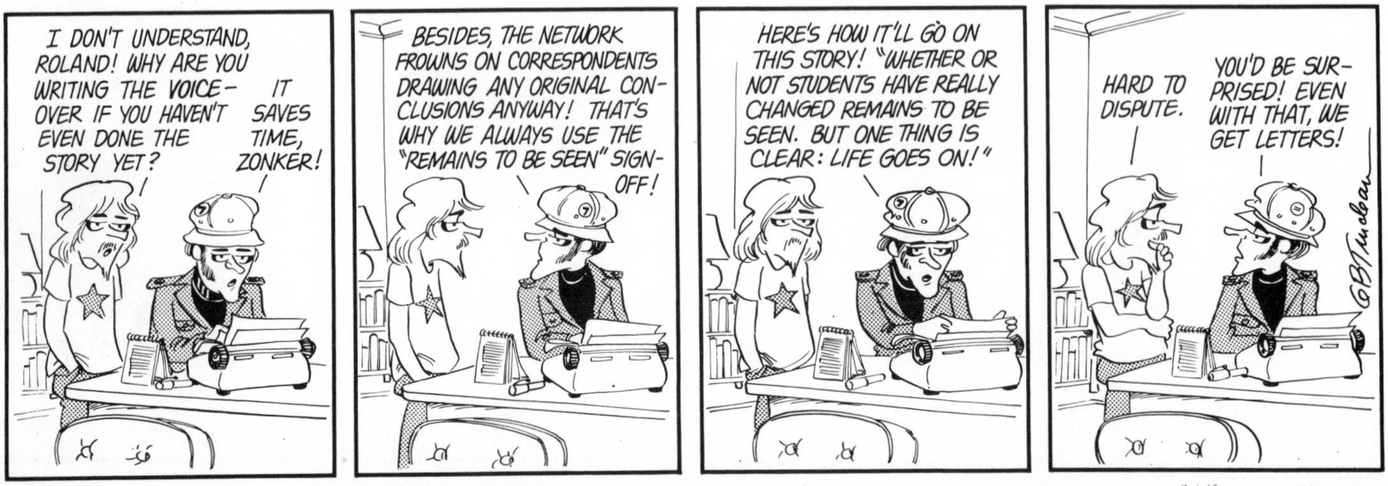
I DON'T UNDERSTAND, ROLAND! WHY ARE YOU WRITING THE VOICE-OVER IF YOU HAVEN'T EVEN DONE THE STORY YET?
IT SAVES TIME, ZONKER!
BESIDES, THE NETWORK FROWNS ON CORRESPONDENTS DRAWING ANY ORIGINAL CONCLUSIONS ANYWAY! THAT'S WHY WE ALWAYS USE THE "REMAINS TO BE SEEN" SIGN-OFF!
HERE'S HOW IT'LL GO ON THIS STORY! "WHETHER OR NOT STUDENTS HAVE REALLY CHANGED REMAINS TO BE SEEN. BUT ONE THING IS CLEAR: LIFE GOES ON!"
HARD TO DISPUTE.
YOU'D BE SURPRISED! EVEN WITH THAT, WE GET LETTERS!
GBTrudeau

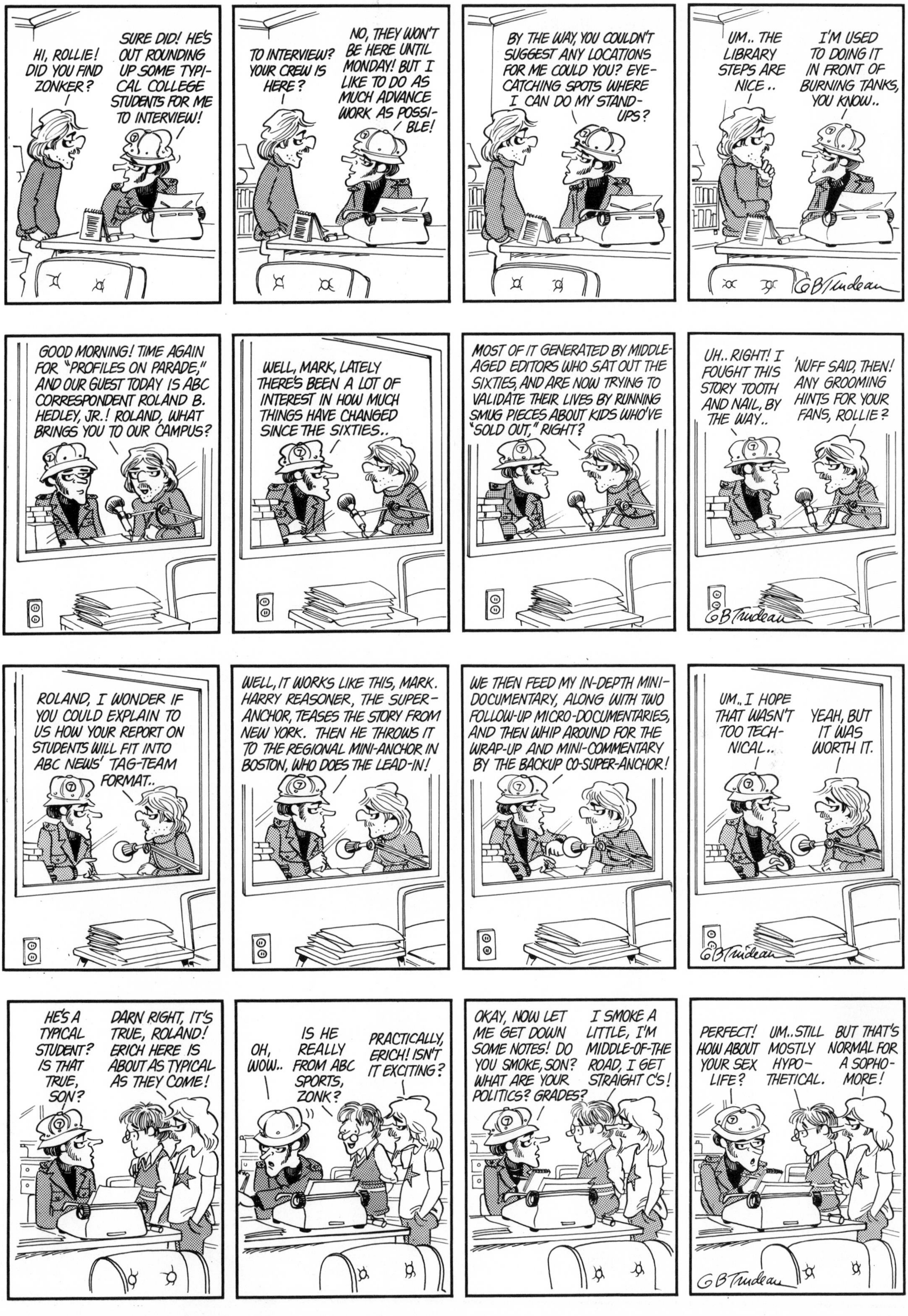
HI, ROLLIE! DID YOU FIND ZONKER?
SURE DID! HE'S OUT ROUNDING UP SOME TYPICAL COLLEGE STUDENTS FOR ME TO INTERVIEW!
TO INTERVIEW? YOUR CREW IS HERE?
NO, THEY WON'T BE HERE UNTIL MONDAY! BUT I LIKE TO DO AS MUCH ADVANCE WORK AS POSSIBLE!
BY THE WAY, YOU COULDN'T SUGGEST ANY LOCATIONS FOR ME COULD YOU? EYE-CATCHING SPOTS WHERE I CAN DO MY STAND-UPS?
UM.. THE LIBRARY STEPS ARE NICE..
I'M USED TO DOING IT IN FRONT OF BURNING TANKS, YOU KNOW..
GBTrudeau
GOOD MORNING! TIME AGAIN FOR "PROFILES ON PARADE," AND OUR GUEST TODAY IS ABC CORRESPONDENT ROLAND B. HEDLEY, JR.! ROLAND, WHAT BRINGS YOU TO OUR CAMPUS?
WELL, MARK, LATELY THERE'S BEEN A LOT OF INTEREST IN HOW MUCH THINGS HAVE CHANGED SINCE THE SIXTIES..
MOST OF IT GENERATED BY MIDDLE-AGED EDITORS WHO SAT OUT THE SIXTIES, AND ARE NOW TRYING TO VALIDATE THEIR LIVES BY RUNNING SMUG PIECES ABOUT KIDS WHO'VE "SOLD OUT," RIGHT?
UH.. RIGHT! I FOUGHT THIS STORY TOOTH AND NAIL, BY THE WAY..
'NUFF SAID, THEN! ANY GROOMING HINTS FOR YOUR FANS, ROLLIE?
GBTrudeau
ROLAND, I WONDER IF YOU COULD EXPLAIN TO US HOW YOUR REPORT ON STUDENTS WILL FIT INTO ABC NEWS' TAG-TEAM FORMAT..
WELL, IT WORKS LIKE THIS, MARK. HARRY REASONER, THE SUPER-ANCHOR, TEASES THE STORY FROM NEW YORK. THEN HE THROWS IT TO THE REGIONAL MINI-ANCHOR IN BOSTON, WHO DOES THE LEAD-IN!
WE THEN FEED MY IN-DEPTH MINI-DOCUMENTARY, ALONG WITH TWO FOLLOW-UP MICRO-DOCUMENTARIES, AND THEN WHIP AROUND FOR THE WRAP-UP AND MINI-COMMENTARY BY THE BACKUP CO-SUPER-ANCHOR!
UM.. I HOPE THAT WASN'T TOO TECHNICAL..
YEAH, BUT IT WAS WORTH IT.
GBTrudeau
HE'S A TYPICAL STUDENT? IS THAT TRUE, SON?
DARN RIGHT, IT'S TRUE, ROLAND! ERICH HERE IS ABOUT AS TYPICAL AS THEY COME!
OH, WOW..
IS HE REALLY FROM ABC SPORTS, ZONK?
PRACTICALLY, ERICH! ISN'T IT EXCITING?
OKAY, NOW LET ME GET DOWN SOME NOTES! DO YOU SMOKE, SON? WHAT ARE YOUR POLITICS? GRADES?
I SMOKE A LITTLE, I'M MIDDLE-OF-THE ROAD, I GET STRAIGHT C'S!
PERFECT! HOW ABOUT YOUR SEX LIFE?
UM.. STILL MOSTLY HYPOTHETICAL.
BUT THAT'S NORMAL FOR A SOPHOMORE!
GBTrudeau

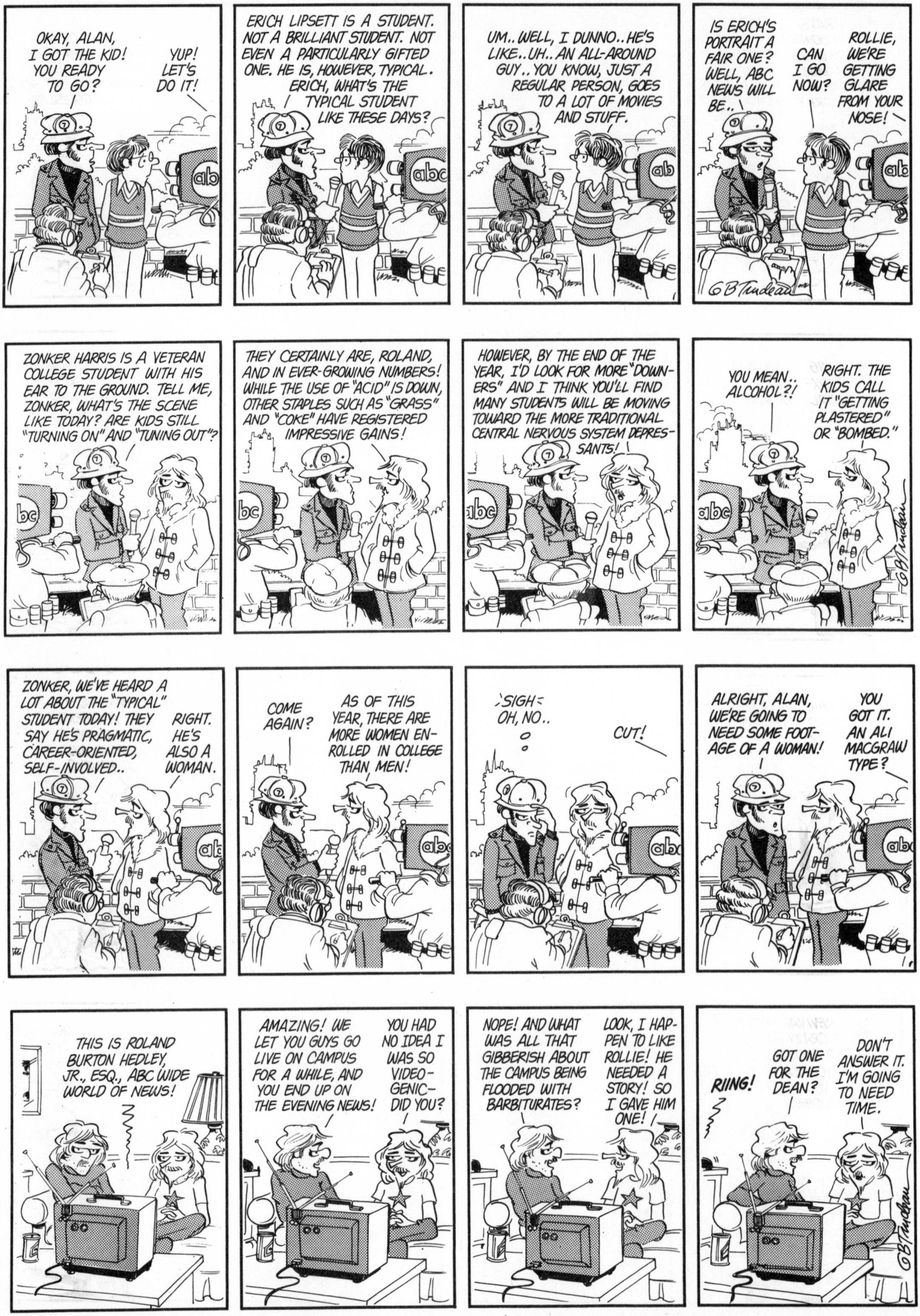
OKAY, ALAN, I GOT THE KID! YOU READY TO GO?
YUP! LET'S DO IT!
ERICH LIPSETT IS A STUDENT. NOT A BRILLIANT STUDENT. NOT EVEN A PARTICULARLY GIFTED ONE. HE IS, HOWEVER, TYPICAL. ERICH, WHAT'S THE TYPICAL STUDENT LIKE THESE DAYS?
UM.. WELL, I DUNNO.. HE'S LIKE.. UH.. AN ALL-AROUND GUY.. YOU KNOW, JUST A REGULAR PERSON, GOES TO A LOT OF MOVIES AND STUFF.
IS ERICH'S PORTRAIT A FAIR ONE? WELL, ABC NEWS WILL BE..
CAN I GO NOW?
ROLLIE, WE'RE GETTING GLARE FROM YOUR NOSE!
G B Trudeau
ZONKER HARRIS IS A VETERAN COLLEGE STUDENT WITH HIS EAR TO THE GROUND. TELL ME, ZONKER, WHAT'S THE SCENE LIKE TODAY? ARE KIDS STILL "TURNING ON" AND "TUNING OUT"?
THEY CERTAINLY ARE, ROLAND, AND IN EVER-GROWING NUMBERS! WHILE THE USE OF "ACID" IS DOWN, OTHER STAPLES SUCH AS "GRASS" AND "COKE" HAVE REGISTERED IMPRESSIVE GAINS!
HOWEVER, BY THE END OF THE YEAR, I'D LOOK FOR MORE "DOWNERS" AND I THINK YOU'LL FIND MANY STUDENTS WILL BE MOVING TOWARD THE MORE TRADITIONAL CENTRAL NERVOUS SYSTEM DEPRESSANTS!
YOU MEAN.. ALCOHOL?!
RIGHT. THE KIDS CALL IT "GETTING PLASTERED" OR "BOMBED."
G B Trudeau
ZONKER, WE'VE HEARD A LOT ABOUT THE "TYPICAL" STUDENT TODAY! THEY SAY HE'S PRAGMATIC, CAREER-ORIENTED, SELF-INVOLVED..
RIGHT. HE'S ALSO A WOMAN.
COME AGAIN?
AS OF THIS YEAR, THERE ARE MORE WOMEN ENROLLED IN COLLEGE THAN MEN!
SIGH
OH, NO..
CUT!
ALRIGHT, ALAN, WE'RE GOING TO NEED SOME FOOTAGE OF A WOMAN!
YOU GOT IT. AN ALI MACGRAW TYPE?
THIS IS ROLAND BURTON HEDLEY, JR., ESQ., ABC WIDE WORLD OF NEWS!
AMAZING! WE LET YOU GUYS GO LIVE ON CAMPUS FOR A WHILE, AND YOU END UP ON THE EVENING NEWS!
YOU HAD NO IDEA I WAS SO VIDEOGENIC- DID YOU?
NOPE! AND WHAT WAS ALL THAT GIBBERISH ABOUT THE CAMPUS BEING FLOODED WITH BARBITURATES?
LOOK, I HAPPEN TO LIKE ROLLIE! HE NEEDED A STORY! SO I GAVE HIM ONE!
RIING!
GOT ONE FOR THE DEAN?
DON'T ANSWER IT. I'M GOING TO NEED TIME.
G B Trudeau

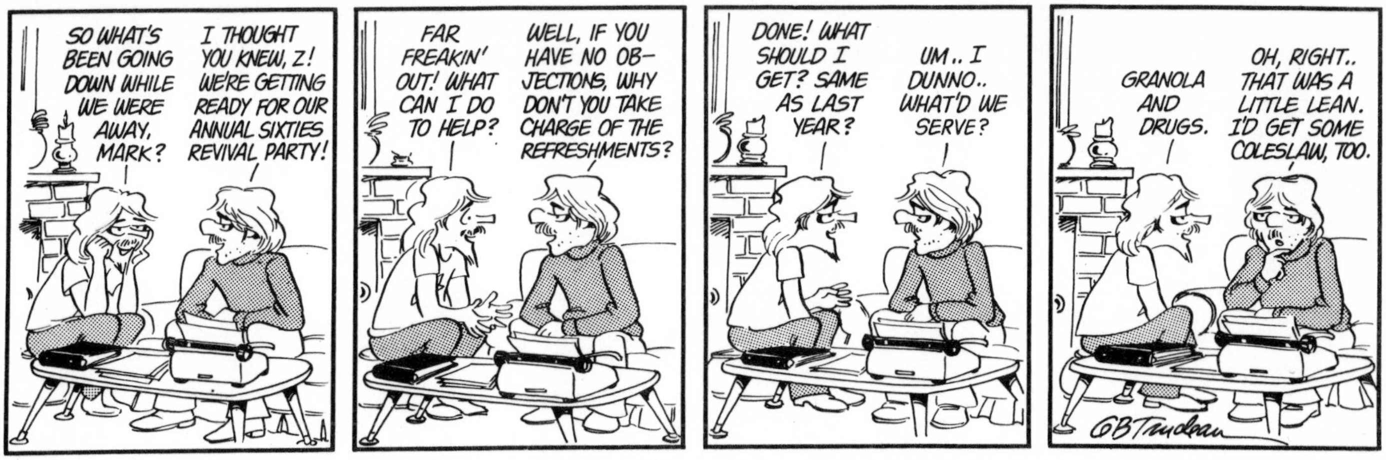
SO WHAT'S BEEN GOING DOWN WHILE WE WERE AWAY, MARK?
I THOUGHT YOU KNEW, Z! WE'RE GETTING READY FOR OUR ANNUAL SIXTIES REVIVAL PARTY!
FAR FREAKIN' OUT! WHAT CAN I DO TO HELP?
WELL, IF YOU HAVE NO OBJECTIONS, WHY DON'T YOU TAKE CHARGE OF THE REFRESHMENTS?
DONE! WHAT SHOULD I GET? SAME AS LAST YEAR?
UM.. I DUNNO.. WHAT'D WE SERVE?
GRANOLA AND DRUGS.
OH, RIGHT.. THAT WAS A LITTLE LEAN. I'D GET SOME COLESLAW, TOO.
GBTrudeau

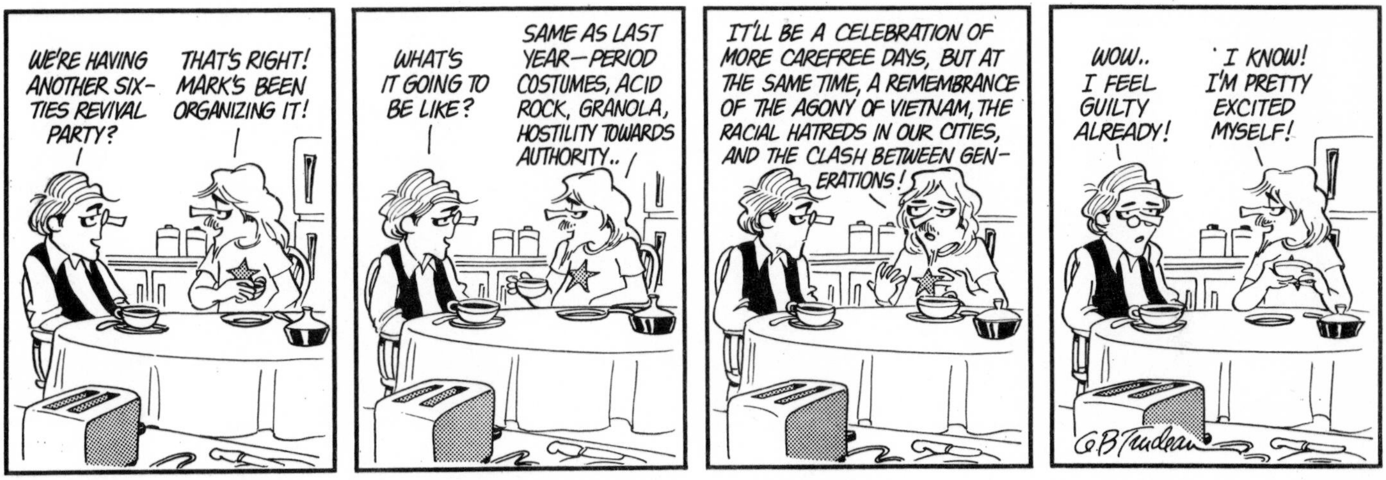
WE'RE HAVING ANOTHER SIXTIES REVIVAL PARTY?
THAT'S RIGHT! MARK'S BEEN ORGANIZING IT!
WHAT'S IT GOING TO BE LIKE?
SAME AS LAST YEAR—PERIOD COSTUMES, ACID ROCK, GRANOLA, HOSTILITY TOWARDS AUTHORITY..
IT'LL BE A CELEBRATION OF MORE CAREFREE DAYS, BUT AT THE SAME TIME, A REMEMBRANCE OF THE AGONY OF VIETNAM, THE RACIAL HATREDS IN OUR CITIES, AND THE CLASH BETWEEN GENERATIONS!
WOW.. I FEEL GUILTY ALREADY!
I KNOW! I'M PRETTY EXCITED MYSELF!
GBTrudeau

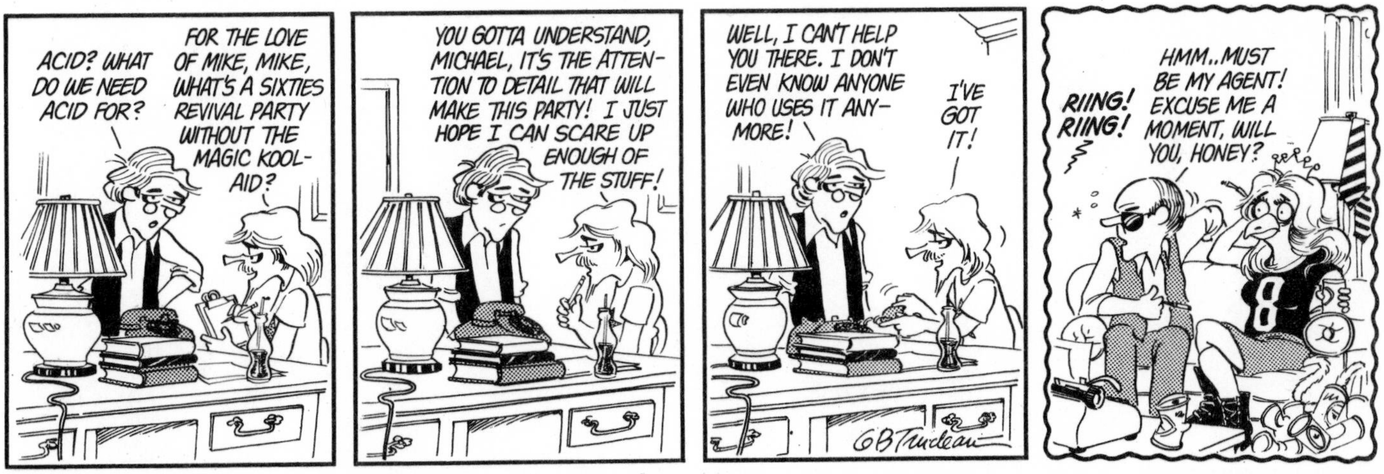
ACID? WHAT DO WE NEED ACID FOR?
FOR THE LOVE OF MIKE, MIKE, WHAT'S A SIXTIES REVIVAL PARTY WITHOUT THE MAGIC KOOL-AID?
YOU GOTTA UNDERSTAND, MICHAEL, IT'S THE ATTENTION TO DETAIL THAT WILL MAKE THIS PARTY! I JUST HOPE I CAN SCARE UP ENOUGH OF THE STUFF!
WELL, I CAN'T HELP YOU THERE. I DON'T EVEN KNOW ANYONE WHO USES IT ANYMORE!
I'VE GOT IT!
GBTrudeau
RIING! RIING!
HMM..MUST BE MY AGENT! EXCUSE ME A MOMENT, WILL YOU, HONEY?

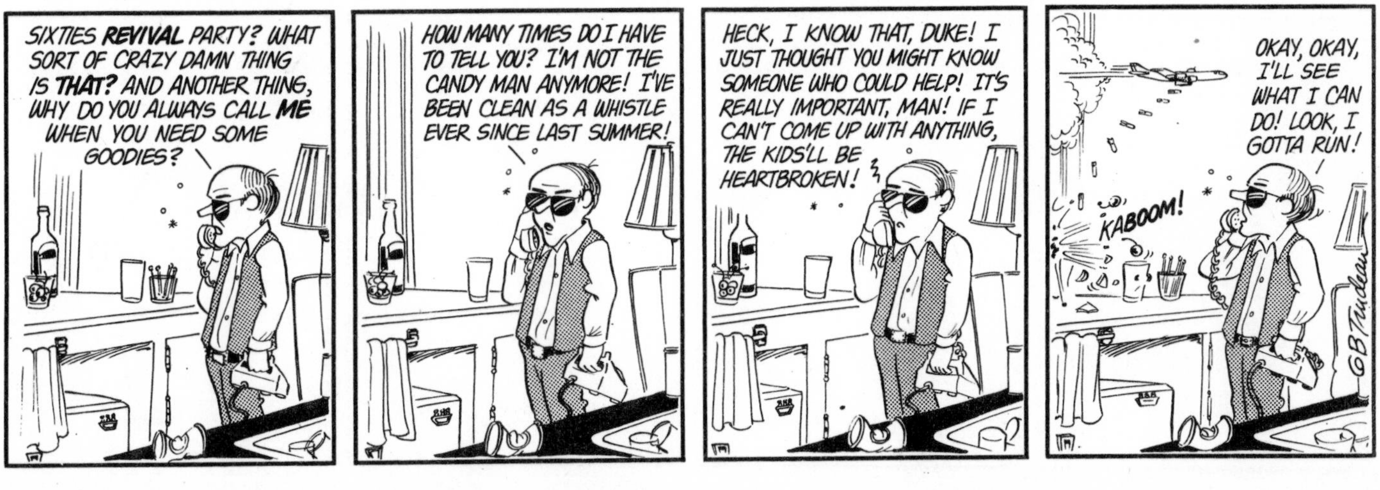
SIXTIES REVIVAL PARTY? WHAT SORT OF CRAZY DAMN THING IS THAT? AND ANOTHER THING, WHY DO YOU ALWAYS CALL ME WHEN YOU NEED SOME GOODIES?
HOW MANY TIMES DO I HAVE TO TELL YOU? I'M NOT THE CANDY MAN ANYMORE! I'VE BEEN CLEAN AS A WHISTLE EVER SINCE LAST SUMMER!
HECK, I KNOW THAT, DUKE! I JUST THOUGHT YOU MIGHT KNOW SOMEONE WHO COULD HELP! IT'S REALLY IMPORTANT, MAN! IF I CAN'T COME UP WITH ANYTHING, THE KIDS'LL BE HEARTBROKEN!
KABOOM!
OKAY, OKAY, I'LL SEE WHAT I CAN DO! LOOK, I GOTTA RUN!
GBTrudeau

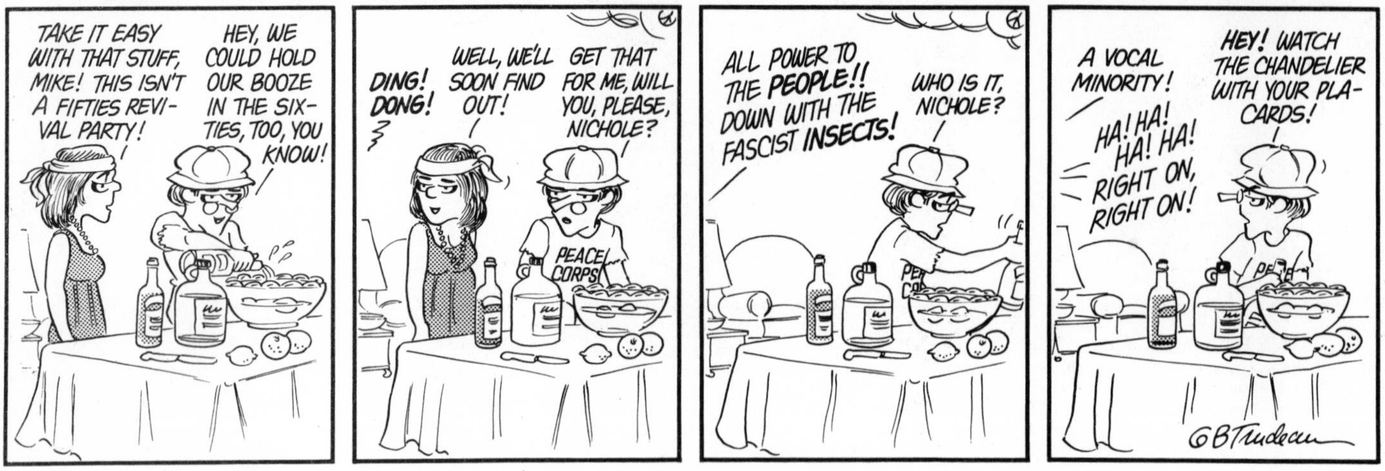
TAKE IT EASY WITH THAT STUFF, MIKE! THIS ISN'T A FIFTIES REVIVAL PARTY!
HEY, WE COULD HOLD OUR BOOZE IN THE SIXTIES, TOO, YOU KNOW!
DING! DONG!
WELL, WE'LL SOON FIND OUT!
GET THAT FOR ME, WILL YOU, PLEASE, NICHOLE?
ALL POWER TO THE PEOPLE!! DOWN WITH THE FASCIST INSECTS!
WHO IS IT, NICHOLE?
A VOCAL MINORITY!
HA! HA! HA! HA! RIGHT ON, RIGHT ON!
HEY! WATCH THE CHANDELIER WITH YOUR PLACARDS!
PEACE CORPS
GBTrudeau

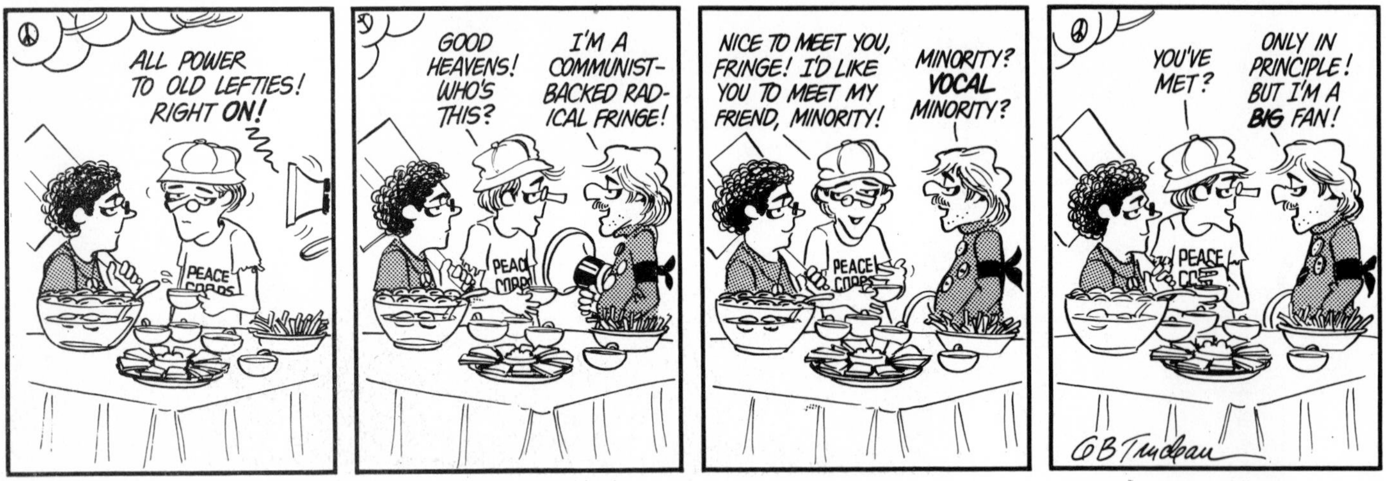
ALL POWER TO OLD LEFTIES! RIGHT ON!
GOOD HEAVENS! WHO'S THIS?
I'M A COMMUNIST-BACKED RADICAL FRINGE!
NICE TO MEET YOU, FRINGE! I'D LIKE YOU TO MEET MY FRIEND, MINORITY!
MINORITY? VOCAL MINORITY?
YOU'VE MET?
ONLY IN PRINCIPLE! BUT I'M A BIG FAN!
PEACE CORPS
GBTrudeau

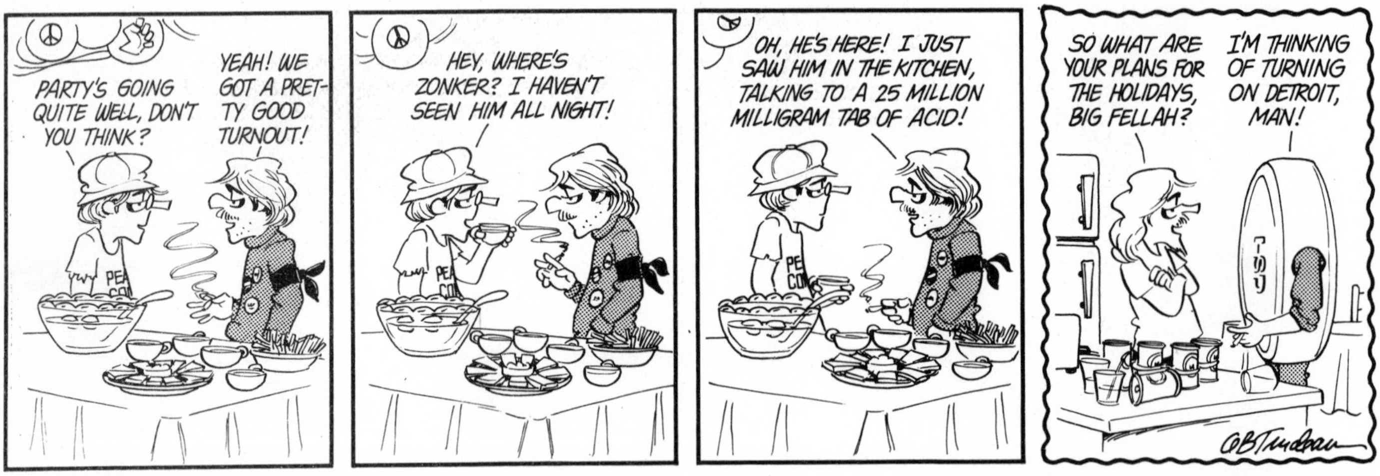
PARTY'S GOING QUITE WELL, DON'T YOU THINK?
YEAH! WE GOT A PRETTY GOOD TURNOUT!
HEY, WHERE'S ZONKER? I HAVEN'T SEEN HIM ALL NIGHT!
OH, HE'S HERE! I JUST SAW HIM IN THE KITCHEN, TALKING TO A 25 MILLION MILLIGRAM TAB OF ACID!
SO WHAT ARE YOUR PLANS FOR THE HOLIDAYS, BIG FELLAH?
I'M THINKING OF TURNING ON DETROIT, MAN!
GBTrudeau

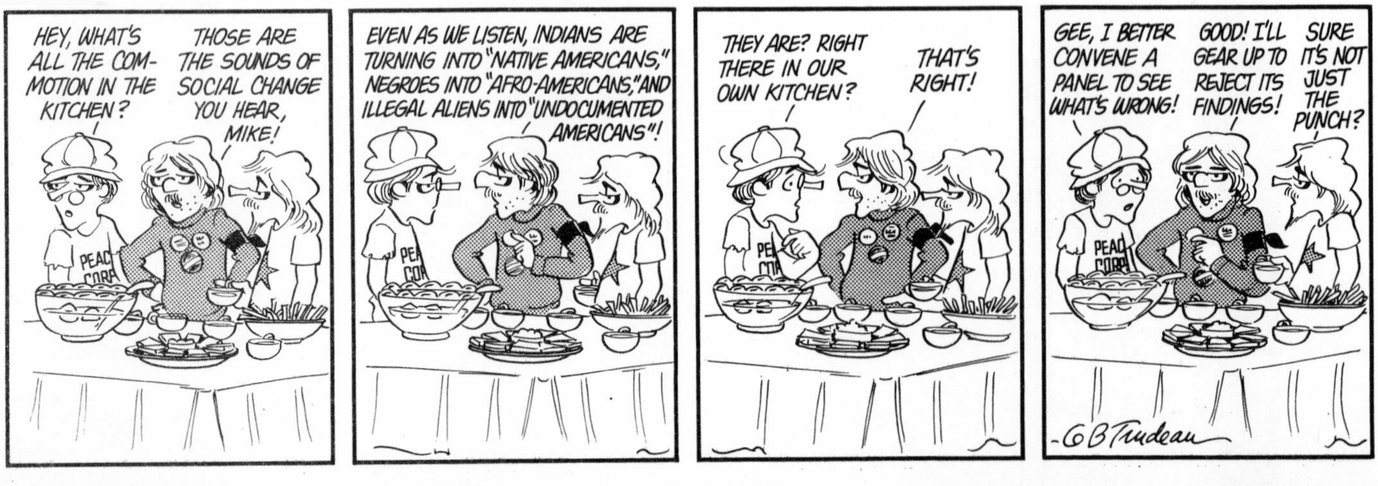
HEY, WHAT'S ALL THE COMMOTION IN THE KITCHEN?
THOSE ARE THE SOUNDS OF SOCIAL CHANGE YOU HEAR, MIKE!
EVEN AS WE LISTEN, INDIANS ARE TURNING INTO "NATIVE AMERICANS," NEGROES INTO "AFRO-AMERICANS," AND ILLEGAL ALIENS INTO "UNDOCUMENTED AMERICANS"!
THEY ARE? RIGHT THERE IN OUR OWN KITCHEN?
THAT'S RIGHT!
GEE, I BETTER CONVENE A PANEL TO SEE WHAT'S WRONG!
GOOD! I'LL GEAR UP TO REJECT ITS FINDINGS!
SURE IT'S NOT JUST THE PUNCH?
GBTrudeau

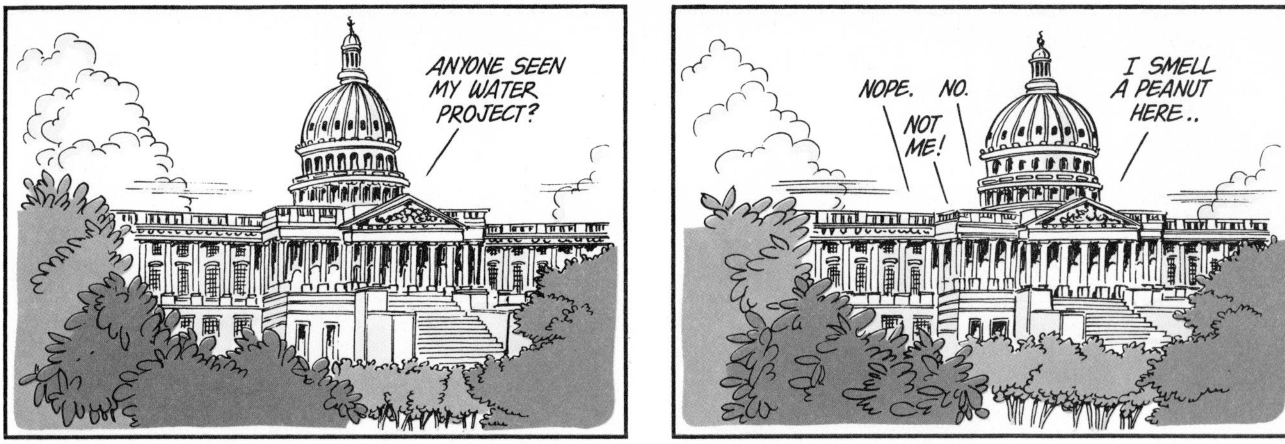
ANYONE SEEN MY WATER PROJECT?
NOPE.
NOT ME!
NO.
I SMELL A PEANUT HERE..

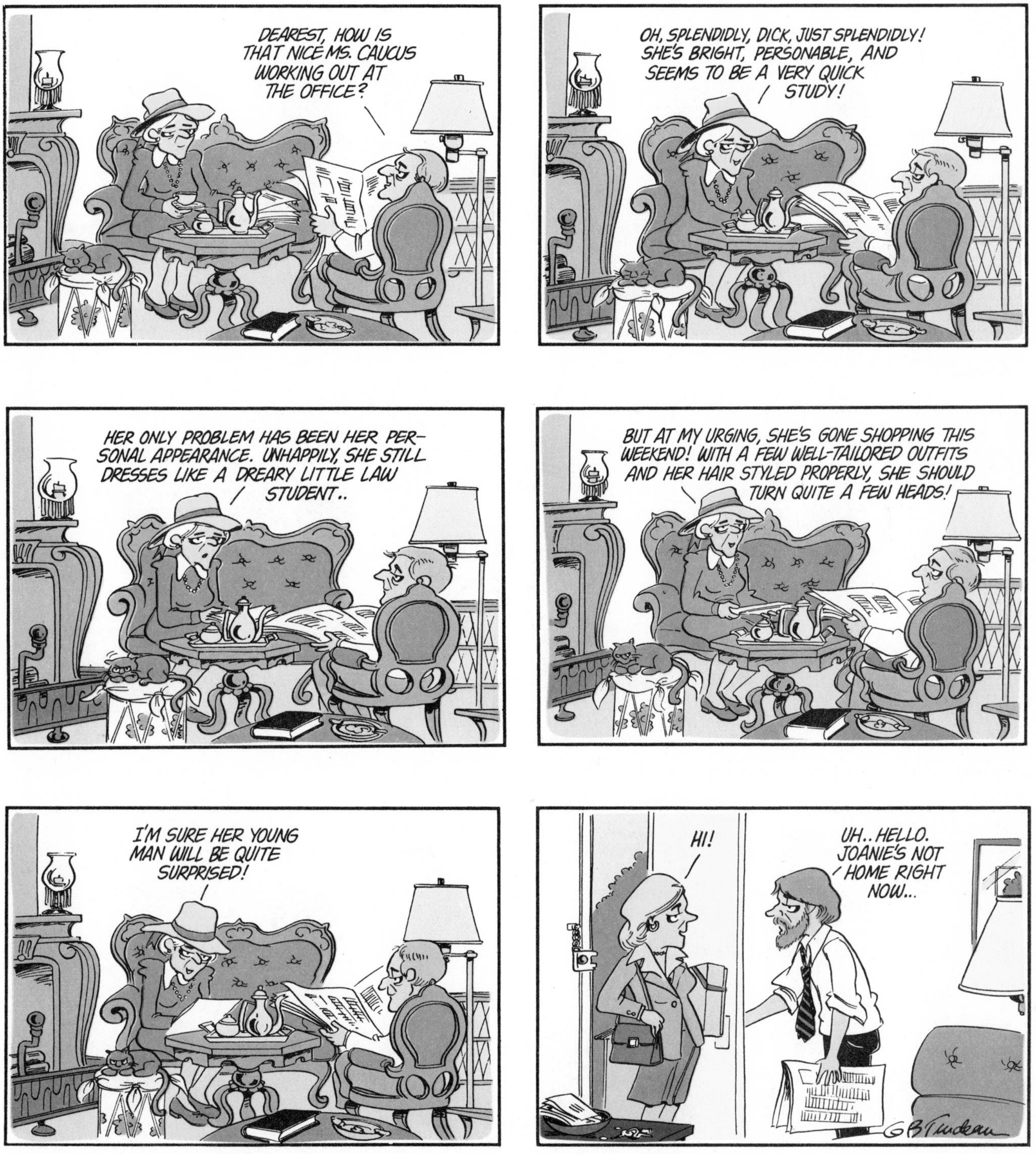
DEAREST, HOW IS THAT NICE MS. CAUCUS WORKING OUT AT THE OFFICE?
OH, SPLENDIDLY, DICK, JUST SPLENDIDLY! SHE'S BRIGHT, PERSONABLE, AND SEEMS TO BE A VERY QUICK STUDY!
HER ONLY PROBLEM HAS BEEN HER PERSONAL APPEARANCE. UNHAPPILY, SHE STILL DRESSES LIKE A DREARY LITTLE LAW STUDENT..
BUT AT MY URGING, SHE'S GONE SHOPPING THIS WEEKEND! WITH A FEW WELL-TAILORED OUTFITS AND HER HAIR STYLED PROPERLY, SHE SHOULD TURN QUITE A FEW HEADS!
I'M SURE HER YOUNG MAN WILL BE QUITE SURPRISED!
HI!
UH.. HELLO. JOANIE'S NOT HOME RIGHT NOW...

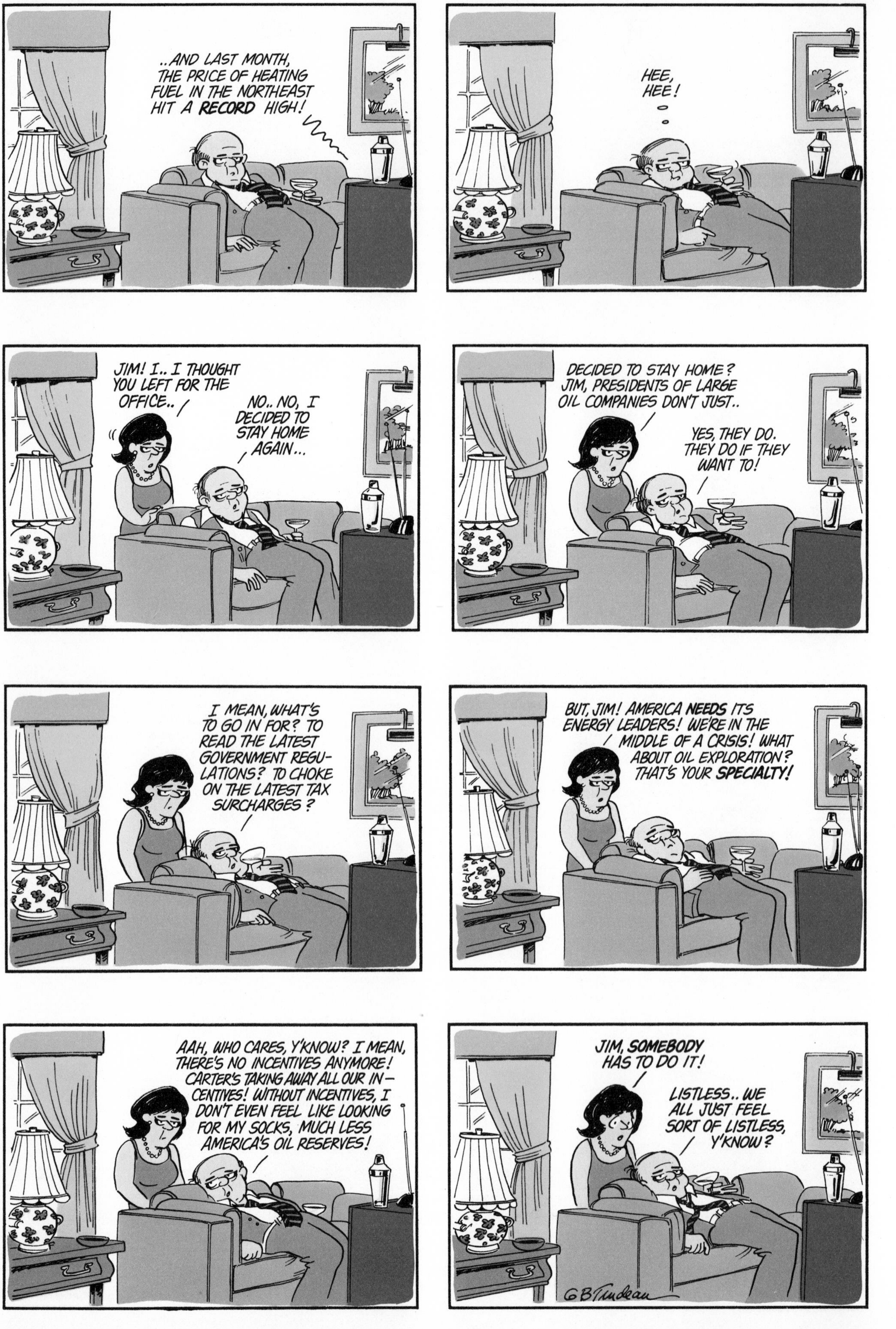
..AND LAST MONTH, THE PRICE OF HEATING FUEL IN THE NORTHEAST HIT A **RECORD** HIGH!
HEE, HEE!
JIM! I.. I THOUGHT YOU LEFT FOR THE OFFICE..
NO.. NO, I DECIDED TO STAY HOME AGAIN...
DECIDED TO STAY HOME? JIM, PRESIDENTS OF LARGE OIL COMPANIES DON'T JUST..
YES, THEY DO. THEY DO IF THEY WANT TO!
I MEAN, WHAT'S TO GO IN FOR? TO READ THE LATEST GOVERNMENT REGU-LATIONS? TO CHOKE ON THE LATEST TAX SURCHARGES?
BUT, JIM! AMERICA **NEEDS** ITS ENERGY LEADERS! WE'RE IN THE MIDDLE OF A CRISIS! WHAT ABOUT OIL EXPLORATION? THAT'S YOUR **SPECIALTY**!
AAH, WHO CARES, Y'KNOW? I MEAN, THERE'S NO INCENTIVES ANYMORE! CARTER'S TAKING AWAY ALL OUR IN-CENTIVES! WITHOUT INCENTIVES, I DON'T EVEN FEEL LIKE LOOKING FOR MY SOCKS, MUCH LESS AMERICA'S OIL RESERVES!
JIM, **SOMEBODY** HAS TO DO IT!
LISTLESS.. WE ALL JUST FEEL SORT OF LISTLESS, Y'KNOW?
GBTrudeau

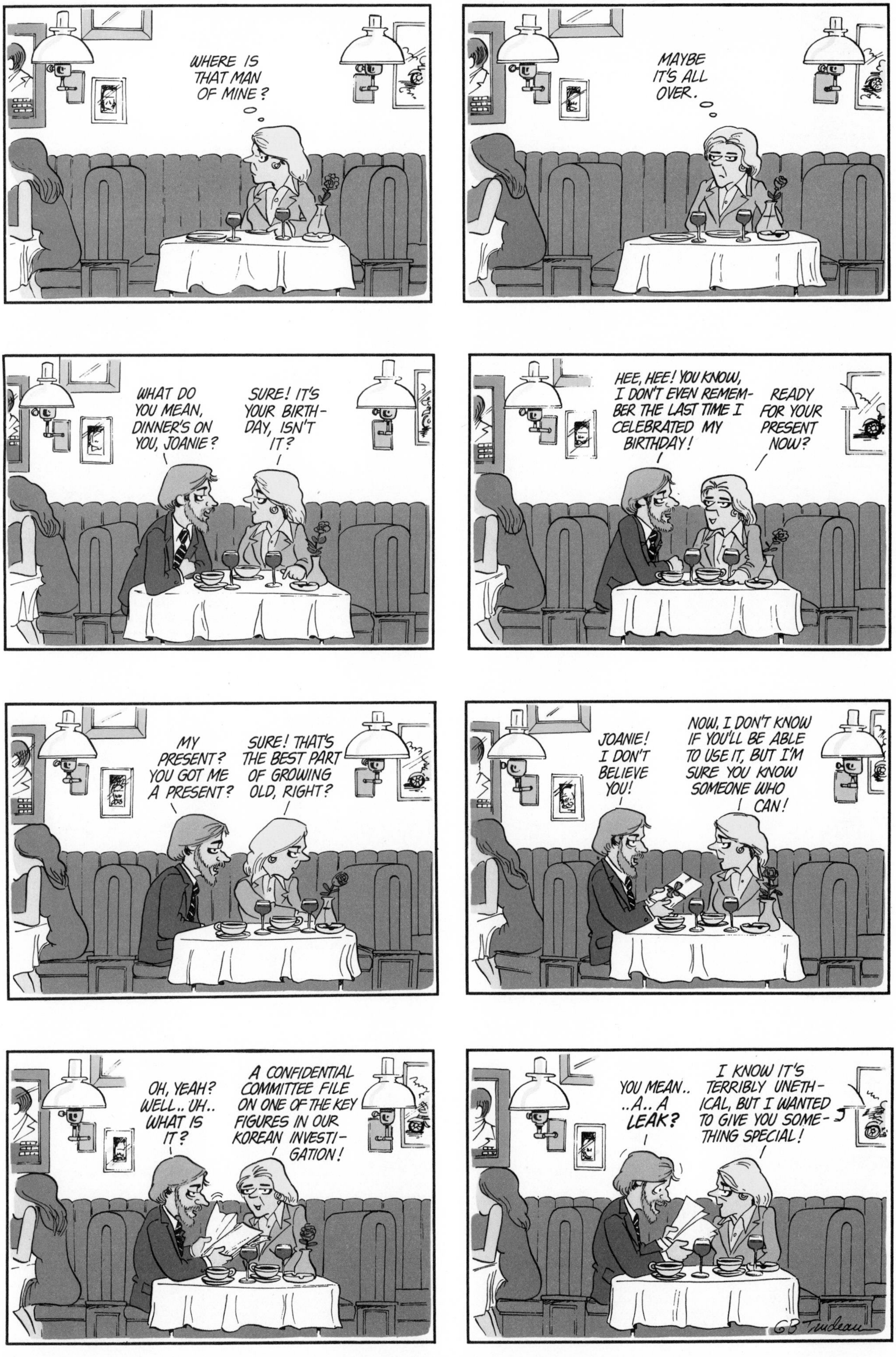
WHERE IS THAT MAN OF MINE?
MAYBE IT'S ALL OVER.
WHAT DO YOU MEAN, DINNER'S ON YOU, JOANIE?
SURE! IT'S YOUR BIRTHDAY, ISN'T IT?
HEE, HEE! YOU KNOW, I DON'T EVEN REMEMBER THE LAST TIME I CELEBRATED MY BIRTHDAY!
READY FOR YOUR PRESENT NOW?
MY PRESENT? YOU GOT ME A PRESENT?
SURE! THAT'S THE BEST PART OF GROWING OLD, RIGHT?
JOANIE! I DON'T BELIEVE YOU!
NOW, I DON'T KNOW IF YOU'LL BE ABLE TO USE IT, BUT I'M SURE YOU KNOW SOMEONE WHO CAN!
OH, YEAH? WELL.. UH.. WHAT IS IT?
A CONFIDENTIAL COMMITTEE FILE ON ONE OF THE KEY FIGURES IN OUR KOREAN INVESTIGATION!
YOU MEAN.. ..A.. A LEAK?
I KNOW IT'S TERRIBLY UNETHICAL, BUT I WANTED TO GIVE YOU SOMETHING SPECIAL!
GB Trudeau

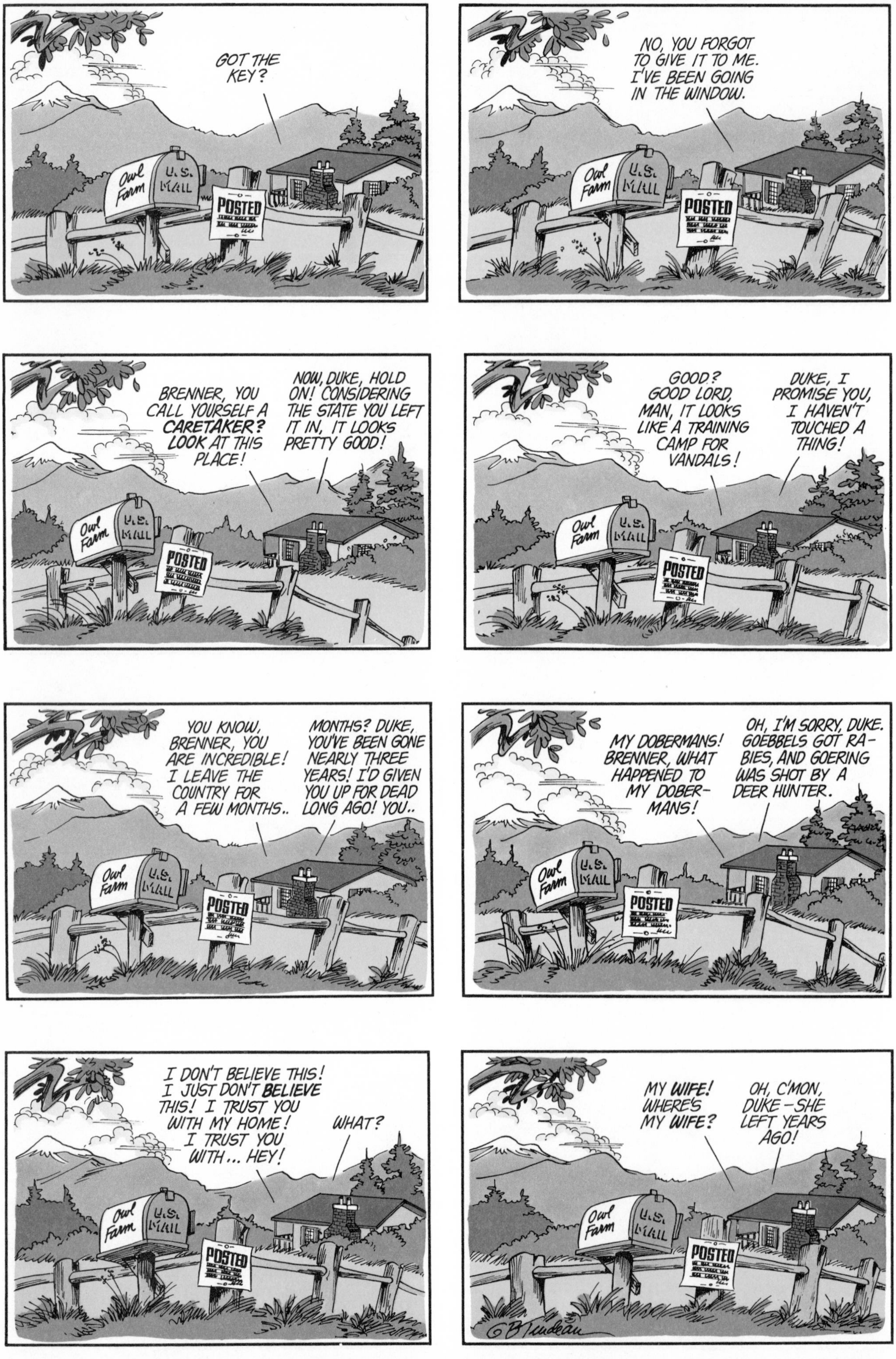
GOT THE KEY?
NO, YOU FORGOT TO GIVE IT TO ME. I'VE BEEN GOING IN THE WINDOW.
Owl Farm
U.S. MAIL
POSTED
BRENNER, YOU CALL YOURSELF A CARETAKER? LOOK AT THIS PLACE!
NOW, DUKE, HOLD ON! CONSIDERING THE STATE YOU LEFT IT IN, IT LOOKS PRETTY GOOD!
GOOD? GOOD LORD, MAN, IT LOOKS LIKE A TRAINING CAMP FOR VANDALS!
DUKE, I PROMISE YOU, I HAVEN'T TOUCHED A THING!
YOU KNOW, BRENNER, YOU ARE INCREDIBLE! I LEAVE THE COUNTRY FOR A FEW MONTHS..
MONTHS? DUKE, YOU'VE BEEN GONE NEARLY THREE YEARS! I'D GIVEN YOU UP FOR DEAD LONG AGO! YOU..
MY DOBERMANS! BRENNER, WHAT HAPPENED TO MY DOBER-MANS!
OH, I'M SORRY, DUKE. GOEBBELS GOT RA-BIES, AND GOERING WAS SHOT BY A DEER HUNTER.
I DON'T BELIEVE THIS! I JUST DON'T BELIEVE THIS! I TRUST YOU WITH MY HOME! I TRUST YOU WITH ... HEY!
WHAT?
MY WIFE! WHERE'S MY WIFE?
OH, C'MON, DUKE—SHE LEFT YEARS AGO!
G B Trudeau

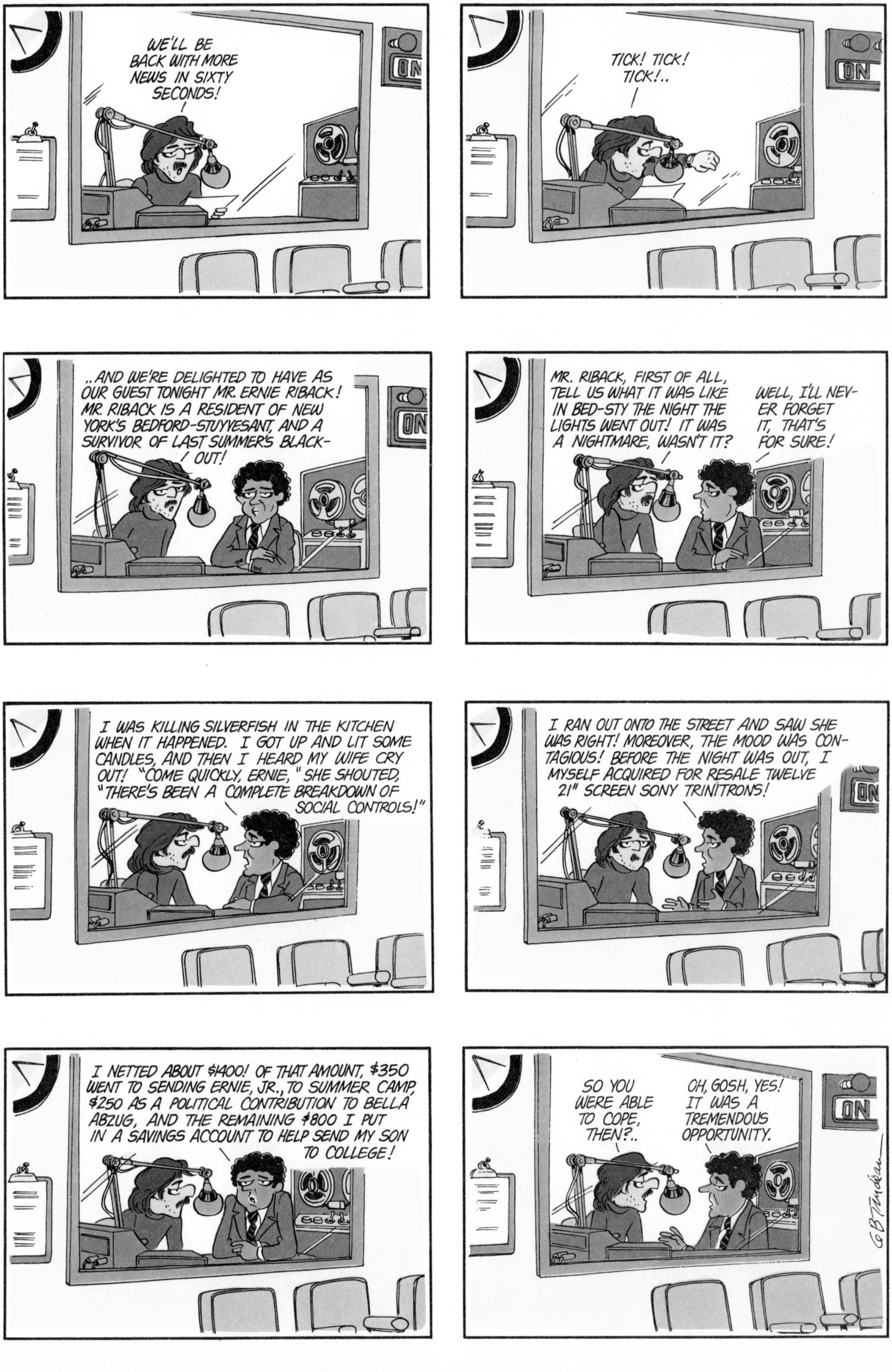
WE'LL BE BACK WITH MORE NEWS IN SIXTY SECONDS!
ON
TICK! TICK! TICK!..
ON
..AND WE'RE DELIGHTED TO HAVE AS OUR GUEST TONIGHT MR. ERNIE RIBACK! MR. RIBACK IS A RESIDENT OF NEW YORK'S BEDFORD-STUYVESANT, AND A SURVIVOR OF LAST SUMMER'S BLACK-OUT!
ON
MR. RIBACK, FIRST OF ALL, TELL US WHAT IT WAS LIKE IN BED-STY THE NIGHT THE LIGHTS WENT OUT! IT WAS A NIGHTMARE, WASN'T IT?
WELL, I'LL NEVER FORGET IT, THAT'S FOR SURE!
I WAS KILLING SILVERFISH IN THE KITCHEN WHEN IT HAPPENED. I GOT UP AND LIT SOME CANDLES, AND THEN I HEARD MY WIFE CRY OUT! "COME QUICKLY, ERNIE," SHE SHOUTED, "THERE'S BEEN A COMPLETE BREAKDOWN OF SOCIAL CONTROLS!"
I RAN OUT ONTO THE STREET AND SAW SHE WAS RIGHT! MOREOVER, THE MOOD WAS CONTAGIOUS! BEFORE THE NIGHT WAS OUT, I MYSELF ACQUIRED FOR RESALE TWELVE 21" SCREEN SONY TRINITRONS!
ON
I NETTED ABOUT $1400! OF THAT AMOUNT, $350 WENT TO SENDING ERNIE, JR., TO SUMMER CAMP, $250 AS A POLITICAL CONTRIBUTION TO BELLA ABZUG, AND THE REMAINING $800 I PUT IN A SAVINGS ACCOUNT TO HELP SEND MY SON TO COLLEGE!
SO YOU WERE ABLE TO COPE, THEN?..
OH, GOSH, YES! IT WAS A TREMENDOUS OPPORTUNITY.
ON

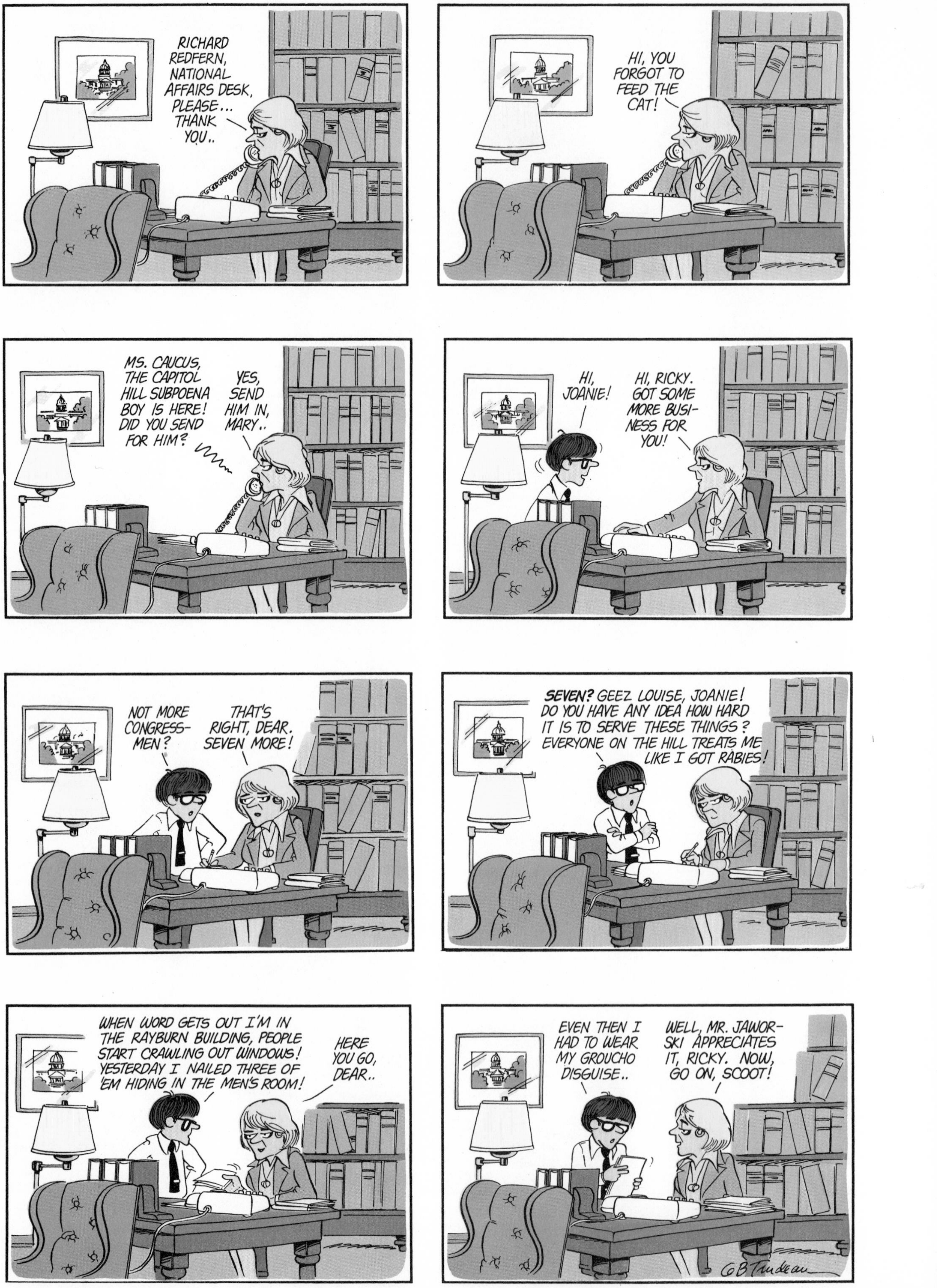
RICHARD REDFERN, NATIONAL AFFAIRS DESK, PLEASE... THANK YOU..
HI, YOU FORGOT TO FEED THE CAT!
MS. CAUCUS, THE CAPITOL HILL SUBPOENA BOY IS HERE! DID YOU SEND FOR HIM?
YES, SEND HIM IN, MARY..
HI, JOANIE!
HI, RICKY. GOT SOME MORE BUSINESS FOR YOU!
NOT MORE CONGRESSMEN?
THAT'S RIGHT, DEAR. SEVEN MORE!
SEVEN? GEEZ LOUISE, JOANIE! DO YOU HAVE ANY IDEA HOW HARD IT IS TO SERVE THESE THINGS? EVERYONE ON THE HILL TREATS ME LIKE I GOT RABIES!
WHEN WORD GETS OUT I'M IN THE RAYBURN BUILDING, PEOPLE START CRAWLING OUT WINDOWS! YESTERDAY I NAILED THREE OF 'EM HIDING IN THE MEN'S ROOM!
HERE YOU GO, DEAR..
EVEN THEN I HAD TO WEAR MY GROUCHO DISGUISE..
WELL, MR. JAWORSKI APPRECIATES IT, RICKY. NOW, GO ON, SCOOT!
GB Trudeau

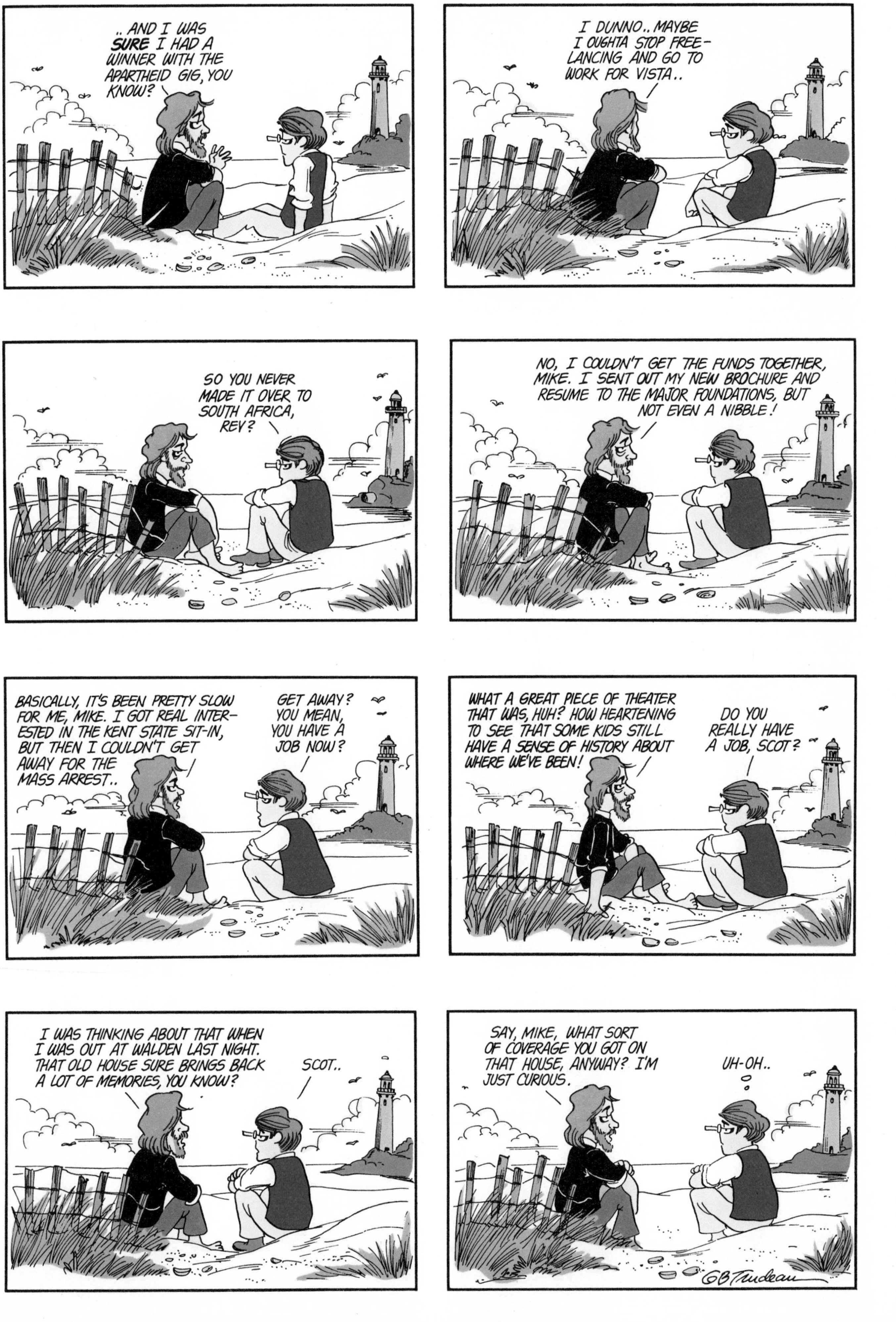

.. AND I WAS **SURE** I HAD A WINNER WITH THE APARTHEID GIG, YOU KNOW?
I DUNNO.. MAYBE I OUGHTA STOP FREE-LANCING AND GO TO WORK FOR VISTA..
SO YOU NEVER MADE IT OVER TO SOUTH AFRICA, REV?
NO, I COULDN'T GET THE FUNDS TOGETHER, MIKE. I SENT OUT MY NEW BROCHURE AND RESUME TO THE MAJOR FOUNDATIONS, BUT NOT EVEN A NIBBLE!
BASICALLY, IT'S BEEN PRETTY SLOW FOR ME, MIKE. I GOT REAL INTER-ESTED IN THE KENT STATE SIT-IN, BUT THEN I COULDN'T GET AWAY FOR THE MASS ARREST..
GET AWAY? YOU MEAN, YOU HAVE A JOB NOW?
WHAT A GREAT PIECE OF THEATER THAT WAS, HUH? HOW HEARTENING TO SEE THAT SOME KIDS STILL HAVE A SENSE OF HISTORY ABOUT WHERE WE'VE BEEN!
DO YOU REALLY HAVE A JOB, SCOT?
I WAS THINKING ABOUT THAT WHEN I WAS OUT AT WALDEN LAST NIGHT. THAT OLD HOUSE SURE BRINGS BACK A LOT OF MEMORIES, YOU KNOW?
SCOT..
SAY, MIKE, WHAT SORT OF COVERAGE YOU GOT ON THAT HOUSE, ANYWAY? I'M JUST CURIOUS.
UH-OH..
GBTrudeau

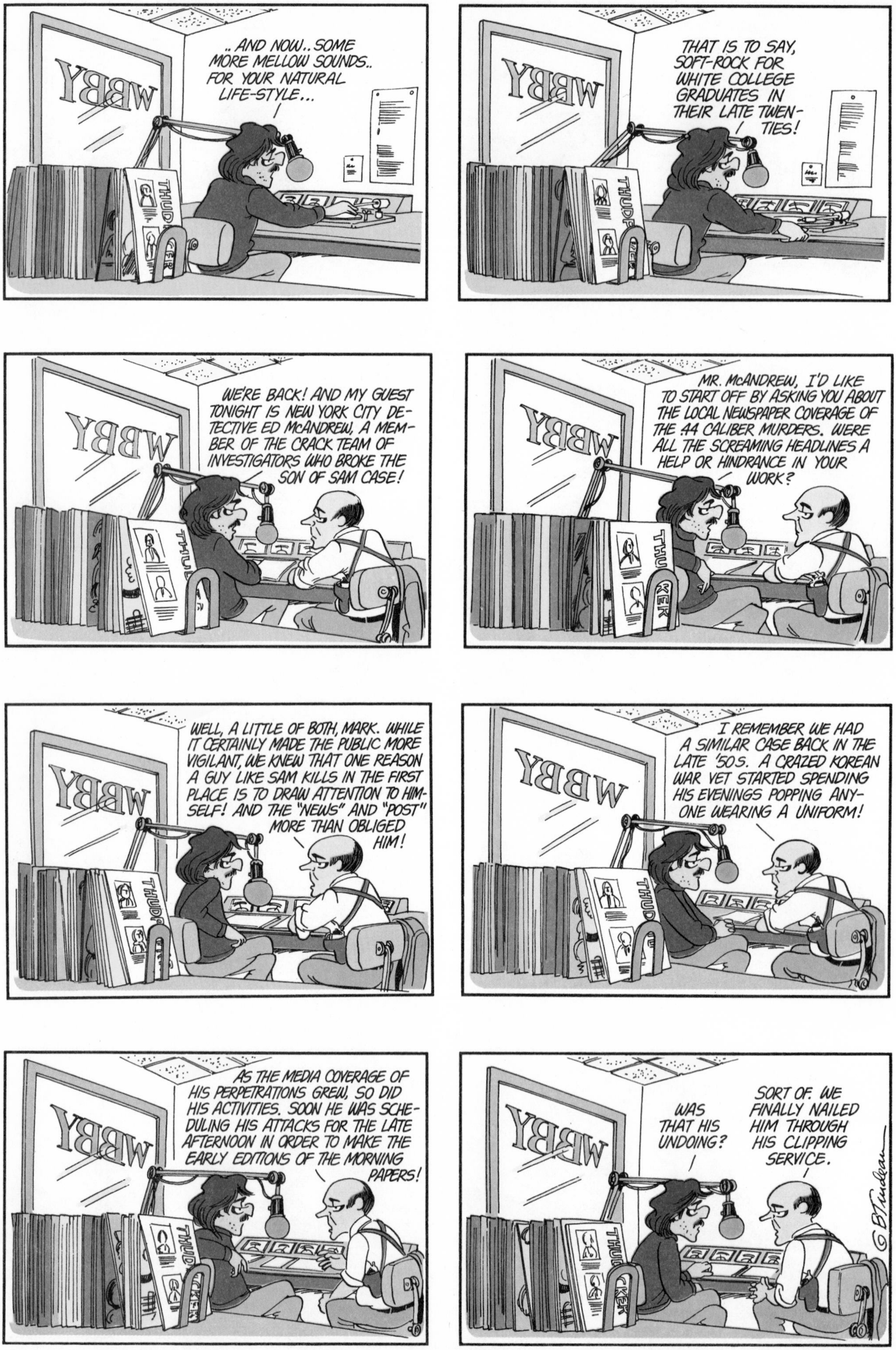
.. AND NOW.. SOME MORE MELLOW SOUNDS.. FOR YOUR NATURAL LIFE-STYLE...
THAT IS TO SAY, SOFT-ROCK FOR WHITE COLLEGE GRADUATES IN THEIR LATE TWEN-TIES!
WE'RE BACK! AND MY GUEST TONIGHT IS NEW YORK CITY DE-TECTIVE ED McANDREW, A MEM-BER OF THE CRACK TEAM OF INVESTIGATORS WHO BROKE THE SON OF SAM CASE!
MR. McANDREW, I'D LIKE TO START OFF BY ASKING YOU ABOUT THE LOCAL NEWSPAPER COVERAGE OF THE .44 CALIBER MURDERS. WERE ALL THE SCREAMING HEADLINES A HELP OR HINDRANCE IN YOUR WORK?
WELL, A LITTLE OF BOTH, MARK. WHILE IT CERTAINLY MADE THE PUBLIC MORE VIGILANT, WE KNEW THAT ONE REASON A GUY LIKE SAM KILLS IN THE FIRST PLACE IS TO DRAW ATTENTION TO HIM-SELF! AND THE "NEWS" AND "POST" MORE THAN OBLIGED HIM!
I REMEMBER WE HAD A SIMILAR CASE BACK IN THE LATE '50S. A CRAZED KOREAN WAR VET STARTED SPENDING HIS EVENINGS POPPING ANY-ONE WEARING A UNIFORM!
AS THE MEDIA COVERAGE OF HIS PERPETRATIONS GREW, SO DID HIS ACTIVITIES. SOON HE WAS SCHE-DULING HIS ATTACKS FOR THE LATE AFTERNOON IN ORDER TO MAKE THE EARLY EDITIONS OF THE MORNING PAPERS!
WAS THAT HIS UNDOING?
SORT OF. WE FINALLY NAILED HIM THROUGH HIS CLIPPING SERVICE.
© B Trudeau

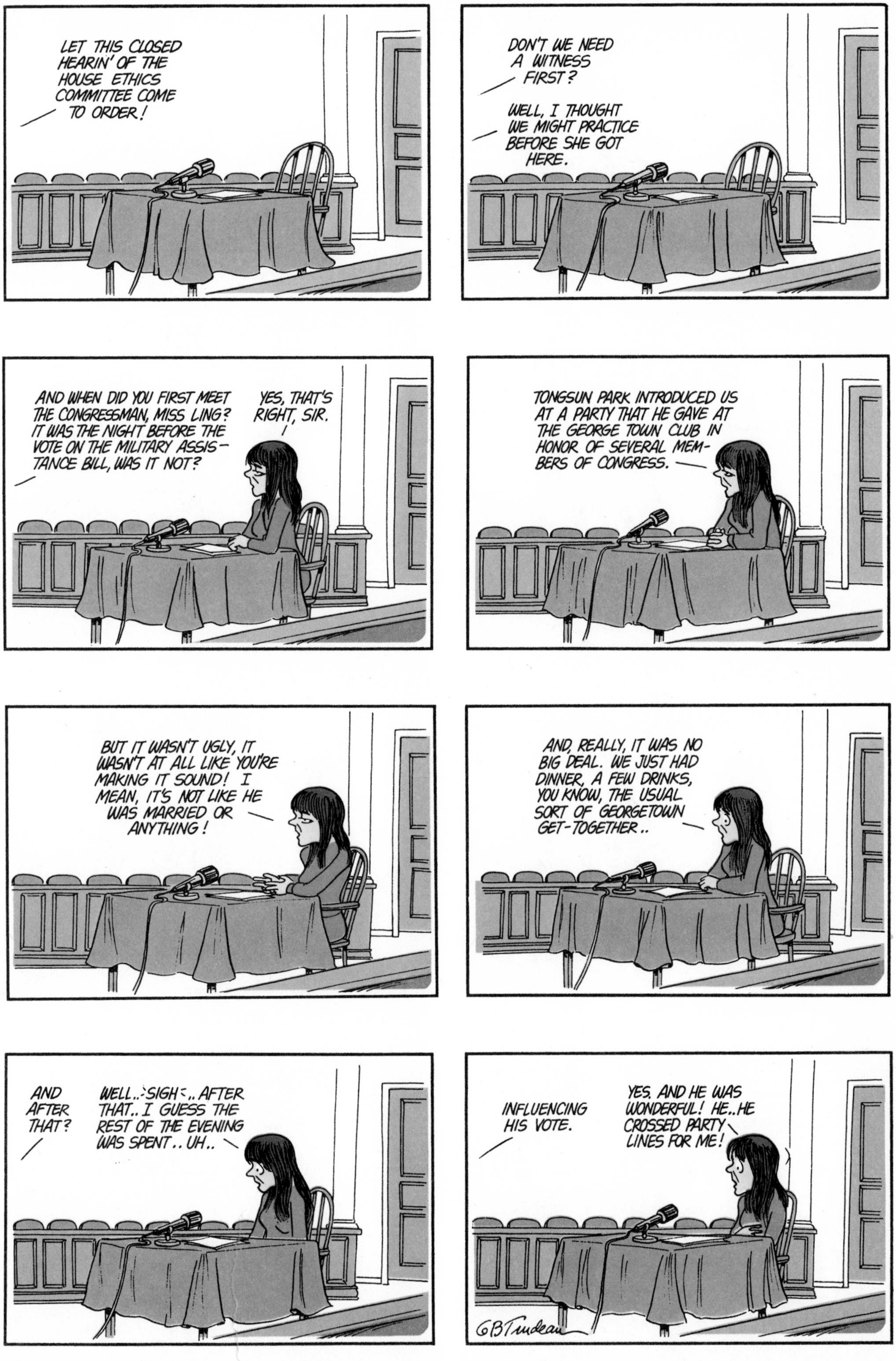

LET THIS CLOSED HEARIN' OF THE HOUSE ETHICS COMMITTEE COME TO ORDER!
DON'T WE NEED A WITNESS FIRST?
WELL, I THOUGHT WE MIGHT PRACTICE BEFORE SHE GOT HERE.
AND WHEN DID YOU FIRST MEET THE CONGRESSMAN, MISS LING? IT WAS THE NIGHT BEFORE THE VOTE ON THE MILITARY ASSISTANCE BILL, WAS IT NOT?
YES, THAT'S RIGHT, SIR.
TONGSUN PARK INTRODUCED US AT A PARTY THAT HE GAVE AT THE GEORGE TOWN CLUB IN HONOR OF SEVERAL MEMBERS OF CONGRESS.
BUT IT WASN'T UGLY, IT WASN'T AT ALL LIKE YOU'RE MAKING IT SOUND! I MEAN, IT'S NOT LIKE HE WAS MARRIED OR ANYTHING!
AND, REALLY, IT WAS NO BIG DEAL. WE JUST HAD DINNER, A FEW DRINKS, YOU KNOW, THE USUAL SORT OF GEORGETOWN GET-TOGETHER..
AND AFTER THAT?
WELL..*SIGH*..AFTER THAT..I GUESS THE REST OF THE EVENING WAS SPENT..UH..
INFLUENCING HIS VOTE.
YES. AND HE WAS WONDERFUL! HE..HE CROSSED PARTY LINES FOR ME!
GBTrudeau

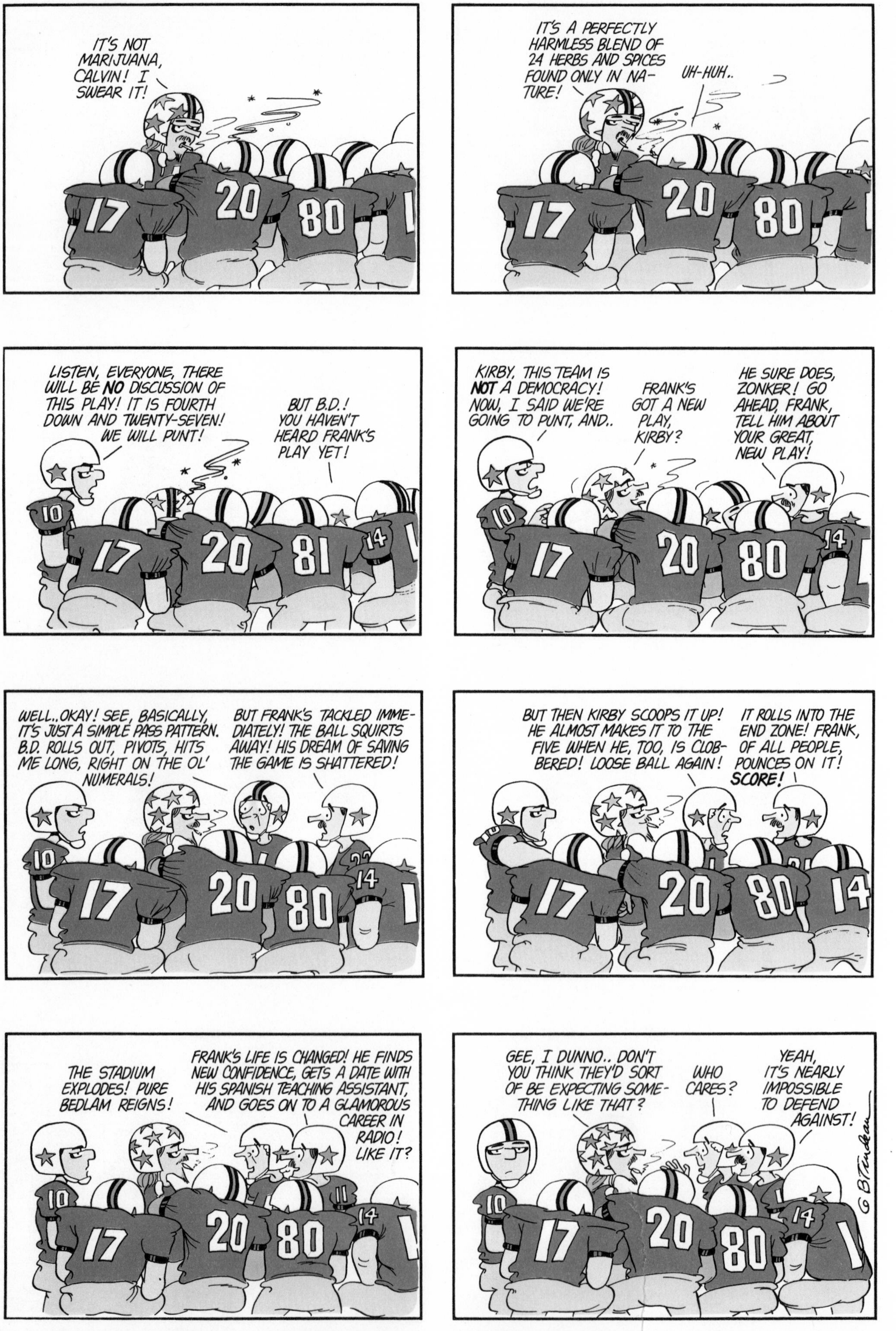
IT'S NOT MARIJUANA, CALVIN! I SWEAR IT!
IT'S A PERFECTLY HARMLESS BLEND OF 24 HERBS AND SPICES FOUND ONLY IN NATURE!
UH-HUH..
LISTEN, EVERYONE, THERE WILL BE NO DISCUSSION OF THIS PLAY! IT IS FOURTH DOWN AND TWENTY-SEVEN! WE WILL PUNT!
BUT B.D.! YOU HAVEN'T HEARD FRANK'S PLAY YET!
KIRBY, THIS TEAM IS NOT A DEMOCRACY! NOW, I SAID WE'RE GOING TO PUNT, AND..
FRANK'S GOT A NEW PLAY, KIRBY?
HE SURE DOES, ZONKER! GO AHEAD, FRANK, TELL HIM ABOUT YOUR GREAT, NEW PLAY!
WELL..OKAY! SEE, BASICALLY, IT'S JUST A SIMPLE PASS PATTERN. B.D. ROLLS OUT, PIVOTS, HITS ME LONG, RIGHT ON THE OL' NUMERALS!
BUT FRANK'S TACKLED IMMEDIATELY! THE BALL SQUIRTS AWAY! HIS DREAM OF SAVING THE GAME IS SHATTERED!
BUT THEN KIRBY SCOOPS IT UP! HE ALMOST MAKES IT TO THE FIVE WHEN HE, TOO, IS CLOBBERED! LOOSE BALL AGAIN!
IT ROLLS INTO THE END ZONE! FRANK, OF ALL PEOPLE, POUNCES ON IT! SCORE!
THE STADIUM EXPLODES! PURE BEDLAM REIGNS!
FRANK'S LIFE IS CHANGED! HE FINDS NEW CONFIDENCE, GETS A DATE WITH HIS SPANISH TEACHING ASSISTANT, AND GOES ON TO A GLAMOROUS CAREER IN RADIO! LIKE IT?
GEE, I DUNNO.. DON'T YOU THINK THEY'D SORT OF BE EXPECTING SOMETHING LIKE THAT?
WHO CARES?
YEAH, IT'S NEARLY IMPOSSIBLE TO DEFEND AGAINST!

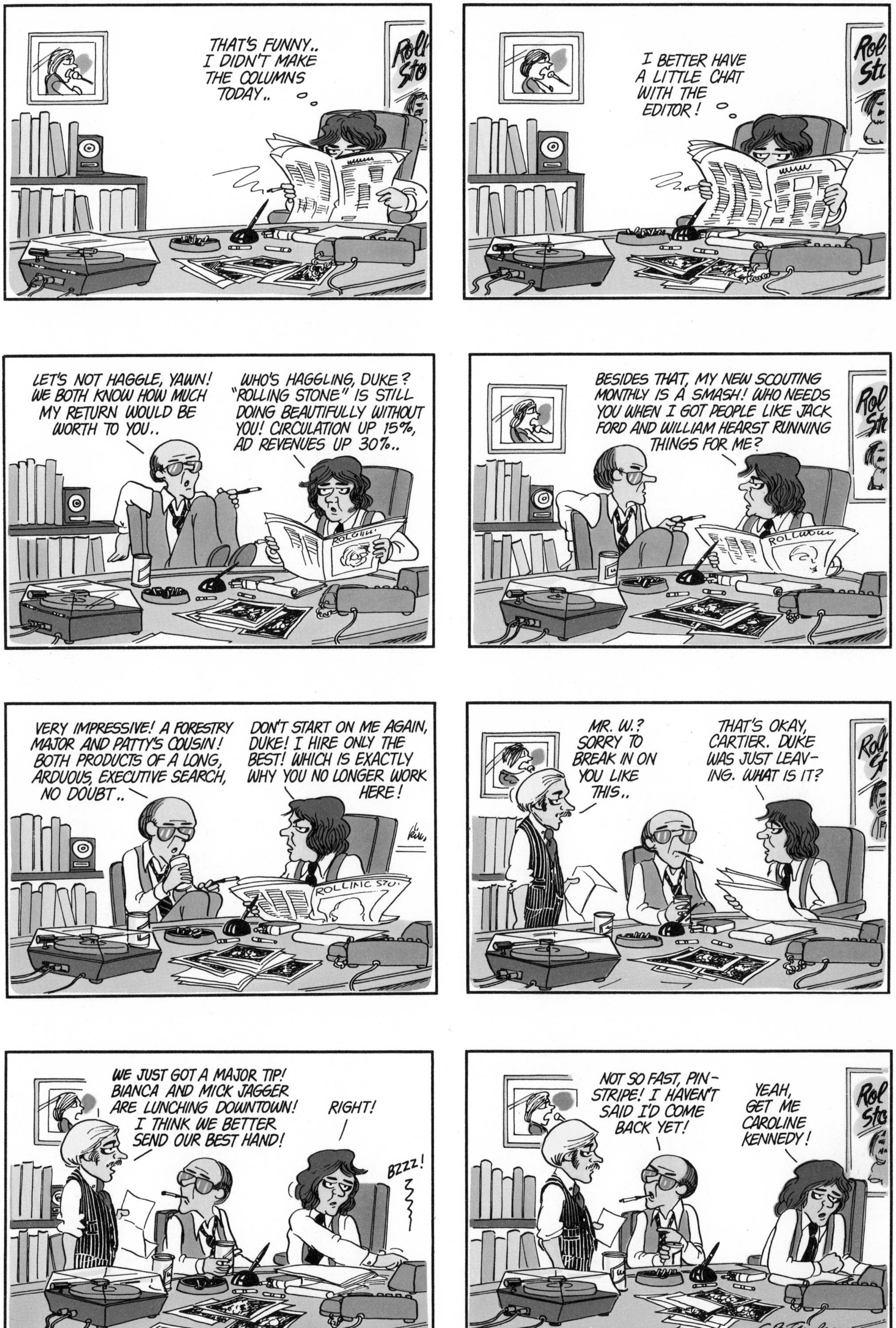
THAT'S FUNNY.. I DIDN'T MAKE THE COLUMNS TODAY..
I BETTER HAVE A LITTLE CHAT WITH THE EDITOR!
LET'S NOT HAGGLE, YAWN! WE BOTH KNOW HOW MUCH MY RETURN WOULD BE WORTH TO YOU..
WHO'S HAGGLING, DUKE? "ROLLING STONE" IS STILL DOING BEAUTIFULLY WITHOUT YOU! CIRCULATION UP 15%, AD REVENUES UP 30%..
BESIDES THAT, MY NEW SCOUTING MONTHLY IS A SMASH! WHO NEEDS YOU WHEN I GOT PEOPLE LIKE JACK FORD AND WILLIAM HEARST RUNNING THINGS FOR ME?
VERY IMPRESSIVE! A FORESTRY MAJOR AND PATTY'S COUSIN! BOTH PRODUCTS OF A LONG, ARDUOUS, EXECUTIVE SEARCH, NO DOUBT..
DON'T START ON ME AGAIN, DUKE! I HIRE ONLY THE BEST! WHICH IS EXACTLY WHY YOU NO LONGER WORK HERE!
MR. W.? SORRY TO BREAK IN ON YOU LIKE THIS..
THAT'S OKAY, CARTIER. DUKE WAS JUST LEAVING. WHAT IS IT?
WE JUST GOT A MAJOR TIP! BIANCA AND MICK JAGGER ARE LUNCHING DOWNTOWN! I THINK WE BETTER SEND OUR BEST HAND!
RIGHT!
BZZZ!
NOT SO FAST, PIN-STRIPE! I HAVEN'T SAID I'D COME BACK YET!
YEAH, GET ME CAROLINE KENNEDY!
G.B. Trudeau

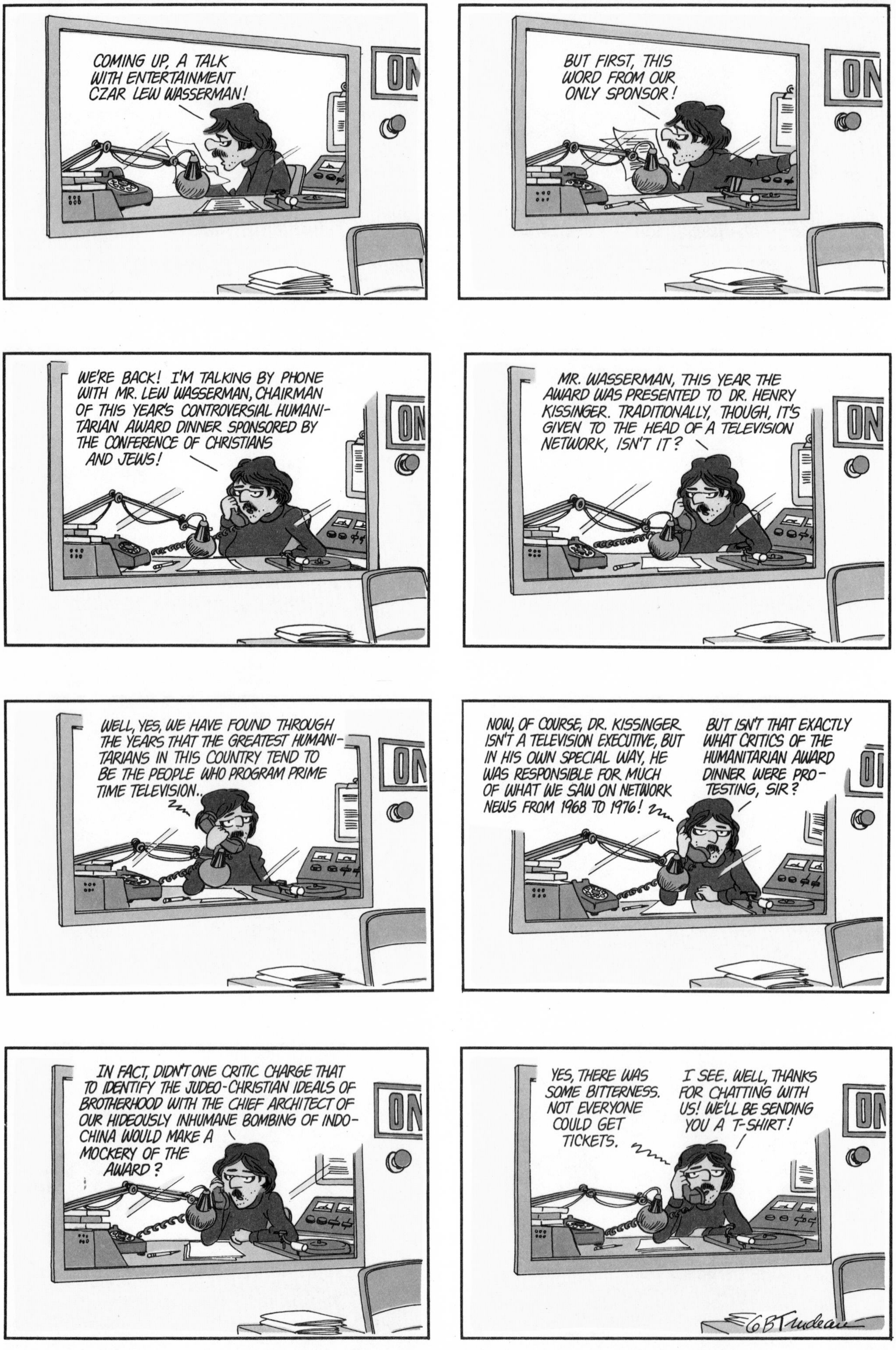

COMING UP, A TALK WITH ENTERTAINMENT CZAR LEW WASSERMAN!
BUT FIRST, THIS WORD FROM OUR ONLY SPONSOR!
WE'RE BACK! I'M TALKING BY PHONE WITH MR. LEW WASSERMAN, CHAIRMAN OF THIS YEAR'S CONTROVERSIAL HUMANITARIAN AWARD DINNER SPONSORED BY THE CONFERENCE OF CHRISTIANS AND JEWS!
MR. WASSERMAN, THIS YEAR THE AWARD WAS PRESENTED TO DR. HENRY KISSINGER. TRADITIONALLY, THOUGH, IT'S GIVEN TO THE HEAD OF A TELEVISION NETWORK, ISN'T IT?
WELL, YES, WE HAVE FOUND THROUGH THE YEARS THAT THE GREATEST HUMANITARIANS IN THIS COUNTRY TEND TO BE THE PEOPLE WHO PROGRAM PRIME TIME TELEVISION..
NOW, OF COURSE, DR. KISSINGER ISN'T A TELEVISION EXECUTIVE, BUT IN HIS OWN SPECIAL WAY, HE WAS RESPONSIBLE FOR MUCH OF WHAT WE SAW ON NETWORK NEWS FROM 1968 TO 1976!
BUT ISN'T THAT EXACTLY WHAT CRITICS OF THE HUMANITARIAN AWARD DINNER WERE PROTESTING, SIR?
IN FACT, DIDN'T ONE CRITIC CHARGE THAT TO IDENTIFY THE JUDEO-CHRISTIAN IDEALS OF BROTHERHOOD WITH THE CHIEF ARCHITECT OF OUR HIDEOUSLY INHUMANE BOMBING OF INDOCHINA WOULD MAKE A MOCKERY OF THE AWARD?
YES, THERE WAS SOME BITTERNESS. NOT EVERYONE COULD GET TICKETS.
I SEE. WELL, THANKS FOR CHATTING WITH US! WE'LL BE SENDING YOU A T-SHIRT!
G B Trudeau

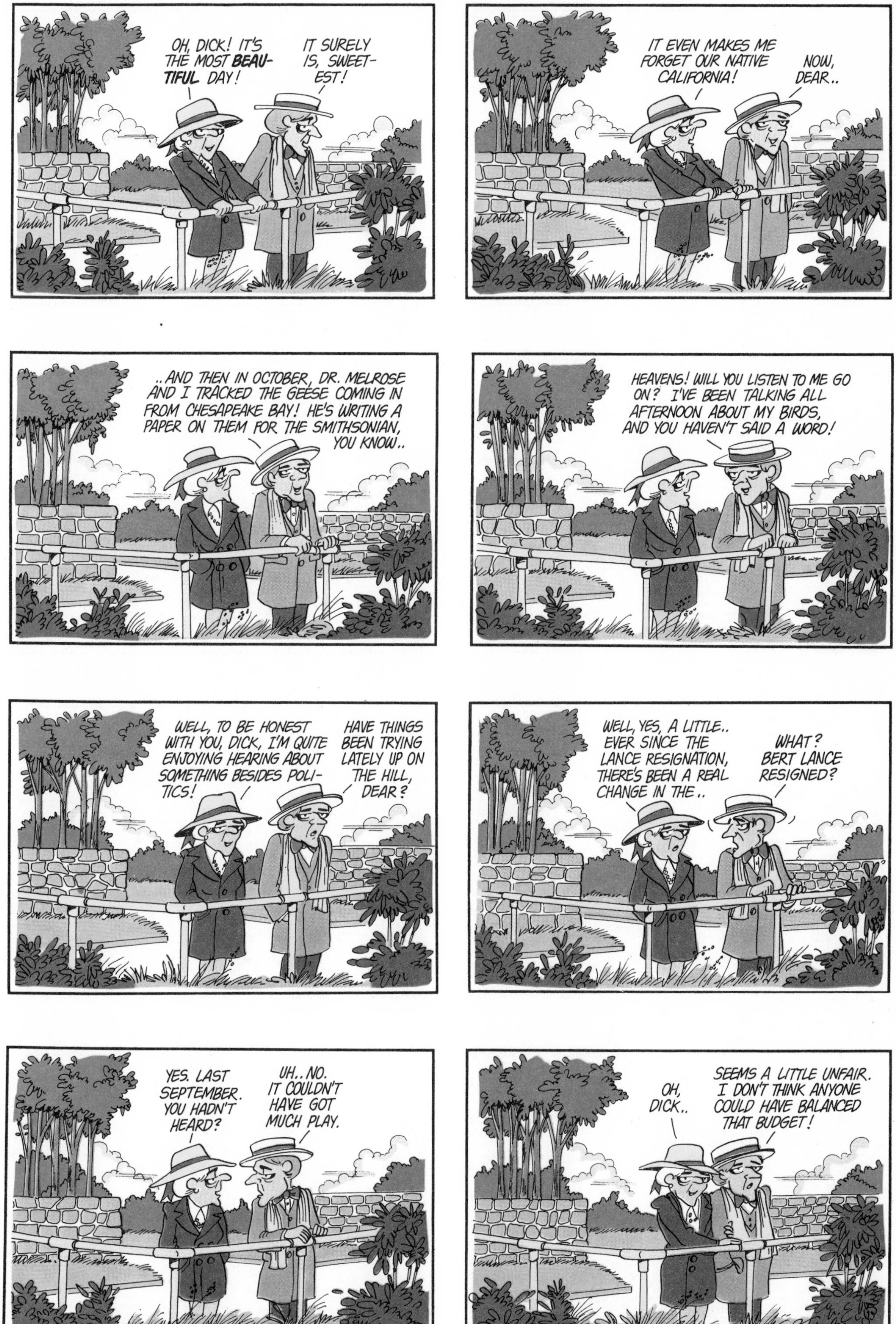
OH, DICK! IT'S THE MOST **BEAUTIFUL** DAY!
IT SURELY IS, SWEETEST!
IT EVEN MAKES ME FORGET OUR NATIVE CALIFORNIA!
NOW, DEAR..
..AND THEN IN OCTOBER, DR. MELROSE AND I TRACKED THE GEESE COMING IN FROM CHESAPEAKE BAY! HE'S WRITING A PAPER ON THEM FOR THE SMITHSONIAN, YOU KNOW..
HEAVENS! WILL YOU LISTEN TO ME GO ON? I'VE BEEN TALKING ALL AFTERNOON ABOUT MY BIRDS, AND YOU HAVEN'T SAID A WORD!
WELL, TO BE HONEST WITH YOU, DICK, I'M QUITE ENJOYING HEARING ABOUT SOMETHING BESIDES POLITICS!
HAVE THINGS BEEN TRYING LATELY UP ON THE HILL, DEAR?
WELL, YES, A LITTLE.. EVER SINCE THE LANCE RESIGNATION, THERE'S BEEN A REAL CHANGE IN THE..
WHAT? BERT LANCE RESIGNED?
YES. LAST SEPTEMBER. YOU HADN'T HEARD?
UH.. NO. IT COULDN'T HAVE GOT MUCH PLAY.
OH, DICK..
SEEMS A LITTLE UNFAIR. I DON'T THINK ANYONE COULD HAVE BALANCED THAT BUDGET!

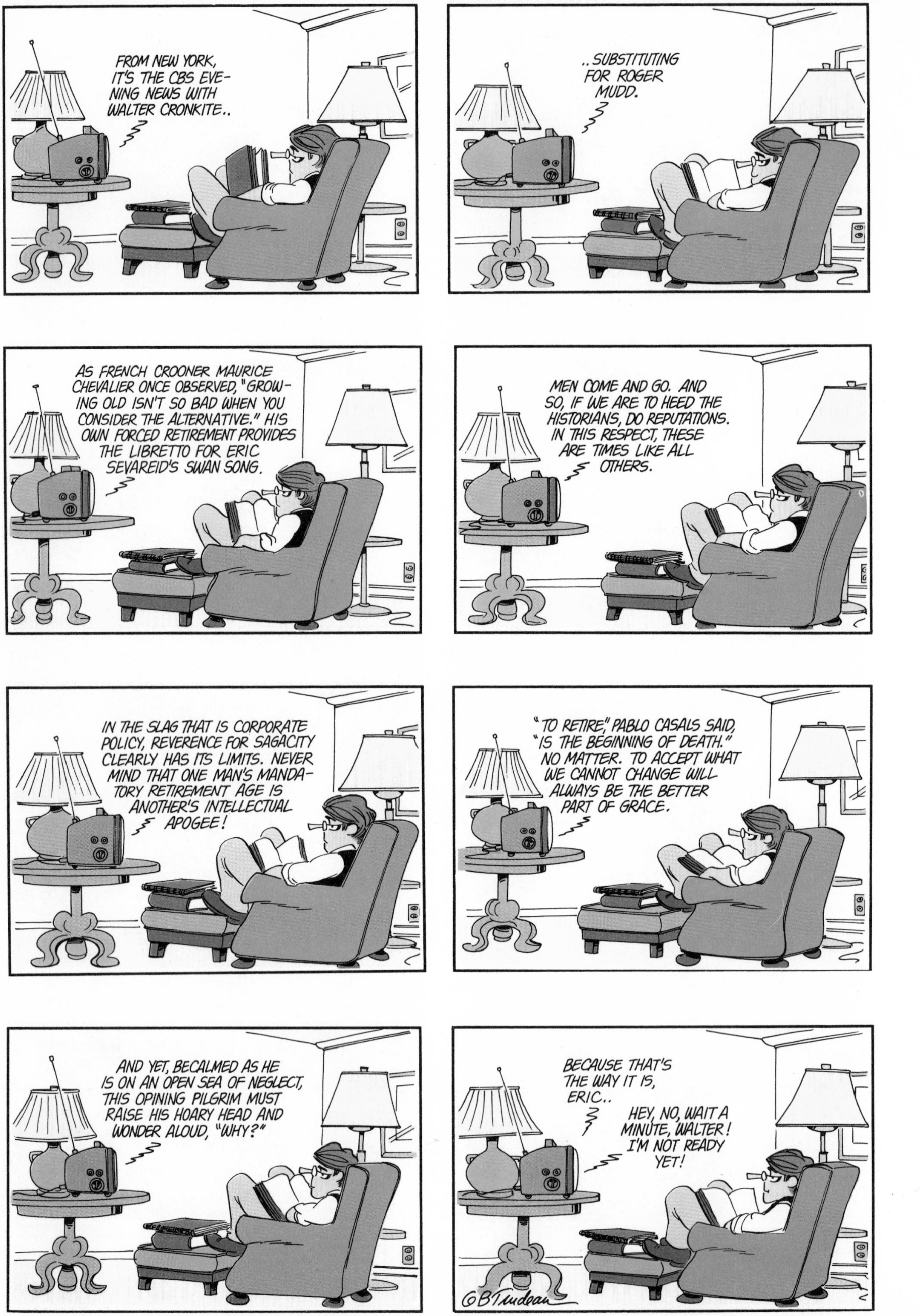
FROM NEW YORK, IT'S THE CBS EVENING NEWS WITH WALTER CRONKITE..
..SUBSTITUTING FOR ROGER MUDD.
AS FRENCH CROONER MAURICE CHEVALIER ONCE OBSERVED, "GROWING OLD ISN'T SO BAD WHEN YOU CONSIDER THE ALTERNATIVE." HIS OWN FORCED RETIREMENT PROVIDES THE LIBRETTO FOR ERIC SEVAREID'S SWAN SONG.
MEN COME AND GO. AND SO, IF WE ARE TO HEED THE HISTORIANS, DO REPUTATIONS. IN THIS RESPECT, THESE ARE TIMES LIKE ALL OTHERS.
IN THE SLAG THAT IS CORPORATE POLICY, REVERENCE FOR SAGACITY CLEARLY HAS ITS LIMITS. NEVER MIND THAT ONE MAN'S MANDATORY RETIREMENT AGE IS ANOTHER'S INTELLECTUAL APOGEE!
"TO RETIRE," PABLO CASALS SAID, "IS THE BEGINNING OF DEATH." NO MATTER. TO ACCEPT WHAT WE CANNOT CHANGE WILL ALWAYS BE THE BETTER PART OF GRACE.
AND YET, BECALMED AS HE IS ON AN OPEN SEA OF NEGLECT, THIS OPINING PILGRIM MUST RAISE HIS HOARY HEAD AND WONDER ALOUD, "WHY?"
BECAUSE THAT'S THE WAY IT IS, ERIC..
HEY, NO, WAIT A MINUTE, WALTER! I'M NOT READY YET!
©BTrudeau

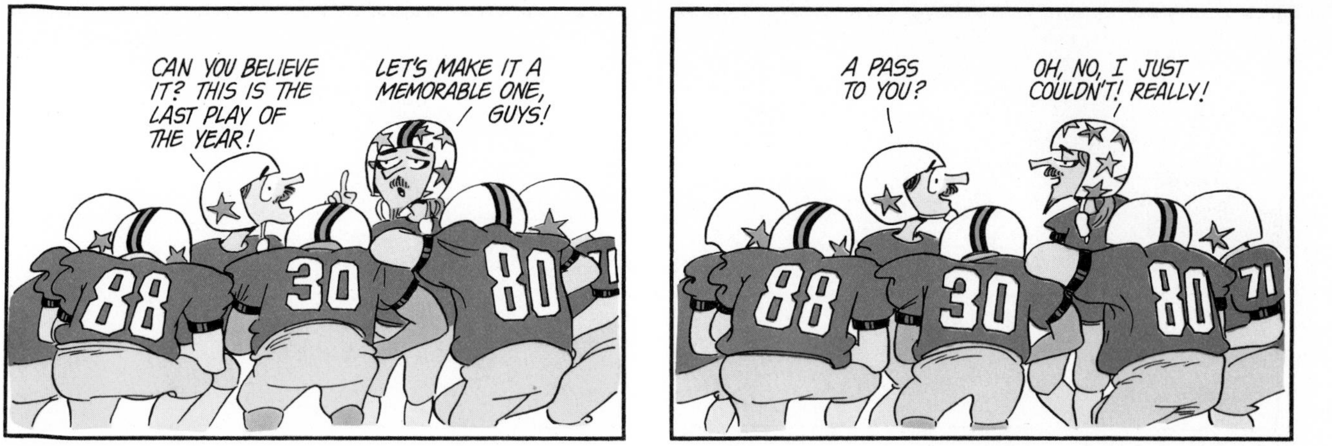
CAN YOU BELIEVE IT? THIS IS THE LAST PLAY OF THE YEAR!
LET'S MAKE IT A MEMORABLE ONE, GUYS!
A PASS TO YOU?
OH, NO, I JUST COULDN'T! REALLY!

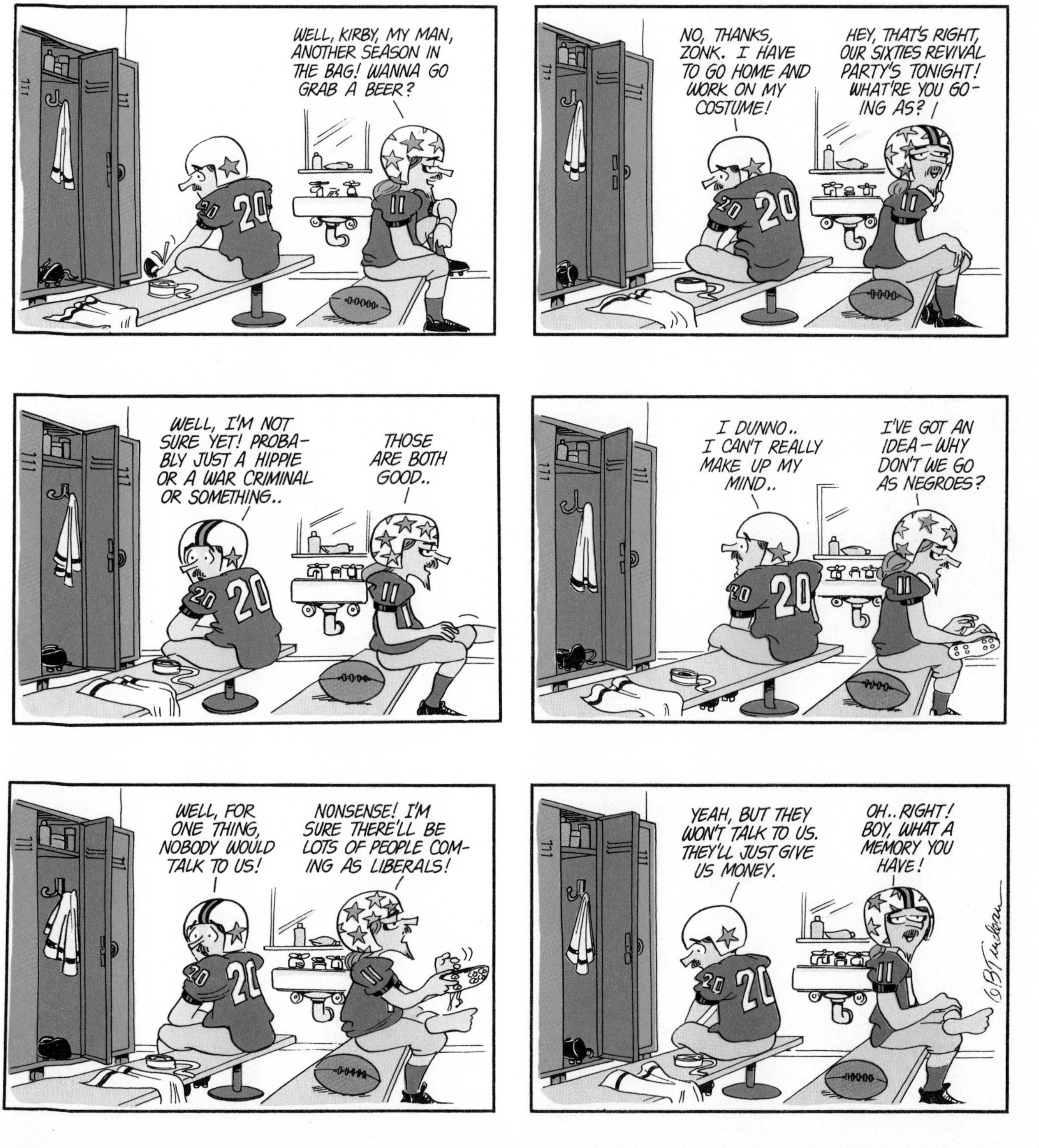
WELL, KIRBY, MY MAN, ANOTHER SEASON IN THE BAG! WANNA GO GRAB A BEER?
NO, THANKS, ZONK. I HAVE TO GO HOME AND WORK ON MY COSTUME!
HEY, THAT'S RIGHT, OUR SIXTIES REVIVAL PARTY'S TONIGHT! WHAT'RE YOU GOING AS?
WELL, I'M NOT SURE YET! PROBABLY JUST A HIPPIE OR A WAR CRIMINAL OR SOMETHING..
THOSE ARE BOTH GOOD..
I DUNNO.. I CAN'T REALLY MAKE UP MY MIND..
I'VE GOT AN IDEA—WHY DON'T WE GO AS NEGROES?
WELL, FOR ONE THING, NOBODY WOULD TALK TO US!
NONSENSE! I'M SURE THERE'LL BE LOTS OF PEOPLE COMING AS LIBERALS!
YEAH, BUT THEY WON'T TALK TO US. THEY'LL JUST GIVE US MONEY.
OH.. RIGHT! BOY, WHAT A MEMORY YOU HAVE!

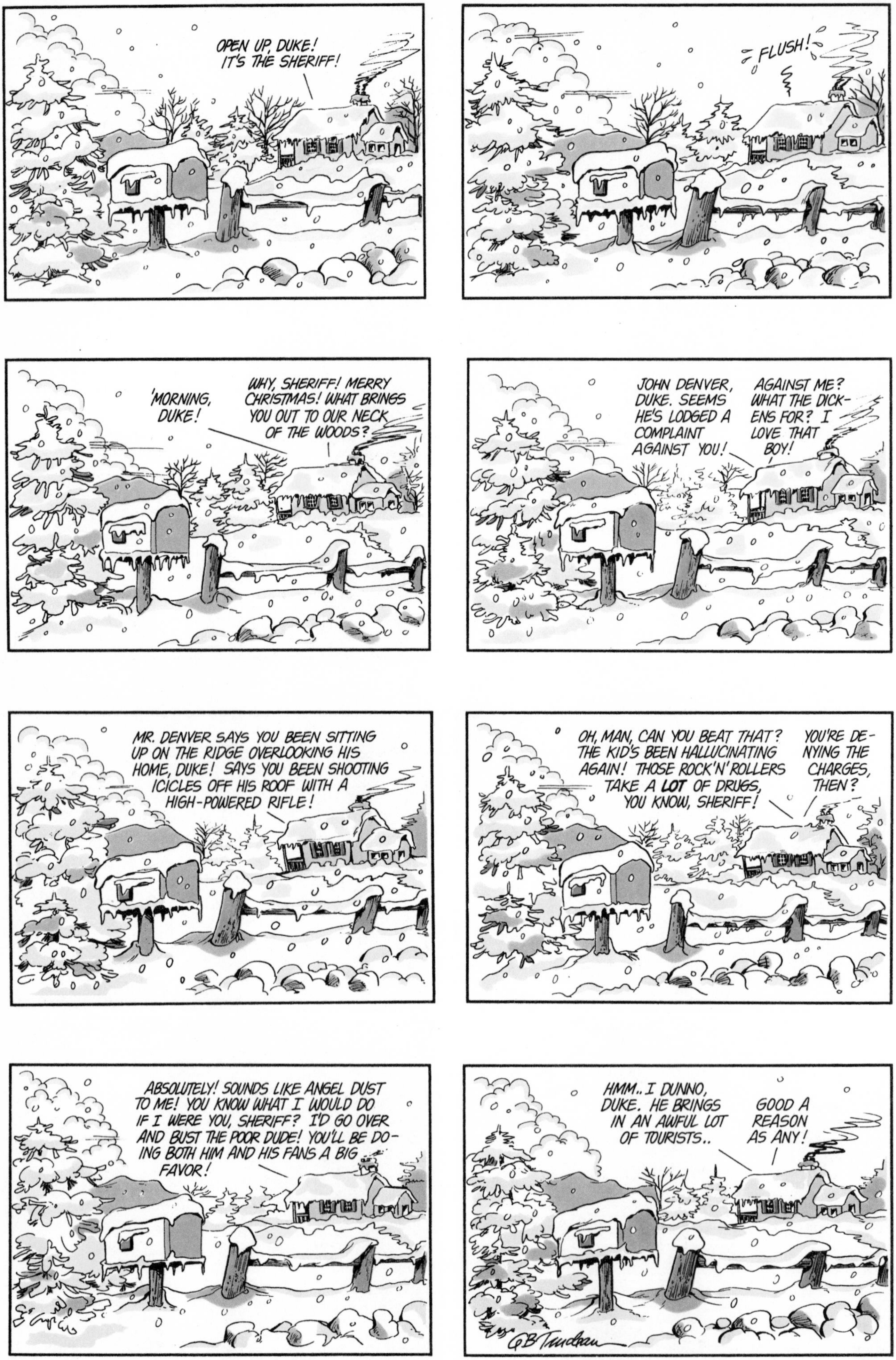
OPEN UP, DUKE! IT'S THE SHERIFF!
FLUSH!
'MORNING, DUKE!
WHY, SHERIFF! MERRY CHRISTMAS! WHAT BRINGS YOU OUT TO OUR NECK OF THE WOODS?
JOHN DENVER, DUKE. SEEMS HE'S LODGED A COMPLAINT AGAINST YOU!
AGAINST ME? WHAT THE DICKENS FOR? I LOVE THAT BOY!
MR. DENVER SAYS YOU BEEN SITTING UP ON THE RIDGE OVERLOOKING HIS HOME, DUKE! SAYS YOU BEEN SHOOTING ICICLES OFF HIS ROOF WITH A HIGH-POWERED RIFLE!
OH, MAN, CAN YOU BEAT THAT? THE KID'S BEEN HALLUCINATING AGAIN! THOSE ROCK'N'ROLLERS TAKE A **LOT** OF DRUGS, YOU KNOW, SHERIFF!
YOU'RE DENYING THE CHARGES, THEN?
ABSOLUTELY! SOUNDS LIKE ANGEL DUST TO ME! YOU KNOW WHAT I WOULD DO IF I WERE YOU, SHERIFF? I'D GO OVER AND BUST THE POOR DUDE! YOU'LL BE DOING BOTH HIM AND HIS FANS A BIG FAVOR!
HMM.. I DUNNO, DUKE. HE BRINGS IN AN AWFUL LOT OF TOURISTS..
GOOD A REASON AS ANY!

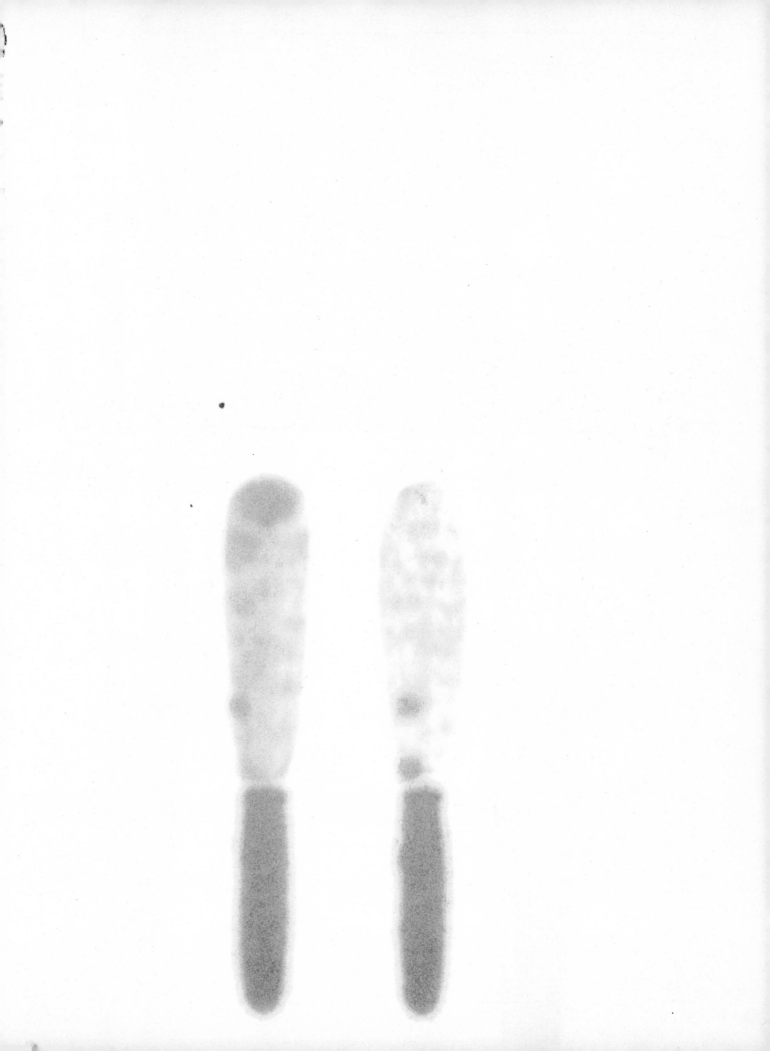